2002

Tax & Financial Guide

for

COLLEGE TEACHERS

and Other College Personnel

■

For filing 2001 tax returns

■

Donald T. Williamson, LLM, CPA
American University
Technical Consultant

Academic Information Service, Inc.

Washington, DC · Bethesda, MD

Academic Information Service, Inc.
Post Office Box 30499
Bethesda, MD 20824

PREFACE

We are pleased to present the 2002 edition of the *Tax & Financial Guide for College Teachers and Other College Personnel*. The Tax Guide is designed to keep College Teachers informed about the latest tax rules that apply to them and tax law changes since the last edition was published. The publication of this edition has been made possible by the interest and support of College Teachers all across the nation for previous editions.

In June 2001, President Bush signed the *Economic Growth and Tax Relief Act of 2001*, the largest tax reduction in twenty years. The reductions are significant and are targeted to individuals. The changes include the enactment of a new 10% tax rate, reductions in the marginal tax rates, marriage penalty relief, increased benefits relating to children (increases in child credit, dependent care credit and adoption credit), education incentives (education IRAs, new pre-paid tuition programs, graduate courses allowed for employer assistance, additional months to deduct interest on educational loans), repeal of the estate and generation skipping taxes, and changes to pensions and individual retirement plans. Most of the relief provisions are phased-in over 10 years due to budgetary constraints and do not start taking effect until 2002 or later years. The tax savings of the lower 10% tax bracket in 2002 was to be refunded to taxpayers in 2001 to help spur the economy.

We want to remind you that the money you save by knowing the tax laws that are described in this guide goes right into your pocket. The dollars you save are not reduced by additional federal and state taxes, social security taxes or retirement deductions, unlike an increase in salary.

We hope you find that this latest edition of the *Tax & Financial Guide for College Teachers and Other College Personnel* is informative and that it contributes to reducing your income tax burden.

Note:

After the tragic events of September 11, 2001, the IRS acted very quickly and announced tax relief for victims and other individuals affected by the events. Most of the states followed the lead of the federal government shortly thereafter. Congress is currently working on legislation for additional tax relief to be effective in 2001 or 2002. As we go to press with this tax guide, tax legislation is being considered. Any such legislation that is passed which concerns college teachers will be posted on the *Tax & Financial Guide* web site: www.taxguide-collegeteachers.com.

TABLE OF CONTENTS

1
Basic Rules

SECTION 1:
BASIC STEPS IN COMPUTING YOUR TAX

The following basic procedure is used to compute your 2001 income tax:

(1) Compute your **total income** subject to tax. This consists of wages, interest, dividends, etc.

(2) Compute your **adjustments to income.** This includes alimony payments you make plus deductible contributions to tax-sheltered IRA and self-employed plans, moving expenses, and other items.

(3) Subtract (2) from (1). This is your **adjusted gross income (AGI).**

(4) Compute your **deductions** by either:

(a) Taking the **standard deduction.** This is a fixed amount depending upon your filing status (single, joint, head of household, or married separate, with extra amounts for those who are at least age 65 and/or blind); or

(b) **Itemizing your deductions.** This is done on Schedule A where you list such things as medical expenses, interest, taxes, casualty losses, charitable contributions, and miscellaneous deductions. Under miscellaneous deductions you include job-related expenses such as travel, books, supplies, professional dues, home office, etc. Certain deductions only apply after a minimum floor has been surpassed — 7.5% of adjusted gross income for medical expenses, 10% for casualty losses, and 2% for the sum total of miscellaneous deductions. (As discussed later in this chapter, the total of itemized deductions for higher-income taxpayers may have to be reduced by the 3% of adjusted gross income phaseout.)

(5) You are allowed a **personal exemption** for each dependent you claim, including yourself, your children, and your spouse. Multiply the number of exemptions by $2,900 in 2001. (As discussed later, this total exemption amount may have to be reduced for higher-income taxpayers by the exemption phaseout.)

(6) Subtract (4) and (5) from (3). The net result is your **taxable income.**

(7) Compute your **tax** by looking up your taxable income in the appropriate tax table or calculating it from the tax schedule.

(8) Subtract **tax credits.** This includes the dependent care tax credit, the credit for excess social security withheld by more than one employer, and the credit for the elderly not fully covered by social security. Observe that tax credits are much more favorable than deductions because they are subtracted directly from your tax instead of from your income.

For 2001 tax returns, the following table shows the amount of the standard deduction for different categories of individuals:

Married filing jointly	$7,600
Married filing separately	$3,800
Head of Household	$6,650
Single	$4,550

Individuals who are at least age 65 or are blind at the end of the year are entitled to a larger standard deduction than given above. The tax form instruction booklet contains a worksheet for computing the standard deduction for such individuals. For 2001, the additional deductions are $900 for married filing jointly or separately and $1,100 for unmarried individuals.

Example

A married couple with 2 dependent children has income of $75,000 and files a joint return. They each make a deductible $2,000 contribution to an IRA, producing a $4,000 adjustment to income. Their itemized deductions total $8,800, which exceeds their standard deduction amount of $7,600. The tax computation proceeds as follows:

(1)	Total Income	$75,000
(2)	Less: Adjustments to Income	−4,000
(3)	Adjusted Gross Income	$71,000
(4)	Less: Itemized Deductions	−8,800
(5)	Less Personal Exemptions: 4 × $2,900 =	−11,600
(6)	Taxable Income	$50,600

The tax is then computed by looking up $50,600 in the appropriate tax table. Finally, the tax credits for child care, excess social security withheld, etc., are subtracted.

Note the two places where expenses are deducted — as *adjustments to income* and as *itemized deductions*. One advantage in deducting expenses as an adjustment to income is that you can still use the standard deduction if it proves beneficial. (Self-employed persons may deduct all their business expenses on Schedule C or Schedule C-EZ. Thus, they are eligible to use the standard deduction and still deduct all their business expenses.)

Another advantage occurs in connection with the floors on various itemized deductions — 7.5% of adjusted gross income for medical expenses, 10% for casualty losses, and 2% for miscellaneous deductions. Claiming an *adjustment to income* reduces your adjusted gross income, thereby lowering these floors. This in turn can raise the amounts you're entitled to deduct in the medical, casualty, or miscellaneous sections of Schedule A [see the *Medical Expenses, Casualty,* and *Miscellaneous Deductions* chapters].

A similar situation occurs in connection with self-employment activities. Income and expenses from such activities are listed on Schedule C or Schedule C-EZ with the net result transferred to the first page of Form 1040 to be used in computing adjusted gross income. Thus, claiming expenses on Schedule C or Schedule C-EZ results in a lowering of adjusted gross income. For the reasons discussed above, this is typically more advantageous than claiming the expenses as an itemized deduction on Schedule A. This is discussed more fully at the end of Section 1 of the *Miscellaneous Deductions* chapter.

Also, reducing adjusted gross income can reduce the phaseouts for itemized deductions and personal exemptions which are discussed in the following paragraphs.

3% Phaseout of Certain Itemized Deductions

This provision, applying to those with adjusted gross income exceeding $132,950 ($66,475 for married filing separately), gradually phases out the write-off for the following itemized deductions: *Taxes, Charity, Moving Expenses, Miscellaneous Deductions,* and *Interest* other than investment interest. (The remaining itemized deductions — Medical, Casualty, and Investment Interest — are not affected by this provision.) Specifically, the above deductions are reduced by 3% of adjusted gross income in excess of the *threshold amount* of $132,950 ($66,475 for marrieds filing separately). However, the reductions cannot exceed 80% of the total of affected deductions. (The deduction for miscellaneous expenses is first reduced by the 2% of AGI subtraction [see the *Miscellaneous* chapter] before the phaseout is calculated.)

Example

Jackson's joint tax return shows the following:

Adjusted gross income $160,750

Deductions for taxes, charity, moving,
    miscellaneous (after 2% of AGI subtraction),
    and non-investment interest...9,000

Jackson's total for the above deductions is reduced by 3% × ($160,750 − $132,950) = $834. Thus, the net total of the above itemized deductions equals $9,000 − $834 = $8,166.

Example

Same as in the previous example, except that the total for the listed deductions is $1,000 instead of $9,000. The 3% of adjusted gross income calculation yields $834 as in the previous example. However, in this example, the reduction cannot exceed 80% × $1,000 = $800. This produces a total write-off for the listed deductions of $1,000 – $800 = $200.

If Jackson's other itemized deductions (medical, casualty, and investment interest) total, say, $5,000, the total for all itemized deductions would equal $5,000 + $200 = $5,200. Because this is less than the standard deduction of $7,600 to which he is entitled, Jackson would simply use the standard deduction instead of itemizing his deductions.

On the other hand, if Jackson's other itemized deductions are greater than $7,400, his total of itemized deductions would exceed $7,400 + $200 = $7,600. In this case, itemizing deductions would yield a higher write-off than the standard deduction.

If your adjusted gross income exceeds $132,950 ($66,475 for marrieds filing separately), you can compute the itemized deduction total to which you're entitled by using the worksheet in the booklet accompanying your tax forms. This amount is then listed on line 28 of Schedule A and transferred to line 36 of Form 1040.

Phaseout of Personal Exemptions

This provision phases out the amount of personal exemptions for high income taxpayers whose adjusted gross income exceeds the *threshold amount.* Specifically, the write-off for personal exemptions ($2,900 per dependent) is reduced by 2% for each $2,500 for married persons filing jointly, single persons, and heads of household but $1,250 for married persons filing separately (or fraction thereof), by which adjusted gross income exceeds the threshold amount.

This *threshold amount* is equal to $199,450 on joint returns, $132,950 on single returns, $166,200 for heads of household, and $99,725 for marrieds filing separately.

Example

Stanley and Alice Barnes have $216,000 adjusted gross income on their 2001 joint tax return. They have 2 dependent children.

On their tax return showing 4 exemptions, their write-off for personal exemptions is $2,900 × 4 = $11,600. Their adjusted gross income exceeds the threshold amount by $216,000 – $199,450 = $16,550. The result of dividing this $16,550 excess by $2,500 is equal (rounding up) to 7, so the phaseout percentage is equal to 7 × 2% = 14%. This means their write-off for personal exemptions is equal to $11,600 – (14% × $11,600) = $9,744.

You can use the worksheet in the instruction booklet accompanying your tax forms to compute the personal exemption phaseout, if it applies to you.

2001 Tax Brackets

The Tax Reduction Act of 2001 lowered the tax rates for all individuals. Beginning in 2001, there is a new 10% tax bracket that will apply to the first $6,000 of taxable income for single individuals, $10,000 for heads of households, and $12,000 for married couples filing joint returns. Also for 2001, the tax rates have been reduced from 28% to 27.5%, 31% to 29.5%, 36% to 35.5%, and 30.6% to 29.1%. Beginning in 2002, tax brackets other than the 15% bracket will be reduced further.

Although the new 10% tax bracket is effective for 2001, Congress wanted to give the benefit of this new tax bracket to taxpayers immediately in the form of a credit based upon their taxable income reported on their 2000 returns. Therefore, in most cases, taxpayers will receive a refund of $300 for single filers [($6,000 × 15%) – ($6,000 x 10%)], $600 for joint filers [($12,000 × 15%) – ($12,000 × 10%)], and $500 for head of household filers [($10,000 × 15%) – ($10,000 × 10%)]. The checks will have been mailed to most taxpayers before the end of 2001.

Because the refund was based upon taxable income on 2000 returns, taxpayers must have filed for 2000 in order to get the refund. Also, no refund will be sent to any taxpayer who was a dependent on another's return. Therefore, most children will not receive a refund.

The IRS began mailing the refund checks in July. The mailings were to be completed by October for all taxpayers who filed their 2000 returns by April 15, 2001. In order to prevent confusions with the 2001 filing season, no refunds will be mailed after December 31, 2001.

Insofar as the refund checks represented a deduction in taxes to be computed on the 2001 return, the credit must be reconciled with the 2001 return filed in 2002. Therefore, if the refund was less than the maximum credit, you can claim the remaining credit on your 2001 return. If the refunded exceeded the credit to which you are entitled on your 2001 return, there is no requirement that you send any of the refund back to the IRS. A worksheet will be required to be attached to your 2001 return to calculate the benefit of the 10% tax bracket and whether the credit matched that benefit.

> **Example**
>
> *In 2000, a married couple filing jointly had taxable income of only $8,000 so that the credit and refund check was $400, i.e. ($8,000 × 15%) – ($8,000 × 10%). If in 2001 taxable income is over $15,000, the joint filers will receive an additional $200 credit on their 2001 return. The taxpayers are entitled to the benefit of the 10% tax bracket on their first $4,000 of income in 2001. They would have already received the benefit of the 10% tax bracket on $8,000 in the form of the $400 rebate check received in 2001.*

The tables below show the tax brackets for different categories of tax returns. (The tables are based on *taxable income*. As discussed earlier, *taxable income* is equal to *adjusted gross income,* less *personal exemptions* and *deductions*.) These brackets apply only to 2001 tax returns, as they are indexed for inflation each year.

2001 TAX BRACKETS

Joint Return		Head of Household	
Taxable Income	Tax Rate	Taxable Income	Tax Rate
$0–$45,200	15%	$0–$36,250	15%
$45,201–$109,250	27.5%	$36,251–$93,650	27.5%
$109,251–$166,500	30.5%	$93,651–$151,650	30.5%
$166,501–$297,350	35.5%	$151,651–$297,350	35.5%
Over $297,350	39.1%	Over $297,350	39.1%

Married Persons Filing Separate Returns		Single Person	
Taxable Income	Tax Rate	Taxable Income	Tax Rate
$0–$22,600	15%	$0–$27,050	15%
$22,601–$54,625	27.5%	$27,051–$65,550	27.5%
$54,626–$83,250	30.5%	$65,551–$136,750	30.5%
$83,251–$148,675	35.5%	$136,751–$297,350	35.5%
Over $148,675	39.1%	Over $297,350	39.1%

What if You Don't Have Enough Money to Pay Your Taxes?

If you do not have the money to pay your tax with your return, you can attach Form 9465, *Installment Agreement Request,* to the front of your return. If the amount of tax due is $25,000 or less and you offer a monthly installment amount that will result in paying off the tax, penalties, and interest within 5 years, the IRS will accept your offer. The IRS will notify you of its acceptance and you should include your first installment payment with the Form 9465 and the return.

The IRS will deduct a $43 processing fee from your first installment payment. The IRS will also charge a one-quarter percent per month late payment penalty on the outstanding liability plus interest of about 7% to 8%.

If you miss a monthly installment payment, the IRS can void the agreement and commence collection action.

Dependents

You get a $2,900 exemption for each dependent, including yourself, which you claim on your tax return. You need to list the social security numbers of all dependents if you wish to deduct them as dependents on your tax return. Be sure to apply for these numbers as soon as possible so you'll have them in time to file your tax return.

The instruction booklet that comes with your tax forms lists the precise rules for determining who qualifies as your dependent. Basically, you must furnish more than 50% of the support of a dependent and the dependent must have gross income of less than $2,900 for the year. However, the $2,900 limitation on earnings does not apply to a child of yours who is either (i) under age 19 at the close of the year or (ii) is under age 24 at the end of the year and was a full-time student during some part of each of 5 months during the year.

You count as support that you provide, the cost of food, medical expenses, health insurance, clothing, telephone, transportation, schooling, etc. You also count the fair rental value of housing that you provide for the child.

In determining whether a dependent has gross income over $2,900, tax-free scholarships or fellowships, social security payments, tax-free interest, disability payments, and other tax-free income are not counted. However, these items are taken into account when determining if an individual has provided more than 50% of another person's support. There is an exception for scholarship or fellowship payments received by a child of yours who is a full-time student in at least 5 months of the year. These payments are disregarded for purposes of the 50% requirement. This is the case even if part of the scholarship or fellowship payments is subject to tax.

In determining whether you have met the 50% support requirement, it is not necessary for the dependent to have used his earnings or savings for his own support. For example, suppose your child earns $3,000 during the year. You provide support (including food, lodging, clothing, use of auto, etc.) of $2,600. If the child saves $600 and uses the remaining $2,400 towards his own support, you will have met the 50% support requirement.

A student loan taken out by a child to use for his support counts as support provided by the child. In some cases, it may be better for the parent to borrow money in his own name and give it to his or her child, in order to preserve the dependency deduction.

A 1980 court case makes it easier to claim an exemption for an elderly parent. This case decided that Medicaid payments as well as benefits from Medicare and private insurance are not counted as support. This makes it easier for a relative to show that he furnished over half the parent's support. [Archer, 73 TC 963]

If a parent could be claimed as a dependent by his grown children except that no child individually provided over 50% of support, they can agree among themselves which one is entitled to the dependency exemption. The child claiming the exemption must have furnished more than 10% of support. The children each fill out Form 2120, which is attached to the tax return of the one claiming the exemption.

A non-relative must be a member of your household for the entire year in order to qualify as a dependent. However, a difficulty arises with friendly, but unmarried taxpayers. If the arrangement violates a state anti-cohabitation law, one partner cannot claim the other as a dependent. This requires some delicate decision-making if the matter is raised in court.

For example, a court ruled against a North Carolina unmarried couple. According to North Carolina law, *"If any man and woman, not being married to each other, shall lewdly and lasciviously associate, bed and cohabit together, they shall be guilty of a misdemeanor."* The court found their friendly cohabitation to violate this statute, thereby ruling out a dependency claim. [Ensminger, 45 AFTR 2nd 80-373]

But a Missouri judge came to a different conclusion. Missouri law forbids *"grossly lewd or lascivious behavior."* And an 1855 court case had declared *"What act can be more grossly lewd or lascivious than for a man and woman, not married to each other, to be publically living together and cohabitating with each other."* However, the judge in this case ruled that times had changed. He declared unmarried cohabitation not to be grossly lewd or lascivious conduct according to today's standards. [Shackelford, 80-1 USTC 9276]

Child Tax Credit

The Tax Reduction Act of 2001 increases the child tax credit to $1,000, phased in over 10 years. For 2001, the credit will be $600 for each such dependent. (This *child* tax credit is entirely separate from the *child care* tax credit discussed in the *Household Services & Child Care* chapter.)

However, the credit phases out once your adjusted gross income ("AGI") exceeds a certain amount. For joint returns, the amount of the credit is reduced by $50 for each $1,000 (or fraction thereof) by which your AGI exceeds $110,000. The phaseout starts at AGI of $75,000 if you file single or head of household.

Because of the AGI limitation on this and other tax breaks [see the *Attending School* and *Tax-Sheltered Plans* chapters], it may pay to shift income or deductions from one year to another. For example, if you file a joint return with one child and have AGI of $122,000, you will lose the entire credit, i.e. $50 of the $600 credit is lost for each $1,000 of AGI over $110,000.

However, if $10,000 of AGI can be shifted to another year, your credit is only reduced by $100. (See Section 8 for a discussion of ways to shift income or deductions from one year to another.)

For 2001, the full tax credit may be reduced because it triggers the alternative minimum tax. Although this tax was intended to apply to the wealthy, even moderate income taxpayers may be affected in this situation [see the final chapter in this *Tax & Financial Guide*].

Mailing in Your Tax Return

If you have a refund coming, mail your tax return in the envelope which is enclosed with the tax return package mailed to you by the IRS. This will speed up the processing of your tax return.

Don't mail more than one tax return in the same envelope, especially if a payment is enclosed. It is common for the IRS to credit a payment to the wrong tax return, resulting in confusion that you'll have to straighten out. Also, you may want to send your return by certified mail.

Direct Deposit of Refund

If you qualify for a refund, you can have it deposited directly into your checking or savings account. Just fill out your account number and the routing number of your bank or savings institution in the *Refund* section towards the bottom of page two of Form 1040. Direct deposit is considered advisable because it's generally safer and faster than waiting for a government check in the mail.

Arranging Your Forms in the Correct Order

When sending in your return, you should arrange the forms in the correct order. Form 1040 goes on top followed by related schedules, A, B, C, etc., in alphabetical order. After that, follow the numerical forms arranged in order of the *attachment sequence number* on the upper right-hand corner of each form. (Using the actual form number will generally not produce the correct sequence.) Finally, you attach any supplemental information you are providing at the end.

The IRS relies upon the tax return being arranged in the above manner. If it is not, an IRS clerk will take apart your return and restaple it in the correct order. (That way, the return can be properly processed by the keypunchers and other employees.) If the clerk mishandles your return while rearranging it, the IRS processing routine may bog down. At the least, this will cause you unwanted correspondence with the IRS in attempting to straighten out the confusion.

Amending Tax Returns of Previous Years

You are permitted to amend tax returns which you filed in previous years. However, you are limited to going back three years if you wish to obtain a refund of back taxes. For example, you may amend your 1998, 1999, and 2000 tax returns if you file on or before April 15, 2002. When you amend your federal tax return, you should amend your state tax return also.

There is a special form, 1040X, which you use for filing an amended return. You also include any applicable schedules or forms. For example, if you want to retroactively claim the child care tax credit, you would submit a Form 2441 along with your Form 1040X. Although not required, it's also a good idea to enclose a copy of the form or schedule as it was originally filed.

If you have overlooked a deduction or tax credit in a previous year, you must file an amended return to rectify the situation. You cannot claim the deduction or credit in a later year to compensate for its omission in the appropriate year.

You can file an amended return as soon as you like after sending in your original return. For example, suppose a week after filing your tax return you realized you overlooked a deduction you could have claimed. You can then file an amended return as soon as you realize the error. The IRS will send you a tax refund incorporating this change.

Similarly, if you discover some unreported income or a deduction you should not have claimed, you can file an amended return. In this case, you should pay the extra tax by using a Form 1040X Payment Voucher found at the end of the instructions for completing Form 1040. This should be done even if the original return showed that a refund was due. The extra tax shown on Form 1040X will be handled separately, not subtracted from the refund shown on the original tax return.

It should be cautioned that amended returns are somewhat more likely to be audited than original returns. If there are questionable items on your original return, you are better off waiting until just before the 3-year limit is about to expire before amending your tax return. Requesting a refund on an amended return does not extend the 3-year period for auditing your original return. Thus, the amended return will not trigger an audit of other items on your original return. The IRS will pay interest on the amount refunded to you.

Notifying the IRS If You Move

If you move, it's a good idea to notify the IRS of your new address, especially if you're waiting for a refund. (The IRS will generally go by the last address used on a tax return of yours.) The IRS has produced an optional form, Form 8822, which you can file with the IRS, specifying your old and new addresses.

Electronic Tax Filing

The IRS allows tax returns to be filed electronically, instead of being submitted on the usual paper forms. You must use the products and services of an organization that qualifies to be a mass user of the electronic filing system. Taxpayers can prepare and e-file their own returns, or use the services of a tax professional. Typically, the charge for e-file services is in the $15–$40 range per tax return.

A new feature in the e-file program for 2001 available to many taxpayers is the Self-Select PIN. It allows taxpayers to electronically sign their e-filed return by selecting a five-digit Personal Identification Number.

The benefit to the IRS is that electronically-filed returns are cheaper to process. This is why they offer and promote this arrangement.

The benefit to the taxpayer is that he or she can get his refund much sooner than filing by mail.

Getting Copies of Tax Returns

If you need a copy of an old tax return, including attachments, you can get it from the IRS. (The IRS keeps tax returns for at least 6 years.) Send in Form 4506 along with a check for $23 to the IRS Service Center where you filed your return. The IRS will send you a copy of the return, including attachments such as schedules and Forms W-2. Miscellaneous work papers, lists, or other extraneous materials will not be copied unless specifically identified and requested. Allow 30 to 60 days for delivery. You can also get a copy, at no charge, of a Form W-2 by filing Form 4506 or other written request with your IRS Service Center. Requests for Forms W-2 take 6 to 8 weeks to process.

You can get free of charge just an information printout of the most important basic items on your tax return, including adjusted gross income and the tax due. (This information is generally kept by the IRS for more than 6 years.) This printout is obtained by calling, faxing, or writing your local IRS office. You can also request that information be sent to a third party. This information can be handy for verifying financial information to a potential lender.

You can also obtain from the IRS a copy of your individual *Master File Transcript* for a given tax year. This transcript will include the date on which the IRS received your tax form, the dates and amounts of any payments you made, and any assessments the IRS made against you. This transcript can be of assistance if you need to straighten out mixups with the IRS. You can obtain your transcript free of charge by writing or calling your local IRS district office. If you write, you should include your Social Security Number and the tax years you want. It's possible that the transcript you receive may be in a form too difficult for you to interpret. If so, you will need to obtain help at your local IRS office in interpreting the transcript correctly.

If you need a current last-minute blank tax form in order to complete your tax return, you can download it from the IRS website at www.irs.gov, or try a local library. Many libraries now make available a portfolio of tax forms which can be photocopied and used in filing your tax return.

IRS Taxpayer Advocate

The IRS has a policy of having at least one ombudsman, now called a *Taxpayer Advocate,* in many IRS offices and service centers. The Taxpayer Advocate is not there to give tax advice but rather to cut through red tape in case you're having trouble getting your refund check or straightening out some other mixup. Check the IRS website (www.irs.gov) for locations and telephone numbers.

If you're expecting a refund, give the IRS ten weeks before making an inquiry. After that time, phone your local IRS office. They can run a computer check to determine what happened and tell you when your refund check will be mailed. If you can't get things straightened out within a reasonable period of time, ask to speak to the Taxpayer Advocate.

IRS Telephone Error Rate

The IRS has a telephone number to "assist" taxpayers with tax questions. However, the IRS has acknowledged in the past an error rate of about 25% by those answering the telephone lines. (For complicated questions, the error rate would be even higher.) Although not a part of the public record, you can be almost sure that the majority of mistakes err on the side of causing more tax to be due rather than less. Also, the IRS answered only some of the calls it received, while the balance either reached busy signals or hung up after being placed on hold.

The IRS has been the subject of many studies in recent years and much criticism. Beginning with the IRS Restructuring Act of 1998, the IRS has been going through a process of modernization with one of the main goals being better service to taxpayers.

It should be pointed out that telephone advice from the IRS is considered to be unofficial. You cannot use it as justification for how you fill out your tax return.

Roundoff

The IRS allows you to round off all figures to the nearest dollar. Note that the detailed tax tables are broken down into bracket intervals of $50, with the same tax applying to everyone in the same bracket. Thus, a difference of 1 cent in income or deductions could, in the worst possible case, throw someone into a higher bracket and increase taxes by as much as $16. If your initial tax computation puts you just over the edge into a new bracket, recheck your rounding.

A similar situation occurs with regard to the phaseout rule for personal exemptions. As discussed earlier in this chapter, the write-off for personal exemptions on a joint return is decreased by 2% for every $2,500 (or fraction thereof) of adjusted gross income in excess of $199,450. The key phrase here is *fraction thereof.*

For example, on a joint return showing 4 exemptions (worth 4 × $2,900 = $11,600) and adjusted gross income of $204,450, the phaseout would be 2 × 2% × $11,600 = $464. But on a return with adjusted gross income one dollar larger, $204,451, the phaseout would be 3 × 2% × $11,600 = $696. This difference of $696 − $464 = $232 in adjusted gross income translates into a tax savings of about $82. In this case, if a roundoff decision was responsible for the extra dollar of adjusted gross income, a change could push the income back into the lower phaseout category and save over $82 in taxes.

The IRS has stated that it prefers taxpayers to round off on their tax returns. For one thing, it helps reduce arithmetic errors. For another, it is easier for the IRS when it keypunches data from tax returns into its computers.

When you round off to whole dollars, you must round all amounts. To round, drop amounts under 50 cents and increase amounts from 50 cents to 99 cents to the next dollar. For example, $1.39 becomes $1 and $2.50 becomes $3.

Extension of Time to File

You can get an automatic extension of 4 months to file your return. To receive this extension, you file Form 4868 with the IRS by April 15. You make an estimate on Form 4868 of the amount of tax that will be due. Then by August 15, file your tax return accompanied by a copy of your Form 4868. Form 4868, along with any payment due, can be filed through the mail, or via the phone or Internet. Payments can be made on a credit card or by authorizing an automatic withdrawal from your bank account. If the 15th falls on a Saturday or Sunday, the time for filing is extended to Monday.

You are expected to enclose payment with Form 4868 of the amount of tax you estimate you owe. However, your extension request will automatically be accepted even if partial or no payment is made. If it turns out you have underpaid by more than 10%, you will be assessed a penalty of one-half of one percent per month plus interest at the going rate. If your total tax payments — withholding, estimated tax, plus payment with Form 4868 — are at least 90% of the tax liability shown on Form 1040, you will only be assessed an interest charge with no extra penalty fee.

However, the estimate you make on Form 4868 must be based on the information you have at your disposal when the estimate is made. Otherwise, the extension request can be ruled invalid. This is illustrated by 2 court cases. In the first case, an individual simply listed $0 on Form 4868 as the estimated amount of tax due, as compared with the true tax liability of $24,433 as computed later on Form 1040. The mere fact she listed $0 as her estimate of tax due was not automatically fatal. Rather, she could not present any reasoning to show that the estimate was a bona fide one based on the information she had at the time. For this reason, the extension request was ruled invalid. [Calhoun, TC Memo 1992-189] In the second case, the amount estimated was paid with the extension request, but the Court objected to the estimate. It did not object just because the estimate turned out to be way off. Rather, it ruled that the taxpayer did not utilize data (such as Forms 1099) readily available to him to generate a properly-made estimate. This meant the extension request was invalid. [Crocker, 92 TC No. 899]

If you file Form 4868 but find you need more than the extra 4 months to file your tax return, you can file for an additional 2 months by using Form 2688. On this form, you give your reasons why you need more time. The IRS will consider the merits of your request and advise you accordingly.

If you file your tax return late without the proper extension, you will be charged interest plus a penalty on the amount of tax due. However, the penalty (but not the interest) can be waived by the IRS if a valid excuse is provided. Such a valid excuse might be the death or illness of yourself or a family member, destruction of records in a fire, failure to receive the required forms after making a timely request from the IRS, etc.

Reporting Interest and Dividends on Your Tax Return

You report interest and dividend payments you receive on Schedule B. The IRS computer will compare the amounts you report with its own records. A mismatch may cause the IRS to seek an additional tax assessment or even conduct an audit of your tax return.

To prevent this from happening, you should report interest and dividend payments separately according to the information slips you receive from the paying institutions; otherwise, the IRS computer will get confused. For example, separate accounts with the same bank should be listed separately. Dividends on stocks held in street name with a broker and reported to the IRS as a total sum received from the broker should be reported that way on your tax return; they should not be reported under the issuing corporations' names unless they were reported to the IRS that way. Dividends on money market funds should be reported as dividends rather than interest. (However, income from money market accounts in a bank or savings & loan is reported as interest.) And deductible fees (not including non-deductible check-writing fees) on interest-paying accounts with a bank should be claimed as a miscellaneous deduction, not subtracted from the amount of interest you report on Schedule B.

Dividends paid on policies issued by mutual insurance companies belong to a separate category. Usually, they just constitute an adjustment of premium overpayment rather than a reflection of investment earnings. As such, they are nontaxable. If you do not receive a Form 1099 from the company reporting taxable dividend payments, this indicates that the payments do not have to be reported on your tax return. You should check with your insurance agent if in doubt.

Frequently, people receive interest or dividends as a nominee; it is for someone else, for example a child, but in your name. This must be reported on your return for matching purposes even if the money was distributed toand reported by others. Show a subtotal of the interest of dividends, from which you subtract the "Nominee Distribution" to arrive at a total carried to page one of your 1040.

Similar reporting is required for tax-exempt interest, an original issue discount (OID), amortizable bond premium, and accrued interest received by the seller of bonds between interest payment dates. Simply change the description of the amount being subtracted to arrive at a total, for example "OID Adjustment."

How Married Couples Should List Their Names on a Joint Tax Return

On joint tax returns, the IRS now provides 2 separate full name lines, one for each spouse. This implicitly recognizes the fact that many wives now keep their maiden names instead of using their husbands'. It doesn't matter which name comes first as long as the first name matches the first social security number. However, once a return is filed using separate names, the same order of names should generally be used on subsequent returns. Switching the order could cause the IRS computer to become confused and result in delinquent notices being sent.

Married women who use their maiden names, especially those with self employment income, are advised to check with the Social Security Administration that their earnings have been properly credited [see Section 4 of the *Retirement* chapter for information on how this is done]. In many cases, due to a mixup, the IRS used their husbands' last names when reporting earnings to the Social Security Administration, causing errors in properly crediting these earnings. Presumably, with the extra line now on tax returns for the listing of both spouses' names separately, this type of error has been eliminated. Also, the name on the tax return must match the name reported to Social Security or your will receive a notice from the IRS.

The Marriage Penalty

Sometimes married couples pay more tax than they would if they were able to file two single-person returns, often called the marriage penalty or the marriage tax. (Married couples cannot file single returns — only joint returns or married-filing-separately returns.) This extra amount of tax is the result of the couple's taxable income being pushed into a higher marginal tax bracket than would apply if the couple were not married. It is also the result of phaseout provisions discussed earlier.

The phaseout threshold for itemized deductions is $132,950 — the same on single returns as on joint returns. And the threshold for the personal exemption phaseout on joint returns is not twice the $132,950 threshold on single returns, but rather $199,450 instead. As illustrated in the next example, this can produce a marriage penalty.

The 35.5% and 39.1% brackets can lead to an even larger marriage penalty for high-income taxpayers. The 35.5% bracket kicks in when income reaches $136,751 on a single return, but only $166,501 on a joint return. And surprisingly, the 39.1% bracket kicks in at the same $297,350 level both on single returns and on joint returns.

Example

Ronald and Mary each have adjusted gross income of $120,000 and itemized deductions of $18,000. They are married with no dependents. Their taxes on a joint return are calculated below, along with what their taxes would have been if they were single.

	Single Person Return		Joint Return	
Adjusted Gross Income		$120,000		$240,000
Itemized Deductions	18,000		36,000	
Phaseout	−0		−3,212	
	18,000	−18,000	32,788	−32,788
Personal Exemptions	2,900		5,800	
Phaseout	−0		−1,856	
	2,900		3,944	
		−2,900		−3,944
Taxable Income		$99,100		$203,268
Tax		$24,878		$54,908

On a joint return, Ronald and Mary show a tax due of $54,908 Had they been single, they could have filed 2 single returns with a combined tax of $24,878 + $24,878 = $49,756. The difference, $54,908 – $49,756 = $5,152, is their marriage tax. This is the extra amount of tax they must pay just because they're married and can't file single person tax returns.

In the above example, part of the marriage penalty was caused by the 35.5% tax bracket that applied on the joint return but not on the single returns. The marriage penalty due to this effect was 5% × ($203,268 – $166,500) = $1,838. The remaining $5,152 – $1,838 = $3,314 was due to the phaseout rules, as discussed above.

When the head-of-household rates apply, the marriage tax can be sharply higher, especially for high-income individuals. For example, a married couple each earning $150,000 could have a marriage tax of $10,000 – $20,000. This is the extra tax they pay by filing a joint return as opposed to being unmarried qualifying for head-of-household rate.

Surprisingly, it is not just higher-income individuals who can get hit by a significant marriage penalty. A low-income couple can pay a marriage penalty of as much as $4,000 because of the way the earned income tax credit works.

Earned Income Credit for Low-Income Individuals

You may know students or other low-income individuals who are supporting a child. They might qualify for the *earned income credit* which in some cases yields a negative income tax. That is, if subtracting the earned-income credit from their tax produces a negative result, the difference is actually paid out to them by the government.

The earned income credit is computed on Schedule EIC. Persons who expect to be eligible for the credit can arrange to have their employers make advance payments to them of the credit. This can amount to a negative withholding rate to go along with the negative income tax.

An individual cannot claim the earned income credit if his *disqualified income* exceeds $2,450. *Disqualified income* consists of interest (both taxable and tax-free), dividends, capital gain net income, net positive rent and royalty income, and net positive passive income that is not self-employment income.

Individuals with One or More Qualifying Children

The highest credit applies to individuals who share the same principal place of abode with qualifying children for more than one-half of the year. Certain temporary absences due to education or illness are disregarded. To qualify, the child must be a son or daughter (or a descendent of either), stepson, stepdaughter, adopted child, or eligible foster child. In addition, the child must be either (1) age 18 or under, (2) a full-time student who is under age 24 at the end of the year, or (3) totally disabled.

If 2 or more persons are eligible to claim the credit for the same child, only the one with the higher adjusted gross income is eligible for the credit. The credit is claimed on the tax return of the parent or other person providing a home for the child — it cannot be claimed on a tax return of the child. Married persons must file a joint return in order to claim the credit.

When there is 1 qualifying child, the credit for 2001 is equal to 34% of earned income up to a maximum of $7,140 of income. If earned income is over $13,090, the credit is $2,428 minus 15.98% of the excess of adjusted gross income or earned income (whichever is larger) over $13,090. The credit is completely eliminated for those with income over $28,281.

When there are 2 or more qualifying children, the credit for 2001 is equal to 40% of earned income up to a maximum of $10,020 of income. If earned income exceeds $13,090, the credit is $4,008 minus 21.06% of the excess of adjusted gross income or earned income (whichever is larger) over $13,090. The credit for those with 2 qualifying children is completely eliminated when income exceeds $32,121.

Individuals with No Qualifying Children

An individual who earned less than $10,710 during 2001 and has no dependent children can claim an earned income tax credit of up to $364, provided that (1) he (or his spouse) is between ages 25 and 64 at year-end, (2) resides in the U.S. for more than half the year, and (3) cannot be claimed as a dependent on someone else's tax return.

For individuals with no qualifying children, the credit for 2001 is equal to 7.65% of earned income up to a maximum of $4,760 of income. If earned income exceeds $5,950, the credit is $364 minus 7.65% of the excess of modified adjusted gross income or earned income (whichever is larger) over $5,950. The credit for those with no qualifying children is completely eliminated when income exceeds $10,710.

Graduate students, in particular, should be alert to this tax credit. Note that the credit can produce a refund to the individual even if no tax was withheld from his salary. A tax return must be filed in order to get this benefit. Many students and other low-income workers lose out on a refund because they are unaware that the earned-income credit exists.

Adoption Tax Credit

The adoption tax credit applies to adoption expenses such as attorney's fees, court costs, adoption fees, and travel expenses including food and lodging. The person being adopted must be under the age of 18 at the time of adoption or be physically or mentally incapable of caring for himself.

For 2001, there is an income limitation that applies to the adoption tax credit. The full credit applies if the taxpayer's adjusted gross income (AGI) is less than $75,000. When AGI exceeds $115,000, the credit is completely eliminated. When AGI is between these limits, a portion of the credit is available related to the amount AGI exceeds $75,000.

On 2001 tax returns, the maximum credit that can be claimed per child is $5,000. This limit was increased to $6,000 for a child with special needs, except in the case of foreign adoptions. The Tax Reduction Act of 2001 increases the adoption credit from $5,000 ($6,000 for special needs children) to $10,000 for all children beginning on 2002 tax returns. The credit is phased-out for taxpayers with incomes over $75,000. Under the Act, the credit is totally phased-out when income exceeds $150,000. The exclusion for employer-provided assistance is increased from $5,000 to $10,000.

The credit applies to adoption attempts, even if the adoption is not consummated. However, foreign adoptions must be consummated before any credit can be claimed.

Discarding the apparently outdated notion of tax simplification, Congress made some complex rules as to when the tax credit is claimed. You do not claim the credit for expenses incurred in the current year until the next year, unless the adoption becomes final in the current year.

Example

In an effort to adopt a child, a couple pays adoption expenses of $4,000 in 2000 and $2,000 in 2001. The adoption becomes final in 2001. For 2001, the couple has AGI of less than $75,000, so the income limitation does not apply. The couple may not claim any adoption expenses as a credit in 2000 because of the one-year delay rule described in the preceding paragraph. However, the 2001 expenses qualify for the credit in the same year because 2001 was the year when the adoption was finalized. Thus, the couple has a total of $6,000 in eligible expenses for 2001. Because there is a $5,000 total limit per child, the adoption credit is $5,000, all claimed on their 2001 tax return. (For a special needs child, the credit would be the full $6,000.)

IRS Locator Service

Here's a little-known service the IRS provides. If an individual needs to be notified of a death, serious illness, inheritance, etc., the IRS can search its database. If the individual is located, the IRS will not notify you directly of his or her whereabouts. Rather, the IRS will forward a letter from you in an IRS envelope. (Your letter will be screened by the IRS to verify that the contents are consistent with the approved purposes.) The individual then has the option of responding to your letter, or not.

To take advantage of this service, write for information to the *Disclosure Officer* at either your local IRS District Office or at the IRS Service Center where you file your tax return. There is no charge for this service.

Section 2:
Basic Rules for Deducting
Business Expenses

You can claim a deduction for expenses which you incur in connection with your profession. These fall under the category of **business expenses.** The basic rule is that such expenses, in order to be deductible, must be both **ordinary and necessary** expenses directly connected with or related to your profession.

On the other hand, not all business expenditures are deductible even though they may be ordinary and necessary. For example, commuting costs to and from work are in most cases not deductible.

The word **"ordinary"** refers to an expense connected with a common and accepted practice in your profession. Thus, attending a professional convention would be an ordinary expense. However, buying a new suit for your boss would probably not be considered an ordinary expense because it is not the accepted practice to do so.

The word **"necessary"** is not used here in its usual meaning of "indispensable." The best definition of a "necessary expense" is one that is **appropriate and helpful** in developing or maintaining your profession.

Fortunately, you do not generally have to interpret principles like the ordinary and necessary rule. There are specific rules and examples that apply to most of the particular business deductions you might have. These are described in the following chapters.

There is one other general restriction on deducting business expenses. You are not allowed to deduct certain expenses if they are considered to be lavish or extravagant. However, it is unlikely you would have to worry about this restriction.

Reimbursable Expenses Are Non-Deductible

If you incur expenses in connection with your employment for which you could have received a reimbursement, these expenses are non-deductible. It makes no difference that you did not apply for the reimbursement and paid the expenses out of your own pocket. For example, a teacher in one court case tried to deduct expenses associated with field trips she took with her students. However, the court ruled that because she could have been reimbursed by her employer, her expenses were non-deductible. [Patterson, TC Memo 1977-107]

Special Form for Deducting Business Expenses

You use either Form 2106 or the simpler Form 2106-EZ for deducting employee business expenses [see the *Miscellaneous Deductions* chapter]. You can obtain these forms by calling your local IRS office or they can be downloaded from the IRS website at www.irs.gov. Self-employed persons deduct their business expenses on either Schedule C or Schedule C-EZ.

SECTION 3:
COMMON MISTAKES

Here's a list of the more common mistakes that are made on tax returns.

1. Failure to Sign Tax Return

Don't forget that two signatures are needed on a joint tax return.

2. Failure to Use Peel-Off Label

The IRS has issued a special request to all taxpayers to use the pre-addressed label that comes with the tax return package sent to you in the mail. This will not only save the government a little money, but it will speed up the processing of your return.

Perhaps even more important are key-punching errors that might occur. Using the pre-addressed label allows the IRS keypuncher to make 13 keystrokes instead of 85, substantially reducing the chance of error. Anyone who has tried to correct a credit card computer mistake will shudder to think of the mess that could ensue if the IRS misplaces your return due to a keypunching error. (The IRS states emphatically that the label contains no special audit codes and its use will not affect your odds of being audited.)

3. Use of Incorrect Tax Table

Double-check to make sure you are using the correct tax table. A common error is the failure of qualified single individuals who maintain a household for a child or dependent to use the special head-of-household table. The head-of-household rate is lower than the single rate, but higher than the rate for joint returns. Note that your household needs to be the child's or dependent's *principal place of abode* only for more than half the year. Don't overlook the fact that the head-of-household rate can apply if a parent qualifies as your dependent, even if the parent does not live with you. Consult the instruction booklet accompanying your tax forms for the basic rules for using the head-of-household rate.

4. Failure to Write Information on Check

You should write your social security number on your check and note what the check is for, e.g., 2001 Form 1040. That way, if your check is separated from your tax return, it will still be possible for the IRS to credit it to the appropriate account.

Also, be sure to write on all checks you send to the IRS, your name, Social Security Number, tax period, and form number. That way if the check gets separated from your tax return in the processing operation, the IRS will be able to handle it without sending you an unwanted notice. It is not uncommon for the IRS to make such errors.

5. Making Check Out to IRS

Make your check out to the Department of the Treasury, not to the IRS. Your check will still be processed if the payee is the Internal Revenue Service or IRS.

6. Not Deducting Medical and Charity Travel

You can deduct travel to doctors, dentists, pharmacies, etc., as well as travel connected with charitable activities. A deduction of 14 cents per mile is allowed for autos used for charitable travel and 12 cents per mile (plus parking fees and tolls) for medical-related auto travel.

7. Failure to Deduct Late Payment Charges

You might be assessed an extra charge for making a mortgage payment late. In most cases, this charge is actually a form of interest and can be deducted as such [see Section 1 of the *Homeowners* chapter]. A survey undertaken by a New York consumer affairs office underlines the fact that this deduction is often overlooked. The office asked eleven tax preparers to fill out a tax return based on financial data which they worked up for a fictitious couple. The data submitted to the tax preparers included a charge for the late payment of a mortgage. The result was unanimous. All eleven of the tax preparers failed to claim the late charge as a tax deduction.

8. Leaving Off Social Security Number of Spouse or Dependent

If you file a joint return, you must include the social security number of yourself and your spouse. Many taxpayers believe that they do not have to include their spouse's social security number if their spouse does not earn any income. This is not the case. Make sure you include the social security number for each dependent listed. Also be sure to check the box for each dependent who is also a qualifying child for the child tax credit.

9. Filing a Joint State Tax Return

In many states, filing a joint return can be a mistake because the same rate schedule is used for joint returns as for single returns. For a married couple each having income, the only effect of filing a joint return is to shift income from a lower bracket to a higher bracket and increase the tax that is due. To illustrate, consider the following example:

Example

A and B, a married couple, have taxable incomes of $30,000 and $20,000, respectively. On a joint return, their taxable income would be $50,000. They live in a state with the following tax rates which are used both for separate returns and for joint returns.

on first $2000	2%
on next $4000	3%
on next $4000	4%
on next $4000	5%
on next $4000	6%
on next $4000	7%
on next $4000	8%
on next $4000	9%
on next $4000	10%
on next $4000	11%
on next $4000	12%
on next $4000	13%
on next $4000	14%
remainder	15%

If A and B file a joint return, their state tax is $4,120. The upper $20,000 of their joint taxable income is taxed at rates from 10% to 14%.

However, if they file separate returns, the outcome is quite different. The $20,000, which was taxed at the higher brackets in the joint return, is shifted to a separate person and is taxed at the lower range brackets of 2% to 7%. A pays the tax of $1,720 on $30,000 and B pays tax of $900 on $20,000. The total $2,620 is a net savings of $1,500 over the tax on a joint return.

If you and your spouse both have incomes, be sure to check if the joint return rate is the same as the separate return rate in your state. If so, you could save taxes by **not** filing a joint return.

Note: In some states, you and your spouse can file separate state tax returns only if you file separate federal tax returns. In this case, you would have to take into account both the state and federal income tax consequences of filing separate returns [see Section 6].

10. Check your math, especially for the child tax credit, earned income credit, taxable social security benefits, total income, itemized deductions or standard deduction, deduction for exemptions, taxable income, total tax, federal income tax withheld, and refund or amount you owe.

11. Be sure to use the correct method to figure your tax. Depending on your income amount and type, you may use the Tax Table, the Tax Rate Schedules, or Schedule D.

12. If you received capital gain distributions but were not required to file Schedule D, make sure you check the box on line 13.

13. Forms W-2 should be attached to the returns along with all other required forms and schedules.

SECTION 4:
CLAIMING THE STANDARD DEDUCTION

As explained in Section 1, the standard deduction is a fixed amount depending only upon the type of tax return being filed. The standard deduction is now equal to $7,600 for joint returns, $4,550 for single returns, $6,650 for heads of household, and $3,800 for returns of married individuals filing separately. (There is an exception, discussed in the next section, for those who can be claimed as a dependent on the tax return of a parent or other individual.) The standard deduction is increased by $900 for married persons over age 64 or blind ($1,800 if both) and by $1,100 for single persons over age 64 or blind.

Note that many of the chapters in this book contain information that still applies even if you claim the standard deduction.

First of all, this chapter contains general information which applies to all taxpayers, whether they use the standard deduction or itemize their deductions. Also of general applicability are the *Divorce, Withholding, Retirement, Foreign Income, Audit, Income-Shifting, Estate Tax,* and *Investing* chapters.

Second, several items can be claimed as an *adjustment to income* or *tax credit* even if the standard deduction is used. This includes household services and child care, alimony, and contributions to IRAs and self-employed plans [see the *Household Services & Child Care, Divorce & Separation,* and *Tax-Sheltered Plans* chapters].

Third, many items ordinarily claimed as an itemized deduction can instead be claimed as a business expense on Schedule C or Schedule C-EZ by those who have some self-employment income [see the *Miscellaneous Deductions* and *Outside Business Activities* chapters]. This would include books, supplies, equipment, home office, auto expenses, entertainment expenses, etc.

Finally, those claiming the standard deduction should also note all the other techniques for reducing tax besides just deducting expenses. For example, they may still be able to participate in a tax-sheltered annuity, deferred compensation, IRA, or self-employed plan. Or, they may be able to claim tax exemption for a grant, make tax-favored investments, shift income to a lower-bracket child, etc. [see the *Tax-Free Grants, Investing,* and *Income-Shifting* chapters].

Section 5:
Tax Returns of Dependent Children

You may have a dependent child with income of his own. If so, he may have to file his own tax return. The following special rules apply in this situation.

First, a child (or other individual) who is eligible to be claimed as a dependent on the tax return of a parent or other person (whether or not actually claimed) cannot use the personal exemption of $2,900 on his or her own tax return.

Second, a dependent child's income is divided into 2 categories for tax purposes — *earned income* and *unearned income*. *Earned income* is income produced by the child's own labor such as a summer or after-school job. The remainder is *unearned income*, including such items as interest, dividends, etc. Gifts and inheritances are in neither category because they are not subject to income tax. Scholarships and fellowships, to the extent subject to tax, are considered to be earned income.

Your dependent child is required to file a tax return if he or she has total income exceeding $750 which includes any amount of unearned income. For example, a child with $10 income from a savings account plus $750 earned income would need to file a tax return. On the other hand, if a child has no unearned income at all, he need not file a tax return unless his or her total income exceeds the standard deduction of $4,550. (However, if taxes were withheld from salary, a tax return should be filed to get this money refunded.)

If your child is too young to fill out his or her own tax return, you as parent (or guardian) are responsible for his or her tax return. The IRS has specified the following format for signing the tax return for say, a child named Jane Doe:

Jane Doe by (your signature), *Parent for minor child*

Be sure to follow the above format. If, for example, you write down "Jane Doe (minor)" instead of just "Jane Doe," you could get a letter from the IRS asking who Jane Minor is. The IRS has actually been making this type of mistake, according to an article in *The Wall Street Journal*.

A dependent child with only *earned income* computes tax in the usual way. The standard deduction for a single taxpayer is $4,550. Because a dependent child cannot claim a personal exemption on his or her own tax return, amounts earned over $4,550 will be subject to tax.

Unearned income is treated differently. At most, $750 of the standard deduction can be used to offset unearned income. Thus, tax will be due whenever a dependent child's unearned income exceeds $750.

If a dependent child has both earned and unearned income, the following basic rule is applied:

The standard deduction on the 2001 tax return of a single individual who can be claimed as a dependent by another taxpayer is $4,550 except that it cannot exceed $750 or $250 plus the individual's earned income, whichever is greater. (Another way to view this is that the standard deduction equals $250 plus earned income, except that it cannot be less than $750 nor more than $4,550.) If an individual's total income is less than or equal to $750, he or she owes no tax and is not required to file a tax return.

To illustrate, the following table shows the standard deduction and taxable income (assuming no personal exemptions) of a dependent child in various situations:

Earned Income	Unearned Income	Dependent's Standard Deduction	Taxable Income
$ 300	$ 700	$ 750	$ 250
800	300	1,050	50
2,400	1,400	2,650	1,150
5,000	200	4,550	650
0	400	750	0
0	1,000	750	250

Example 1

A dependent child has $800 earned income and $1,500 unearned income during 2001 — a total of $2,300. According to the rules discussed above, his standard deduction is equal to $1,050. Thus, his taxable income is $2,300 – $1,050 = $1,250. This is taxed at the child's 15% tax bracket — 15% × $1,250 = $188.

The above discussion assumes that the dependent child does not have itemized deductions exceeding $750. If in fact his itemized deductions do exceed $750, the tax forms will lead through a different computation procedure, taking these deductions into account.

Children Under Age 14 with Unearned Income Exceeding $1,500

A special rule applies to a child who has not reached age 14 by the last day of the year and has unearned income exceeding $1,500. Namely, this excess is not taxed at the child's tax bracket, but rather at the parent's tax bracket, if higher. This is commonly referred to as the *Kiddie Tax*. (If the parents are married filing separate returns, the tax bracket of the spouse with the higher taxable income is used. In the case of unmarried parents, it is the tax bracket applying on the return filed by the custodial parent that counts. This is the case even if the custodial spouse files a joint return with a new spouse who is not a parent of the child.)

This proviso was enacted into law to curb the practice of transferring assets to a young child in order that income earned on these assets be taxed at the child's lower rate rather than at the parent's rate. However, it applies to all unearned income of the child, whether or not due to assets given to the child by his parents.

Form 8615 is used for a dependent child under age 14 who has unearned income in excess of $1,500. The tax on this excess amount is computed as though it had been earned by the parent on top of the income reported on the parent's tax return. The child's remaining income (i.e. earned income plus the first $1,500 of unearned income) is taxed at the child's tax rate.

Because the first $750 of income is offset by the standard deduction, the following would be the tax treatment of a dependent child under age 14 with only unearned income:

Unearned Income	Tax Treatment
$0-$750	Exempt from Tax
$751-$1,500	Taxed at child's rate
Over $1,500	Taxed at parent's rate if higher than child's rate

Form 8615 is attached to the *child's* personal tax return, not the parent's. Form 8615 makes a *what if* calculation. It determines how much extra tax the parent would have to pay if the child's unearned income over $1,500 had been earned by the parent. However, after this computation is made, it is the child who actually owes the taxes, not the parent. If there is more than one child with unearned income over $1,500, Form 8615 calculates tax as if all the excess income were earned by the parent and it distributes the tax among the personal returns of the children.

Example 2

A child has $800 in earned income and $1,700 in unearned income. His parents' highest tax bracket is 27.5%.

The excess of unearned income over $1,500, ($1,700 – $1,500 = $200), is taxed at the parents' tax rate — $200 × 27.5% = $55. The remainder, $800 of earned income and $1,500 of unearned income, is subject to tax of $188 as shown in the preceding example. Thus, the child's total tax would be $55 + $188 = $243.

The Form 8615 attached to the child's tax return requires the taxable income figure shown on the parent's tax return to be entered on line 6 of that form. If this figure is not available when the child's tax return is due, the IRS says you can use the figure shown on the previous year's tax return or other reasonable estimate of the parent's taxable income. You should enter *"Estimated"* on line 6 of Form 8615 next to the estimated amount. If you later determine that your estimate was so off the mark that the wrong tax bracket was used, an amended return should be filed for the child correcting the amount of tax due [see Section 1].

When income on the child's return is taxed at a parent's tax rate using Form 8615, the parent's tax return is not affected. For example, the 7.5% and 2% floors on medical and miscellaneous deductions are not changed.

Unearned income of children who are age 14 or older as of the last day of the year is not taxed at the parent's tax bracket even if it exceeds $1,500. Instead, it is taxed along with earned income at the child's tax bracket in the usual way as discussed earlier.

Child's Payment of Own Medical Expenses Can Save Taxes

If your child incurs substantial medical expenses not covered by insurance, it may save taxes for him or her to pay the cost out of his or her funds. For example, suppose your child has $2,000 of income, all unearned, and that he or she runs up an orthodontia bill of $1,000. Let's say that you cannot deduct this on your own tax return because 7.5% of your adjusted gross income exceeds your family's total medical bills [see the *Medical Expenses* chapter].

However, if your child pays the $1,000 bill out of his own funds, the story is different. He or she would be entitled to a medical deduction of $1,000 − (7.5% × $2,000) = $850. Compared with the standard deduction of $750 applying to the child, this reduces taxable income by an extra $100, resulting in a lower tax bill. (You aren't supposed to directly provide the $1,000 to the child for him or her to turn over to the orthodontist.)

Form 8814 Eliminates Filing a Child's Tax Return

Filing a tax return for a child is a nuisance. This is especially true if he or she is under age 14 and has unearned income exceeding $1,500, requiring the inclusion of Form 8615, along with the child's Form 1040 and Schedule B.

However, there is a simplified procedure which allows you to include your child's unearned income on your own personal tax return, instead of filling out a separate return for your child. This is done by listing your child's income on Form 8814, which you attach to your own tax return. (However, as discussed below, this can cost you extra taxes.)

Not everyone can use this simplified procedure. In order to qualify to report your child's income on Form 8814 attached to your tax return, the following conditions must be satisfied:

(1) The child's income is comprised entirely of interest, dividends, and capital gain distributions;

(2) The child's income is between $750 and $7,500;

(3) No estimated tax payments have been made in the child's name and social security number;

(4) No overpayment from the previous year's return was applied to the current year; and

(5) No backup withholding has been made for the child.

You fill out a separate Form 8814 for each child whose income you are including on your own tax return.

Note the strictness of Requirement (1). If your child has even one dollar of earned income, this requirement is not satisfied. Also note that the $750 figure in Requirement (2) actually has no restrictive effect. No tax is due and no tax return needs to be filed if income does not exceed this level.

If you and the child's other parent are married, but file separate returns, the spouse with the higher taxable income must report the child's income on Form 8814 attached to his or her tax return. This also applies to households where the custodial parent has remarried and files separately. If divorced, it is the custodial spouse who attaches Form 8814 to his or her tax return.

Should You Use Form 8814?

Filing Form 8814 with your 2001 tax return produces the same basic tax as filing Form 8615 in your child's name. However, there are several possible disadvantages to using Form 8814 that can cause the total tax to exceed that produced when Form 8615 is used.

First, under the computation procedure on Form 8814, your child's unearned income exceeding $1,500 is added to your adjusted gross income on Form 1040 (so that it becomes taxable at your income tax rate). By increasing your adjusted gross income, your deductions for medical expenses and miscellaneous deductions can be decreased because they are subjected to 7.5% and 2%, respectively, of adjusted gross income subtractions [see the *Medical Expenses* and *Miscellaneous* chapters].

Also, there are several other provisions in the law that are negatively affected by an increase in adjusted gross income. The deduction for IRA contributions can be decreased or eliminated [see Section 2 of the *Tax-Sheltered Plans* chapter], the passive loss write-off for rental property can be decreased [see Section 2 of the *Investing Your Money* chapter], and the Child Care Tax Credit (for those with adjusted gross income less than $28,000) can be reduced [see the *Household Services and Child Care* chapter]. Also, the phaseouts for itemized deductions and personal exemptions can increase when adjusted gross income increases [see Section 1].

Another disadvantage of using Form 8814 is that the child's itemized deductions can't be claimed. However, this disadvantage only occurs when the child's total deductions exceed $750. Otherwise, the $750 standard deduction applies.

A final disadvantage applies to those who live in states which tie their income taxes to the federal taxes. In such states, if you file a federal tax return which includes a child's income, you might have to do the same on your state tax return. Since your child's tax bracket will be less than yours (perhaps even zero), this may cause an increase in taxes. For example, in Virginia, a child can have Virginia-adjusted gross income up to $5,000 without paying taxes. But if this $5,000 is included on the parent's federal tax return, it must be included on the parent's state return as well. Virginia's basic tax rate is 2% on the first $3,000 plus 3% of income over $3,000. This would result in extra tax of ($3,000 × 2%) + ($2,000 × 3%) = $120. (In a state with a top marginal bracket of 10%, the extra tax would be $5,000 × 10% = $500. Because some states such as Maryland allow a subtraction for the child's income taxed on the federal return, you should check the instructions for your state in determining whether additional state tax will result from reporting your child's income on your tax return.

Why You Should Give $15,000 to Each of Your Children

As discussed above, the first $750 in investment income received by a child is exempt from tax. The next $750 is taxed at the child's rate of 15%. Thus, up to $1,500 can be received by the child with a tax of no more than $113. If the $1,500 were received by the parent instead of the child, the tax in the 27.5% bracket would be $413, a difference of over $300.

To take advantage of this difference in rates, parents should consider placing as much as $15,000 into the name of each child. The income on this amount would generally be less than $1,500 and therefore be subject to the lower tax rate. [See the *Income-Shifting* chapter for a discussion of the ways of placing money in the hands of minor children.]

The above discussion applies chiefly to children under the age of 14. At age 14 or older, all of a child's income is taxed at the child's rate. This means that far more than $15,000 placed in the hands of the child can produce income taxed at the lower 15% rate.

Section 6:
Separate vs. Joint Returns

As you no doubt know, there are several different tax rates depending upon your marital status. Single people may use either the ordinary single taxpayer rate or the lower head-of-household rate if they maintain a household for a child, grandchild, or other dependent and satisfy the rules as stated in the instruction booklet accompanying the tax forms.

Married people may file a joint return on which they list all their combined income. Alternatively, each of them may file his or her own return subject to a special tax rate for married people filing separate returns. This special rate is designed so that a married couple, each with X dollars of taxable income, pays the same tax by filing separate returns as by combining their income in a joint return with 2X dollars of taxable income. In theory, the graduated feature of the income tax rates would then guarantee that people with unequal amounts of taxable income pay at least as much by filing separate returns with X and Y dollars of taxable income respectively as they would by filing a joint return with X + Y dollars of taxable income.

However, this situation has been changed by the relatively "flat" tax rate schedule now in effect. Many married couples will now find that the joint return tax table yields little tax advantage over the table for separate returns.

In fact, as discussed later in this section, there is a *neutral zone* where the basic tax table for a joint return yields no tax advantage at all. This would mean that if any of the following tax advantages of filing separate returns applies, this would produce a lower total tax than filing a joint return. (This presumes that the possible disadvantages of separate returns discussed below do not outweigh the advantages.)

Advantages of Separate Returns

The following is a list of situations where filing separate returns can yield a tax advantage over filing a joint return.

(A) If one spouse pays substantial medical expenses. The reason for this is that only medical expenses in excess of 7.5% of adjusted gross income are deductible.

For example, suppose a married couple each has an adjusted gross income of $25,000. He paid medical expenses totalling $3,400, while she paid none. On a joint return showing $50,000 adjusted gross income, they would have to subtract 7.5% × $50,000 = $3,750 from the amount of medical expenses, i.e. they would get no deduction. But on a separate return, he would only have to subtract 7.5% × $25,000 (his adjusted gross income) from his medical expenses. He would then have a medical expense deduction of $3,400 – (7.5% × $25,000) = $1,525.

However, if you live in a community property state, you might be required to split all medical expenses on separate returns. This could destroy any benefit that might be obtained by separate returns. (The apportioning of income and deductions on separate returns is discussed later in this section.)

(B) If one spouse has substantial miscellaneous deductions while the other does not. The reason for this is that only miscellaneous deductions in excess of 2% of adjusted gross income are deductible.

For example, suppose a married couple each has an adjusted gross income of $30,000. She has miscellaneous deductions of $1,000 while he has none. On a joint return showing $60,000 adjusted gross income, they would have to subtract 2% × $60,000 = $1,200 from their total of miscellaneous deductions, i.e. they would get no deduction. But on a separate return, she would only have to subtract 2% × $30,000 = $600. This would leave her with a net miscellaneous deduction of $1,000 – $600 = $400.

(C) If one person sustains a substantial casualty loss. Because only casualty losses in excess of 10% of adjusted gross income can be deducted, separate returns might be advantageous for the same reason as illustrated in (A) for medical expenses or (B) for miscellaneous deductions.

(D) If you are required to file separate federal returns to benefit from favorable state separate returns. A number of states allow couples to file separate state returns only if they file separate federal returns. And some of these states have lower taxes for couples who file separately [see the last item in Section 3]. Thus, a married couple might be better off filing separate returns if the state tax benefits exceed any federal return disadvantage. (However, don't forget that saving on state income taxes is less valuable than saving on federal income taxes because state income taxes are deductible on federal tax returns, but not conversely.)

(E) If one spouse earns less than $10,000 and wishes to contribute to an IRA and the other spouse is a participant in a retirement plan, the lower paid spouse can claim a deduction for the contribution. If both spouses have lived apart for the entire year, they each would apply the rules for single individuals for purposes of deducting IRA contributions.

Disadvantages of Separate Returns

One benefit that cannot be claimed on a separate return is the tax credit for household services and child care. A married couple can generally claim this credit only if they file a joint return [see the *Household Services and Child Care* chapter].

Another disadvantage of separate returns applies to those who are receiving social security benefits. Their social security benefits might be taxed on a separate return but untaxed on a joint return [see Section 4 of the *Retirement Plans* chapter].

A third disadvantage applies to those couples who own rental property that they actively manage. On a joint return, they might be entitled to deduct up to $25,000 of net losses under the *passive loss* rules [see Section 2 of the *Investing Your Money* chapter]. This $25,000 allowance doesn't apply to married couples filing separate returns.

A fourth disadvantage occurs if one spouse has capital gains and the other has capital losses exceeding $1,500. On a joint return, the losses could be subtracted from the gains, producing a lower tax than on separate returns [see Section 1 of the *Investing Your Money* chapter].

A fifth disadvantage can apply to married couples with combined adjusted gross income less than $53,000 who wish to make a deductible IRA contribution. They can do so on a joint tax return even if one or both spouses are active participants in a retirement plan. But on separate returns, any available IRA deduction might be reduced or eliminated altogether. [See Section 2 of the *Tax-Sheltered Plans* chapter.]

Reporting Income and Deductions on Separate Returns

If you and your spouse file separate returns, you must allocate your income and deductions between the two of you. You and your spouse must either both itemize your deductions or both claim the standard deduction.

Income which you earn is reported on your tax return. So is interest or dividends on securities of which you are the sole owner. Your spouse's separate return contains his or her earnings and personal investment interest. Income from investments which you own jointly with your spouse is split evenly between your 2 separate tax returns.

When you file separate returns, you must claim your own $2,900 personal exemption. If you have dependents supported by common funds of you and your spouse, you may divide their exemptions between you in any way you choose. However, you can't split the exemption of any one dependent between you. Each dependent's $2,900 personal exemption must be claimed one way or the other — either on your tax return or your spouse's.

Expenses connected with earnings must be reported on the tax return containing these earnings. For example, your job-related expenses would be claimed on your tax return. Similarly, expenses incurred to produce separate business or investment income are deducted by the spouse who owns the income, provided they're paid from that spouse's separate funds.

Expenses that are not attributable to any specific income, such as medical expenses, are deductible by the spouse who pays them. If the expenses are paid from joint funds, the deduction is divided equally between both spouses. This makes it important for many couples to pay for deductible expenses in such a way that taxes are minimized when separate returns are used.

This is particularly true for medical expenses and miscellaneous expenses because they are subject to 7.5% and 2% of AGI subtractions, respectively. For example, if one spouse, preferably the lower-earning spouse, pays all the medical bills for the family, the 7.5% of AGI subtraction will do the least harm. It may even keep from losing the entire deduction, as discussed earlier in the subsection outlining the possible advantages of filing separate returns.

Another advantage of planning can occur if spouses are in differing tax brackets on separate returns. In this case, it is generally best for the higher-bracket spouse to pay deductible items such as charitable contributions. The higher the tax bracket, the greater tax-lowering effect a deduction will produce.

If you and your spouse are splitting the income on separate returns from a joint savings account or other joint investment, you should pay attention to the Form 1099 you receive after year-end reporting this income. If all the income is reported under your Social Security number, the IRS computer matching program is likely to detect a discrepancy and kick out your return for examination. To prevent this, show the full amount of interest on your separate return as it appears on the Form 1099. Under that, subtract 1/2 of that amount, stating *"1/2 reported by spouse"* followed by the name and social security number of your spouse.

There may be peculiarities in state law that affect how income and expenses are allocated to husband and wife. For example, you might be surprised to hear about a Massachusetts case in which the Court ruled that all income and expenses on rental property owned jointly as *tenants by the entireties* by a husband and wife must be reported on the husband's federal tax return. Under Massachusetts law, property purchased prior to 1980 fell under the *"common law rule that the husband during coverture and as between himself and his wife had the absolute and exclusive right to the control, use, possession, rents, issues and profits of property held as tenants by the entirety."* [Springmann, TC Memo 1987-474]

Advantage of Separate Checking Accounts

As discussed above, it can prove beneficial to control which spouse pays certain deductible expenses. The best way to accomplish this is to maintain separate checking accounts. A check drawn on an account in the sole name of one spouse is the best indication that the expenditure is attributable to that spouse alone. In contrast, a payment made by a check drawn on a joint account will generally be attributed 1/2 to each spouse and reported that way on separate tax returns.

Community Property States

Different rules apply to those who live in one of the community property states: Arizona, California, Idaho, Louisiana, Nevada, New Mexico, Texas, Washington, or

Wisconsin. In these states, income earned by one spouse legally belongs ¹/₂ to each spouse and would be reported that way on separate tax returns. (In the last 4 of the states listed above, income from most separate investment property is similarly split between the spouses.) Expenses connected with the production of that income would be similarly divided, ¹/₂ on each spouse's tax return. This provides the ideal situation because the taxable income on each spouse's separate return will be comparable, likely placing them in the *neutral zone*. By having one spouse pay all medical or remaining miscellaneous expenses out of personal funds, tax savings might be obtained as discussed above.

Individual state laws determine which are considered community funds belonging to both spouses and which are personal funds belonging only to one spouse. Generally, personal funds are those stemming from bank accounts or investments owned prior to the marriage, or property acquired by gift or inheritance.

Estimated Taxes

The best way for a married couple to handle estimated tax payments they make [see the *Withholding* chapter] is to indicate they are being made as joint filers. That way, when income tax time comes around, estimated tax payments can be allocated as you choose on separate tax returns. Any portion of the total payments can be allocated to one spouse, with the remainder allocated to the other spouse.

When Should a Married Couple File Separate Returns?

The flatness of the tax tables comes from the wide range of the 27.5% and 30.5% tax brackets. This leads to a two-segment *"neutral zone"* where the tax rate schedules produce the exact same total tax on a joint return as on separate returns. If incomes fall into the neutral zone, filing separate returns will produce a lower tax when any of the separate return advantages A – E discussed above apply. (This presumes the possible disadvantages discussed above do not outweigh any advantages.)

Specifically, a married couple falls into the *neutral zone* for 2001 if either:

(1) Each spouse has taxable income between $22,000 and $54,625, with adjusted gross income less than $66,475; or

(2) Each spouse has taxable income between $54,625 and $83,250, with adjusted gross income less than $99,725.

(*Taxable Income* equals *Adjusted Gross Income,* less *Deductions* and *Personal Exemptions.*)

(The reason the neutral zone stops at $99,725 is that this is when the phaseout of personal exemptions kicks in on separate returns. This phaseout occurs at twice the rate on separate returns as on joint returns — 4% for each $2,900 above the threshold rather than 2%. As a result, separate returns can produce a higher tax bill when this threshold is exceeded.)

Example 1

X and Y are a married couple with 2 children. Their income and deductions are divided as follows:

	X	Y	Joint
Adjusted Gross Income	$40,000	$50,000	$90,000
Deductions (for Charity, Interest, & Taxes)	–3,000	–5,000	–8,000
Personal Exemptions ($2,900 each)	–5,800	–5,800	–11,600
Taxable Income	$31,200	$39,200	$70,400

The taxable incomes of X and Y fall into the neutral zone. The tax computations using the rate schedules for joint and separate returns given earlier are as follows:

	Separate Return of X		Separate Return of Y		Joint Return	
Tax Bracket	Income	Tax	Income	Tax	Income	Tax
15%	$22,600	$3,390	$22,600	$3,390	$45,200	$6,780
27.5%	8,600	3,365	16,600	4,565	25,200	6,930
	$31,200	$5,755	$39,200	$7,955	$70,400	$13,710

Thus, filing separate returns produces a total tax of $5,755 + $7,955 = $13,710, which is exactly the same tax as produced on a joint return. In effect, the 15% rate and the 27.5% rate are each applied to the same amount of income under either the separate returns or joint return computation, producing the same total tax either way.

Example 2

X and Y are a married couple with no dependents. Their income and deductions are divided as follows:

	X (Separate Return)		Y (Separate Return)		X & Y (Joint Return)	
Adjusted Gross Income		$85,000		$70,000		$155,000
Deductions (for Charity, Taxes & Mortgage Interest)	8,000		5,000		13,000	
Phaseout of Deductions	–556		–106		– 662	
	7,444		4,894		12,338	
		–7,444		–4,894		–12,338
Personal Exemptions		–2,900		–2,900		–5,800
Taxable Income		$74,656		$62,206		$136,862
Tax		$18,306		$14,510		$32,816

> *The above taxable incomes place X and Y into the neutral zone applying to couples each with taxable income between $54,625 and $83,250 and adjusted gross income less than $99,725. Using the rate tables in the manner illustrated in Example 1, X would owe tax on a separate return of $18,306 and Y would owe tax on a separate return of $14,510. The total $18,306 + $14,510 = $32,816 is precisely the same as the tax that would be due if they filed a joint return.*

As the above examples show, when incomes of a married couple are in the neutral zone, there is no difference provided by the basic tables in the amount of tax due using separate returns as compared to filing a joint return. This means that the presence of other factors favoring separate returns will yield a lower tax.

Example 3

Same as Example 2, except that Y incurred $3,100 of unreimbursed deductible job-related expenses. These are miscellaneous deductions subject to the 2% of AGI (adjusted gross income) subtraction. On the Joint Return showing $155,000 AGI, the miscellaneous deduction would be equal to $3,100 – (2% × $155,000) = $0, so the tax on the Joint Return would remain the same as in Example 2. Of course, the tax for X remains the same because there are no changes on X's tax return. However, the tax computation for Y improves as follows:

Separate Tax Return of Y

Adjusted Gross Income		$70,000
Deductions		
Charity, Taxes & Mortgage Interest	5,000	
Miscellaneous Deductions		
$3,100 – (2% × $70,000) =	1,700	
	6,700	
Phaseout of Deductions		
3% × ($70,000 – $66,475) =	–106	
	6,594	
		–6,594
Personal Exemptions		–2,900
Taxable Income		$60,506

Thus, the taxable income on the separate return of Y has been reduced by $62,206 – $60,506 = $1,700. This lowers Y's tax by $519. Thus by filing separate tax returns rather than a joint return, X and Y save $519 in taxes.

In the above examples, a married couple's income fell into the neutral zone where the basic tax tables produced the same tax on 2 separate returns as on a joint return. This meant that any of the advantages A – E of separate returns discussed earlier would make separate returns beneficial. (This assumes that none of the disadvantages discussed earlier offsets the advantages.)

However, falling into the neutral zone is not necessary. The bubbles caused by the phaseouts of itemized deductions and personal exemptions [see Section 1] destroy the absolute flatness of the basic rates at higher-income levels. However, the variation in rates is still relatively small. The question then becomes whether or not the advantages provided by A – E for separate returns outweigh the leveling effect of the joint return tax bracket structure. Generally speaking, the closer the incomes are to falling within the neutral zone, the more likely this is to be the case.

Also, there are isolated cases when one of the phaseout rules actually provides an advantage to separate returns, even if none of the basic advantages A – E apply. This can happen when the lower-income spouse has adjusted gross income close to the separate return threshold amount ($99,725 in 2001) for the phaseout of personal exemptions.

For many couples, the above guidance suffices to determine whether separate returns are better than a joint return. For others, there will be no easy way. In such cases, it will be necessary to compute taxes both ways to see which is best.

Note: The above discussion only takes into account *federal* income taxes. In some states, the filing of separate federal tax returns forces you to file separate state tax returns. In this case, you would have to take into account both the federal and state tax consequences of filing separate returns.

Section 7:
Recordkeeping

In order to substantiate your deductions, you are required to keep records of what you spend. Generally, you should retain any cancelled checks or receipts that verify expenditures. In addition, there are special recordkeeping rules which apply to certain specific types of deductions, e.g. travel expenses. These special rules are discussed in later chapters.

Except for an overall listing of your expenditures broken down into appropriate categories, you do not include your records with the income tax return which you file. It is only if your return is chosen for audit that you will be asked to produce these records.

Special Recordkeeping Requirements

The 1986 Tax Reform Act brought with it a number of special recordkeeping requirements. These are listed below. (Details are provided in later chapters of this *Tax & Financial Guide.*)

(1) **Interest.** Interest connected with owning a home or investing your money is usually fully deductible, while personal interest (e.g. an auto loan) is no longer deductible. To get the full deduction to which you are entitled, you need proper records which place interest payments into the most favorable category. [See the *Interest* chapter and Section 1 of the *Homeowners* chapter.]

(2) **Home Improvement Records.** You need to keep records of any improvements you make to your home. These may be needed to back up a deduction for interest secured by your home and may also be needed to figure any capital gains tax due when your home is eventually sold. [See the *Homeowners* chapter.]

(3) **Tax-Free Interest.** You need to keep track of tax-free interest from municipal bonds or municipal bond mutual funds. Even though untaxed, this interest must be reported on line 8b of your tax return. [See the *Interest* chapter.]

(4) **IRAs.** If you contribute to IRAs on a non-deductible basis, you need to maintain records for the life of the IRAs. These records are needed to minimize tax due when you receive payouts from the IRAs. [See Section 2 of the *Tax-Sheltered Plans* chapter.]

(5) **Travel.** You need to keep travel records which separate out your meal expenses, because they are only 50%-deductible on your tax return. [See the *Travel* chapter.]

(6) **Carryovers.** You might be prevented from claiming a loss due to home office expenses, investment interest paid, or losses on rental property or other passive activities. These losses may be carried over to be deducted on future tax returns if you have kept records backing up your expenses. [See the *Home Office, Interest*, and *Investing Your Money* chapters.]

IRS Says Cancelled Checks or Credit Card Slips Are Not Always Necessary

The IRS recently issued a ruling which will make it easier for some persons to substantiate deductible payments that they have made. Under this ruling, there are circumstances under which neither cancelled checks nor credit slips are needed.

In particular, you do not have to retain a cancelled check as proof of payment if you have sufficient other evidence such as *"an invoice marked 'paid,' a check register or carbon copy of the check, and an account statement that shows the check number, date, and amount."*

To save money, your bank may not be returning cancelled checks to you. You are allowed to prove payment if the statement the bank sends to you shows (1) the check number, (2) the amount of the check, (3) the date the check was posted, and (4) the name of the payee. If this information is not on the statement, you would have to ask the bank to send you a copy (front and back) of the check, if you need to substantiate payment.

Similarly, you do not need a credit card slip if the monthly credit card statement shows (1) the amount of the charge, (2) the date of the charge, and (3) the name of the payee. The same would be true if payment is made by electronic transfer instead of by credit card. [IRS Rev.Proc. 92-71]

The above only refers to proving that a payment was made. You still need to be able to establish the deductible nature of the payment. For example, if you have verified that a check or credit card payment was made to a drug store, you would still need a receipt, sales slip, charge slip, etc., to show that the items purchased were drugs or deductible medical supplies.

What If You Didn't Keep Records?

You may still be able to deduct your expenses even if your return is audited. If you can establish that you are entitled to a certain business deduction, you may be allowed to estimate your actual expenses in the absence of records. However, you can be sure that the auditor of your tax return will agree to a low estimate at best. If you should end up in Tax Court, the Court may make its own estimate of your expenses under what is called the **Cohan Rule** which permits such estimates. Once again, the estimate will probably be on the low side. So you should do yourself a favor and keep records in the future if you have not done so in the past.

Exception: The Cohan Rule does not apply to travel, entertainment expenses or gifts nor to the deduction for *listed property* [see the *Depreciation* chapter] such as certain home computers.

Loss of Records Beyond Your Control

If you lose your records due to circumstances beyond your control such as a fire or earthquake, you will get a break. In this case, you probably will be allowed a reasonable estimate of your expenses.

How Long to Keep Records

You should keep records associated with your tax return for at least 6 years. Records which show how much you paid for property and the cost of improvements should be kept indefinitely, as should records relating to IRAs.

Don't make the mistake of throwing away your records too early just because the IRS sends you a refund check. That's what Robert Wells, a college biology teacher in Florida, did as reported in the following Tax Court case. He claimed a deduction for an automobile he used to gather specimens and perform other tasks connected with his job. As the Court explained it,

> "After Robert filed his tax return . . . on which he asked for a refund, further information was requested by the Internal Revenue Service about the claimed automobile depreciation. Before this matter was straightened out between Robert and the Internal Revenue Service, Robert was sent a refund check. Assuming that that was the end of the matter, Robert just disposed of all [his] literature on it and ... was grateful that I.R.S. had recommended in the favor of a legitimate taxpayer and had gone on to other matters."

However, the refund check just reflected the ordinary processing procedure. It did not signify that the IRS official checking his return had accepted it as filed. Because Robert no longer had the required records, his deduction was not allowed. [Wells, TC Memo 1976-52]

SECTION 8:
YEAR-END STRATEGIES FOR LOWERING TAXES

The end of the year often presents special opportunities to adjust one's financial affairs in order to reduce taxes.

Medical Expenses

Only medical expenses exceeding 7.5% of your adjusted gross income are deductible. If your medical bills will not exceed this amount, they will give you no deduction this year. Instead, you should shift the expenses to the following year by delaying payment until after the first of the year. You can also delay getting optional items like new eyeglasses, etc. In this way, you will get a deduction in case your medical expenses exceed the 7.5% limitation the next year.

If your medical expenses exceeded the 7.5% limitation this year, but you are not sure they will do so the next, the opposite strategy is called for. You will want to pay all your medical bills before the end of the year to avoid losing a deduction for them the following year because of the 7.5% floor.

Miscellaneous Deductions

A 2% of adjusted gross income (AGI) floor applies to the total of miscellaneous deductions claimed on your tax return [see the *Miscellaneous Deductions* chapter]. The same expense-shifting maneuver discussed above with regard to the 7.5% of AGI floor on medical expenses applies with respect to the 2% floor on miscellaneous deductions.

To illustrate with a simple example, suppose you have annual AGI of $50,000. In this case, the floor on the total miscellaneous deductions is $2\% \times \$50,000 = \$1,000$. If you have $1,000 of miscellaneous deductions both this year and next, you lose out on any deduction in either year. However, if you can shift, say, $300 from one year to the other, you will wind up with miscellaneous deductions totalling $1,300 in one year and $700 in the other. Applying the 2% of AGI floor, this will yield a net deduction of $300 in the year to which the expenses are shifted.

In line with the above discussion, if it looks as though you might exceed the 2% of AGI floor this year but probably not the next, you will want to shift expenses from next year to this year. On the other hand, if you will not exceed the 2% floor this year, a shift to next year when the floor might be exceeded can possibly save the deduction.

For example, you can time the purchase of job-related items such as books, supplies, equipment, journals, professional dues, etc., so they occur in the year producing the best tax result. The same goes for investment-related expenses like safe deposit rentals, subscriptions to financial publications, etc.

Travel expenses are also amenable to such treatment. For example, suppose you are planning a trip early in the year for which you are entitled to a deduction. You have the option of buying the airline tickets either in the year of travel or in the preceding year. The deduction belongs to the year in which you purchased the ticket.

In fact, the Tax Court ruled that the year of purchase is the only year in which you may claim the deduction. In this case, an individual claimed a deduction for a trip made in January to oversee some investment property. But because she had purchased the tickets the previous December, she was denied a deduction. By the time of the trial, it was too late to file an amended return claiming the deduction in the proper year. [Lyman, TC Memo 1984-115]

Using the Standard Deduction

Deduction-shifting may be advantageous when your deductions total near the standard deduction. For example, suppose the standard deduction to which you are entitled is $4,550. As of November 30, your deductions total $2,700 and you estimate another $800 of deductible expenses for the remainder of the year. These anticipated expenses will do you no good on this year's tax return because your total deduction of $3,500 would still be less than the standard deduction. It would be better to shift these deductions to the following year when your total deductions might exceed the standard deduction. This is accomplished by delaying payments until after the first of the year.

Conversely, if your deductions are exceeding the standard deduction one year but might not the next, transferring deductions to the earlier year might prevent their loss as a tax benefit. This is accomplished by paying early before the year's end.

When Are Payments Considered Made?

Generally, you make a payment when you write a check and place it in the mail (or deliver it in person). It does not matter that it isn't received until the next year. The deduction will be allowed for the year appearing on the date of the check unless there is some strong indication it was mailed in a different year.

Expenses charged on credit cards are deductible in the year they're charged, not in the year the charge is paid. This applies to cards issued by third parties, e.g. VISA, MasterCard, American Express, etc. Other charge arrangements are deductible in the year paid.

Sometimes, payments are made under a "pay-by-phone" arrangement whereby a bank or savings institution pays bills upon receiving telephone instructions from depositors. In the following month, the depositor receives a statement of bills paid on his account. The payment dates shown on the statement determine when payments can be deducted by the depositor. [Rev Rul 80-335]

Tax-Sheltered Plans

If you plan to take advantage of the tax-sheltered plans for which you're eligible, be sure to observe the appropriate deadlines [see the *The Tax-Sheltered Plans* chapter]. Note in particular that you must actually establish your self-employed plan before December 31 even though payment does not have to be made until April 15 or the extended filing date. Note also that payments to a Tax-Sheltered Annuity are only deductible in the current year if made by December 31.

Capital Gains and Losses

If you own stocks or bonds, tax considerations may call for a sale of some of these assets prior to December 31. [See the *Investing Your Money* chapter for the basic rules.] For example, you may wish to sell stocks that have decreased in value in order to offset capital gains or produce a deductible loss on your tax return.

SECTION 9:
IRS MATCHING PROGRAM

The IRS has a master computer, located in West Virginia, which matches figures reported on your tax return with Forms W-2, 1099, etc., sent to it by your employer, savings bank, etc. If a mismatch is detected, your tax return will be kicked out for examination. This will result in a letter sent to you by the IRS or a full-scale audit of your tax return.

At one time, the IRS was not able to input all the Forms W-2, 1099, etc., into the computer. In particular, most forms it received on paper, rather than on magnetic tape, were simply not processed. But now, with optical scanners for paper forms and improved efficiency overall, you can be almost certain that any discrepancy will be detected by the IRS computer.

This means that you must take care that the figures you report on your tax return agree with Forms W-2, 1099, etc., which the IRS receives from your employer, savings bank, etc. This will substantially improve the odds that your tax return won't be selected for examination.

If you receive a Form 1099 which is in error, contact the issuer to issue an amended form, copies of which will be sent to you and the IRS. The IRS requires that Forms 1099 contain the telephone number of the issuer. If you get no response, just go ahead and file your return with the figures you believe to be correct. If the IRS contacts you about the discrepancy, you should simply write back that your figures are correct and the 1099 is in error. Under a new amendment to the Taxpayer Bill of Rights, the burden of proof in this instance shifts to the IRS. The IRS must then come up with proof other than the incorrect 1099 that your figures are incorrect. Otherwise, presumably, the amounts you stated will be honored.

The following is a list of items to be aware of that the matching program might pick up.

Interest and Dividends

Be sure to report your interest and dividends exactly as shown on Forms 1099 that are sent to you, because the IRS computer will be digesting the copies of these forms sent to the IRS. For example, if your stock broker sends you a Form 1099 reporting dividends on stocks which he is holding for you in "street name," the stock broker's name should be listed as the payer on Schedule B where you report your dividends.

Also, take care if you have income from money-market or bond mutual funds. The income received from these funds is considered as dividends, not interest. If you report this income as interest, the IRS computer will think you haven't reported dividends that you received.

Married persons filing separate returns should take special care if they split income from jointly held savings accounts, stocks, etc. In this situation, you should examine each Form 1099 you receive after year-end which reports such income. If the income is reported under your social security number, the IRS computer matching program is likely to detect a discrepancy if you split the income between your tax return and that of your spouse. To prevent this, show the full amount of interest on your separate return Schedule B as it appears on the Form 1099. Under that, subtract ½ of that amount, stating *"½ reported by spouse"* followed by the name and social security number of your spouse.

Reimbursed Job-Related Expenses

You may have incurred job-related expenses for which you received a reimbursement from your employer. Check to see if these reimbursements were included as taxable income on your year-end Form W-2. If so, don't just subtract this from the total income amount you report on line 7 of your Form 1040. This will cause a mismatch that the IRS computer will detect, kicking out your tax return for examination.

Instead, include the reimbursement in the total income that you report on line 7. Then, claim the expenses for which you received a reimbursement in Step 1 of Form 2106. This is discussed in more detail in the *Miscellaneous Deductions* chapter.

Moving Expenses

The same discussion above for reimbursed job-related expenses applies to reimbursed moving expenses which are included in taxable income on your Form W-2.

Tax-Free Grants

You may have received a scholarship, fellowship, or other grant which qualifies, in whole or in part, for tax-free treatment. Sometimes, these grants are reported on Forms W-2 as taxable income.

In such a case, don't just omit the tax-free portion of your grant from your tax return. This will cause a discrepancy that will make the IRS computer unhappy, causing your tax return to be selected for examination.

Instead, report the full amount appearing on your Form W-2 on line 7 of your Form 1040. Then, list the tax-free portion of your grant as a negative entry on line 21, *Other Income.* This will produce the same adjusted gross income, but will not create a mismatch that makes the IRS computer unhappy. In 1987 and 1988, over 20,000 graduate students were harassed for back taxes, precisely because they were unaware of this method of avoiding a computer mismatch. [see the *Tax-Free Grants* chapter]

Capital Gains and Losses

On Schedule D, *Capital Gains and Losses,* you are required to report the total proceeds from the sale or redemption of stocks, bonds, etc. This should equal the total you obtain from adding up the amounts of the sales reported on Forms 1099 you receive. If it doesn't, be sure to read Section 1 of the *Investing Your Money* chapter to see if the alternate way of taking commissions into account applies.

If the totals still don't agree, you should attach an explanation of the mismatch to your tax return. The IRS computer may still kick out your return, but the human who examines the kicked-out return will be able to see the justification for the discrepancy.

Section 10:
Free or Low-Rent Housing

Some colleges and universities provide housing to faculty members or administrators either rent-free or at a reduced rent. Where the housing is a condition of employment and is used in a substantial way for college-related functions, this does not generate taxable income. This tax-free fringe benefit typically applies only to Chancellors, Presidents, or other head administrators. [IRS Private Letter Rulings 7823006, 7823007]

In other cases, the rental value of qualified campus lodging is considered to be equal to 5% of its appraised value (as appraised by an independent qualified appraiser). To the extent a faculty member pays less than this amount in rent, such shortfall becomes a taxable fringe benefit. However, if the rent paid is equal to or greater than 5% of value, no extra tax is due. Qualified campus lodging is lodging furnished by an educational institution to an employee, spouse, or dependents for use as a residence. The lodging must be located on, or in proximity to, the campus. The employee cannot be required to receive the lodging as a condition of employment to perform his or her duties.

This same benefit applies to certain medical research institutions even if they don't have traditional students.

Ordained ministers are entitled to a special tax break if they receive housing allowances (called parsonage allowance) provided as part of their pay as a regular faculty member. Such allowances are tax-free to the extent they are actually used for housing costs, e.g. rent or ownership costs including down payments, mortgage payments, utilities, interest, taxes, and repairs. To qualify for this tax break, the school at which the minister teaches must be an integral agency of a religious organization under the authority of a church or church denomination.

A 1984 court case illustrates how this can apply to faculty members who qualify. Sixteen teachers at a Christian college in the South were also ministers within the Church of Christ. The teachers owned or rented their own homes and reported their housing costs to the college. The college then designated part of their pay to cover these costs as housing allowances. The Court ruled that they could exclude from tax, housing allowances equal to their expenses. [Reed, 82 TC 208]

2

Books, Supplies, and Equipment

You are entitled to a deduction for the cost of books, periodicals, supplies, equipment, home computers, and other items which you use in your profession or for other business purposes. Those items which have a definite short life span such as paper or pencils are deducted in the year they are purchased. For items which will be used for a number of years, such as a typewriter or desk, there are two options, the **expensing option** and the **depreciation option.**

Under the *expensing option,* you deduct the cost of the items, up to a total deduction of $24,000, in the year they are placed into service. Under the *depreciation option,* a specified percentage of the cost is deducted in each year of the depreciation period. Generally, the depreciation period for books, equipment, and furniture is 5 years or 7 years. For most individuals, the expensing option is preferable to depreciation. A complete discussion of the two options for deducting business items is contained in the *Expensing and Depreciation* chapter. As explained there, both options require the use of Form 4562 which you attach to your tax return. (You do not use Form 4562 for short-lived items such as periodicals, paper, or other supplies.)

Special Rules for Computers and Entertainment Items

There is a specified category of items, called *Listed Property*, to which special depreciation and recordkeeping rules apply. *Listed Property* includes the following items:

Listed Property

1. Automobiles and other passenger vehicles.

2. Home Computers (except for employer-owned computers used exclusively at a regular business establishment or computers used exclusively in a home office qualifying for deduction as described in the *Home Office* chapter).

3. Property of a type generally used for entertainment, recreation, or amusement, e.g. video recorders, cameras, etc., except for such property used either (i) exclusively at your regular job location or deductible home office, or (ii) in connection with your principal job or business.

4. Cellular telephones.

Special Depreciation Rules for Listed Property

Special rules apply for depreciation of listed property. Under these special rules, such items must be *required by the employer* in order for an employee to obtain any deduction. Also, if such items are used 50% or less for business purposes, a special stretched-out depreciation table must be used instead of the regular depreciation table or expensing option. Details are contained in the *Expensing and Depreciation* chapter.

Recordkeeping Rules for Listed Property

There are special recordkeeping regulations that apply to listed property. These regulations apply to all listed property for which a deduction is claimed, no matter when the property was purchased.

Formerly, listed property was subject only to the same basic rules applying to any other deduction. That is, the better your records, the more likely your deduction would stand up to IRS scrutiny. But no explicit standards applied. In fact, even in the absence of any records, taxpayers could often qualify for a deduction by making a reasonable estimate of business use.

However, now an estimate is no longer sufficient to support a deduction for an item of listed property. Instead, there must be adequate records to support your deduction. This means you must maintain a diary or similar written record which, for each job or business/investment use of the item, contains the following information:

1. Date;

2. Business purpose (unless this is evident from the surrounding facts and circumstances); and

3. Length of time the item was used.

Your records do not have to conform to any specific format. You can keep a diary, log book, journal, etc. Or, you can use a calendar on which you write down all the required data.

If you use an item of listed property both for personal and business purposes, you must keep track of the total amount of time the item was in use. This will enable you to substantiate the percentage of time the item was used for business purposes.

Your records should be maintained in a *timely* manner. According to the IRS, this means you write down each entry soon enough that you have *"full present knowledge"* of all the details. You are not required to make daily entries; IRS regulations state that it is all right to record your usage at the end of each week. However, even if your records are updated weekly, they should still give a daily breakdown of each separate period of use.

You do not need to maintain your records by hand. IRS regulations specifically allow you to use a home computer to keep a log of business and personal use.

If your business use percentage is relatively constant during the year, IRS regulations provide that a suitable sampling technique can be used instead of keeping records for the entire year. The following 2 examples are adapted from these regulations. [IRS Reg. §1.274-5T]

Example 1

You use a home computer during the year both for personal and business purposes. You keep adequate records for the first 3 months of the year which show that 60% of the time your computer is used, it is used for business purposes. Assuming you can establish that your business usage continues at approximately the same rate for the remainder of the year, your records support a deduction based on 60% of the cost of the computer.

Example 2

Same as Example 1 except that you keep adequate records during the first week of each month. As long as it is established that these are "representative" weeks, you can base your deduction on the business use percentage determined for the sample weeks.

Note that the preceding recordkeeping rules only apply to *listed property*. This does not include home computers if they are used in a home office which meets the deductible rules described in the *Home Office* chapter. For such computers, only the usual purchase receipts need be kept. This is illustrated by the following 1996 court case.

Court Case

Zeidler conducted a consulting activity out of his home. He used one room exclusively and regularly for business purposes. In this room he kept a computer which he purchased and used solely for business purposes.

The IRS allowed Zeidler a home office deduction. However, it denied a deduction for the computer. The IRS claimed that because Zeidler had not kept the listed property usage records (as described earlier in this Section), a deduction was ruled out.

However, the Court ruled the IRS to be in error. Because the IRS had allowed a home office deduction, the computer used in this office was not listed property. Because Zeidler had a purchase receipt for the computer and the Court was satisfied the computer was used solely for business purposes, a deduction was allowed for the computer. [Zeidler, TC Memo 1996-157]

Questions on Tax Return

On your 2001 tax return, the following two questions must be answered on Form 4562, Part V, Section A concerning your deduction for listed property:

1. Do you have evidence to support the business/investment use percentage claimed?

2. If "Yes," is the evidence written?

Note that it is possible to answer yes to the above questions, yet not satisfy the recordkeeping requirements of the law. For example, you might create a written record at the end of the year. This would enable you to answer *yes* to the above questions so your tax return would not be spotlighted for audit. But such a record would fail the *timely* requirement described earlier. If your deduction actually were audited, it would likely be disallowed for failure to keep adequate records.

Deductible Items

The following is a list of items which are legitimate professional expenses. You may be able to think of others. Bear in mind that whether any particular item is an acceptable deduction depends on whether you use it in your professional capacity.

Books

You may deduct for the cost of books used in connection with professional duties. Those books which are only useful for a year or less are claimed as a miscellaneous deduction when purchased. Books of more lasting value are either expensed in the year of purchase or depreciated over a 7-year period unless they are expensed under IRS Section 179 [see the *Expensing and Depreciation* chapter].

It is generally assumed that books have lasting value unless there is some particular reason to regard them as having only short-term value, such as being an annual edition of a regularly updated publication, containing information which will soon be out-of-date, etc.

To deduct the full amount you spent during the year on books with a lasting value, the law requires you to *expense* these items on Form 4562, as described at the beginning of this chapter. If you simply deduct the cost as a miscellaneous deduction without also using Form 4562, the IRS can force you to depreciate the cost over a 7-year period. After the filing deadline (including extension) for your original tax return has expired, it is too late to elect the *expensing option*.

The importance of using Form 4562 is illustrated by the following court case.

> **Court Case**
>
> *Cadwallader was a Psychology Professor at a public university in the Midwest. In addition to teaching, advising, and other university-related duties, he was actively engaged in research. During the year, he spent $747 for books connected with his professional duties. He simply claimed this amount as a miscellaneous deduction, without electing the* expensing option *on Form 4562.*
>
> *The IRS did not quarrel with Cadwallader's right to a deduction for his books. However, because the* expensing option *was not elected on a Form 4562 attached to the original tax return, Cadwallader would have to depreciate the cost over a period of years. Under the depreciation rules at the time, this meant he was entitled to a deduction in the year of purchase of only $112. The remainder, $747 – $112 = $635, could only be deducted in future years over the remaining lifetime in the depreciation period.* [Cadwallader, TC Memo 1989-356]

The deduction for books can be sizable, as illustrated by the following recent court case.

> **Court Case**
>
> *Mathes was a History Professor at a major California university. He amassed a huge collection of books related to Mexican colonial history, his area of specialization. He kept these books in an office he maintained at home. The Court did not allow Mathes a home office deduction because it felt his facilities at the university were adequate [see Section 1 of the Home Office chapter]. However, it did allow a depreciation deduction for his books. The amount allowed was less than Mathes had claimed, but it was still large — $7,156 in one year and $8,051 the next.* [Mathes, TC Memo 1990-483]

Supplies

You may deduct the cost of pens, pencils, paper, tape, maps, records, computer disks, slides, film, sheet music, staples, desk blotters, briefcases, record books, etc. These items fall into the short lifetime category and are deducted in the year of purchase. The cost of such items can add up to a significant sum, no matter what the level of teaching. According to an article in the *Wall Street Journal*, a survey of members of the Texas Teachers Federation turned up an average annual expenditure of $242 for supplies used in the classroom.

But sometimes, a much larger amount for supplies can be justified. A court case shows the IRS allowing an art teacher to deduct $1,529 for art supplies used in her teaching. The auditor allowed this high deduction when the teacher was able to provide receipts backing up her purchases. [Starr, TC Memo 1995-190]

Periodicals

You may deduct subscriptions to journals, periodicals, etc. connected with your job.

However, if you pay in advance for a subscription that extends for more than one year, the IRS states that you should spread out your deductions accordingly. For example, suppose that in December 2001, you paid $300 for a 3-year subscription to a job-related journal to begin in 2002. Only $100 of this amount would be deductible on your 2001 tax return. The remainder would be deducted in future years — $100 on your 2002 return and $100 on your 2003 return.

On the other hand, suppose the $300 subscription prepaid in December 2001 is not a new subscription, but rather is a 3-year extension of a subscription, expiring at the end of March 2004. Then only $75 of the prepayment — covering the 3/4 of the year from April to December 2001 — will be deductible for 2001. The remaining $225 will be deductible in portions for 2002 ($100), 2003 ($100), and 2004 ($25), reflecting the termination of the subscription at the end of March 2004.

The above prorating of multi-year subscriptions was found by the IRS to prevent the shifting of deductions from a lower tax-rate year to a higher tax-rate year. As a practical matter, it is doubtful the IRS will single out such a deduction for examination unless the adjustment arising from the proration is substantial.

Newspapers and Magazines

Newspapers and magazines can be deductible if they are sufficiently connected with your job. This is true even if the periodical is aimed at the general public rather than at members of your profession. This is illustrated by the following 2 court cases.

The first case involved a public relations executive. He usually bought at least two newspapers daily and magazines such as *Time* and *Newsweek*. He also purchased local newspapers and magazines when he traveled. These magazines and newspapers were needed by him in connection with his work. No record was kept of his purchases but he estimated that he spent one dollar per day for a total of $360 for the year. The Court allowed the deduction but reduced the amount to $250 because of a lack of records. [Conley, TC Memo 1977-406]

The second 1991 case involved a college counselor with a masters degree in psychology. Despite IRS objection, the Tax Court allowed a $50 deduction for a subscription to *Psychology Today*. The deduction was allowed even though *Psychology Today* was a magazine aimed at the general public. [Drake, TC Memo 1991-628]

As the above two cases show, a deduction for general circulation magazines can stand up in court if there is sufficient business reason to subscribe. In fact, the IRS is not likely to challenge your deduction unless the adjustment would be substantial.

The above advice is underscored by a court case involving a consultant who claimed a deduction for books and journals connected with his profession. The IRS allowed him a $200 deduction even though he presented no documentation to back up his deduction. [Kannas, TC Memo 1980-127]

Teachers, in particular, should take note of the above. Many teachers use current information from newspapers and magazines in their teaching. And other teachers use such information in connection with their professional research. In such cases, a deduction for these items might be justified.

In addition to job-related publications, you can deduct the cost of magazines and newspapers if they are sufficiently connected with your investment activities. This would include the *Wall Street Journal, Forbes Magazine,* etc.

Special Clothing

The cost of uniforms or other clothing, including their cleaning, laundering, repair, etc., is deductible if the clothing is (1) required in your job and (2) not adaptable to general wear. Such items might include laboratory coats and safety equipment, aprons, caps and gowns, etc. However, you cannot deduct ordinary street clothes even if you wear them only at your job.

Telephone Expenses

You can deduct your professional telephone expenses (including installation charges, repair costs, equipment fees, etc.) if you need to make business-related calls from your home.

However, there is one item connected with telephone use that you cannot deduct. Namely, you cannot deduct any portion of the monthly base charge (including related sales or excise tax) for local service on the first telephone line in your residence.

This restriction is rather limited. It does not apply to the cost of business-related long distance charges, equipment rental or purchases, optional services such as call waiting or call forwarding, or charges attributable to additional telephone lines. The restriction applies only to the basic service charge on your first telephone line.

If you have a choice of several basic telephone packages, it may pay to select the lowest priced package. This minimizes the amount that is non-deductible under the above restriction. The extra cost of additional telephone calls, above the amount provided by the basic package, would be deductible to the extent connected with business usage.

The best way to substantiate your business-related long distance calls is to go through and single them out on the listing you receive from your telephone company. If this is not possible, you'll have to make the best estimate you can.

Rather than go through your entire year's telephone bills, you might be able to use a sampling technique if you make substantial business use of your phone. This is illustrated by a 1986 court case involving an engineer who designed and supervised rehabilitation projects of industrial offices. He made extensive use of his home telephone to call prospective employers, headhunters, and job shops throughout the U.S. and the world, chiefly in order to find work. Instead of plowing through the entire year's telephone bills, the Court agreed to use just the January bill as a representative sample of the business use percentage of his telephone. The Court estimated that 40% of the telephone calls during January were for business purposes. Since his total telephone bills for the year came to $4,216, he was allowed a deduction of 40% × $4,216 = $1,686 for the year. [Payne, TC Memo 1986-93]

Note that your telephone calls can be deductible even if you are not permitted a home office deduction for failure to satisfy the stringent rules described in the *Home Office* chapter.

As long as telephone calls are business-related, it makes no difference to whom they're made. Even if made to a relative or friend, the calls can be deductible. This is illustrated by a 1989 court case. In this case, an individual ran into financial difficulty with a farm that he owned. During the year, he made over 150 long distance calls to his sister, seeking financial and business advice regarding his continuing financial and legal difficulties. His sister was a retired Air Force cost accountant and had been raised on a farm.

The Court ruled that he could deduct $1,678 for business-related calls. According to the Court,

"If the expense was incurred for a business purpose that bears a reasonably close relationship to the taxpayer's trade or business, it will be properly deductible . . . Petitioner's contemporaneous telephone bills and other records corroborate his testimony as to a continuing course of communication with his sister regarding attempts to save his farm. He did not claim that all calls to his sister were business related, and he deducted the cost of only those identified on his monthly

bills as business calls. We conclude, therefore, that there is sufficient documentation of expenses on the record to justify allowing petitioner a business expense deduction for these telephone calls." [Lewis, TC Memo 1989-78]

Equipment and Furnishings

You may be able to deduct for the cost of tape recorders, cameras, projectors, home computers, typewriters, calculators, etc., which you use in connection with your job either at work or at home. In one case, the IRS even allowed a teacher to deduct for a radio used for job-related purposes [Reilly, TC Memo 1979-253] . You have to prorate the expenses if these items are also used for personal activities. You may also deduct for office furnishings such as desks, chairs, lamps, etc., which are used in a home office for which you're entitled to a deduction. [See the *Expensing and Depreciation* chapter for details on how to deduct for equipment and furnishings.]

Another case shows how camera equipment can qualify for deduction. A Professor of Management spent $1731 on a Canon A-1 camera, tripod, auto bellows, and lenses. He testified that he used the equipment only in connection with his teaching duties—to take pictures and make slides to show during his lectures. He presented slides showing computer equipment and programs for use in his course in computer programming, slides of Mexico for use in his course on tourism development, and slides of Austrian coins, a passport, an international driving permit, and mountain ranges for use in his tourism course.

The Court allowed full depreciation deductions for the cost of the camera equipment. It believed the Professor's claim that he made no personal use of the equipment, noting that he also owned a different camera, a 10-year old Mamiya Sekor, for use in taking personal or family photographs.

In the above case, the ownership of a second camera was probably an important factor. In another recent case, the Tax Court denied a deduction to an elementary school teacher for the purchase of a Minolta 35-millimeter camera with wide angle lens. He used the camera to take pictures of students, to take photographs for the school yearbook, and to teach darkroom techniques to his science class. There was no evidence that the teacher owned a second "personal" camera. In this case, the Court felt that the camera was basically a personal item used only occasionally for job-related activities. Therefore, no deduction was allowed. [Cardwell, TC Memo 1982-453]

Home Computers

Home computers, including peripheral equipment, can be expensed or depreciated to the extent the computer is used for business rather than personal purposes. In addition, the cost of electricity to operate the computer is deductible.

Software which is bundled together with your original purchase of the computer is considered part of the original cost. Software which is itemized separately or purchased at a different time can generally be deducted in the year of purchase. Although the official IRS position is that software is an intangible item which should be amortized over a period of three years, most experts disagree. And the IRS is not expected to enforce its position for the relatively small purchases of home computer software.

Home computers fall under the special rules for *listed property* described in the *Expensing and Depreciation* chapter. Unless used only in a deductible home office, the use of such a computer must be *"for the convenience of the employer and required as a condition of employment."* Otherwise, no deduction is allowed. As discussed in the *Expensing and Depreciation* chapter, IRS regulations state that in order to satisfy this requirement, the use of the computer *"must be required in order for the employee to perform the duties of his or her employment properly."* The following example illustrates a case where this requirement is not met.

Example 3

D is employed as an engineer with Z, an engineering contracting firm. D occasionally takes work home at night rather than working late in the office. D owns and uses a computer which is virtually identical to the one she uses at the office to complete her work at home. D's use of the computer is not for the convenience of her employer and is not required as a condition of employment. [IRS Reg. §1.280F-6T]

The above example taken from IRS regulations would suggest, at least implicitly, that the regular use of a home computer for valid work-related duties qualifies for deduction, provided adequate facilities are not available at work. This suggestion is also present in an official IRS Revenue Ruling.

This revenue ruling concerned an individual with a doctorate in aerospace engineering who had a research position with a private corporation. His job description, like the job descriptions of all engineers and scientists who worked for the corporation, provided that he seek to accomplish the research objectives by whatever means he and the corporation determined were necessary.

He purchased a computer and kept it at home. He purchased it because the computers at work were often used by other employees during working hours and he often performed job-related work at home. He did not use the computer for any other purpose than his job-related work.

The IRS denied a deduction because of failure to satisfy the *condition of employment* test. However, the reason given for the denial was that adequate computer facilities existed at work. In the words of the IRS,

"In order to satisfy the requirement that a home computer is required as a condition of employment there must be a clear showing that the employee cannot perform properly the duties of employment without it. That clear showing is lacking in this situation because there is no evidence that the computers supplied [at work] are insufficient to enable him properly to perform the duties of his employment." [Rev. Rul. 86-129]

The above revenue ruling based its denial on the fact that it was not shown that the computing facilities at work were insufficient to properly perform the job. This was the feature the IRS chose to focus upon in its official public ruling on the subject.

However, we had advised our readers not to be overly deterred from claiming a deduction. We felt that future court cases might overturn such treatment of the home computer deduction. This advice has been borne out by the following two recent court cases. In the first case, decided in 1996, an employee needed her home computer so she could tap into her employer's data base using a modem after hours.

In the second case, a college teacher did not stop when the IRS originally denied his deduction. Feeling strongly that his deduction was justified, he did not go to the informal small case tax court which does not establish legal precedence [see the *Audit* chapter], but went to the regular tax court itself. He thereby established a precedent that will prove valuable to others in a similar situation.

Court Case

A sales manager employed by Pacific Bell purchased a computer and printer for $3,689 which she used in her home. The computer was used exclusively for job-related purposes to write various reports required for Pacific Bell and to keep up with the volume of work associated with her position as sales manager. She was able to tap into her employer's computer system for information she needed after hours by using the modem connected to her computer.

The only issue at trial was whether her purchase of the computer was "for the convenience of her employer and required as a condition of employment." The Court decided this issue in her favor. Referring to her as the "petitioner," it ruled:

> *"Because of her heavy caseload and the number of sales representatives she managed, it was necessary for petitioner to purchase a computer and printer. Petitioner used the computer and printer to complete various reports she was required to submit to her supervisors at Pacific Bell. [Her boss] testified that sales managers could access information at home via modem and that by using computers at home sales managers were able to work efficiently and keep on top of the volume of work. [Her boss] further testified that only third level management could enter the building after hours and that petitioner was considered second level management. Thus, petitioner was unable to use the office computer after business hours. We find, based on the facts and circumstances presented, that petitioner's purchase of the computer and printer was for the convenience of her employer and required as a condition of employment. Accordingly, petitioner is entitled to a deduction for the computer and printer based on their cost of $3,689.* [Mulne, TC Memo 1996-320]

Court Case. Professor Wins Home Computer Victory

Thomas Cadwallader was a Professor of Psychology at a large midwestern university. His wife, Judy Douglas, was the chief transportation planner for a local governmental agency.

Cadwallader and Douglas purchased an IBM-compatible home computer costing, together with peripherals and software, $2,597. The computer was used at home, almost entirely (98% of the time) for job-related purposes.

Cadwallader used the computer in connection with his scholarly activities. He was an active researcher into the history of American psychology. He used the computer for the management of historical data connected with this research. He also used the computer for word processing and other document preparation purposes when writing papers which were published in professional journals. While there were a few computers on campus he might have had some access to, these were far from adequate. He needed to have his own home computer to accomplish the research and writing which he performed during the year.

Douglas also used the computer in connection with her job as a transportation planner. She was required to do planning which involved extensive number crunching. Much of this work previously had been done on a mainframe computer owned by the state, but the state eliminated access to this computer. Her office lacked the funds to purchase a computer of its own. And were it to ask for extra funds to make such a purchase, it would take too long a period of time even if the purchase were authorized.

The IRS objected that the purchase of the computer was not an explicit requirement of the job for either Cadwallader or Douglas. They did not need to purchase the computer either to obtain or keep either of their jobs. Neither of them had a statement from the employer stating that a computer was a necessity of the job. Thus, according to the IRS, under the listed-property rules for computers purchased by employees after June 18, 1984 [see the Expensing and Depreciation *chapter], no deduction should be allowed.*

However, Cadwallader and Douglas pointed to the IRS's own language in Rev. Rul. 86-129 [as quoted earlier in this subsection]. There did not have to be an absolute requirement to purchase the computer. It was necessary only that "there be a clear showing that the employee cannot perform properly the duties of employment without it." As he and his wife testified, this was clearly shown in both their cases. He also cleverly argued that the purchase of a microcomputer could not have been an absolute requirement of his job since microcomputers weren't even invented when he obtained his current position. (He had tenure so he couldn't be fired for not making the purchase later.)

The Court sided with Cadwallader and Douglas. It stated,

> *"In order for the 'condition of employment' requirement to be satisfied, petitioners' employers need not explicitly require them to use a computer. . . . Instead, it is only necessary that petitioners' use of the computers be required in order for them to properly perform the duties of their employment. . . . We conclude that this requirement is satisfied. . . .*

> *"We also conclude that the 'convenience of employer' requirement is satisfied. Here the computer purchase spared petitioners' employers the cost of providing them with suitable computer equipment with which to engage in their job responsibilities."*

Since the 2 basic requirements for deducting listed property were satisfied [see the Expensing and Depreciation *chapter], the Court allowed a deduction for the home computer.* [Cadwallader, TC Memo 1989-356]

In the above case, a college teacher was able to deduct his use of a home computer because he used it extensively in connection with his job-related research. But what if a teacher uses a home computer just for teaching-related activities? The following 2 recent court cases shed light on this question.

Court Case. Deduction for Teaching-Related Computer Use Denied

Bryant was a teacher at a private lower school in the East. Her school decided to stop using hand-written report cards and evaluations. Instead, the teachers were required to enter this information on a disk compatible with Macintosh computers.

Although the school had 8 Macintosh computers available for faculty and student use, Bryant purchased a computer of her own. She claimed there were an insufficient number of computers available at school for the faculty to use in preparing their reports. Also, there were security and confidentiality problems involved in using the school computers which were also used by the students. And after-school use would be dangerous because the school was located in a dangerous area, across the street from an area of drug activity. As a result, she contended she needed her own computer to prepare her reports in a timely and adequate manner. This indicated the computer was required as a condition of her employment, *meaning a deduction should be allowed.*

However, the Court did not agree. A number of other teachers were able to prepare their reports on the school's computers. This meant the purchase of the computer was not a condition of employment. *And her purchase of her own computer did not result in the school purchasing less computers than it otherwise would. This meant the computer was purchased for the* convenience of the taxpayer, *not the* convenience of the employer. *As a result, Bryant's deduction for her home computer was denied.* [Bryant, TC Memo 1993-597]

Court Case. Deduction for Teaching-Related Computer Use Approved

Starr was an art teacher employed by a large county school system. She purchased a Macintosh computer for $2,084 which, according to the Court record, was used for "teaching purposes." Most interestingly, the IRS did not object to her taking a deduction for her computer. The only issue it raised at the trial was the fact that Starr had not elected to expense *the computer by filling out Part I of Form 4562 [see Section 2 of the* Expensing & Depreciation *chapter]. This meant she was entitled to a 20% x $2,084 = $417 depreciation deduction for the year of purchase, with the remaining 80% x $2,084 = $1,667 deducted over the succeeding 5 years according to the Regular Depreciation Table [see Section 3 of the* Expensing & Depreciation *chapter].* [Starr, TC Memo 1995-190]

In the preceding case, the Court itself did not rule on whether the home computer qualified for a tax writeoff. The interesting fact is that the IRS did not object to a writeoff when Starr's tax return was being audited. No details were given of Starr's computer usage in the record of the court case, because it was not an issue at trial. This indicates that, in practice, IRS agents may be more liberal in allowing home computer deductions during an audit than the officials who write the rulings. If you believe a deduction for your home computer can be supported, you should not be unduly deterred from claiming a deduction.

Note that the above discussion only applies to computers which are **not** used in a deductible home office. If you are eligible to deduct for a home office in which you use a computer, the computer does not need to satisfy the listed property requirement that it be for the *convenience of the employer and required as a condition of employment.* (Computers which you own and use at work where you are employed are not treated as home office computers; in order to be deductible, they must satisfy the *listed property* requirements stated in the preceding sentence.)

If you use a computer in a home office which qualifies for deduction, it is not considered to be a fixture of the home office. Thus it can be deducted, even if the deduction exceeds the income received from the activity for which the home office is used [see the *Home Office* chapter].

If you can claim a deduction for your computer, *Condition 2* described in Section 1 of the *Expensing and Depreciation* chapter applies. Namely, if business use does not exceed personal use, a special stretched-out depreciation table must be used. Of course, in any event, you're only entitled to a deduction for that percentage of cost equal to the percentage of time the computer is used for business rather than personal purposes. For example, if a $2,000 computer is used 60% for business purposes and 40% for personal purposes, your deduction would be based on the cost attributable to business use — 60% × $2,000 = $1,200. However, you can still deduct the full cost of software for business or investment applications, even if the computer itself is used partly for personal purposes.

As discussed near the beginning of this chapter, special recordkeeping rules apply to use of a home computer. However, no matter what the nature of your records, the IRS may question whether your claimed business use is legitimate. Here are a number of steps you can take to safeguard your deduction:

1. **Establish a clear business purpose.**

   To deduct a home computer, you should use it for specific business purposes — either connected with (i) your regular job, (ii) an outside business activity, or (iii) managing your investments. Of these three activities, the latter two are the safest justifications to use. The IRS is generally tougher about expenses incurred by an employee than it is about expenses incurred by a business owner or active investor.

   It's a good idea to purchase specific business-related software in the same year you purchase your computer. Purchase of such programs as word-processing, portfolio analysis, spread sheet analysis, etc. will give credence to your claim that the computer is being used for business-related purposes. Similarly, subscriptions to data banks like the Dow Jones Information Service would point to an investment business use.

2. **Don't have personal software listed on the same invoice as your computer or business software.**

   Of course, you should not be deducting that fraction of the cost of the computer corresponding to your use for personal purposes such as game playing.

But you don't have to stir up doubts by having game software intimately connected with your computer. If your computer deduction is questioned, you would want to be able to present invoices which point to your business use of the computer, not your personal use.

3. Buy a bigger rather than a smaller computer.
Popular inexpensive computers are more questionable than higher-power, more expensive computers. The inexpensive computers are often used for game playing while the more expensive computers are typically purchased with a business purpose in mind.

4. Buy a different computer than the one available at work.
The type of home computer most easy to deduct is one which is different than any computer available at work. This is illustrated by Example 3 discussed earlier in this chapter.

5. Save your output.
If you have a printer, save as much output as you can which illustrates your business usage. This is concrete proof that you're making substantial business use of your computer.

Insurance
You can deduct the cost of extra insurance you purchase to cover items you own. Ordinary homeowners' insurance policies usually exclude or have a special limitation on items used for business purposes. You must purchase extra insurance if you wish to cover these items. There is even special insurance you can take out on home computers to cover the extra calamities that occur such as power surges which damage equipment or software.

Where Do You Deduct Books, Supplies, and Equipment?
Items used in your professional capacity as an employee, whether deducted immediately or depreciated over their useful life, are deducted under the *Miscellaneous Deductions* section of Schedule A. These items, when aggregated with your other miscellaneous deductions, are subjected to a 2% of adjusted gross income floor [see Section 1 of the *Miscellaneous Deductions* chapter].

Items used in connection with a self-employment activity are deducted as a business expense on Schedule C or Schedule C-EZ. In this case, the items escape the purview of the 2% of adjusted gross income floor and can be claimed even by those who use the standard deduction. In any event, if items are used partly for personal purposes, you must prorate the expenses accordingly.

Form 4562 is used to list items with a useful life of more than one year which are being expensed or depreciated. There is a special Part V on Form 4562 for computing your depreciation or expensing deduction for *listed property*. This Part V is used for all listed property for which a deduction is being claimed, no matter when the property was purchased. You do not need to use Form 4562 if your only depreciation deduction is for items which were not listed property and were first placed into service prior to 2001. [See the *Expensing and Depreciation* chapter for further details.]

Deducting for Books or Other Items Purchased in the Past

Suppose you purchased books or other depreciable items in a prior year but did not claim a deduction. Can you get any deduction now? The answer is yes.

As long as you still own the items, there is a new procedure for claiming all the past depreciation you missed or under-reported, going back any number of years [IRS Revenue Procedure 99-49]. This procedure is accomplished by filing Form 3115 with the IRS. More details are contained in Section 3 of the *Expensing and Depreciation* chapter.

Miscellaneous Materials

The deduction for miscellaneous materials used in connection with your teaching duties might yield a sizable deduction. This is illustrated by the following court cases.

Court Case

Gardner was a Professor of Education at a university in the South. The university did not provide all the supplies and educational materials which she used in her classes. As is typical with many teachers, she dug into her own pocket to pay for certain materials she felt were needed in her classroom teaching. According to the Court, *"The furnishing of supplies and materials to supplement those provided by a school may constitute an ordinary and necessary business expense."* In Gardner's case, the Court allowed a deduction of $856 for the cost of supplies and course materials purchased during the year.

Furthermore, this was not the only miscellaneous deduction allowed in connection with her duties as professor. She was allowed a deduction of $695 for depreciation, $78 for typewriter repair, and $300 for secretarial assistance. The sum of these job-related items which could be claimed as *miscellaneous deductions* was $1,929. [Gardner, TC Memo 1983-541]

Court Case

Mathes was a History Professor at a large university, with duties including both teaching and research. He conducted his research in his office at school and in his home office. His home office was ruled non-deductible because the Court felt his on-campus facilities were adequate [see Section 1 of the *Home Office* chapter]. But his deduction for the supplies he used was allowed. The Court did not accept the large amounts he initially claimed, but it did allow a deduction for supplies of $1,069 in one year and $668 the next — a total 2-year deduction of $1,737. [Mathes, TC Memo 1990-483]

If you are like most people, you haven't kept complete records of all the miscellaneous supplies you purchased for use in connection with your job. This does not rule out a deduction on a reasonable estimate. For example, in one court case, a teacher was allowed a $125 deduction for miscellaneous educational materials, even though he had no records or receipts [TC Memo 1978-299]. (Because this case was decided a number of years ago, the $125 figure would correspond to a larger figure now. In this connection note the survey, discussed earlier in this section, in which an average expenditure of $242 was spent by teachers for supplies used in the classroom.)

However, where the out-of-pocket expenses that are deductible do not exceed the 2% of AGI threshold, you should consider donating the supplies to the school and deducting them as a charitable contribution.

3

Home Office

SECTION 1
WHEN CAN YOU DEDUCT FOR A HOME OFFICE?

College faculty members often find it necessary to do a substantial amount of work at home. At one time, most of these college faculty members were able to claim a deduction on their tax returns for this use of a "home office." A number of years ago, however, Congress passed tough legislation severely restricting the home office deduction. An employee must satisfy the following rules in order to claim a deduction for a portion of his home used as an office during the tax year.

Rule 1. The portion of his home must be used **exclusively and regularly** for business purposes.

Rule 2. The home office must be the **taxpayer's principal place of business**.

Rule 3. The use of the home office must be for the **convenience of the employer.**

Exceptions to Rule (2). If the home office is a *"separate structure which is not attached to the dwelling unit,"* Rule (2) does not need to be satisfied. However, Rules (1) and (3) still apply. Another exception when Rule (2) does not apply is when the office is used *"by patients, clients, or customers in meeting or dealing with the taxpayer in the normal course of his trade or business."*

In a case to be discussed below, the Supreme Court in *Soliman* ruled that the meaning of "principal" for this purpose required that the home office be the most important place where the taxpayer earned his income from his trade or business. This may be based on time spent at different locations or where most of the income is actually earned. Congress amended the law, effective for years beginning in 1999, defining "principal" to include the place where a taxpayer conducts the administration or management of the business.

Exclusive Use of Home Office on a Regular Basis

The *exclusive use* requirement of Rule (1) means that there must be a specific part of the home used solely for business or professional purposes. No deduction is allowed for a den or other area which is used both for business and personal purposes. The area set aside must be *regularly* used for business purposes. No deduction is allowed for incidental or occasional business use, even if the area is used for no other purpose.

It is not necessary for the home office to be a separate room or partitioned-off area. This is illustrated by the following court case.

Court Case

A college professor used a portion of his bedroom as a home office. This portion was

> *"furnished with a desk, a chair, two file cabinets, and three bookcases. In the other portion or area of the bedroom petitioner had his bed and a dresser. He insisted that although the two areas were located within a single room, they were separate and discrete areas. However, the two areas of the room were not separated by any wall, partition, curtain, or other physical demarcation."*

The IRS claimed that the professor had not met the *exclusive use rule* because the home office was not an entire room or an area physically separated from the rest of the bedroom. But the Court found nothing in the law which supported this requirement. If the home office occupied a specific area of the home and this area was not used for other purposes, the *exclusive use requirement [Rule (1)]* was met, even if the area was not physically separated from the rest of the home. *(The Court disallowed the home office deduction for other reasons discussed below but carefully pointed out that the exclusive use requirement was met in this case.)*
[Weightman, TC Memo 1981-301]

A separate court case shows that a home office need not be located in an ordinary "room." In this case, the Court ruled that a large walk-in closet would qualify as a home office, if all the other requirements for deduction were met. [Hughes, TC Memo 1981-140]

Home Office as Principal Place of Business

Rule (2), which requires that a home office be the *principal place of business,* is the most difficult for teachers to satisfy. This rule has undergone several different interpretations by the courts over the past few years.

Originally, the Tax Court settled upon the *focal point* test. That is, it defined the principal place of business to be the *focal point* of a taxpayer's activities.

Then, after being overruled by several different Courts of Appeal, the Tax Court introduced an easier test to satisfy. Under this test, a home office satisfied the *principal place of business* requirement if (1) the taxpayer spent a substantial amount of time in his home office, (2) the home office was essential to the taxpayer's work, and (3) no other location was available to perform the office functions [Soliman, 94 TC No. 20]. This opinion of the Tax Court was upheld by the Court of Appeals in the area where the taxpayer resided [Soliman, 935 F.2d 52].

However, this interpretation did not last long. The IRS appealed the case to the Supreme Court. In a 1993 decision [506US 168], the Supreme Court discarded the previous interpretations and came up with its own 2-part test for satisfying the *principal place of business* requirement.

Supreme Court Test

According to the Supreme Court in 1993, the following were the two primary considerations in deciding whether a home office satisfies the *principal place of business* test:

(1)   the relative importance of the activities performed at each business location;

(2)   the time spent at each place.

(The Court stated that each case *"turns upon its particular facts"* and that *"no one test is always determinative."* In other words, the above two criteria are to be used when possible, but will not necessarily decide every case.)

The Court singled out one situation where determining the *relative importance* criterion in (1) would be relatively straightforward. Namely when goods or services are involved, *"the point where goods and services are delivered must be given great weight in determining the place where the most important functions are performed."*

The written decision does not explicitly state which of the above 2 conditions is the more important or whether they have equal importance. However, it appears from reading the entire Court opinion that the first condition is the more important. In other words, if the activities at one location are determined to be more important than the activities at any other location, this location will typically be considered the principal place of business, no matter what the time spent at each location. Only when there is relatively equal importance assigned to each location does the time spent at each place have significant importance. In fact, this is the interpretation the IRS has adopted in the 4 examples, discussed later in this Section, contained in the most recent IRS ruling on this issue.

Below is a more detailed discussion of the Soliman case in which the home office policy of the Supreme Court is spelled out.

Soliman Court Case

Soliman was an anesthesiologist at several hospitals in the Washington, D.C. area. Because none of the hospitals provided him with an office, he used one bedroom in his 3-bedroom home as an office.

Soliman used his home office solely for activities connected with his professional duties — recordkeeping, reading medical books and journals, telephoning patients and other doctors, preparing monthly lectures he gave to nurses, etc. He didn't see any patients at his home office. Soliman spent an average of 2 to 3 hours a day working in his home office. This constituted about 30% of his total working hours.

When Soliman deducted his home office, the IRS objected. The "focal point" of his professional activities was where he administered anesthesiology to patients, not where he performed his office chores. And a distinct minority of his working time — only 30% — was spent in his office at home. According to the IRS, this meant the home office was not the "principal place of business," ruling out a deduction.

The Tax Court — upheld by the Court of Appeals — sided with Soliman, ruling that his home office could be deducted. It based its decision on 3 conditions satisfied by Soliman which it felt were sufficient to justify a home office deduction, namely that Soliman spent a substantial amount of time in his home office, his home office was essential to his work, and no other location was available to perform his office functions.

The Supreme Court overturned this decision, and ruled that Soliman's home office expenses were not deductible. However, Congress changed the law so that managerial and administrative duties can qualify a home office to be deductible.
[Soliman, 506 US 168]

In the 1997 Tax Reduction Act, Congress believed that the Supreme Court's decision in *Soliman* unfairly denied a home office deduction to a large number of taxpayers who manage their business from home and overturned the decision. Starting in 1999, the phrase "principal place of business" includes a place of business used solely by the taxpayer for administrative or management purposes of any trade or business activities if there is no other office made available by the employer. [Code Sec. 280A(c)(1)]

Congress went a step further in outlining circumstances in which taxpayers perform administrative or management activities in places other than the home office and fail to meet the *principal place of business* requirement but may take the deduction under these unique circumstances (Congress liberally interpreted management activities):

1. Taxpayers who do not conduct administrative or management activities in a fixed location other than the home office, but have an outside third party perform administrative or management activities at a location outside of the home office (e.g. billing services).

2. Taxpayers who carry out administrative or management activities at a location other than a fixed location (e.g. car or hotel) in addition to performing the activities in the home office.

3. Taxpayers who perform minimum administrative or management activities in a fixed location other than the home office.

4. Taxpayers perform substantial non-administrative or non-management activities in a fixed location other than the home office, (e.g. meeting or providing services to clients).

With respect to professors, under the 1997 Tax Reduction Act, professors are eligible for a home office deduction if they do not have a fixed office location at the school in which they are employed or do not have adequate office facilities and conduct all of their administrative or management activities from their home (i.e. research, lesson plans, etc.).

In addition, a professor may take a home office deduction if his office at home is utilized for a business outside of the scope of his school employment such as writing or research for outside business activities. However, if the professor has an office at the school, any use of the home office for school activities would be considered non-business use and, therefore, no deduction for an office in the home would be allowed.

In essence, under the new law enacted by Congress, the taxpayer in *Soliman* would be entitled to a home office deduction because he used his home office for administrative and management activities associated with his anesthesiology practice.

The above discussion only applies to the case of an employee who uses his home office in connection with his job-related duties. It is different when a home office is used in connection with a separate self-employment activity such as writing a profit-making book, consulting, etc. In that case, a home office deduction is much easier to obtain. This situation is discussed later in this section.

The following 1990 court case shows that even when a home office does not qualify as the *principal place of business* of an individual's business activities taken as a whole, it still might qualify as a deductible home office for one of these activities.

Court Case

Hoye was a surgeon on the staffs of 2 hospitals in the Midwest. In addition to his surgery practice, he set up a laboratory in the basement of his home. He used the laboratory to perform specialized biopsies on tissue samples from his patients and from patients of other doctors. The fees he received for his laboratory work amounted to about $9,000 per year.

The question was whether or not the laboratory qualified as a deductible home office. The laboratory was the principal place of business for the laboratory work. However, it would not be the principal place of business for his medical activities as a whole.

The Court ruled that the 2 activities could be separated. The surgical activities constituted one business and the laboratory a second distinct business. Because his laboratory satisfied the home office rules for his laboratory business, it qualified for deduction.

The IRS had objected that the surgical and laboratory work were closely related and therefore should be considered as one business. But the Court did not agree. It stated, "In fact, the operation of two trades or businesses by a taxpayer is more likely to be in fields which are closely related."

Although Hoye could claim a home office deduction, he could not deduct the cost of driving between his home and the hospital where he performed surgery. To deduct the cost of traveling between a home office and a location of a different business activity, the home office must be the site of the most important activity [see Example 9 in Section 2 of the Travel chapter]. In Hoye's case, the most important activity was his surgical, not his laboratory work. However, he could deduct the cost of traveling between his home office and other locations directly connected with the laboratory business for which the home office was used (e.g. suppliers, the bank, etc.). [Hoye, TC Memo 1990-57]

Example 1

Joe is an English professor at a local university and also writes novels for publication. He does all of his research and writing in his home office as well as all of the administrative duties. He also spends time in the home office writing lesson plans for his college courses. Joe has an office at the university where he can work on his lesson plans but works at home in order to be able to spend time with his young children. The use of the home office to prepare lesson plans is considered personal because Joe has an office at the school. Joe's use of the home office is not for the convenience of his employer. Therefore, the home office is not used exclusively for writing novels and Joe cannot deduct any of the expenses for the home office. If Joe only used the office for writing novels, his expenses would be deductible.

Example 2

The facts are the same as in Example 1 except that Joe does not have an office available to him at the university. The university is overcrowded and offices are not available to all staff. Offices are assigned by seniority and Joe has not been at the university long enough to get an office. Because Joe does not have an office at the university, his use of the home office for preparing lesson plans, grading papers, etc., is not considered personal use. Therefore, Joe would be entitled to deduct all of the expenses attributable to the home office.

Home Office Used for Two Separate Activities

Sometimes a home office is used for 2 separate business activities. In this situation, as the Tax Court case below confirms, both uses must qualify under the home office rules in order for any deduction to be allowed. In particular, the home office must be the *principal place of business* for each of the activities.

Although the following case concerns only a single individual using a home office for 2 different purposes, the same principle would apply to 2 people sharing a home office.

Court Case

Hamacher was a professional actor, working in the theatre as well as doing radio and television commercials. In addition to his acting, he was the administrator of an acting school. The school provided office space which Hamacher could use.

Hamacher used one room in his six-room apartment as a home office. He used the office both in connection with his acting duties and his duties as school administrator.

The Court examined Hamacher's activities. He had 2 separate "business" activities — one as actor and the other as administrator. His home office was used for each of these activities.

The Court ruled that for the home office to be deductible, it must be the principal place of business for each of the business activities taking place in the home office. In this case, it would need to be the principal place of both Hamacher's acting and administrating duties. However, Hamacher had a suitable office at the school where he was administrator. This office, not the home office, was the principal place of his administrating 'business.'

Because the home office failed the test for one of the business activities for which it was used, it did not qualify for deduction. Even if it met the basic rules to be deductible in connection with his acting activities, this would not matter. No deduction could be claimed. Nor could any travel between home and other local job locations be deducted. (The result, presumably, would have been different had the claimed home office usage been only in connection with his acting activities.) [Hamacher, 94 TC 348]

Home Office Used for Secondary Business Activity

For most employees, the *principal place of business* requirement rules out a deduction for a home office used in connection with their main job. But the use of a home office connected with a secondary business activity can be deducted, as long as the home office is the principal location of that activity. It does not matter that an individual's main job is located elsewhere. For example, the use of a home office for writing a profit-making book, consulting, tutoring, running a side business, etc., would qualify. However, as discussed in Section 2, the deduction for a home office used as the principal place of business for a secondary business activity cannot exceed the gross income from that activity.

Court Case

Samuel was a full-time education teacher, working on a master's degree at a nearby university. His wife was a former teacher and was also working on a master's degree at the same University. Together, they decided to develop and manage a sales business in order to earn extra money. They operated this business solely out of an office in their home and claimed a $2,500 deduction on their tax return. In the Court's words,

> *"Samuel testified that within petitioner's three-bedroom apartment, two children slept in one room, an infant child slept in petitioner's bedroom, and the third bedroom was used as an office. They also testified that there was a desk and a telephone in the third bedroom and that the closets were used to store the sales products. Samuel testified that he did not use the room to prepare for his teaching job or his university studies."*

The IRS objected that the room was not used exclusively as the principal place of their sales business. But the Court did not agree with this objection, stating,

> *"In our opinion, the evidence is sufficient to establish that petitioners exclusively used the office in their home on a regular basis as the principal place of their sales business. The room was not used for recreational purposes, and petitioners used local libraries and university facilities to study for their courses at the university. [The IRS] has presented no evidence to the contrary. Therefore, we hold that petitioners may deduct expenses incurred in maintaining the office in their home."*

That was the good news. Had the sales business produced a reasonable amount of income, they would have obtained substantial benefit from their home office deduction. But the bad news was that they only had $46.50 in sales for the year. Not only was this a business disappointment, but under the rules described in Section 2, this meant their home office deduction could not exceed $46.50. [Taylor, TC Memo 1985-499]

You cannot get around the home office limitation by renting your home office to your employer or to an entity for which you are providing services as an independent contractor. This was ruled out by a provision in the 1986 Tax Reform Act. This loophole was eliminated in response to an accountant who, under prior law, rented his home office to the accounting firm for which he worked, converting an office that was secondary to his job into a primary place of business of his "rental business."

Also, a home office deduction cannot be claimed for purely investment activities — reading financial periodicals, clipping bond coupons, etc., because these do not qualify as *trade or business* activities. (In order to be in the *trade or business* of investing, one must be a short-term active *trader* rather than a long-term *investor.*) But this restriction does not apply to overseeing rental properties if it involves active management duties. This is illustrated by the following court case.

Court Case

Curphey was a dermatologist, employed 40 hours per week by a hospital in Hawaii. He owned 6 single-family residential properties which he managed himself. He lived in a two bedroom condominium and

> *"used one bedroom exclusively as an office for bookkeeping and other activities related to management of his rental properties. That room was furnished with a desk, a bookcase, a filing cabinet, calculators, and a 'code-a-phone answering service'. There was no television, sofa, or bed in that room and petitioner did not allow guests to stay there. The closet of that room was used only to store items related to the rental properties such as lamps, carpets, and other furnishings, signs which petitioner used to advertise the units for rent, cleaning materials which he needed to prepare a rental unit for a new tenant, and a tool box."*

Because Curphey was actively involved in the management of his properties, his efforts constituted a trade or business activity *rather than just an* investment activity. *And since his home office was used regularly as the principal business location for this activity, it qualified for deduction.* [Curphey 73 TC 766]

Home Office For Convenience of Employer

Rule (3) on the first page of this chapter requires that the home office be for the *convenience of the employer.* This requirement does not apply to self-employment activities because there is no *employer* involved. For employees, this requirement means there must be a genuine need for you to have a home office. If you have an office at work, you will be required to show why the facilities there are inadequate.

Two recent court cases underscore this requirement. In one case, Professor Cadwallader made extensive use of his home office in connection with his research into the history of American psychology. He was able to deduct the cost of his books and a computer which he used in his home office [see the *Books, Supplies, & Equipment* chapter]. But he was not allowed to deduct his home office, because he had adequate office space at school in which he could have conducted his research. In its decision, the Court gave an up-to-date summary of the *convenience of employer* requirement,

> *"Research and writing are the principal work of most university (as distinct from college) professors, including Professor Cadwallader. If, therefore, the university failed to supply him with adequate office facilities, this would imply that it expected him to equip his home with a suitable office. If he did so, and used the home office exclusively and on a regular basis for his scholarly research and writing, then he would be entitled to the home office deduction. But if he is given adequate facilities on the campus to conduct the major part of his scholarly research and writing there, the fact that he chooses to work at home instead does not entitle him to a deduction. It is then not the convenience of the employer but the professor's own convenience, and perhaps his tax planning, that induces him to maintain a home office."* [Cadwallader, 919 F2d 1273 (1990)]

The other case concerned a History Professor who had a reputation as one of the top researchers at the University where he worked. The University provided him with an office which while *"sufficient in size to perform some research, as well as administrative work (such as the grading of exams), it could not accommodate the extensive collection of materials he used in his work. Had petitioner requested additional space at the University, he would not have been able to obtain it."* Because his facilities at school were inadequate, he performed most of his research out of his home office which was large enough to contain his very large collection of books. This would seem sufficient to satisfy the *convenience of employer* requirement. But no. The Court ruled that he could have used the extensive selection of materials which the Professor stated were at his school's library. This meant his home office was for his personal convenience rather than for the convenience of his employer. Presumably, had the library not contained such an extensive collection, the result would have been different. [Mathes, TC Memo 1990-483]

Vacation Office Ruled Deductible

The following court case shows how a vacation home office can qualify for deduction, even when used only a small portion of the year.

Court Case

Heineman was the chief executive officer of a large corporation in Chicago. He spent his summers in Wisconsin where he owned property overlooking Lake Michigan. The property contained a vacation residence plus a separate structure which was furnished as an office. The office was used by Heineman each August for long-range corporate planning. The rest of the year, the office was unused.

The Wisconsin office was more suitable than the Chicago office because Heineman could avoid the interruptions of daily business that would occur in Chicago. By using his Wisconsin office during August, he could find the isolation he wanted for concentrating on long-range planning.

The IRS objected to Heineman's home office deduction. It claimed that the office was simply a personal convenience, not a necessity of the job; he could have just stayed in Chicago and worked in his regular office.

The Court did not buy this objection. It found that "there was a business reason for performing the review of the long-term plans away from the Chicago office, and the expenses of the office for performing that work are not made nondeductible because the petitioner chose to perform the work in an environment more suitable to him."

The IRS also objected that Heineman had not asked his employer to reimburse him for the cost of constructing his home office. But the Court overruled this objection too. There was no evidence that he could have been reimbursed. And, even if he could have been reimbursed, he did not want his company to have a claim on any of his Wisconsin property.

Consequently, the Court allowed Heineman a home office deduction. This included a full year's depreciation on the cost of constructing the office, even though it was used only one month a year. [Heineman 82 TC 538]

The above case opens the door for individuals with summer property who perform work-related duties there. Note, however, that in the above case, the home office was in a separate structure not attached to the residence. This exempted it from the *principal place of business* test as described earlier in this section. Home offices which are not located in detached structures fall under the *principal place of business* requirement.

Items Used in a Home Office

As discussed in the next section, the home office deduction includes the basic cost of providing office space (including depreciation, furniture, utilities, etc.) plus the cost of auxiliary items such as equipment and telephone service. But even if you don't qualify for the home office deduction, a deduction for the auxiliary items used in the home office may still be permitted.

The cost of providing telephone service, except for the basic monthly service charge for your primary residential phone line, is an example of this [see the *Books, Supplies, & Equipment* chapter]. In several court cases, a deduction for business use of a home telephone was permitted at the same time the basic deduction for a home office was ruled out. [Shepherd, TC Memo 1976-48; Barry, TC Memo 1978-250]

Supplies and equipment such as a typewriter or calculator would also qualify for deduction independent of the basic home office deduction. For example, in one court case a deduction for the rental of a typewriter and calculator was permitted, even though these items were used in the person's residence at night and there was no deduction allowed for the basic cost of providing these residential facilities. [Hicks, TC Memo 1960-48]

Payments for Services

Even if you don't qualify to deduct your home office, you can still get a deduction for services performed in the office if connected with a legitimate business activity. This is shown by a recent court case concerning an individual who used a home office in connection with a real estate business he had established. His business produced no income for the year, so he was not entitled to any home office deduction under the rules that applied for that year. However, he claimed $1,300 paid to relatives for cleaning the home office, answering the telephone, and filing.

The amount paid for cleaning was considered a direct home office expense, therefore nondeductible. But answering the telephone and filing were ordinary business expenses, not direct home office expenses, even though performed in the home office. As a result, the Court, estimating that $1/3$ of the amounts paid to the relatives was for answering the telephone and filing, allowed a Schedule C deduction of $1/3 \times \$1,300 = \$433$. [Dollar, TC Memo 1987-346]

Office Decorating

The cost of cleaning, decorating, and furnishing your home office is deductible, as long as the home office meets the requirements described above.

Pictures and other works of art do not qualify for a deduction because they do not wear out. However, in one court case, deductions of $445 were allowed for the cost of framing pictures which were then hung in a home office. [Fanning, TC Memo 1980-462]

But beautifying your regular office at work might not qualify for deduction. A court case disallowed a deduction to a government worker for a live plant and framed print she purchased for her office at work. Her employer had provided all the furnishings considered necessary to do her job. The cost of beautifying her office was ruled to be a personal rather than a business expense. [Henderson, TC Memo 1983-372]

Lawn Care & Landscaping

According to a 1988 court case, a portion of your lawn care and landscaping expenses might be claimed as part of your home office deduction. In this case, a couple ran an audio-visual business out of their home. Because clients regularly visited their home, the Court allowed them to deduct a portion of their expenses for lawn care, landscaping, and driveway repair corresponding to the percentage of their home used as a deductible home office. The deduction was allowed because the appearance of the residence and grounds was a factor in creating the proper impression for their clients [Hefti, TC Memo 1988—22]. (However, if a home office is used only by the owner, without regular visits by clients or customers, the cost of such items would not be deductible.)

Travel from a Home Office to Another Business Location

If you have a home office which is the principal location of a business activity, you can deduct the cost of traveling from your home office to another location in connection with that business activity. The following cases were decided under prior law; however, the relevant travel rules were the same as under current law.

Court Case

Wickler was an anesthetist at a small hospital in the South. She was not considered an employee of the hospital, but rather was an independent contractor. The hospital billed patients for her fees and deducted an agreed percentage of the fees and remitted the balance to the anesthetist.

Under prior law, the Court found her home office to be her principal place of business in which a substantial part of her work was performed. In such a case, travel between her home office and another business location (in this case, the hospital where she worked) is deductible. Because 90% of her automobile mileage was incurred traveling between her home and the hospital, she was permitted to deduct 90% of her automobile operating expenses and depreciation for the year. [Wickler, TC Memo 1986-1] *The conclusion would be the same under the new law.*

A similar conclusion was reached in a 1987 court case concerning an attorney associated with a law firm. He received cases referred to him by the law firm and was considered an independent contractor because of the degree of independence he had in his work. He spent most of his time working in his home office, but went to the law firm's office when he needed administrative support from the law firm's staff. Because his home office was his principal place of business, he was permitted to deduct his travel to and from the law firm. [Wollesen, TC Memo 1987—611]

Even if a home office deduction cannot be claimed because there are no expenses, a deduction may still be allowed for travel to and from the home office. That's the conclusion of the Tax Court in the following 1990 case.

Court Case

Kahaku was a self-employed guitarist who performed 8–12 hours per week at a seafood restaurant in Honolulu. He lived in his father-in-law's house. He paid no rent to his father-in-law.

One room in the house was set aside for Kahaku's exclusive use as an office or studio. In this room, he maintained all of his business records, practiced approximately 30 hours per week, recorded music, and listened to music.

Under the law applying at the time, Kahaku's home office was ruled to be his principal place of business. However, Kahaku was not entitled to a deduction for his home office because he was using it rent-free and had no expenses to deduct. That was not the issue. Rather, because the home office met all of the basic qualifications for deduction, he could deduct the cost of driving between his home and the restaurant where he performed. Also deductible were trips to music stores and audition sites. The total deduction, including depreciation and actual expenses on his auto, amounted to $17,201 over a 2-year period. [Kahaku, TC Memo 1990-34]

If your home is a *secondary* location of a business activity, you cannot deduct the cost of traveling to the principal place of that business activity. Such travel is considered nondeductible commuting. A possible way around this restriction in certain cases is to make an intermediate business stop. For example, picking up business mail at a post office, making a business-related purchase, depositing business receipts at a bank, etc., might qualify. The cost of traveling between such a stop and your principal place of business for the related activity would then generally be deductible.

Also, if you travel from your home to a temporary job location, you may be able to deduct your travel expenses even if your home is not the principal place of business. The rules for deducting this type of travel are discussed in Sections 3 and 4 of the Travel chapter.

SECTION 2:
COMPUTATION OF HOME OFFICE EXPENSES

If you have an allowable home office deduction, you may deduct a pro rata portion of the expenses incurred in the general maintenance of the home. The list of allowable home expenses includes:

1. rent (if residence is rented)

2. depreciation (if residence is owned)

3. cost of heat and light

4. cleaning expenses (including salary for cleaning person)

5. painting the outside of the house

6. premiums on home insurance

7. general house repairs (e.g. repairing the gutters)

8. extermination and termite inspections

9. mortgage interest

10. property taxes

Note that if you claim a portion of your mortgage interest and property taxes as a home office deduction, you cannot claim these same amounts again as itemized deductions elsewhere on Schedule A.

Be on the alert for any expenses which you think are relevant. For example, in one case a taxpayer was allowed to depreciate a pro rata portion of the cost of a vacuum cleaner because it was used in cleaning his home office.

Expenses relating solely to the use of your office may be deducted in full, such as the cost of painting only the office or the cost of furniture used in the office. You may not deduct expenses relating only to portions of the house excluding the office, such as painting the living room.

How Is the Pro Rata Proportion Computed?

Suppose that you have a room set aside for use as a home office. There are two methods to determine what proportion of home expenses can be attributed to your home office. The primary method is to divide the area occupied by the home office by the total area of the entire home. Thus, if the office occupies 140 square feet and your home has a total area of 2,500 square feet, then you can deduct 140/2,500 = 5.6% of the allowable home expenses.

If the rooms in your house are about the same size, you can divide the number of rooms used for your home office by the total number of rooms in the home. For example, if you use one room of a five room house as your office and the rooms are about the same size, you may deduct 1/5 of the allowable home expenses. [IRS Publication 587] (There is a court case which indicates you don't have to count every area as a full room; in this case, a kitchen in a house was counted only as 1/2 of a room, resulting in a deduction equal to 1/5.5 of the home expenses. [Moretti, TC Memo 1982-552])

Example

You use one room of a 6 room house you own as a home office for which you are entitled to a deduction. If the rooms are about the same size, you can deduct 1/6 of the following expenses:

Depreciation on house	$2,000
Electricity for light and air conditioning	490
Gas for heating	250
Repair of the roof	300
Fire insurance	100
Cleaning person	390
Mortgage interest	2,500
Property taxes	800
TOTAL	$6,830

Thus, your home office deduction is 1/6 × $6,830 = $1,138. In addition, you can deduct for the cost of furnishings or equipment used in the home office [see the Expensing and Depreciation chapter].

Home Office Can Be More Than One Room

The following court case illustrates that the home office deduction need not be limited to a single room or even two rooms.

Court Case

Greenway was a professor of anthropology, specializing in ethnomusicology. He was also an author, having written several published books and numerous articles.

He set aside 3 rooms of his house as a home office. He used 3 rooms in order to keep separate projects on which he was working simultaneously and did not use those rooms for any other purpose. Under the rules in effect at the time, he was entitled to a deduction for the use of his home office.

The IRS allowed him a deduction for the full use of all 3 rooms. The only home office question among the issues that came up at the trial was a secondary one concerning the amount of depreciation that should be allowed.
[Greenway, TC Memo 1980-97]

Home Office Deduction Cannot Produce a Loss

If a home office deduction would result in a loss on your tax return, you cannot deduct this loss. The way to proceed in such a case is as follows:

Start with the gross income produced by the business activity for which you are using the home office. From this, subtract expenses other than home office — supplies, salaries, travel, etc. Next, subtract home office expenses in the following steps:

1. Interest and Taxes

2. Operating Expenses such as repairs, utilities, insurance, cleaning, etc.

3. Depreciation

If the result of step 1 is zero or a loss, do not go on to steps 2 or 3. You get to deduct the interest and taxes, but are not allowed any deduction on this year's tax return for operating expenses or depreciation.

If the result of step 1 is positive, then you go on to steps 2 and 3. If a loss results at either of these steps, you must stop; in this case, the business activity produces a net result of $0 for the year.

If you are disallowed from deducting expenses by the rules in the preceding paragraphs, all is not lost. You may be able to carry over these deductions to future years as described later in this chapter.

Of course, in the above list you only subtract that pro rata portion of interest and taxes, etc., corresponding to the percentage of the home used as an office. The remainder of interest and taxes is deducted on Schedule A in the usual way. The following illustration is adapted from an example published by the IRS. [Prop. Reg. §1.280A-2(i) (7)]

Example

X operates a consulting business out of his home office for which he is entitled to a deduction. X has a special telephone line for the office and occasionally employs secretarial assistance. X determines that his home office occupies 20% of his home. On the basis of the following figures, X determines that the sum of the allowable business deductions for the use of the office is $1,050:

Income from consulting services.		$4,000

Expenses for secretary	$ 500
Business telephone	250
Supplies	350
	$1,100

Total expenses other than home office	−1,100
Net income derived from use of home office	$2,900

1. Interest and Taxes:	**Total**	**Allocable to Office**
Mortgage interest	$6,000	$1,200
Real estate taxes	2,000	400
	$8,000	$1,600

Amount allowable	−1,600
Limit on further deductions	$1,300

2. Operating expenses:	**Total**	**Allocable to Office**
Insurance	$ 250	$ 50
Utilities	2,500	500
Repairs	250	50
Cleaning	500	100
		$700

Amount allowable	−700
Limit on further deductions	$ 600

3. Depreciation:	**Total**	**Allocable to Office**
Depreciation on house	$5,500	$1,100

Amount allowable in current year	$ 600
Remainder (carried over to future years as described below)	$ 500

X may claim the remaining $6,400 ($8,000 − $1,600) paid for mortgage interest and real estate taxes as itemized deductions on Schedule A.

Home Office Losses Carried Over to Future Years

As illustrated above, a home office deduction is not allowed to the extent it creates a net loss from the business activity to which it is attributable. However, such a disallowed amount can be carried over to the following year to the extent it does not produce a net loss for the business activity in that year. There is no time limit on the carryover. Any amounts disallowed can continue to be carried over until there is a net profit from the business activity they can be deducted against.

Example

Smith operates a consulting business from his home office which generated gross income of $6,000. Business expenses that are not attributable to the home office itself (e.g. secretarial services, telephone, supplies, etc.) total $4,000. Home office expenses (interest, taxes, utilities, depreciation, etc.) total $3,000. Thus, Smith has a net loss of $1,000 ($6,000 – $4,000 – $3,000) for the year. This $1,000 loss cannot be deducted in the current year, but must be carried over to the following year.

In the next year, Smith has gross income from his consulting business of $9,000, home office expenses of $2,500, and other expenses of $3,500. The result, as reported on his 2002 Schedule C, would be as follows:

A.	Gross Income	$9,000
B.	Expenses other than home office:	–3,500
C.	A – B:	5,500
D.	Home office expenses for 2002:	–2,500
E.	C – D:	3,000
F.	Carryover from 2001:	–1,000
G.	Net profit reported on Schedule C:	$2,000

In the above example, E ($3,000) exceeded the $1,000 carryover from the previous year. Had it not, any excess would continue to be carried over until there was a year in which the consulting business had a profit. For example, suppose that in the above, E equaled $600 instead of $3,000. In this case, $600 of the $1,000 carryover would be applied to reduce the net profit to $0. The remaining $400 would continue to be carried over into the future.

It is important to remember that you can deduct mortgage interest and real estate taxes in the year incurred no matter if there is a loss on the Schedule C. The remaining amount of loss must be carried over to the following year.

Sometimes it is possible to shift income or expenses in such a way that the carryover provision can be used to obtain a deduction that might otherwise be lost altogether.

Example

Jones anticipates the following income and expenses from a self-employment activity run out of his home:

Year	2001	2002
Income	$6,000	$6,000
Expenses other than Home Office	−6,000	−6,000
	0	0
Home Office Expenses	1,000	1,000
Deductible Tax Loss	0	0

The reason there was no taxable loss during either 2001 or 2002 was because of the limitation on deducting home office expenses discussed above.

But now suppose $2,000 of income is shifted from 2001 to 2002, say, by delaying issuing a bill for services rendered. The result would be as follows:

Year	2001	2002
Income	$4,000	$8,000
Expenses other than Home Office	−6,000	−6,000
	−2,000	2,000
Home Office Expenses	1,000	−1,000
Home Office Expense Carryover from 2001		−1,000
		0
Deductible Tax Loss	$2,000	0

By shifting income to 2002, an extra $2,000 tax loss is achieved that would otherwise be carried over to future years or simply lost if not offset by future income from the business.

Moving Your Home Office

If you move from one residence to another, you may deduct the cost of moving the furnishings, books, etc., in your home office. You are not restricted by the mileage limitation which applies to general moving expenses.

Where is the Home Office Deduction Claimed?

Employees claim their home office used for job-related activities as a *miscellaneous deduction* on line 20 of Schedule A. When aggregated with other miscellaneous deductions, it is subject to the 2% of adjusted gross income floor that applies.

As discussed below, *self-employed* persons claim their home office expenses on Form 8829, with the total home office deduction transferred to Schedule C. (The simplified Schedule C-EZ cannot be used when a home office deduction is claimed.) These expenses can be deducted even if the standard deduction is used. And there is no 2% of adjusted gross income floor.

Home Office Form 8829 for the Self-Employed

Form 8829 must be used by those with self-employment income who claim a home office deduction on Schedule C. Employees who claim their home office as a miscellaneous itemized deduction on Schedule A do not have to fill out Form 8829.

How to Avoid Capital Gains Tax If You Sell Your Home

You do not pay capital gains tax upon sale of your principal residence, provided you satisfy the rules described in Section 3 of the *Homeowners* chapter. But this does not apply to that portion of your house used as a home office. For example, if part of your house is being used as a home office, capital gains tax would be due on an appropriate fraction of the profit at the time of sale plus any depreciation you had claimed in prior years.

If you sell or exchange your home you may be able to exclude up to $250,000 ($500,000 for married filing a joint return) of the gain. See Chapter 9, *"Tax Deductions for Homeowners,"* Section 3, for more detail.

4

Expensing and Depreciation

SECTION 1:
INTRODUCTION

This chapter concerns non-trivial job-related, business, or investment items which will be used for more than one year. Such items now generally fall into one of 3 classes.

The **real estate class** consists of houses, apartments, and other buildings. Land is not included because it generates no deduction based on its "wearing out."

The **5-year recovery** class consists of (i) automobiles and trucks, (ii) computers and peripheral equipment, calculators, typewriters, and copiers, and (iii) items used for research and experimentation.

The **7-year recovery** class includes books, furniture, and office equipment not included in the 5-year class.

For items in the real estate class, you are not allowed to deduct the cost all at once. Instead, you must apportion the cost over a period of years. This is called **depreciation.**

For items in the 5-year or 7-year recovery class (e.g. books, equipment, furniture, etc.), you can **expense** the item, that is, deduct the entire cost in the year it is first used. This option is limited to $24,000 worth of items purchased in 2001. This *expensing method* is discussed in Section 2.

You can also *depreciate* books, equipment, furniture, etc., over either 5 years or 7 years, depending upon the recovery class to which the item belongs [see Section 3].

Expensing is almost always preferable to depreciation because, other things being equal, a tax writeoff is more valuable the earlier it is used because of the time value of money. However, there are certain cases when the depreciation method should be used for 5-year or 7-year recovery class items.

First, an item must be used more than 50% for business purposes throughout the entire recovery class period. Otherwise, the item should be *depreciated* rather than *expensed*. If the expensing method is used for an item purchased in 2001 and then in a later year within the recovery class period, business use falls below 50%, the IRS can *recapture* a portion of the expensing deduction that was claimed [see Section 2].

Second, the expensing method should not be used on automobiles which cost more than $15,500. Because of special rules that apply, depreciation is superior to expensing for such automobiles [see the *Automobile Expenses* chapter].

Third, depreciation might be preferable to expensing in some cases where your business use percentage is expected to increase in future years.

Fourth, items used for investment purposes (e.g. a computer used just for tracking stocks) cannot be expensed, but must be depreciated.

Finally, there are special rules which apply to certain home computers, photo and video items, cellular telephones, and automobiles which are considered *listed property*. As discussed below, sometimes depreciation is the only allowable writeoff method for these items.

Form 4562 is the basic form on which the items being depreciated or expensed are listed. (However, as discussed near the end of this chapter, Form 4562 is not required if all the items were purchased prior to 2001.) For employees, their total job-related depreciation or expensing deductions are included under *Miscellaneous Deductions* on Schedule A. (As discussed in Section 1 of the *Miscellaneous Deductions* chapter, a 2% of adjusted gross income floor applies to the sum total of all miscellaneous deductions claimed on Schedule A.) Self-employed individuals claim these deductions on Schedule C or Schedule C-EZ, escaping the 2% of adjusted gross income floor.

Special Rules for Autos, Computers, Cellular Telephones, and Entertainment Items

There are two special conditions that apply to the following items, called *Listed Property* by the IRS:

Listed Property:

1. Automobiles and other passenger vehicles.

2 Home Computers (including peripherals), except for employer-owned computers used exclusively at a regular business establishment or computers used exclusively in a home office qualifying for deduction as described in the *Home Office* chapter.

3. Property of a type generally used for purposes of entertainment, recreation, or amusement (e.g. video recorders, cameras, etc.), except if used either (i) exclusively at your regular job location or deductible home office, or (ii) in connection with your principal job or business.

4. Cellular Telephones.

Condition 1: Listed Property Purchased by an Employee Must Be Required by His Employer.

In order for listed property purchased by an employee in connection with his job to be deductible, the law states that its use must be *"for the convenience of the employer and required as a condition of employment."* According to IRS regulations, the phrase *"condition of employment"* refers to the proper performance of an employee's duties. Quoting from these regulations,

"In order to satisfy the 'condition of employment' requirement, the use of the property must be required in order for the employee to perform the duties of his or her employment properly. Whether the use of the property is so required depends on all the facts and circumstances. Thus, the employer need not explicitly require the employee to use the property. Similarly, a mere statement by the employer that the use of the property is a condition of employment is not sufficient." [IRS Reg. §1.280F-6T]

The IRS has not similarly interpreted the phrase *"for the convenience of the employer."* However, this phrase would appear to be superfluous in this context. It is hard to produce an example where the *condition of employment* requirement would be satisfied without the *convenience of the employer* requirement being satisfied also.

The IRS regulations give three examples which apply to the use of automobiles or other personal transportation vehicles. In two cases where the employer did not provide a vehicle but the employee had to travel to various jobsites, the *condition of employment* requirement was satisfied. But in the third case, the *condition of employment* standard was not satisfied where the employer made a car available to the employee, but the employee chose to use her own car and receive reimbursement instead.

The IRS regulations also contain an example concerning the use of a home computer. This example is discussed in the *Books, Supplies, and Equipment* chapter.

Condition 2:   Listed Property Must Be Used More than 50% for Business Purposes — Otherwise a Special Depreciation Table Applies.

Listed property which is used 50% or less for business purposes cannot be expensed. Instead, a special *Listed Property Depreciation Table* [see Section 3] must be used to determine the annual writeoffs. This special table stretches out the deductions over a longer period of time than under the regular depreciation table.

Listed property which is used more than 50% for business purposes is not subject to this restriction. The expensing method (or regular depreciation table) applies to these items.

However, no matter what the percentage of business use, Condition 1 above must still be satisfied. Otherwise, no expensing or depreciation deductions can be claimed.

Maximum Limitations on Autos

There are extra limitations on the amounts that can be deducted for expensing or depreciation on an automobile. These are described in the *Automobile Expenses* chapter.

SECTION 2:
EXPENSING METHOD

On your 2001 tax return, you can deduct in full, instead of depreciating, up to $24,000 worth of items in the 5-year or 7-year recovery classes which you placed into service during 2001. These categories include automobiles, calculators, equipment, furniture, etc., but not buildings or other real estate. However, this option does not always apply to certain *listed property* as discussed in Section 1.

The $24,000 limit applies to single or joint tax returns. For married persons filing separately, the $24,000 limit is allocated equally between the two separate returns unless a different allocation is elected.

The procedure of deducting the cost in the first year of use instead of depreciating is called *expensing*. To qualify for expensing, the items must be used in connection with your job or self-employment activity. Items which are used just for investment-related activities do not qualify for the expensing option, but must be depreciated as discussed in Section 3.

> **Example 1**
> *You bought a $300 printer in 2001 which is used only for job-related purposes. Under the expensing option, you deduct the full $300 on your 2001 tax return. There are no further deductions for the printer in future years.*

If more than $24,000 worth of items was purchased in 2001, the expensing option is limited to $24,000, with the remainder depreciated as discussed in Section 3.

> **Example 2**
> *You purchased a $200 fax machine and $26,000 worth of computer equipment during 2001, all of which are used in an outside business activity. You can use the expensing option on up to $24,000 worth of purchases, say, the entire $200 fax machine and $23,800 of the computer. The remaining $26,000 – $23,800 = $2,200 of the computer is depreciated over the 6-year period 2001-2006, as described in Section 3. The total deductions in each year are as follows:*
>
> | Year | Deduction | |
> |------|-----------|--|
> | 2001 ....$24,000 (expensing limit) + 20% × $2,200 = | | $24,440 |
> | 2002..32% × $2,200 = | | 704 |
> | 20034..19.2% × $2,200 = | | 423 |
> | 2004..11.52% × $2,200 = | | 253 |
> | 2005..11.52% × $2,200 = | | 253 |
> | 2006..5.76% × $2,200 = | | 127 |
> | | | $26,200 |

If an item is used partly for business purposes and partly for personal purposes, the expensing option is applied to the appropriate fraction of the item's cost.

Example 3

You purchased a $100 calculator in 2001 which is used 90% for job-related purposes and 10% for personal purposes. You can deduct 90% × $100 = $90 of the cost on your 2001 tax return.

Election to Use Expensing Option

Technically speaking, depreciation is considered to be the "regular" method with the expensing option a secondary method which you can elect to use instead of depreciation. To elect this option, you fill out Part I of Form 4562. The total cost of property you are expensing (referred to as Section 179 property on Form 4562) is listed on line 2. If you do not make the appropriate *election to expense*, the IRS could require you to use the depreciation option. This form should be included with the original tax return you file, not an amended return.

Items Converted to Personal Use

Suppose you purchase an item which is used for business purposes the first year, but is used primarily for personal purposes thereafter. Under the expensing option, you would deduct the full cost in the first year, thereby giving you a total write-off for an item which is used overall only partly for business purposes. To prevent this "distortion," Congress enacted into law a special recapture provision affecting the expensing option.

This provision applies if the item is *not used predominantly in a trade or business* at anytime within the period of the recovery class to which the item belongs. Under this provision, the IRS is authorized to *recapture* a portion of the expensing deduction which was claimed. That is, you would be required to report as taxable income in a later year a part of the expensing deduction you claimed in the year of purchase.

SECTION 3:
DEPRECIATION

This section describes the depreciation rules that apply to items placed into service after 1986. For items placed into service prior to 1987, different rules apply [see previous editions of this *Tax & Financial Guide*].

Depreciation Methods for 5-Year and 7-Year Property

As discussed in Section 1, items other than real estate generally fall into either the 5-year recovery class (e.g. autos, computers, fax machines, research items, etc.) or the 7-year recovery class (e.g. books, furniture, etc.). For both of these categories, there are 2 choices of depreciation methods — the **accelerated** method and the

straight-line method. (The accelerated method is sometimes referred to as the *prescribed* method, abbreviated PRE, or the *double-declining* balance method, abbreviated DDB, in IRS forms. The straight-line method is abbreviated SL.) For either of these categories, you must use the same method for all items purchased during a given year. However, you may use the straight-line method for all items in one category and the accelerated method for all items in the other. You will be able to make a different choice of methods for items purchased in future years.

For items purchased in 2001, the following table shows the percentage that would be deducted each year under the accelerated and straight-line methods. The percentages are applied to the full cost of an item (including sales tax, delivery charges, etc.), assuming it is used entirely for business-related purposes. Observe that the accelerated method will be the best choice for most people because it yields the most rapid write-off. (As discussed later in this section, a different table applies to certain *listed property* [see Section 1] used 50% or less for business purposes.)

REGULAR DEPRECIATION TABLE

5-Year Property

(autos, computers, fax machines, etc.)

Year	Accelerated Method	Straight-Line Method
2001	20 %	10%
2002	32 %	20%
2003	19.2 %	20%
2004	11.52%	20%
2005	11.52%	20%
2006	5.76%	10%
	100%	100%

7-Year Property

(books, furniture, etc.)

Year	Accelerated Method	Straight-Line Method
2001	14.29%	7.14%
2002	24.49%	14.29%
2003	17.49%	14.29%
2004	12.49%	14.28%
2005	8.93%	14.29%
2006	8.92%	14.28%
2007	8.93%	14.29%
2008	4.46%	7.14%
	100%	100%

Observe that in the above table, it makes no difference when during the year the item was placed into service. Thus, for example, the same deductions are produced by an item purchased in January as by one purchased in December. The tables are constructed on the basis of an item being placed into service at the midpoint of 2001 and being used, say, in the case of 5-year property, until the midpoint of 2006 — a total of 5 full years. That is why, for example, it takes an extra 6th year to fully depreciate an item in the 5-year recovery class.

Example

You purchased a fax machine in 2001 for $300. Using the first column in the table for items in the 5-year category, the following would be the annual depreciation deductions:

Year	Deduction	
2001	20% × $300 =	$ 60
2002	32% × $300 =	96
2003	19.2% × $300 =	58
2004	11.52% × $300 =	35
2005	11.52% × $300 =	35
2006	5.76% × $300 =	16
		$300

In the above example, it is assumed the fax machine was used 100% for business purposes. If used partly for personal purposes, the above deductions would be reduced accordingly. For example, if the fax machine were used 60% for business purposes and 40% for personal purposes, the basic depreciation percentages would be applied to 60% × $300 = $180. In this case, the deductions for each of the 6 years in the table would be 20% × $180 = $36, 32% × $180 = $58, etc.

Listed Property

As discussed in Section 1, special rules apply to automobiles, cellular telephones, and certain home computers or entertainment items which fall into the *Listed Property* category. If such items qualify for deduction but are used 50% or less for business purposes, neither the expensing method nor the regular depreciation table applies. Instead, a special *Listed Property Depreciation Table* must be used.

Depreciation begins in the year an item starts being used by you for business purposes and is based on its original cost (or market value at the time of initial business use, if lower). The percentages in the table are applied to the fraction of the cost of an item attributable to business use. You report depreciation for Listed Property in Part V of Form 4562.

LISTED PROPERTY DEPRECIATION TABLE

(Applies to Listed Property purchased in 2001 used 50% or less for business purposes)

Year	Autos	Computers	Entertainment Equipment
2001	10%	10%	4.17%
2002	20%	20%	8.33%
2003	20%	20%	8.33%
2004	20%	20%	8.33%
2005	20%	20%	8.33%
2006	10%	10%	8.33%
2007			8.34%
2008			8.33%
2009			8.34%
2010			8.33%
2011			8.34%
2012			8.33%
2013			4.17%
	100%	100%	100%

Example

A home computer was purchased for $3000 in 2001 and is used 30% of the time for job-related research required by an employer. The computer is used at home, but not in a deductible home office. Because the computer is used 30% for business purposes, the preceding Listed Property Depreciation Table is applied to 30% × $3000 = $900. Thus, the annual depreciation deductions are as follows:

Year	Deduction
2001	10% × $900 = $ 90
2002	20% × $900 = 180
2003	20% × $900 = 180
2004	20% × $900 = 180
2005	20% × $900 = 180
2006	10% × $900 = 90
	$ 900

Varying Percentage of Business Use

The business use of an employer-required *listed property item* purchased in 2001 may vary from year to year. In such a case, the regular depreciation table applies, provided business use exceeds personal use in each year of the write-off period indicated in the *listed property depreciation table,* i.e. 6 years for autos, 6 years for computers, and 13 years for entertainment equipment.

Example

An automobile was purchased for $10,000 in 2001. It is used for employer-required business purposes as follows: 60% during 2001, 70% during 2002, 80% during 2003 and later years until sold. The following would be the depreciation deductions according to the regular depreciation table for 5-year property described earlier in this section.

Year			Deduction		
2001	20% ×	60% ×	$10,000	=	$1,200
2002	32% ×	70% ×	10,000	=	2,240
2003	19.2% ×	80% ×	10,000	=	1,536
2004	11.52% ×	80% ×	10,000	=	922
2005	11.52% ×	80% ×	10,000	=	922
2006	5.76% ×	80% ×	10,000	=	461

For automobiles which cost more than $15,500, there are special limitations which might alter the above computation procedure. Details are contained in the *Automobile Expenses* chapter.

If listed property is not used more than 50% for business purposes in each year of use during the time period indicated in the listed property depreciation table, the special listed property depreciation table must be used throughout the entire depreciation period.

Example

An automobile was purchased in 2001 for $10,000. It is used 60% for business purposes each year except that in 2004, it is used only 40% for business purposes. The 40% usage in one year of the 6-year period in the listed property depreciation table disqualifies it from the regular depreciation table. Thus, the special listed property depreciation table must be used as follows:

Year			Deduction		
2001	10% ×	60% ×	$10,000	=	$600
2002	20% ×	60% ×	$10,000	=	1,200
2003	20% ×	60% ×	$10,000	=	1,200
2004	20% ×	40% ×	$10,000	=	800
2005	20% ×	60% ×	$10,000	=	1,200
2006	10% ×	60% ×	$10,000	=	600

As discussed above, the depreciation method to be used depends upon the business usage percentage not just in the current year, but in future years as well. This means you have to predict in advance what this percentage will be in order to determine which table to use. If you use the regular table because you think your business use will remain above 50% but that turns out not to be the case, a *recapture* provision will come into play. Under this provision, you are supposed to pay back the difference between the deductions yielded by the regular table and the listed property table by including this difference in taxable income. (You may always use the listed property table for a given class of items instead of the regular table if you choose. No adjustments are made if it turns out you qualified to use the regular table because the business use percentage remained above 50%.)

Items Used for Investment Purposes

As discussed in Section 1, there is a special rule (Condition 2) which requires business use to exceed 50% in order to qualify listed property for depreciation under the regular table. In deciding if this condition is satisfied, business use does not include use in connection with investment activities. However, once the correct depreciation table is determined, investment use can be taken into account. The following example illustrates this situation.

Example

A home computer is purchased in 2001 for $3000. The computer is used at home, but not in a deductible home office. The computer is used 40% of the time for job-related research and 30% of the time for managing investments.

Not counting investment use, business use does not exceed 50%. Therefore, the listed property depreciation table must be used. However, the investment use is taken into account when applying the table. That is, the percentages in the table are applied to the cost attributable to business plus investment use, 70% × $3000 = $2100. Thus, the depreciation deductions are as follows:

Year	Deduction
2001	10% × $2100 = $210
2002	20% × 2100 = 420
2003	20% × 2100 = 420
2004	20% × 2100 = 420
2005	20% × 2100 = 420
2006	10% × 2100 = 210
	$2100

Special Recordkeeping Rules for Listed Property

There are special recordkeeping rules which apply to *listed property*. Details of these recordkeeping rules are contained in the *Automobile Expenses* and *Books, Equipment, & Supplies* chapters.

Items Purchased Late in the Year

The preceding depreciation tables provide the same deduction no matter what date during the year an item was purchased. This is because the tables treat all items as though they were purchased at the midpoint of the first year of use. For example, the 5-year regular depreciation table would yield a 20% of cost first year deduction for an auto placed into service on December 31 even if driven for only a few miles. To prevent such a "distortion," Congress has provided a special *40%-rule* when too much is purchased in the last three months of a given year.

The 40%-Rule

Suppose you buy one or more items during the year (other than buildings or other real estate) for which you claim depreciation. If 40% or more of the total cost is attributable to items purchased in the last 3 months of the year, the usual depreciation tables given earlier in this section cannot be used. Instead, the 40%-rule states that each item must be depreciated according to the quarter (i.e. 3-month period) during which the item was placed into service. The 40%-rule does not apply when you use the expensing option described in Section 2 instead of depreciation.

The following table gives the first four years regular or listed property depreciation percentages under this 40%-rule according to the quarter in 2001 during which an item was placed into service. (These tables cannot be used unless the 40%-rule applies.)

DEPRECIATION IN FIRST 4 YEARS WHEN 40%-RULE APPLIES

(Use column according to quarter of the first year during which the item was placed into service.)

	Year	Quarter 1	Quarter 2	Quarter 3	Quarter 4
Regular (i.e. Non-Listed Property)					
5-year property					
accelerated	1	35%	25%	15%	5%
	2	26%	30%	34%	38%
	3	15.6%	18%	20.4%	22.8%
	4	11%	11.4%	12.2%	13.7%
straight-line	1	17.5%	12.5%	7.5%	2.5%
	2	20%	20%	20%	20%
	3	20%	20%	20%	20%
	4	20%	20%	20%	20%
7-year property					
accelerated	1	25%	17.85%	10.71%	3.57%
	2	21.43%	23.47%	25.51%	27.55%
	3	15.31%	16.76%	18.22%	19.68%
	4	10.93%	11.98%	13.02%	14.06%
straight-line	1	12.5%	8.93%	5.36%	1.79%
	2	14.29%	14.29%	14.29%	14.29%
	3	14.28%	14.28%	14.28%	14.28%
	4	14.29%	14.29%	14.29%	14.29%
Listed Property					
Autos or Computers	1	17.5%	12.5%	7.5%	2.5%
	2	20%	20%	20%	20%
	3	20%	20%	20%	20%
	4	20%	20%	20%	20%
Entertainment Equipment	1	8.75%	6.25%	3.75%	1.25%
	2	10%	10%	10%	10%
	3	10%	10%	10%	10%
	4	10%	10%	10%	10%

Example

An individual depreciates a computer purchased for $1,200 on March 25, 2001, and peripheral equipment purchased for $900 on December 20, 2001. These items fall into the listed property category. Over 40% of the total cost is due to purchases made in the last 3 months, as is verified by the following computation:

Quarter Purchased	Item	Cost
1	Computer	$1,200
4	Peripherals	900
		$2,100

$900 / $2100 = 43%

Thus, the special 40%-rule tables are used — the 1st quarter column for the computer and the 4th quarter column for the peripherals.

2001 Deduction

Computer	17.5% × $1,200 =	$210
Peripherals	2.5% × 900 =	23
		$233

2002 and 2003 Deductions

Computer	20% × $1,200 =	$240
Peripherals	20% × 900 =	180
		$420

Observe that if the 40%-rule had not applied, the deduction for 2001 obtained by using the listed property depreciation table would have been 10% × $2,100 = $210 instead of $233. Thus, the 40%-rule in this case yields a higher deduction than under the ordinary rules. The reason for this is the increased deduction for the first quarter purchase of the computer. Had the computer been purchased later in the year, the 40%-rule would have produced a lower deduction than under the regular rules.

Due to the events of September 11, 2001, taxpayers may elect not to apply the 40%-rule for their 2001 tax year if the third quarter of that year includes September 11. This one-time election can be made by anyone, even if they were not affected by the terrorist attacks.

To elect not to apply the 40%-rule, "Election Pursuant to Notice 2001–70" should be written across the top of Form 4562. The election should not be made without determining if using the 40%-rule produces higher depreciation than not using the 40%-rule. There may not be any saving if assets placed in service early in the year have longer recovery periods than those placed in service during the last half of the year.

Houses and Other Real Estate

The *real estate class* is divided into 2 categories — the *residential rental category* and the *non-residential category.* The residential rental category consists of houses, apartments, etc., which are rented out as a personal residence. The non-residential category consists of other real estate such as office buildings, home offices, retail stores, etc. Land is not included because it cannot be depreciated on the basis that it doesn't "wear out."

There are 2 depreciation tables — one for residential rental real estate and the other for non-residential real estate. These tables, given below, provide far less generous depreciation deductions than under the law prior to 1987. These tables apply to real estate which you first placed into business service in 1987-2001, even if purchased and used as a personal residence before 1987.

RESIDENTIAL RENTAL PROPERTY
FIRST PLACED INTO BUSINESS SERVICE IN 1987 – 2001

(Use column for the first month in the year the property is used for business purposes.)

Year	Jan	Feb	Mar	Apl	May	Jun	Jly	Aug	Sep	Oct	Nov	Dec
1	3.48	3.18	2.88	2.58	2.27	1.97	1.67	1.36	1.06	.76	.45	.15
2-27	3.64	3.64	3.64	3.64	3.64	3.64	3.64	3.64	3.64	3.64	3.64	3.64
28	1.88	2.18	2.48	2.78	3.09	3.39	3.64	3.64	3.64	3.64	3.64	3.64
29	-0-	-0-	-0-	-0-	-0-	-0-	.05	.36	.66	.96	1.27	1.57

NON-RESIDENTIAL REAL ESTATE
FIRST PLACED INTO BUSINESS SERVICE IN JAN. 1, 1987 – MAY 12, 1993

Year	Jan	Feb	Mar	Apl	May	Jun	Jly	Aug	Sep	Oct	Nov	Dec
1	3.04	2.78	2.51	2.25	1.98	1.72	1.46	1.19	.93	.66	.40	.13
2-31	3.17	3.17	3.17	3.17	3.17	3.17	3.17	3.17	3.17	3.17	3.17	3.17
32	1.86	2.12	2.39	2.65	2.92	3.17	3.17	3.17	3.17	3.17	3.17	3.17
33	-0-	-0-	-0-	-0-	-0-	.01	.27	.54	.80	1.07	1.33	1.60

NON-RESIDENTIAL REAL ESTATE
FIRST PLACED INTO BUSINESS SERVICE IN MAY 13, 1993 – DEC. 31, 2001

Year	Jan	Feb	Mar	Apl	May	Jun	Jly	Aug	Sep	Oct	Nov	Dec
1	2.46	2.24	2.03	1.82	1.60	1.39	1.18	.96	.75	.53	.32	.11
2-39	2.56	2.56	2.56	2.56	2.56	2.56	2.56	2.56	2.56	2.56	2.56	2.56
40	.10	.32	.53	.74	.96	1.17	1.38	1.60	1.81	2.03	2.24	2.45

Example. Residential Property

In April 2001, you purchased a house for $100,000 (not including the price of the land) which you rent out at a fair market price. To determine the depreciation deduction each year, you use the April column in the above table. Thus, the annual depreciation deductions would be as follows:

Year	Deduction	
2001	2.58% × $100,000 =	$2,580
2002	3.64% × $100,000 =	$3,640
2003	3.64% × $100,000 =	$3,640
etc.		

If you stop using the item for business purposes before the end of a given year, you claim depreciation for that year based on the number of months the item is used, applying a mid-month convention (i.e. the month of disposition is counted as $1/2$ of a month). For example, in the above calculation if you withdrew the house from the rental market on March 2, 2003, the deduction for 2003 would be $2.5/12 \times \$3,640 = \$758$.

If you claim a deduction for an office in a home you own [see the *Home Office* chapter], then along with your other expenses, you deduct a pro rata proportion of the depreciation of your home. Similarly, you deduct depreciation for a home you rent out to others with a profit-making intent [see the *Homeowners* chapter]. You begin the depreciation calculation at the time you first start using the home for business purposes.

Example. Non-Residential Property

In 1984, you purchased a house for $100,000 (not including the price of the land). In March 2001, you converted a room into a home office qualifying for deduction [see the Home Office chapter]. The home office constitutes $1/7$ of the home, so $1/7 \times \$100,000 = \$14,286$ is the cost eligible for depreciation. Because the room was first placed into business service in 2001, the above tables apply. You must use the table for non-residential property because you are using that particular room as a business office rather than as a residence. Because the March column applies, the following would be the annual depreciation deductions:

Year	Depreciation		
2001	2.03%	× $14,286 =	$290
2002	2.56%	× $14,286 =	$366
2003	2.56%	× $14,286 =	$366
etc.			

As in the preceding example, if you sell the house or otherwise stop using the room as a home office, you claim depreciation based on the number of months the item is used, applying a mid-month convention. For example, if you sold the house in September 2003, the deduction for 2003 would be $9.5/12 \times \$366 = \$290$.

Real Estate Placed Into Service Before 1987

For real estate placed into business service prior to 1987 that you are continuing to so use, you would just continue with the same depreciation method you have been using under the old rules. The following tables show the most rapidly permitted depreciation deductions in the initial years for real estate placed into business service between January 1, 1981 and December 31, 1986. (For further information on items first placed into business service before 1987, especially if purchased before 1981, see previous editions of this *Tax & Financial Guide*.)

RESIDENTIAL & NON-RESIDENTIAL REAL ESTATE
FIRST PLACED INTO BUSINESS SERVICE 1981-1986

Property Purchased 1/1/81-3/15/84

(Use column for the first month in the year the property is used for business purposes.)

Year	Jan	Feb	Mar	Apl	May	Jun	Jly	Aug	Sep	Oct	Nov	Dec
1	12	11	10	9	8	7	6	5	4	3	2	1
2	10	10	11	11	11	11	11	11	11	11	11	12
3	9	9	9	9	10	10	10	10	10	10	10	10
4	8	8	8	8	8	8	9	9	9	9	9	9
5	7	7	7	7	7	7	8	8	8	8	8	8
6	6	6	6	6	6	7	7	7	7	7	7	7
7	6	6	6	6	6	6	6	6	6	6	6	6
8	6	6	6	6	6	6	5	6	6	6	6	6
9	6	6	6	6	5	6	5	5	5	6	6	6
10	5	6	5	6	5	5	5	5	5	5	6	5
11-15	5	5	5	5	5	5	5	5	5	5	5	5
16	0	0	1	1	2	2	3	3	4	4	4	5

Property Purchased 3/16/84-5/8/85

(Use column for the first month in the year the property is used for business purposes.)

Year	Jan	Feb	Mar	Apl	May	Jun	Jly	Aug	Sep	Oct	Nov	Dec
1	9	9	8	7	6	5	4	4	3	2	1	.4
2	9	9	9	9	9	9	9	9	9	10	10	10
3	8	8	8	8	8	8	8	8	9	9	9	9
4	7	7	7	7	7	8	8	8	8	8	8	8
5	7	7	7	7	7	7	7	7	7	7	7	7
6	6	6	6	6	6	6	6	6	6	6	6	6
7	5	5	5	5	6	6	6	6	6	6	6	6
8-12	5	5	5	5	5	5	5	5	5	5	5	5
13	4	4	4	5	4	4	5	4	4	4	5	5
14-17	4	4	4	4	4	4	4	4	4	4	4	4

Property Purchased 5/9/85-12/31/86

(Use column for the first month in the year the property is used for business purposes.)

Year	Jan	Feb	Mar	Apl	May	Jun	Jly	Aug	Sep	Oct	Nov	Dec
1	8.8	8.1	7.3	6.5	5.8	5.0	4.2	3.5	2.7	1.9	1.1	0.4
2	8.4	8.5	8.5	8.6	8.7	8.8	8.8	8.9	9.0	9.0	9.1	9.2
3	7.6	7.7	7.7	7.8	7.9	7.9	8.0	8.1	8.1	8.2	8.3	8.3
4	6.9	7.0	7.0	7.1	7.1	7.2	7.3	7.3	7.4	7.4	7.5	7.6
5	6.3	6.3	6.4	6.4	6.5	6.5	6.6	6.6	6.7	6.8	6.8	6.9
6	5.7	5.7	5.8	5.9	5.9	5.9	6.0	6.0	6.1	6.1	6.2	6.2
7	5.2	5.2	5.3	5.3	5.3	5.4	5.4	5.5	5.5	5.6	5.6	5.6
8	4.7	4.7	4.8	4.8	4.8	4.9	4.9	5.0	5.0	5.1	5.1	5.1
9	4.2	4.3	4.3	4.4	4.4	4.5	4.5	4.5	4.5	4.6	4.6	4.7
10-14	4.2	4.2	4.2	4.2	4.2	4.2	4.2	4.2	4.2	4.2	4.2	4.2

Example

In April 1986, you purchased a house for $80,000 (not including the price of the land) which you rent out at a fair market price. To determine the depreciation deduction each year, you use the April column in the above table. Thus, the annual depreciation deductions would be as follows:

Year			Deduction
1986	6.5%	× $80,000 =	$5,200
1987	8.6%	× $80,000 =	$6,880
1988	7.8%	× $80,000 =	$6,240
1989	7.1%	× $80,000 =	$5,680
1990	6.4%	× $80,000 =	$5,120
1991	5.9%	× $80,000 =	$4,720
1992	5.3%	× $80,000 =	$4,240
1993	4.8%	× $80,000 =	$3,840
1994	4.4%	× $80,000 =	$3,520
1995	4.2%	× $80,000 =	$3,360
1996	4.2%	× $80,000 =	$3,360
1997	4.2%	× $80,000 =	$3,360
etc.			

If you stop using the item for business purposes before the end of a given year, you claim depreciation for that year based on the number of months the item is used, applying a mid-month convention (i.e. the month of disposition is counted as $1/2$ of a month). For example, in the above calculation if you withdrew the house from the rental market on March 2, 2001, the deduction for 2001 would be $2.5/12 \times \$3,360 = \$700$.

Basis

When you compute depreciation on a used home or other building, you actually use a figure called the **basis** as the starting cost. It is used in place of "original cost" in the above examples illustrating the depreciation methods. If you start using a home for business purposes as soon as you purchase the home, the basis is just the original price you paid for the home (including legal fees and other settlement costs that can't be deducted). However, if you start using it for business purposes in a later year than the one in which you purchased the home, the basis is the lesser of

(1) Your original purchase price plus the cost of any improvements, or

(2) The fair market value of the home at the time you started using it for business purposes.

The purchase price in (1) refers to the original purchase price when you bought the home. It is not dependent upon your down payment or your monthly mortgage payments.

You cannot depreciate the value of the land on which your home is situated because land doesn't wear out. Thus, (1) and (2) above refer to the price of the home only, excluding the value of the land on which it is situated. You must estimate what cost was due to the home and what cost was due to the land and depreciate only the cost due to the home. Don't use a round number for estimating the cost of the house alone. Tax auditors use this as a tip-off that you haven't reduced the price by the esti-mated percentage attributable to the value of the land.

A court case indicates how such an allocation between structure and land can be made. In this case, the Tax Court permitted an individual to use his property tax assessment, even though it was from a later year than the one at issue. Because the assessment indicated that 12.17% of the total value of the property was due to the land, he was permitted to base his depreciation deduction on the remaining 87.83% due to the structure [Kahle, TC Memo 1991-203]. However, if a more reliable document such as an engineering report indicates a different allocation, this should be used to make the allocation instead of the property tax assessment. [IRS Private Letter Ruling 9110001]

The same rules described above for computing the basis of a home apply to other items as well. For example, if you start using an automobile for business purposes which you purchased at an earlier date, you would use the lesser of (i) original cost, or (ii) market value as the starting cost figure. In this case, the mar-ket value would presumably be the required lesser figure.

Improvements

An improvement is a repair or addition which adds to the value or prolongs the life of the home. Ordinary maintenance or repair expenses are not improvements and cannot be depreciated. (Of course, if you incur these maintenance expenses at a time when the home is being used for business purposes, you get an appropriate deduc-tion for these expenses.)

For example, adding central air-conditioning, replacing the roof, panelling the den, installing permanent storm windows, landscaping, new plumbing, installing new shelving, etc., are improvements. However, the cost of painting, cleaning, fixing a broken air-conditioner, etc. are ordinary maintenance expenses.

Form 4562

If you claim any expensing or depreciation deduction, you must fill out Form 4562 and include it with your tax return. On the first page of this form, expens-ing is claimed in Part I, while depreciation is claimed in Parts II and III. Part II calls for you to list in column (e) the *"Convention"* and in column (f) the *"Method."* When you use the accelerated method in the regular depreciation table for 5-year or 7-year property, you would enter "HY" in column (e) [for *half-year convention*] and "200DB" in column (f) [for *200% Declining Balance Method*].

Your expensing deduction cannot exceed your *taxable income limitation* which you list on Line 11 of Form 4562. According to regulations issued by the IRS in 1992, this limitation includes all active trades or businesses (including those as an employee), not just the one producing the expensing deduction. Thus, an employee can use the expensing deduction in connection with an outside business activity, even if it produces a net loss for that activity.

Form 4562 May Not Be Required

If you (1) do not claim depreciation for items first placed into service in 2001, (2) do not claim depreciation for any listed property items, and (3) do not claim the standard mileage allowance for an automobile used for self-employment purposes, the situation is different. You do not have to fill out Form 4562 at all. You just list the total depreciation amounts on Form 2106, Schedule C, Schedule E, or other appropriate place on your tax return, depending upon the type of business use.

What If You Neglected to Take Depreciation in the Past?

You may have overlooked depreciation deductions you could have claimed in the past. Perhaps you failed to claim depreciation on a rental house, deductible home office, or personal computer which you still own. In the past, there was nothing you could do to regain this depreciation except file amended tax returns for the preceding 3 years.

Now, however, the IRS has a procedure which allows you to claim past depreciation you missed, going back any number of years, on items you still own [IRS Revenue Procedure 99-49]. Under this procedure, you must attach Form 3115 to your timely filed (including extensions) federal income tax return for the year of change. A copy of the application must be filed with the national office no earlier than the first day of the year of change and no later than when the original is filed with the federal income tax return for the year of change. On that return, you will claim all the depreciation you overlooked at one time. You are also allowed to claim under-depreciation in the same manner.

Form 3115 runs 8 pages and contains lots of accounting terminology. You'll probably need to get professional assistance to properly complete this form.

5

Interest

Under the law prior to 1987, the basic tax rule for interest paid was simple — namely, all interest payments were equally deductible on your tax return. (The only major exception was for debts used to purchase tax-free investments such as municipal bonds.)

Those were the good old days. Under current law, some interest is better than others. Depending upon the use of the debt on which interest is paid, the interest might be non-deductible, currently deductible, or deductible in the future.

These rules apply to all debts existing in 2001, even if originated prior to January 1, 1987, when the new rules went into effect.

There are now 5 separate categories of interest:

(1) *interest on your home,*

(2) *personal interest,*

(3) *passive interest,*

(4) *trade or business interest,*

          and

(5) *investment interest.*

The basic tax treatment for each type of interest is described below.

Except for interest on a personal residence, the categorization depends upon how the proceeds of the underlying loan are *used* rather than *secured.* For example, suppose you take out a loan, secured by stocks you own, which you use to purchase an automobile. The interest you pay on the loan falls into the *personal interest* category because the loan was used for the personal purpose of buying an automobile. The fact that it was secured by stocks does not place it into the *investment interest* category.

If an interest payment is due on a loan, you can't borrow more money from the original lender to cover the payment. Otherwise, you lose out on the interest deduction. The IRS has stated that it *"will disallow any deduction claimed for interest paid on a loan if the payment was made with funds obtained from the original creditor through a second loan, an advance, or any other financial arrangement similar to a loan"* [News Release 83-93]. In such a case, no actual payment is considered made — just a renewed promise to pay the original lender. However, if money is borrowed from a different lender to pay the interest due on the original loan, a deduction can be allowed. While common sense may point to this as an irrelevant distinction, the courts have upheld this distinction as a matter of law [Roberts, TC Memo 1987-235].

1. Interest on Your Home

You can deduct interest you pay on a loan secured by your primary home or a second home. The loan can be a traditional first or second mortgage. Or, it can be a home-equity loan taken out to purchase a car or other personal item. As long as the loan is *secured* by your home, it falls into this category. The *second home* need not be an ordinary house, condominium, or cooperative, but can be a mobile home, boat, or other property as long as it contains basic living accommodations, including sleeping space, toilet, and cooking facilities.

There are limits on how much interest you can deduct on loans taken out after October 13, 1987. Generally speaking, the limit on debt used to purchase or construct a home is $1,000,000 and the limit on home-equity debt is $100,000. Details on the rules for loans secured by your home are contained in Section 1 of the *Homeowners* chapter.

Under the current law, home-equity loans have become the debt of choice for many persons. With a typical home-equity loan arrangement, you can set up a line of credit with a bank or savings institution, secured by your equity in your house. You can then draw upon this line of credit anytime you choose. For example, if you need financing to purchase an auto, you can use a fully deductible home-equity loan. This will be better than a loan taken against the value of the auto, which would generate personal interest, not qualifying for deduction as discussed below.

Because home-equity loans are better secured, they offer lower interest rates than most any other type of loan — typically 1/2% below or 2% above the prime lending rate. However, the flip side of this for the borrower is the danger that ownership of his home could be jeopardized if he defaults on the loan. Also, the origination fees for a home-equity loan may offset the savings in taxes and additional interest, especially when the loan amount is on the low side.

2. Personal Interest

The personal interest category includes all interest not falling into any of the 4 other categories discussed in this chapter. Thus, for example, it includes interest paid in 2001 on credit cards, auto loans, late utility or tax payments, etc. Interest paid on past due Federal or State income taxes is considered personal interest, even if there is investment income reported on the tax return. (Underpayment *penalties*, such as the penalty for late filing of a tax return or underpayment of estimated tax, are not even considered to be interest and yield no deductions.) Under the current law, *personal interest* cannot be deducted. Only interest in one of the other categories can now be eligible for deduction.

3. Interest on Passive Activities

There is a category of human financial endeavor invented by the drafters of the 1986 Tax Reform Act, called *passive activities.* The *passive activities* category includes investments in limited partnerships or other business enterprises in which neither you nor your spouse participates on a regular, continuous, and substantial basis. It also includes investments in real estate, no matter what the extent or nature of your participation.

There is a limit on the deductibility of *passive interest,* i.e. interest connected with passive activities in which you have invested. Namely, this interest (along with other expenses) is fully deductible only against the total income produced by your passive activities.

If a net loss is produced because interest plus other expenses exceeds income, this loss cannot be deducted on your 2001 tax return. The remainder can be carried over to be deducted in future years when either there are passive profits, or your ownership of the passive activity is disposed of.

There is an exception that applies to rental real estate owned by individuals with adjusted gross income not exceeding $100,000. Losses arising from such activities can be fully deducted up to $25,000, provided the individual is involved in basic decision-making connected with the rental activity. The $25,000 limit is phased out for those with income between $100,000 and $150,000.

Details on these passive activity rules are contained in Section 2 of the *Investing Your Money* chapter.

4. Trade or Business Interest

You may deduct in full any interest you pay in connection with a trade or business activity (other than as an employee) in which you are a *material participant.* To be a *material participant*, you must perform services on a regular, continuous, and substantial basis.

For example, suppose you have a self-employment consulting practice. You would be able to deduct any interest payments you make in connection with this consulting business. This would include interest on loans for operating capital, mortgage payments on office facilities, etc. You would deduct your interest payments in the usual way as an expense item on Schedule C or Schedule C-EZ.

5. Investment Interest

Income from investments that do not fall into either the passive activity or trade or business activity categories discussed above are considered to be investment income. This includes stock dividends, bond interest, savings account interest, etc. (It generally does not include capital gains.) It also includes any interest paid by the IRS on tax overpayments you made. [IRS Private Letter Ruling 9307005]

If you incur debt in order to purchase stocks, bonds, or other investments, the interest you pay on this debt falls into the category of *investment interest* (sometimes called *portfolio interest*). Investment interest is fully deductible only against investment income, not against earnings or passive income. The way this restriction works is as follows:

a. You first determine your *net investment income* by subtracting investment losses from investment income. You can get the appropriate income and loss figures from Schedule B, Schedule D, etc., of your tax return.

b. Next, you total up the interest paid on any loans which were taken out to make investment purchases. If the total investment interest for the year is less than or equal to the total investment income, you deduct the entire amount of interest you paid on Line 13, *Investment Interest,* of Schedule A.

c. If the total investment interest you paid in 2001 exceeds your total investment income, the difference is your *excess investment interest*. This excess investment interest is nondeductible on your 2001 tax return, but can be carried over to future years when there is investment income against which it can be deducted.

There is a special Form 4952 for computing your deduction for investment interest. If you have paid interest on loans used for investment purposes, you should fill out this form and attach it to your tax return.

Example 1

Cooke has a margin account with his stockbroker which he uses to purchase stocks and bonds. His 2001 investment income (including dividends, interest, etc.) totals $6,000 and he has a net capital loss for the year of $2,000. He pays $5,000 in interest during 2001 on his margin account.

Cooke's *excess investment interest* is computed as follows:

A.	Investment Interest		$5,000
B.	Investment Income	$6,000	
C.	Less: Investment Losses	−2,000	
D.	Net Investment Income (B − C):		$4,000
E.	Excess Investment Interest (A − D):		$1,000

Cooke may claim the amount on line D, $4,000, as an itemized deduction on line 13 of Schedule A. The remaining $1,000 on line E is carried over to a future year in which there is investment income.

Interest to Carry Tax-Free Bonds

There is another type of interest for which no deduction is allowed. Namely, you cannot deduct interest on a loan where the purpose of the loan is to purchase or carry tax-free municipal bonds.

For example, if you use municipal bonds as collateral for a loan, interest on the loan would be entirely non-deductible. The same is true if you use the proceeds of a loan to purchase tax-free bonds. In these 2 situations, a direct connection can be made between the loan and the carrying of tax-free bonds.

In more indirect situations, the deductibility of the interest is a judgment call. The question becomes whether or not the *purpose* of the borrowing was to purchase or carry tax-free bonds.

For example, suppose you have 2 brokerage accounts — one a margin account which you use to purchase stocks and the other a cash account which you use to purchase tax-free bonds. The IRS would generally disallow a deduction for interest on the borrowings in the margin account to the extent you could have sold the tax-free bonds instead of borrowing to purchase the stocks [IRS Private Letter Ruling 8637061].

The situation is different for ordinary personal loans such as mortgages on personal residences. The carrying of tax-free bonds will not generally affect the deductibility of interest on these loans. The personal purpose of taking out such a loan predominates over the investment purpose of holding tax-free securities.

The above applies to the question of deductibility of interest you *pay* on loans you have taken out. No matter what the situation, you do not pay federal income tax on the interest you *receive* on tax-free municipal bonds.

While there are restrictions on borrowing to purchase or carry *tax-exempt* investments as described above, the same is not necessarily true for certain *tax-deferred* investments. For example, if you borrow money to contribute to an IRA or self-employed plan, the IRS has informally stated that interest on such borrowing would be *investment interest,* deductible against taxable investment earnings outside the IRA or self-employed plan. However, the same restriction on borrowing to purchase tax-exempt investments applies to the purchase of single-premium insurance policies or annuities from insurance companies.

Allocation of Interest

As discussed above, the tax treatment of interest you paid during the year depends upon which of the categories the interest falls into. According to the IRS, it is the *use* of the loan proceeds that determines into which category the interest is placed.

For example, suppose you borrow $10,000 from a bank, putting up stocks you own as collateral. You use the $10,000 to purchase an automobile for personal purposes. In this case, the interest paid on the loan falls into the *personal interest* category. Putting up your stocks as security did not cause the interest to fall into the investment interest category. Conversely, if you take out a personal loan and invest the proceeds, interest paid on the loan is *investment interest.* The *use* of the funds you borrowed, not the *security* for the loan, is what counts.

Exceptions

First, interest on loans secured by your primary home or a second home is fully deductible within certain basic limits. In this case, the use to which the loan is put does not matter [see Section 1 of the *Homeowners* chapter].

A second exception applies if you take out a loan and wait for a period of time before spending the money. Until you write the first check on the account into which you deposited the loan, the interest you pay on the loan is considered *investment interest.* For example, suppose you deposit an $8,000 loan into a checking account on February 1. The first check you write after February 1 on this account is on May 1 for $8,000 to purchase a personal auto. The interest paid on the loan from February 1 to May 1 is considered *investment interest,* fully deductible against investment income. After May 1, the interest becomes nondeductible *personal interest.*

Tracing the Proceeds of the Loan

As described above, the category to which interest belongs generally depends on the use to which the borrowed money is put. This involves "tracing" the loan from the time it is received by you until the time it is put to use.

There are 3 basic ways you can control the linkage between a loan and an expenditure for purposes of placing interest into the category you want. First, you can make the purchase with the loan check, appropriately endorsed. Second, you can set up a new account into which only the loan is deposited. Or third, you can satisfy the 30-day rule discussed below by spending the proceeds of the loan for its intended purpose within 30 days of receipt.

For example, suppose you receive the loan in a check which you endorse over to another party from whom you are buying an interest in a passive activity. Or, suppose you open a bank account into which only the loan proceeds are deposited and later, you write a check on this account to buy into a passive activity. In either case, you have a direct tracing of funds from the time of the loan to the time of purchase. Any interest on the loan belongs to the *passive interest* category.

There are rules which handle more complicated situations when there is more intermingling of funds from various sources. In this situation, you should seek accounting assistance to make the proper allocations. In general, what happens is that the loan proceeds deposited in your bank account are considered to be spent in the order you write checks [see Example 5], unless the 30-day rule, discussed below, can be applied.

30-Day Rule

You do not need to have a direct trace like the ones discussed in the preceding two paragraphs. Instead, you can take advantage of the *30-day rule.*

Under the *30-day rule,* if you deposit the loan proceeds into your regular bank account, you can make a direct connection between the loan and any expenditure made within 30 days before or 30 days after the date of deposit. The expenditure need not be made from the same bank account, but can be made with a check drawn on a different account or with cash. (The date on a check is generally considered to be the date of the expenditure, as long as an unreasonable amount of time has not elapsed between the date on the check and the date the check cleared.)

Example 2

You borrow $5,000 from a bank on September 3, which you deposit into your regular checking account. On September 26, you write a $5,000 check on this account to purchase U.S. Savings Bonds. In the meantime, you have made a number of deposits into and withdrawals from the account.

Under the *30-day rule,* you are allowed to make a direct connection between the loan and the investment in Savings Bonds. Thus, interest on the loan can be placed into the *investment interest* category.

Example 3

Same as in Example 2, except that the purchase of the Savings Bonds was made on August 10 with a check drawn on a different bank account than the one into which the loan proceeds were deposited on September 3.

In this case, the *30-day rule* applies the same as in Example 2, even though the purchase was made prior to the loan out of a different checking account than the one used to receive the loan proceeds. Thus, the interest on the loan can be placed into the *investment interest* category.

> **Example 4**
> *Same as in the preceding example, except that only $4,000 is used to purchase Savings Bonds. The remaining $1,000 is spent on personal items.*
> *In this case, only $4,000 of the $5,000 loan is linked to the investment. Thus, 4/5 ($4,000/$5,000) of interest payments on the loan falls into the investment interest category. The remainder is personal interest.*

If the 30-day rule is not applied, loan proceeds deposited in your bank account are considered to be spent in the order you write checks.

> **Example 5**
> *There is $3,000 in your checking account. On September 3, you borrow $5,000 and deposit the funds into this checking account. On September 10, you purchase $2,000 worth of furniture. On October 25, you purchase $4,000 in U.S. Savings Bonds. These are the only transactions in your checking account during this period.*
> *The 30-day rule does not apply to the October 25 purchase. Therefore, the $5,000 loan is considered as having been spent $2,000 for furniture, with the remaining $3,000 spent towards the Savings Bond purchase. Thus, 2/5 ($2,000/$5,000) of interest payments on the loan constitute personal interest, with the remaining 3/5 investment interest toward the purchase of the Savings Bonds.*

The above tracing rules are considerably relaxed in the case of money used to purchase, construct, or improve a personal residence. Details are contained in Section 1 of the *Homeowners* chapter.

Student Loans

For 2001, interest up to $2,500 paid on student loans is deductible. The deduction is allowed only for interest payments made during the first 60 months (whether consecutive or not) in which interest payments are due. Months during which the loan is in deferral or forebearace do not count against the 60-month period. The original loan and all refinancings are counted as one loan. The limit on the number of months during which interest paid on a qualified educational loan is deductible is repealed beginning in 2002.

The deduction applies to loans for higher education of the taxpayer, his spouse, or an individual who was the taxpayer's dependent at the time the debt was incurred. The loans can be used for tuition, fees, room and board, and related expenses such as books and supplies. The student must be taking a work load of at least one-half the normal full-time load for the course of study that the student is pursuing. The student must be enrolled in a degree, certificate, or other program leading to a recognized credential at an institution of higher education.

To yield deductible interest, the loan cannot be received from a related party such as a family member or certain trusts controlled or financed by family members. Also, an individual (such as a minor or other dependent student) cannot claim the deduction if he can be claimed as a dependent by another taxpayer (such as a parent).

Married taxpayers must generally file a joint tax return to get a deduction. Also, if a taxpayer deducts interest on a home-equity loan taken out to finance an education, he cannot also deduct interest as *student loan interest.*

The write-off for *student loan interest* is actually an adjustment to income, rather than an itemized deduction. This means it can be used by those who use the standard deduction, as well as by those who itemize their deductions [see Section 1 of Chapter 1].

Limitations

There are two further restrictions. First, the $2,500 limitation is to be reduced by certain other nontaxable educational benefits. This includes qualified scholarships and educational assistance allowances, as well as amounts received from an employer as a tax-free educational benefit. It also includes U.S. Bond interest excluded from tax as an educational benefit, and amounts excluded from tax using the new Education IRAs [see Section 1 of the *Attending School* chapter].

Second, there is a relatively stringent income restriction. Joint filers get no student loan deduction if their adjusted gross income (AGI) exceeds $75,000, and there is a reduced deduction when AGI is between $60,000 and $75,000. For single persons, the $75,000 figure is replaced by $55,000 and the $60,000 figure by $40,000. (These figures are raised starting in 2002.) To make matters more complicated, AGI must be *"adjusted"* in the preceding sentences by certain other tax benefits such as deductible IRA contributions and excluded social security benefits.

For parent(s) who exceed the above limits, it may be better for the student to take out the loan and pay the interest. That way, he could obtain the deduction for *student loan interest.* However, for this to be of benefit, he would need to have sufficient earnings to file a tax return. Also, as noted earlier, the student loan deduction cannot be used by someone who is claimed as a dependent on someone else's tax return.

How You Should Handle Future Loans

The following describes a number of steps you can take to arrange that your borrowings become deductible to the fullest extent permitted under the law.

1. Keep separate accounts for personal, business, and investment activities. Although this might entail some extra fees, this is the most surefooted way to allocate borrowings to deductible categories. For example, if you place borrowed money into your "investment account" from which all your investments are purchased, interest on the borrowings can be deductible as investment interest no matter what the timing of your borrowings and purchases.

2. If you don't maintain separate bank accounts, make sure debts incurred for investment can be connected to the investment by **observing the 30-day rule** described earlier in this chapter. Another way to make the connection is to receive the borrowings in the form of a check made out directly to your stockbroker.

3. Take out a home-equity loan and use the proceeds to pay off your auto loans, student loans, credit card balances, etc. This can convert personal interest into fully deductible home-equity interest.

4. If you purchase a home, **establish a home-equity credit line at the same time you take out a first mortgage loan** from a bank. The bank may waive its usual fees for appraisal and other services that would just duplicate services required for the first mortgage. With a home-equity line of credit, you have a low cost source of tax-deductible borrowing for your future needs.

5. Pay any deductible interest you owe before year-end. This will give you a deduction in the current year rather than the next year. Shifting deductions forward is generally a tax-savings strategy [see Section 8 of Chapter 1]. Note that the date appearing on your check is what determines the year of payment (unless the IRS should notice an unusually long period of time between the date on the check and the date it was cashed).

6. If you purchase a new home, consider taking out a larger mortgage. This initial mortgage fixes the amount of debt qualifying as fully-deductible *home acquisition debt.* Further amounts that are borrowed against your home cut into the $100,000 *home-equity debt* ceiling, unless used to substantially improve the home. While this ceiling may seem more than adequate now, who knows what future inflation in auto prices, college tuition for your children, etc., may bring.

Even if you don't need the full amount borrowed at the time of purchase, it may still be worthwhile to borrow the maximum in the event of future needs. In the meantime, you can probably invest the unneeded funds, say, in a tax-free bond fund, offsetting the extra cost of the borrowed funds, after considering the tax deduction this provides. Of course, you must be willing to experience the uncertainty of favorable or unfavorable price changes in the bond fund as interest rates vary [see Section 5 of the *Investing Your Money* chapter]. You may want to check with a financial advisor before doing this.

7. Generate investment income to cover investment interest. If you have borrowed to purchase stocks or other investments, your interest is deductible as long as you have sufficient investment income, as discussed earlier in this section. It may pay to sell securities producing a capital gain or shift some investments to interest-paying taxable bonds in order to generate enough investment income to qualify your investment interest for deduction.

8. If your employer permits you to **borrow from your retirement plan,** you may be able to get a full deduction on the interest, even if the loan proceeds are used for personal purposes. The trick is to provide your home as additional collateral on the loan. Because the assets in your retirement plan will generally be more than enough to cover the loan you're permitted to take, there should be no additional home appraisal or other fees required. Although your employer would tap your retirement assets to cover any loan defaults, the fact that the loan is additionally "secured" by your home should establish it as fully-deductible *home-equity debt.* (In the case of 401(k) deferred compensation plans or tax-sheltered annuity plans [see the *Tax-Sheltered Plans* chapter], for the interest to be deductible, the loan should not also be secured by elective contributions made to the plan. Also, there are restrictions that apply to owners, officers, or certain other *key employees.*)

Formalities should be observed in documenting the loan. Specifically, (1) the debt should be secured by a recorded deed of trust or mortgage, (2) an appraisal should be made, (3) the loan together with other home debt should not exceed 90% of appraised value, and (4) the interest rate should be based on prevailing commercial rates for similar loans at the time the loan is made.

9. If you have borrowed all you can on your personal residence, **borrow additional amounts against any rental property you own.** The interest can be fully deductible as passive interest if you fall within the $25,000 exemption discussed earlier in this chapter. And, even if you don't satisfy the exemption, disallowed passive interest, unlike personal interest, can still be carried over to be deducted in future years.

10. If you own stocks or other securities, **use margin loans to make purchases.** However, you can't simply borrow against your stocks to make a personal purchase of, for example, a $15,000 auto. If you do, the interest would be *personal interest* because it is the *use* to which the funds are put that determines the category of interest. Under the law as currently written, however, this is how you can proceed instead.

First, sell $15,000 worth of stock and use the money to buy the auto. Then, using a margin account with your broker, repurchase the stock with funds borrowed from your broker. Interest on the margin account then becomes investment interest because the funds were used to purchase the stock.

Of course, you must take into account capital gains tax and commissions to see if this maneuver makes economic sense. Your stockbroker will be more than willing to expedite this type of transaction for obvious commercial reasons. Some even have set up special arrangements to promote this strategy. Note that the interest rate on a margin loan is probably lower than the rate on any other type of loan available to you.

The same trick works if, instead of stock, you have $15,000 in an interest-bearing or other type of bank account. In this situation, you buy the auto with the $15,000 in your bank account. Then you borrow money on the auto and use the money to re-deposit in your bank account. Interest on the loan then becomes investment interest because the proceeds of the loan were placed into a bank account, which is considered to be an investment vehicle.

11. Pay off all your credit card balances. Interest on these balances is nondeductible personal interest. If you don't have the funds to pay off these balances, try taking out a deductible home equity loan. If this is not possible, you should at least consider using a cash advance on one credit card to pay off your balances on another. Of course, this does not affect the amount you owe, nor does it change the tax picture. But there is often a difference of up to 5% between the rate charged on credit card purchases and the rate charged on cash advances.

Don't Let Your Credit Card Limits Get Too High

It is not uncommon these days for credit card companies to periodically raise the borrowing limits to higher and higher levels. If you have a number of credit cards, the total of these limits might reach a high value. And this in turn could affect your ability to take out a deductible home-equity loan or mortgage on your home. The reason for this is that lenders don't like to see an unusually large amount of available credit. They worry that if this credit were used, it might affect your ability to make timely payments on your loan. For this reason, you should cancel credit cards you do not need and perhaps even ask that your borrowing limits on credit cards you keep be reduced in line with your needs.

Also, if you receive an unwanted credit card in the mail, don't simply discard it. The card's credit line, perhaps thousands of dollars, may still appear on your credit report. Instead, mutilate the card and return it to the issuer with a request that your account be closed.

6

Medical Expenses

SECTION 1:
DEDUCTION FOR MEDICAL EXPENSES

Schedule A includes a deduction for medical expenses that you pay for yourself, your spouse, and your dependents. This includes doctor bills, transportation, medical insurance, medical devices, etc., plus the cost of prescription medicine and insulin. You cannot deduct non-prescription medicine such as aspirin, laxatives, etc.

From your total of medical expenses, you subtract 7.5% of your adjusted gross income (AGI) to arrive at your medical deduction. Schedule A leads you through the appropriate computation.

Getting Around the 7.5% of AGI Limitation

For most taxpayers, the 7.5% of AGI limitation severely restricts their medical deduction.

Here are some strategies for coping with this limitation:

1. Bunch your medical expenses into a single year.

To take a simple example, say your adjusted gross income is $40,000 in each of two successive years, and that your family's medical expenses over this 2-year period amount to $6,000. If these expenses are spread evenly, $3,000 in each year, you lose out on any medical deduction. The medical deduction floor (7.5% × $40,000 = $3,000) wipes out the deduction in each year.

However, if expenses are shifted from one year to the other, you get a deduction. For example, if the $6,000 expenses are split up with $3,600 in the first year and $2,400 in the second, you wind up with a $600 medical deduction in the first year.

Certain elective procedures can be timed so they bunch up in one year. For example, if your family members go to the eye doctor every other year and typically need new eyeglasses, synchronize the appointments so they all occur in the same year. Similarly, non-critical elective surgery can be timed appropriately. This may be especially beneficial in the case of elective dental procedures, e.g. the pulling of wisdom teeth, because the typical medical insurance policy does not cover dental expenses.

You may also be able to arrange for a doctor or dentist to bill you all at once for work done over a period of time. For example, if your child needs $2,500 worth of orthodontia work over a 2 or 3 year period, you might be better off if you're billed for the entire amount up front rather than spreading it out over the period the work is done. However, you can't simply voluntarily pay in advance. To get a deduction, you must actually incur the financial obligation by the year you make the payment. In this example, the orthodontist would be only too happy to send you a bill showing the entire amount due in advance, and may even give you a discount for early payment.

2. Set up a medical plan under which all expenses become deductible.

This is the best idea of all because the 7.5% of AGI subtraction is totally eliminated. However, this works only if you or your spouse has income from a self-employment activity (e.g. writing, consulting, editing, reviewing, tutoring, etc.). A full deduction can be achieved by incorporating the self-employment activity and setting up a corporate medical plan to pay all expenses. Or, more simply, an individual can "employ his spouse in the business" and set up a plan which pays all the medical expenses of his spouse's family (including himself). Under either arrangement, a business deduction is obtained for the full amount of the family's medical expenses with no initial 7.5% of AGI subtraction. Also, a self-employed person might be able to set up a medical plan, without employing his spouse, which covers 40% of the cost of medical insurance for his family. [See Section 2 of the *Outside Business Activity* chapter for further details.]

3. Claim medical items as a business expense.

If you can't claim a medical deduction because of the 7.5% of AGI limitation, perhaps you can claim a medical item as a business expense. For example, suppose you need special eyeglasses which you use only at work. You might be able to claim the cost of such an item as a job-related *miscellaneous deduction* rather than as a *medical deduction*.

4. Pay attention to the rules covering divorced couples.

Divorced couples should take note of the rule concerning the deduction for their children's medical expenses. Namely, either spouse may claim medical expenses which he actually pays for his children. It makes no difference that the other ex-spouse may have custody of the children or that the ex-spouse is claiming dependency exemptions for them.

Because of this rule, it may be better to give an ex-spouse money to pay for your children's medical expenses rather than pay the expenses directly. This situation can occur when your total expenses do not exceed the 7.5% of AGI floor. Further details are given in the *Divorce and Separation* chapter.

5. Shift Medical Expenses to a Lower-Earning Spouse

It can sometimes pay to have the lower income-earning spouse pay all the medical bills. This, coupled with filing separate returns, can result in a tax savings.

For example, suppose you have adjusted gross income of $50,000 and your spouse has adjusted gross income of $20,000. Your family has medical expenses totalling $5,000 for the year.

On a joint return with adjusted gross income of $70,000, the medical expenses floor, 7.5% × $70,000 = $5,200, wipes out the entire medical deduction. Alternately, if you paid all the expenses yourself, and you file a separate return, your medical deduction would equal $5,000 – (7.5% × $50,000) = $1,250. However, if your spouse paid all the medical bills, the medical deduction on your spouse's separate return would equal $5,000 – (7.5% × $20,000) = $3,500, a big increase over the other two alternatives.

Of course, taking advantage of this tax-saving option requires a married couple to file separate returns instead of a joint return. Whether or not this is an advantageous thing to do is discussed in Section 6 of Chapter 1.

Deductible Medical Expenses

Doctors, Dentists, etc.

You can deduct for doctors, dentists, optometrists, chiropractors, osteopaths, podiatrists, psychiatrists, psychologists, physical therapists, and acupuncturists. The medical expense deduction also includes nursing services for a sick or disabled individual, but not for a healthy baby. The services need not be rendered by a professional nurse in order to be deductible.

Medical Insurance

Deductible medical insurance includes hospital and health insurance, whether paid directly by you or withheld from your paychecks. It does not include life insurance or disability insurance except for those portions specifically designated as covering medical expenses. It also does not include insurance payments made by your employer or withheld from your paychecks under an eligible *tax-free* plan.

Medical Aids and Devices

Hearing aids, dentures, eyeglasses, crutches, wheelchairs, orthopedic shoes, elastic stockings, etc., are deductible medical expenses. The IRS has also ruled that if one foot is smaller than the other because of a medical condition, the extra cost of buying 2 pairs of shoes instead of one is deductible. [IRS Private Letter Ruling 8221118]

Birth Control Pills, Legal Abortions, and Vasectomies

The IRS has ruled that these items are deductible medical expenses. A deduction is also generally allowed for other birth control items when prescribed by a doctor.

Medical Charge Portion of School Tuition & Retirement Home Fees

Many colleges and private schools include a charge for medical expenses as part of their tuition or fees. This is deductible, provided that the tuition bill or other statement from the school indicates the amount which is attributable to such medical fees. You should ask the school to provide you with such a statement if they do not do it automatically.

Similarly, payments to a retirement home might include a fee for health care. This fee is deductible in the year paid, even if payment is made in advance for lifetime health care. If a refund is received in a later year, say, because the individual leaves the retirement home, such a refund would then be includable in taxable income. [Rev. Rul. 75-302]

The IRS took a liberal position on how to figure the amount to be considered a health care fee in a ruling issued to a representative of a retirement community. The retirement community provided life care to its residents in return for a one-time admission fee plus a monthly service charge. This life care included access to a 31-bed medical center that was part of the facility.

The IRS ruled that the portion of the fees allocable to medically-related expenses was deductible at the time the fees were paid. In this connection, medical-related expenses included not only salaries of medical personnel and the cost of medicine plus supplies, but also *"expenses allocable to the medical facility such as house-keeping, maintenance and utilities, a proportionate share of interest on indebtedness, real estate taxes, insurance, and depreciation."* The IRS also stated that it would be appropriate to make the allocation of fees by using the financial history of a comparable facility. [IRS Private Letter Ruling 8630005]

Long-Term Care for the Chronically Ill

Starting with the 1997 tax year, unreimbursed amounts paid for long-term care services of an individual, his spouse, or dependent are deductible as medical expenses whether or not the person is in an institution. The services need not actually be medical in character. Deductible expenses are those for necessary diagnostic, preventative, therapeutic, curing, treating, mitigation and rehabilitative services, and maintenance or personal care services required by a chronically ill individual.

Amounts paid to relatives for long-term care services are not deductible unless the relative is a licensed professional with respect to the services rendered.

Premiums on long-term care insurance are deductible within limits. The amount of long-term care premiums that can be deducted is limited to: under age 40, $230; age 40-50, $430; age 51-60, $860; age 61-70, $2,290; age 71 or older, $2,860. The amounts has been indexed since 1997.

Employers can provide long-term care insurance as a tax-free benefit like regular health insurance. If benefits are structured as a per diem payment, only $190 per day is covered, unless expenses are actually being paid out at the time premiums are being paid.

Drugs and Medicine

You **can deduct** the cost of prescription medicine and insulin which you purchased. You **cannot deduct** the cost of non-prescription medicines such as aspirin, laxatives, etc. Even if your doctor recommends an over-the-counter drug, it is not deductible if it does not actually require a prescription to obtain.

Medical Expenses of Non-Dependents

If you satisfy all the requirements of claiming a dependency for a qualifying relative, except that the relative earned more than $2,900, you may still claim a deduction for medical expenses. For example, if you furnish more than 1/2 the support for a parent, you can deduct medical expenses which you pay on his or her behalf. This is the case even though your parent's earnings may disqualify him or her from being your dependent.

To obtain the deduction, payments must be made out of your own funds. However, it is permissible for, say, a parent to give money to a child who then pays medical expenses for the parent, thereby obtaining the deduction. This is illustrated by a court case in which an individual paid the medical bills of his mother out of funds she had given to him. A Court of Appeals ruled that he was entitled to the deduction because the payments were made from funds which belonged to him at the time. However, it should be clear that funds are actually given to the one making the medical payments. In this case, it was necessary to go all the way to a Court of Appeals to win the deduction. The mother had just given her son a power of attorney over her funds instead of an outright gift. The Court had to sift through state law to determine that this constituted a valid no-strings-attached gift of the funds to her son. [Ruch, 718 F2d 719 (1983, CAJ), rev. TC Memo 1982-493]

When you pay the medical expenses of a parent or other individual, be sure to make the payments directly. If you just give money to a parent who uses it to pay medical expenses, you lose the deduction.

Travel

You can deduct your transportation expenses incurred in connection with obtaining medical services. Thus, you can deduct your transportation costs to and from the doctor, dentist, optician, etc. You can also deduct transportation costs to and from the drug store if you are going there in order to pick up medicine. If you use your automobile, you may deduct your actual operating expenses (such as gas, oil, tolls, and parking, but not depreciation or insurance) or deduct 12 cents per mile. Medical travel can include more than just the usual trips to the doctor, dentist, or drug store. For example, the following have been ruled deductible: trips to attend meetings of Alcoholics Anonymous and trips to a swimming pool by a boy suffering from rheumatoid arthritis.

According to a recent IRS ruling, there is another item you can deduct in addition to the 10 cents per mile or actual operating expenses. Namely, you can deduct a pro rata portion of taxes you pay on the automobile. [Rev Proc 89-66] For example, if 15% of your annual mileage is for medical purposes, you can claim 15% of the taxes as a medical deduction.

According to two IRS rulings, transportation costs for relatives of the person receiving medical treatment are deductible when these are necessary. One ruling allowed a wife to deduct her costs in accompanying her wheelchair-confined husband to an out-of-town location to receive treatment. [IRS Private Letter Ruling 7928088] Another ruling permitted parents to deduct the cost of attending consultations at a psychiatric hospital concerning their son who was a patient there. [IRS Private Letter Ruling 7931059] However, the cost of ordinary family visits to a patient in a hospital is not deductible.

If an individual travels out-of-town to obtain outpatient medical care at a licensed hospital or similar institution, up to $50 per day of lodging expenses (but not meals) are deductible. A separate $50 limit applies to someone who is needed to accompany the patient. For example, a parent accompanying a child could deduct up to an additional $50 per day for his lodging expenses. To obtain this lodging deduction, there can be no significant element of personal pleasure, recreation, or vacation in the away-from-home travel.

Childbirth Classes

Most couples now take "childbirth classes" prior to the birth of a child. An IRS Private Letter Ruling indicates the tax status of tuition paid for these classes. Costs allocable to preparing the mother for the childbirth itself are deductible. This would include Lamaze techniques, labor and delivery procedures, birthing positions, etc. Not deductible would be instruction in feeding and newborn care, general study of prebirth developmental stages, adjusting to becoming a parent, etc. When both types of instruction are included, you are supposed to make an allocation between deductible and nondeductible items based on the number of hours devoted to each type of instruction.

Usually, the fee (if any) will cover attendance of both the prospective mother and father (or coach). In this case, the IRS asserts that only the cost of the mother is deductible (even if the father chooses not to attend). Thus, for example, if the cost of such childbirth instruction is $100, only $50 of this cost allocable to the mother would qualify for deduction. [IRS Private Letter Ruling 8919009]

Special Diet

If your doctor orders you to go on a special diet, you can deduct the excess of what the special food costs over what regular food would cost. For example, the extra cost of special food for an individual on an ulcer diet can be deducted. Also, whiskey taken for the relief of angina pains can be deducted when recommended by a doctor's prescription. [Rev. Rul. 55-261]

Two court cases illustrate the deduction for special foods. In the first case, a couple had to eat organic food because they were allergic to regular chemically-treated food. They were permitted to deduct half the cost of their food as a medical deduction. The couple used Labor Department statistics for their area to establish the extra cost of food purchased in health stores. [Randolph, 67 TC 481]

The second case involved an individual who was placed on a high protein diet by her doctor. She kept records of what she spent for food, compared the total with that spent by a friend, and deducted the difference. The Court allowed her a deduction for 30% of her total grocery bill as the excess amount due to her special diet. [Von Kalb, TC Memo 1978-366]

Special Equipment (Including Air Conditioning)

Under doctor's orders, you might need special equipment in your house to take care of an existing medical condition or disease. This equipment can qualify for a medical deduction. For example, the IRS has ruled that the cost of a special mattress and plywood bed boards was deductible when recommended for the relief of an arthritic condition. Another IRS ruling was issued to a family with a son suffering from allergies. Upon prescription from the son's allergist, the following items were all ruled deductible: air conditioning for the home and automobile, electrostatic air cleaner, and humidifier. [IRS Private Letter Ruling 8009080] And in a 1981 case, the Tax

Court allowed a deduction for health club equipment added to the home of a Las Vegas casino dealer as a result of a doctor's advice that it would help relieve the pain of severe arthritis suffered by his wife. [Keen, TC Memo 1981-313] However, in another ruling, the IRS stated that exercise equipment could not be deducted when prescribed in order to prevent possible future heart disease, rather than to treat an existing medical condition. [IRS Private Letter Ruling 8019025]

Under special circumstances, the cost of installing a swimming pool can qualify as a medical deduction. For example, the IRS ruled in 1983 that an individual with severe osteoarthritis could deduct the cost of constructing an indoor pool in his house when his doctor prescribed a treatment of swimming several times a day. [Rev Rul 83-83] Of course, the IRS will be quite skeptical when it is claimed that the construction of a pool is primarily for medical purposes rather than for personal purposes. In the above ruling, the IRS was influenced by the fact that the pool was only 8 feet wide by 36 feet long and no deeper than 5 feet — designed for lap swimming rather than general recreational use. However, the pool need not be specially designed to warrant a deduction if all the facts and circumstances point to medical rather than personal reasons for use of the pool. [Cherry, TC Memo 1983-470]

When deducting medical equipment, you must first subtract any increase in value which the equipment adds to your house. For example, if you purchase central air conditioning for $3,000 and this adds $2,000 to the value of your house, then you can only deduct the difference, $3,000 – $2,000 = $1,000. This $1,000 is deducted in the year of purchase, not depreciated over its useful life. However, you are entitled to a full deduction for equipment added to a rented house or for portable equipment such as a room air conditioner. In any event, you can deduct the full cost of servicing and operating the equipment, e.g. electricity, repairs, service contract, etc. Note that the IRS can be tough about allowing deductions for medical equipment. You may need an appraiser's report on how much the equipment added to the value of your house. In the absence of such a report, the IRS can throw out the deduction altogether. For example, in one case, a court disallowed the full $4,000 cost of air conditioning because of the failure to get an appraiser's report. [Wallace v. U.S., 439 F2d 757 (1971 CA8)]

Special Schooling

According to IRS Regulations, medical expenses include

"the cost of attending a special school for a mentally or physically hand-icapped individual, if his condition is such that the resources of the institution for alleviating such mental or physical handicap are a principal reason for his presence there. In such a case, the cost of attending such a special school will include the cost of meals and lodging, if supplied, and the cost of ordinary education furnished which is incidental to the special services furnished by the school. Thus, the cost of medical care includes the cost of attending a special school designed to compensate for or overcome a physical handicap, in order to qualify the individual for future normal education or for normal living, such as a school for the teaching of braille or lip reading. Similarly, the cost of care and supervision, or of treatment and training,

of a mentally retarded or physically handicapped individual at an institution is within the meaning of the term 'medical care.' [Reg. §1.213-1(e)(1)(v)(<u>a</u>)]

"Where an individual is in an institution, and his condition is such that the availability of medical care in such institution is not a principal reason for his presence there, only that part of the cost of care in the institution as is attributable to medical care. . .shall be considered as a cost of medical care; meals and lodging at the institution in such a case are not considered a cost of medical care for purposes of this section." [Reg. §1.213-1(e)(1)(v)(<u>b</u>)]

The above regulations are illustrated by a Private IRS Ruling. This ruling allowed parents to deduct the full cost of private schooling for their daughter with a learning disability. The school was a special school attended only by children with learning disabilities. The ruling stated that the parents could deduct not only the full tuition, but also transportation to and from the school *"to the extent such transportation expenses are primarily for and essential to the medical care"* of the daughter. Presumably, this means they were allowed to deduct 10 cents per mile (or alternate actual costs as described in the *Automobile Expenses* chapter) for each day's commute to and from school. [IRS Private Letter Ruling 8401024]

In contrast, 2 other court cases have dealt with learning disabled children who attended schools which enrolled regular students, but had a separate program to aid the learning disabled. In both these cases, the extra cost of the special program was deductible, but not the regular tuition. [Sims, TC Memo 1979-499, and Fay 76 TC No. 32] In another case, however, the Court allowed no deduction for the cost of a private school attended by a boy with a learning disability. The boy was sent to the school because he would benefit by the highly structured environment and the personal treatment afforded by a 4-1 student-faculty ratio. But because the school had no special program geared to the learning-disabled, the cost was non-deductible. [TC Memo 1980-572]

A 1992 Court Case shows the extent to which items connected with the schooling can be deducted. In this case, a 17-year old boy with behavioral problems due to habitual drug use was enrolled in a special college-preparatory boarding school located about 500 miles away from home. The school curriculum was designed to address both the educational and emotional needs of its students. The program included community interaction, peer support, and therapy sessions with the student and his family members. The Court allowed not just the cost of tuition, room, and board, but also the cost of maintaining a required "allowance account" for the student, the cost of air travel and auto rental connected with his family attending therapy sessions, and the cost of long distance telephone therapy calls with their son and the staff at the school. [Urbauer, TC Memo 1992-170]

Weight Reduction Programs and Health Clubs

The IRS has ruled that a taxpayer can't deduct the cost of a weight reduction program if the purpose of the program is to improve the general health and well-being of the participant. Similarly, membership in a health spa cannot be deducted (contrary to what those selling memberships may tell you) if you join just to lose weight or keep fit, rather than to combat a specific medical condition.

However, if a weight reduction program is part of the treatment of a specific medical condition or disease, it can be deducted. This was the conclusion of the IRS in a ruling issued to an individual suffering from hypertension and hearing problems. Because her doctors had recommended the weight reduction program for the alleviation of specific illnesses, the cost was deductible as a medical expense. [IRS Private Letter Ruling 8004111]

Similarly, the IRS allowed an individual to deduct the cost of participating in an intensive 13-day special exercise and diet program. The individual was advised to participate in the program as part of treatment for his hypertension and arteriosclerosis. [IRS Private Letter Ruling 8251045]

Also, an IRS ruling permitted a deduction for the cost of swimming recommended by a doctor for a child who suffered from rheumatoid arthritis. This included the cost of a membership fee to use the pool plus the cost of transportation to and from the pool. [IRS Private Letter Ruling 8326095] However, the cost of swimming to maintain general health or fitness would not be deductible.

Aids to the Handicapped

Individuals suffering from handicaps can claim medical deductions for expenses incurred in dealing with their handicap. For example, a blind child was permitted to deduct the cost of braille books in excess of the cost of regular editions. Similarly, the salary paid to an individual to accompany a blind child throughout the school day was ruled deductible. [Rev. Rul. 64-173]

Some recent private letter rulings indicate that the IRS will allow a wide variety of items if they are designed to aid the handicapped. For example, the cost of installing a liftgate in a van for an individual confined to a wheelchair is deductible. [IRS Private Letter Ruling 8034084] Similarly, the IRS ruled that an adapter for closed captioning of television programs could be deducted by a hearing-impaired individual. [IRS Private Letter Ruling 8112030] And in a third ruling, the IRS allowed a hearing-impaired individual to deduct the cost of maintaining a cat because the cat was trained *"to respond to unusual sounds in an instantaneous and directional manner."* [IRS Private Letter Ruling 8033038]

Expenses incurred by a handicapped person for removing structural barriers in his residence are fully deductible. These are not considered to increase the fair market value of the residence. According to a recent IRS ruling, this includes constructing entrance ramps, widening doorways or hallways to accommodate a wheelchair, making bathroom modifications, lowering kitchen cabinets, adjusting electric outlets or fixtures, modifying smoke alarms, changing door hardware, modifying entranceways and grading of ground to provide access to the residence, etc. [Rev. Rul. 87-106]

Cosmetic Procedures

Cosmetic surgery or other procedures are only deductible if necessary to ameliorate a deformity arising from a congenital abnormality, a personal injury resulting from an accident or trauma, or disfiguring disease. The surgical procedure for correcting nearsightedness, *radial keratotomy,* qualified as a medical expense. It is not regarded as cosmetic surgery, according to the IRS. [IRS Private Letter Ruling 9625049]

Alcoholics Anonymous Meetings

The cost of attending meetings of Alcoholics Anonymous, pursuant to competent medical advice, is deductible. This includes the cost of transportation to and from the meetings. [Rev. Rul. 63-273] The cost of attending meetings of other similar rehabilitative organizations would also be deductible.

Disability Income

You might receive payments from your employer while sick or temporarily disabled. These payments are fully taxable even if made under a special sick pay plan. However, worker's compensation is tax exempt.

If you are permanently disabled, you may be able to exclude disability payments made from a plan to the extent that you contributed to the plan. In addition, there is a tax credit, computed on Schedule R, Form 1040, which may exclude a portion of employer-provided permanent disability payments from tax. According to the IRS, *"an individual shall be considered to be disabled if he is unable to engage in any substantial gainful activity by reason of any medically determinable physical or mental impairment which can be expected to result in death or to be of long-continued and indefinite duration."*

Non-Traditional Medical Treatment

Deductions for medical care are not limited to traditional medical procedures. In accord with this policy, deductions have been allowed for holistic medical care, Navajo Indian healing ceremonies, acupuncture, etc.

SECTION 2:
MEDICAL SAVINGS ACCOUNTS

Medical Savings Accounts (MSAs) are a relatively new tax-sheltered method of paying for medical care (starting in 1997). The Community Renewal Tax Relief Act of 2000 renamed MSAs as "Archer MSAs" and extended the time for which such accounts can be created through 2002. This type of account only applies to those who are not covered by a basic service medical plan, including HMOs, etc. However, catastrophic medical insurance is not only permitted, but is required as discussed below.

MSAs bear a similarity to IRAs (see Section 2 of the *Tax-Sheltered Plans* chapter). An individual can deduct contributions made to a medical savings account in his name, and no tax is due on investment earnings from funds left in the account. Furthermore, amounts can be removed from the account to pay for eligible medical expenses, with no tax due. (With an IRA, any amounts withdrawn are subject to ordinary income tax, plus a possible penalty tax in the case of early withdrawals.)

Eligibility

Two types of individuals are eligible to set up an MSA. First are self-employed individuals and their spouses. Second are employees of a small employer who averages 50 or fewer employees and has established a medical savings account program covering all his employees. (Employees of such employers should get detailed information from the employer.)

To set up an MSA, an individual must be covered by a high-deductible plan (often called a *catastrophic insurance* plan) bought outside the MSA. The deductible specified in the plan must be between $1,600 and $2,400 for individual coverage or between $3,200 and $4,800 for family coverage applying to more than one person. (Family policies must have only the overall family deductible with no separate deductibles for family members.) In addition, the annual out-of-pocket expenses under the plan cannot exceed $3,200 for individual coverage or $5,850 for family coverage. Out-of-pocket expenses include deductibles, co-payments, and other amounts the individual must pay for covered benefits, but do not include insurance premiums.

To be eligible for an MSA, an individual cannot be covered by medical insurance other than the required high-deductible insurance described above. However, this prohibition does not apply to coverage for accidents, disability, dental care, vision care, long-term care, insurance for a specified disease or illness, insurance that pays a fixed amount per day (or other period) of hospitalization, or insurance under which substantially all of the coverage provided relates to liabilities from workers' compensation laws, torts, or ownership or use of property (such as automobile insurance).

Contribution Limits

There is a maximum limit on how much can be contributed to an MSA each year. This limit is 65% of the high-deductible insurance amount for individuals and 75% of the high-deductible amount for families. For example, if an individual has a high-deductible policy covering only himself with a deductible amount of $1,800, he could contribute 65% × $1,800 = $1,170 to the MSA. With the maximum family deductible of $4,800, the maximum contribution would be 75% × $4,800 = $3,600.

There is another limitation. A self-employed person or the spouse of a self-employed person cannot make deductible contributions to an MSA which exceed the amount of self-employment earned income for the year.

Contributions up to the above maximums are deductible on an individual's tax return. This deduction is actually an *adjustment to income* and serves to lower adjusted gross income. This is better than an *itemized deduction* for the reasons described in Section 1 of Chapter 1. In particular, a person who uses the standard deduction can still write off his MSA contributions. And the 7.5% reduction for those itemizing their medical expenses does not apply to MSAs.

Contributions for a given year can be made all at one time or broken up into multiple pieces. All contributions for a given year must be made by April 15 of the following year.

When Can Distributions be Made?

Distributions from an MSA can be made at any time an individual chooses. No tax is due to the extent the distributions are made to cover medical expenses. The MSA can pay the medical bills directly, or can reimburse you if you pay the bills directly from your own funds. Here, medical expenses include the items discussed in Section 1 except for the cost of insurance other than long-term care insurance, premiums for *COBRA-type* health care continuing coverage, or premiums for health care coverage while an individual receives unemployment compensation.

Income tax is due on MSA distributions which are not used to pay for medical expenses. In addition to the regular income tax, a 15% penalty applies. However, this 15% penalty does not apply after the original account holder becomes age 65, becomes disabled, or dies.

Upon death, an individual's MSA passes to the beneficiary he has named. No tax is due on this passage if the beneficiary is a spouse, and the spouse may continue the plan as his or her own. Other beneficiaries must receive a distribution of the amounts in the MSA at death and pay income tax at the ordinary tax rates applying to the beneficiary.

How to Set Up an MSA

Most MSAs are set up through independent insurance agents. They can provide the necessary high-deductible insurance policy and enable you to set up a suitable bank or other account into which your contributions will be made. At a later time, you can transfer your MSA account into one operated by another bank, mutual fund, etc. This will become a more valuable feature as more institutions choose to sponsor MSAs. Any institution that currently sponsors IRAs automatically qualifies to sponsor MSAs if it chooses to do so.

The bank or other financial organization in possession of your MSA assets does not supervise expenditures or withdrawals from your account. You are solely responsible for keeping records of the medical bills which you pay and for making sure all your withdrawals qualify under the rules described in this section.

Technically, the IRS can cut off the opening of new MSAs if there is too great a demand for them. You would find out if such a limit is in force when you attempt to open up your plan with an insurance agency. This restriction is unlikely to come into force because the volume of established plans is running far below IRS expectations.

Seniors on Medicare will be able to establish an MSA called a "MedicarePlus Choice MSA" through 2002 under rules similar to the above. This will be a pilot program open to 390,000 seniors on a first-come, first-served basis.

MSAs as a Tax-Shelter

In addition to providing a tax break for medical expenses, MSAs can be used as a tax-shelter. Although tax-free withdrawals can be used to pay medical expenses, there is no explicit requirement making these withdrawals mandatory. An individual could apparently pay all medical expenses out-of-pocket and leave his MSA alone. That way, investment earnings would compound year after year on a tax-free basis.

In fact, MSAs are similar to IRAs (see Section 2 of the *Tax-Sheltered Plans* chapter), but have a few advantages that IRAs do not. First, there is no age limit beyond which distributions must be made. Second, the maximum contribution to an MSA can reach $3,600 per year as discussed earlier in this Section, while the basic limit on IRAs is $2,000. Finally, of course, tax-free withdrawals for medical expenses can be made out of an MSA, while such withdrawals from IRAs are generally taxed.

7

Charitable Contributions

You **can deduct** contributions you make to the following nonprofit agencies:

1. **Religious Organizations.** This includes annual dues, seat charges, and assessments, as well as ordinary contributions.

2. **Charitable Organizations.** Examples include the American Heart Association, Salvation Army, YMCA, Travelers Aid Society, etc.

3. **Governmental Bodies** where the contribution is for some public purpose such as education, public works, civil defense, etc.

4. **Educational Organizations.** This includes colleges, universities, research organizations, etc.

5. **Civic Organizations** such as non-profit hospitals, veterans organizations (e.g. American Legion, VFW, DAV), youth organizations (e.g. Boy Scouts, Girl Scouts), volunteer fire departments, PTAs, organizations to support the Olympic games and other athletic competitions, and societies for the prevention of cruelty to animals.

6. The cost of **benefit tickets** sold by charitable organizations. If these tickets are for some commercial production such as a play or concert, you can deduct only the excess of the price of your tickets over the regular admission price. Similarly, you can deduct the excess cost of purchasing items from a charity (e.g. Christmas cards over value received). The IRS is now requiring charities to state how much of the cost of a ticket or other item represents a charitable contribution, and how much represents the regular price.

7. **Contributions Required to Purchase College Athletic Tickets.** At some colleges and universities, if a person makes a specified contribution to the school or tax-exempt fund run by the school, this qualifies the person to purchase tickets to an athletic event held in the school's facilities. Because the contribution yields a *benefit* to the contributor (namely the right to purchase athletic tickets), it cannot be fully deducted. Instead, 80% of the specified contribution needed to qualify for the ticket-purchasing privilege can be claimed as a charitable deduction. The remaining 20% is non-deductible. (This 80%-rule applies whether or not the tickets are readily available for purchase by non-contributors.) No deduction is allowed for the actual cost of the tickets.

8. **Exchange Students.** You can deduct the cost of maintaining an elementary or high school student (other than a dependent or relative) in your home under a program sponsored by a charity. This deduction is limited to $50 per month.

You **cannot deduct** as charitable contributions:

1. Contributions to foreign charities except as provided otherwise in treaties. However, contributions to domestic charities which distribute funds abroad are deductible.

2. Contributions to organizations which devote a substantial portion of their time in attempting to influence legislation.

3. Contributions to political organizations and candidates.

4. Contributions to homeowners associations.

5. Donations which give you a direct benefit such as tuition to a church-related school.

6. Contributions to civic leagues, social and sports clubs, labor unions, and chambers of commerce.

7. Contributions to fraternal groups except when the contribution is to be used only for charitable or other qualifying purpose.

8. The cost of raffle tickets, even if a majority of the proceeds goes to charity.

If in doubt, you can simply ask the organization in question whether contributions qualify for tax-deductible status. In questionable cases, they will probably have already received a ruling from the IRS.

Where Do You Deduct Charitable Expenses?

Charitable expenses are claimed as an itemized deduction on line 15 of Schedule A for donations of money or line 16 for donations of property. Only those who itemize their deductions can deduct their charitable contributions.

Recent IRS rules have made it easier to tell when a contribution will be deductible on your tax return. When tax-exempt organizations solicit you for contributions by mail, phone, TV, or radio, they must inform you in a *conspicuous and easily recognizable format* if the contributions do **not** qualify as a charitable deduction. This applies to social welfare organizations, labor unions, trade associations, social clubs, and political organizations with annual gross receipts exceeding $100,000. Thus, if you do not receive a disclaimer from such an organization, it is almost guaranteed that your donation will be tax-deductible.

Donation of Services

You **cannot** deduct the value of services you perform for a charitable or other organization, nor can you deduct for the cost or rent of property or equipment you own which you allow a charity to use. You **can** deduct the out-of-pocket costs for telephone calls, materials, supplies, and the cost of operating equipment. You can also deduct the cost of ingredients or materials that go into something you donate, e.g. food cooked for a church supper. Similarly, you can deduct the cost of buying and maintaining special clothing such as choir robes or scout leader uniforms.

You can also deduct your charitable travel costs. This includes the cost of getting to and from the charity and for charitable activities. It also includes expenses incurred in attending a convention of a qualified charitable organization, provided that you attend as an official delegate. (Meal expenses connected with attendance at such a convention are subject to the same 50%-rule described in Section 1 of the *Travel* chapter; that is, only 50% of the cost of such meals can be claimed as part of your charitable deduction.)

In order for travel expenses to be claimed as a charitable deduction, there must be no significant element of personal pleasure, recreation, or vacation in the travel. The tax-writing committee of Congress described this requirement as follows:

> "In determining whether travel away from home involves a significant element of personal pleasure, recreation, or vacation, the fact that a taxpayer enjoys providing services to the charitable organization will not lead to denial of the deduction. For example, a troop leader for a tax-exempt youth group who takes children belonging to the group on a camping trip may qualify for a charitable deduction with respect to his or her own travel expenses if he or she is on duty in a genuine and substantial sense throughout the trip, even if he or she enjoys the trip or enjoys supervising children. By contrast, a taxpayer who only has nominal duties relating to the performance of services for the charity, or who for significant portions of the trip is not required to render services, is not allowed any charitable deduction for travel costs."

Further examples were given in a 1987 IRS notice:

> "For example, a taxpayer who sails from one Caribbean Island to another and spends eight hours a day counting whales and other forms of marine life as part of a project sponsored by a charitable organization generally will not be permitted a charitable deduction. By way of further example, a taxpayer who works on an archaeological excavation sponsored by a charitable organization for several hours each morning, with the rest of the day free for recreation and sightseeing, will not be allowed a deduction even if the taxpayer works very hard during those few hours. In contrast, a member of a local chapter of a charitable organization who travels to New York City and spends an entire day attending the organization's regional meeting will not be subject to this provision even if he or she attends the theatre in the evening. This provision applies whether the travel expenses are paid directly by the taxpayer or by some indirect means such as by contribution to the charitable organization that pays for the taxpayer's travel expenses." [Notice 87-23]

If your **automobile** is used, you can either deduct 14 cents per mile or compute your actual cost of operating the automobile, including gas and oil, but not insurance, depreciation, or general repairs such as tune-ups, lubrication, etc. With either method, you can deduct parking and tolls in addition.

According to an IRS ruling, there is another item you can deduct in addition to the 14 cents per mile or actual operating expenses. Namely, you can deduct a pro rata portion of taxes you pay on the automobile. [Rev Proc 89-66] For example, if 15% of your annual mileage is for charitable purposes, you can claim 15% of the taxes as a charitable deduction. Your travel is deductible if you are actually rendering services to a charitable organization, but not if your travel is for personal purposes. For example, travel to attend church choir rehearsals or to attend scout meetings as a troop leader is generally deductible. However, travel just to attend church services or drive your children to their scout meetings is not.

Babysitting as a Charitable Expense

Suppose you hire a babysitter to watch your children so you can perform volunteer services for a charitable organization. Can you claim the cost of the babysitter as a charitable deduction?

The answer is not settled. The IRS ruled in 1973 that the cost of such babysitting is not deductible. [Rev.Rul. 73-597] But five years later, the Tax Court, not bound by IRS Rulings, granted a deduction for such charity-related babysitting. [Kingsley, TC Summary Opinion 1978-74] However, this case was tried in the *Small Case* division of the Tax Court and therefore cannot be cited as legal precedent the way ordinary cases can [see the *Audits* chapter]. As a result, the IRS is able to rely upon its revenue ruling and deny charity-related babysitting costs, should the issue come up in an audit. But an individual who claims such a deduction can take some comfort because of the above Tax Court case and the possibility the deduction could hold up in a regular Tax Court case. However, because the donation would be contrary to a revenue ruling, it should be disclosed on Form 8275 to avoid a penalty if challenged.

Gifts of Appreciated Property

The best way to make a substantial donation to charity, generally, is to give *appreciated property*, i.e. property (including stocks, bonds, etc.) that has risen in value since the time you purchased it. You can get a deduction for the full market value of the property, avoiding the capital gains tax that would be due if you were to sell the property, rather than give it away. In effect, your charitable contribution is increased by the capital gains tax that has been avoided. If you were to sell the property first, you would have that much less to give to charity after paying the capital gains tax due.

If you have a stock certificate for, say, 100 shares of a company, but only want to donate 40 shares to charity, there is a simple way to handle this situation. Send the certificate into the appropriate agent of the company and ask that your stock be split into two certificates, one for 40 shares and the other for 60 shares. You then can donate the 40-share certificate to the charity.

If the property to be donated would result in a capital loss, you should sell it and donate the cash. By doing so, you can deduct the loss.

There are some restrictions that apply. First of all, to deduct the full market value of appreciated property, you must have owned the property for at least 12 months. Second, *tangible property* such as furniture, art objects, jewelry, etc., must be directly related to the charitable purpose of the organization to which they were given (e.g. books given to a library). If the full market value cannot be deducted, you are allowed to deduct only the original price (or other basis) you paid for the item.

Under the 1993 Tax Act, gifts of appreciated property are no longer a *tax preference* for purposes of the *minimum tax* [see the *Alternative Minimum Tax* chapter].

Recordkeeping Rules

The IRS has regulations concerning the documentation you need to back up your deduction for charitable contributions. For contributions of money, you need either a cancelled check, receipt, or suitably maintained record as described below.

For contributions of clothing or other property, you do not need to keep written records as was once required. Instead, you must generally have a proper receipt from the charity. As discussed below, the receipt must describe the items donated, but is **not** required to assign a monetary value to the items.

You do not include receipts or written documentation with the tax return that you file. Rather, you keep these with your own records in case your tax return is challenged by the IRS. However, as discussed later, detailed information does need to be provided as part of your tax return in the case of large contributions.

Donations of Money

For charitable contributions of money of less than $250.00, you are required to maintain either:

(i) a cancelled check;

(ii) a receipt (which can be a letter or other communication) from the charity showing the name of the charity, date of the contribution, the amount, and your name. For small amounts, an emblem, button, tag, or other evidence which indicates a donation has been made will suffice; or

(iii) in the absence of a cancelled check or receipt from the donee organization, other reliable written records showing the name of the donee, the date of the contribution, and the amount of the contribution.

No specific recordkeeping format is required by the IRS under (iii). However, the most preferred form of record would be a diary in which the information concerning each contribution is recorded *contemporaneously* (i.e. at or soon after the contribution is made). According to IRS regulations,

"The reliability of the written records . . . is to be determined on the basis of all the facts and circumstances of a particular case. In all events, however, the burden shall be on the taxpayer to establish reliability. Factors indicating that the written records are reliable include, but are not limited to:

(A) The contemporaneous nature of the writing evidencing the contribution.

(B) The regularity of the taxpayer's recordkeeping procedures. For example, a contemporaneous diary entry stating the amount and date of the donation and the name of the donee charitable organization made by a taxpayer who regularly makes such diary entries would generally be considered reliable."

Note that the above rules require each contribution to be separately documented. For example, a written diary must list each individual contribution as it is made. A monthly listing, say, of just the total amounts given that month would not satisfy the above rules.

Despite the apparent severity of the documentation rules, there is a favorable side as well. Normally, a taxpayer must be able to substantiate his itemized deductions by receipts or cancelled checks. However, the regulations now specifically allow charitable deductions to be backed by an appropriate written diary in the absence of cancelled checks or other receipts. This could be a boon to those who make a large number of cash donations during the year.

For example, say a family usually places a $20 bill in the collection plate each Sunday at church and makes other miscellaneous cash donations during the year. A tax auditor would ordinarily balk when looking at such a large total of charitable contributions unsupported by receipts or cancelled checks. But under the above rules, as long as the family has kept an appropriate written diary listing each contribution, it will have satisfied the new IRS recordkeeping requirement.

Of course, it's still best to have receipts or cancelled checks whenever possible. Even though an appropriate written diary is a permissible option, the larger the total of otherwise undocumented amounts listed in the diary, the more scrutiny the IRS will give to the reliability of the diary.

There is no official format specified for the written diary of charitable contributions. Even a properly kept kitchen calendar can suffice in some circumstances. This is illustrated by the following recent case.

Court Case

Burns worked as an auto assembler, earning an annual salary of over $32,000. She claimed charitable contributions of $3,462, mostly to her church.

The substantiation she had for her charitable contributions was not the best. The church didn't keep any records of the contributions, nor did it issue receipts. And she didn't even have a regular checking account, so all her contributions were made with cash. However, she did keep track of her contributions by recording them on a calendar hanging in her kitchen. This was the only written substantiation she provided to the Court.

Despite the lack of receipts or cancelled checks, the Court allowed her to deduct almost the entire amount–$3,282. The Court disallowed only a few items, mainly where it was not convinced that the contributions were made to a qualified charity.

The charitable deduction was allowed despite a decided negative factor in her record. Burns had filed an initial return as a "tax protester," claiming she owed no tax because her earnings were offset by a *"Cost basis (fair market value) of labor Received as Gift from Creator."* The Court usually deals harshly with persons who make such frivolous claims.

However, there were several positive features in Burns' favor. Her pastor testified that he personally observed several $150 contributions she had made which correlated with her kitchen calendar records. Also, the next year, she moved to a new church which did keep records showing that she made contributions of similar size to the ones claimed in the year at issue. These factors supported the reliability of her records.

While her records were found reliable, the Court indicated in a footnote that it was not endorsing the absence of receipts or cancelled checks in all cases. Here, it was partly influenced by the fact that the IRS had not made an objection on these grounds. [Burns, TC Memo 1988-536]

Contributions of $250 or More

If you make a charitable contribution of $250 or more, a cancelled check alone is not enough documentation. To back up a deduction, you must have a written acknowledgement of the donation from the charity. You are supposed to have this acknowledgement in your possession before you file your tax return. However, you do not include the acknowledgement with your tax return, but keep it with your records in case your tax return is audited.

There is no specific format for the acknowledgement. For example, letters, postcards, or computer-generated forms can be used. If the donation is a cash contribution, the acknowledgement must list the amount of the donation. If the donation is in the form of property, the acknowledgement must describe the property, but does not have to place a value on it. It is your responsibility to place a value on the donation.

Separate contributions are regarded as independent payments in determining whether the $250 threshold has been exceeded. For example, if you make two $200 contributions on successive Sundays, the special documentation rule for contributions over $250 does not apply. However, you can't simply write multiple checks on the same day to get around the requirement. For example, two $200 checks written to the same charity on the same date would generally be treated as one $400 contribution.

There is a provision which large charities may use to report contributions directly to the IRS. If you have been informed that this has been done, you do not need to have an individual acknowledgement in your possession.

Also, there is a special provision for handling contributions made by payroll deductions. You can substantiate such contributions by a combination of two documents. The first would be a pay-stub or W-2 Form issued by your employer containing the amount withheld from your wages. The second is a document prepared by the charity stating that it doesn't provide goods or services as whole or partial consideration for any contribution made by payroll deduction. Because deductions made from separate paychecks are ordinarily not aggregated, it is only when $250 or more is deducted from a given paycheck that the extra documentation rules come into play.

Items Worth More Than $500

If you donate an item worth more than $500, you should have a written record which shows how you acquired it (e.g. by purchase, gift, inheritance, etc.), the approximate date you acquired it, and, for items other than publicly traded securities, its cost (or other basis).

If there are unusual circumstances involved in the donation of property, these must be described in the written records you keep, e.g. if you have donated only a partial interest in the property, if there are "strings attached" to the use of the donated property, if the use of the property is unrelated to the charitable activities of the recipient, or if you held the property for a year or less and are valuing it at more than you paid for it.

If you made noncash contributions totaling more than $500 in value, you must fill out Form 8283 and attach it to your tax return. You are also required to attach a qualified appraiser's report if you donated property (other than listed securities) worth more than $5,000.

Court Allows Charitable Deduction Without Documentation

As discussed above, the IRS has specific recordkeeping requirements for backing up the deduction for charitable contributions. In practice, however, the Tax Court has not been as strict. In three cases, it has allowed a charitable deduction, despite the lack of any written documentation, when the deduction consists of small donations made on a regular basis. And remarkably, the amount allowed in these three cases was identical — $500.

In the first case, an insurance adjuster managed and sang in a gospel group that gave concerts at various churches during the year. He made cash contributions to his own church and to the churches at which he performed. The Court found his oral testimony that he made contributions to be credible. As a result, it allowed him a deduction of $500 for these contributions, despite a lack of any recordkeeping. This amount could be deducted in addition to about $2,000 in contributions to his own church for which there was verification. [Foster, TC Memo 1990-427]

The second 1991 case concerned a counselor at a community college. He claimed that he attended church regularly and tithed $25 each Sunday. He also donated two large bags of clothes and shoes to Goodwill. The language of the Court hinted that it was less than totally convinced of the value of contributions which were made. With no documentation whatsoever, it allowed a charity deduction of $500. [Dawkins, TC Memo 1991-225]

And in the third 1991 case, an electrical engineer made contributions to two churches, the Smithsonian Institution, and public radio and TV. The Court believed the engineer had made contributions, but did not accept the amount he had claimed. Without any documentation, the Court allowed a charitable deduction of $500 in one year and another $500 the next. [Tavano, TC Memo 1991-237]

It is not clear how the IRS will react to the Tax Court's apparent policy of allowing undocumented charitable contributions of as much as $500. Of course, to get the maximum deduction, it's best to keep the required records which document your contributions. However, if no records have been kept, a deduction of $500 would still seem in order in light of the above court cases. Of course, you're not entitled to this amount unless you actually made the contributions. In each of the above cases, the Court was convinced by oral testimony that contributions of at least this amount were made, despite the lack of written proof.

Contributions for Which Something Is Received in Return

If you receive an item from charity as a result of a donation you made, then you can't deduct the full amount you donated. Instead, you must subtract the market value of the item. For instance, if you pay $70 to attend a charity banquet and the meal is worth $50, then you can only deduct $70 – $50 = $20. This is the case even if you don't show up at the banquet.

However, there is a way to get a full deduction in the above situation. Return the banquet ticket to the charity and ask them to give it to someone else. As long as you return the ticket to the charity ahead of time, you can deduct the full amount because you have given away your right to attend.

Contributions Exceeding $75

If you make a contribution exceeding $75 and receive goods or services in return, you must obtain a disclosure statement from the charity to back up your deduction. This statement must estimate the value of the goods or services that you received. You then subtract this estimate from the amount of your contribution to determine your deduction.

For example, suppose you paid $100 to attend a charity dinner. The charity sends you a required statement valuing the dinner at $40. You would then deduct $100 – $40 = $60 as a charitable deduction on your tax return.

You do not include the statement from the charity with your tax return. Rather, you keep it with your records in case your tax return is audited.

There are three circumstances when the charity need not provide a disclosure statement. First, when the goods or services have *insubstantial value* as defined in the next subsection.

Second, when there is no "donative element" involved in a particular transaction with a charity. An example of this would be with a purchase made at a museum gift shop. Because this generates no charitable contribution, no statement is required from the charity.

Third, no statement needs to be issued when only an intangible religious benefit is provided. An example of when this would apply would be admission to a religious ceremony. This would not apply to such items as tuition for education leading to a recognized degree, travel services, or consumer goods.

Insubstantial Items Received from a Charity

There is an exception to the above rules if the value of an item received from a charity is "insubstantial." In such a case, the full donation can be deducted. Donated items are presumed to have *insubstantial value* if one of the following three conditions is satisfied:

(1) The fair market value is less than 2% of the amount contributed. (This applies to contributions up to $3,800);

(2) The donation is $38.00 or more and the only benefits received in connection with the donation are token items, such as bookmarks, calendars, key chains, tee shirts, etc., bearing the organization's name or logo; or

(3) The items were received, unsolicited by the recipient, from the charity as part of a money-raising program and can be kept whether or not a contribution is made.

In (2) and also in (3) above, the total cost to the charity of the items an individual receives must be less than $7.60. [Rev. Proc. 2001-13]

In the above rules, newsletters or program guides that are not available to the public generally are ignored unless they contain advertising or they pay for articles.

In practice, it is the charity's duty to determine if any of the above rules apply. They are supposed to inform you if any portion of a contribution you made is not deductible.

Used Clothing or Other Property

For each donation of clothing or other property, except cash, the IRS requires you to have a receipt from the charitable organization. In the words of the IRS regulations, the receipt should show all of the following information:

(i)   *The name of the donee;*

(ii) *The date and location of the contribution; and*

(iii) *A description of the property in detail reasonably sufficient under the circumstances. Although the fair market value of the property is one of the circumstances to be taken into account in determining the amount of detail to be included on the receipt, such value need not be stated on the receipt. A letter or other written communication from the donee acknowledging receipt of the contribution, showing the date of the contribution, and containing the required description of the property contributed constitutes a receipt for purposes of this paragraph.*

Note that the above regulation explicitly states that the receipt does not need to place a value on the items donated to the charity. This means that you can assign the fair market value yourself. Of course, if the charity does agree to assign a value on the receipt, this would likely be accorded more weight should your deduction be examined.

Exception

The IRS regulations contain the following exception to the receipt-keeping requirement:

"A receipt is not required if the contribution is made in circumstances where it is impractical to obtain a receipt (e.g., by depositing property at a charity's unattended drop site). In such cases, however, the taxpayer shall maintain reliable written records with respect to each item of donated property . . ."

The written records should include the following information:

(A) The name and address of the donee organization to which the contribution was made;

(B) The date and location of the contribution;

(C) A description of the property in detail reasonable under the circumstances (including the value of the property), and, in the case of securities, the name of the issuer, the type of security, and whether or not such security is regularly traded on a stock exchange or in an over-the-counter market; and

(D) The fair market value of the property at the time the contribution was made, the method utilized in determining the fair market value, and if the valuation was determined by appraisal, a copy of the signed report of the appraiser.

In addition to the written record of each contribution, you should also have a receipt or letter from the charity, with date and location of the contribution, which details the property contributed.

Evaluating Used Items

You are entitled to deduct the *fair market value* of used clothing or other items which you donate to the Salvation Army, Goodwill, church rummage sales, etc. Most charities will give you a receipt for the donated items, but will refuse to appraise their value. This means that you must determine the value yourself.

In practice, it is difficult to assign a value based on the current *market value* because the market for used clothing and other items is so variable. However, a 1980 court case gives some guidance. An individual gave the Salvation Army 12 pairs of trousers, 3 suits, 2 coats, 2 shirts, 1 pair of cowboy boots, and 2 pairs of shoes, all less than 3 years old. These items were purchased new at a total cost of $710. The Court ruled that the individual was entitled to a charitable deduction of $250 — about 35% of the value of the items when new. [Patch, TC Memo 1980-11]

If there is expert testimony as to the value of donated merchandise, a larger deduction can be obtained than normally allowed. This is illustrated by a court case concerning a woman who was *"extravagant in purchasing clothing for herself and her children."* She donated much of this clothing to a local charity and claimed several thousand dollars in charitable deductions over a period of years. Ordinarily, the Court would be expected to trim the amount of deductions claimed. However, the woman had worked for a period of time in the charity's clothes resale shop. Because of this, her estimate of the value of the clothing was considered expert testimony and the deduction was allowed in full. [Haseltine, TC Memo 1979-325]

Another court case, in contrast, shows that an unsubstantiated assignment of high value to used clothing can backfire. An individual claimed a deduction for 2/3 of the new value for used items donated to Goodwill and the Salvation Army. The Court found the values assigned to the items to be *"clearly exaggerated to put it mildly."* Because his appraisal was so lacking in credibility, the Court simply accepted the IRS estimate and allowed the individual a deduction for only about 10% of what he had originally claimed. [Sylvester, TC Memo 1978-461]

As the above indicates, the IRS will disagree with an unsubstantiated high valuation based on too high a percentage of the original cost of items given to charity. However, the result may be different if a valuation is based on a large number of donated items.

This is illustrated by a 1987 court case concerning a donation to the Salvation Army. The donation consisted of a large number of used items which had been stored in an individual's garage. The individual donated the items after he and his first wife were divorced.

According to the Court, *"He had not purchased the items donated, and was unable at trial to itemize the donated property or describe it, except for a stove, which he could describe only generally. The receipt from the Salvation Army showed the donor's declared value to be $3,000 . . ."* However, the receipt did not purport to reflect the actual value of the donated property other than the individual's own valuation, nor did it list the items contributed. Additionally, the receipt bore the notation that *"a value for contributed property could not be determined by the receiving attendant."*

The Court did not allow a full $3,000 deduction. However, despite the meager documentation, the IRS had still allowed a rather generous deduction of $950 for the donated items. The Court accepted this figure as the proper charitable deduction. [Goldstein, TC Memo 1987-47] (However, note that under current law, you must document a donation of items to charity on Form 8283 if you claim a deduction for them of over $500.)

As the above discussion indicates, used clothing and other items usually generate a charitable deduction which is considerably less than their value when new. This is because these items are generally given away only after they are worn out, damaged, or seriously out of style. However, perhaps you donate items which are still in good condition. Maybe you are moving, have lost or gained weight, etc. If so, the value of the merchandise might be considerably higher.

There is a court case that illustrates this point. This case did not involve a charitable deduction, but rather a deduction for loss due to theft. However, the identical question arises in determining both these deductions, namely deciding the fair market value of used items for which ownership has just changed hands.

The stolen items consisted of clothing, cash, a radio, and a camera. The total purchase price of these items was $1,512, with half of the total due to the clothing. The age of the items ranged from 2 years old to only a few months old. The Court placed a value of $1,054 on the items when stolen — a full 70% of the stated original price.
[Harris, TC Memo 1978-332]

Court OK's Deduction for Giving Journals and Books to Charity

In the past, there has been uncertainty surrounding the deduction for giving books to charity, in particular when the books were received free to begin with. For example, when an elementary school principal tried to claim a charity deduction in a case decided a number of years ago, he was essentially rebuffed. In a controversial interpretation of the law, it was ruled that because the principal had received the books free, his charity deduction would be cancelled out by taxable income equal to the value of the books he received free from the publishers.

However, the following court case changed the picture. In this case, a professor donated a collection of books and journals to a research institute. Despite the fact he had received many of these items free, the Court allowed a charitable deduction based on the fair market value, with no offsetting taxable income. However, the charitable deduction had to be decreased by any deductions claimed for the books and journals in previous years as job-related expenses.

Court Case

Wehausen was a Professor of Engineering Science for many years at a distinguished public university in the West. Prior to this employment, he served as the editor of *Mathematical Reviews*, a mathematics abstracting journal. Through subscriptions, gifts, and professional activities over the years, he assembled an extensive collection of mathematical journals and publications.

Nearing retirement age, he donated his collection of mathematical journals to a newly established mathematics research institute. He then claimed a charitable deduction on his tax return.

Both the IRS and the Court agreed with Wehausen that he was entitled to a deduction. And there was no disagreement as to the general method of determining the amount of the charitable deduction. Over the years, Wehausen had previously deducted a total of $1,805 in subscription fees for journals included in his donated collection. Everyone agreed that the amount of the charitable deduction should equal the *fair market value* of the journals at the time of donation, minus the $1,805 total of previously claimed tax deductions.

The only dispute at trial was how to determine this *fair market value*. On hand were 2 different appraisal figures, one of $5,245 provided by the research institute to which the donation had been made, and the other of $19,900 provided by an appraiser hired by Wehausen.

The Court did not accept the methodology used in the $19,900 appraisal. The appraiser testified that for domestic journals, he "*simply looked in the backs of the journals, looked at the price of back issues and added them up.*" However, the Court rejected this procedure. The main objection was the lack of evidence as to the condition of the journals donated by Wehausen.

"The most apparent flaw in [Wehausen's] valuation method is its failure to recognize that the demand for and value of a secondhand periodical may differ from that of a publisher's back issue (which in absence of evidence to the contrary, we presume to be unused or of a very high quality). While we recognize that secondhand periodicals may resemble the condition and quality of back issues, and may in fact be of comparable value, petitioners bear the burden of showing this to be the case. Absent evidence of comparability, we will not assume that a publisher's back-issue subscription price represents the fair market value of a secondhand periodical. Our review of the record reveals no persuasive evidence that petitioner's donated collection of secondhand periodicals was comparable to the quality and value of the back-issue prices used as the basis for his appraisal. And as no secondhand catalog, back-issue subscription list or evaluation of the collection's quality was produced, we are unable to independently determine whether the values assigned accurately represented those of the secondhand market."

Thus, the Court accepted the alternate appraisal for domestic journals provided by the research institute. For foreign journals, on the other hand, the appraiser's valuation was accepted. For these journals, he did not just use the back-issue price, but based his appraisal on *"his long experience of what out of print Russian, Polish, Italian or Japanese periodicals fetch on the American market."* The fact that the appraiser did not use past sale figures for the mathematical journals in question was acceptable to the Court, which stated,

"We recognize from the outset that foreign mathematical journals may well have an even more limited market than their domestic counterparts. Consequently, while direct evidence of actual sales of similar periodicals would furnish us with the best evidence of fair market value, it is understandable that petitioners did not produce evidence of recent sales."

Thus, for domestic journals, the Court accepted the appraisal figure provided by the research institute, while for foreign journals, it accepted the figure of the appraiser hired by Wehausen. Putting together these 2 valuations, the Court came up with a total for the donated collection of $6,628. Subtracting the $1,805 previously deducted by Wehausen, this produced a charitable deduction of $6,628 – $1,805 = $4,815. [Wehausen, TC Memo 1988-460]

As required in the above court case, you are supposed to reduce the value of books and journals donated to charity by any job-related deductions you claimed for these items in previous years. However, like many persons, you may not have kept sufficiently detailed records on exactly which items you have previously deducted.

In such a case, it is advised to make the best estimate you can based on your recollection. The recordkeeping requirements described earlier do not ask you to state whether a deduction has previously been claimed. In fact, your receipt or written record only needs to show the name, date, recipient, and description of the donated item. Whether you received the item free or paid and deducted for it are not part of the recordkeeping requirement. If you have the required charity records and your deduction is not unusually large, you are unlikely to be challenged.

As noted earlier, if you donate an item worth $500 or more, you are required to record how the item was acquired. However, this $500 figure applies on an item by item basis. For example, even if you donate more than $500 worth of books, you do not fall under this requirement because no single book is worth more than $500. (However, you still must fill out Form 8283 — it is just the acquisition information on lines 1(d), (e), (f) that you can ignore.)

Donating Your Old Car to Charity

Here's a deduction that's often overlooked. Instead of selling or trading in your old car, you can donate it to Goodwill or another charity and receive a deduction at the same time. And the amount of the deduction can be greater than the price you would have received upon sale or trade-in. Here's why.

The full market price of the car can be determined by reference to its "Blue Book" value. This can be obtained from a library, car dealer, etc. This Blue Book value is generally the price the car would be sold for by a used car dealer. This amount will often exceed the price you could get with a private sale or trade-in. In fact, the charitable deduction can sometimes be more financially advantageous than a sale.

For example, an old car that would get you only $100 from a junk yard might have a Blue Book value of, say, $400. For someone whose highest tax bracket (combined federal and state) exceeds 25%, the $400 deduction reduces taxes by more than the $100 sale price.

You can get a receipt from the charity specifying the car you have contributed. However, you will probably have to look up the Blue Book value yourself. There are websites available on the Internet where you may obtain the fair market value or "Blue Book" value for the automobile that you donate to charity. These sites include:

Edmunds   www.edmunds.com

Kelly Blue Book   www.kbb.com

Donating Used Computer Equipment to Charity

If you have computer equipment you are no longer using, donate it to charity and claim a tax deduction. You will have to place a value upon the equipment you donate. One way to do this is to consult newspaper and magazine ads for used computer equipment.

One organization which recycles computers to give them to rural and inner-city schools and other non-profit entities is SCROUNGE. This organization is run by students at Penn State University. [SCROUNGE; 101 South Frear Laboratory; Penn State; University Park, PA 16802; Telephone No. 814-863-7688.]

There are many organizations accessible through the Internet that are seeking donations of computer equipment. There are also websites that provide a directory of these organization. Listed below are some websites that may be helpful in locating an organizations that is looking for donations of used computer equipment:

Organization	Website
Share the Technology	www.sharetechnology.org
Give Spot.com	www.givespot.com/donate/computers
PEP National Directory of Computer Recycling Programs	www.microweb.com/pepsite

Limitations

There are a number of rules which place an upper limit on the amount of charitable contributions you can deduct in any one year. If you make contributions in excess of 20% of your adjusted gross income, you should check the special rules which apply. These special rules may be found in Publication 526, which may be obtained at no charge from your local IRS office or downloaded from the IRS website at www.irs.gov.

Other Charitable Gifts

There are several methods of making charitable contributions that are beyond the scope of this publication. Generally, these methods involve split-interest gifts that can have a significant impact on your income and estate tax. These methods can be used to generate income, give away income, and, at the same time, garner an income tax deduction. They affect the estate tax because after the death of the income beneficiaries, the asset goes to a named charity. These methods involve charitable lead trusts or charitable remainder trusts. Please consult a tax advisor for more information about these techniques.

8

Household Services and Child Care

You may qualify for a tax credit equal to a percentage of payments made to a babysitter, maid, housekeeper, day care center, nursery school, etc.

The exact percentage of the tax credit depends upon your adjusted gross income as explained later in this chapter. Like other tax credits, the credit for household services and child care is subtracted directly from your final tax liability instead of from taxable income. Thus, it is more valuable than a deduction of the same amount. [see Chapter 1, Section 1]

Note that although it is required that there be dependents under 13 (or disabled dependents of any age) in the household, the tax credit still can apply when no child-watching services are performed. For example, payments to a maid or housekeeper can qualify even if no one is home the entire time services are being performed.

Qualification Rules

In order to qualify for the household services and child care tax credit, the following rules must have been satisfied:

(1) Your expenses were necessary to enable you to be gainfully employed during the period the expenses were incurred. Unpaid volunteer work or work for a nominal salary does not count. However, active search for gainful employment does qualify. If you are married and living with your husband or wife, either (i) both of you were gainfully employed, or (ii) one of you was gainfully employed and the other was disabled or was a full-time student during 5 or more months of the year. In addition, married couples who live together must file a joint return;

(2) You maintained a household including a dependent under age 13 or a disabled spouse or disabled dependent of any age. (Qualification is determined on a daily basis. For example, if you have a child who turns age 13 on August 23, you can claim the tax credit for services rendered through August 22); and

(3) Your payment for the service was not made to a child under age 19 of yours (or of your spouse) or to a person who can be claimed as your dependent.

Payments to Relatives

At one time, payments to close relatives for child care generally did not qualify for the child care tax credit. However, now the only restriction is in Rule (3) above. In particular, payments to a child's grandparent qualify for the tax credit.

Especially with the high personal exemption and standard deduction amounts [see Chapter 1], many retired persons over age 65 will pay little or no income tax. The child care tax credit offers a way to transfer money to such persons and achieve a net reduction in tax. Note that there is no specific ceiling on the hourly rate that can be paid for child care, although the IRS might object if it were too far out of line. However, because this information isn't called for on the tax form, IRS objection is unlikely.

Which Expenses Qualify for the Child Care Tax Credit?

If you qualify under the preceding rules, then the following expenses qualify for the household services and child care tax credit.

1. Expenses Within the Home

The tax credit applies to expenses for ordinary and usual household services performed in and about the home. These services must be necessary to the running of the home and must be of benefit to a qualifying dependent or disabled spouse. This includes the services of a housekeeper, maid, or babysitter, but not a gardener. The tax credit applies also to the cost of meals furnished to a qualifying household worker. However, the cost of lodging is not deductible except to the extent you incur expenses beyond what you would have normally paid if you had not provided lodging. [Rev Rul 76-288]

All of your expenses for housework are eligible for the tax credit even if only part of them are for a qualifying dependent.

Example
You pay a housekeeper to care for your 9-year-old and 15-year-old children so that you can work. The housekeeper spends most of the time doing the regular household work, cleaning, and cooking, and spends 30 minutes a day driving you to and from work. The entire expense of the housekeeper is a work-related expense. You do not have to subtract any amount for being driven to and from work, because the time involved is minimal. You do not have to subtract any amount for the care of the 15-year-old child (not a qualifying dependent) because the household expense is partly for the care of the 9-year-old child, who is a qualifying dependent.

In the above example, the housekeeper had some child-watching duties in addition to her main duty of taking care of the house. While this established that the housekeeper performed services of benefit to the child, the law does not specify that child-watching services be performed. All that's required is that the child directly benefit from the services. This can be the case where a housekeeper, maid, or cook, at least part of the time, cleans the child's room, cooks food which the child eats, etc.

However, note the first qualification rule on the first page of this chapter, namely that the expenses must be necessary to enable you to be gainfully employed. Ordinarily, this requirement is not difficult to satisfy. However, the following 1990 court case gives an example where it was not satisfied.

Court Case

Brian and Suzanne Knutson were a married couple, he an accountant and she a teacher. They had three children, all of whom were under age 15, the qualifying age during the year in question. They hired a cleaning service which sent a team of 5 or 6 workers once a week to clean the house. No direct child-care duties were performed.

When the Knutson's household services and child care tax credit was challenged, they wound up in Tax Court. And the Court denied the tax credit. It did not believe that the hiring of a cleaning service was necessary to enable the Knutsons to work, stating,

> *"Brian testified both petitioners were very busy with numerous household improvement projects and programs with the children. We find the cleaning service was employed to make life easier for petitioners and to allow them to spend their leisure time in pursuits they enjoyed rather than cleaning their home. While the Court understands petitioners' desires, we do not believe Congress intended other taxpayers to subsidize the expenses related to a cleaning service in this instance."* [Knutson, TC Memo 1990-440]

There are two things to note in the above court case. The first pertains to the type of cleaning service that was employed. The cleaning was performed only once a week for a brief period of time by a team of 5 or 6 workers. This meant that the cleaners would not be available to perform extra services a housekeeper might provide, such as waiting for repairmen, accepting deliveries, letting children in the house after school, etc. Such extra services, one might argue, could not be performed personally and therefore would be beneficial in enabling one to work.

Second, the couple in the above case made the mistake of emphasizing how busy they were with household projects and activities with the children. The judge took this to mean they could have done the cleaning if they had wanted to do so. They did not hire the cleaning service because it was necessary in order to work, but rather because they wanted time for other activities. If the couple's spare time had been filled with work-related or essential non-discretionary activities, the result could have been different.

2. Expenses Outside the Home

The tax credit applies to the cost of care for children under 13 outside the home, such as in a day care center, nursery school, day camp, babysitter's home, etc. Benefits incident to the care (food, education, etc.) are, strictly speaking, not child care costs. However, if a payment covers incidental benefits inseparably as part of the care, the entire cost will ordinarily be considered as being for child care. Thus, the credit applies to the full amount paid to a day care center or nursery school even if it includes lunch or educational activities. However, tuition for a child in the first or higher grade does not qualify, nor does the cost of transportation between your home and a child care location.

The tax credit also applies to outside-the-home care of a disabled spouse or disabled dependent over 12 who regularly spends at least 8 hours per day in the taxpayer's household. Dependent care centers which care for more than 6 persons per day must comply with all applicable local regulations to qualify for the credit.

Vacation Trips

As the following court case shows, expenses connected with sending your child on an out-of-town trip can qualify for the child care tax credit.

Court Case

Mr. and Mrs. Zoltan were both employed full-time. During a span of 2 years, they sent their 11-year-old son on a school-related Easter trip to Washington, D.C., and to France for 2 months to visit his older sister. The Zoltans claimed the child care tax credit for the cost of the trip to Washington, D.C., and for $350 in payments made to the sister in France for taking care of the boy. The Court considered these trips separately.

Easter Trip to Washington, D.C.

The Court found that the trip to Washington, D.C. was "primarily undertaken for the son's well-being and protection." (It noted that the cost of hiring a housekeeper to watch over the son would have been at least as expensive as the cost of the trip.) And, although transportation costs to a child care location do not qualify for the credit, that was not pertinent here. The child care began when they delivered their son to the tour sponsor at the bus depot in their home town. Thus, the bus trip was part of the basic child care, not auxiliary transportation.

However, the Court felt that a substantial portion of the trip was for educational purposes, not just child care. Thus, an allocation had to be made between the child care services and the educational services provided by the trip. The Court ruled that only $35 of the $116 expense could be deducted. Had the trip been to a less educational place than Washington, D.C., presumably the amount allocated to child care would have been higher.

Trip to France to Visit Sister

Under the law that applied at the time, payments to close relatives did not qualify for the child care tax credit. For this reason only, the Zoltans were not entitled to a credit for the $350 they paid to their son's sister for taking care of him in France. However, this payment to relatives restriction no longer applies, except as provided in Rule (3) on the first page of this chapter. Presumably, the $350 would have been allowed as a child care expense had the case been decided under current law. [Zoltan, 79 TC 490]

As the above case shows, the cost of sending a child on an out-of-town trip can qualify for the child care tax credit. Technically, it is required that the *principal purpose* of the trip be to insure your child's *well-being and protection*. But if you need to provide child care in order to work, you could almost always claim this is your principal purpose in sending your child out of town. Because the above Court decision ruled this was the case even for an Easter trip to Washington, D.C., it is hard to conjure up a situation which would not have satisfied the *principal purpose* requirement.

In the above case, the bus trip to Washington, D.C., was considered an integral part of the child care activities qualifying for the tax credit. The key was that the work performed by the ultimate care providers started with the bus trip.

However, in a 1989 court decision, the cost of transportation did not qualify for the child care tax credit. In this case, a married couple sent their children by airplane to visit their grandparents over a school holiday period. While payments made to the grandparents would qualify for the child care tax credit, the cost of airplane tickets would not. Although the children were cared for on the flights by cabin attendants, the court ruled *"There is nothing in the record to indicate that the cabin attendants were under the direction of [the grandparents], the service providers in the instant case."* Presumably, had a grandparent actually accompanied the children on the plane flight, a deduction would have been allowed. [Perry, 92 TC 470]

Summer Camp

The cost of sending your child to overnight camp does not qualify for the child care tax credit. This is the case even if the camp replaces child care that would have qualified for the credit.

However, the cost of sending a child to day camp still qualifies for the child care tax credit under the same conditions that applied in prior years. Namely, if there is a significant educational component to the camp (as there would be with a computer or baseball camp), an allocation would have to be made between non-deductible educational costs and deductible child care costs. However, no allocation need be made if the day camp provides only incidental instruction (e.g. in swimming, archery, etc.) in an unstructured fashion. When the educational activities are only incidental to the child care aspect of the camp, the entire cost of the camp can be deducted. This would include the cost of food and recreational services that are *"incident to and inseparably a part of his care."* [Zoltan, 79 TC 490]

Similarly, out-of-town trips apart from overnight camp are not ruled out. As illustrated in the preceding court case, costs connected with an out-of-town sightseeing trip or visit with a relative can qualify for the child care tax credit.

Private Schooling

You may feel it necessary to send a child to private school in order to allow you to be gainfully employed. The following court case supports your right to a child care tax credit for a portion of the expenses you incur.

Court Case

A woman and her son moved from Maryland to Philadelphia where he was enrolled in the Wagner Junior High School. However, he was not able to adjust to his environment at Wagner. "Unlike his Maryland school, Wagner was fraught with classroom disorders and teacher strikes. Gang fights took place after school, and petitioner was concerned for her son's safety. . . . Petitioner felt that she could not work while her son was attending Wagner because she had to remain constantly prepared to pick him up if problems arose at school."

As a result, she enrolled her son in a private boarding school. She then claimed a tax credit for that portion of the cost which was not allocable to the cost of education. The IRS objected, claiming the private schooling was not necessary to enable her to work. Other mothers sent their children to Wagner and were able to work without incurring any child care expenses.

But the Court overruled the IRS objection. "Petitioner considered herself unable to work while her son was at Wagner. However, no doubt many Wagner students did have working mothers. It was not objectively impossible to be employed while a child was at Wagner. However, we do not believe that the statute requires us to test the correctness of the parent's conclusion that child care is required to obtain employment, but only the sincerity of that conclusion. Different parents will apply different standards for what risks they are willing to put their children to. One parent may feel a . . . boy could be left alone at home after school hours; another would disagree. The statute requires the prescribed purpose; it does not impose a test of objective necessity."

The IRS also objected that the dominant motive in sending her son to boarding school was not to enable her to work, but to provide for his education. But the Court tossed aside this objection also. " . . . if the parent could not have accepted the job without having sent the child to boarding school, she is deemed to have incurred the expense in order to be able to accept gainful employment . . . Since one of petitioner's reasons for sending her son to boarding school was to be able to take a job, and since she could not have taken a job without such child care arrangement, she is entitled to a child care deduction for some part of the cost of sending him to [private school]. We adopt in other words a 'but for' test. If the care was required to permit the taxpayer to work, and if one motive for obtaining the care was to permit gainful employment, the concurrent existence of other motives will not cause the expenditure to fail the statutory test. The employment motive must be present. It need not be exclusive or even dominant."

Thus, the Court ruled in favor of the taxpayer. The portion of the cost of the private school which went for education, tuition, books, supplies, etc., would not qualify as a child care expense. However, "incidentals that go with providing well-being and protection such as room, board, and supervision before and after the normal school day" *would qualify for the child care tax credit.* [Brown, 73 TC 156]

In the above case, the cost of education did not qualify because the child was in the "first or higher grade." For younger children, the full cost may be claimed as a tax credit. For example, a 1980 court case allowed a tax credit based on the entire cost of private school because the child was only 4 years old. The school was considered a nursery school, so the full cost could be claimed as described earlier in this chapter. [Christre, TC Memo 1980-64]

Interestingly, while the regulations allow a tax credit for nursery school and forbid a tax credit for education in the first or higher grades, they do not spell out the situation for kindergarten. Presumably, a tax credit could be claimed for the cost of a private kindergarten which provided more nursery school, type activities than formal schooling found in the first or higher grades.

Amount of Credit

The tax credit is equal to 30% of expenses on tax returns showing an adjusted gross income of up to $10,000, decreasing to 20% for those with adjusted gross incomes over $28,000. The following table shows the exact percentage to be used at each income level, subject to the limitations described below.

Adjusted Gross Income	Applicable Percentage
Up to $10,000	30%
$10,001–12,000	29%
$12,001–14,000	28%
$14,001–16,000	27%
$16,001–18,000	26%
$18,001–20,000	25%
$20,001–22,000	24%
$22,001–24,000	23%
$24,001–26,000	22%
$26,001–28,000	21%
$28,001 and over	20%

Limitations

1. The overall limitation

The household and child care tax credit is subject to a maximum limitation. The maximum amount of 2001 expenses to which the credit can be applied depends upon the number of *qualifying dependents* (i.e. dependents under age 13 and disabled dependents or spouse over age 12) as follows:

(a) $2,400 if there is one qualifying dependent; or

(b) $4,800 if there are 2 or more qualifying dependents.

Thus, for those with adjusted gross incomes less than $10,000, the credit cannot exceed in case (a), $720 (30% × $2,400); or in case (b), $1,440 (30% × $4,800); while for those with adjusted gross incomes greater than $28,000, the credit cannot exceed in case (a), $480 (20% × $2,400); or in case (b), $960 (20% × $4,800).

Under (b), you are entitled to the credit on up to $4,800 of expenses as long as there are at least 2 qualifying dependents, even if a majority of this amount was spent for the care of only one child. For example, if you spent $3,000 for nursery school for your 4-year-old child and $300 for incidental care of your 12-year-old, you would apply the credit to $3,300 of expenses. The $2,400 limit under part (a) would not apply, but rather the $4,800 limit under part (b).

The Tax Reduction Act of 2001 increased the dependent care tax credit beginning in 2002. The maximum amount of expenses used to compute the credit is increased from $2,400 to $3,000 for one child and from $4,800 to $6,000 for two or more children. The percentage used to determine the maximum amount of the credit is increased from 30% to 35%, with the reduction to 20% for taxpayers with adjusted gross income of more than $43,000.

2. The earned income limitation

The expenses to which the credit is applied cannot exceed your earned income. For married couples filing a joint return, the expenses to which the credit is applied cannot exceed either your earned income or your spouse's earned income, whichever is lower. Earned income includes income produced by an individual's own work, whether it be as an employee or as a self-employed person. It does not include income from investments, such as stocks, bonds, rented property, savings accounts, etc.

In some cases, it pays to "put a spouse on the payroll" in order to boost the earned income of the lower-earning spouse and obtain a larger tax credit. For example, this might be possible for an individual with an outside business activity in which the spouse can be of assistance. This is discussed more fully in Section 3 of the *Outside Business Activity* chapter.

3. Reduction for tax-free amounts received as a fringe benefit

The law allows employers to set up a *dependent care assistance program* under which employees can receive, as a tax-free fringe benefit, reimbursement for up to $5,000 of child care expenses incurred during the year. (Such reimbursements will be reported on 2001 year-end W-2 Forms.) This program is often set up as part of a larger *flexible spending account* that allows employees to select among various available fringe benefits. [see Section 6 of the *Tax-Sheltered Plans* chapter] Amounts received under such a program must now be subtracted from the amount of child care expenses to which the child care tax credit is applied. If total child care expenses exceed the overall limitation of $2,400 or $4,800, this overall limitation is reduced by the reimbursements received under a dependent care assistance program. Form 2441 will lead you through the appropriate computation.

Sometimes, dependent care assistance programs are set up under a *salary-reduction agreement.* With such an arrangement, you agree to have your salary reduced by the amount you will be receiving as a reimbursement. You wind up receiving the same total amount from your employer, but now a portion of this amount is exempt from tax. Because such dependent care reimbursements reduce the amount to which you can apply the tax credit, you essentially must choose between a reduction in taxable income and a tax credit of 20% (assuming adjusted gross income exceeds $28,000). If your income reaches into the 28% tax bracket or above, the salary reduction is more beneficial. In the 15% tax bracket, the 20% tax credit is more valuable.

Special Rule for Students

The preceding earned income limitation would permit no tax credit if one spouse were a student with no earned income. However, because Congress wanted to make the tax credit available to married couples in which one spouse is a student, they included the following special rule:

A spouse who is a student is treated for purposes of the earned income limitation as though

(1) He earned $200 per month for each month he was a full-time student during the year, if there was one qualifying dependent; or

(2) He earned $400 per month for each month he was a full-time student during the year, if there were two or more qualifying dependents.

The above amounts only serve to raise the limit on the amount of expenses to which the household services and child care tax credit is applied. They don't affect the adjusted gross income, which is the basis for the table showing what percentage to use.

Example

A married couple has two children under age 13 for which they incur $5,000 in child care expenses. One spouse earns $25,000 for the year, while the other has no earnings but is a full-time student for 10 months during the year. They file a joint return showing an adjusted gross income of $25,000. Thus, as determined by the table given earlier, the applicable tax credit rate is 22% of expenses. The student is deemed to have earned $400 for each of the 10 months in school, or a total of $4,000 earned income for the year. Because the amount of expenses to which the credit is applied cannot exceed this amount, their credit for the year is equal to 22% × $4,000 = $880.

What If You Are Separated or Divorced?

Special provisions are made for couples who are divorced or separated under a written agreement. In this case, the household services and child care tax credit can be claimed only by that parent who has custody of a qualifying child for a longer period of time than the other parent. (This is the case even if the dependency exemption was transferred to the other spouse on Form 8332 as discussed in the *Divorce and Separation* chapter.) The child must be in the custody of one or both parents for half of the year and must receive over half of his support from his parents.

Ordinarily, married couples must file a joint return in order to claim the household services and child care tax credit. However, there are the following exceptions to this rule for separated couples.

An individual who is legally separated from his spouse under a decree of divorce or of separate maintenance can claim the credit on a separate tax return. An individual who simply does not live with a spouse for the last 6 months of the year can also claim the household services and child care tax credit on a separate tax return. In this case, the qualifying child's principal home must have been with the individual for more than half of the year and the individual must have furnished over half the cost of maintaining the home.

Where is the Tax Credit Claimed?

You use Form 2441 to claim your Household Services and Child Care expenses. This form will lead you through a step by step computation of the appropriate tax credit.

You must report the name, address, and SSN (Social Security Number) or TIN (Taxpayer Identification Number) of any provider of child care or household services for which you're claiming a tax credit. You list these three items on the Form 2441 which you use to claim the tax credit. If the provider is a tax-exempt organization (charity, church, etc.), no identification number needs to be reported. You would just enter *"tax exempt"* in the space provided for the identification number.

If you are unable to obtain the child care provider's Social Security or Taxpayer Identification Number, all is not lost. You can still claim the tax credit by showing you exercised "due diligence" in attempting to obtain the number. To this end, you should include a statement with the Form 2441 which you file, explaining that you requested the number but it was not provided.

There is a special form, Form W-10, which the child care provider can fill out giving the required information. This form is not filed with the IRS. Rather, you keep this form with your records to back up your tax credit claim in case of IRS challenge. This form is obtainable from your local IRS office or by calling 1-800-829-3676. It is best to have the provider fill out this form when hired. If you wait until tax preparation time, you might not be able to track down a provider you are no longer using.

The use of Form W-10 is not mandatory. In its place, the IRS permits you to have either:

1. a photocopy of the provider's social security card or driver's license showing the social security number;

2. a recently printed letterhead or printed invoice that has on it the provider's name, address, and social security or taxpayer identification number; or

3. a copy of a completed Form W-4 (Employee's Withholding Allowance Certificate) if the provider is the individual's household employee.

Note that the child care provider is actually required by law to furnish you with a correct social security or taxpayer identification number. The provider is liable for a $50 penalty for each failure to furnish a correct number.

Social Security and Other Taxes

If you regularly employ a babysitter, maid, etc., inside your home, these are employees of yours governed by the social security laws. This means that you are supposed to pay social security tax if any of these employees earned $1,300 or more during 2001. The social security tax rate (including the Medicare portion) was equal to 7.65% for the employer and for the employee. You could withhold the employee's 7.65% from his paycheck or you could pay both portions yourself. You do not have to pay social security taxes for an outside contractor such as a day care center, outside babysitting service, etc. Also, you do not have to pay social security taxes on a domestic worker under age 18, unless the worker is not a student and his principal occupation is domestic work.

You only pay social security tax on actual wages. Food, clothing, and lodging given to household workers aren't subject to social security tax even when the extra cost of these items qualifies for the household services and child care tax credit. Note that any social security taxes you pay are considered to be part of your costs. That is, these taxes are included in the total expense figure on which you compute the tax credit.

You do not have to report social security payments due on domestic workers on a separate Form 942, as was once required. Instead, you can report these amounts on Schedule H which you include with your 2001 tax return, due April 15, 2002. Any amounts due are then added into the tax computation made on Form 1040. Further details are contained in Section 4 of the *Retirement Plans* chapter.

In addition to social security tax, here are your other obligations when you hire a domestic worker.

A. Federal Unemployment Tax (FUTA)

If you paid a total of $1,000 or more to all your domestic employees during any one calendar quarter in the current or preceding year, you must also pay Federal Unemployment Tax (FUTA). This tax applies only to the first $7,000 paid to each employee during the year. The Federal Unemployment Tax rate is 6.2%. However, you get a credit against this tax for payments that you make toward state unemployment taxes. (The state unemployment tax generally equals 5.4 percent of taxable wages, but the exact amount of credit depends on your state.)

FUTA payments which you owe are computed on Schedule H and become part of your Form 1040 taxes, as discussed earlier in this subsection and in more detail in Section 4 of the *Retirement* chapter.

B. Federal Income Tax Withholding

Even if your employee is a family member, all wages to domestic helpers are subject to federal income tax. However, you do not have to withhold this income tax from wages unless you and your employee both want it withheld. If you do not withhold the federal income tax, the employee is then responsible for paying any tax that is due when he or she files their income taxes. (The employee may also be required to pay quarterly estimated taxes.) If you do withhold income taxes, the employee must fill out Form W-4, *"Employee's Withholding Allowance Certificate."* This shows the number of exemptions that the employee is claiming. Amounts withheld during 2001 are reported on Schedule H which you attach to your 2001 Form 1040 due April 15.

C. State Unemployment Insurance

If you pay a domestic helper $1,000 or more in any quarter, then you must pay state unemployment tax. You should contact your state unemployment insurance tax office for information on how to file the state tax return and get a state employer ID number if needed. (Every state has a limit on the amount of wages that are subject to unemployment insurance tax. Most limits are higher than the $7,000 federal unemployment tax limit.)

D. W-2 Form

You must issue a W-2 Form to each household employee who earned more than $1,300 for the year, listing wages and any amounts withheld. You send a copy of this form to the Social Security Administration. For further details, see the *Instructions to Form W-2,* obtainable from the IRS.

E. Advanced Payment of the Earned Income Credit

Some employees with low family income will qualify for the earned income tax credit against their federal income taxes. See Section 1 of Chapter 1 for further details.

F. States' Compensation Laws

Some states require household employees to be covered by Workers' Compensation Insurance. Even if such insurance is not required in your state, you may want to be insured against unforeseen accidents.

G. Immigration Laws

All employers must verify that anyone hired is eligible for employment in this country. Immigration laws require an employee to complete an Immigration and Naturalization Service Form I9 no later than the first day of work. This form is available at your local Immigration and Naturalization Service office. As a part of filling out this form, the employee must show to the employer documents that verify both the employee's identity and employment eligibility. The employer must look at these documents and keep records on certain information in them. This includes such things as the name of the document, the expiration date, etc. It is a good idea to photocopy the document.

Form I9 is to be kept by the employer for at least three years after the employee starts working. If the employment is terminated, the employer must keep the document for a year after termination. It should be noted, however, that the penalties for violating the above immigration requirements, while they can range up to approximately $2,000, are rarely enforced.

9

Tax Deductions for Homeowners

We have discussed in a separate chapter how to deduct expenses connected with using a home office. The purpose of this chapter is to discuss the other deductions to which a homeowner is entitled simply through the use of a house as a residence. Throughout this chapter, the word *house* or the word *home* refers not just to a free-standing structure, but includes cooperative apartments, condominiums, which you own.

In order to deduct interest or taxes on a home, you must actually own the home. Otherwise, the deduction is lost. For example, suppose you live in a home owned by your parents and you make the mortgage payments which include interest and taxes. In this situation, neither you nor your parents can claim a deduction. If you had paid your parents rent and they had made the payments, they would have been entitled to the deductions.

SECTION 1:
INTEREST

As described in the *Interest* chapter, some interest is non-deductible. For example, there is no longer any deduction for interest on consumer purchases.

However, the deduction for interest on loans secured by your home remains fully deductible—within certain basic limits described below. This is the case even if the proceeds of the loan are used for consumer purchases or any other purpose. This special treatment applies to loans on your primary home and on a second home. The loans can be first or second mortgages, home-equity loans, or any other loans secured by your primary or second home. Also, late payment charges on such loans are generally considered to be interest on the loans because they are payments for the "use" of money.

The second home need not be an ordinary home, condominium, or cooperative, but can be a mobile home, boat, or other property as long as it contains basic living accommodations, including sleeping space, toilet, and cooking facilities. If you rented out the second home during part of the year and also made personal use of it, the home will qualify if your personal use of it is both (i) more than 14 days and (ii) more than 10 percent of the number of days during the year that the home was rented out at a fair rental. (If the home was not rented out at all, it can qualify as a second home no matter what personal use you made of it. This includes rent-free use by a relative or friend.)

If you have more than one possible second home, you can choose any one you wish to be your *second home* for the year. Next year, you can make a different choice of *second home.*

A married couple filing separate returns can claim home interest only on 2 homes between them. Each one can take into account only one residence unless they both consent in writing to one of them taking into account both residences.

To qualify under the home interest rules, the debt must be secured by the home under a legally binding agreement. If a loan is used to make payments on a home but the loan is not actually secured by the home, it does not qualify.

This is illustrated by several IRS Private Letter Rulings. In one ruling, an individual took out a loan from a savings and loan association, using funds on deposit as collateral. He then used the loan proceeds to make payments on the mortgage on his home. The IRS ruled that interest on the loan from the savings and loan association was not deductible as home mortgage interest. Even though the loan was used to make payments on a home, it was not *secured* by the home and therefore could not generate deductible home interest. [IRS Private Letter Ruling 8802056] In another ruling, the IRS vetoed a deduction for interest on a loan used to purchase a personal residence because the debt was secured only by stocks and bonds, not by the residence itself. [IRS Private Letter Ruling 8906031]

In most cases, a portion of your monthly mortgage payment goes toward paying interest on a home loan while another portion goes toward paying off the principal. Only the interest portion can qualify for deduction. You cannot deduct the portion which goes toward paying off the principal. Commercial lenders provide an annual statement which shows what portion of your payments is attributable to interest costs.

If an interest payment is due on a loan, you can't borrow more money from the original lender to cover the payment. Otherwise, you lose out on the interest deduction. [IRS News Release 83-93] In such a case, no actual payment is considered made — just a renewed promise to pay the original lender. However, if money is borrowed from a different lender to pay the interest due on the original loan, a deduction is allowed. While common sense may point to this as an irrelevant distinction, the courts have upheld this distinction as a matter of law. [Roberts, TC Memo 1987-235]

Limit on Deductible Home Mortgage Interest

Debt secured by a home is divided into 2 categories — *acquisition debt* and *home-equity debt.* The following shows the maximum amount of each type of debt that generates fully deductible home interest. These limits apply to the combined debt on a primary and second home.

Acquisition Debt:	$ 1,000,000
Home Equity Debt:	$100,000

The above amounts are halved for married persons filing separate returns.

Acquisition debt consists of debt incurred to purchase, construct, or substantially improve a residence. If such debt is later refinanced, the new debt is still considered acquisition debt to the extent it does not exceed the balance of the old debt at the time of refinancing. (If you refinance for a larger amount, taking out the extra amount in cash, this extra amount is not considered *acquisition debt* but becomes *home-equity* debt as discussed below.)

However, under a grandfathering provision, debt on a home incurred before October 14, 1987, is considered acquisition debt (and the $1,000,000 limit is not applied to such debt), no matter for what purpose the debt was incurred. For example, even a home-equity loan taken out before October 14, 1987, is considered *acquisition debt* rather than *home-equity debt*. As such, it is not counted against the $100,000 limitation that applies to *home-equity debt* taken out after this date. Furthermore, the grandfathering rule still applies if such debt is refinanced on or after October 14, 1987, to the extent the new debt does not exceed the old debt at the time of refinancing. Under this grandfathering provision only, the final payment date of the new debt cannot extend beyond the final payment date of the old debt. (In the case of a "balloon" mortgage acquisition debt that is not amortized over its term, the grandfathering provision applies for the term of the first refinancing, but not for more than 30 years after that first refinancing.)

For determining whether or not a loan is considered *acquisition debt,* the tracing rules described in the *Interest* chapter are relaxed. If you take out a loan within 90 days before or after you purchase a home, you may treat the loan as *acquisition debt* to the extent of amounts spent to purchase the home. Or, if you construct or substantially improve a residence, loans taken out during the period from 24 months before completion of the construction to 90 days after may similarly be considered acquisition debt.

You may treat a loan as "taken out" on the date you make a written application to incur the debt, provided the debt proceeds are actually disbursed within a reasonable time (30 days is a reasonable time) after approval of the application. In particular, these new rules allow you to purchase or construct a house for all cash and still have *acquisition debt* when you proceed to finance the house within 90 days after purchase or construction.

If you borrow money under the above rules to purchase, construct, or improve a residence, the debt does not become *acquisition debt* until it is actually secured by the residence via a deed of trust or other legal document. Before that time, it is generally *personal interest* (see the *Interest* chapter). [IRS Notice 88-74]

Home-equity debt consists of all other debt secured by your primary or second home other than acquisition debt. Note that it makes no difference to what purpose the home-equity debt is put. To the extent the debt does not exceed the $100,000 limit, all interest on such debt is fully deductible as home mortgage interest, no matter how the debt proceeds are spent.

Example 1

Kramer bought a personal residence in 1984 for $90,000, putting down $25,000 cash and taking out a first mortgage for $65,000. By July 1, 2001, his home had appreciated in value to $200,000.

Case 1: On July 1, 2001, Kramer took out a second loan secured by the home (second mortgage, home-equity loan, etc.) for $80,000.

The initial $65,000 loan is *acquisition debt* and the $80,000 loan taken out on July 1, 2001 is *home-equity debt.* Because the home-equity debt of $80,000 does not exceed the $100,000 home-equity limit, all interest payments on both loans are fully deductible as *home interest.*

Case 2: Kramer took out a second loan in 2001 with an average 2001 balance of $120,000.

Since this loan exceeds the $100,000 limit, only 5/6 ($100,000/$120,000) of the loan is considered home-equity debt. Thus, Kramer can deduct as *home interest* all the interest on his first mortgage (acquisition debt) plus 5/6 of the interest on the second loan (home-equity debt). The remaining 1/6 of the interest on the second loan is nondeductible *personal interest,* unless qualifying as investment or business interest as discussed in the *Interest* chapter. (See the text following Example 2 for the definition of the term *average balance.*)

Case 3: Kramer took a second loan for $120,000 before October 14, 1987.

In this case, the second loan comes under the grandfathering rule and is considered *acquisition debt.* Thus, Kramer can deduct the full interest on both the first and second loans as *home interest* Furthermore, interest on any additional home loans up to $100,000, taken out after October 14, 1987, will be fully deductible *home-equity interest.*

Example 2

Cooper purchased a home for $60,000 in 1980, putting down $10,000 and taking out a first mortgage for $50,000. On January 1, 2001, the house had risen in value to $180,000 and the first mortgage balance was paid down to $30,000. On this date, Cooper refinanced the first mortgage for $155,000. The *average balance* of this refinanced loan during 2001 was $150,000.

Because the balance of the first mortgage on the date of refinancing was $30,000, $30,000 of the new mortgage is considered to be *acquisition debt.* The remaining $120,000 ($150,000 − $30,000) is *home-equity debt.* Of this $120,000, $100,000 falls within the home-equity limit. Thus $130,000 of the refinanced loan ($30,000 + $100,000) qualifies for deduction. That is, 13/15 ($130,000/$150,000) of the interest on the loan is fully deductible as *home interest.* The remaining 2/15 of interest is nondeductible *personal interest* unless it falls into the investment or business interest category as described in the *Interest* chapter.

In the preceding example, the **average balance** of the refinanced loan during 2001 was compared to the balance of the old loan just before refinancing to see if the $100,000 limitation on home-equity debt was satisfied. Most mortgage lenders now provide this *average balance* figure on the statement they send to you after year-end, reporting the taxes and interest you paid during the year. Or, there are a number of methods for computing an average balance figure yourself which are described in the instructions to Form 1040. For example, one method that can be used under the appropriate circumstances is to add the 2000 year-end balance plus the 2001 yearend balance and divide by 2.

Example 3

Wilson bought a home on February 15, 1991, for $200,000. He paid all cash, taking out no loans on the home at the time of purchase because he expected interest rates to fall. On September 1, 2001, he took out a first mortgage which had an average balance during 2001 of $150,000.

Case 1: None of this money was used to substantially improve the home.

Wilson has no acquisition debt on the home, because the first mortgage was taken out more than 90 days after purchase. The $150,000 is considered to be home-equity debt. Only $100,000 of this debt generates fully deductible home interest. Thus, Wilson deducts 2/3 ($100,000/$150,000) of the interest payments on the loan as home interest. The remainder is nondeductible personal interest, unless it qualifies as investment or business interest as discussed in the *Interest* chapter.

Case 2: Out of the proceeds of the loan, $20,000 is used for making substantial improvements to the home. The remainder is used for personal purposes.

In this case, there is acquisition debt of $20,000. The remaining $130,000 ($150,000 – $20,000) is considered home-equity debt, $100,000 of which generates fully deductible home interest. Thus, Wilson deducts 4/5 [($20,000 + $100,000) / $150,000] of his interest payments as fully deductible home interest. The remaining 1/5 is nondeductible personal interest.

Warning to Homebuyers — Take Out Large Mortgage at Time of Purchase

If you are planning to buy a home, pay particular attention to Example 3. You might consider as large a loan as you will need at the time of purchase. This will establish the loan amount as a fully deductible acquisition debt. As Example 3 illustrates, a loan taken out at a later time might not qualify for a full deduction if the deductible limit for home-equity debt is exceeded. In effect, the tax law encourages home buyers to take out the largest initial mortgage with the smallest down payment possible. Then, you can use any available money to pay for the purchase of consumer items (personal auto, appliances, etc.) where any interest incurred would not be deductible.

Similarly, it may be unwise to prematurely "pay off" your existing mortgage. A refinancing of your existing mortgage is generally considered to be acquisition debt. But once all debt is paid off, any new loan is considered home-equity debt, subject to the $100,000 limitation. Again, use the extra cash to pay for consumer items.

Example 4

You have a primary home and a second home, both of which you own debt-free because you have paid off your mortgages. On December 1, 1993, you borrowed $60,000 on your primary home and on January 1, 2001, you borrowed $80,000 on your second home. (Both loans were balloon mortgages.) The proceeds of these loans were used for personal purposes.

You are limited to a $100,000 total on the amount of home-equity debt qualifying for deduction. You can deduct in full the interest on the earlier $60,000 loan and $1/2$ [$40,000/$80,000] of the second loan. Or you can lump the 2 loans together and deduct in full $^{10}/_{14}$ [$100,000/($60,000 + $80,000)] of the total interest paid on the 2 loans during the year. In either case, the remaining interest is nondeductible personal interest.

Does It Pay to Refinance Your Home?

It may pay for you to refinance the current mortgage on your home, i.e., replace it by one bearing the current rate of interest. This will be the case if the current interest rate is sufficiently lower than the interest rate you're paying on the existing mortgage. Because of the large fluctuation in interest rates that occurred during the past few years, tens of millions of homeowners have refinanced their mortgages, in most cases lowering their monthly payments. And as rates continued to plunge, many homeowners refinanced their homes for a second or even a third time.

The chief deterrent to refinancing is the closing costs which banks charge when you take out a new mortgage. These closing costs include not just points on the new loan, but also fees for appraisal, credit reports, title insurance, legal services, mortgage recording, etc.

Refinancing an existing mortgage pays if you plan on holding it past the *crossover point.* This is the point in time when you have saved in lower interest costs an amount equal to the extra closing costs on the new loan. This is illustrated by the following examples.

Example 5

Parks has an existing mortgage on his home with a remaining balance of $100,000 and bearing a fixed interest rate of $10^{1}/_{2}$%. He has the opportunity to refinance with a new $100,000 loan bearing an interest rate of 9%. Closing costs would consist of $2,000 in points and $1,500 in other fees — a total of $3,500.

The interest payments on the existing mortgage are $875 per month. The refinanced mortgage would have monthly interest payments of $750, a savings of $125 per month.

The crossover point is determined by dividing the closing costs by the monthly savings in interest, $3,500/$125 = 28 months. That is, after 28 months have elapsed, Parks will have accumulated $125 × 28 = $3,500 in interest savings, - exactly counteracting the $3,500 closing costs. If Parks plans to move before this 28 months crossover point, then he would accumulate less in interest savings and should not refinance. If he stays in his house for longer than 28 months, the interest saved by refinancing will outweigh the closing costs incurred.

The above example ignored the fact that interest payments on a home mortgage are deductible. The next example shows how this is factored into the equation for those who itemize their deductions.

Example 6

Same as the preceding example, except that the deductibility of the monthly mortgage interest is taken into account. We assume in this example that Park's effective tax rate — federal, state, and local combined — is 36%.

As in the above example, Parks pays $875 in interest under the existing mortgage and $750 under the refinanced mortgage. However, because these amounts can be deducted, they represent after-tax amounts of $875 – (36% × $875) = $560 and $750 – (36% × $750) = $480. Thus, the after-tax interest savings is $560 – $480 = $80.

The crossover point in this example is obtained by using this $80 figure instead of the $125 figure in the preceding example: $3,500/$80 = 44 months. If Parks plans to move before 44 months, he should not refinance. If he stays longer than 44 months, the interest saved by refinancing will exceed the closing costs, making a refinancing profitable.

Although the above example includes the effect of income tax on the interest payments, there are 2 additional factors that may need to be taken into account to make a more exact computation.

The basic computation compared the $3,500 paid at closing with the $80 per month interest savings produced by a refinancing. However, this direct comparison ignores the fact that the $3,500 is paid at the beginning, while the $80 payments are spread out over the course of the loan. If the "time value of money" (i.e. the ability of the $3,500 to produce investment income) is accounted for, the crossover point would be lengthened.

However, counteracting this factor is the fact that $2,000 of the closing costs are points, deductible as discussed later in this Section. The deductibility of the points reduces the after-tax cost of closing to an amount lower than $3,500. This factor shortens the crossover point.

In Examples 5 and 6, these two factors — the up-front nature of the closing costs and the deductibility of points — cancel each other out for the most part. However, to make an exact comparison, they would have to be included in the computation.

Finally, there is the "aggravation factor." Even if refinancing produces a small advantage on paper, it probably should be avoided. The drudgery of filling out an application, the bother of getting an appraisal, etc., all raise the "cost" of refinancing. In addition, there is the possibility that rates will go lower. This would mean losing out on perhaps several thousand dollars by not waiting to refinance. If refinancing now would produce only a small savings, the odds would suggest waiting to be a better gamble. Of course if a current refinancing could produce a large savings, this savings could diminish if rates move higher before the refinancing is executed.

The above analysis applies only to *fixed-rate loans,* i.e. loans on which the interest rate remains fixed throughout the duration of the loan. This is the most popular type of loan because most people like the security of knowing what their financial obligations will be in future years. In contrast, interest payments on *variable-rate loans* change according to the variation in market interest rates. Variable-rate mortgages generally carry a lower interest rate than fixed-rate mortgages at the time of issue, but this can reverse if interest rates rise. However, for those who don't mind the gamble, adjustable-rate mortgages could turn out to be the best choice.

What to Look for in a Home-Equity Loan

As discussed earlier in this Section, the tax code enshrines home-equity loans as a privileged borrowing vehicle, no matter what the status of the borrower or purpose to which the loan is used. A millionaire who takes out a $100,000 home-equity loan to throw an African Safari party for his close friends gets a full deduction for interest on the loan. Meanwhile, the less affluent individual who borrows on an automobile needed to get to work gets no deduction.

If you are a homeowner, you need to take cognizance of this bias in the law. You should lean toward taking out a home-equity loan rather than use other forms of consumer credit such as auto loans, credit card debt, etc.

Of course, factors other than tax treatment must also be considered when comparing a home-equity loan with other types of debt. On the plus side is the fact that home-equity loans generally offer a lower interest rate than other types of consumer loans — often significantly lower.

On the negative side are the fees that may be required to take out a home-equity loan. Such fees might include origination fees, appraisal fees, legal fees, title insurance, etc. Because of the competitive nature of the home-equity market, shopping around for the best deal might save considerable amounts on such fees.

Lenders are required to hold cash reserves to cover the value of credit lines that borrowers have not yet drawn upon. Because of this, most banks will charge a fee based on the total line of credit which you obtain, not just on the amount currently borrowed. Even before this reserves requirement went into effect, many banks had been charging a closing fee of 1%-3% (sometimes termed "points") on the total credit line. Now, this type of fee or an "inactivity fee" is widespread. In the presence of such fees, you should not establish a credit line in excess of the amount you actually anticipate borrowing unless fees are based only on the amount actually borrowed.

You should also beware of "teaser rates" which seem much lower than normal. When you read the fine print, these teaser rates only apply for a short period of time, with a higher rate applying thereafter.

One last caveat is to remember that home-equity loans are secured by your home. In case of default, ownership of your home could be jeopardized. Particular care should be taken with floating interest rates under which required payments can increase if certain benchmark interest rates rise.

Consumer Protection Rules on Mortgage Errors

Because of the recent flood of mortgage refinancing, a higher number of errors are being made than before. Such errors might include failures to credit mortgage payments, mistakes in escrow accounts, errors generated when the mortgage is sold to another company, etc.

Fortunately, Congress recently passed a law which protects an individual's rights in correcting such mistakes. Provided you make your complaint or inquiry in the proper way, the lender or mortgage servicer must acknowledge your communication in writing within 20 business days of receipt, and to correct or clarify the problem within 60 days of receipt. If this is not done, federal civil penalties may apply.

The proper method of communication is a separate distinct written correspondence from you to the lender or the company currently servicing your mortgage. The correspondence must include your name, address, account number, and your inquiry or complaint. Do not simply write a note on your monthly payment coupon. This would not be a proper method of communication under the law.

If your mortgage dispute involves an allegation of unpaid funds, the above 20-60-day rule gives you an added protection. During the 60 business day period after receipt of your letter, the mortgage lender or servicer is prohibited from informing credit bureaus of your alleged delinquency. Without the 20-60-day rule applying, in contrast, your lender can tell anyone checking your credit that you're delinquent on your mortgage — even if it later turns out you're not.

Late Payment Charges

If you are late in making a monthly mortgage payment, you will probably be assessed a *late payment charge*. In most cases, such a charge represents additional interest and is deductible as such. However, in some cases, this late payment charge takes the form of a service charge and is not deductible. This is the conclusion of the Tax Court in a 1991 court case.

In this court case, a 4% late payment charge was assessed when a mortgage payment was late. The court ruled that the nature of the charge indicated it was not interest. In particular, the 4% fee was independent of how long the payment went unpaid. No matter if the delinquent period was 1 day or 2 years, the same 4% charge applied. Furthermore, the bank's internal records indicated that the bank *"assessed the late charge, primarily, to recoup costs (telephone costs, letters, supervisory reviews, field visits, loan workouts, and note revisions) attendant to its attempt to collect the delinquent loan."* As a result, the court ruled the late payment fee to be a nondeductible service charge rather than a deductible interest payment. [West, TC Memo 1991-18]

Points

When you buy a house, you might have to pay "points" in order to be able to obtain the loan. Because these points represent money you are paying to a lender in order to borrow money, they are actually a form of interest and are deductible as such. However, *fees* incurred in obtaining the loan such as appraisal fees, settlement fees, notary fees, etc., are not considered to be interest and cannot be deducted as such.

FHA or VHA points paid by a buyer which are designated as *loan origination fees* are considered to be interest and therefore eligible for deduction. But to the extent that FHA and VHA points are designated as *service charges*, they are nondeductible fees.

When you obtain your mortgage loan, the lender can tell you about the tax status of any points being charged. Only points which are paid to purchase your *principal* residence and which do not exceed what is generally paid in your area can be deducted immediately. Other points must be deducted ratably over the period of the loan.

In order to be deducted immediately, the points must be paid when you purchase your principal residence. Points on a second home or investment house cannot be deducted in the year of purchase, but must be deducted rateably over the period of the loan, as discussed later in this Section.

According to a 1999 IRS ruling, the following 5 conditions must be satisfied in order for points to be deducted immediately:

1. The Settlement Sheet must clearly designate the amounts as points incurred in connection with the loan, for example as *"loan origination fees," "loan discount,"* or *"points."* (Mortgage broker commissions also qualify when calculated the same way as other points.) Other charges such as appraisal fees, inspection fees, title fees, attorney fees, and mortgage insurance are not deductible;

2. The points must be computed as a percentage of the loan amount;

3. The points must not exceed what is generally paid in the area in which the home is located;

4. The points must be paid in connection with the acquisition of your principal residence.

5. The loan must be secured by that residence; and

6. The points must be *paid directly* by you. This does not mean you have to issue a check in the amount of the points. Rather, this condition will be satisfied as long as the funds you provide before or at closing — including down payments, escrow deposits, earnest money, and funds actually paid at closing — at least equal the amount of the points. [Rev Proc 94-27]

Any points paid upon purchase of a home which do not meet the preceding conditions cannot be deducted in the year of payment, but must be "amortized" over the period of the loan in the same way as refinancing points discussed below.

The lender who issues you a mortgage on your principal residence will send you a Form 1098 at the end of the year reporting the interest you paid. A copy of this form will also be sent to the IRS.

There is a special box on Form 1098, labeled *"Points paid directly by payer(s)/borrower(s) on purchase of a principal residence."* The lender is supposed to report in this box the points which you are entitled to deduct immediately. Be sure that the amount reported in this box includes all the points you're entitled to deduct under the rules as described above. If the lender has under-reported the points you're entitled to deduct, it's best to contact the lender and have him issue an amended Form 1098 reporting the correct figure.

Refinancing

You cannot claim a current deduction for points paid on a refinanced home mortgage when a new mortgage simply replaces an existing mortgage. Instead, you must deduct the points ratably over the period of the loan. For example, if you pay $4,800 in points on a 20-year loan replacing an existing mortgage and involving 240 monthly payments, you can deduct $4,800 / 240 = $20 for each payment that was due during the tax year.

However, if part of the loan proceeds is used for improving your principal residence, points allocable to that part of the loan can be currently deducted, provided the points meet the rules described earlier for purchasing a home. However in this case, you should pay the points directly, rather than having the points added to the loan or paid from the loan proceeds. To illustrate the allocation method, suppose that in the loan example in the preceding paragraph, the amount refinanced was equal to $100,000, of which $40,000 was used to improve your house. Because 40% of the loan was for improvements, you may currently deduct 40% × $4,800 = $1,920 in points. The remainder of the points, $4,800 − $1,920 = $2,880 must be deducted ratably over the period of the loan, $2,880 / 2440 = $12 per month.

An exception to the general rules can occur when an original purchase or home improvement mortgage is designed to be refinanced a short period of time later. An example of this is given in a 1990 court case. In this case, an individual purchased a house, financed by a 3-year first mortgage of $122,000. Before this mortgage expired, he refinanced with a 30-year mortgage, paying off the previous loan. As part of the refinancing, he paid a total of $4,440 in points.

Because the original loan expired in only 3 years, it was obviously contemplated at the time that it would be refinanced within the 3-year period. For this reason, the Eighth Circuit Court of Appeals ruled that the refinancing was sufficiently connected with the original purchase of the home. The same would be true with a refinancing of a bridge loan, construction loan, or similar short-term loan. [Huntsman, 66 AFTR 2d 90-5020, reversing 91 TC No. 57]

Although the IRS announced that it did not agree with the above court decision [this means it could challenge a deduction for points on any type of refinancing outside the 7-state area comprising the Eighth Circuit (Ark., Iowa, Minn., Mo., Neb., ND, SD)], recent cases have cited the Huntsman favorably.

If a new loan is taken out on a personal residence in part to refinance an existing loan and in part to pay for improvements, points allocable to the part used for improvements can be deducted immediately. The amount allocable to the refinancing is prorated over the lifespan of the loan.

Example

Jacoby has an existing long-term mortgage on his home with a current balance of $80,000. He refinances in 2001 with a new 25-year $100,000 loan, using the extra $20,000 to pay for improvements to the home. He is required to pay $4,000 in points when he takes out the new loan.

Of the $100,000 new loan, 20% is used to pay for improvements. This means that 20% of the points, 20% × $4,000 = $800, can be deducted in 2001. The remaining $3,200 is prorated over the 25-year lifespan of the loan at the rate of $3,200/25 = $128 per year. Thus, Jacoby deducts $800 + $128 = $928 in points on his 2001 tax return, with $128 deducted in each of the remaining 24 years of the loan.

Deducting Remaining Points When Mortgage Is Paid Off

If you are required to deduct points ratably over the period of the loan, any undeducted points become deductible if the loan is paid off early via a refinancing or otherwise. For example, if the $4,800 loan discussed above were paid off after 40 months, you would deduct the remaining points, $4,800 – (40 × $20) = $4,000 in the year of payoff. [IRS Private Letter Ruling 8637058]

Points Paid by Seller Can Be Deducted by Buyer

The IRS issued a ruling in 1994 under which the purchaser of a home can deduct points even if paid by the seller. Under this ruling, seller-paid points are considered to lower the selling price of the home, with the points treated as paid by the purchaser. [Rev Proc 94-27]

Example

Breyer purchases a home from Selbert for $120,000, making a down payment of $20,000 and taking out a mortgage for $100,000. As reflected on the settlement sheet, Selbert paid 2 points equal to $2,000. Breyer is entitled to deduct the $2,000 in points on his tax return. The official selling price of the home is lowered by this $2,000: $120,000 – $2,000 = $118,000. This $118,000 figure is the one which will be used in any capital gains computation that might occur when Breyer sells his home in the future.

To qualify for deduction as in the above example, points must satisfy the same rules as discussed earlier for deducting points in the year of purchase. In particular, points must be properly shown on the settlement sheet, must be computed as a percentage of the loan amount, and must be the going rate in the area where the home is located. Also, the points must be used to purchase the buyer's *principal residence.*

Deducting Points on a Home Refinanced More Than Once

Because of fluctuating interest rates in recent years, many homeowners have refinanced their homes more than once. When a second refinancing occurs, a hidden deduction can be generated. If you have been ratably deducting points paid on a refinancing over the period of the loan, you may deduct immediately any remaining amounts upon undergoing a second refinancing. The following example shows how to compute this deduction.

Example

You refinanced your home in 1993, taking out a new 20-year mortgage of $150,000. As part of the settlement costs, you paid 3 points equal to $4,500. Over the 8-year period 1993-2000, you deducted $4,500 / 20 = $225 in points each year, a total of $8 \times $225 = $1,800$.

You refinanced your home again in 2001. Because this effectively means you have paid off the previous $150,000 mortgage, you can now deduct the remainder of the points on this mortgage. This would produce an interest deduction of $4,500 – $1,800 = $2,700 which you claim on your 2001 tax return.

To obtain a deduction as shown in the previous example, the second refinancing should not be obtained from the same lending institution that provided the first refinancing. When the same lending institution provides both refinancings, it is the IRS position that the first refinanced mortgage has not actually been repaid, meaning the remainder of the points would not be deductible.

Points to Be Reported to IRS by Lender

The lending institution will generally report the amount of points you paid on the interest-reporting form it sends the IRS after year-end. The form will specify whether you paid the points from separate funds as opposed to the points being withheld from the loan disbursement. The IRS plans to use this information to uncover home buyers who are deducting points which were not handled properly.

Discount Loans

Sometimes, loans are issued under a discount arrangement under which you receive less than the face amount of the loan, with the difference representing the interest. FHA mortgage loans and home improvement loans are common examples of this. The following example shows how to treat this type of loan.

Example

You borrow money from a bank in order to make a home improvement. The face amount of the loan is $10,000. However, you receive only $8,000 and are required to pay back the face amount of $10,000 in 40 equal monthly installments of $250 each. The interest on the loan is the difference between the $10,000 you pay back and the $8,000 you received, namely $2,000. This is paid over the 40 months. Thus, $2,000/40 = $50 of each monthly payment is deductible as interest. If you made 12 such payments during the year, you would have a $50 \times 12 = $600 interest deduction for the year.

In the above example, the $10,000 which you paid back all went to the lender as payment for the loan. However, often the loan will include mandatory insurance payments. These insurance payments are not deductible except in connection with home office or other business expenses. In the above example, if each of the 40 monthly payments had included $5 for insurance, you would actually be paying $200 in insurance and only $9,800 back to the lender. Thus, your interest deduction would be $9,800 – $8,000 prorated over the 40-month period. Your loan agreement will state any insurance charges that are included in your monthly payments.

Graduated Payment and Adjustable Rate Mortgages

Some mortgages are structured so that payments in early years are artificially low, increasing during later years. That is, the early payments do not cover all the interest due on the mortgage; the principal due on the loan increases by an amount equal to the unpaid interest. A similar situation can arise on certain adjustable rate mortgages when the interest rate is adjusted upward, but mortgage payments remain fixed below the amount required to cover the total interest due.

In such cases, you can only deduct the amount of interest actually paid. You cannot deduct the unpaid interest which was added to your mortgage balance. (The statement received from the bank or mortgage company holding your mortgage will generally show the amount actually paid.)

However, an IRS Private Letter Ruling contains a little-known fact. If you pay off or refinance the loan with another institution, you can then deduct the deferred interest which increased the principal balance on your mortgage. In this ruling, an individual borrowed $55,400 on his home under a graduated payment mortgage. Because his payments for the first few years did not cover the amount of interest on the loan, his principal balance had grown by $3,300 to $58,700 after two years. He then refinanced his house with another lending institution, paying off the $58,700 balance with the original lender. The IRS ruled that he could deduct the $3,300 at the time he refinanced the loan as a payment of deferred interest on the original loan.

The IRS noted that had he refinanced with the same institution, the $3,300 could not have been deducted at that time. In such a case, he has made no actual payment but just promised to pay again. While this may seem a distinction without a real difference, the courts have upheld this distinction. [IRS Private Letter Ruling 8346015]

Seller Financing Restricted

When you sell your house, you may consider helping the buyer finance the purchase by lending part of the purchase price at a below market rate. You could finance most of the purchase price as a first trust or only part to help with the down payment as a second trust. For a sale to another individual who will also use the house as a principal residence, there is no minimum interest rate that you must use. As long as the interest rate is more than you would get from leaving the funds in a bank account, you are ahead.

With other types of loans, IRS requires you to charge interest at a minimum stated rate. Interest rates are published monthly for short-term (1 to 3 years), mid-term (3 to 9 years) and long-term (more than 9 years). There are certain exceptions to these rules: no interest has to be charged on loans of less than $10,000 or $100,000 if the borrower has less than $1,000 of investment income (interest, dividends, capital gains). There is also an exemption for loans to a *continuing care facility* up to a maximum loan of $144,100 in 2001 for you and your spouse aged 65 or older. The limit is increased annually.

Penalty Payments for Prepayment of Mortgages

Many mortgage contracts provide for a penalty payment if you prepay part or all of your mortgage. These payments are deductible as interest.

Deducting 13 Monthly Interest Payments Instead of 12

Typically, the 2001 statement from the institution holding your home mortgage will reflect the 12 monthly payments due on the first day of each month during the year. You would then be entitled to deduct the total interest portion of these payments.

However, there is a way to squeeze an extra month's interest deduction on your 2001 tax return. This is done simply by sending in your January 1, 2002, mortgage payment early so it's received by the lender during December 2001. Because this payment is actually for the use of money during December 2001, you're entitled to deduct this on your 2001 tax return.

The validity of this extra month's interest deduction, although not entirely clear from the law, is supported by an example that appears in the official IRS Audit Manual. In this example, an individual's tax return under audit contained a number of interest deductions, some of which are being denied. However, the IRS actually increased the deduction for mortgage interest by $880. The individual had deducted only 12 mortgage payments, but he deserved a deduction for the 13 payments he actually made during the calendar year. [IRS Audit Manual, MT 4231-74]

This extra deduction could be substantial. For example, if your mortgage payment includes, say, $1,000 in interest each month, you would get an additional deduction of $1,000 for 2001.

It's possible that the statement you receive from the lender might not show this extra payment, even if received prior to year-end. In such a case, it's best to request the lender to issue a corrected statement to be sent to you and the IRS. This will eliminate the possibility of an IRS computer letter asking you to explain a discrepancy. Otherwise, you should deduct the extra interest on Schedule A for interest not reported on the Form 1098.

Where Do You Deduct Interest Payments?

Interest payments on a primary or second home are deducted on line 10 of Schedule A. You cannot deduct interest payments on a personal residence if you claim the standard deduction.

If you make interest payments on a home mortgage to an individual rather than a bank or other lending institution, Schedule A requires you to list that individual's name, address, and social security number. This gives IRS computers the capability of checking that the individual receiving the payments reports them on his tax return.

Section 2:
Taxes

The real estate taxes which you pay on your home are deductible. Often, you do not pay these directly to the local government, but instead pay them as part of your monthly mortgage payment. What usually happens to these tax payments is this. The mortgage company accumulates these payments during the year in an escrow account. Then, when a year's worth of payments has been accumulated, the mortgage company pays your real estate taxes for the next year to the local government.

You can deduct the real estate taxes only when they are actually paid to the local government. The mortgage company which places your payments into escrow is considered to be acting as your agent. Thus, the IRS does not consider that you have paid your taxes by sending money to the mortgage company. They must actually be delivered to the taxing agency.

> **Example**
>
> Your local tax year begins on July 1 and runs through June 30 of the following year. From July 2000 through June 2001, you pay $100 per month for local property tax as part of your mortgage payment to your bank. The bank accumulates these payments into an escrow account and pays your real estate tax bill of $1,200 on July 1, 2001. You can deduct this $1,200 on your 2001 tax return. The tax portion of your mortgage payments from July through December 2001 is not deductible on your 2001 return. These amounts are being placed in escrow and will become deductible on your 2002 return when the bank pays your July 1, 2002, tax bill.

In its yearly statement to you, the institution holding your mortgage will state how much real estate tax it paid on your account the previous year. This is the figure you use in deducting your taxes. Do not simply multiply your current tax payments by 12, because the tax rate might have been changed recently.

Your taxes are deducted on Schedule A along with the rest of your itemized deductions. You cannot claim a deduction for taxes on your personal residence if you claim the standard deduction.

Special Assessments

If an assessment is paid for the purpose of building or improving some facility, it is a non-deductible item. For example, assessments for sewers, street paving, etc., are non-deductible. The law regards such items as capital expenditures, that is, expenditures which tend to increase the value of your property. Even if you could show that no increase in value actually took place, it would do you no good. It would not change the non-deductible category into which the IRS places these expenditures.

If a portion of an assessment represents a maintenance charge or interest expense associated with an improvement, this portion is deductible if it is levied *against an interest in real property,* as opposed to being a *user charge* for some service or benefit. While this distinction is not always easy to make, an IRS ruling has described 3 situations which illustrate the difference. In situation 1, the city assesses a front-foot benefit charge against abutting property that is benefited by the construction of a water system. In situation 2, a city water authority imposes a 2-part charge upon its customers, one part being a metered per-gallon fee and the other a flat uniform charge for maintenance and interest on the water system facilities. And in situation 3, a sewer authority imposes a flat charge per unit for each year on all residential customers. In situations 2 and 3, no deduction is permitted because the charges are considered to be merely fees paid for receipt of water and sewer services. But in situation 1, the charge is considered to be an assessment *"imposed because of and measured by some benefit inuring directly to the property against which the assessment is levied."* Thus, it is an assessment *"against the property"* and the portion representing interest and maintenance is deductible. [Rev. Rul 79-201]

Observe that in situation 3, had the sewer services been paid from revenue derived from a general local tax such as a property tax, the entire tax would still be deductible. It is only when the charges are singled out as user fees for services that they become non-deductible.

You will have to check with your local government to determine if any percentage of your water or sewer bill is attributable to deductible assessments. Sometimes this information will be distributed to all city residents. However, in surprisingly many cases, the local government is unfamiliar with the tax law and cannot give this breakdown. All you can do in such a case is to refer the appropriate government official to the above cited revenue ruling and pressure for this information to be provided.

How Do You Apportion Taxes When a House Is Sold?

When a house is sold, the real estate taxes are considered apportioned according to the date the property is transferred to the new owner. The following example illustrates how this is done.

Example
You buy a house and sign the final settlement papers on February 1, 2002. The real estate tax year in your locality runs from July 1 through the following June 30.

The settlement sheet includes real estate taxes in two places. First of all, the previous owner had paid one year's taxes in advance on July 1, 2001. (This payment was actually paid by the mortgage company from money placed into escrow taken from monthly payments from July 2000 through June 2001.) Since you are occupying the house from February 1, 2002 through June 30, 2002, you must reimburse the previous owner for this 5-month portion of the tax bill which he already paid for.

The second place where real estate taxes appear is in replacing the tax escrow account of the previous owner. Money had been placed in escrow from July 2001 through January 2002. This money needs to be available in July 2002 when your new mortgage company has to pay the real estate taxes for the year beginning July 1, 2002. The tax portion of your mortgage payments will be added to your tax escrow account to pay the taxes for the next year, July 1, 2002 through June 30, 2003.

The taxes for the period July 1, 2001 through January 31, 2002, belong to the seller of the house. Because he paid these taxes in advance on July 1, 2001, his deduction is claimed on his 2001 tax return. The purchaser of the house deducts on his 2002 return, the taxes from February 1, 2002 through June 30, 2002, which he paid at settlement plus the full next year's taxes paid on July 1, 2002, by the mortgage company out of the escrow account.

The preceding example shows how taxes are divided for the purpose of determining how much tax deduction goes to the seller and how much to the buyer. The actual settlement sheet may not reflect this division correctly. For example, the seller may have paid part of the taxes attributable to the period after transfer. However, this does not count. The IRS considers this as a disguised way of reducing the price of the house. The seller can only deduct the taxes for the period when he owned the house. The buyer deducts the taxes for his period of ownership, even if he did not actually pay them.

Transfer Taxes

When you buy a house or other real estate, the settlement charges include various transfer and recordation taxes. These taxes can add up to several thousand dollars in some localities. These taxes are **not** deductible. Only those local taxes which are specifically designated in the tax code can be deducted. And this does not include real estate transfer or recordation taxes.

Transfer and recordation taxes are considered to be part of the cost of the property. If the property is used for business or investment purposes (e.g. rental real estate, home office, etc.), those taxes will be written off over a period of years as part of the depreciation on the property [see the *Expensing and Depreciation* chapter].

SECTION 3:
CAPITAL GAINS ON SALE OF A HOUSE

If you sell your house for a higher price than the one at which it was purchased, you may have a capital gain. This capital gain is computed by subtracting the original purchase price of the house and the cost of any improvements from the amount realized by the sale. You also add back any deductions you have claimed for casualty losses.

On the other hand, if you sell your personal residence for a lower price than the one at which it was purchased, there is no tax consequence. You do not get a capital loss to write off against any capital gains you might have.

The **amount realized by the sale** means the actual sales price less the cost of expenses directly connected with making the sale. Such expenses include the cost of advertising, commissions, legal fees, transfer taxes, and points or loan placement fees charged to the seller.

You do not include the cost of furnishings such as rugs, drapes, washing machine, etc., in the price of the house. You are supposed to pay capital gains tax in the unlikely event that you receive more for these items than you paid. However, you cannot claim a capital loss if you sell these items at a lower price.

The **purchase price** of a house includes not only the cost of the house itself, but also expenses connected with buying the house such as legal fees, title fees, transfer and deed-recording fees, etc.

An **improvement** is a replacement or addition which adds to the value or prolongs the life of your house. This is distinguished from an ordinary maintenance or repair expense. For example, adding central air-conditioning, replacing the roof, panelling the den, new plumbing, new furnace, installing permanent storm windows, landscaping, assessments for capital items, etc., are improvements. Similarly, the cost of blacktopping a driveway, replacing gutters, new doors, waterproofing the basement, installing built-in shelving, etc., can generally be regarded as improvements. However, the cost of painting, cleaning, fixing a broken air-conditioner, etc., are ordinary maintenance expenses.

Sometimes a repair can be converted into an improvement by working it into a major remodeling project. This can provide a tax advantage because improvements reduce the capital gains tax that might become due when the house is sold. For example, the cost of wallpapering and painting can be included as part of an overall improvement plan of remodeling or renovation. Independent of such a plan, however, wallpapering and painting do not constitute improvements. [Bayly, TC Memo 1981-549]

Special Rules When Personal Residence Is Sold

There is a special break from the general capital gains tax when a personal residence is sold. (Vacation houses, second homes, rental homes, etc., do not qualify.) An individual may exclude from tax up to $250,000 ($500,000 on most joint returns) of capital gain realized on the sale of a personal residence.

To qualify for the $250,000 exclusion from capital gains tax on a personal residence you sell, the following 3 rules must be satisfied:

Rule 1: Ownership. You must have *owned* the residence for an aggregate of 2 years out of the 5 years preceding the sale;

Rule 2: Occupancy. You must have *occupied* the residence as a personal residence for an aggregate of 2 years out of the 5 years preceding the sale; and

Rule 3: Prior Sale. You must not have applied the exclusion from capital gains to a previous sale within the prior 2 years.

In Rules 1 and 2 above, the 2-year periods need not be consecutive, as long as periods of ownership or occupancy add up to at least 2 years.

Married Individuals

A $500,000 exclusion (instead of $250,000) applies to married individuals, provided all of the following conditions are satisfied:

(i)   A joint tax return is filed;

(ii) Either spouse satisfies Rule 1;

(iii) Both spouses satisfy Rule 2 (if only one spouse satisfies Rule 2, the $250,000 exclusion applies); and

(iv) Both spouses satisfy Rule 3.

Example

Mr. and Mrs. Mitchell purchased a home on January 1, 1998 for $200,000. They used the home as a personal residence until it was sold on September 1, 2001 for $240,000. Both of them satisfy Rules 1 – 3, so the $500,000 capital gains exclusion applies. Since the gain, $240,000 – $200,000 = $40,000, does not exceed $500,000, the entire $40,000 gain is excluded from taxation.

Sales Due to Changes in Employment and Health

You might have to sell a home because of a change in place of employment or a change in health. In this case, if any of Rules 1 – 3 are satisfied for shorter periods than the required 2-year periods specified in the Rules, then a partial exclusion can be claimed. The amount of the exclusion is that fraction of the gain (as computed under the basic rules) equal to the fraction of the 2-year period that the Rule is satisfied. If more than one Rule is satisfied for less than the 2-year requirement, the Rule producing the smallest exclusion is applied.

Adjustment If Depreciation Has Been Claimed on the Home

You may have claimed depreciation on your home during a period when it was rented out, or when part of the home was used as a home office. In this case, if your home is sold at a gain, the total depreciation allowed after May 6, 1997 is not eligible for the exclusion. That is, a taxable capital gain equal to this depreciation will be realized when the home is sold.

Special Rules for Spouses Who Lived Separately or Are Divorced

Some spouses live apart in separate principal residences. If each spouse satisfies Rule 1 – 3 individually, then they are each entitled to a $250,000 exclusion. These can be claimed on separate returns or added together to produce a $500,000 exclusion on a joint return.

If a single person marries someone who has used the exclusion within 2 years prior to the marriage, the newly married person can claim the $250,000 exclusion if he or she satisfied Rules 1 – 3. Once 2 years have passed since either spouse has claimed an exclusion, they are eligible for the $500,000 exclusion under the rules applying to couples filing jointly.

If a residence is transferred to an individual incident to a divorce, the individual can count the time his former spouse owned the residence as part of the 2-year ownership period required in Rule 1. Also, a taxpayer can count towards the 2-year occupancy required by Rule 2, periods when his spouse or ex-spouse is given use of the residence under the terms of a divorce or separation. (See Chapter 20, *"Divorce and Separation."*)

Nursing Home Residents

If an individual is incapable of self-care, time spent in a nursing home (or similar licensed facility) is counted as time spent in the individual's home for purposes of Rules 1 and 2. To qualify for this special treatment, the individual must have owned the home while in the nursing home, and have used the home as a personal residence for at least 1 year during the 5 years preceding the sale.

Property Used Partly for Business or Rental During the Year of Sale

In the year of sale, you may have used part of your property as your home and part of it for business or to produce income. Examples are:

- A house with a room used as a home office;

- An apartment building in which you lived in one unit and rented the others; and

- A store building with an upstairs apartment in which you lived.

If you sell the entire property, you should consider the transaction as a sale of two properties. The sale of the part of your property used for business or rental is reported on Form 4797, *Sale of Business Property.*

To determine the amounts to report on Form 4797, you must divide your selling price, selling expenses, and basis between the part of the property used for business or rental and the part used as your home. In the same way, if you qualify to exclude any of the gain on the business or rental part of your home, divide your maximum exclusion between that part of the property and the part used as your home. You generally can exclude gain on the part of your home used for business or rental if you owned and lived in that part of the home for at least 2 years during the 5-year period ending on the date of the sale (except you have to pay tax on the depreciation previously deducted).

However, the rules are slightly different for home offices. If the room is not used as an office in the year of sale or it is used partly as an office and partly for personal use, so that it does not qualify for a deduction, only the depreciation is taxable in the year of sale, rather than the pro rated percentage of the gain.

Property Used Exclusively for Rental During the Year of Sale

Even if you meet the ownership and use tests for excluding gain on the sale of your home, you may have to recognize and pay tax on the gain if the home is being rented in the year of sale. The main consideration in determining whether or not you must recognize the gain is *intent*. A taxpayer who rents his/her home only temporarily should still qualify for the exclusion, while a taxpayer who rents his/her home on a more permanent basis would not qualify for the exclusion. Examples are:

- A professor who takes a one-year sabbatical to travel overseas and rents his home during the year that he is away would qualify for the exclusion as long as he meets the ownership and use tests.

- A person who wants to move to a new home, but is unable to sell his/her present home due to adverse market conditions rents the home for a year and then attempts to sell it when the market conditions are more favorable. He/she would be allowed to exclude the gain as long as he/she meets the ownership and use tests.

- The same taxpayer decided to move to a new home during a period of favorable market conditions and kept the second home as a rental property. The gain would not be excludable, even if the taxpayer fulfills the ownership and use requirements.

Example

Brian Smith, a single person, bought a home in Maryland in 1990. He lived in the home until May 31, 2000, when he accepted a one-year temporary work assignment in Texas. He moved out of the home and put it up for rent. He rented the home to a tenant under a one-year lease that expired on May 31, 2001, at which time Brian intended to move back to the home. On April 15, 2001, Brian was offered a permanent position in Texas and decided to sell his Maryland home and permanently relocate to Texas. Brian sold his home on September 23, 2001, at a gain of $89,672. He had claimed depreciation of $5,457 on his tax return during the period that the home was rented. Because Brian's intent when he moved out of his home was to rent it only temporarily, and because he meets the ownership and use tests, Brian qualified for an exclusion. The only gain that Brian must report on his 2001 tax return is $5,457, which is the amount of depreciation that Brian claimed on his home during the rental period.

In the above example, if Brian's original work assignment in Texas had been permanent and he decided to keep his Maryland home as a rental property, he would have to recognize the entire gain of $89,672 on his tax return in the year he sold the home, regardless of whether or not he met the ownership and use tests.

Reporting the Gain

If you are able to exclude all of the gain on the sale of your main home, you do not need to report the sale on your tax return. If you have any taxable gain on the sale of your main home that cannot be excluded, report the entire gain on Schedule D. Report it on line 1 or line 8 of Schedule D, depending on how long you owned the home. If you qualify for a partial exclusion, show it on the line directly below the line on which you report the gain. Write "Section 121 exclusion" in column (a) of that line and show the amount of the exclusion in column (f) as a loss (in parentheses).

Report any gain from the business part of your home in Part III of Form 4797. The exclusion amount should be entered on line 2 of Form 4797.

Example

Emily White, a single person, sold her home on December 1, 2001. She had bought the home in 1991 and had owned and lived in it the entire 5-year period ending on the date of sale. For the first 2 1/2 years of that period, Emily used the entire home as her main home. For the last 2 1/2 years, she used 75% of the house as her main home and 25% of the house for business. Her records show the following:

Purchase Price	$ 80,000
Depreciation (on business part, after 5/7/97)	1,363
Selling Price	160,000
Selling Expenses	10,000

Because she meets the ownership and use tests for the entire house, she can claim the exclusion for both the home and business parts. She starts by finding the adjusted basis of each part. She determines that 75% of the purchase price was for the part used as her home; 25% was for the part used for business.

	Personal 75%	Business 25%
Purchase Price	$ 60,000	$ 20,000
Minus: Depreciation	—	1,363
Adjusted Basis	$ 60,000	$ 18,637

Next, she figured the gain on each part, dividing her selling price and selling expenses between the two parts.

	Personal 75%	Business 25%
Selling Price	$ 120,000	$ 40,000
Minus: Selling Expenses	7,500	2,500
	$ 112,500	$ 37,500
Minus: Adjusted Basis	60,000	18,637
Gain	$ 52,500	$ 18,863

Then, to figure her taxable gain and exclusion on each part, she fills out Schedule D Worksheet 2 (Part 2) for each part, dividing her maximum exclusion between the two parts. Because she is single, her maximum exclusion is $250,000.

	Personal **75%**	**Business** **25%**
6) Depreciation after May 6, 1997	$ -0-	$ 1,363
7) Subtract line 6 from gain	52,500	17,500
8) Maximum exclusion	$ 187,500 [1/]	62,500
9) Exclusion (smaller of line 7 or line 8)	52,500	17,500
10) Taxable gain (gain minus line 9)	-0-	*
11) Smaller of line 6 or line 10	-0-	*

*   Lines 10 and 11 do not need to be filled out for the business parts.

[1/]   This represents 75% of the $250,000 exclusion for single persons.

The gain from the part used as her home does not have to be reported on her return, because she can exclude all of it. She would report the gain from the business part ($18,863) in Part III of Form 4797.

However, if Emily had stopped using part of her home for business purposes in a year prior to the year of sale, she would have only had to report gain in the amount of depreciation claimed.

Do You Need to Keep Records under the New Law?

You should retain the settlement papers which show how much you paid for your current residence. When this residence is sold, your capital gain will be equal, roughly, to the sales price minus the purchase price you paid originally. If this difference does not exceed $250,000 ($500,000 on joint returns), no tax is due.

If you keep records of improvements, these can be used to reduce the capital gain, helping to keep it below the $250,000 or $500,000 limit. Whether these records will be needed depend upon a number of factors, such as how expensive your home is, how long you plan to own it, and what the rate of inflation will be.

SECTION 4: RENTING A HOME TO OTHERS

If you rent out a home you own, you report the rent as income and you take the expenses associated with the rental as a deduction against the income. Special rules cover the situation when expenses exceed income. As discussed later in this Section, these rules may prevent you from claiming a loss in this situation.

There are also special *passive loss* rules that can restrict the ability to deduct losses on rental activities. However, these passive loss rules do not apply to losses up to $25,000 incurred by persons with income under $100,000, provided they sufficiently participate in managing the rental. This $25,000 limit is phased out for those with income in the $100,000 — $150,000 range. [see Section 2 of the *Investing Your Money* chapter for details on these *passive loss* rules.] In the remainder of this section, we assume that these passive loss rules do **not** affect your total deduction because of this $25,000 exemption or the existence of off-setting passive profits.

Deductible expenses include advertising costs, legal fees, utility bills you pay, homeowner's insurance, management fees, interest, and taxes. You can also deduct depreciation according to the rules described in the *Expensing and Depreciation* chapter. You compute your depreciation starting from the point you first rent your home as described in the *Expensing and Depreciation* chapter. That is, your depreciation is based on the original purchase price of the house plus the cost of improvements (less any casualty losses you have claimed) or else on the fair market value of the house when you start renting it out, whichever is lower.

Depreciating Your Furniture

If you rent out your home furnished, you can deduct depreciation on the furnishings and appliances. Because used furniture and appliances are usually worth less than their original purchase price, you will have to estimate their current fair market value and use this as the basis for depreciation. You can use either the straight-line or accelerated depreciation method for 5-year property as described in the *Expensing and Depreciation* chapter. The depreciable life for furniture was changed from 7 years to 5 years by IRS Announcement 1999-82.

How Are Rental Income and Expenses Reported?

You report your rental income and expenses on Schedule E. Note that expenses connected with renting a home are not considered itemized deductions. Thus, they may be deducted even if the standard deduction is claimed.

Example

Jones rents out a house from September 1, 2001 until December 31, 2002, a total of 16 months.

Depreciation Calculation on House

Jones originally paid $80,000 for the house when he purchased it in 1985 and later added central air conditioning at a cost of $4,000. Because the sum of these two amounts, $84,000, is less than the current fair market value, this sum is used as the basis for depreciation.

The following depreciation calculation is made according to the procedure explained in the *Expensing and Depreciation* chapter.

(1) Depreciation for 4 months from
   9/1/01 to 12/31/01 ....1.06% × $84,000 = $ 890

(2) Depreciation for year from
   1/1/02 to 12/31/02..3.64% × $84,000 = $3,058

Depreciation Calculation on Furniture

Jones estimates that the furnishings and appliances in the house have a current value of $6,000. Because $6,000 is less than his original cost, it is used as the basis for depreciation. He uses the accelerated method for 7-year property, as described in the Expensing and Depreciation *chapter.*

(1) Depreciation for 2001 .... 20.0% × $6,000 = $1,200

(2) Depreciation for 2002 .... 32.0% × $6,000 = $1,920

Total Expenses

Jones pays $500 per month in mortgage interest. He also pays $1,200 per year in property taxes and $120 per year in insurance. In order to make the appropriate allocations to 2001, these latter two amounts are prorated on a monthly basis — $100 per month for taxes and $10 per month for insurance.

Expense Summary

	2001		2002
Depreciation on house:	$ 890		$3,058
Depreciation on furniture:	1,200		1,920
Interest:	$500 × 4 mo. = 2,000		$500 × 12 mo. = 6,000
Taxes:	$100 × 4 mo. = 400		$100 × 12 mo. = 1,200
Insurance:	$ 10 × 4 mo. = 40		$10 × 12 mo. = 120
Advertising:	25		0
Legal expenses:	40		137
Totals:	$4,595		$12,435

Rent

Jones rents out his house for $625 per month. The tenants pay the cost of utilities. Thus, Jones receives rent of $625 × 4 months = $2,500 in 2001 and $625 × 12 months = $7,500 in 2002.

Net Result

For 2001, Jones has rental income of $2,500 and expenses of $4,595, a net loss of $2,095 for 2001.

For 2002, Jones has rental income of $7,500 and expenses of $12,435, a net loss of $4,935 for 2002.

The depreciation deductions illustrated in the above example apply to houses placed into rental service after 1986. Houses placed into rental service in 1986 or earlier come under more generous rules [see the 1987 edition of this *Tax & Financial Guide*], even if the rental period extended into 1987 and beyond.

Profit Motive Needed to Establish Loss

As in the above example, it may turn out that your expenses exceed the rental income, producing a net loss. In order to deduct the loss on your tax return, you should have a profit motive when you rent out the house. To begin with, you must charge the going rate for rent in your locality. However, even if you charge this "fair market rate," the IRS may still question your profit motive.

This is confirmed by IRS Private Letter Ruling 7826006 concerning a college professor who rented out his house when he went away on leave of absence. The professor had listed his house with a rental agency and charged the fair market value for rent in his area. Advice was sought from the National Office on what additional factors should be considered in deciding whether a loss should be allowed.

The IRS ruling stressed that the Professor must have a profit motive. If he was just renting out his house to lessen the loss that would occur if the house were left unrented, this would not suffice. He must have actually intended to make a profit on the transaction. Beyond this, the IRS ruling did not give much further guidance, telling the local IRS office that, *"The question of whether the taxpayer had a profit-making objective is a determination to be made by you based upon all the surrounding facts and circumstances."*

According to letters we have received from readers of prior editions, the IRS has in fact been challenging the profit motive of individuals when they rent out their personal residences while temporarily located away from home. Because there is often no chance that the rental income will exceed the taxes, interest, and other expenses, the IRS simply claims that there could be no profit motive. The taxpayer is often stymied as to how to counter this logically simple objection.

However, there is a strong argument that can be made by the taxpayer in this situation. Namely, the profit motive in owning a rental house comes from the appreciation in the value of the house that will occur over the period of time the house is rented out. In fact, investors who buy houses for the sole purpose of renting them out are often in precisely this situation. Their expenses exceed their rental income, but they look to the profit that will be made eventually when the house is sold for more than its purchase price.

A Tax Court case supports this position. An individual owned some property which he rented out at substantial annual losses. The IRS challenged the deduction of his losses, claiming that these large losses showed there could be no profit motive present.

However, the Tax Court permitted the losses to be deducted. It ruled that considering the anticipated appreciation of value of the property, a profit motive was present. In permitting the eventual increase in property value to be considered, it quoted the Income Tax Regulations as follows:

> *"The term 'income for [these purposes] includes not merely income of the taxable year but also income which the taxpayer has realized in a prior taxable year or may realize in subsequent taxable years, and is not confined to recurring income but applies as well to gains from the disposition of property. For example, if defaulted bonds, the interest from which if*

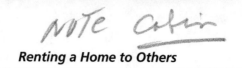

received would be includable in income, are purchased with the expectation of realizing capital gain on their resale, even though no current yield thereon is anticipated, ordinary and necessary expenses thereafter paid or incurred in connection with such bonds are deductible. Similarly, ordinary and necessary expenses paid or incurred in the management, conservation, or maintenance of a building devoted to rental purposes are deductible notwithstanding that there is actually no income therefrom in the taxable year, and regardless of the manner in which or the purpose for which the property in question was acquired." [Clancy, TC Memo 1978-85]

Home Rented Out for Part of the Year

If you rent out a home for less than 15 days during the year, it is considered that no business transaction took place. In this case, you neither report the rental income nor deduct any expenses. You deduct your taxes and interest on Schedule A as though no rental had taken place.

If you rent out your home for at least 15 days during the year, and use it for personal purposes part of the year, you cannot deduct a rental loss if the following condition is satisfied:

The home was used for personal purposes both:

(i) more than 14 days, and

(ii) more than 10% of the number of days during the year on which the home is rented out.

However, if the above condition applies, the home qualifies as a *primary* or *second home* under the rules discussed in Section 1. This means that all interest attributed to your personal use of the home can be deducted as *home interest* on line 10 of Schedule A.

However, if you do not satisfy the above condition, you have not used the home enough to qualify it as your *primary* or *second* home. This means that the interest attributed to your personal use of the home is considered nondeductible *personal interest* [see the *Interest* chapter]. However, in this case, because of your minimal personal use, you would qualify to deduct a loss from the rental activity.

Exception

For a home which is rented out for part of the year and used as your principal residence the remainder of the year, the above restriction on deducting rental losses does not apply if either:

(1) The rental period consisted of at least 12 consecutive months (not necessarily all in the same calendar year); or

(2) The rental period was a consecutive period of less than 12 months ending in the sale of the residence.

For example, if you rent out your home from June 1, 2001 through May 31, 2002, and use it as your principal residence the remainder of 2001 and 2002, the consecutive 12-month rental period satisfies the above exception.

If you are planning to be out of town for an extended period of time, you should take careful note of the above exception. By making sure you rent out your house for at least 12 consecutive months, you might become eligible to deduct a rental loss on your tax return. As shown by the preceding example, this could make a significant difference in your taxes.

This exception permitting losses on rental houses to be deducted can be used on a *primary or second home* [see Section 1] even if the passive loss rules, as discussed in Section 2 of the *Investing Your Money* chapter, would otherwise apply. More specifically, any interest disallowed under the passive loss rules can be claimed as primary or second home interest on line 10 of Schedule A. To qualify, you must use the home during the year for personal purposes both (i) more than 14 days, and (ii) more than 10% of the number of days during the year for which the home is rented out.

What Happens If a Loss Cannot Be Deducted?

If you are prevented from deducting a loss on a rental house for the reasons above, you must use the following procedure for offsetting your rental income with your expenses: Start with the *gross rental income*. This equals the rent you receive from tenants minus the costs of obtaining these tenants (advertising, rental agency fees, etc.). From this amount, (a) first subtract taxes and interest, (b) second, subtract rental expenses such as maintenance, insurance, utilities, etc., and (c) third, subtract depreciation. If a loss results, you cannot deduct the loss. The rental simply produces no tax result — neither a gain nor a loss. Of course in (a), (b), (c), you deduct only that proportion of the annual expense which corresponds to the proportion of time the house is rented out.

Note that the above order of deducting expenses forces you to deduct taxes and interest first. This prevents you from using the other expenses in (b) and (c) first to offset the rental income and then claiming the full amount of taxes and interest as an ordinary itemized deduction on Schedule A. However, if the allowable tax and interest expenses should exceed your rental income, the excess is deductible in the usual place on Schedule A. In any event, you still deduct on Schedule A that proportion of interest and taxes corresponding to the percentage of time the home is used for personal purposes.

Any rental losses on a residence rented out for part of a year which cannot be deducted as described above can be carried over to a future year. That is, these losses can be deducted against any rental income you receive on the residence in a future year.

Example Revisited

In the preceding example, net losses resulted both in 2001 and 2002. Because the home was not used for personal purposes in 2002, the full loss of $4,485 is reported on the 2002 tax return. According to the 12-month exception described above, the $1,753 loss is also deductible on the 2001 tax return, provided the home is used as a principal residence for the period preceding the rental.

However, let us now suppose that the home was rented out only for the 4-month period Sept. 1, 2001–Dec. 31, 2001, and used for personal purposes the remainder of 2001. In such a case, the restriction on deducting losses would apply. The rental would produce neither a net gain nor a net loss on the 2001 tax return. However, the $1,753 loss that cannot be deducted in 2001 can be carried over to a future year.

Note that because the $2,000 interest and $400 taxes attributable to the rental period total less than the $2,475 gross rental income ($2,500 rent minus $25 advertising cost), these amounts are used up in offsetting the rental income according to the (a), (b), (c) priority described above. Thus, these amounts cannot be deducted in the Interest *or* Taxes *Sections on Schedule A. However, the interest and taxes attributable to the period the house was used for personal purposes can be deducted as itemized deductions on Schedule A.*

Where Are Rental Income and Expenses Reported?

You report rental income and expenses for a home you own on Schedule E. Note that Schedule E expenses are not itemized deductions, but rather serve to lower adjusted gross income on Page 1 of your Form 1040. This means you can claim these expenses even if you use the standard deduction.

The above paragraph applies if you are renting with a *profit motive,* as discussed earlier in this Section. If you do not have a profit motive (for example, say, when you rent to a relative at below the market rate), rental income goes on line 21 of Form 1040, *Other Income,* and expenses are claimed as an itemized deduction on Schedule A, line 22.

Note: The above discussion is meant to give general guidance on the proper treatment of homes that are used both for personal and rental purposes. Especially if the passive loss rules come into play [see Section 2 of the *Investing Your Money* chapter], professional assistance should be sought to handle your write-offs in the proper way.

10

Automobile Expenses

Many types of auto travel can be deducted as described in the *Travel* chapter — convention trips, travel to and at a temporary job, travel between two jobs, travel to obtain education, etc. In addition, you can deduct for miscellaneous automobile travel connected with your employment such as travel from your office to libraries to do research, travel to pick up official visitors at an airport, etc.

There are two basic methods to deduct for business use of an automobile which you own. The first method is to deduct a *standard rate* per mile plus parking and tolls. The second method is to compute your *actual expenses*. As discussed below, the second method can prove superior because it includes a write-off for the cost of the automobile in addition to operating costs.

If business does not exceed 50% of the total use of the automobile, a special depreciation table applies as illustrated in Chapter 4, "*Expensing and Depreciation.*" Also, an employee must use the standard mileage unless his/her employer requires the use of the automobile.

Where on the Income Tax Form Do You Deduct Auto Expenses?

An employee uses Form 2106 or Form 2106-EZ, *Employee Business Expenses,* on which to list his automobile expenses. The total of automobile expenses is then entered as a *miscellaneous deduction* on Schedule A. As discussed in the *Miscellaneous Deductions* chapter, the sum total of travel expenses plus other miscellaneous deductions is subjected to a 2% of adjusted gross income floor.

Self-employed persons claim auto expenses on Schedule C or C-EZ, the same as any other business expense related to their self-employment activity. Thus, these expenses escape the 2% of adjusted gross income floor that applies to miscellaneous deductions; also, non-itemizers as well as itemizers get to deduct their auto expenses on Schedule C or Schedule C-EZ.

If, as discussed later, expensing or depreciation is claimed for an auto, Form 4562 must be filled out also [see the *Expensing and Depreciation* chapter]. If a person claims auto expenses in connection with a self-employment activity and is not required to use Form 4562, Part IV of Schedule C or Part III of Schedule C-EZ must be filled out.

Recordkeeping Rules

You are required to maintain adequate records to support your deduction for auto expenses.

AUTO MILEAGE & EXPENSE RECORD

| Date | Destination/Business Purpose | Odometer | | (Round Trip) Mileage | | | | Parking/ |
		Start	End	Job	Invest.	Med.	Char.	Tolls
1/1	Beginning Odometer Reading	7168						
1/5	Dr. Jones—appointment	7216	7237			21		
1/6	Drop off Goodwill donation	7237	7259				22	
1/10	Seminar at State Univ.	7342	7371	29				$3.00
1/12	Pick up Dr. Smith (Visiting Consultant) at Airport	7410	7462	52				
1/16	Church Choir Rehearsal	7531	7543				12	
1/18	Pick up Medicine at Drug Store	7571	7579			8		
1/20	Consult with Stockbroker	7612	7632		20			
12/31	Ending Odometer Reading		15,641					
	TOTALS			1,264	124	212	314	$146
	CENTS/MILE ALLOWED			34½	34½	12	14	
	TOTAL DEDUCTIONS			$436	$43	$25	$44	$146

In general, this means you must maintain a diary or similar written record which, for each job or business use of your auto, contains the following information:

1. Date;

2. Business purpose of trip; and

3. Business mileage traveled.

You should also keep track of the total mileage your auto was driven during the year by writing down the odometer readings at the beginning and end of each year.

If you are deducting your actual expenses rather than using the standard mileage rate, you must also record the date and amount of each expenditure for gasoline, repairs, etc. You can take the sum of such expenses and prorate this sum based on the percentage your auto was driven for business purposes. For example, if your auto was used 60% for business purposes and you spent $1,000 for gasoline during the year, you would be entitled to a deduction of 60% × $1,000 = $600 for gasoline (assuming you are deducting your actual expenses rather than using the standard mileage rate).

Your records should be maintained in a *timely* manner. This means you write down each entry soon enough that you have full recall of all the details. However, it is no longer required that your records be contemporaneous with business use. According to the IRS, it is acceptable to record your usage or expenses at the end of each week. However, even if your records are kept weekly, they should still give a daily breakdown of each separate period of business use.

It is not necessary to write down information in a diary (or other record) which duplicates information reflected on a receipt as long as your diary and receipts complement each other in an orderly manner. And you do not have to write down the business purpose of your travel if it is evident from the surrounding facts and circumstances.

On the previous page is a suggested recordkeeping format for an auto for which you use the standard mileage rate. You can use a different format as long as the requisite information is recorded.

Sampling Rule for Local Auto Travel

The type of detailed records normally expected for out-of-town travel do not have to be kept for local auto travel of a recurring nature. The regulations state that it is permissible to use a "sampling technique" for deducting such travel on your tax return. [IRS Reg. §1.274-5T] The following examples are adapted from the regulations.

Example 1

You work at 2 different business locations and often drive from one location to the other on the same day. You should record the date of each trip at or near the time of each trip. However, you need to record the distance between the 2 business locations only once, not each time you drive. You also should record the total number of miles your auto is driven overall. This will satisfy the recordkeeping requirement for this travel.

Example 2

You use your auto during the year for miscellaneous business travel, e.g. travel between job locations, to seminars, to libraries, etc. You keep adequate records for the first 3 months of the year which show that this business mileage is 15% of the total mileage put on your auto. You also record the beginning and final odometer readings for the year which show your auto was driven for 10,000 miles during the year. Assuming it is established that your business usage continues at approximately the same rate for the remainder of the year, your records support a deduction for 1,500 miles (15% × 10,000 miles) of business auto travel for the year.

Example 3

Same as Example 2, except that you keep adequate records during the first week of each month which show your auto is used 15% for business travel. As long as it is established that these are "representative" weeks, your records support a deduction for 15% of the total mileage for the year.

Observe that in both Examples 2 and 3, the sampling period constitutes about ¹/₄ of the year. The IRS specifically states that this can be an adequate sampling period. However, the IRS has not stated what the shortest acceptable sampling period would be. For example, if records were kept only during one or two months of the year, there is no current guidance as to whether or not this would constitute an acceptable sampling period.

Information Required on Tax Return

You do not include your mileage or expense records when you send in your tax return. Rather, you keep these records in case your tax return is audited. Employees must answer the following questions (stated in slightly different words) for all auto travel (local and out-of-town) on Part II of Form 2106 or Part III of Form 2106-EZ. Self-employed persons answer similar questions either on Part IV of Schedule C, Part III of Schedule C-EZ, or else on Part V of 4562 when expensing or depreciation is being claimed.

1. When was the vehicle first placed into service?

2. How many miles was the vehicle driven for business purposes?

3. Was the vehicle used for commuting? If so, what was the total commuting mileage for the year?

4. How many miles was the vehicle driven for non-commuting personal purposes?

5. Was another vehicle available for personal use?

6. Was your vehicle available for use during off-duty hours?

7. Do you have evidence to support your deduction? If so, is the evidence written?

Note that the purpose of asking the above questions on tax returns is twofold. First, the existence of these questions (in particular, question number 7) will discourage carelessly made estimates, rather than more careful recordkeeping. Second, if the IRS examines the answers to these questions, indication of an unjustified deduction may be spotlighted. For example, if the answer to question 3 indicates the auto was used a high percentage for non-deductible commuting, this may be inconsistent with the percentage of business use claimed. Or, if the answer to question 7 is "no," this will raise a red flag concerning the ability to justify the auto deduction claimed.

Note that a written re-creation of your business travel made at the end of the year might entitle you to answer "yes" to question 7 above, thereby avoiding spotlighting your return for audit. However, should your return actually be audited, such a re-creation would not actually satisfy the recordkeeping requirement discussed earlier in this chapter.

The Standard Mileage Rate

Under the standard rate method, you deduct 34$\frac{1}{2}$ cents per mile for each mile of business use in 2001. In addition, you may deduct parking fees and tolls.

The standard mileage rate is not meant to cover interest or taxes on the auto. These might be able to be deducted separately according to the rules discussed in the *Interest* and *Taxes* chapters. However, note that sales tax cannot be claimed as an itemized deduction. Instead, it is considered a part of the purchase price, perhaps boosting an expensing or depreciation calculation based on the cost of the auto.

Your employer may reimburse you at a mileage rate less than the allowable 34$\frac{1}{2}$ cents per mile. In this case, you are allowed to deduct the difference as an employee business expense on Form 2106 or Form 2106-EZ.

For example, suppose you use your automobile 1,000 miles for job-related purposes and that your employer reimburses you at the rate of 25 cents per mile. You can deduct the 1,000 miles of travel at the rate of 34$\frac{1}{2}$ cents – 25 cents = 9$\frac{1}{2}$ cents per mile. This produces a deduction of $\$.095 \times 1,000 = \$95$, which is claimed on Form 2106 or Form 2106-EZ.

There are some restrictions which the IRS has placed on the use of the standard mileage rate. First of all, if you use the standard rate, it must be used right from the beginning of business use. That is, you cannot use the standard rate on an automobile for which you have deducted your actual expenses in a prior year.

Secondly, once you use the standard rate on an automobile, you cannot use the usual depreciation method on that automobile in a later year. Instead, you must continue to use the standard rate, or else compute your actual expenses using an appropriate straight-line depreciation method.

Third, if you lease a vehicle and elect to use the standard mileage in lieu of actual expenses, you must use the standard mileage rate for the entire lease period.

Extras in Addition to the Standard Rate

According to the IRS, the standard rate is used *"in lieu of all operating and fixed costs of the automobile allocable to business purposes. Such items as depreciation, maintenance and repairs, tires, gasoline (including all taxes thereon), oil, insurance, and registration fees are included in operating and fixed costs. However, parking fees and tolls attributable to use for business purposes may be deducted as separate items."* [Rev. Proc. 2000-48]

According to a 1984 court case, the above quote is not interpreted as restricting the extras that may be deducted to the *parking fees and tolls* described in the third sentence above. Other items not covered by the first two sentences can be deducted also. In this case, an individual used his automobile 50% for business purposes for which he claimed the standard mileage rate. During the year, he incurred towing expenses of $173.25.

The Court ruled that these towing costs were not part of the operating and fixed costs covered by the standard mileage rate. It ruled,

> *". .under the standard rate method, petitioners are also entitled to deduct certain additional amounts actually incurred, such as parking and tolls. We believe that petitioners' towing costs which respondent has conceded were substantiated fall within this category."*

Because the individual's automobile was used 50% for business purposes, the Court allowed a deduction of 50% × $173.25 = $86.62 for towing costs. The allocation was not based on the nature of auto use when the towing costs were actually incurred. [Alcalen, TC Memo 1984-334]

No indication is given as to what items besides towing costs would be allowed in addition to the standard rate covering *"operating and fixed"* costs. Clearly, garage rental fees could be considered parking fees. However, other extras (e.g. auxiliary auto supplies) are neither clearly included nor excluded. What the above court case suggests, for the first time, is that an individual can use the standard rate and still be entitled to deduct extras besides parking and tolls which can also be considered neither *operating* nor *fixed* costs.

Computing Your Actual Auto Expenses

Instead of the standard mileage rate, you can deduct your actual automobile expenses. This includes gas, oil, repairs, insurance, etc. — plus parking and tolls. It also includes a portion of the cost of the automobile. It is here that a substantial deduction can be claimed.

To write off the cost of the automobile, you use the appropriate expensing or depreciation procedure as described in the *Expensing and Depreciation* chapter. However, there are special maximum limitations, described below, that apply only to automobiles.

Also, as described in Section 1 of that chapter, expensing or depreciation can be claimed by an employee for job-related use of an auto purchased only if such use is required by his employer. Otherwise, the standard mileage rate must be used.

Interest on an auto owned by an employee is considered nondeductible personal interest even if the auto is used for job-related purposes.

According to a court case, there are circumstances where a deduction for automobile expenses will be allowed, even if a reimbursement is received from your employer. This is discussed in Example 6 of the *Miscellaneous* chapter.

Expensing and Depreciation Rules for Autos

There are special **maximum limitations** on the total of expensing plus depreciation deductions that can be claimed for a given automobile in any one year. The following table gives the maximum limits on annual deductions that can be claimed for an automobile placed into service in 1991–2001. (For autos placed into service before

1991, different limitations apply. [see previous editions of this *Tax & Financial Guide*] These limits were designed to affect only "luxury" automobiles costing more than $15,300 in 2001. However, because of the expensing option, the initial first year limit can affect the deduction for any automobile purchased in 2001 costing more than $3,060.

Maximum Annual Deductions for Autos Placed into Service in 1991

Year	Maximum Deduction
1991	$2,660
1992	4,300
1993	2,550
each succeeding year	1,575

Maximum Annual Deductions for Autos Placed into Service in 1992

Year	Maximum Deduction
1992	$2,760
1993	4,400
1994	2,650
each succeeding year	1,575

Maximum Annual Deductions for Autos Placed into Service in 1993

Year	Maximum Deduction
1993	$2,860
1994	4,600
1995	2,750
each succeeding year	1,675

Maximum Annual Deductions for Autos Placed into Service in 1994

Year	Maximum Deduction
1994	$2,960
1995	4,700
1996	2,850
each succeeding year	1,675

Maximum Annual Deductions for Autos Placed into Service in 1995 or 1996

Year	Maximum Deduction
1	$3,060
2	4,900
3	2,950
each succeeding year	1,775

Maximum Annual Deductions for Autos Placed into Service in 1997

Year	Maximum Deduction
1	$3,160
2	5,000
3	3,050
each succeeding year	1,775

Maximum Annual Deductions for Autos Placed into Service in 1998

Year	Maximum Deduction
1	$3,160
2	5,000
3	2,950
each succeeding year	1,775

Maximum Annual Deductions for Autos Placed into Service in 1999

Year	Maximum Deduction
1	$3,060
2	5,000
3	2,950
each succeeding year	1,775

Maximum Annual Deductions for Autos Placed into Service in 2000 & 2001

Year	Maximum Deduction
1	$3,060
2	4,900
3	2,950
each succeeding year	1,775

The above limitations apply to an auto used 100% for business purposes. They are reduced proportionately for autos used partly for personal purposes. For example, the upper limit on an auto used 60% for business purposes would be 60% of the above amounts.

If the maximum limitations come into play, the full value of the automobile can still be written off — the write-off period is just extended. Examples 3 and 4 illustrate this situation.

When the expensing method is used, the remainder not expensed is depreciated according to the usual 5-year table [see the *Expensing and Depreciation* chapter]. However, the total expensing plus depreciation deductions for a given year are subject to the maximum limitations described above. This can lead to an unexpected pitfall. [Temp. Reg. §1.280F-2T]

To illustrate, suppose that an automobile was purchased for $10,560 in 2001 and the maximum expensing deduction of $3,060 is claimed in the first year. The remainder, $10,560 − $3,060 = $7,500, would then be depreciated according to the 20%, 32%, 19.2%, 11.52%, 11.52%, 5.76% percentages provided by the 5-year depreciation table. Because the maximum $3,060 write-off has been used up by the expensing deduction, no depreciation deduction is allowed for the first year. The depreciation deductions for the remaining years are as provided in the following table. Observe that an extra 7th year is now required to achieve the full $10,560 write-off for the cost of the auto.

Year	Deduction		
2001		$3,060	expensing
2002	32% × $7,500 =	2,400	depreciation
2003	19.2% × $7,500 =	1,440	depreciation
2004	11.52% × $7,500 =	864	depreciation
2005	11.52% × $7,500 =	864	depreciation
2006	5.76% × $7,500 =	432	depreciation
2007	Remainder =	1,500	depreciation
		$10,560	

It is possible to avoid the above pitfall of spilling over the auto write-off into a 7th year. The key is to claim an expensing deduction of less than $3,060, with the remaining depreciation deductions filling out the normal depreciation period for 5-year items. This can generally be done for automobiles costing less than $15,300 by using the following formula to compute the optimal Expensing amount E:

$$E = \frac{\$15,300 - \text{Cost of Auto}}{4}$$

For autos costing $15,300 or more, the depreciation method alone should be used, with no expensing deduction.

Example 1. Auto Costing Less Than $15,300

An auto is purchased in 2001 for $11,000 and is used entirely for business purposes. According to the formula above, the following amount E should be expensed:

$$E = \frac{\$15,300 - \$11,000}{4} = \$1,075$$

The remainder, $11,000 − $1,075 = $9,925, is depreciated via the usual 5-year depreciation table.

Year	Expensing	Depreciation		Deduction
2001	$1,075 +	20% × $9,925	=	$3,060
2002		32% × $9,925	=	3,176
2003		19.2% × $9,925	=	1,906
2004		11.52% × $9,925	=	1,143
2005		11.52% × $9,925	=	1,143
2006		5.76% × $9,925	=	572
				$11,000

Example 2

Same as Example 1, except that the auto is used 60% for business purposes. In this case, the amount to be written off is 60% of the cost, namely 60% × $11,000 = $6,600. In the formula for E, the $15,300 is similarly multiplied by 60%: 60% × $15,300 = $9,180. Thus, the expensing deduction E in this situation is:

$$E = \frac{\$9,180 - \$6,600}{4} = \$645$$

The remainder, $6,600 − $645 = $5,955, is depreciated via the usual depreciation table for 5-year property.

Year	Expensing	Depreciation		Deduction
2001	$645 +	20% × $5,955	=	$1,836
2002		32% × $5,955	=	1,906
2003		19.2% × $5,955	=	1,143
2004		11.52% × $5,955	=	686
2005		11.52% × $5,955	=	686
2006		5.76% × $5,955	=	343
				$6,600

Note that the deduction for 2001 is equal to the maximum limitation that applies, namely 60% × $3,060 = $1,836.

Example 3. Auto Costing $15,300 or More

An auto is purchased in 2001 for $19,000 and is used 100% for business purposes. Because the auto costs more than $15,300, the deduction produced by the 5-year depreciation table would exceed the maximum limitations ($3,060 is less than 20% × $19,000 = $3,800; $4,900 is less than 32% × $19,000 = $6,080, etc.). Thus, the depreciation deductions for each year are equal to the maximum limitations until the final year, when the amount used is chosen to fully depreciate the $19,000 cost:

Year	Deduction
2001	$3,060
2002	4,900
2003	2,950
2004	1,775
2005	1,775
2006	1,775
2007	1,775
2008	990
	$19,000

In the above example, it is presumed that the automobile continues to be owned through the end of 2008. Under any depreciation method, for items in the 5-year or 7-year category placed into service in 2001, half a year's depreciation is allowed in the year of disposition. Thus, in the above example, if the automobile were disposed of in 2005, the depreciation deduction for 2005 would be $1/2 \times \$1,775 = \$888$. The automobile would produce no further deductions after 2005, the year of disposition.

Also, in the above example, it was assumed the automobile is used 100% for business purposes. The following example illustrates a situation where business usage is less than 100%.

Example 4

Same as the previous example, except that instead of 100%, the business use percentage is 60% for 2001–2004., and 55% for 2005–2008. In this case, the amounts in the previous example are multiplied by these percentages to arrive at the depreciation deductions for each year.

Year	Depreciation Deduction
2001	60% × $3,060 = $1,836
2002	60% × $4,900 = 2,940
2003	60% × $2,950 = 1,770
2004	60% × $1,775 = 1,065
2005	55% × $1,775 = 976
2006	55% × $1,775 = 976
2007	55% × $1,775 = 976
2008	55% × $ 990 = 495

Comparing the Actual Expenses Method with the Standard Mileage Rate

The following examples illustrate the use of the actual expenses method and compare the results with the standard mileage rate.

Example 5

You purchased an automobile in February 2001 for $11,000. You drive the automobile 10,000 miles per year for each of the years 2001–2006. Of these 10,000 miles, 6,000 (60% of the total) are for business purposes.

Actual Cost Method

Your operating expenses per year are as follows:

Repairs and parts	*$650*
Insurance	*250*
Car washing	*50*
Gas and oil	*700*
License (including driver's license)	*75*
Motor club membership	*40*
Garage rent	*150*
Total	*$1,915*

Because your auto is being used 60% for business purposes, the amount of operating expenses attributable to business use is 60% × $1,915 = $1,149.

The expensing and depreciation deductions for this situation have already been calculated in Example 2. Thus, the total deductions for each year are as follows:

Year	Expensing/ Depreciation		Operating Expenses		Total Deduction
2001	$1,836	+	$1,149	=	$2,985
2002	1,906	+	1,149	=	3,055
2003	1,143	+	1,149	=	2,292
2004	686	+	1,149	=	1,835
2005	677	+	1,149	=	1,835
2006	343	+	1,149	=	1,492
					$13,494

(In addition to the above amounts, parking fees and tolls incurred in business-related travel are deductible.)

On a per business mile basis, the figures above become:

2001:	$ 2,985/6,000 business miles =	50 cents per mile
2002:	$ 3,055/6,000 business miles =	51 cents per mile
2003:	$ 2,292/6,000 business miles =	38 cents per mile
2004:	$ 1,835/6,000 business miles =	31 cents per mile
2005:	$ 1,835/6,000 business miles =	31 cents per mile
2006:	$ 1,492/6,000 business miles =	25 cents per mile
Overall:	$13,494/36,000 business miles =	37 cents per mile

(The above figures were based on a purchase price of $11,000 and will change according to any change in purchase price. For example, for an auto costing $15,300 or more, the overall cents per mile figure in this example for the period 2001–2006 would be 45 cents instead of 37 cents.)

Standard Mileage Rate

The standard mileage rate is 34$^{1}/_{2}$ cents per mile. This is less than the amount computed under the actual cost method. However, when an employee uses an auto purchased for job-related travel, such use must be required by his employer in order for the actual cost method to be used [see the Expensing and Depreciation chapter]. Otherwise, the standard mileage rate must be used.

Comment. Observe that under the expensing/depreciation option, the higher the percentage of business use, the higher will be the deduction. Thus, it pays you to limit your personal use of an auto which is used for business purposes in order to increase the percentage of business use. For example, if you own two automobiles, use one of them (as much as possible) for business purposes and the other (as much as possible) for your personal activities.

As described in Section 1 of the *Expensing and Depreciation* chapter, special rules apply to automobiles which are not used more than 50% for business purposes in each of the first 6 years of ownership. For such automobiles, the special *Listed Property Depreciation Table* must be used [see Section 3 of the *Expensing and Depreciation* chapter].

Example 6

You purchased an automobile in March 2001 for $12,000. You drive the automobile 10,000 miles during each year of 2001–2006. Of these miles, 30% are for business purposes each year. Because the automobile is used 30% for business purposes, the cost attributable to business use is 30% × $12,000 = $3,600.

Your operating expenses (not including expensing or depreciation) total $1,200 per year. Because your auto is being used 30% for business purposes, the amount of operating expenses attributable to business use each year is 30% × $1,200 = $360.

Actual Cost Method

Because business use does not exceed 50% in each of the first 6 years, the expensing method cannot be used. And depreciation is limited to the amounts in the Listed Property Depreciation Table in the "Expensing & Depreciation" chapter. Thus, the annual deductions for 2001–2006 are as follows:

	Depreciation		**Operating Expenses**		**Total Deduction**
2001:	10% × $3,600	+	$360	=	$ 720
2002:	20% × 3,600	+	360	=	1,080
2003:	20% × 3,600	+	360	=	1,080
2004:	20% × 3,600	+	360	=	1,080
2005:	20% × 3,600	+	360	=	1,080
2006:	10% × 3,600	+	360	=	720
					$5,760

(In addition to the above amounts, parking fees and tolls incurred in business-related travel are deductible.)

To see how this works out on a per mile basis, the calculation is as follows:

Total mileage, 2001–2006:	60,000 miles
Business miles:	30% × 60,000 = 18,000 miles
Total expenses, 2001–2006:	$5,760
Per mile deduction:	$5,760/18,000 = 32 cents per mile

Standard Mileage Rate

As in the preceding example, the standard mileage rate of 34$\frac{1}{2}$ cents per mile can be used instead of the actual cost method. (The standard rate is mandatory if the use of the auto is not required by the employer.)

Taxes and Registration Fees

The annual fee you pay to register your automobile and receive your new license plate or sticker is deductible to the extent the automobile is used for business purposes.

For an automobile used for personal purposes, this annual fee is generally not deductible. However, in some states, part of the fee is based on the value of the automobile and constitutes a form of personal property tax. In such a case, the part of the fee that qualifies as a personal property tax is deductible under *Taxes* on Schedule A.

Interest

If you borrow money to purchase a personal automobile, interest on the loan is considered nondeductible personal interest [see the *Interest* chapter]. The same situation applies to an *employee* who uses his automobile for deductible job-related travel, whether he deducts his actual auto expenses or uses the standard mileage rate. That is, all interest paid on the automobile is still considered nondeductible personal interest. (An exception would occur if the auto was financed by a home-equity loan, in which case the interest could be fully deducted as discussed in Section 1 of the *Homeowners* chapter.)

The opposite is true if the auto is used in connection with a self-employment activity. In this case, any interest attributable to such use is fully deductible on Schedule C or Schedule C-EZ as interest paid in connection with a trade or business. This interest is deductible in addition to the regular automobile deduction computed under either the actual expenses or standard mileage rate method.

For example, suppose you use an auto 30% for self-employment activities and that you paid $1,000 interest on an auto loan during the year. You would claim $300 as a *business interest* deduction on Schedule C or Schedule C-EZ. The remaining $700 would be nondeductible.

Allocating Repair Expenses

A 1980 court case shows how to allocate repair expenses when an auto is used both for personal and for deductible purposes. You do not have to establish which repairs are directly attributable to your deductible travel. Instead, just multiply the total of your repair bills for the year by the fraction: deductible mileage/total mileage for the year. [Goodman, TC Memo 1980-122]

Leasing an Automobile

If you lease an automobile, payments under the lease are deductible to the extent the automobile is used for business purposes. For example, if a leased automobile is used 30% of the time for business or deductible job-related purposes, 30% of the lease payments are deductible.

If the lease period extends 30 days or longer and the automobile is worth more than about $15,500, a special rule applies. In this case, the IRS requires an adjustment to be made which adds back to taxable income an amount representing the "excess luxury value" of the automobile. This amount is included as part of gross income on Schedule C or Schedule C-EZ (for the self-employed) or listed on line 24b of Form 2106 (for employees). The amount to be included depends upon the fair market value of the automobile and can be looked up in a table at the back of Publication 463, available from the IRS.

Trading In Your Old Automobile

Suppose that you trade in your old automobile when you purchase a new one. If you did not claim a deduction for your old automobile, your old automobile does not enter into the computation of depreciation for your new automobile. Thus, you use the full price of your new automobile (without subtracting the trade-in value of your old automobile) in calculating your depreciation the same way as if you had no trade-in.

If you trade in an automobile that was used for business on another automobile that will be used for business, the IRS in Notice 2000-4 has taken a more liberal approach in computing depreciation. The Notice treats the taxpayer as if he owns two automobiles for depreciation purposes:

(1) The old automobile which is continued to be written off as if the trade-in never took place; and

(2) The new automobile with a cost equal to the purchase price of the new automobile less the adjusted basis in the old automobile.

Example 7

You bought a $20,000 auto in 1997 and trade it in for a new $20,000 auto on Jan. 1, 2001. The old auto has a trade-in value of $6,250, so you pay $13,750 cash for the new auto. You claimed a total of $12,985 in depreciation for 1997 through 2001, leaving an adjusted basis of $7,015 ($20,000 less $12,985). Your basis in the *new auto is $20,765 (adjusted basis in old plus $13,750 cash). Under the notice, you are treated for depreciation purposes as if you (1) still own the old $20,000 auto, and can write off the remaining depreciable basis over 2001 through 2003; and (2) bought a new auto in 2001 for $13,750 ($20,765 basis in the new auto less $7,015 remaining basis in the old auto), which is depreciable over 2001 through 2006. Depreciation deductions are:*

$4,525 for 2001 (5th year depreciation of $1,775, plus 1st year depreciation of .20 × $13,750).

$6,175 for 2002 (6th year depreciation of $1,775, plus 2nd year depreciation of .32 × $13,750).

$4,415 for 2003 (7th year depreciation of $1,775, plus 3rd year depreciation of .192 × $13,750).

Trading in your old automobile on a new automobile can prove better than selling your old automobile and purchasing a new one in two separate transactions. In a majority of states, when you trade in your old automobile on a new one, you pay sales tax on the purchase price minus the value of a trade-in. On the other hand, if you purchase a new automobile after selling your old one, you'll pay sales tax on the full purchase price of the new automobile.

For example, suppose you have an old automobile worth $2,000 which you trade in on a new $10,000 automobile. In this case, you would pay sales tax based on the net price, $10,000 – $2,000 = $8,000. However, if you sell your old automobile and purchase a new automobile in separate transactions, you will pay sales tax based on the full $10,000 purchase price.

Auto Used for Job-Hunting

You are allowed to deduct the expenses of an automobile which you use to look for a new job, as long as you look for work in the same field as your previous job [see Section 2 of the *Miscellaneous Deductions* chapter]. There is no restriction on the type of automobile or length of time of the job search. For example, in a court case, a $3,861 deduction was allowed for depreciation of a Cadillac used 70% of the time during the year for job-hunting activities. [Campana,TC Memo 1990-395]

11

Income Shifting

Basic Principle

The basic principle behind income shifting is simple. You are in a certain tax bracket and your child is in a lower (usually zero) tax bracket. If you can shift some of your income from yourself to your child, then you will have reduced or eliminated altogether the income tax due on such amounts.

Actually the beneficiary need not be your child, but could be a parent, relative, or other person to whom you desire to transfer property or money. However, you generally cannot use the methods described here to shift money to your spouse.

It should be pointed out that income shifting can have the negative effect of reducing the amount of financial aid your child will receive when he attends college. If this is a relevant consideration, see Section 1 of the *Expenses of Attending School* chapter.

What Kind of Income Can Be Shifted?

You cannot transfer income you earn as a salary to someone else and relieve yourself of tax. You are always liable for the tax on your own earned income. But unearned income produced by investments such as stocks, bonds, savings accounts, and royalties can be shifted. However, you can't just assign the income on such investments to someone else. In order to shift the tax burden, you must also transfer the property (real estate, stocks, bonds, royalty contract, money, etc.) which produces such income.

If you wish to transfer income-producing property to someone else, you can make an outright gift of that property. However, if the recipient of your gift is a minor child, an outright gift can cause difficulty. Because your child lacks legal responsibility, it may be impossible to control the property. For example, a broker may be unwilling to sell a security and buy another, because he is concerned about the lack of legal obligation of the minor to pay.

Gifts to Minors

Gifts to minors are generally made under the Uniform Gifts to Minors Act. This Act provides a simple way to transfer securities (or life insurance policies or money) to a minor and still retain the power to buy, sell, and reinvest these items on behalf of the minor. You buy the securities in your child's name with yourself or your spouse declared as custodian. (Your broker or banker will know how to handle such a transaction.) You then have the power to reinvest (into other securities, savings accounts, etc.) as you choose, providing you do so for the benefit of the child. When the child reaches majority age, he or she then assumes complete ownership and control over the investment and your custodianship ends.

Recently, many states have switched over from the *Uniform Gifts to Minors Act (UGMA)* to the *Uniform Transfers to Minors Act (UTMA)*. The UGMA and UTMA are basically the same, except for 2 provisions. In most states, under the UGMA, the assets automatically come under control of the child when he reaches 18, the age of majority. Under the UTMA, distribution of the assets to the child can be delayed to a later age, generally 21. Also, the UTMA permits the custodianship to own a wider array of properties such as real estate, partnerships, royalties, etc.

Under either the UGMA or UTMA, the income earned on the investments is taxed to the child. (Make sure you obtain a separate social security number for your child so the income won't be taxed to you.) But there is one important exception. If the income is used to discharge your legal obligation to support the child, then you must pay the tax on the amounts so used. See the subsection later in this chapter on what constitutes support.

Tax on Children's Income

Special rules apply to children under the age of 14. Under these rules, discussed in Section 5 of Chapter 1, unearned income in excess of $1,500 is taxed at the parent's tax rate rather than at the child's. These rules were designed by Congress to prevent large scale income-shifting to young children. As a result, there is no current tax savings to transferring property to a child under age 14 if this child produces income in excess of $1,500 per year.

Another feature of the current law is that a child cannot claim a personal exemption if he is eligible to be claimed as a dependent on a parent's tax return. This means that only the first $750 of unearned income is now exempt from tax. Amounts between $750 and $1,500 are taxed at the child's rate (10% for 2001). The remainder of unearned income may be subject to tax at the parent's rate, depending upon whether or not the child is under age 14.

Although large scale income-shifting to young children has been eliminated, this does not mean income-shifting is dead. For one thing, the first $1,500 of unearned income each year is taxed to the child. Under the 2001 tax tables, the tax on this amount would be only $75, no doubt less than if taxed at the parent's top tax bracket.

Second, the income of a child age 14 or older is still taxed at the child's rate. Only children under age 14 are affected by the rule taxing unearned income at the parent's rate. Thus, income-shifting to an older child or other relative remains intact. Furthermore, by choosing appropriate investments, advantage can be taken of the potential for income-shifting to an older child, even if the child is currently under age 14. This is done by choosing investments which pay off in a future year when the child will be at least age 14.

One example of such an investment would be U.S. Series EE savings bonds. The interest on these bonds need not be reported until the year in which the bonds are redeemed, which can be arranged to occur after the child has reached age 14 [see Section 3 of the *Investing Your Money* chapter].

A second example would be stocks chosen for growth rather than for dividends. If the stocks are sold after the child has reached age 14, the entire capital gain will be taxed at the child's tax bracket. (However a stock mutual fund might not serve the same purpose because it would declare periodic capital gains distributions.) For example, if the child's taxable income does not exceed $27,050 in 2001, the long-term capital gain will be taxed at 10% rather than 15%.

Further examples of investments which delay income to future years might be real estate, deeply discounted bonds, insurance policies, and gold or other precious metals.

Trusts

Another way to shift income is to set up a *trust* for the benefit of your child. You then transfer money or other assets into the trust. The trust can then accumulate the income produced by these assets.

There is a tax advantage to income earned by the trust which is not distributed to the beneficiary. Namely, the first $1,800 is taxed at the lowest 15% rate. However, the rate structure rises sharply to equal 39.1% on income exceeding $8,900 in 2001.

The trust can be set up to distribute money to a child at some later time, e.g. when the child goes to college. Or, arrangements can be made to delay distributions of remaining funds until the child reaches age 21 or some later age. These distributions are taxed at the child's rate as long as the child is at least age 14 and the distributions are not used to discharge your legal obligation to support the child.

In addition to allowing income-shifting on earnings up to $1,800 (the 15% tax bracket for 2001), setting up a trust has another advantage over making an ordinary gift. Namely, a trust allows you to maintain control over the funds until your child reaches an age you regard as being sufficiently mature. In contrast, under the Uniform Gifts to Minors Act, the child gets automatic control over all the funds when he reaches the relevant age of majority, typically age 18.

For example, suppose an individual wishes to set aside $20,000 towards a child's college education. He is reluctant to make a gift under the Uniform Gifts to Minors Act because the money would come under the complete control of the child when he reaches age 18. He is not sure he can adequately predict how his child will use such a large sum of money received at a relatively young age.

Instead, the individual could set up a trust with his spouse as trustee. The money in the trust can be spent for the child's benefit, but only at the direction of his spouse, the trustee. Eventually, when the child reaches a sufficiently mature age any remaining funds in the trust can be turned over to him.

Another trust arrangement that is available is a Section 529 trust. Assets are gifted to the trust, the growth is not taxed currently, and if the assets are used to pay for higher education expenses, no tax will be paid on the growth.

What Constitutes Support?

As stated above, tax shifting isn't allowed on amounts used to discharge your legal obligation to provide support. But the definition of what is included in this legal obligation depends upon the state where you live. In most states, only the necessities such as food, shelter, and clothing are considered support so that income-shifting can be used for the cost of private school, music lessons, summer camp, etc. In other states, support includes all that is commensurate with the parents' wealth and social position, possibly including a college education. However, in most states, a child reaches majority at age 18, after which there may be no support obligation.

Hiring a Child or Spouse

One of the best ways to shift income to a child (or spouse) is to hire him in connection with an outside business activity. A dependent child can earn up to the amount of the standard deduction ($4,550 in 2001) before any tax is due. Earned income above this amount is taxed at the child's tax bracket [see Chapter 1]. The child could use such funds to save for college, fund an IRA or a Roth IRA or for any other use he/she chooses. Typically, a spouse is hired to provide income to fund a retirement account or an IRA.

Examples of work he might do include operating a computer, clerical work, cleaning a home office, etc. This type of arrangement is discussed more fully in Section 3 of the *Outside Business Activity* chapter.

Stock Investment Plans

A number of companies offer special *dividend reinvestment plans* under which dividends are automatically invested to purchase additional shares of stock. These plans are particularly useful for investing funds held in your child's name because the dividends are automatically reinvested without any action required on your part. Furthermore, under some of these plans, the reinvested dividends purchase additional shares at a 3% or 5% discount. Your stockbroker won't tell you about these plans because the purchases are made directly through the companies with no commission costs whatever. Many plans even permit further purchase of stock to be made without commission charges. Ordinarily the charge for purchasing a small number of shares of stock would be quite high.

Most of the dividend reinvestment plans have the following features. First of all, in order to participate, an individual must already be a stockholder in the company. However, you do not have to own any specific amount of stock. Ownership of just one share entitles you to full participation in the plan.

There are two features to the plan. The first feature is that you can choose to have all or a portion of your dividends on company stock automatically reinvested to purchase further shares of the company. These shares are purchased with little or no commissions or service charges. Also, there may be a discount of up to 5% of market price. Full reinvestment of dividends is made possible because the plan permits fractions of shares to be issued.

The other feature of the plan is that at any time, additional funds can be mailed in to purchase further shares of the company at the full market price. Once again, no commissions are charged and the issuance of fractional shares allows the full amount to be invested. However, there is an upper limit, typically $3,000–$5,000, that can be invested in any one quarter (3-month period).

Recordkeeping is all done by the company. Unless you request otherwise, no certificates will be issued. Instead, purchases will be credited to your account with statements mailed to you periodically. At any time, you can request to have certificates issued to you in the amount of your account.

You can get a list of companies that offer dividend reinvestment plans by calling Standard & Poors at 1-800-977-1450. In addition, the *Value Line* advisory service, found in many libraries, can be used to check whether a given company offers a stock purchase plan. You can also find a significant amount of information about dividend reinvestment plans by visiting www.dripcentral.com on the World Wide Web. If a company does have such a plan, this fact will be noted at the bottom of the page description of that company. If a discount on reinvested dividends is offered, this will be indicated in the note. You can then write to the company itself for full details of the plan.

Dividend reinvestment plans should be considered especially when accounts are maintained for children or other dependents. The automatic reinvestment feature, the simplified recordkeeping, the ability to invest small amounts, and the discount of up to 5% all combine to make these plans very attractive.

Rules for Interest-Free Loans

At one time, interest-free loans could be used as a means of income-shifting between family members. For example, a child could have received an interest-free loan from a parent and then earned interest on the money. The interest would have been taxed at the child's lower tax bracket rather than at the parent's higher bracket.

But Congress has severely restricted this technique. Now, if an individual makes an interest-free loan of more than $10,000 to another person who invests it at a lower tax bracket, the IRS will "impute" interest income to the lender at the going interest rate. For example, suppose a parent makes an interest-free loan of $12,000, payable on demand, to a child who invests the money in his own name in a certificate of deposit. If the short-term U.S. Treasury interest rate is 4%, then the IRS will impute interest to the parent of 4% × $12,000 = $480. This amount will have to be included in the taxable income of the parent and may be deductible by the child. Effectively, this eliminates the tax-shifting of the interest-free loan.

For loans made at a below-market interest rate, a similar provision applies. In this case, the difference between the going Treasury rate and the interest actually charged will be imputed to the lender.

The above rules apply to interest-free gift loans made in order to shift income to a lower tax bracket. For other interest-free gift loans, where the avoidance of tax is not *"one of the principal purposes,"* the rules are different. In such a case, you can make up to $10,000 of loans to an individual who has less than $1,000 of investment income such as interest and dividends without the imputed interest rules coming into play. (For example, parents could loan money interest-free to a child to buy a home, attend school, etc.) In this situation, if the recipient earns some income on the money, interest can still be imputed to the lender if the purpose of the loan is tax avoidance. The amount imputed is either the going Treasury rate or the actual amount of income earned, whichever is lower.

12

State and Local Taxes

You **can deduct** the following taxes imposed by a state or local government:

- Property tax [see the *Homeowners* chapter]
- Income tax
- Personal property tax

You **cannot** deduct:

- Sales tax
- Beverage tax
- Cigarette tax
- Admission tax
- Gasoline tax
- Driver's license fee
- Dog license
- Fishing or hunting license

Also, you cannot deduct a passport fee unless it qualifies as a legitimate business expense. (For example, a passport fee for a business-related trip would be deductible, but not for a pleasure trip.) Automobile registration fees are deductible only to the extent the auto is used for business purposes or the fees are based on the value of the automobile and, therefore, qualify as a personal property tax [see the *Automobile Expenses* chapter].

Generally, the deduction for state and local taxes is only available to the taxpayer who incurs the taxes. For example, a child may have a state tax liability on income he receives. Even if the parents pay the tax, they get no deduction on their federal tax return. Such a payment is considered to be a gift to the child followed by payment of the tax by the child. Thus the child, not the parents, gets the deduction for state taxes paid.

In most cases, the child will not be able to use the deduction for state and local taxes paid. A dependent child is entitled to a 2001 standard deduction of at least $750, even if he has only unearned income. Thus, unless a child has at least $750 in deductions, including the deduction for state and local taxes, he will use the standard deduction instead of itemizing. This means the deduction for state and local taxes will not be usable [see Section 5 of Chapter 1].

Payroll Taxes

In some places, contributions to unemployment or disability funds are deducted from employees' paychecks. The IRS will allow contributions to state disability funds in New York, California, New Jersey, and Rhode Island to be deducted as a tax on Schedule A. (Contributions to private disability funds remain nondeductible.) Also, the IRS has ruled that amounts withheld from wages for contribution to the West Virginia unemployment fund are deductible taxes [Rev Rul 89-16].

Transfer Taxes

When you buy stocks, bonds, real estate, etc., you may have to pay transfer taxes. These tax payments are not deductible. Instead, they are considered to be part of the purchase price. As such, they reduce any capital gains (or increase losses) in the year of sale and increase annual depreciation write-offs in the case of investment real estate [see the *Expensing and Depreciation* chapter].

Sales Tax

Prior to 1987, you were permitted to claim a deduction for state and local sales tax you paid during the year. Generally, this deduction was obtained from an IRS-provided table, based on your income and the state where you lived. But this deduction was eliminated.

However, sales tax is still deductible on items for which you are claiming a deduction, such as a trade or business expense. For example, if you are deducting for supplies purchased in connection with your job, you would deduct the full amount you paid for the supplies, including any sales tax charged. Similarly, if you purchase an item such as an automobile or typewriter which you are deducting as described in the *Expensing and Depreciation* chapter, then you use the full cost of the item, including any sales tax charged, as the basis for your expensing or depreciation deduction.

State and Local Income Taxes

Schedule A includes a deduction for state and local income taxes which you pay. These taxes are deductible in the year in which they are paid by being withheld from your paychecks or by direct payment. For example, amounts withheld from your paychecks during 2000 and credited toward your state income tax due April 2001 were deductible on your 2000 federal tax return. If you made an additional direct payment toward these taxes in 2001, then this payment becomes deductible on your 2001 tax return.

On the other hand, you may have received a state or local tax refund during 2001 because of overwithholding during 2000. In this case, the full amount withheld during 2000 should have been deducted on your 2000 tax return and you report the refund as income on line 10 of your 2001 tax return. (The refund is still reported as income even if you have it credited against your current tax rather than having a refund check mailed to you.) This is illustrated in Example 1 below.

For example, suppose you claimed the standard deduction on your 2000 tax return. This means that you did not get any federal tax benefit from the **deduction** for state taxes withheld from your paychecks. In such a case, you would not have to report a 2001 tax refund as income. This is illustrated in Example 2 below.

Example 1

In 2000, $2,000 in state income tax was withheld from your paychecks which you deducted on your 2000 federal tax return along with $6,000 in other deductions. When you filled out your 2000 state tax return, you computed $1,500 as the amount of state income tax for the year. Because $500 too much was withheld during 2000, the state sent you a refund check for that amount in 2001. Because you deducted the $2,000 withheld on your 2000 federal tax return but received $500 of this amount back, you're really entitled only to a net $1,500 deduction. To compensate for the extra benefit you obtained by deducting $2,000 instead of the $1,500, you report the $500 refund as income on your 2001 federal tax return.

In the above example, the $500 state tax refund received in 2001 was due to over-withholding in 2000. Because the overwithholding produced an extra tax benefit on your 2000 tax return — a $2,000 deduction instead of a $1,500 deduction — the $500 refund had to be included as income on your 2001 return to offset the extra benefit.

However, you do **not** have to report a 2001 tax refund as income to the extent it was due to overwithholding during 2000 from which you derived no federal tax benefit. For example, suppose you claimed the standard deduction on your 2000 tax return. This means that you did not get any federal tax benefit from the **deduction** for state taxes withheld from your paychecks. In such a case, you would not have to report a 2001 tax refund as income. This is illustrated in Example 2 below.

Example 2

In 2000, $1,000 in state tax was withheld from Smith's paychecks. His other deductions amounted to $800. Because $1,000 + $800 = $1,800 was less than the standard deduction, Smith did not itemize his deductions on his federal tax return but used the standard deduction instead. Smith received no federal tax benefit from the $1,000 withheld in state taxes because he didn't itemize his deductions.

Now suppose Smith received a state tax refund in 2001. This refund resulted from the fact that the $1,000 withheld in 2000 was too much. But because he claimed the standard deduction, this overwithholding produced no federal tax benefit on his 2000 return. Therefore, he does not have to include the refund as income on his 2001 federal tax return.

In the above example, Smith received no federal tax benefit from the state tax overwithheld from his paychecks because he used the standard deduction. Therefore, the state tax refund which resulted from this overwithholding did not have to be reported as income in the following year.

However, sometimes an individual receives a **partial** benefit from state tax overwithholding. This can occur only when an individual's other deductions are less than the standard deduction, but when the state tax is added in, the total exceeds the standard deduction. In this situation, you report as income on line 10 of your 2001 tax return that portion of the overwithholding during 2000 (which you received in 2001 as a refund of state tax) from which you derived a tax benefit.

In practice, you compute this amount by filling out the worksheet in the instructions to Form 1040. However, Example 3 illustrates the basis behind this computation.

Example 3

C and D filed joint federal income tax returns for 2000 and 2001. For 2000, their state income tax deduction (equal to the amounts withheld from their 2000 paychecks) was $1,000 and their other itemized deductions were $6,500. On their 2000 state tax return, they computed their state tax to be $600. This meant that $400 of state tax had been overwithheld during 2000, resulting in a $400 state tax refund received in 2001. However, only a portion of this $400 overwithholding had actually produced a tax benefit on their 2000 federal tax return. This portion is computed as follows:

(1) Total deductions actually claimed on 2000 federal tax return:
$6,500 + $1,000 = **$7,500**

(2) Total deductions that would have been claimed on 2000 federal tax return had there been no state tax overwithholding. [The greater of (i) $6,500 + $600 = $7,100 or (ii) the Standard deduction for 2000, $7,350]: **$7,350**

(3) Tax benefit on 2000 federal tax return resulting from state tax overwithholding, (1) – (2): **$7,500 – $7,350 = $150**

The amount computed in (3) above, $150, is the portion of the $400 refund which yielded a tax benefit the preceding year. Thus $150 is reported on line 10 of their 2001 federal tax return.

The above examples concern refunds of state or local income taxes. However, the same principle would apply to refunds of property taxes. Thus, a 2001 refund of property taxes overpaid in 2000 would be reportable as income only to the extent it pushes deductions over the standard deduction as illustrated in the above examples. IRS instructions have been misleading on this matter.

Tax Refunds Reported on Form 1099-G

If you received a state or local income tax refund during the year, you may receive a statement of this amount on Form 1099-G which is mailed to you by the payer of the refund. The IRS will also receive a copy of the Form 1099-G.

Don't make the mistake of automatically including the amount reported on Form 1099-G on your tax return. If this amount is exempt from tax according to the discussion above, then you do not report any of this amount on your return. If partially exempt, you only report the amount that is taxable on line 10 of Form 1040. It is alright if this amount does not agree with the amount reported on Form 1099-G.

However, it is advisable to attach a statement to your tax return explaining any discrepancy. This will protect against being questioned on this issue should the IRS matching program kick out your tax return because of the discrepancy.

Some states allow you to contribute, by means of a check-off on your state tax return, to one or more special funds, e.g. funds for veterans' benefits, wildlife conservation, etc. These check-offs might reduce the amount of the state tax refund you receive. In such a case, the amount reported on Form 1099-G will probably exceed your actual refund — it will report the refund you would have received without any check-offs. You would then use the higher amount reported on Form 1099-G as the basis for reporting your tax refund on line 10, and deduct the amounts checked off as a charitable contribution on Schedule A.

———13———
Tax-Sheltered Plans

SECTION 1:
BENEFIT OF TAX-DEFERRAL

A number of different types of tax-sheltered plans are available under the current tax laws, including IRAs, self-employed retirement plans (formerly Keogh plans), tax-sheltered annuities, flexible spending accounts, and deferred compensation plans. Of particular note are the remarkable *Defined-Benefit Plans* discussed in Section 3. With such plans, those with self-employment income can often **shelter up to 100% of this income from current tax.**

The principle behind most of these tax-sheltered plans is the same. First, you place a certain amount of money that you earn this year into one of these plans. You do not generally pay any current income tax on this money. That is, it is subtracted from your adjusted gross income on this year's tax return. (Three exceptions to this are non-deductible payments to an IRA [Section 2A], payments to a Roth IRA [Section 2B], and payments to a variable annuity [Section 7]. Although not subject to current income tax, these amounts are subject to self-employment taxes.

Second, after the money is placed into the plan, it is invested in savings certificates, stocks, bonds, or other securities depending upon the type of plan it is. As income is earned on the investment, no tax is paid. Year after year, the interest or other investment income compounds without the interference of any amount being taken out to pay taxes. If instead of placing an amount of money into such a plan, you were to invest it yourself, you would have to pay the tax as you went along. Any amount taken out in tax would no longer be available to earn investment income for you. In effect, the tax-sheltered plan is letting you use these amounts you would have to pay in tax as an interest-free loan to invest for your benefit.

Finally, you must pay tax as the money is withdrawn from the plan. Thus, you have not avoided tax but simply deferred it. But this deferral can result in a tremendous benefit because of all the extra interest, interest on interest, etc., you have earned on that amount of money not taken out in tax.

The table below illustrates the monetary advantage of a tax-sheltered plan. It examines the options of an individual with $1,000 who wishes to invest at the end of year 1. The table assumes that the individual's highest federal tax bracket remains at 31% and that there is an additional effective marginal state tax rate of 6%.

Column A shows the yearly total accumulation of original investment plus all income earned, assuming that the individual first pays the tax due on $1,000 ($370) and invests the remainder ($630) herself. Column B shows the yearly total, assuming the $1,000 is placed in a tax-sheltered plan. Column C shows the amount the individual would receive if distribution of the accumulated funds were subject to tax at the same rate used throughout the table. All three columns assume the funds earn 9% annually. This, of course, assumes you are disciplined enough to invest the tax savings on an annual basis.

Year	Column A Invested by individual; all taxes paid	Column B Invested in tax- sheltered plan; tax not paid	Column C Invested in tax- sheltered plan; all taxes paid
1	$ 630	$ 1,000	$ 630
5	786	1,412	889
10	1,035	2,172	1,368
15	1,364	3,342	2,105
20	1,796	5,140	3,239
25	2,367	7,911	4,984
30	3,118	12,172	7,668
35	4,108	18,728	11,799
40	5,413	28,816	18,154

For some, the above table understates the advantage of tax-sheltering. If a person's income tax rate rises through the years, the Column A accumulations might decrease markedly. The Column C distribution would not be affected nearly as much because there is no compounding effect caused by the annual application of a higher tax rate. Also, the Column C distribution might be greater than indicated if the individual's tax rate drops after retirement, if she elects an annuity option which further defers tax, or if she can use the special lump sum averaging provision discussed later in this chapter.

Contributing to Tax-Sheltered Plans Can Raise Other Deductions

Generally, contributions to tax-sheltered plans reduce your AGI (adjusted gross income). This happens directly when wages are reduced by the amount of the contributions [see Sections 4-6] or when contributions can be claimed as an adjustment to income [see Sections 2 and 3].

This reduction in AGI can have a favorable secondary effect of raising certain other deductions. In particular, the deduction for miscellaneous expenses is reduced by 2% of AGI [see the *Miscellaneous Deductions* chapter]; thus, reducing AGI raises the deduction for miscellaneous deductions. The same situation applies to the deductions for medical expenses and casualty losses since these are subject to 7.5% and 10% of AGI income subtractions, respectively [see the *Medical Expenses* and *Casualty Losses* chapters].

Another benefit of lowering AGI is to permit deductible IRA contributions to be made by some individuals. For example, as discussed in Section 2, a married individual who is a participant in a retirement plan cannot make a deductible contribution to a regular IRA for 2001 if his AGI is $63,000 or more. And he can obtain only a partial deduction if his AGI falls into the $53,000-$63,000 phase-out range. Thus, for example, if a married individual with AGI of $63,000 reduces his AGI by making a $5,000 contribution to a self-employed retirement plan, tax-sheltered annuity, deferred compensation, or other tax-sheltered plan, his AGI would be reduced to $58,000. This would give him an additional $1,000 deduction if this amount is contributed to an IRA.

SECTION 2:
INDIVIDUAL RETIREMENT ACCOUNTS

Individual Retirement Accounts (IRAs) are individual tax-sheltered savings plans set up with a mutual fund, savings institution, insurance company, etc. Funds in an IRA can be invested as an individual wishes (except most collectibles are prohibited) with all investment income exempt from tax. It is this ability to compound income over a period of time in a tax-free manner that makes contributing to an IRA desirable.

There are two basic types of IRAs. IRAs of the first type are sometimes called *regular IRAs*. If the basic rules are satisfied, an individual can deduct up to $2,000 for the tax year 2001 when contributed to a regular IRA. Tax is only due when funds are withdrawn at a later time.

For the tax year 2002, the maximum IRA contribution is rasied from $2,000 to $3,000. For individuals who are at least 50 years old, the limitation is increased further by $500 to $3,500.

IRAs of the second type, called *Roth IRAs* or sometimes *back-end IRAs*, came into effect in 1998. The rules for this type of IRA are a twist of the old rules. You do not deduct contributions made to a Roth IRA, but instead qualified withdrawals are entirely exempt from tax. In many cases, Roth IRAs are superior to regular IRAs, as discussed later in Section 2C.

Why did Congress invent a whole new type of IRA instead of just liberalizing the rules for the old IRAs? The answer is simple. Roth IRAs have no impact on the agreement to balance the budget in 5 years, because there is no current deduction for contributions. The budgetary impact will only come later after the current Congress is gone, when distributions are tax-free instead of being taxed under the old IRA rules.

This Section is divided into 3 parts. Section 2A discusses the rules for regular IRAs, Section 2B discusses the rules for Roth IRAs, and Section 2C discusses the rules applying to both regular IRAs and Roth IRAs. (There is another type of IRA, the *Education IRA*, which is discussed in the *Expenses of Attending School* chapter.)

A. Regular IRAs

As in prior years, you can deduct up to $2,000 in 2001 (increasing in 2002 and later years) for contributions made to a regular IRA, provided you satisfy **any** of the following conditions:

Condition A: Neither you nor your spouse is covered by another retirement plan; *or*

Condition B: The total adjusted gross income (ignoring IRA contributions) on your tax return is less than $53,000 on a joint return or $33,000 on a single person's or head of household's return; *or*

Condition C: One spouse is covered by another retirement plan and total adjusted gross income (AGI) is not greater than $160,000. The deductible portion of the IRA under this condition is phased out for AGI between $150,000 and $160,000.

(The above conditions apply to the 2001 tax year. For the 2002 tax year, the $53,000 figure in Condition B is raised to $54,000 and the $33,000 figure to $34,000.)

To satisfy Condition A, you must not be an *active participant* at any time during the year in a *retirement plan*. Here, the term *retirement plan* includes tax-favored plans sponsored by your employer such as a pension, profit-sharing, deferred compensation, 401(k), or stock bonus plan. It also includes tax-sheltered annuities [sometimes called 403(b) plans] and self-employed retirement plans. However, it does not include social security, nor does it include unfunded deferred compensation plans established by a government or tax-exempt organization.

Your employer will determine whether or not you are an *active participant* in a retirement plan which it sponsors. In some cases, this determination can rest upon certain technical factors. However, in general, you are an *active participant* in a plan if any contributions were made **to** the plan on your behalf during the year. (Receipt of annuity payments **from** the retirement plan does not cause an individual to be classified as an active participant.) However, if you are covered by a retirement plan with a specific defined benefit (e.g., an amount based on salary and length of service), you are automatically considered to be an *active participant,* even if no contributions were made on your behalf that year. Furthermore, you can be an *active participant* in a plan even if you have not been in the plan long enough to be vested (meaning you have the right to receive some or all of your share of the funds). Your employer is required to inform you on your year-end Form W-2, by marking the *Pension Plan* checkbox, if you were an *active participant* in one of its plans during the year.

If you satisfy Condition A, Condition B, or Condition C, you can deduct any regular IRA contributions totalling up to $2,000 for the 2001 tax year, provided the total does not exceed your own *earned income.*

Earned income means income produced by your own work, whether as an employee or as a self-employed person. It does not include income on investments such as stocks, bonds, savings accounts, rental property, etc., nor does it include income which is exempt from tax.

Tainted Spouse Rule

To satisfy Condition A for the 2001 tax year, neither you nor your spouse can be an active participant in a retirement plan. This is colorfully called the *tainted spouse rule*. Even if you are not an active participant in any plan, you can still fail Condition A because of the taint of your spouse's participation. This is the case even if you and your spouse file separate tax returns.

There is a loophole in the tainted spouse rule for married couples filing separate returns where one spouse earns less than $10,000. That spouse can make a deductible contribution under the phase-out rules described on the next page, no matter what the earnings amount or retirement plan status of his spouse [see Example 6 for an illustration of this situation]. However, there is also a loophole for married couples where one spouse is covered by a plan and the other is not. The non-covered spouse is allowed to make a deductible IRA contribution if the AGI shown on the return is less than $150,000. The deductibility of this IRA contribution is phased out for AGI between $150,000 and $160,000. For example, if AGI is $155,000, only $1,000 of the IRA contribution would be deductible.

There is also a special rule for married couples who live apart for the entire year. On a separate return, either spouse can choose to ignore the other spouse's earnings or retirement plan status and choose to apply the regular IRA rules for single persons. Under these rules, a deductible $2,000 IRA contribution can be made by a person if either he alone is not covered by a retirement plan or has AGI on his separate return of $33,000 or less [see Example 6].

If you divorce during the year, then the tainted spouse rule does not apply. Because the basic tax rules look to your marital status as of the end of the year, you are considered a single person for the entire year. As such, you file a single tax return under the rules applying to single taxpayers.

Spousal IRAs

If your spouse has no earned income, you can contribute up to $2,000 to a Regular IRA in your spouse's name. If you have earnings of at least $4,000, you can contribute $2,000 to your IRA and another $2,000 to your spouse's IRA.

However, you must still satisfy Condition A, Condition B, or Condition C in order to make a deductible contribution to your or your spouse's Regular IRA. For example, if you are covered by another retirement plan and the AGI shown on your 2001 tax return is $160,000, you cannot make deductible contributions to any Regular IRAs.

Phase-Out Range

The individual limit for deductible IRA contributions is phased out if AGI (ignoring IRA contributions) falls into the *phase-out range*. The phase-out range for the 2001 tax year is $53,000 – $63,000 for joint filers and $33,000 – $43,000 for singles.

For joint filers in the $53,000 – $63,000 phase-out range, the maximum amount that can be deducted is given by the formula: $20\% \times (\$63,000 - \text{AGI})$. As can be seen from the formula, the maximum IRA deduction for joint filers is $2,000 if AGI is $53,000, and $0 if AGI is $63,000, with an intermediate amount between the phase-out endpoints of $53,000 and $63,000.

Analogous formulas apply to singles and marrieds filing separately. The following table gives the formulas and phase-out ranges for these formulas:

PHASE-OUT TABLE FOR 2001 TAX RETURNS

COLUMN I Type of Tax Return	COLUMN II Maximum Deduction for IRA Contributions	COLUMN III Phase-Out Range for which Column II Applies
Joint	20% × ($63,000 – AGI)	$53,000 – $63,000
Single	20% × ($43,000 – AGI)	$33,000 – $43,000
Married filing separately	20% × ($10,000 – AGI)	$0 – $10,000

For the 2002 tax year, the numbers in the above table are raised.

PHASE-OUT TABLE FOR 2002 TAX RETURNS

COLUMN I Type of Tax Return	COLUMN II Maximum Deduction for IRA Contributions	COLUMN III Phase-Out Range for which Column II Applies
Joint	20% × ($64,000 – AGI)	$54,000 – $64,000
Single	20% × ($44,000 – AGI)	$34,000 – $44,000
Married filing separately	20% × ($10,000 – AGI)	$0 – $10,000

In the above tables, you round up to a multiple of $10 after using Column II to determine the maximum IRA deduction that applies. For example, if you compute $1,488 using Column II, you round this up to $1,490. Also, if you compute a deduction limit of less than $200 but more than $0, you are allowed to use $200 as the deduction limit.

Example 1

Morgan files a 2001 joint tax return showing AGI of $70,000. Neither he nor his wife is covered by a retirement plan.

In this case, Condition A applies. Morgan can deduct a contribution to his regular IRA of any amount of his earned income up to $2,000. His spouse can also deduct a contribution to a separate regular IRA of any amount up to $2,000.

Example 2

Scott files a 2001 joint tax return showing AGI of $70,000. He is covered by a retirement plan provided by his employer.

Scott can get no deduction for contributing to a regular IRA. Neither Condition A nor Condition B applies. Furthermore, his AGI is above the $53,000-$63,000 phase-out range given in the above Phase-Out Table for 2001 tax returns. Scott's spouse, however, could make a $2,000 deductible IRA contribution to her own IRA. She in effect borrows $2,000 of Scott's earned income in order to qualify. This would be a deductible contribution because the AGI is less than $160,000.

Example 3

Farley files a 2001 single tax return showing AGI (ignoring IRA contributions) of $36,560.

Case 1. Farley is covered by his employer's retirement plan. Using the appropriate formula in Column II of the Phase-Out Table, Farley's regular IRA deduction cannot exceed 20% × ($43,000 − $35,560) = $1,288, which is rounded up to $1,290.

Case 2. Farley is not covered by any retirement plan. In this case, Condition A applies. This means that Farley can deduct any amount up to $2,000, when contributed to a regular IRA.

Example 4

John and Mary file a 2001 joint tax return with AGI of $55,000 (ignoring IRA contributions). Mary is covered by her employer's retirement plan.

Case 1. John and Mary each earn $27,500. To compute the maximum IRA deduction for each spouse, the Column II formula for joint returns is applied:

$$20\% \times (\$63,000 - \$55,000) = \$1,600.$$

Thus, each spouse can deduct a regular IRA contribution of up to $1,600 — a total of $3,200 for the couple.

Case 2. John earned $1,500 and Mary earned $53,500. In this case, Mary can deduct a regular IRA contribution of up to $1,600, the same as in Case 1. John's deductible IRA contribution is limited to $1,600, the amount of his earned income ($1,500) plus $100 of earned income borrowed from Mary.

Example 5

You and your spouse file a 2001 joint tax return with AGI (ignoring IRA contributions) of $55,000. Your spouse has no earned income. Both spouses are covered by a retirement plan provided by their employers.

You use the Phase-Out Table to compute your own deduction limit:

$$20\% \times (\$63,000 - \$55,000) = \$1,600.$$

You can also contribute to a spousal IRA in your spouse's name, if you wish. The contribution is not restricted to the same $1,600 limit that applies to your regular IRA. Thus, your total contributions to regular IRAs equals $1,600 + $2,000 = $3,600.

Example 6

Sam and Jane, a married couple, have earned income in 2001 of $155,000 and $6,000, respectively. They have no unearned income. Sam is covered by a retirement plan, but Jane is not. If they file a joint tax return, then the fact that their combined AGI exceeds $160,000 and Sam is an active participant in a retirement plan rules out a deductible regular IRA contribution both for Sam and for Jane (because of the tainted spouse rule).

If they file separately, then Sam still cannot deduct an IRA contribution on his separate tax return. But the situation for Jane is different. She is still covered by the tainted spouse rule which rules out a full $2,000 deduction. But because the income shown on her tax return lies in the $0-$10,000 phase-out range for separate returns, she can make a deductible regular IRA contribution of the following amount [see Column II of the Phase-Out Table]:

$$Deduction = 20\% \times (\$10,000 - \$6,000) = \$800$$

The above assumes that Sam and Jane lived together. If they did not live together at any time during the year, then Jane could apply the regular IRA rules for single individuals. Because the AGI on her separate return is under $33,000, she could make a $2,000 contribution to a regular IRA, fully deductible on her separate return.

Where Is the Deduction for Regular IRA Contributions Claimed?

The deduction for regular IRA contributions is claimed as an adjustment to income on line 23 of Form 1040. Because it is an *adjustment to income* rather than an *itemized deduction,* it can be claimed by those who use the standard deduction as well as by those who itemize.

Non-Deductible Contributions

If you do not qualify for the full $2,000 IRA deduction in 2001, you can make *non-deductible contributions* to a regular IRA. Although these IRA contributions are not deductible, all *earnings* on these funds compound entirely free from tax until distributions are made.

The total of all your IRA contributions (deductible and non-deductible) for 2001 cannot exceed $2,000, nor can it exceed earned income. For example, if you were not allowed a deductible IRA contribution, you can make a $2,000 non-deductible contribution; if you were allowed an $800 deductible IRA contribution, you can make an additional $1,200 non-deductible contribution.

On the other hand, if you make a $2,000 *deductible* contribution to your IRA, you cannot make any *non-deductible* contribution for the year to the same or different IRA in your name.

You make non-deductible contributions to a regular IRA in exactly the same way you make deductible contributions — i.e., you just deposit funds into the IRA account. You can mingle deductible and non-deductible contributions in the same regular IRA. No purpose is served by segregating these 2 different types of contributions into different IRAs.

At the time you contribute to a regular IRA, you do not need to specify to the institution managing your IRA what the tax nature of the contribution is. However, you do you need to specify what percentage of your total contribution for the year is deductible and what percentage is non-deductible.

For example, you can make a $2,000 contribution to your regular IRA at the beginning of the year, even if you don't know what your tax situation will be for the year. You will determine what percentage is deductible when you fill out your tax return after the end of the year. And, as discussed later, you can even cancel any contributions for the year that you wish to retract by making withdrawals before the tax-filing deadline.

To illustrate the rules for making non-deductible contributions, let us revisit the previous examples in this section. In Example 1, if Morgan makes the maximum deductible IRA contribution of $2,000, a non-deductible contribution cannot be made to an IRA in his name. On the other hand, in Example 2, because no deductible contribution is allowed, a $2,000 non-deductible contribution could be made.

Form 8606

If you make a non-deductible contribution to a regular IRA in 2001 (or in 2002 for the year 2001), you must fill out Form 8606 and include it as part of your 2001 tax return. Only a few lines on this form need to be filled out. Basically, you list the value of all your IRAs on December 31, 2001, and the amount of non-deductible contributions you made for the 2001 tax year. You will automatically receive this information from the institution managing your IRA. They are required by law to send you a Form 5498 reporting the December 31, 2001, balance of your IRA account and any contributions you made during 2001.

Your spouse must file a separate Form 8606 if any non-deductible contributions were made to a regular IRA in your spouse's name.

If you made a non-deductible contribution to a regular IRA for 2001, you are supposed to keep a copy of your 2001 tax return until you no longer have an IRA in your name. You are also supposed to retain the Form 5498 sent to you by the institution managing your IRA for each year you either make a contribution to or receive a distribution from an IRA. The maintenance of these records may be required to back up your claim of non-taxability for a portion of regular IRA distributions received in later years. When you withdraw funds from your regular IRA(s), the more non-deductible contributions you have made, the larger the portion of the withdrawal that is exempt from tax [see Example 7]. Without any records, you would not be able to back up the fact that you made non-deductible contributions to your regular IRA. This would mean that if challenged by the IRS, all distributions received from your regular IRA might be subject to tax as if you had made no non-deductible contributions.

When Are Your IRA Contributions Due?

You can choose any schedule you want for making contributions. You can make periodic contributions or make one big contribution. You are under no obligation as to the amount you contribute in any given year, as long as your contributions do not exceed the maximum allowable amount. You have until the filing date of your tax return to establish or make contributions to an IRA. Thus, contributions for 2001 can be made until April 15, 2002, regardless of when you file your tax return. However, the April 15 deadline for your IRA contribution applies even if you are relying on an extension to file your return after this date.

According to a 1986 IRS ruling, if you mail in your IRA contribution, the postmark date is what counts. In this ruling, a person mailed a contribution on April 11 that the bank did not receive until April 16, one day after the deadline. The IRS ruled that because the envelope was postmarked April 12, three days before the April 15 deadline, the payment could be deducted as an IRA contribution. [IRS Private Letter Ruling 8611090]

If you make an IRA contribution and later change your mind, you can withdraw the contribution before the due date of your tax return, with no penalty. You should also withdraw any investment income earned by the withdrawn funds while in the IRA. However, this withdrawal privilege does not apply to lump-sum distributions rolled over into an IRA as described at the end of this Section.

Contributing After Age 59 1/2

Suppose you don't want to contribute to an IRA because you want to have the funds readily available to spend if you need them. If you are age 59 1/2 or older, an IRA is generally a no-lose proposition, because you can withdraw funds at any time with no IRS penalty. You can use the IRA simply as a tax-free savings account in which you want to keep readily available emergency funds.

Can Regular IRA Contributions Be Made After Age 70 1/2?

The general rule is that you cannot contribute to a regular IRA for the year you reach age 70 1/2 or any year thereafter. However, if you have reached age 70 1/2 and are still working, you may contribute to a regular IRA for your non-working spouse as long as your spouse is less than age 70 1/2 at the end of the tax year. Also, you can roll over a lump sum distribution from a pension plan (see below), even though you have reached age 70 1/2, provided you begin distributions as required.

When Is Money Withdrawn from a Regular IRA?

You may start withdrawing money from your regular IRA anytime after the age of 59 1/2. After that age, you may take as much money out of your IRA each year as you choose.

However, you must begin the distribution of money from your regular IRA by April 1 of the year following the year in which you reach age 70 1/2. You don't have to retire from your ordinary job in order to receive payments. You can choose to receive the entire account in one lump sum or receive the amount in periodic payments spread out over a number of years. For example, if you turn 70 1/2 during 2001, you must make your initial withdrawal for the 2001 tax year by April 1, 2002. This distribution is taxable in the year received. Distributions for each future year must be made by December 31 of that year. In particular, your distribution for the 2002 tax year must be made by December 31, 2002. This means that distributions for both 2001 and 2002, if received in 2002, are taxed in the same year. If this bunching of income would shift you into a higher tax bracket, then you should advance the 2001 distribution so it's received before December 31, 2001, and will be reported as income on your 2001 tax return instead of on your 2002 tax return.

If you have more than one regular IRA when you reach age 70 1/2, then application of the basic rules would require using the total of all IRAs to compute the minimum annual distributions to be made. Instead of making withdrawals out of each IRA, you may choose to make a withdrawal from just one of the IRAs, as long as the total amount withdrawn is at least as much as the sum total required to be distributed under the basic rules [per IRS Proposed Regulations dated January 12, 2001]. This is of particular benefit if one of the IRAs consists of a long-term certificate of deposit or other investment that would produce a financial penalty if cashed in early.

It is permissible for you to withdraw money from a regular IRA before reaching age 59 1/2. However, as discussed later in this section, an extra 10% penalty tax may apply to such early withdrawals.

How Are IRA Distributions Taxed?

If you have never made any non-deductible contributions to an IRA, then the taxation rules for distributions are simple. Namely, any withdrawal of funds from the IRA is taxed at your ordinary income tax rate along with your other income. Thus, you will probably want to spread out payments over a number of years instead of receiving a lump-sum distribution. Note that lump-sum distributions do not qualify for the special averaging rule that applies to regular retirement plans or to self-employed retirement plans [see the *Retirement Plans* chapter].

Distributions of Non-Deductible Contributions

If you have made non-deductible contributions to a regular IRA, a portion of any distributions you later make from the same or a different regular IRA in your name is not taxed. (You have already paid tax when you earned the money to make the non-deductible contribution.) Also, the 10% penalty tax on early withdrawals before age 59 1/2, discussed later, does not apply to a return of non-deductible contributions. Thus, the portion of a distribution attributed to non-deductible contributions escapes not only the ordinary tax, but the additional 10% penalty tax as well.

To determine the non-taxable percentage of a distribution, you divide the total non-deductible contributions you have made over the years by the value of your IRA at the end of the year of distribution. The *value* of your IRA is the year-end account balance, adding back any distributions made during the year. If you have more than one regular IRA in your name, you group them together and treat them as if they were all part of one big IRA.

Example 7

You made the following contributions to a regular IRA:

	Deductible	Non-Deductible
1997	$2,000	
1998	1,500	
1999	1,000	$1,000
2000	1,000	1,000
	$5,500	$2,000

On October 31, 2001, you make a withdrawal of $3,000. Let's say that at the end of 2001, the total in the IRA account is $7,000.

The percentage of your account that is due to non-deductible contributions is:

$$\frac{\$2,000}{\$3,000 + \$7,000} = 20\%.$$

Thus, 20% of the $3,000 distribution is tax-free: 20% × $3,000 = $600. The remaining $2,400 ($3,000 − $600) is included in taxable income on your 2001 tax return.

As can be seen from the above example, the tax treatment of a distribution depends upon the percentage of your regular IRA derived from non-deductible contributions — the higher the percentage, the larger the portion of the distribution that is exempt from tax.

If you have a choice, you are better off concentrating non-deductible contributions in one spouse's regular IRA and deductible contributions in the other spouse's IRA. That way, if you want to make a withdrawal, you can do so from the IRA in which the non-deductible contributions are concentrated. Because amounts attributable to non-deductible contributions are not taxed upon withdrawal, this will maximize the amount of the withdrawal that is exempt from tax.

Example 8

You have one regular IRA in your name, and your spouse, who also works, has none. The account balance in your IRA at the end of the year (due to contributions in previous years plus interest) is $10,500. You wish to make a $1,500 non-deductible contribution on this date and intend to make a $1,000 distribution one year later. We will assume an interest rate of 10% for this one-year period.

Case 1. You make a $1,500 non-deductible contribution to your own regular IRA.

This brings your account balance to $10,500 + $1,500 = $12,000. Under the 10% interest assumption, this rises to $13,200 by the end of the next year when you make the $1,000 distribution. Under the rules illustrated in Example 7, the percentage of the distribution that is untaxed (as a partial return of non-deductible contributions) is $1,500 ÷ $13,200 = 11%. Thus, 11% × $1,000 = $110 is untaxed, with the remaining $890 subject to tax in the year of distribution.

> **Case 2.** **You make the $1,500 non-deductible contribution into a regular IRA set up in your spouse's name.**
>
> Under the 10% interest assumption, the account balance of $1,500 rises to $1,650 by the end of the next year when the $1,000 distribution is made. Following the method illustrated in Example 7, the percentage of the distribution that is untaxed is $1,500 ÷ $1,650 = 91%. Thus 91% × $1,000 = $910 is untaxed, with only $90 remaining to be taxed in the year of distribution. When compared with Case 1, this is a decrease in current taxable income of $890 – $90 = $800.

Are Non-Deductible Contributions Worthwhile?

Before making non-deductible contributions to a regular IRA, you should exhaust all the tax-deductible plans for which you are eligible — self-employed retirement plans, tax-sheltered annuities, and deferred compensation plans [see the remaining sections in this chapter]. For the 2001 tax year, you should also invest as much as you're eligible for in a Roth IRA[see Section 2B]. Contributions to a Roth IRA are better than non-deductible contributions to a regular IRA because Roth distributions are completely tax-free, while non-deductible contributions to a regular IRA result in only partly non-taxable distributions.

If you still have money left that you wish to invest on a long-term basis, then non-deductible contributions to a regular IRA may make sense. The ability of the IRA to compound earnings without paying current tax is valuable, especially over a long period of time. However, you should make a comparison with other tax-sheltered investments before making non-deductible contributions to a regular IRA. In particular, you should take a look at *variable annuities* [see Section 7 of the *Tax-Sheltered Plans* chapter] and *tax-managed mutual funds* [see Section 5 of the *Investing Your Money* chapter]. Both of these investments offer tax-sheltering of investment income, but no deduction when funds are put into the investments.

If you expect to make withdrawals from your regular IRA before many years have passed, you should be careful about making non-deductible regular IRA contributions when you already have an existing regular IRA. The reason for this is illustrated in Case 1 of the preceding example. In that case, a non-deductible contribution of $1,500 was followed the next year by a $1,000 withdrawal — leaving a net $500 addition to the IRA. Because there was a substantial amount already in a regular IRA, a tax was triggered on $890 of the withdrawal. If we assume the tax on this $890 amounts to $300, the withdrawal would yield $700 in after-tax money.

However, instead of making the full $1,500 contribution, it would have been better to hold on to $700 and contribute the remaining $800 to the IRA. This leaves you with the same in-pocket $700, but the IRA winds up with an extra $800, which is $300 more than the net $500 addition in the preceding paragraph. (Investment income was ignored in the preceding analysis because its inclusion would not affect the basic comparison.)

Can Money Be Withdrawn Before Age 59 1/2?

Yes. However, the purpose of the legislation creating the IRAs was to provide a retirement vehicle. Thus, there is a penalty for early withdrawals. If you do withdraw money before age 59 1/2, and you have never made any non-deductible contributions to a regular IRA, there is a **10% penalty tax** on the amount of the distribution that you withdraw. This is in addition to the ordinary income tax that applies.

If you have ever made a non-deductible contribution to a regular IRA, then as discussed above, only a portion of any distribution is subject to ordinary income tax. The 10% penalty tax only applies to this taxable portion. The remaining portion of the distribution attributed to non-deductible contributions is not subject to ordinary income tax nor to the 10% penalty tax.

Note that the 10% penalty is not so severe as to absolutely limit the use of an IRA to those seeking a retirement vehicle. You still might be better off setting up an IRA and making a premature withdrawal than you would had you invested the money outside an IRA.

For example, suppose you could make a $1,000 deductible contribution to a regular IRA or invest without tax protection. If you were in the 28% tax bracket, then investing the funds yourself would mean you could put $720 to work earning interest or other income. But the IRA would have an extra $280. Over a period of years, the extra income earned on the $280 would be sufficient to compensate for the 10% penalty. In addition, the fact that your money is compounding entirely tax-deferred in an IRA instead of being taxed each year provides a further advantage.

Assuming no non-deductible contributions have been made, the break-even point is generally around 7 years. That is, you are generally better off with a regular IRA if the money is left in for about 7 years or more and then withdrawn prematurely (with 10% penalty) than you would have been with a comparable investment outside the IRA. However, the exact break-even point depends upon the interest rate earned by funds in the IRA and your upper tax bracket (federal plus state and local). For example, assuming an 8% interest rate and 33% tax bracket, the break-even point is 7 years; but assuming a 10% interest rate and 40% tax bracket, the break-even point is reduced to 5 years.

In the case of non-deductible contributions to a regular IRA, the break-even point is about twice as long. For example, assuming an 8% interest rate and 33% tax bracket, the break-even point is 13 years. This presumes there have been no deductible contributions made to regular IRAs over the years. Otherwise, because of the complex distribution tax rules, the break-even point is even longer.

For example, if substantial deductible contributions have been made, the break-even point can be as much as 23 years under the previous assumptions. The reason for this increased break-even period is that in this case, a small distribution from a regular IRA can be almost fully taxable, whereas with only non-deductible contributions, a significant part of the distribution is exempt from tax.

Because of the extended break-even point, it is not generally advisable to make non-deductible contributions to a regular IRA if you plan to withdraw funds before reaching age 59 1/2.

Exceptions to the 10% Penalty Tax

For the 2001 tax year, a distribution received from an IRA before age 59½ is exempt from the 10% penalty tax if it is either:

(1.) Due to death or disability;

(2.) Used to pay medical expenses exceeding 7.5% of AGI;

(3.) Used to pay health insurance premiums by an individual who has received unemployment compensation for at least 12 weeks;

(4.) Used for qualified first-time home purchases. The first-time homebuyer can be yourself, your spouse, or any child, grandchild, or ancestor of you or your spouse. To be a "first-time homeowner" for this purpose, an individual (and his spouse, if married) must not have been a full or part owner of a principal residence during the 2-year period ending with the date the purchase contract is signed or the date when construction of the new home begins. IRA amounts used for qualified first-time home purchases by an individual are limited to a $10,000 lifetime maximum;

(5.) Used to pay for qualified college costs of yourself, your spouse, and children of you or your spouse. Included in qualified costs are tuition, room and board, fees, books, supplies, and equipment. Total costs must be reduced by any tax-exempt scholarship payments received; *or*

(6.) Made in the form of periodic payments, prorated over your life expectancy or the joint life expectancy of yourself and a beneficiary. If you wish, these annuity payments can be stopped after 5 years, provided you are at least age 59½ at that time. This early withdrawal privilege will be useful to some who have fixed payments they have to make over a period of years. This would include mortgage payments, tuition payments, and alimony or child support.

If you have more than one IRA, each is treated independently of the other with regard to item (6) above, the *periodic payment* rule. You can choose to take payments from one of the IRAs according to the guidelines above, while the other remains untouched. If you wish, you can divide an existing IRA into 2 separate IRAs and withdraw funds from only one of them.

The IRS has issued a ruling indicating the appropriate methods that are permissible in determining how much can be paid out under the *periodic payment* rule above. The institution managing your IRA can advise you of the exact amount in your situation, depending upon your age, the age of the beneficiary you name, and the prevailing interest rate. However, an example in the IRS ruling gives an indication of what to expect.

In this example, a 50-year-old individual with a $100,000 account balance was permitted to receive annual distributions of $9,002 per year. This amount was based upon using a then-*"reasonable interest rate"* of 8% and a life expectancy of about 33 years. [IRS Notice 88-25]

If the individual in the above example continued this payout rate over a 5-year time period, he would receive a total of about $45,000 — 45% of the original $100,000 account balance. After reaching age 59 ½, he could either continue with the payments or halt them, letting the income continue to compound inside the IRA.

It should be pointed out that in the above example, the payout each year was exactly the same. However, this is not the only type of payout method that is permitted. It is permissible to make an annual recomputation based on the new remaining account balance and a new life expectancy figure. This recomputation procedure permits payments to continue until death, instead of possibly running out, as can happen with a fixed payout schedule.

Hidden IRA Bonus

When contemplating how much to contribute to a regular IRA , take note of the extra bonus you get if you also are claiming a medical deduction. Only medical expenses in excess of 7.5% of your AGI are deductible on your 2001 tax return. But your IRA contribution is an "above the line" *adjustment to income* which reduces your AGI, thereby raising your medical deduction.

For example, if you make a deductible contribution of $2,000 to a regular IRA in 2001, your AGI is reduced by $2,000 which in turn can raise your medical deduction by 7.5% × $2,000 = $150 — a 7.5% bonus.

A similar situation occurs with the 2% of AGI floor discussed in the *Miscellaneous Deductions* chapter. A $2,000 deduction for a regular IRA contribution in 2001 can raise the deduction for miscellaneous expenses by $40.

Switching Funds from One IRA to Another

The IRS allows you to switch your funds from one regular IRA into another. There are two ways to make such a switch — by direct transfer or by rollover.

A *direct transfer* (sometimes called a *trustee-to-trustee transfer*) is accomplished by having the institutions managing the IRAs transfer the funds between them. You do not take possession of the funds at any time. There is no limit on the number of direct transfers that can be made during any period of time.

A *rollover* is an investment switch which you make yourself. You withdraw the funds out of an existing regular IRA account and invest them in your new regular IRA. As long as the reinvestment is made within 60 days after receipt of the funds, no tax is paid. You must notify the institution from which you are withdrawing funds that you're planning to make a rollover.

The 2001 Tax Reduction Act allows for exceptions to the rule that rollovers must be re-contributed to a qualified plan or IRA within 60 days in the case of a casualty, disaster or other events beyond the reasonable control of the individual. This exception to the 60-day requirement begins in 2002.

You are limited to one such rollover of an existing IRA during any 12-month period. You keep and pay tax on any income earned on funds during the period the funds have been removed from the first IRA and not yet rolled into the second IRA.

You can make more than one rollover during a 12-month period if different funds from different IRAs are involved. For example, if you have 2 separate regular IRAs, you may consolidate by rolling over the funds from each of these IRAs into a third regular IRA. [IRS Private Letter Ruling 8731041]

There is no tax due at the time a switch is made by either a direct transfer or a rollover. And you can elect to have no withholding on funds switched out of the original IRA. This is in contrast to the mandatory withholding that applies when funds are switched from a retirement plan into a regular IRA (as discussed at the end of this Section), using a rollover (there referred to as a *personal rollover*).

Partial rollovers of amounts withdrawn from a regular IRA are permitted. This enables you to defer tax on that portion which is rolled over. The portion withdrawn which is not rolled over is includible in your ordinary income.

Most (but not all) institutions will permit you to switch out of their IRAs at any time. If you want the switch made with dispatch, a rollover may be better than a direct transfer. Institutions can take several months to complete a direct transfer because of delays in processing the paperwork.

There may or may not be a small switchover fee, depending upon the institution. And if your money is invested with a bank in a certificate of deposit, there will usually be a penalty (typically 3 or 6 months loss of interest) if a switch is made before the certificate matures.

You can avoid the bother of making a direct transfer or rollover by investing with a large no-load family of funds. Typically, you will then be allowed to switch between funds just by making a toll-free telephone call whenever you wish. You can also apportion up your IRA among several different funds as you choose.

Borrowing from Your IRA

You might need to borrow money for a short time to meet an unexpected emergency. Your regular IRA can come in handy for this purpose. Even though your IRA cannot make a formal loan to you, the same effect can be obtained by using the rollover privilege.

Under the rollover privilege described above, you can withdraw funds from your regular IRA anytime you choose. You then have 60 days in which to deposit the funds in a new regular IRA. This gives you 60 days use of the money to cover a temporary emergency. Of course, the money should be redeposited in an IRA within the 60-day period, otherwise tax (plus 10% penalty if under age 59 1/2) will be triggered on the withdrawn amount. According to a 1990 IRS ruling, you do not need to set up a new regular IRA, but can simply redeposit the money in the same IRA from which it was withdrawn [IRS National Office Advice Memorandum 9010007]. As mentioned above, these funds cannot be rolled out again until 12 months have elapsed since the previous rollout.

If the IRA holds property other than cash and this property is received from an IRA, the identical property must be transferred to the new IRA.

> **Example**
>
> *An individual withdrew funds from an IRA and invested in stock. Within 60 days the stock was contributed to the IRA. Because the same property was not contributed to the new IRA, the rollover failed and the entire amount was taxable.* [Lemishou, 110 TC 110]

What If You're Short of Cash to Fund Your IRA?

You may want to contribute to a regular IRA for 2001 but are temporarily short of cash to contribute as much as you wish. Here are some ways to get around this difficulty.

1. Borrow from a bank or savings institution

You are permitted to borrow funds to make your IRA contribution. You get a deduction for the IRA contribution and can still deduct the interest as *investment interest* under the rules described in the *Interest* chapter. Ordinarily, you can't deduct interest on any loan if the proceeds are used directly to make a tax-exempt investment. But the IRS has ruled that this restriction does not apply to IRAs because the income earned by IRA funds is not strictly *exempt* from tax as with, say, municipal bonds. Rather, this income is tax-deferred because tax will have to be paid on IRA earnings when money is withdrawn at some later date [IRS Private Letter Ruling 8527082]. It is best to borrow from a different institution than the one with which your account is established so the IRS can't construe that you're using your IRA as collateral for the loan.

2. "Borrow" from an existing IRA

As discussed in the previous subsection, you can "borrow" from an existing regular IRA for a period of 60 days or less. If you are short of funds, you can use this 60-day rollover period to pay this year's IRA contribution out of an existing IRA from a previous year. For example, suppose you file a tax return on March 15, 2002, showing that you're due a refund of $1,000. Let's say you listed a $1,000 IRA deduction on the tax return but didn't have the money to make the contribution (which is due by April 15).

On April 10, you roll $1,000 out of an existing regular IRA and deposit it in your checking account. You then write a $1,000 check to open a new regular IRA for the 2001 tax year. When you receive your $1,000 tax refund, you can write a $1,000 check to your new IRA, which is regarded as completing the rollover started on April 10.

The period from March 15 to 60 days after April 10 (when the rollover must be completed) is sufficient time to receive your refund unless there is a foul-up. However, since the rollover needs to be completed within 60 days, you might want to have a backup source of emergency funds to avoid the situation of making a premature withdrawal should your refund be inordinately delayed.

3. Contribute your tax refund to your IRA

You must make your regular IRA contribution by April 15, 2002 in order for it to be deductible on your 2001 tax return. However, you may take the deduction on your 2001 tax return even if you have not yet contributed to or even opened your regular IRA in 2001. As long as your contribution is eventually made by the April 15 deadline, you're alright.

For example, suppose you want to make a $2,000 deductible contribution to your 2001 IRA but only have $1,200 on hand. Let's say you fill out your tax return by February 10, 2002, which shows a large refund due to you. In this situation, you can do the following:

Contribute the $1,200 to your regular IRA, but claim a $2,000 IRA deduction on your tax return. Then mail in your tax return promptly. Because the IRS usually sends refunds within 4-6 weeks, you should receive your refund before April 15, 2002. You then contribute the remaining $800 to your IRA out of the refund money you receive from the IRS.

This procedure has been officially approved by the IRS. Your regular IRA does not even have to be opened at the time you mail in your tax return. As long as you eventually contribute the amount claimed on your 2001 tax return by April 15, 2002, your deduction is proper. [Rev. Rul. 84-18]

However, if April 15, 2002, rolls around and you don't have enough money to make the contribution claimed on your 2001 tax return, you'll have to file an amended tax return. This is done by filling out Form 1040X [see Chapter 1, Section 1], on which you report the actual IRA contribution made and recompute your taxes with this new lower figure as your IRA deduction instead of the old one. You should enclose a check for the extra tax due when you mail your Form 1040X to the IRS.

Why Two IRAs Can Be Better than One

There are several reasons why an individual might want to have his money split into two (or more) regular IRAs instead of one.

One consideration is the ability to use your regular IRA as a short-term source of money as described earlier in this Section. With one IRA, you can borrow money in this manner only once in any 12-month period. But, under regulations proposed by the IRS, each IRA is considered separately for purposes of this 12-month rule. For example, suppose you have two regular IRAs, IRA 1 and IRA 2. If you roll over IRA 1 into a new regular IRA 3, you cannot roll over this money again until 12 months have elapsed. But this does not restrict withdrawals from IRA 2. You can use the rollover privilege to withdraw funds from IRA 2 without regard to the rollover of funds from IRA 1. In effect, you have had the use of IRA money for two 60-day periods instead of one.

If you contemplate an IRA as a backup source of emergency cash, you might want to have 2 IRAs for a different reason. You would want one IRA in a liquid investment such as a mutual fund required to disburse funds upon request with no penalty.

The remainder of your money could be placed in a less liquid investment such as a bank certificate of deposit requiring an interest penalty on premature withdrawals.

Finally, of course, is investment diversification. Spreading money out in different investments is typically recommended to lessen market risk. This benefit alone, however, may not be sufficient to outweigh the extra bother of maintaining more than one account, especially if the amounts are small relative to your overall financial picture.

Choosing a Beneficiary

When you set up your regular IRA, you will be asked to choose a beneficiary in case you die before all funds are distributed to you. Tax-sheltering can then continue over the life of the beneficiary. In fact, some individuals will want to change their beneficiary from a spouse to a child to take advantage of these rules. If distributions from the IRA have not begun, the options permitted by the IRS are as follows:

(1) Starting no later than December 31 of the year following the year of death, annual payments can begin to the beneficiary based on his life expectancy. For example, a beneficiary with a life expectancy of 60 years would receive at least 1/60 of the value of the IRA the first year, 1/59 (approximately) the second, etc. The remaining funds continue to earn tax-deferred income in the IRA. There are several other payout options on which the institution managing your IRA can give you information. However, if the beneficiary is a spouse, payments do not have to begin until December 31 of the year the deceased would have reached age 70½ and they can be spread out over the life of the spouse.

(2) If no beneficiary is named in the plan documents or your will, the entire balance must be distributed to a beneficiary within 5 years after death.

(3) In any event, income tax is due on any payments received by beneficiaries from the regular IRA.

According to (1) above, naming a young child or grandchild as beneficiary allows the IRA to continue sheltering funds from tax for a long period of time. Naming a spouse as beneficiary means distributions need not begin until a later time. Which option has a stronger tax-savings effect depends upon the ages of the various people involved.

It's not a good idea to name a spouse and a child as joint beneficiaries of a regular IRA. The payouts will be keyed off of the life expectancy of the spouse and an age no more than 10 years younger than the spouse, meaning that the IRA may be depleted before the child reaches a mature age. Instead, divide the IRA into 2 separate IRAs, with the spouse as beneficiary of one and the child beneficiary of the other. When the child inherits the IRA, payments can extend over the longer life expectancy, thereby maximizing the amount of tax-sheltering of income in the IRA.

There is a pitfall to be aware of when a non-spouse is named beneficiary of a regular IRA. The existing IRA should simply be renamed to reflect the new ownership. It should not be rolled over or transferred into a new IRA in the beneficiary's name. And no further contributions should be made to that IRA. Otherwise, a tax could be triggered. [Rev Proc 89-52]

This is illustrated by a 1990 IRS private letter ruling. In this ruling, an individual took a regular IRA which she inherited (not from a spouse) and rolled it over into a new IRA in her name. According to the IRS, this simple shift caused the entire IRA to be taxed to the beneficiary [IRS Private Letter Ruling 9014071]. If you have named a non-spouse as beneficiary of your IRA, it is important to inform that beneficiary of this pitfall. Also, keep in mind that the beneficiary may take all funds sooner than over his/her life expectancy. This can be avoided by naming a trust as the beneficiary with the individuals named as beneficiaries of the trust.

According to a 1995 IRS ruling, there's a way for a surviving spouse who inherits an IRA to keep the IRA going over a long period of years as a sort of tax-sheltered trust fund for a beneficiary. To accomplish this, the surviving spouse rolls over the inherited IRA into a new IRA in his or her own name. When the new IRA is set up, a beneficiary can be selected with a long life expectancy, say a grandchild. The new IRA will make payouts to the surviving spouse until death, and then continue payments over the lifetime of the grandchild. In this way, the IRA can continue to earn tax-free income on funds for perhaps 60 or more years. (As described above, non-spouse beneficiaries of an IRA cannot take advantage of this maneuver because they are not permitted to roll over an inherited IRA into an IRA in their own name.) [IRS Private Letter Ruling 9311037]

The above only refers to the *income tax* consequence of inherited IRAs, not to the *estate tax* consequence. If your estate will be large enough to fall under the estate tax rules [see the *Estate Tax* chapter], professional estate planning should be sought to minimize that tax also.

Naming a Charity as Beneficiary of Your IRA

If you plan to leave money to charity in your will, then here's a tax saving idea approved in a recent IRS Letter Ruling. Name a charity to be beneficiary of a regular IRA that you own. Unlike a human beneficiary, the charity will pay no income tax on amounts received from the IRA. In contrast, if you had willed just an amount of money to the charity and willed the IRA to a relative, your relative would have to pay income tax on distributions from the IRA. (On the other hand, if the relative is young, you may prefer to leave the IRA to him so that tax sheltering of earnings can continue for a long time.)

Rolling Over a Retirement Plan Distribution into an IRA

You might receive a distribution of part or all of the money credited to your account in the retirement plan where you work. (The typical case when this occurs is when a person leaves his job, but this need not always be so.) This distribution is subject to tax along with your other earnings for the year. The special averaging rule and capital gains treatment [see Section 2 of the *Retirement Plans* chapter] lessen this tax burden substantially but your money is no longer sheltered. Any future investment income is subject to tax.

A special *rollover provision* in the law allows you to avoid the above situation. Under this provision, you can roll over a retirement plan distribution you receive into a regular IRA without paying tax on the distribution. You can also make a rollover into a new qualified pension plan instead, if the new plan permits such transfers.

Under the rollover provision, any distribution or part of a distribution from a retirement plan can be rolled over, tax-free, into a regular IRA (or into a different retirement plan) with the following two exceptions: First, the distribution must not be part of an annuity arrangement. More specifically, it must not be one of a series of substantially equal payments made over your life (or life expectancy), the joint lives (or joint life expectancy) of you and a beneficiary, or a specified period of 10 years or more.

Second, you must exclude from the rollover: (1) your own non-deductible employee contributions to the plan, and (2) *minimum distribution amounts* that must be paid to you if you are over age 70½.

If you receive a distribution from a tax-sheltered annuity, similar rules apply. With the same restrictions as discussed above, all or part of the distribution can be rolled over into a regular IRA or into a different tax-sheltered annuity. Tax-sheltered annuities cannot be rolled over into other types of retirement plans.

If you have rolled over a retirement distribution into a regular IRA, you can choose at a later time to place part or all of this IRA into the retirement plan of a new employer, if the employer's plan permits such rollovers. If this is done, the special averaging rule and capital gains treatment will become applicable again. Similarly, tax-sheltered annuity distributions rolled over into a regular IRA can be rolled back into a tax-sheltered annuity plan provided by a new employer.

However, it may pay to have a retirement distribution taxed currently rather than use a rollover IRA. This is done if you qualify for the special averaging rules discussed in Section 2 of the *Retirement Plans* chapter.

When you roll over a retirement distribution into a regular IRA, you should set up a new IRA to be a recipient of the funds. (If you roll over the distribution into an IRA with existing funds in it, you will not be allowed to later roll over funds from the IRA into the retirement plan of a new employer.) Also, you should use a different IRA if you make personal contributions in the future.

Spouses of employees may also benefit from rollover IRAs. If an employee dies and his spouse receives a retirement fund distribution, all or part of this distribution can be placed into a regular IRA and continue to grow tax-sheltered.

Note that the contribution limits, active participation requirements, and earnings tests discussed at the beginning of this section do not apply to IRA rollover contributions. Any amount may be rolled over without paying tax. However, you cannot include your own non-deductible contributions that you made to your retirement plan. These amounts must be subtracted from the total distribution before being transferred to the IRA. No tax is due on the return of your own contributions because you have already paid tax on these amounts when they were earned [see the *Retirement Plans* chapter].

Before deciding to use the rollover feature of a regular IRA, be sure to examine whether or not the loss of the special averaging rule and capital gains treatment will make such use unwise. However, the ability to continue a tax-free shelter for a number of years usually outweighs the loss of the averaging rule and capital gains treatment.

Also, if a new employer will accept the distribution into his retirement plan, then the rollover feature probably should be used. Similarly, if your original employer allows you to leave your money in his plan even though you terminate employment, this may be the best arrangement of all. This is especially true because your own contributions to the plan remain tax-sheltered.

However, there are cases when people will prefer to have their money in an IRA rather than a regular retirement plan. The flexibility of being able to make premature withdrawals (although subject to a possible 10% penalty tax), the ability to choose your own investment vehicle, and the ability to precisely determine the payout rate during retirement may create such cases.

Two Types of Rollovers

There are two types of rollovers, *direct rollovers* and *personal rollovers*.

Direct rollovers are rollovers executed by a direct trustee-to-trustee transfer. The employer transfers funds directly from the retirement plan to the trustees of the IRA or new retirement plan by wire or by mail. It is permissible for you to personally deliver a check from the employer to the trustee, but the check must be made out to the trustee, not to you personally. No tax is paid when a direct rollover is made and there is no withholding on funds when they are passed from your employer to the new trustee.

Personal rollovers are executed by you personally. You receive a distribution check from your retirement plan which you can deposit into your bank account. You then have 60 days to redeposit the money into a regular IRA or into a new retirement plan. No tax is due if the rollover is properly executed. However, if you fail to redeposit the entire rollover amount within 60 days, the funds not redeposited will become subject to income tax along with your other income. In addition, there is an extra 10% penalty tax that generally applies if funds are received before you are age 59$\frac{1}{2}$ (or age 55 if you are leaving your job).

While there is no tax due upon making a personal rollover, there is withholding. Your employer is required to withhold 20% of amounts distributed to you which are eligible for a rollover. (Withholding is only required when a rollover is made out of a retirement plan, not when it is made out of an IRA into another IRA or qualified plan, as discussed earlier in this Section.) This withholding is not a tax, but rather is treated the same as any other withholding. That is, you will get back any excess withholding as a refund after you file your income tax.

This withholding requirement does not eliminate rollovers, but rather makes them more inconvenient. The following example illustrates the basic difficulty in using a personal rollover.

Example

You wish to roll over a $100,000 retirement plan distribution into a regular IRA during the 60-day period after the distribution. Your employer will withhold 20% × $100,000 = $20,000 and you will receive the remaining $80,000.

You can roll over the $80,000 into a regular IRA. In this case, no tax is due on the $80,000 rollover. However, tax and the 10% early withdrawal penalty will still be due on the $20,000 that was credited to you but withheld rather than paid out to you. The $20,000 withheld by your employer is not entirely lost. It will be turned over to the IRS and credited towards your tax liability for the year.

A second possibility is for you to come up with $20,000 from other funds and combine this with the $80,000 you received to produce a total of $100,000, which you contribute to your regular IRA. In this case, no extra tax is due on the distribution because the entire amount before withholding was rolled over into your IRA. As in the preceding paragraph, the $20,000 withheld from the distribution is treated the same as any other withholding. You will get this amount back after your taxes are computed, the same way any excess withholding produces a tax refund.

When you make a personal rollover, you can divide the rolled over funds into more than one regular IRA or qualified retirement plan, if you wish. With a direct rollover, you can also divide the proceeds into more than one regular IRA or plan, provided your employer is willing to do the extra paperwork involved. If not, you can make the rollover into a single IRA to begin with, and then roll over into any number of IRAs you wish. The latter rollovers would not be subject to withholding because they are rollovers from one regular IRA to another, not rollovers out of a retirement plan.

Due to the complexity of the rules, professional advice should be sought before making any retirement distribution decisions.

B. Roth IRAs

Roth IRAs are a type of tax-sheltered plan instituted by the *1997 Tax Reduction Act*. It is much easier to qualify for a Roth IRA than a regular IRA, because there is no restriction for individuals who are covered by another pension plan.

Roth IRAs are sometimes called *back-end IRAs* because contributions are nondeductible, while distributions are generally non-taxable. In contrast, contributions to a regular IRA are deductible while distributions are taxable.

However, there is no difference in the tax treatment of funds while in either type of IRA; namely, earnings on these funds are not subject to any tax. As discussed in

Section 2C, regular IRAs and Roth IRAs produce about the same investment result, with the advantage to Roth IRAs if an individual's tax rate remains about the same.

Who Can Contribute to a Roth IRA?

An individual can contribute up to $2,000 of his earned income to a Roth IRA for the tax year 2001 (increasing to $5,000 as previously noted). There is no age limit after which an individual can no longer make contributions. (In contrast, an individual can no longer make contributions to his regular IRA in the year he reaches age 70½ or thereafter.) *Earned income* means income produced by your own work, whether as an employee or as a self-employed person. It does not include income on investments.

The $2,000 annual limit for 2001 applies to all IRAs owned by an individual, whether Roth IRAs or regular IRAs. For example, if you make a $600 contribution to a regular IRA, you are limited to $1,400 in contributions to a Roth IRA for 2001.

Adjusted Gross Income Limitation

While Roth IRAs have no age restrictions and no restriction on participation in another pension plan, there is an AGI limitation. If you file a joint tax return, you can't contribute to a Roth IRA if the total AGI shown on the return exceeds $160,000. This restriction is phased out between $150,000 and $160,000 so that if AGI is below $150,000, the full $2,000 contribution in 2001 can be made. On single tax returns, the $160,000 figure becomes $110,000 and the $150,000 figure becomes $95,000. No Roth IRA contributions are permitted if you are married filing separately unless you have lived apart for the entire year, in which case you are treated as single for Roth purposes.

Although an individual may be able to make a contribution to a Roth IRA of as much as $2,000, he gets no deduction for this contribution. The tax advantage of a Roth IRA is the absence of tax either on investment earnings in the IRA or on distributions from the IRA.

Distributions from Roth IRAs

A distribution from a Roth IRA is tax-free if

1. the distribution is made 5 tax years or more after the first contribution was made to the Roth IRA; and

2. the distribution was made after age 59½, or because of death or disability, or was applied toward qualified first-time home purchases. A qualified first-time home purchase occurs when a home purchaser (and his or her spouse, if married) did not own an interest in a principal residence during two years prior to the purchase.

Withdrawals from Roth IRAs that do not meet the above two conditions are included in taxable income except as discussed in the following subsection.

Tax-Free Withdrawals of Contributions

Roth IRAs have a special feature that allows you to withdraw at any time an amount up to or equal to your total contributions, free of tax. (This feature would generally be applied after either of the other two tax-free withdrawal rules discussed above are used.) All of an individual's Roth IRAs are aggregated for this purpose.

Example

Walker contributes $2,000 to a Roth IRA in 1999 and $1,000 to another Roth IRA in 2000. In 2001, the first IRA has increased in value to $2,500 and the second to $1,500. At that point, Walker closes out the first IRA and receives the full $2,500. Because this $2,500 does not exceed the total $3,000 in contributions he made to Roth IRAs, the entire $2,500 withdrawal is exempt from tax.

Withdrawals that exceed all the exceptions described above are subject to ordinary income tax. In addition, a 10% penalty tax generally applies. However, the same exceptions to the 10% penalty tax described in Section 2A for regular IRAs would apply to Roth IRAs.

When Are Contributions to a Roth IRA Made?

The timing rules for making contributions to Roth IRAs are the same as for regular IRAs as discussed in Section 2A. Thus, you can make contributions for the 2001 tax year anytime until April 15, 2002. Contributions for the 2002 tax year can be made anytime between January 1, 2002 and April 15, 2003.

When you open a new Roth IRA, you must specify that it is a Roth IRA rather than a regular IRA.

Why Your Child Should Open a Roth IRA

Because of the Kiddie Tax [see Section 5 of Chapter 1], investment earnings received by a child might be taxed at the parents' highest tax bracket instead of at the child's. However, if the underlying investment is held by an IRA in the child's name, then no current tax is due on the earnings. This can make it worthwhile to set up an IRA for a child.

To illustrate, suppose you pay $2,000 to your 9-year-old child in 2001 for performing chores, e.g. cleaning, lawn care, babysitting, etc. This can be considered *wages* received by the child if the amount is similar to what would have been paid to an unrelated person for the same work. Furthermore, these wages are exempt from social security tax [see Section 3 of the *Outside Business Activity* chapter] and from income tax as well because of the standard deduction that applies to earned income [see Section 5 of Chapter 1].

Next, have the child contribute the $2,000 for 2001 to a Roth IRA in his name. Earnings on this money will now be tax-sheltered as long as it remains in the IRA. A considerable tax savings could be achieved, especially if the Kiddie Tax would otherwise apply [see Section 5 of Chapter 1]. The child could later withdraw the money to pay for college tuition. Little or no tax is paid on this withdrawal.

Additional tax savings would be achieved if the child performs chores — cleaning, filing, etc. — connected with a business activity of a parent. In this case, the parent actually gets a tax deduction for the payments made to the child. This situation is discussed further in Section 3 of the *Outside Business Activity* chapter.

C. Rules Applying to Both Regular IRAs and Roth IRAs

Annual Limit on Total IRA Contributions

The total amount of earned income an individual can contribute to all his IRAs (regular plus Roth) for 2001 cannot exceed $2,000. For a married couple, the total contributions to all their IRAs (regular plus Roth) for 2001 cannot exceed $4,000. If their combined earned income is less than $4,000, then their total IRA contribution is limited to this lesser amount. Rollovers into IRAs are not included in the above limitations.

Comparing Regular IRAs with Roth IRAs

Over a period of years, Roth IRAs have a small advantage over regular IRAs, assuming your tax rate remains the same. This is best seen by considering the following example.

Example 1

You have $2,000 in 2001 that you plan to invest in an IRA for 25 years and then withdraw the money. We assume you earn 7% on the invested funds. We also assume you are in the 28% tax bracket throughout this period.

Case 1. You invest the $2,000 in a Roth IRA. Over a 25-year period with a 7% annual return, the $2,000 grows to $10,854. You withdraw this amount with no tax due because it satisfied the tax-free withdrawal rules for Roth IRAs.

Case 2. You invest the $2,000 in a regular IRA. Because you deduct this $2,000 at your 28% tax rate, you save $2,000 × 28% = $560 in taxes. In effect, this gives you an extra $560 that you invest outside the IRA at the same 7% rate. (However, this 7% investment rate is reduced by taxes each year.) At the end of the 25 years, this $560 has grown to $1,914. At this time, you withdraw the $10,854 from your IRA and pay taxes of $10,854 × 28% = $3,039, leaving you with a net $10,854 – $3,039 = $7,815 from the IRA. Thus, the total you have after 25 years equals $1,914 + $7,815 = $9,729.

Conclusion. The Roth IRA gave you a net result of $10,854 after 25 years while the comparable figure for the regular IRA was $9,729. This means that the Roth IRA yielded 11.6% more than the regular IRA. If a 10- (instead of 25-) year holding period is assumed, the 11.6% Roth IRA advantage computed above becomes 5.0%. For a 9%-yield assumption (instead of 7%), the Roth advantage becomes 14.2% over 25 years and 6.2% over ten years. If you can't save and invest the tax savings from the deductible IRA for the 25 years, then the Roth advantage becomes much greater.

In the above example, it was assumed that your tax rate remained at 28% when it came time to withdraw your money. If you anticipate being in a lower bracket at retirement, then this generally negates the financial advantage of a Roth IRA, because less tax will be taken out from the regular IRA. However, while many advisors assume a lowering of tax bracket after retirement, this may not happen. The income from retirement plans, social security payments, investment earnings, etc., often puts seniors into the same tax bracket they were in before retirement.

There are several advantages of Roth IRAs over regular IRAs that do not center around the amounts received in later years. (These are all discussed in more detail elsewhere in this Section 2.) First, far more people are eligible to contribute to Roth IRAs than to regular IRAs. Second, there are no forced withdrawals from Roth IRAs as there are from regular IRAs at age 70½. And third, you can always withdraw without penalty your contributions from a Roth IRA, but not generally from a regular IRA if you are under age 59½.

Rollovers from Regular IRAs into Roth IRAs

You may roll over all or part of a regular IRA into a Roth IRA, provided your AGI is not more than $100,000 for the year of the rollover. Married persons filing separately who have not lived apart all year cannot make such a rollover. (If you wish to roll over all the funds in a regular IRA, you may be able to have the institution sponsoring the regular IRA officially convert it into a Roth IRA, without any movement of money.) Rollovers do not fall under the annual limitation applying to ordinary contributions to IRAs. As discussed in the next paragraph, these rollovers are **not** treated like the tax-free rollover of funds from one regular IRA to another regular IRA, as discussed in Section 2A.

When you roll over funds from a regular IRA into a Roth IRA, you must pay tax on these funds as if they were distributed to you from the regular IRA instead of being rolled over. (The $100,000 AGI limitation described in the preceding paragraph is computed without regard to amounts rolled into a Roth IRA.) However, the extra 10% penalty tax on IRA withdrawals made before age 59½ does not apply when the amount withdrawn is rolled into a Roth IRA. The most economic advantage is gained by using non-IRA dollars to pay the tax and allow the full amount of the IRA to be rolled over.

There was a special break if a rollover was made in 1998. In this case, the tax due on the funds rolled out of the regular IRA could be spread out evenly over the 4-year period 1998-2001, with no interest due. The 2001 tax return is the fourth year of this break.

Is Rolling Over a Regular IRA into a Roth IRA a Good Idea?

If you have money in a regular IRA, should you roll it into a Roth IRA? The same considerations apply here as in the comparison between regular IRAs and Roth IRAs discussed earlier. Consider the following example, using the same calculations as in Example 1.

Example 2

You have a regular IRA with current balance of $2,000. You plan to keep this money tax-sheltered until 25 years from now when it will be withdrawn. We assume you earn 7% on invested funds and are in the 28% tax bracket throughout this period.

Case 1. You roll over your $2,000 regular IRA into a Roth IRA. *You pay an additional $560 out-of-pocket (28% × $2,000) to cover the tax due when such a rollover is made. Just as in Example 1, Case 1, the $2,000 grows to $10,854 in 25 years, which you withdraw without any tax due.*

Case 2. You leave the $2,000 in your regular IRA. *To make this comparable with Case 1, we assume you take $560 out-of-pocket and invest it outside the IRA at the same 7% interest rate. After 25 years, you are in the exact same situation as in Example 1. That is, your $560 investment has grown to $1,914 and your IRA has grown to $10,854, which is worth $7,815 after taxes are paid upon withdrawal. In total, you have $1,914 + $7,815 = $9,729.*

Conclusion. *As in Example 1, Case 1 produces a financial advantage of 11.6% over Case 2. That is, under the assumptions given above, rolling over your regular IRA into a Roth IRA improves your investment result by 11.6%. If you can't save and invest the tax savings from the deductible IRA for 25 years, the Roth advantage becomes much greater.*

The above example only illustrates the financial advantage a rollover can yield under the assumption your tax rate remains constant. As discussed after Example 1, a different situation applies if this is not the case. The comments after Example 1 regarding non-financial advantages also apply when considering if a rollover of a regular IRA into a Roth IRA is to your advantage. Also, if you experience a year in which your tax bracket is lower than normal, then making a rollover that year is a good idea, because the rollover will be taxed at a lower rate. You can also gain a spread of the tax over a number of years by rolling a percentage of your IRA to a Roth each year.

IRA Contribution Based on Alimony Payments

A special rule applies to alimony payments. As long as these payments qualify as alimony [see the *Divorce & Separation* chapter], taxable to the recipient, they can be considered the same as *earned income* for purposes of IRA rules. The person paying the alimony still gets to make his normal IRA contribution based on his income.

Custodial Fees

Many institutions charge a set-up fee or an annual maintenance fee. If these fees are separately billed, they can be deducted in addition to the maximum allowable IRA contribution which you make. For example, suppose you are eligible to make a $2,000 deductible IRA contribution with an institution charging a $25 custodial fee.

You could pay the institution $2,000 for the IRA contribution, which you deduct on line 23 of Form 1040, plus the $25 fee that you deduct as a miscellaneous deduction on Schedule A. You should pay the fee with a separate check so you're not accidentally credited with an excess contribution.

However, you can't separately deduct brokerage commissions connected with the purchase and sale of securities in your IRA.

What Kinds of IRA Plans Are Available?

Most financial institutions have set up IRA plans in which you can invest your money. The following is a general discussion of the types of plans being offered by different institutions.

Banks

Generally, IRAs managed by *banks* place your money into a certificate of deposit. Most of these institutions give you a choice of several types of certificates. The choice will usually include both fixed-rate certificates and variable-rate certificates. The rate on a *fixed-rate certificate* is set at the time of purchase and remains the same during the entire certificate period. The rate on a *variable-rate certificate* is adjusted periodically, usually once a month, based on a formula tied to the going rate on Treasury bills or other standard. Some institutions set a floor below which the interest on a variable-rate certificate cannot fall. This can be a valuable feature if short-term interest rates drop a significant amount.

Each institution is free to set its own interest rate according to any method it chooses and to select which kinds of certificates it will offer. This means that you will have to shop among your local banks and savings institutions if you want to get the best deal. When you inquire about the interest rate being offered, be sure to ask for the **effective annual yield.** This takes into account the effect of the compounding method used by the institution, e.g. daily, monthly, etc., and therefore is an accurate standard of comparison. Also, be sure to inquire whether money can be added to an existing account and whether there are any fees for opening or maintaining an account.

Many institutions allow you to add funds to an existing IRA account, with the maturity date remaining the same. This is a particularly useful feature because it avoids the unwieldy situation of having numerous IRA accounts, each with a separate maturity date.

A number of institutions allow additional funds to be added at the original interest rate, regardless of rates being paid on new IRA accounts. This can be a valuable feature if interest rates fall.

IRA accounts with a bank are backed by the same Federal Deposit Insurance applying to regular accounts. The minimum amount that can be invested varies among institutions from as little as $1 to as much as $1000 or more. Most banks do not charge a fee to open or maintain an IRA account. Most other investments offered through the bank's brokerage service are not FDIC insured.

Like regular certificates of deposit, there is generally an interest penalty if funds are withdrawn prior to maturity. However, an institution may waive the penalty if funds are withdrawn early from a certificate of deposit at age 59 1/2 or thereafter or upon death or disability. A majority of institutions (but not all) will make such a waiver as a general policy.

If you receive a promotional item such as a toaster or free checking account when you deposit money into an IRA, you need not worry. The IRS had been claiming that the receipt of such items could be considered as "prohibited transactions" causing a penalty tax to be assessed. But in 1990, the IRS announced that it would find such promotional items acceptable and would not assess any penalty. This assumes that the promotional items are reasonable in value and the interest rate paid on the IRA account is within normal range. [IRS Announcement 90-1]

Mutual Funds

Nearly every money-market or other mutual fund can be used as an IRA by filling out the appropriate form with the fund's sponsor. The typical minimum investment to open an IRA with a mutual fund is $500, although some have lower minimums. There is generally an annual custodial fee of about $10 charged by the mutual fund for managing your IRA.

There are mutual funds that concentrate on virtually any type of investment, e.g., long-term bonds, growth stocks, money-market instruments, etc. If you invest in a no-load mutual fund managed by one of the major fund institutions, you can switch money from one type of fund to another just by making a toll-free telephone call. See Sections 4-6 of the *Investing Your Money* chapter for further information on investing in mutual funds.

Mutual funds that concentrate on bonds and other securities issued by the U.S. Government have a slight disadvantage when held by an IRA. The interest on these securities is exempt from state income tax, and presumably the interest rate is a bit smaller because of this advantage. Because this exemption is wasted by the tax-exempt IRA, an alternate fully-taxable investment might be preferable. The same applies to U.S. government securities held directly in a self-directed IRA. Tax-exempt and tax-deferred investments should not be placed in an IRA or other retirement account because the earnings become taxable when withdrawn.

Stockbrokers

Most stockbrokers offer *self-directed IRA accounts*. These are used like ordinary brokerage accounts to buy stocks, bonds, etc. You can also make more esoteric purchases such as limited partnerships in real estate or oil drilling ventures. You instruct your broker which securities to buy and sell with the money in your account. There are usually fees connected with self-directed IRA accounts. These vary widely from one brokerage house to another, but a typical fee structure might be a one-time $50 set-up charge plus an annual $50 maintenance charge. In addition, the usual brokerage commissions would apply.

Because of the custodial fees and commission charges, self-directed plans are not suitable for most individuals with less than $5000 in an IRA. Unless they have a particular investment strategy in mind, they are better off with an IRA managed by a bank, savings institution, or a no-load mutual fund.

In addition to self-directed accounts, many stockbrokers and banks offer IRAs which place money into mutual funds. The custodial fees may be lower for this type of account than for a self-directed account. However, most of the mutual funds used by stockbrokers are *load funds* which impose a sales charge of up to 7.5%. If you want to invest in a mutual fund, you would be better off with a no-load fund offered directly by the sponsoring organization, because no sales fee is imposed.

Insurance Companies

Insurance companies offer annuity plans into which you can place your IRA money. Many of these plans offer a choice of several investments, including money-market or other mutual funds. Other plans may guarantee a certain rate of return for a short period of time but after that, the rate could drop substantially.

Insurance company IRAs usually have significant fees associated with their use. These fees can include an "up-front" sales charge or a "back-loaded" fee for withdrawing money within 7-10 years after investment. Or, the "fee" could take the form of a lower interest rate or lower payout calculation than would be justified by market conditions or actuarial calculations. Because of the fees that are charged by insurance company IRAs, most individuals will be better off with an IRA run by a bank or mutual fund.

Gold and Silver Coins

Under prior law, IRA contributions could not be invested in *collectibles* such as art, coins, antiques, stamps, etc. But now, there is an exception for certain U.S. minted gold and silver coins and for certain coins issued under the laws of individual states. These coins can be purchased for an IRA, provided they are held for you by a trustee such as a broker, banker, etc.

If you are planning on holding coins over a long period of time, it may not be worthwhile to hold them as part of your IRA portfolio. Since coins yield no income until they are sold, there is no need to hold them in a tax-deferred plan. On the other hand, if you think you will buy and sell your coins over time, the ability to keep capital gains tax-deferred will be of value.

SECTION 3:
SELF-EMPLOYED RETIREMENT PLANS

A self-employed retirement plan (formerly called a Keogh plan) is a tax-sheltered retirement plan that can be used to shelter self-employment income from tax. Self-employment income includes earnings resulting from personal services that are not employee wages (i.e., the type from which social security is withheld).

This might include income from consulting, royalties from writing a book, fees for editing or reviewing, sales from an invention, income from tutoring, honorariums for lecturing, commissions from real estate sales, director's fees, or any other income earned from a side business or as a private contractor. Sometimes an employee can rearrange his agreement with a current employer so as to become a self-employed private contractor. Self-employment income does not include investment income such as interest and dividends.

Each year, you can contribute a certain portion of your self-employment income (as reported on Schedule C or Schedule C-EZ) into your plan. These contributed amounts are tax deductible in the year of contribution. You get this benefit even if you claim the standard deduction. Furthermore, no tax is paid on the investment income as it is earned by the amounts you contribute. Only when money is withdrawn from the plan is any tax paid.

Note that you do not have to specifically withhold your contributions from the earnings you receive. You can contribute any funds you have to a plan within the maximum limitations described below. For example, you can make a contribution by taking money out of a savings account and placing it in your plan. You still get a tax deduction for the amount shifted to the plan and furthermore, your savings are now shielded by the umbrella of a tax-sheltered plan.

The basic way self-employed plans work is the same as for regular IRAs. And the same types of plans can be set up for a self-employed plan as for an IRA as discussed in Section 2. The chief differences between self-employed plans and regular IRAs are the eligibility requirements and contribution limitations. In addition, there is a special averaging rule that generally applies to lower the tax on lump-sum distributions from self-employed plans, but not from IRAs [see Section 2 of the *Retirement Plans* chapter]. Also, if your self-employment activity requires you to hire other employees who work either more hours than you or at least one thousand hours per year, you may have to make contributions to your plan on their behalf.

How Much Can Be Contributed?

The maximum that can be contributed to a self-employed plan is 20% of self-employment income received during the year up to a maximum contribution of $30,000. For example, if self-employment income totals $10,000, the maximum contribution is 20% × $10,000 = $2,000. The 20% figure applies to net self-employment earnings. That is, business expenses are subtracted from income before multiplying by 20%.

The contribution limit for defined contribution plans has increased from $35,000 to $40,000. In addition, you will now be able to deduct 100% of compensation rather than 25%. This applies to employment other than educational institutions and will be effective beginning in 2002.

The 20% limit applies in full only to those who owe no social security tax. Others get to claim one-half of the social security tax paid on their self-employment income as a special deduction on Line 26 of Form 1040. Self-employment earnings must be reduced by this deduction before applying the 20% factor to determine the self-employed plan deduction.

Example

You have self-employment earnings of $10,000 in addition to salary from your regular job of $40,000. Your total earnings of $50,000 is less than the basic social security ceiling. This means the entire amount of your self-employment earnings will be subject to the maximum social security rate on Schedule SE, $10,000 × .9235 × 15.3% = $1,413. One-half of this amount is allowed as an adjustment to income on Line 27 of Form 1040, 1/2 × $1,413 = $707. [The .9235 factor is a technical adjustment that appears on Schedule SE to take into account this adjustment to income.]

Your maximum self employed plan contribution is computed as follows:

Net self-employment earnings (Schedule C, line 31) $10,000

Less: social security adjustment (Form 1040, line 26)...................... − 707

$9,293

Maximum self-employed plan rate × 20%

Maximum self-employed plan contribution $1,859

In the above example, the maximum contribution was $1,859, or 18.59% of the $10,000 self-employment earnings. This will be true in general. That is, for anyone whose total 2001 earnings do not exceed $80,400, the maximum plan contribution is 18.59% of self-employment earnings. If total income exceeds $80,400, this percentage as computed above will be between 18.59% and 20%.

There is a worksheet in Publication 560, available from the IRS, that you can use for computing your maximum allowable plan contribution.

The above limits apply to regular self-employed plans. There is a special type of plan, called a *defined benefit plan,* to which far more can be contributed — in many cases, **up to 100% of a person's net self-employment earnings.** This type of plan is discussed later in this section.

The above limitations are maximum levels of contribution. You may contribute less than these maximums if you choose. Furthermore, you do not have to be consistent from year to year. You might contribute differing amounts in different years or none at all.

In order to make a plan contribution for the 2001 tax year, the plan must be in existence on December 31, 2001. If your plan has been established by December 31, you have until April 15 of the following year to make contributions. If you qualify for an extension of time to file your tax return [see Chapter 1], you have until the extended due date to make a contribution. Of course, the earlier you make a contribution, the sooner your funds are put to work earning tax-deferred income.

Those with incomes from both a regular job and an outside business activity should apportion their expenses judiciously if they want to make full use of the plan limitations. Swing items, such as professional books, may best be taken as a miscellaneous employee deduction connected with the regular job rather than as a business expense against self-employment income. (This assumes that the 2% of AGI floor discussed in the *Miscellaneous Deductions* chapter has already been exceeded.) This will keep net self-employment income as high as possible, maximizing the contributions that can be made to a self-employed retirement plan. (However, if extra social security tax is triggered by an increase in self-employment income, this may not be the best strategy.)

What if You Missed the December 31 Deadline?

If you missed the December 31, 2001 deadline for opening a plan to shelter your 2001 earnings, all is not lost. There is another type of plan, called a SEP (simplified employee pension) which is similar to a self-employed plan but which can be opened up until April 15, 2002 (or extended filing date of your tax return). SEPs were designed to be simplified pension systems for small businesses with more than one employee but can be used by individual self-employed persons as well. Ordinarily, a self-employed plan is preferable to a SEP because the contribution limitations are more generous and the lump-sum averaging privilege could apply. However, in the case where the self-employed plan deadline is missed, a SEP can be the remedy. There is no continuing funding requirement for a SEP, and a self-employed plan can be set up starting the next year. Most banks, mutual funds, etc., can set up a SEP for you upon request.

How Is a Regular Self-Employed Plan Established?

The simplest procedure is to choose a mutual fund, bank, or savings institution of your choice. They will have the appropriate forms you need to establish your plan. All investment income will then be automatically reinvested in the mutual fund, savings account, etc. Insurance companies also sell plans that combine investment features with insurance features.

When you set up your self-employed plan, you will probably be asked to specify what percentage of self-employment income you wish to contribute. Self-employed plans that specify such a percentage are sometimes called *money-purchase* plans. If in a later year, you wish to change the percentage, you can make a simple "amendment," specifying the new percentage. However, if you do not want to contribute more than about 12% of your net self-employment income, you can set up your plan as a *profit-sharing* plan. Profit-sharing plans let you contribute any amount you wish each year within the legal limits, without specifying a particular percentage.

To achieve maximum flexibility without the need for making any "amendments," some persons set up both types of plans, one *money-purchase* plan and one *profit-sharing* plan. This type of arrangement can specify that each year, 8% of net self-employment income be contributed to the money-purchase plan and that any desired amount, not causing the overall limit (discussed earlier in this Section) to be exceeded, be contributed to the profit-sharing plan. An individual with this arrangement can then contribute any amount between 8% and the upper limit (about 18.59%–20%) of net self-employment income each year, without any amendment provision coming into play. After 2001, it will be possible to have only a profit-sharing plan that will be able to accept the maximum allowable contribution.

Self-employed plans set up with banks or savings institutions generally invest money in higher-paying certificates of deposit rather than in passbook accounts. With most institutions, the waiting period before such certificates can be cashed in does not apply when money is withdrawn after an individual is age 59 1/2 or over.

Individuals should shop around before choosing a plan. There are differences between plans set up with savings institutions or banks. Some require an annual service charge while others do not. And the top interest rate can vary depending upon the manner in which the interest is compounded. According to the IRS, you can have your plan funds transferred from one institution to another without incurring any tax penalty.

It is also possible to set up a plan in such a way that you control the investment of the funds. One way to maintain indirect control is to set up a *self-directed* plan with a bank or stockbroker. The bank or stockbroker acts as custodian and agrees to invest the funds as you direct. You can deduct any custodial fees you pay as a separate business expense in addition to the actual contributions to the plan which you make.

At one time, a Form 5500 or 5500-EZ had to be filed with the IRS each year the plan was in force. But the IRS has been steadily reducing this requirement. Now, plans covering only one person do not have to file any form as long as the assets in the plan do not exceed $100,000. (If your plan does not meet this condition, check with the institution managing your plan to give you information for filing the proper form.) However, a Form 5500 or Form 5500-EZ does need to be filed for the year a plan is terminated.

Defined Benefit Plans

Because of a change in the law a few years ago, a tremendous opportunity has become available to those with self-employment income. Instead of being bound by the limitations on a regular self-employed plan as described above, they can set up a more generous *defined benefit plan.*

Defined benefit plans, in their present form, came into being after a new "pension parity" law went into effect. Congress decided that persons with self-employment income should be placed on a par with individuals operating under the shell of a corporation (e.g., physicians who list the initials P.A. or P.C. after their name). Because the laws for corporations allow for the funding of such generous pensions, those with even a modest amount of self-employment income have now been handed this big tax break.

Defined benefit plans work like other tax-sheltered plans, such as IRAs, tax-sheltered annuities, or regular self-employed plans. You get a full deduction on your tax return for any contributions (not exceeding the self-employment income of that year) made to your plan. And the money in your plan is invested, with all interest, dividends, etc. compounding entirely exempt from tax until withdrawn from the plan. Also, the same special averaging break that applies to lump sum distributions from regular self-employed plans may apply to your defined benefit plan as well.

The chief advantage of defined benefit plans is that far more can be contributed (and deducted) than to a regular self-employed plan. The exact amount is calculated by an enrolled actuary and is based on a person's age, sex, marital status, and self-employment earnings. (As with regular self-employed plans, *self-employment earnings* here means *net self-employment earnings* after related business expenses have been subtracted.) As an illustration, here's a rough estimate of the maximum contribution range for a married man if the plan is set up the right way:

Age	Maximum Deductible Contributions as a Percentage of Self-Employment Earnings
40	40% — 70%
45	50% — 75%
50	55% — 100%
55	55% — 100%

The contribution limit for defined contribution plans has increased from $140,000 to $160,000 and the salary that can be used to determine the contribution was increased from $170,000 to $200,000 by the 2001 Tax Reduction Act. This also applies to compensation from employment other than educational institutions and is effective beginning in 2002.

A history of prior self-employment earnings will place the maximum allowable contribution in the upper end of the range in the table above, in many cases 100% of self-employment earnings. For example, suppose a 50-year old married man anticipates self-employment earnings of $10,000 during 2001. Let's say he had self-employment earnings from 1995-2000 which averaged $4,000 or more per year. In such a case, he could generally contribute (and deduct) any amount up to 100% of these earnings, namely $10,000.

Under a regular self-employed plan, the above individual would be limited to a contribution of no more than 20% × $10,000 = $2,000. Thus, the defined benefit plan in this case permits a deduction of 5 times as much as a regular self-employed plan.

A person with no self-employment earnings prior to 2001 might be restricted to the lower percentage figure in the table for his age. However, this percentage can be boosted — perhaps up to 100% — if the person "employs his spouse" in the business activity. Any legitimate employee activity will do, e.g., clerical work, typing, answering business calls, etc., as long as wages (subject to social security tax) are actually paid to the spouse. Because of a special provision in the law for employees, even a small wage paid to a spouse can increase the percentage of earnings that can be contributed to the plan. (Employing a spouse to perform some business activities can have another beneficial effect. This might enable you to set up a plan to pay all medical and dental expenses of your employee-spouse and family, including yourself. In this way, you get a full medical deduction for your family's medical expenses, with no initial 7.5% of adjusted gross income subtraction. [See the *Outside Business Activity* chapter for further details.])

The figures in the above table represent the **maximum amounts** that can be contributed, with an individual's exact amount to be determined by an actuary. With a properly structured plan, you have the option of making any contribution amount you choose as long as it doesn't exceed the maximum allowable and is not below the minimum needed to meet funding standards. Each succeeding year, you can contribute any portion of your self-employment income you choose that year, as long as the maximum contribution level is not exceeded. If there are contributions to a tax-sheltered annuity or other self-employed plan, these may, in certain circumstances, lower the contributions you are permitted to make to your defined benefit plan.

An important extra benefit is that you can serve as manager of your defined benefit plan, in complete charge of all the money in your plan. You directly control the investments in and disbursements from the plan. On the other hand, you may prefer to delegate investment responsibility to a professional investment advisor, stockbroker, etc. The choice depends upon you.

To take advantage of a defined benefit plan to shelter 2001 earnings, you must set up your plan before the end of 2001. (However, the earlier in the year you set up such a plan, the better.) These plans are more complicated to set up and run than regular self-employed plans because an actuary must be involved in making the appropriate calculations and sending in the appropriate certification forms each year to the IRS. Fees for such services are tax-deductible as a business expense.

How Do You Set Up a Defined Benefit Self-Employed Plan?

To get further information on how to set up a defined benefit plan, write to *Academic Information Service, Inc.,* at the address on the back cover of this book with the envelope marked *Attention: David Harry.* This information will include the name of an actuarial firm to whom we have been referring readers. If you wish, this firm can handle all the details of setting up and maintaining your plan.

When May Funds Be Withdrawn?

You may start withdrawing money from your plan anytime after the age of 59 1/2. However, you must begin withdrawing money by April 1 of the year following the year in which you reach age 70 1/2. It is possible to contribute to a plan after age 70 1/2 even though, as required, you are withdrawing funds at the same time.

If you turn 70 1/2 during 2001, you must make your initial withdrawal for the 2001 tax year by April 1, 2002. This distribution is taxable in the year received. Distributions for each future year must be made by December 31 of that year. In particular, your distribution for the 2002 tax year must be made by December 31, 2002. This means that distributions for both 2001 and 2002, if received in 2002, are taxed in the same year. If this bunching would shift you into a higher tax bracket, then you should advance the 2001 distribution so it's received before December 31, 2001. That way, it will be reported as income on your 2001 tax return instead of on your 2002 tax return.

If you withdraw penalty funds prior to age 59 1/2, such funds are taxed along with your other income that year. In addition, an extra 10% tax is imposed on the amount of the early withdrawal, except in the case of death or disability. The 10% penalty tax will be waived if either (i) the withdrawal is used to pay medical expenses in excess of 7.5% of your adjusted gross income, (ii) the distribution is made after you stopped working and is part of a series of substantially equal periodic payments intended to extend over your lifetime or the joint lives of you and your spouse, or (iii) you have retired after reaching age 55.

As a general rule of thumb, even if you have to pay the extra 10% tax prior to age 59 1/2, the tax advantage of sheltering your savings under a plan puts you ahead if the funds withdrawn were in the plan for 7 years or more.

How Are the Proceeds of Your Plan Taxed?

You can take your money out of a plan in the form of a lump-sum distribution. Lump-sum settlements can receive favorable tax treatment provided that you have been a plan participant for at least 5 tax years before the tax year of the distribution and provided you were 50 years of age or older on January 1, 1986.

This favorable tax treatment is provided by a special averaging rule that applies to most or all of the lump-sum distribution. For example, this rule applied to $100,000 of distribution yields a tax rate of about 15%. Furthermore, the tax rate is totally independent of your other taxable income. This averaging rule is described in Section 2 of the *Retirement Plans* chapter.

Except in the case of death or disability, you can use the averaging rule for a plan you maintain only after reaching age 59 1/2 and then can use it only once. If you withdraw any money from your plan prior to age 59 1/2, this might destroy your right to use averaging at a later time when you otherwise would qualify [IRS Private Letter Ruling 7726047]. Also, if you have made contributions to a plan prior to 1974, special capital gains rules may apply to a portion of the lump-sum distribution [see the *Retirement Plans* chapter].

You do not need to take a lump-sum settlement. It is often advantageous to elect to receive the distribution over one of the following periods:

(a) your lifetime;

(b) the joint lifetime of you and your spouse;

(c) a period not extending beyond your life expectancy; *or*

(d) a period not extending beyond the joint life expectancies of you and your spouse.

The advantage of receiving the distribution over an extended period of time, such as the joint life expectancy of you and your spouse, is that the balance of the funds remains in the plan, compounding investment income entirely tax-deferred. The distributions you take out from the plan this way are taxed as ordinary income.

Can You Combine a Self-Employed Plan with Other Plans?

Yes. You can contribute to a self-employed plan even if you participate in some other type of retirement plan, IRA, or tax-sheltered annuity. A contribution to any of these plans cannot exceed the individual limit on that plan. Of course, your contributions to the self-employed plan are based only on your self-employment income. And your combined contributions to an IRA and a self-employed plan cannot exceed your earned income.

Comparing Self-Employed Plans with IRAs

If an individual with self-employment income does not wish to contribute the maximum amounts to both a regular individual self-employed plan and an IRA, he will have to make a choice. Which is better? Operationally, there is little difference — the usual investment choices can be made with either type of plan. And the requirement to begin distributions between ages 59 ½ and 70 ½ applies to both types of plans. However, there is one distinguishing feature, namely the special lump-sum averaging rule described above. This feature applies to self-employed plans but not to IRAs. Because of this, a self-employed plan is generally preferable to an IRA.

Where Do You Deduct Payments to Your Self-Employed Plan?

Payments on your behalf to your self-employed plan are deducted on line 29 of Form 1040 as an *Adjustment to Income*. Contributions made on behalf of any employees covered under your plan are deducted on line 19 of Schedule C or line 2 of Schedule C-EZ.

SECTION 4:
TAX-SHELTERED ANNUITIES

A *tax-sheltered annuity* is a special type of plan available only to employees of educational institutions and certain other non-profit organizations. (Tax sheltered annuities are often called *"403(b) plans"* after the Tax Code section under which they are authorized.) Most of these institutions maintain a list of one or more of these plans which are available to their employees. Generally, all employees are eligible to participate, including administrators, librarians, clerical help, etc. In fact, under nondiscrimination rules, tax-sheltered annuity plans must be available to employees generally (except students working less than 20 hours per week), rather than just to higher paid employees.

Employees of state or local departments of education are also eligible unless they are holding a public office such as a trustee or board of education member. For example, the IRS has ruled that an electrical engineer qualified for a tax-sheltered annuity because he worked for a state Department of Education. [IRS Private Letter Ruling 8137067]

The actual rule is that only an employer's contribution to such a plan is not taxable. However, the usual policy is to permit an employee to reduce her current or next year's salary by an amount equal to that being contributed to the annuity plan.

Thus the employer incurs no cost but the employee may still take advantage of the tax-saving feature of the plan.

For example, suppose a teacher's annual salary is $45,000 and she wishes to contribute $1,000 toward the purchase of an annuity. She would agree with her school to take a reduction of $1,000 in salary. Her annual salary would then officially be $44,000 and her school would contribute $1,000 toward the purchase of an annuity. The teacher would pay tax based on her $44,000 salary but not on the amount contributed to her annuity until she retired and started receiving annuity payments.

Note that an institution may have a regular retirement plan and still provide its employees the opportunity to participate in tax-sheltered annuities.

In order to get a tax break for contributions to a tax-sheltered annuity, the appropriate *reduction-in-salary* agreement must be signed prior to the date compensation is available to the employee. Failure to sign the appropriate form can ruin the entire arrangement. This was learned the hard way by a New Jersey teacher in a recent court case.

The teacher authorized her employer to withhold part of her salary and place it into a tax-sheltered annuity. But she failed to sign the appropriate reduction-in-salary agreement. This meant that the contributions to the annuity plan were not technically made from her employer's funds, but rather from her funds. The court was sympathetic but ruled against the teacher as a matter of law. As the written court opinion stated,

> *"The Court recognizes that the myriad of statutory and administrative provisions may be confusing. Nevertheless, plaintiff did not comply with the base provision that the contributions be made 'by' the employer."* [Bulletin vs U.S., 38 AFTR 2nd 76-5712]

There is a credit of up to $1,000 for contributions to certain pension arrangements including an annuity purchased by an educational institution. The credit is phased out for income over $15,000 for single filers, $22,500 for heads of households and $30,000 for joint filers. The credit begins in 2002 and ends in 2006 per the 2001 Tax Reduction Act.

Making Changes in Midyear

Prior to 1996, a signed reduction-in-salary agreement for a given year could not be altered during the year without tax consequence, unless you terminated it altogether. After 1995, this restriction was eliminated and in fact multiple reduction-in-salary agreements can be used.

Example

Professor Barnes is paid $6,000 per month by the college where he works. At the beginning or sometime later in the year, he enters into a 10% salary reduction agreement yielding a monthly tax-sheltered annuity contribution of $600. Later in the year, he signs a new salary reduction agreement increasing his 10% contribution to 12%, an additional monthly contribution of 2% × $6,000 = $120.

Under prior law, Professor Barnes would owe tax on the additional $120 monthly contributions because of the midyear change in his original salary reduction agreement. But now, no such extra tax is due. Professor Barnes can exclude all the contributions made during the year to his tax-sheltered annuity.

Withdrawals from Tax-Sheltered Annuities

Previous law did not require there to be any restrictions on when you were first allowed to withdraw funds from a tax-sheltered annuity. However, now an extra 10% penalty tax applies to withdrawals made from a tax-sheltered annuity prior to the date an individual reaches age 59 1/2, dies, or becomes disabled. The 10% penalty tax will be waived if either:

(i)   the withdrawal is used to pay medical expenses in excess of 7.5% of adjusted gross income;

(ii) the individual has retired from his job after reaching age 55;

(iii) the distribution is part of a series of substantially equal periodic payments intended to extend over the life of the employee or the joint lives of the employee and a beneficiary;

(iv) the distribution is part of a divorce settlement under a qualified Domestic Relations Order; or

(v)   the distribution is used to settle an IRS levy under Internal Revenue Code, Section 6331.

The exception in (iii) can be used to withdraw amounts before age 59 1/2 and escape the 10% penalty tax. For example, an individual could begin receiving his annuity payments at age 50. As long as the distribution method provides for substantially equal lifetime payments as described in (iii), the 10% penalty tax does not apply.

Furthermore, the individual can alter the distribution agreement after reaching age 59 1/2 as long as no change is made in the first 5 years other than by reason of death or disability. For example, an individual can start receiving payments at age 50 and alter or stop the payments after reaching age 59 1/2. Or, he could start receiving payments at age 57, continuing for 5 years until he reached 62. In either case, the 10% penalty tax is waived. (However, observe the rules below for contributions and earnings after 1988 under which the ability to receive distributions prior to age 59 1/2 is restricted.)

There is an exemption from the 10% penalty tax for individuals who, as of March 1, 1986, had separated from employment and elected to start receiving a scheduled series of specified benefit payments.

There is also a mandatory distribution rule that applies to benefits accruing in 1987 or later years. Distributions of such benefits from a tax-sheltered annuity must start by April 1 of the year following the year in which you reached age 70 1/2. (However, if you are still working for the same employer who set up the plan, you can wait to start withdrawals until you stop working for that employer.) This mandatory distribution rule does not apply to benefits accrued before 1987. (However, there may be a mandatory distribution requirement imposed by the particular tax-sheltered annuity plan to which you have contributed.)

If you have more than one tax-sheltered annuity, then annual distributions need not be made out of each separate annuity. You can determine the total amount required to be distributed that year from all your tax-sheltered annuities under the basic rules described later in this section and withdraw this amount out of just one (or more) of the tax-sheltered annuities as you choose [IRS Notice 88-38].

There is a special restriction on the ability to withdraw funds from a tax-sheltered annuity, with or without the 10% penalty. Specifically, withdrawals from tax-sheltered annuities can be made only after an employee leaves his job, attains age 59 1/2, becomes disabled, dies, or encounters *financial hardship*. However, this restriction only applies to voluntary contributions (under a reduction-in-salary arrangement) made after 1988 and to earnings both on those contributions and on amounts held as of December 31, 1988. Hardship withdrawals will be restricted to contributions invested in the annuity under a reduction-in-salary agreement, excluding any earnings earned by the investments. An employee will be considered to encounter a *financial hardship* only to the extent he has *"an immediate and heavy bona fide financial need and does not have other resources reasonably available to satisfy the need."*

Borrowing From Your Tax-Sheltered Annuity

There is a way to tap the funds in your tax-sheltered annuity early without running into the restrictions on withdrawals made before age 59 1/2. Namely, you may be able to borrow money from your tax-sheltered annuity account.

The IRS has specifically allowed tax-sheltered plans to offer loan privileges to its participants, subject to certain limitations on the amount and duration of the loan. The basic maximum loan amount is the lesser of $50,000 or 50% of the present value of the not-for-profit benefit under the plan. However, this limitation may be reduced by previous loan balances during the preceding 12 months. And the duration of the loan cannot exceed 5 years unless used to purchase the employee's personal residence.

Interest on loans secured by your elective deferral amounts in your tax-sheltered annuity plans is not deductible. This is the case even if the loan is used for normally deductible purposes, although interest to purchase a residence or make investments may be deductible [see the *Interest* chapter]. Congress did not want an employee to be able to earn tax-free interest on money in a tax-sheltered annuity plan at the same time he was deducting interest payments on amounts borrowed from the plan.

Note that the above information only describes possible loan rules permitted by the IRS. A given tax-sheltered annuity plan may or may not offer loan privileges to its participants. If you want to be able to borrow money from a tax-sheltered annuity, it may be necessary (if possible) to transfer your funds to an annuity plan which in fact does offer these privileges.

What Types of Tax-Sheltered Annuity Plans Are Available?

Many different types of plans exist. Most eligible non-profit institutions select several different plans that they make available to their employees. Some of them provide investment in fixed income securities such as bonds, and others provide investment in common stocks as well. Some plans require that you wait until retirement whereupon the amount accumulated in your account is used to purchase an annuity. Others allow you to withdraw the cash value of your account before retirement. This latter feature is attractive for those who wish to put aside money to be received in an otherwise low income year.

To get further information on the plans available to you, contact the personnel office where you work. They will have a list of those plans in which you can participate and either provide you with descriptive brochures or give you the addresses of where to write for these brochures. Be sure to obtain and read these brochures carefully. Different plans have different combinations of features. You will want to select the plan which best meets your own personal objectives.

Some institutions allow their employees to choose any commercially available plan. You can get a sampling of available plans by contacting a few of the large mutual fund organizations [see Section 5 of the *Investing Your Money* chapter for addresses and toll-free telephone numbers], writing to TIAA-CREF [see the discussion later in this Section], and contacting some major insurance companies.

When selecting which tax-sheltered annuity plan to invest in, be sure to examine the options available for the withdrawal of funds. Some plans allow more withdrawal opportunities than others. And some plans provide for a fixed annuity payout after retirement while others gear the payout to the performance of stocks or other securities in their portfolio. Also, different options may be offered governing the period during which payments are made, as well as different survivorship options under which payments continue to a beneficiary after the death of the individual.

It is possible to have part or all of your funds in one tax-sheltered annuity plan transferred to another plan with no tax consequence, provided the two plans permit such a transfer. The IRS has ruled that such a transfer can be made as long as the new plan has distribution restrictions as stringent as the original plan. The ability to have one's funds transferred from one tax-sheltered annuity into another applies not just to current employees, but to retirees and beneficiaries as well [Rev. Rul 90-24]. An individual who wishes to make such a transfer should contact his employer or the organization providing the tax-sheltered annuities to arrange the transfer without having any funds pass through his hands.

Choosing a Beneficiary

When you set up a tax-sheltered annuity, you will be asked to name a beneficiary in case you die before funds are distributed to you. The tax rules are the same as for beneficiaries of an IRA.

Rolling Over Your Tax-Sheltered Annuity into an IRA

There is one further option which some plans may provide, namely the right to receive the funds credited to an individual's account in a lump-sum payment. Due to a little known provision in the law, this could be the most beneficial option of all.

Distributions of part or all of the funds in your tax-sheltered annuity can be rolled over into a regular IRA. This is a special type of account set up with a mutual fund, savings institution, or brokerage house. The funds placed into a regular IRA continue to earn income entirely free from tax. Only when funds are withdrawn is income tax paid.

Rollovers from tax-sheltered annuities are governed by the same rules as rollovers from retirement plans, as described in Section 2A of this chapter. As discussed there, 20% of the rollover will be withheld unless the rolled-over funds are transferred directly to the IRA (for example, via a check made out directly to the trustee of the IRA). Distributions from a tax-sheltered annuity can also be rolled over into another tax-sheltered annuity, but not into any other type of retirement plan.

The advantage of an IRA over an annuity is the flexibility and individual control it provides. Your funds can be placed into virtually any type of investment you choose. Often, funds can earn a higher interest rate than would be credited to your account under a fixed annuity arrangement. And you can switch your funds from one type of investment to another as your goals change.

Governmental and educational institution plans will be treated the same as other pension plans for purposes of rollovers from IRAs or other pension plans beginning in 2002 per the 2001 Tax Reduction Act.

Finally, you can control the payout of funds from a regular IRA. Each year, you can withdraw any portion of the funds you choose. Or, you can leave the funds alone and let the tax-free income build up, subject to the restrictions discussed in Section 2A.

TIAA-CREF Supplemental Retirement Annuities

A supplemental retirement annuity (SRA) is a type of tax-sheltered annuity plan run by TIAA-CREF (Teachers Insurance and Annuity Association–College Retirement Equities Fund; address: 730 Third Avenue, New York, NY 10017-3206; www.tiaa-cref.org). An attractive feature of SRAs is the low annual fee charged by TIAA-CREF — about 1/4 of 1% of assets in your account. Note that your institution does not have to be part of the TIAA-CREF regular retirement program in order for you to purchase an SRA.

SRAs have the same general features as the regular TIAA-CREF plans. Currently, there are 8 choices you can make on how your money will be invested. See Section 3 of the *Retirement Plans* chapter for information concerning the investment choices, withdrawal privileges, and tax treatment of TIAA-CREF plans.

Unisex Mortality Tables

Because of a Court decision, TIAA-CREF will use a unisex mortality table to compute pensions for individuals retiring after May 1, 1980. This decreases benefits for men in some cases with a corresponding increase for women [see the discussion in the *Retirement Plans* chapter]. However, only those annuity payments which are an integral part of the plan are affected. If you receive the benefits in a lump sum that you use to purchase a commercial annuity, the Court ruling does not apply. Unless the law is changed, the commercial annuity can generally be based on mortality tables that are differentiated by sex.

Women benefit from plans based on unisex mortality tables if they are planning to select a single-life annuity at retirement [see the *Retirement Plans* chapter]. For example, TIAA-CREF, which will pay the same annuities to men and women per dollar invested, becomes more attractive than a plan that lets the individual select only a commercial annuity paying less to women than to men. For women, unisex annuities can also be more attractive than the do-it-yourself withdrawals provided by rolling over a tax-sheltered annuity into an IRA. This is because these annuities are based on a life-expectancy assumption which is shorter than that expected by the average woman.

Social Security Tax

Amounts contributed to a tax-sheltered annuity under a reduction-in-salary agreement are subject to social security tax. The social security tax is withheld from the employee and matched by an employer's contribution.

Contribution Limits for Tax-Sheltered Annuities

There are three basic limitations on how much can be contributed to a tax-sheltered annuity, the *elective deferral limitation,* the *annual limitation,* and the *overall limitation.*

The **elective deferral limitation** requires that the total voluntary contributions made by an individual to tax-sheltered annuities under a reduction-in-salary agreement cannot exceed $10,500 in 2001 ($11,000 in 2002 and increasing to $15,000 in 2006). The $10,500 limit in 2001 is reduced by deductible contributions made to a SEP [see Section 3] or by amounts deferred under a 401(k) deferred compensation plan [see Section 5].

The $10,500 limit in 2001 will be raised to as much as $13,500 (increasing to $18,000 by 2006) for individuals who have worked for their current employer for at least 15 years, provided their previous contributions to tax-sheltered annuities with their current employer averaged less than $5,000 per year. For such long-term employees, the $10,500 limit in 2001 is raised by the lesser of (i) $3,000, or (ii) the excess of $5,000 multiplied by the number of years of service with the current employer over the total voluntary contributions made in prior years to tax-sheltered annuities with that employer.

The extra amounts provided by this rule cannot total more than $15,000 over a lifetime. Thus, if a person voluntarily contributes $12,500 under this rule for each of

5 years, his lifetime maximum of $15,000 would be used up. His voluntary contributions for 2001 could then not exceed $10,500.

Example

Smith has worked for his current employer for 20 years. During each of the first 10 of these years, he made voluntary contributions of $3,000 to his tax-sheltered annuity, and during the last 10 years, $6,000 per year. His total voluntary contributions for these 20 years add up to (10 × $3,000) + (10 × $6,000) = $90,000. This is subtracted from 20 × $5,000 = $100,000 as required in (ii) in the above discussion: $100,000 − $90,000 = $10,000. Since this exceeds the $3,000 figure in (i), the maximum allowable voluntary contribution under the elective deferral limitation is $10,500 + $3,000 = $13,500.

The above $10,500 (or $13,500) limit applies only to *voluntary* contributions that you elect to have made to your tax-sheltered annuities. It does not apply, for example, to contributions that are a fixed percentage of compensation and are required to be made as a condition of employment.

In contrast, the *annual limitation* and the *overall limitation,* apply to the *total* contributions made during any one year, whether the contributions are voluntary or required. Thus, contributions that are required to be made to a pension plan set up under the tax-sheltered annuity rules (and thereby exempted from current tax) are included in computing the *annual limitation* and the *overall limitation,* but not included in the *elective deferral limitation.*

The **annual limitation** states that contributions in any given year cannot exceed 25% of your reduced salary. Your reduced salary is the amount you are paid after the annuity contribution is deducted from your original salary.

Example

Your annual salary is $40,000 before any contributions to tax-sheltered annuities are made. The annual limitation in this case would be $8,000. This yields a reduced salary of $40,000 − $8,000 = $32,000. Then $8,000 = 25% × $32,000, verifying that $8,000 is the annual limitation. (Observe that $8,000 is equal to 20% of the unreduced salary of $40,000; this same 20% would apply in general no matter what the actual salary figure.)

To determine if this year's contributions to your tax-sheltered annuity satisfy the **overall limitation** you perform the following steps:

(1) Subtract this year's contributions (voluntary and required) to your tax-sheltered annuities from your salary to obtain your *reduced salary.*

(2) Take 20% of your reduced salary and multiply this by the number of years you have worked for your current employer. (Count part-time work in proportion to the fraction of the full-time load you worked.)

(3) Under your current employer, add up the total of all amounts that have been contributed to your tax-sheltered annuity plus the amounts contributed by your employer to your regular retirement plan, including this year's contribution. Also, add any salary that your employer deferred under a Governmental deferred compensation plan.

(4) If (3) does not exceed (2), you have satisfied the overall limitation.

Example

You have worked for your current employer for 5 years. Your initial salary was $30,000 and you received a $2,000 raise in each of the succeeding years. In each of these years, your employer contributed 6% of your salary to your regular retirement plan. In addition, you arranged to have $4,000 of your salary contributed to a tax-sheltered annuity in each of the first 4 years. For the 5th year, the overall limitation restricts your tax-sheltered contribution to $5,900. This is verified according to the following computation.

Year	Salary	Employer's Contribution to Retirement Plan	Contribution to Tax-Sheltered Annuity	Reduced Salary
1	$30,000	$1,800	$4,000	$26,000
2	32,000	1,920	4,000	28,000
3	34,000	2,040	4,000	30,000
4	36,000	2,160	4,000	32,000
5	38,000	2,280	5,900	32,100
		$10,200	$21,900	

To verify that the $5,900 contribution in year 5 falls within the overall limit, note that $10,200 (Retirement Plan Contributions) + $21,900 (Annuity Contributions) = $32,100 does not exceed 20% × $32,100 (reduced salary) × 5 (number of years on job) = $32,100.

We have presented the above rules for your information in planning for the future. In most cases, your employer will, at your request, compute for you the maximum amount that can be placed tax-free into your tax-sheltered annuity for any given year. TIAA-CREF will also make this computation for its participants.

Reduction of the Annual Limitation

This reduction rule only applies if you are covered by a "defined contribution" pension plan with the same employer under which you are having contributions made to your tax-sheltered annuity. A **defined contribution** plan is one that computes your retirement benefit strictly on the basis of how much was contributed to your account. If your retirement plan provides a pension based on a percentage of your salary during a certain period of time, then it is **not** a defined contribution plan. Most governmental and private pension plans are not defined contribution plans. However, pension plans run by TIAA-CREF are defined contribution plans so the reduction rule would apply.

The reduction rule states that in computing the 25% annual limitation, you must add your employer's contribution to your retirement plan plus certain other amounts such as forfeitures credited to your account. If you are covered by a defined contribution plan, you'll have to check with your employer to determine the precise limitation in your case.

Options Which Permit an Increase in the Annual or Overall Limitations

Believe it or not, the above are only the basic rules that apply to contribution limits for tax-sheltered annuities. The law provides several options you are permitted to adopt which may increase the contributions that can be made to your tax-sheltered annuity. (If you don't wish to contribute more than the regular rules allow, you don't have to concern yourself with these options.) These options provide alternatives to either the annual limitation or the overall limitation. They do not affect the elective deferral limitation. In all cases, your annual voluntary contributions to a tax-sheltered annuity cannot exceed $10,500 (or $13,500 for certain 15-year employees as described earlier) in 2001.

Each of the following three options for 2001 may serve to increase the amount you can have contributed to your tax-sheltered annuity with the tax-exempt educational, charitable, or religious organization for which you work. Once you utilize one of these options, you cannot use any of the other options in a later year.

Option #1. You can choose to forget entirely about the overall limitation. You would still be restricted by the annual limitation, which provides a 25% ceiling on contributions, as well as by the $10,500 (or $13,500) elective deferral limitation.

Option #2. You can raise the annual limitation by $4,000. If you adopt this option, your annual contributions are still subject to the overall limitation plus a third limitation of $15,000. Also, the elective deferral limitation would still apply.

Option #3. For your final year of employment, you can disregard the annual limitation altogether and be restricted by the overall limitation where you take into account only the last ten years. However, the $10,500 (or $13,500) elective deferral limitation would still apply.

Discussion of the Options

Option #1 is of little use to the average individual. It would only come into use if someone wishes to make consistently high contributions to a tax-sheltered annuity during his entire employment period. Most people would not be able to afford such contributions in their earlier years so that the overall limitation does not come into force. However, those switching to a new job late in their careers might benefit from this option.

Example

Jones obtains a new position three years from retirement age. He wishes to contribute the maximum possible amount to a tax-sheltered annuity. Jones adopts Option 1. He can then have 25% of his reduced salary contributed each year (provided the elective deferral limitation is satisfied). Under the basic rules or the other options he would be restricted to 20%. However, note that Option 3 provides a limitation based on 20% of the final year's salary. Thus, if his salary were to go up substantially, this could turn out to be the best choice.

Option #2 might be chosen if you wish to make large contributions now but have made low contributions in the past.

Example

Stirling has 5 years left until retirement and will earn $25,000 in each of these years. He has held his current job for the past 15 years and has not participated in a tax-sheltered annuity to date. During these 15 years, his total salary has added up to $200,000. By selecting Option 2, he could have $8,200 per year contributed to a tax-sheltered annuity for his remaining 5 years with the remainder, $25,000 − $8,200 = $16,800 being his reduced salary. Since he is in no danger of exceeding the overall limitation, the 25% + $4,000 limitation of Option 2 applies: $8,200 = $4,200 + $4,000 where $4,200 is 25% of the reduced salary of $16,800.

Option #3 represents an opportunity for anyone who wishes to defer tax on a substantial portion of his final salary and spread it out via an annuity over his lower-bracket retirement years.

Example

Rodgers has been working for the same employer for 20 years and decides to quit. His employer has annually contributed $1,000 to his regular retirement plan. In addition, during the last 10 years, he had a total of $14,000 contributed to a tax-sheltered annuity. His final salary was $30,000. Under Option 3, Rodgers can have $12,000 contributed to a tax-sheltered annuity in his final year (assuming the elective deferral limitation is satisfied). This is verified as follows:

Salary in final year...$30,000

Contribution to tax-sheltered annuity $12,000

Reduced Salary $18,000

Allowable total contributions:
$18,000 × 20% × 10 years = ...$36,000

The total contributions made by his employer to the regular retirement plan plus the total of all contributions to a tax-sheltered annuity do not exceed this allowance, as verified by the following computation:

Employer's contribution to retirement plan:	
$1,000 × 10 = ...	$10,000
Previous contributions to tax-sheltered annuity	$14,000
Final year contribution to tax-sheltered annuity	$12,000
Total	$36,000

There is no special form to file with the IRS to elect one of the above options. You just arrange with your employer to withhold the appropriate amount. You are considered to have elected an option when it is needed to justify the extra amounts being contributed to your tax-sheltered annuity. In subsequent years, you can elect the same option or apply the regular limitations, but not elect a different option.

SECTION 5:
DEFERRED COMPENSATION PLANS

Some employers permit deferral of income under a *Deferred Compensation Plan.* Under such a plan, typically, salary is set aside instead of being paid out currently. The money set aside is invested on behalf of the employee, with the accumulated funds paid out after retirement, usually in the form of an annuity.

Deferred compensation plans may not have the same legal status as regular retirement plans or tax-sheltered annuities. In particular, they may be *unfunded* instead of *funded* plans. This means that the employee's claim to the funds owed him has the same status as any other creditor's claim instead of having the preferred status that applies to regular retirement plans.

Deferred compensation plans offered by private companies vary from organization to organization. Each organization sets its own limits (within IRS guidelines) on how much pay can be deferred. Many private companies will match part of their employees' contributions, making these plans particularly attractive. The special lump-sum averaging rule [see the *Retirement Plans* chapter] can apply to plans run by private companies. Details should be available from the personnel office where you work.

Note that the 1986 Tax Reform Act placed a ceiling on contributions to deferred compensation plans known as 401(k) plans run by private companies. This ceiling is reduced by deductible contributions to an IRA and by an individual's contributions to a tax-sheltered annuity made under a salary reduction agreement. The ceiling for 2001 is $10,500. However, the IRS may require particular company plans to have a lower ceiling if not enough lower-paid company employees participate in the plan.

Contributions to 401(k) plans will be increased from the current maximum of $10,500 to $11,000 in 2002, increasing to $15,000 on a phased-in basis through 2006.

For individuals age 50 or older, there is a catch-up contribution beginning in 2002. The additional contribution in 2002 is $1,000 and goes up in increments of $1,000 a year through 2006 when the catch-up is $5,000.

Withdrawal Rules

The IRS has issued rules concerning the ability to withdraw funds from deferred compensation plans (called 401(k) plans after the relevant section of the Tax Code) maintained by private companies. These rules affect so-called *hardship withdrawals.*

Ordinarily, the same general withdrawal rules that apply to other types of retirement plans also apply to 401(k) deferred compensation plans. That is, withdrawals attributable to contributions you elected to make can be made only upon separation from service (including retirement, death, or disability) or after reaching age 59 ½. However, there is an extra provision that allows you to make such withdrawals if you need the money because you have a *financial hardship.* (Under the usual rules, you will be required to pay ordinary income tax on the amount of any withdrawals, plus the 10% penalty tax if applicable.)

The IRS issued regulations on what qualifies as a hardship distribution. The basic requirement is that it must have been made because of *an immediate and heavy financial need.* The following are examples of such financial needs:

1. Medical expenses of the employee, spouse, or dependents;

2. Purchase of a principal residence (not including mortgage payments);

3. Tuition and fees for the next 12 months of college education for the employee, spouse, or dependents;

4. Payments to stave off eviction from or foreclosure on a principal residence; and

5. Federal and state income taxes and penalties on the amount of the withdrawal.

To demonstrate a need for the funds, the general requirement is that you weren't able to obtain the funds elsewhere such as from insurance, reasonable liquidation of assets, distributions or nontaxable loans from other retirement plans, or borrowing from commercial sources on reasonable commercial terms. However, the rules provide for an exception to this general rule if your deferred compensation plan includes certain *safe harbor* rules. These safe harbor rules are satisfied if:

1. The distribution does not exceed the amount of the need;

2. The employee has obtained all available distributions and nontaxable loans from all plans maintained by the employer; and

3. The employee cannot make further elective contributions to any plan maintained by the employer for at least 12 months after the hardship distribution. For 2002 and thereafter this time period has been reduced to six months.

If the above safe harbor rules are satisfied, the employee need not exhaust his other resources before making a hardship withdrawal.

Loans

Many deferred compensation plans have a provision under which you can borrow a certain percentage of your account balance. Generally, such loans are issued for periods of 5 years or less. Longer-term loans may be issued if the funds are used to acquire your principal residence.

Tax-Exempt Organizations (Section 457 Plans)

Different rules apply to deferred compensation plans run by tax-exempt organizations. The basic rule for such plans is as follows:

> *During any given year, the amount of salary set aside cannot exceed either $7,500 or 33 1/3% of an individual's full salary before reduction. If the employee participates in a tax-sheltered annuity, this limitation applies to the total amount contributed to both plans.*

There is an exception to the above limitation that allows catch-up contributions to be made. During each of the 3 years prior to normal retirement age, an employee may defer up to $15,000 per year. However, this catch-up provision only applies to the extent that full utilization was not made of the full limitations in prior years going back to 1979. In other words, the total amounts set aside over the life of the plan still cannot exceed the total amounts that would have been set aside had the individual made full use of the $7,500 or 33 1/3% of salary contribution each year starting in 1979.

Details concerning any deferred compensation plans available to you should be obtained from the personnel office where you work.

SECTION 6:
FLEXIBLE SPENDING ACCOUNTS

The tax-sheltered plan that is rapidly becoming one of the most popular is the so-called *Flexible Spending Account* (FSA) — sometimes called a *cafeteria plan*. The name comes from the fact that under this type of plan, you can choose from a selection of different tax-sheltered benefits according to your needs.

Under a typical FSA plan you are permitted to set aside a certain portion of your salary — which goes untaxed — to go towards paying certain benefits you select from a list provided under the plan. Such benefits can include:

1. medical and dental expenses (other than health insurance)

2. child care expenses (for dependents under age 13)

3. deferred compensation arrangement

4. group term life insurance

5. extra vacation days

6. group legal services

7. employee portion of health insurance

8. long-term care insurance

9. adoption assistance

10. disability insurance

To illustrate, let's take the example of a FSA plan that includes the first 2 benefits listed above and that permits you to set aside up to $2,000 of your salary towards these expenses. At the beginning of the year, you designate how to apportion this $2,000 (assuming you choose to set aside the maximum amount). For example, let's say you designate $500 towards child care expenses and $1,500 towards medical expenses for yourself, your spouse, and dependents. As you incur these expenses during the year, you submit the bills to your employer who will reimburse you up to the $500 maximum for child care expenses and $1,500 maximum for medical expenses.

To pay for these reimbursements, your employer will withhold the $2,000 from your paychecks during the year. However, you do not have to wait until sufficient amounts have been withheld. For example, you could get reimbursed for $2,000 worth of expenses incurred in January even though only a fraction of the $2,000 had been withheld up until that point.

The advantage comes from the tax treatment. The $2,000 withheld from your paychecks is exempt from tax. Thus, your taxable income is reduced by $2,000. If you had received this amount in salary and then paid the expenses yourself, you would have had to pay both income tax and social security taxes as well. In particular, this is an inferior outcome if you can't otherwise get a tax deduction or tax credit for these expenses because of the limitations that apply [see the *Medical Expenses* and *Child Care* chapters].

And in the case of child care expenses, the tax reduction produced by a flexible spending account will generally outweigh the benefit of the child care tax credit, provided a sufficient amount of expenses are covered. You should report any child care expenses reimbursed under a flexible savings account on Part III of Form 2441, even if you owe no tax on the reimbursement.

Under many FSA plans, you would have complete flexibility as to the allocation of the $2,000 each year. You could choose an allocation like that illustrated above, or you could choose to receive part or all of this amount in salary instead.

The main catch in FSA plans is the *use it or lose it* rule. That is, if you do not use up the initially designated amounts before the end of the year, then these amounts are lost to you. You cannot receive a refund nor carry over the amounts to the following year.

Thus, in the above example, if you incurred only $400 in child care expenses and $1,000 in uninsured medical expenses, you would be reimbursed for these amounts only. The remaining $600 would revert to the employer or be spread out among all the participants in the plan. Thus, you will not want to allocate funds unless you are fairly certain expenses will be incurred. This is usually not a problem for families, which can count on a certain minimum of medical (including dental) expenses, child care expenses, etc.

FSA plans are of particular benefit to working couples. Often, there is a duplication of benefits under typical fringe benefit arrangements. For example, one spouse's medical insurance plan may be just a duplication of the other spouse's plan — causing a loss of benefits. However, under a FSA plan that included medical insurance as only one of several options, there would be no loss of benefit. The funds could be allocated towards paying for other benefits such as uninsured medical or dental expenses, child care, or perhaps be contributed to a deferred compensation plan instead.

It pays to check into any FSA plan for which you might be eligible. Because FSA plans are relatively new, many employees are still unaware of how beneficial they can be. In fact, fewer than 25% of employees whose employers offer FSAs take advantage of them.

SECTION 7
VARIABLE ANNUITIES

A *Variable Annuity* is basically a mutual fund investment which is imbedded in an insurance policy. The reason for this embedding is the special tax status of insurance. Namely, investment income earned on cash value amounts in insurance policies are exempt from tax. This allows amounts in variable annuities to accumulate income like a mutual fund, but without paying current tax on the earnings.

As discussed later, the insurance component of variable annuities is minimal. This means that variable annuities are basically mutual fund investments with a slight alteration to qualify for the special tax treatment afforded insurance policies.

Most major mutual fund companies and insurance companies offer variable annuity investments. In a typical variable annuity investment, you write a check and designate into which fund you wish your money invested. You generally can choose between stock funds, bond funds, and a money-market fund. There is often a minimum initial investment amount of $2,500 or $5,000, with a lower minimum of $500 or $1,000 for additions to your account.

Your investment grows according to the performance of the mutual fund you have chosen. If the fund does well, the value of your variable annuity account will prosper accordingly. And no tax will be paid on dividends or capital gains earned by the mutual fund. On the other hand, if the fund does poorly, so will your variable annuity account.

You are usually allowed to switch part or all of your funds from one mutual fund to another. You can also transfer funds from a variable annuity offered by one company to another offered by a different company, provided the companies permit such transfers. No tax is due when these switches are made in the appropriate manner.

You are permitted to cash in part or all of your variable annuity account at any time you wish. Each withdrawal will be allocated into a tax-free part and a taxable part. For example, suppose that your investment has quadrupled in value. Approximately one-fourth of the withdrawal would be non-taxable, representing a return of your original investment. The remaining three-fourths would be taxable as ordinary income.

If you withdraw funds before reaching age 59½, you generally must pay an extra 10% penalty tax in addition to the ordinary income tax that applies. This is the same penalty tax that applies to early withdrawals from IRAs and self-employed plans [see the *Tax-Sheltered Plans* chapter]. On the other hand, an individual generally does not need to make any withdrawal from his variable annuity until reaching age 85. This compares favorably with regular IRAs and self-employed plans, where withdrawals must begin by age 70½.

If you wish, you can choose to have payments made from your variable annuity in the form of an annuity. This means you would receive regular payments over your lifetime or other specified period. There is typically a wide choice in the types of annuities you are allowed to choose.

When you open your account, you name a beneficiary to receive the appropriate amounts after your death. If you have not made any withdrawals, your beneficiary will receive at least as much money as you invested. This protects against a decrease in the value of the investment vehicle you have chosen. This *insurance* against the possibility your portfolio will have shown an overall net loss at the time of your death is what makes variable annuities qualify under the tax-exempt rules applying to insurance policies.

Fees

There are three types of fees charged by variable annuities. First is the investment fee. This is the same type of fee charged by any mutual fund for operating expenses and management fees. Annual investment fees typically range from 0.2% to 3% of net assets.

The second type of fee is an insurance fee to cover the mortality risk and insurance company operating expenses. As discussed above, the *mortality risk* covers the expected loss that would occur if the value of your account when you die is less than your total investments. This fee typically ranges from an annual charge of 0.55% to 1.50% of net assets. Because the mortality risk is actually quite low, it is fair to regard this charge as more of a fee than as payment for an extra benefit.

The third type of fee is a sales charge. This charge is only made by insurance companies and load mutual funds which must compensate salesmen or other agents. Variable annuities offered by no-load mutual funds do not generally impose any sales charges. There are different types of sales charges that can be imposed. One type is an up-front charge of 4% – 8% on any amounts invested. A more common type of fee is a surrender charge. A typical surrender charge might levy a 7% fee on amounts withdrawn within one year of investment, 6% within two years, etc., phasing out after seven years have elapsed.

How Do You Select a Variable Annuity?

Perhaps the most important thing to look for in a variable annuity are the total fees it charges. Investment and insurance fees can total from about 1% to 3% or more. Fees at the higher end of this range will generally negate the tax savings benefit involved. And if sales charges are levied, the picture is even worse. (However, the negative effect of sales charges is mitigated when they are in the form of surrender fees that decrease with time.)

The lowest fees can be found among the variable annuities offered by no-load mutual funds. Of these, the Vanguard Variable Annuity Plan (800-522-5555) charges the lowest total fees — about 1% of annual assets, with no sales charges. The Scudder Horizon Plan (800-SCUDDER, Ext. 2268) charges total fees of about 1.4%, also without sales charges. The average fees charged by variable annuities, not counting sales charges, total a whopping 2.24%.

Of course, the ultimate objective is strong investment performance. Each week *Barron's,* available at most newsstands and libraries, contains a listing of available variable annuities. This listing includes the current *unit price* of each variable annuity investment as well as total investment returns over the most recent 4-week and 52-week periods. The listing is organized according to the underlying insurance company, not the mutual fund company or stockbroker. This means you may have to browse a bit to find the variable annuity plan in which you are interested.

To get information on available variable annuity plans, you can contact mutual fund companies, stockbrokers, and insurance companies. A listing of toll-free telephone numbers for some major no-load mutual fund companies can be found in Section 5 of the *Investing Your Money* chapter. The prospectuses you receive will contain a breakdown of the fees that are charged and past performances for each of the mutual fund investment options.

Of course, some variable annuity funds will show better investment performances than others, even when similar portfolio types are compared, e.g., bond funds, stock funds, etc. However, this should not be the only criterion to be examined. With mutual funds in general, studies have turned up little correlation between past performances and future performances.

Theoretically, the average mutual fund investment inside a variable annuity should slightly outperform the average mutual fund outside, ignoring the difference in fees. The reason for this is that the ordinary mutual funds are subject to random waves of investments and redemptions which can cause extra transaction fees. Investors in variable annuities invest and withdraw with much less frequency.

Another item that is reported in the prospectus is the quality rating of the insurance company. Of course, the higher the rating, the better. However, as the prospectus will disclose, the underlying mutual fund may be insulated as a separate investment pool, with assets unavailable to general creditors of the insurance company.

14

$\sum_0^t G_t = cum$ **Estate and Gift Tax**

includes
$\sum (G_t - Ex_t)$ per person

SECTION 1:
INTRODUCTION

Basic Gift and Estate Tax Law

Prior to 1977, there were two separate taxes, one on estates and one on gifts. The estate tax was levied on property passing from one individual to another upon the death of the first individual. To prevent an individual from escaping estate tax simply by giving away his property before death, a separate gift tax applied to the **giver** of substantial amounts.

The 1976 Tax Reform Act combined these two taxes into a new Unified Estate and Gift Tax. To determine the amount of gift tax due under this law, a cumulative total of all gifts made by an individual during his lifetime is kept. When total taxable gifts exceed a certain minimum amount, gift tax becomes due. Excluded from this cumulative total are gifts totalling up to $10,000 per year per recipient and gifts made in any amount to a spouse. Also excluded from taxable gifts are payments made directly to the provider by the donor for tuition or medical care of the donee and any gifts to qualified charities.

The tax rate is graduated with the rate determined by the cumulative lifetime total of gifts. For example, if a person has made gifts worth X amount in prior years and gives Y amount of gifts this year, the gift tax rate that applies is the one in the X to X + Y bracket. A credit is then granted against the tax on the amount of gifts X for any tax paid on the X amount of gifts in prior years.

The maximum estate and gift tax is reduced from 55% to 50% in 2002. The maximum rate is reduced further — 49% in 2003 to 45% in 2007 until totally repealed in 2010.

The federal estate tax is repealed for decedents dying after December 31, 2009. However, the repeal sunsets (expires) as of December 31, 2010 unless Congress re-enacts this provision before it sunsets.

To determine the amount of estate tax due, the deceased's taxable estate is first computed by subtracting certain adjustments (as explained in Section 3) from the sum total of all property passing to his heirs. The tax on this estate is then obtained by using the same tax schedule that applies to gifts. The cumulative total of all taxable gifts made during the individual's lifetime determines which tax bracket applies. For example, if a person has made gifts worth G during his lifetime and his taxable estate is worth E, then the tax rate used is the one that applies to the bracket G to G + E.

In summary then, the Unified Estate and Gift Tax applies to the sum total of all taxable gifts made during one's lifetime plus the value of the taxable estate. However, no tax is due unless this total exceeds $675,000 for 2001. The unified credit exemption (the amount of a decedent's estate exempted from estate tax) is increased from $675,000 to $1,000,000 per person beginning in 2002. The exemption increases to $3,500,000 in 2009, after which the estate tax is repealed.

SECTION 2:
GIFT TAX

If one person makes a substantial gift to another, then the giver may have to pay a gift tax. The recipient pays no gift or income tax. The gift tax is computed by adding the cumulative total of all gifts made during an individual's lifetime to other individuals. There are two exemptions which are excluded from this cumulative total.

(1) Each year you may exempt gifts totalling up to $10,000 to any one person if that person has the right to use the cash or property immediately. You get a separate $10,000 exemption for each person to whom you make a gift. If your spouse consents, you can regard a gift to a third person as being ½ from each of you and give $20,000 tax-free to each person.

Simply writing a check and giving it to the recipient is not sufficient to establish that a gift has been made that year. The check must actually be cashed or presented to the bank for deposit by the recipient before the end of the year. This was the conclusion of the Tax Court in a 1993 case [Metzger, 100 TC 204]. (However, presumably a gift by certified check would be considered completed at the time of certification.). Note that this treatment of gifts differs from the treatment of charitable contributions [see the *Charitable Contributions* chapter]. Charitable contributions are considered made when a check is written and either placed in the mail or delivered to the recipient, or is charged on your credit card.

(2) In addition to (1), you may exempt any gifts made during your lifetime to your spouse. Also, you can exempt any amounts paid on behalf of any donee directly to a school for tuition or to a health care provider for medical services.

The following is a sampling of the 2001 tax rates that would apply to different amounts of lifetime gifts:

Lifetime Total of Taxable Gifts	Tax
$ 675,000	$ 0
$ 750,000	$ 27,750
$1,000,000	$125,250
$2,000,000	$560,250

The above schedule is not applied separately to each year's gifts, but instead is applied to the sum total of all taxable gifts you have made in your lifetime. For example, suppose that (after subtracting exclusions) you have made taxable gifts totalling $200,000 in previous years and have paid gift tax (under prior law) totalling $7,800. If you now make a taxable gift of $550,000, this will bring your lifetime total of gifts up to $750,000. Because the tax on $750,000 is $27,750 in 2001 and you have already paid $7,800 tax in previous years, you must now pay the difference, $27,750 – $7,800 = $19,950.

Gift Tax Return

12,500

Taxpayers who make taxable gifts during the year (gifts in excess of $10,000 per donee in any year or $20,000 if married and gift splitting is elected) that must be reported to the IRS should file Form 709, *United States Gift (and Generation-Skipping Transfer) Tax Return*. A gift tax return has the same due date as the individual income tax return and may be extended.

The maximum amount of gifts that will not be subject to the gift tax is increased to $1,000,000 beginning in 2002 and is capped at this amount both before and after the repeal of the estate tax.

Example — Gift Tax Formula

During the year, David Brown made gifts to his five children and to selected charities totaling $252,400. He gifted $188,400 to his children and $65,000 to charities. The tax computation for 2001 is computed below

Gifts at fair market value		$ 253,400
Less: Charitable gifts	$ 65,000	
Annual $10,000 exclusion per donee	50,000	(115,000)
Taxable gifts		138,400
Gift tax computed on total taxable gifts		35,320
Less: Unified credit exemption		(220,550)
Gift tax due for current year		$ 0

SECTION 3:
ESTATE TAX

The Gross Estate

The first step in computing the estate tax of a deceased person is to determine the gross estate. The gross estate includes the fair market value of all property held by the decedent at death which includes the following:

- Home and other owned real estate

- Cash and debts owed to the deceased

- Stocks and bonds

- Personal belongings and household furnishings (including automobiles)

- Life insurance

- Annuities and death benefits

In order for you to estimate the size of your estate, let us consider the above items separately.

Your Home and Real Estate

Include the value of all your real estate holdings, including your own home and real estate in other countries. If you have a mortgage on your property, then the amount of the unpaid balance will be subtracted from the value of the estate. If you own property jointly, see the subsection on jointly-held property.

Cash and Amounts Owed to You

Include money you have in banks and savings accounts as well as currency on hand. Also include any amounts owed to you via a note, mortgage, etc., which you hold.

Stocks and Bonds

All stocks and bonds you own are subject to estate tax. This includes U.S. savings bonds, income-tax-free municipal bonds, stocks in foreign countries, etc. These are valued at their current fair market value, with publicly traded securities valued at the average of the high and low on the date of death. If you own a piece of a small business, then your executor will, at your death, evaluate your shares according to what an appraiser thinks a willing buyer would pay for them.

Life Insurance

If you own a life insurance policy on your life, the face amount of the insurance is included in your estate. However, there is a way to avoid having this insurance included in your estate. If the insurance goes to a beneficiary and if that beneficiary or other individual owns the policy, then the insurance is not included in your estate. However, that person must have complete control of the policy. You must not possess any "incident of ownership" in the policy such as the right to borrow on the policy, to surrender it for cash, or change the beneficiary. There is also a problem if the policy was transferred to the beneficiary within 3 years prior to the death of the insured.

There is another restriction which forbids you from having a "reversionary interest" in the policy. Roughly speaking, this restriction states that you should have less than a 5% chance of getting back the policy or its proceeds because of your beneficiary dying before you. This restriction can be satisfied by having your beneficiary name someone other than yourself to inherit the policy in the event the beneficiary dies before you.

Jointly-Owned Property

There are two basic ways in which property can be jointly owned. The first way, called tenancy-in-common, means that each of the owners has a share of the property and can dispose of that share as he or she chooses. Upon death, his or her share passes to whomever is named in the will. If there is no will, all property will pass according to the inheritance laws of the state.

Under tenancy-in-common, your share of the ownership would be included in your estate. For example, if you own an equal share of a house under tenancy-in-common with another person, then your estate would include 1/2 the value of the house. It would make no difference who had contributed the funds to buy the house.

The second and more prevalent type of co-ownership is called joint tenancy. Under this type, when one of the co-owners dies, the property passes automatically to the other co-owner. It cannot be willed to another individual.

Your estate includes 1/2 the value of any property held in joint tenancy with your spouse. For property held in joint tenancy with a non-spouse, your estate includes that portion of the joint property which represents the fraction you paid for.

There is a special type of joint tenancy available only to husband and wife, called **tenancy-by-the-entireties.** Under ordinary joint tenancy, one party alone can demand to dissolve the tenancy and retrieve his share. But under tenancy-by-the-entireties, generally, husband and wife must agree on any dissolution of the ownership. In most states, tenancy-by-the-entireties is available only in joint ownership of real estate. There is no difference between ordinary joint tenancy and tenancy-by-the-entireties as far as estate tax is concerned.

Tenancy-by-the entireties has the extra advantage that it is not subject to judgements by creditors unless they are creditors of both spouses. For example, if only one spouse is sued for malpractice, a house held in tenancy-by-the-entireties is not affected.

Annuities and Death Benefits

Many annuities and pension plans have a survivorship feature which pays a beneficiary either a lump sum or periodic payments upon the death of the original participant. Also, tax-sheltered annuities, self-employed retirement plans, and IRAs may make payments to survivors. The value of such payments is generally included in the estate.

Owners of Small Businesses

Starting in 1998, a special deduction became available to the estates of small business owners. If more than 50% of the value of the estate consists of family-owned business interests, a portion of the value of that business may be deducted in arriving at the taxable estate. For estates of decedents dying in 2001, the exclusion cannot exceed $675,000. In 2002 and 2003, the maximum exclusion is $300,000. This provision was repealed for estates of decedents dying after 2003 based on the recent changes to estate and gift tax law in the 2001 Tax Reduction Act.

Deductions from the Gross Estate

To compute the taxable estate, the following deductions are subtracted from the gross estate:

(1) The marital deduction

The full value of all property left to a spouse is deductible from the estate. Thus, if the entire estate is left to a spouse, no estate tax is due. Special rules apply if the spouse is not a U.S. citizen.

(2) Funeral expenses, administration expenses, and debts

This includes undertaker charges, the cost of a burial plot and tombstone, and any personal debts that must be settled by the estate. Also deductible are the costs of settling the estate—attorney fees, court costs, executor fees, and appraiser fees.

(3) Charitable contributions

The full market value of any bequest made to charity is deductible. Sometimes, bequests are made in a form other than an outright donation. For example, income-producing property might be left in trust with the provision that the income from such property be paid to a child, upon whose death the property is given to charity. In such a case, an actuarial computation is made to determine how to allocate the benefits between the child and the charity. The estate would get a deduction for the value allocated to charity.

Computation of the Estate Tax

The estate tax is computed as follows: First, the taxable estate is computed by subtracting allowable deductions from the gross estate. Then, the total of lifetime taxable gifts is added in and the tax computed on this amount. Next, any gift taxes that have already been paid are subtracted from the tax bill. Last, there are several tax credits which are subtracted to reduce the tax bill further.

Tax Credits

(1) State death tax credit

You can subtract state death taxes up to a certain maximum amount. There is also a credit for death taxes paid to a foreign country on property in that country not to exceed the U.S. tax attributable to the foreign property. The credit for state death taxes is gradually reduced beginning in 2002.

(2) Credit for prior federal estate tax

Suppose one person inherits part of an estate on which estate tax was paid and then dies soon after the inheritance. The estate of the second person to die might then be hit by a second estate tax. To reduce the effect of this double taxation, a credit is allowed on the estate tax of the second person to die if death occurs within ten years of the first death — the longer the time, the less credit allowed.

Estate Tax Return

If the value of the gross estate of a decedent who died during the year 2001 exceeds $675,000 (the 2001 Unified Credit Exemption, Form 706, *United States Estate (and Generation-Skipping Transfer) Tax Returns* must be filed. This return is due exactly nine months after the date of death.

Example — Estate Tax Formula

Gross estate		$2,500,000
Less: Allowable deductions, including administration expenses, taxes, charitable bequests, debts, etc.		(500,000)
Taxable estate		2,000,000
Add: Post-1976 taxable gifts		138,400
Tax base		2,138,400
Tentative tax on total transfers		848,616
Less: State death tax credit	986,000	
Unified credit	220,550	320,100
Estate tax due		$ 528,466

State Inheritance or Estate Taxes

Virtually all states have some type of inheritance or estate tax. These taxes differ widely from state to state both in the size of the tax and the manner in which they are applied. Many states vary the rates according to the relationship between the deceased and the beneficiary — the closer the relationship, the lower the tax.

How Is the Estate Settled?

The rules differ according to state law but the basic procedure is the same. Property which is owned in joint tenancy passes directly to the surviving owner. Property in certain types of trusts remains governed by the trust agreement. Other property is distributed to the heirs as provided in the will. If there is no will, state law governs how the property is distributed.

A court will be responsible for supervising the distribution of the estate. In the will, an executor is named who has the responsibility of evaluating the assets, paying the appropriate taxes, and distributing the property according to the will. If there is no will, an executor will be appointed by the court. If the estate is simple, a family member or friend may be named as executor. In more complicated estates, an individual or bank trust department specializing in such matters will often be the executor or personal representative. In such cases, executor fees typically range in the neighborhood of 5% of the value of the estate governed by the will.

Making a Will

Anyone with even a modest amount of assets should have a will. In the absence of a will, your assets will be distributed according to an arbitrary formula given by state law. The distribution formula may not be what you want. For example, in some states, the estate of a married individual with no children would be distributed 50% to the individual's parents and 50% to the spouse. Elsewhere, the estate of a married individual with children might be distributed 1/3 to the spouse and 2/3 to the children. This could impose a hardship on the spouse who might actually have to go to court to get permission to use the children's share for their benefit.

If there are children, a will should be drawn up which includes the appointment of a guardian in case both the parents die. Otherwise, the court would be in charge of appointing a guardian. Even if there are no children and all property is held in joint tenancy, a will may be called for. To illustrate what can happen without a will, suppose an individual with no children owns all property in joint tenancy with a spouse. If the two of them die in a joint accident, without a will the property would pass from the first to die to the second to die and then to, say, the parents of the second party. The family of the first to die would get nothing.

You should have your will reviewed by a qualified attorney whenever your circumstances change significantly — for example, if you divorce or change permanent residence to another state.

Note that the cost of drawing up a will isn't deductible as such. However, if your will includes provisions designed to reduce estate tax, the cost of working out these provisions is deductible. Ask your lawyer to itemize the bill to show that portion of his fee attributable to estate tax planning.

Revocable Living Trusts

A *revocable living trust* is an arrangement under which you transfer assets — real estate, bonds, stock, etc. — to a trust. True to its name, the trust can be revoked by you at any time or you can otherwise alter the terms of the trust. You can serve as trustee and manage the assets yourself. After your death, a successor trustee — friend, relative, attorney, bank, etc. — distributes the assets to your beneficiaries as specified in the trust document. You can change the successor trustee or any other provision of the living trust at any time you choose.

A revocable living trust can be used to avoid *probate*. When you die, the assets registered in your name will be distributed to the beneficiaries specified in your will, under the supervision of a probate judge. However, those assets transferred to the living trust do not go through probate.

The avoidance of probate has several major *advantages.* The most important advantage is the escape from probate fees. The legal fees and court costs can amount to about 5% of the estate, although this percentage can decline with larger estates.

A second advantage is the speed-up of the distribution of your assets to your beneficiaries. The probate process generally takes from 6 months to 2 years to distribute the assets. This can cause a hardship for beneficiaries who might need funds in the interim. In contrast, there is no delay with a living trust. The successor trustee can distribute the assets anytime after your death.

Third, under the probate process, an unknown judge unfamiliar with your family will divide up the assets. In contrast, with a living trust, the successor trustee that you have named will do the distribution. Presumably, this trustee will be more familiar with your family situation and can sort out which assets should go to which beneficiary in a more knowing manner.

Another advantage of a living trust is that a provision can be made to manage your assets in case you become disabled. In the trust document, you can name who you want to preside over your affairs if you become disabled.

Also, living trusts offer privacy. Under the probate process, your will becomes a matter of public record, available at the county courthouse. But the living trust is a private document, not made public except if a beneficiary or other party convinces the judge that he might have been shortchanged.

The above describes some benefits offered by living trusts. However, there are several *disadvantages* as well.

First, living trusts are not free. You will have to pay a lawyer $500 – $3,000 or more to draft the trust according to your specifications. This is a one-time fee unless you later choose to make amendments. However, this fee can be far less than the cost of probate. And according to a recent court case, part of the cost of setting up a revocable living trust can be deductible to the extent there is any tax planning involved [Wong, TC Memo 1989-683]. As long as all income from the trust is distributed to you and reported on your tax return (the usual situation), no extra tax return needs to be filed for the trust.

Second, living trusts entail complexity. You will want to re-register most or all of your assets in the name of the trust instead of in your personal name. Stocks and bonds can be re-registered by filling out the appropriate form that the companies will send you upon request. Real estate is more difficult. You will probably need a lawyer to re-title real estate at a charge of about $100 – $200 per property.

Third, there is a nonadvantage that is often misrepresented by those selling living trust information. Namely, living trusts do not affect federal or state estate taxes. The same amounts will be due whether assets are distributed under the probate process or via the provisions of a living trust. The savings is only in the elimination of probate costs.

The above gives a sketch of the advantages and disadvantages of a living trust. If your assets are held mostly in joint name, then this joint property automatically bypasses probate, so a living trust will not save money. However, if you have -

significant assets in your name only, you may wish to talk over the value of a living trust with one of the many professionals specializing in estate planning.

Finally, if you use a living trust to dispose of your estate, you will still need a simple will that gives all property not in the name of the living trust to such trust.

What Can Be Done to Minimize Estate Tax?

There are many strategies for reducing estate tax. If your estate will be sizable, then you should consult an estate planning professional such as a lawyer or CPA specializing in such matters to design a plan to minimize your estate tax. In fact, many people claim that the main effect of the estate tax is not to raise significant amounts of money for the Treasury, but to force people to arrange their affairs in such a way as to avoid or minimize the tax.

Here are just three of the basic techniques used for reducing estate tax:

A. Give property away before death.

The annual exemptions of up to $10,000 per recipient per year ($20,000 if married) can be used to transfer a substantial amount over a period of years. Gifts of income-producing property can also have the advantage of reducing income tax by shifting income to a lower-bracket taxpayer.

Sizable gifts made to minors are usually made under the Uniform Gifts to Minors Act or Uniform Transfer to Minors Act [see the *Income Shifting* chapter]. Under these acts, a custodian is named who controls and invests the funds until the minor reaches majority age whereupon he/she assumes control of the funds.

For property transferred prior to death, the recipient takes the basis and holding period of the donor. Under current law, assets received from an estate receive a step-up in basis to fair market value at date of death. Under the new law taking effect after 2009, the step-up to fair market value of property acquired from a decedent will be limited to a total of $1,300,000 (plus an additional $3,000,000 for property passing to a surviving spouse).

B. Use trusts to avoid double estate tax.

A common device used in estate planning for large estates is to make use of a *bypass or credit shelter trust.* Typically the situation is this: An individual wants to leave funds first to his spouse and then, after the death of his spouse, to his children. If the funds were left outright to the spouse, these funds would escape estate tax at that time but would be subjected to estate tax at the death of the spouse. The second estate tax is usually more severe than the first because the second estate does not qualify for the marital deduction (unless the surviving spouse remarried) and is generally larger in amount.

To lessen the taxation of the spouse's estate, most planned estates leave a certain portion of the funds to a *bypass or credit shelter trust.* Such a trust, for example, might be directed to pay the interest earned by the funds to the spouse as long as the spouse is living. Upon death of the spouse, the funds would be transferred to the children. The trust could also provide that in case of emergencies, the spouse is to receive part of the principal in addition to the interest.

The value of the funds placed in such a *bypass or credit shelter trust* is included in the first estate. But, since the spouse never has control of the funds, there is no second estate tax upon the death of the spouse. The principal simply passes automatically over to the children without a second estate tax being paid.

C. Make charitable gifts.

There is an estate tax deduction for any funds left to charity. However, an individual may want to benefit a charity, but is worried that an outright bequest would leave a surviving spouse or child without adequate support.

A common approach is to leave funds to a charitable trust. For example, a trust might be directed to pay all annual income earned by the funds to a spouse or child. Upon death of the spouse or child, the remaining principal is given to charity. The estate gets a charitable deduction based on an actuarial computation of the present value of the future gift to charity.

Caution. We have only briefly touched upon some of the basic principles involved in estate planning. The only proper way to plan an estate is to consult with a lawyer or CPA who specializes in such matters.

15

Investing Your Money

SECTION 1:
CAPITAL GAINS AND LOSSES

Most of the income you receive, whether salary from your job, stock dividends, interest on a savings account or bond, rent from property you own, etc., is considered **ordinary income.**

But if you buy an item at one price and sell it at a higher price, then the resulting profit is not considered ordinary income but falls into a special category called a **capital gain.** The item could be a bond, stock, real estate, or any other type of property or security, tangible or intangible.

The same distinction exists with respect to losses. If you lose money in a business venture or rental property because expenses exceed income, etc., then you have an **ordinary loss.** This ordinary loss is generally just subtracted from your ordinary income when you compute your tax. But if you sustain a loss because you sell an investment item at a lower price than the one at which you purchased it, then you have a **capital loss.** This capital loss cannot always just be subtracted from your income, but is treated according to the special rules below.

The main break is that assets held more than 12 months are taxed at at a capital gains rate of 20% (10% if you are in the 15% bracket) unless the capital gains arises from certain real estate transactions (the portion of the gain equal to depreciation claimed as a deduction is taxed at 25%) and the gain from the sale of collectibles.

In all cases, assets held less than 12 months (short-term assets) that are sold at a profit get no special capital gains rate, but produce ordinary taxable income when sold. This is if a net gain is produced after netting short-term gains and losses and long-term gains with short-term losses.

If assets acquired after January 1, 2001 are held for at least five years, the capital gains rates are reduced from 20% to 18% and from 10% to 8%.

Capital Losses

If you have capital losses, they will serve to offset the amount of gains on which you have to pay tax. Short-term capital gains and losses are netted against each other and long-term capital gains and losses are netted against each other. Long-term gains offset short-term losses and short-term gains are reduced by long-term losses. Net short-term gains are taxed at your regular tax rate and long-term gains are taxed at 20% (10% if you are in the 15% bracket).

Example 1 — Net Short-Term Capital Gain

Kimberly has two transactions involving the sale of capital assets during the year. As a result of the transactions, she has a short-term capital gain of $5,000 and a short-term capital loss of $3,500. Kimberly's net short-term capital gain is $1,500 ($5,000 – $3,500) and her adjusted gross income increases by $1,500.

Example 2 — Net Long-Term Capital Gain

Justin has two transactions involving the sale of capital assets during the year. As a result of the transactions, he has a long-term capital gain of $5,000 and a long-term capital loss of $3,500. Justin's net long-term capital gain is $1,500 ($5,000 – $3,500), and his adjusted gross income increases by $1,500.

Example 3 — Net Long-Term Capital Gain

Angelina has four transactions involving the sale of capital assets during the year. As a result of the transactions, she has a short-term capital gain of $6,000, a short-term capital loss of $8,000, a long-term capital gain of $12,000 and a long-term capital loss of $4,000. After the initial netting of short-term and long-term gains and losses, Angelina has a net short-term capital loss of $2,000 ($8,000 – $6,000) and a net long-term capital gain of $8,000 ($12,000 – $4,000). Because the net long-term capital gain exceeds the net short-term capital loss by $6,000 ($8,000 – $2,000), her net long-term capital gain is $6,000.

In addition, the IRS has ruled that short-term capital losses, after first offsetting short-term capital gains, offset 25% capital gains (for real estate depreciation) first and then 20% capital gains. This is a favorable benefit for taxpayers.

If your total capital losses exceed your total capital gains, then the result is your *net capital loss*. (You include in this computation all gains and losses, whether short-term or long-term.) You deduct this net capital loss from your ordinary income if it does not exceed $3,000. If it exceeds $3,000, you deduct $3,000 on your 2001 tax return and carry over the excess into the future.

For example, if you have a net capital loss of $7,000, then you deduct $3,000 on your 2001 tax return and carry over $7,000 – $3,000 = $4,000 to be deducted on future tax returns.

Collectibles

As a general rule, collectibles held for more than twelve months do not qualify for the lower long-term capital gain rates. For example, long-term capital gains on antiques, gems, stamps, and most coins are taxed at the maximum rate of 28%. An exception is certain minted gold and silver coins issued by the U.S. and coins issued under state law, which qualify for the lower long-term capital gains rates.

Depreciable Real Estate

If you own rental housing or other depreciable real estate, then you deduct depreciation each year in addition to your operating expenses. When you sell the building, you will have to pay capital gains tax on your profit plus the total depreciation you have claimed. The capital gain representing the total amount of depreciation claimed is taxed at 25%. The remainder can qualify for the lower long-term capital gain rate.

Example
You sold a rental house on November 1, 2001, which you purchased a number of years ago. The house was purchased for $50,000 and sold for $150,000, a profit of $100,000. Over the years, you claimed depreciation deductions totaling $30,000. Thus, your capital gain is $100,000 + $30,000 = $130,000. You have to pay a maximum tax on the $30,000 of 25% x $30,000 = $7,500. The remaining $100,000 is subject to a maximum capital gains tax rate of 20%.

Unrealized Capital Gains and Losses

The above rules only come into force when you actually sell the item in question. Until you sell, you pay no tax on your capital gains and get no deduction for your losses.

Example
You buy 100 shares of common stock at $10 per share and the price doubles to $20 per share. You have a profit of $1,000, but it is an unrealized gain (sometimes called a "paper profit") and generates no tax liability. If you were to sell, then you would realize a $1,000 gain and would have to pay tax on the gain.

50% Capital Gains Reduction for Small Business Stock

The 1993 Tax Act instituted a new capital gains break on certain small business stock originally issued after August 10, 1993. When such stock is held at least 5 years, 50% of any capital gains realized on the sale of the stock is exempt from tax. (No extra tax break is available in case of a capital loss.)

To qualify for this tax break, the corporation must have issued the stock to you. However, the corporation issuing the stock need not be newly founded. An established corporation can issue new stock qualifying for the tax break.

There are a number of restrictions on the type of corporations whose stock qualifies for this tax break. The major restrictions are as follows:

1. The corporation's gross assets must not exceed $50 million at any time between August 10, 1993, and the date the new stock is issued.

2. No more than 10% of the corporation's assets can consist of real estate not used in the active conduct of its business. (For this purpose, owning, dealing in, or renting real estate does not qualify as the active conduct of a trade or business.)

3. At least 80% of the corporation's assets must be used in a business activity *other than* those involving:

   a. The performance of services in health, law, engineering, architecture, accounting, actuarial science, performing arts, consulting, athletics, financial services, brokerage services, or any trade or business in which the principal asset is the reputation or skill of one or more of its employees;

   b. Banking, insurance, leasing, financing, investing, or similar businesses;

   c. Farming businesses or businesses involving the production of products for which percentage depletion is allowable; or

   d. Operating a hotel, motel, restaurant, or similar business.

The above list represents the major restrictions that apply to this tax benefit. There are a number of other technical requirements that a corporation must satisfy for its stock to qualify for the 50% reduction in capital gains tax. Your stockbroker or the corporation issuing the stock can advise you if all these requirements have been met.

If you take advantage of the 50% capital gain exclusion, the remaining 50% is taxed at 28%, not at the lower 20% rate.

You can exclude gains only to the extent the sales price doesn't exceed 10 times the purchase price. Also, if you have substantial capital gains in any one year, you might fall under the provisions of the complicated alternative minimum tax [see the *Alternative Minimum Tax* chapter]. This affects the 50% reduction in capital gains tax benefit. It probably won't eliminate this benefit altogether, but typically can cut it in half.

You can sell qualifying small business stock which you held for at least 6 months and purchase different small business stock within 60 days of the sale. If this is done, no capital gain tax is due on the sale and the 5-year holding requirement runs from the purchase date of the original stock. To exclude all the proceeds of the first sale from tax, the new stock must cost at least as much as the proceeds from the sale.

Special Election for Capital Assets Acquired Prior to January 1, 2001

If capital assets acquired after January 1, 2001, are held for more than five years, the 20% capital gains rate is reduced to 18% and the 10% rate to 8%. However, you can also use this provision for capital assets acquired before January 1, 2001 and plan to hold for five more years. On your 2001 return, you can make an election to treat capital assets as if you sold them at their fair market value on January 1, 2001 (this is known as a "deemed sale") and report the gain on Schedule D. You will pay tax on the gain at the 2001 capital gains rates.

The election should probably only be made for 2001 if you have or little or no gain on the deemed sale and plan to hold the assets for the required five years. It would not be financially prudent to make the election and pay a substantial amount of tax on the gain in 2001 to save 2% on the tax rates five years from now. You cannot make the election for assets with a loss or for your personal residence. However, you could consider gifting the stock to children age 14 and over before the end of

2001 and have them sell the stock and only pay the tax at the 10% long-term rate (as long as they are in the overall 15% tax bracket.)

Where Are Capital Gains and Losses Reported on Your Tax Return?

You use Schedule D to report your capital gains and losses. This schedule will lead you through the appropriate computations. You use Form 4797 to compute the gain on the sale of depreciable assets. This form will help determine the gain subject to the 25% rate mentioned above.

Reconciliation with Broker's Statements

If you sold stocks, bonds, etc., during the year, you will receive a Form 1099-B at the end of the year from your broker, mutual fund, etc., reporting the pro ceeds from the sales. The total of all amounts reported on Forms 1099-B and Forms 1099-S that you receive should match the total sales prices shown in the sections on Schedule D where you compute your capital gains and losses on stocks, bonds, etc. You must attach a statement to your tax return explaining any discrepancy.

The Form 1099-B which you receive from your stockbroker reporting transactions will show the amount being reported to the IRS as the *total proceeds* from your sales of securities. It will also indicate whether these proceeds are the *gross proceeds* or the *gross proceeds less commissions* you paid on the sales.

If your broker reported the *gross proceeds* to the IRS, you list the gross amounts received on each sale before commissions are subtracted in column (d), *Sales price,* on Schedule D. You then add the commissions to the amount reported in column (e), *Cost or other basis.* Thus, the amount reported in column (e) will include your purchase price plus the commissions paid both on the purchase and the sale of the security. In this way, when the amount in column (e) is subtracted from the amount in column (d), your true monetary gain or loss will be calculated, including the effect of the commissions you have paid.

If your broker reported the *gross proceeds less commissions* to the IRS, then these are the amounts you report in column (d). The amount in column (e) will then be your purchase price plus the commissions you paid on the purchase, but not including the commissions you paid on the sale which were already taken into account in the figure reported in column (e).

Wash Sales

You may own stocks or other securities which are selling at a lower price than when purchased. Tax considerations might call for a sale of such securities in order to create a currently deductible tax loss. However, if it is desired to still own the securities while producing a tax loss, you can't just sell securities at a loss and then buy them right back. Any purchase of the same securities within 30 days before or after the sale negates any losses. To get around this restriction, you can purchase similar but not identical securities to the ones sold. Or, in the case of bonds, you can achieve the same result by making a swap through a brokerage house. The broker can also advise you of more exotic methods of achieving the same result, such as using appropriate short sales or options transactions.

Brokerage Fees

You cannot deduct brokerage commissions or other charges related to the purchase or sale of securities or other assets. Instead, as discussed above, these fees serve to lower the capital gain or increase the capital loss computed on Schedule D when you make a sale.

Custodial or management fees you pay on investments are deductible as a *miscellaneous deduction* on your tax return. For example, a fee charged by a bank for management of a money-market account would be deductible (unless it represented a normal check-processing fee).

Special Treatment for Inherited Property

Inherited property such as real estate, stocks, bonds, etc., is given a *fresh start* or *stepped up* basis when inherited. This means that, for purposes of future capital gains tax computations, it is treated as though it were purchased at its market value at the time of inheritance. Thus, when you sell property which was acquired by inheritance, tax is due only on the appreciation in value since the time it was inherited. No tax is ever paid on the increase in value that took place when the property belonged to the previous owner. The gain on the sale of inherited property is always treated as long-term gain no matter how long you or the decedent owned the asset.

Shifting Profits to Different Years

When you sell property on which you have a profit, you may wish to shift some or all of this profit to later years. This can be done by making an *installment sale,* whereby you agree to receive at least some part of the money due you in more than one year. Then you would report the proportionate profit in the years you receive the various payments from the buyer. There are no restrictions on the number of payments or on the size of the initial payment.

The installment sale reporting procedure does not apply to the sales of stocks or securities that are traded in an established marketplace. Also, there are restrictions that apply to the sale of real estate for more than $150,000 when the seller owes any business-related debts. These restrictions do not generally apply to the sale of a personal residence.

If you receive delayed payments, you must charge interest. You can't simply regard all money received as part of the selling price and thereby convert interest into capital gains. Check with the IRS website to determine the minimum acceptable interest rate to charge at the time of sale.

The law prevents tax reduction by using an installment sale to a very close relative as an intermediate step. For example, suppose you sell property on which you have a profit to your father with payments to be made in future years and he resells it for the same price within the next two years. You would have to include the entire profit on your tax return in the year of sale, not as you received the payments from your father. In addition, losses on sales between related taxpayers are never deductible.

You do not have to use the installment reporting procedure described above. If you wish, you may make an election to report the entire profit in the year the sale is consummated, even if payments are to be made in future years.

Section 2:
Passive Loss Rules

In the past, many high-earning individuals sought *tax-shelter* investments that were designed to produce a current loss rather than a profit. This loss could then be used on the individual's tax return to cancel out earnings which otherwise would have been taxed at a high-bracket rate of as much as 50%. Ideally, a tax-shelter investment would mostly generate "paper losses" produced by the tax law rather than an actual cash loss.

For example, the most common of these tax shelters were investments in rental real estate. The paper losses in real estate came from the annual depreciation allowances permitted under the law. (Depreciation can be claimed as a deduction even if the property is increasing in value.)

The 1986 Tax Reform Act cracked down on tax-shelter investments by restricting losses produced by *passive activities*. The basic idea is that losses produced by a *passive activity* cannot be used to offset either *earned income* or *investment income* from stocks, savings accounts, etc. These losses can only be used to offset income from other passive activities. As enacted by Congress, the rules apply not just to passive activities which produce a paper loss, but also to activities which produce cash losses as well.

What Is a Passive Activity?

A *passive activity* is a limited partnership or other business activity in which neither you nor your spouse participates on a regular, continuous, and substantial basis. However, any rental activity is automatically considered to be a passive activity no matter what the level of personal participation.

In contrast to *business* activities, *investing* in stocks, bonds, savings accounts, etc., is not considered to be a passive activity. Also, there is a special exception for oil and gas working interests in which there is no limit on the taxpayer's liability.

Limit on Passive Losses

Losses produced by a passive activity cannot be used to offset income from active sources such as salary from a job or profits from a business run by the taxpayer. And it cannot be used to offset *investment income* such as dividends or interest. Rather, losses from passive activities can only be used to offset income from the same or other passive activities, or are deductible in the year the activity terminates.

The way this restriction on passive losses works is as follows. You first total up the profits and losses from all your passive activities. This includes any capital gains or losses generated by the sale of a passive activity. It also includes interest on debt used to buy into the passive activity as well as interest expenses incurred by the activity itself. It does not include any portfolio income such as dividends or interest on securities, even if connected with a passive activity.

Next, you compare the total profits with the total losses produced by the passive activities. If the total profits exceed the total losses, then you have a net *passive profit* for the year. In this case, the passive loss rules do not apply. The profits and losses from your passive activities are treated in the same manner as other income.

However, if the losses exceed the profits, then you have a net *passive loss* for the year, which cannot be deducted on your tax return. However, losses not currently deductible may be carried over to future years, as discussed later in this section.

Exceptions

There is an exception to the above disallowance rule for passive losses. This exception for rental real estate losses applies to anyone whose adjusted gross income does not exceed $100,000 (ignoring IRA contributions, taxable social security benefits, and passive activity losses). Such an individual can exempt up to $25,000 of her/his net losses produced by rental real estate from the passive loss disallowance rule. To qualify for this exception, the individual (together with her spouse) must own at least 10% of the rental real estate and must be an *active participant* in the rental activity. To qualify as an *active participant,* the individual need not manage the property personally. But she needs to be involved in basic decision-making activities such as choosing tenants, approving repairs, etc. (The rental property exception also can apply to a vacation home which is rented out, on average, for periods of 7 days or less. Here the $100,000 and $25,000 limitations do not apply. However, in this case, the owner must either be the only one performing services connected with the rental or meet a *material participation* standard requiring a minimum number of 100 hours of service.)

The $25,000 passive loss exemption for rental real estate is phased out at the rate of 50 cents for each dollar of income over $100,000. For example, an individual with adjusted gross income of $110,000 could exempt $20,000 of rental real estate losses. The exemption is entirely phased out for those with adjusted gross income of $150,000 or more.

For married persons filing separately, the $25,000, $100,000, and $150,000 figures above are halved, provided they lived apart for the entire year. If they did live together and are filing separately, the $25,000 exemption is eliminated altogether.

Carry-Over Provisions

There are 2 carry-over provisions which cushion the passive loss rules. First, any passive losses which are disallowed in a given year may be carried over to be deducted against passive profits in future years. Second, in the year you sell your entire remaining interest in a passive activity to an unrelated party, any unused passive losses connected with this activity can be deducted. Thus, the passive loss rules do not really *deny* deductions, so much as *delay* these deductions until a future time.

What Should You Do If You Have Disallowed Passive Losses?

Seek help. You will need professional assistance if you are caught in the web of the passive loss rules. For one thing, you may be able to negate the effect of these rules by investing in other suitable passive activities which produce a profit. Or, you may want to sell or abandon a passive activity in order to be able to claim any unused losses under the carry-over provisions.

There is a Form 8582 to be filled out if there are passive activities with net losses. This form will carry you through the appropriate computation. In addition, there are special instructions on Schedules A, C, D, and E of Form 1040 that may apply if you have passive losses.

You are exempted from the requirement to file Form 8582 if you satisfy the exception for rental real estate losses described above. For this filing exemption, your adjusted gross income must actually be less than $100,000, not in the phase-out range above $100,000. Also, your only passive losses must be from rental real estate activities in which you materially participate.

If you own a home that you rent out for part of the year and live in for part of the year, then the passive loss rules may result in disallowance of interest expenses on your tax return. If this is the case, any interest disallowed in connection with the passive activity may still be deductible as interest on a primary or second home [see Section 4 of the *Homeowners* chapter].

SECTION 3:
U.S. TREASURY SECURITIES

When you purchase U.S. Treasury Securities (sometimes just called *U.S. Treasuries*), you are making a loan to the U.S. Government. These securities fall into one of three categories according to their maturity lengths. *Treasury bills* have maturity lengths of 3 to 12 months; *Treasury notes* from 2 to 10 years; and *Treasury bonds* of 30 years. The minimum purchase amount for Treasury bills is $10,000; for Treasury notes with maturities less than 4 years, $5,000; and for Treasury notes and bonds with maturities 4 years or longer, $1,000. (U.S. Savings Bonds fall into a different category and are discussed at the end of this Section.)

U.S. Treasuries offer the following advantages:

1. Safety

U.S. Treasuries are the safest securities you can own, being backed by the full faith and credit of the U.S. Government. You are guaranteed to receive all interest payments due in addition to the full principal upon maturity.

This guarantee is stronger than the one backing bank and savings & loan deposits up to $100,000 per account. When a bank or savings & loan goes under, an agency of the U.S. Government will assure that your deposits are returned to you plus interest earned up to the date of default. However, you may have to wait a period of time before receiving any money and can lose interest on your funds for the duration of this period.

U.S. Treasuries, however, are subject to the same market risks as other securities. That is, if the prevailing market interest rate goes up, the value of the securities goes down. This risk is the strongest for long-term securities like 30-year Treasury bonds and the smallest for short-term securities like 3-month Treasury bills.

2. Competitive Interest Rates

Interest rates on short-term U.S. Treasuries are competitive with interest rates paid on certificates of deposit. In fact, sometimes the yield on a U.S. Treasury will exceed the rate you can get from your bank or savings & loan on a C.D. with the same maturity. As discussed later in this section, you can use the U.S. Treasury rates reported in the newspaper to make an exact comparison with the rates paid by your local bank or savings & loan.

Because they are guaranteed by the government, long-term U.S. Treasuries do not pay as high an interest rate as bonds issued by private corporations. However, the spread is not as great as one might expect. For example, long-term U.S. Treasuries were recently paying interest rates of about 3/4% less than high quality corporate bonds.

3. Liquidity

Because there is a huge market in U.S. Treasuries, they are very easy to buy or sell. *The Wall Street Journal* and major daily newspapers contain a listing of the quotes each day and most any bank or stockbroker can execute a purchase or sale at the going rate. (Also, there is a lower spread between bid and ask prices than on stocks or bonds traded on major stock exchanges.)

4. No Unwanted Calls

Many corporate and municipal bonds have a "call" provision which allows the issuer to buy back your bond. This comes into play if market interest rates go down. In this case, if the issuer calls your bond, you are unable to earn the same interest rate as you have been receiving. In contrast, the vast majority of U.S. Treasuries cannot be called early. If interest rates go down, you continue earning the higher interest rate until the date of maturity.

A similar comparison can be made with federally-backed mortgage securities like GNMAs. When interest rates fall, more people pay off their mortgages, causing a larger payout of principal. Once again, you are unable to earn as high an interest rate as you were before.

5. Freedom from State and Local Income Tax

Interest you receive on Treasury securities is exempt from state and local income tax (but not from federal income tax). This gives it an advantage over competing investments, such as certificates of deposit and corporate bonds, which are subject to state and local income tax.

Income from mutual funds which invest only in Treasury securities is also free of state and local income tax in most states. However, there are some states which do tax such income.

How to Purchase Treasury Securities

There are 2 basic ways to purchase Treasury securities:

1. Purchase Through a Bank or Stockbroker

You can purchase existing securities through a bank or stockbroker. The commission on such a transaction is about $50. This is a prohibitive 5% commission on a $1,000 purchase, but only a 1/10 of one percent commission on a $50,000 purchase. You can sell Treasuries before maturity through a bank or stockbroker also.

You can find a listing of the Treasury yields for various maturities in the *Wall Street Journal* or other daily newspaper. The *yield* column is the one you want to look at. It shows the annualized yield to maturity, which is the figure that should be used to compare competing investments.

The yield should not be confused with the *coupon rate*. The coupon rate is based on the rate at the time of issuance. When buying a Treasury security after issuance, you are paying that price which will produce the quoted yield. This price will be more or less than the original cost depending on which way interest rates have moved.

Treasury bills have the peculiarity of being purchased on a *discount basis*. This means, for example, that a 10% one-year bill with face value of $10,000 would actually be purchased for $9,000 and redeemed one year later for $10,000. This produces an annualized yield of ($10,000 − $9,000)/$9,000 = 11.11%, a higher rate than the quoted 10% rate. This is the general situation. When purchasing a Treasury bill, you need to check out the *annualized yield* figure in the newspaper if you want to make a comparison with other investments. Keep in mind that Treasury bills are not a capital asset, so the capital gains rates never apply to earnings you receive.

2. Purchase Directly from U.S. Government

Treasury Securities can be purchased directly from the government without paying any commissions. This is done through a *Treasury Direct* account which you can open with the government by mail. When you open this account, you must designate a checking or savings account at a financial institution into which interest and principal payments are deposited. Once deposited, these funds are fully available to you by writing checks or making cash withdrawals. The government does not send any checks directly to you.

A convenient feature of the Treasury Direct system is the ease with which part or all of the money received at maturity can be reinvested. Well before maturity, a letter will be sent to remind you that your securities are coming due. The letter will explain your reinvestment options, and you indicate your choice by return mail.

In some cases you are allowed to indicate future automatic investments. For example, with 3-month bills, you can designate that automatic reinvestments be made every 3 months over a 2-year period. You can cancel the reinvestment designation by giving notice at least 20 days prior to any of the maturity dates.

You can purchase U.S. Treasury notes or bonds by mailing a cashiers check or a personal check. For Treasury bills, a personal check must be certified. This means you will have to lose a few days' interest until the purchase is officially consummated. If you prefer, you can deliver cash or check to a Federal Reserve Bank in person.

When individuals purchase U.S. Treasuries directly from the government, they usually do so on a *noncompetitive* basis. This means that they will accept the market yield determined when the government auctions the bills. This will be the lowest yield needed to sell all the securities to meet the government's needs. If you wish, you can also make a competitive bid specifying the yield you wish to receive. If the market yield set by the auction equals or exceeds the yield you have specified, your purchase will go through. Otherwise, your money will be returned to you.

To set up a Treasury Direct account for the purchase of U.S. Government securities, you can write to: *Bureau of Public Debt; 1300 C Street, S.W.; Washington D.C. 20239.* They will send you an application form plus the appropriate informational material. According to this material, thousands of government checks are lost or stolen in the mail each year. But with Treasury Direct, this is not a problem because funds are transferred electronically.

Instead of writing, you can call 202-874-4000. This will get a recording which gives you a menu of options for listening to various informational tapes. As the recording will indicate, when you press the appropriate button on a touch tone telephone, you will be connected to a human being if you call during regular business hours. This person can answer questions you may have and will mail application forms and informational material you need.

Instead of contacting Washington, D.C., you can call, write, or visit the Federal Reserve Bank servicing your area. You can even make purchases in person at one of these banks, if you don't want to transact business by mail. Your local bank should be able to give you the address and telephone number of the nearest Federal Reserve Bank.

You can also obtain information and forms for opening an account on the Internet at www.publicdebt.treas.gov/sec/sectrdir.htm.

Inflation-Indexed U.S. Bonds

In 1997, the U.S. Government began issuing bonds that are guaranteed to provide a positive yield after inflation is taken into account. At the time of issuance, a basic real interest rate is determined (around 3.5% annually in 2000). Every 6 months, the bond principal is adjusted upward for inflation, and the basic interest rate is applied to the enlarged principal. The following example illustrates this procedure.

Example

Smith purchases a $1,000 10-year inflation-indexed U.S. Bond when it is issued at the beginning of the year. The basic annual interest rate on the bond is 3.5%. During the year, the annual inflation rate is 4%. Because the inflation adjustment is made twice a year, the semiannual rate is 4% ÷ 2 = 2%.

At midyear, the principal is adjusted upward by the semiannual 2% inflation factor, $1,000 x 1.02 = $1,020. An interest payment is made to Smith based on the increased principal and the basic semiannual interest rate of 3.5% ÷ 2 = 1.75%. This payment to Smith equals $1,020 x 1.75% = $17.85.

At year-end, the principal is adjusted upward again, $1,020 x 1.02 = $1,040. The interest payment made to Smith at year-end equals $1,040 x 1.75% = $18.20.

A similar calculation is made each 6 months until the end of the 10-year maturity is reached. At that time the final interest payment will be made and the entire upward adjusted principal paid out to Smith. In real (after inflation) dollars, when Smith received the final principal payment, he gets back the same amount he originally invested. Plus, he had received real interest payments at an annual rate of 3.5%.

In the above example, Smith received interest payments of $17.85 + $18.20 = $35.95. Also, the principal on the bond increased by $1,040 – $1,000 = $40. This increase in principal is deemed to be additional interest, not a capital gain. As a result, Smith reports interest income on his tax return of $35.95 + $40 = $75.95. Thus, Smith will be paying tax not only on the $35.95 income he received, but also on the $40 which he didn't receive as a cash payment. Smith will not have to pay any capital gains tax when the bond matures because he has already made tax payments annually on the increase in principal value.

Inflation-indexed U.S. Bonds with 10-year maturities are sold in denominations of $1,000. You can buy these bonds directly from the government when they are issued every 3 months. (For information, call the Bureau of the Public Debt at 202-874-4000 or visit the above-mentioned website.) These bonds also trade in the market after the issue date. You can make purchases at any time through stockbrokers or some banks.

U.S. EE Savings Bonds

U.S. EE Savings Bonds fall into a different category from the U.S. Treasury Securities discussed above. For one thing, they are aimed at the "little guy," with a minimum purchase of only $25 and a maximum purchase per person per year of $15,000.

Second, the rate structure is different. The rules have been changed for bonds issued after April 30, 1997. Bonds issued after this date earn interest at 90% of the rate on 5-year Treasury securities averaged over the preceding 6 months. Interest is credited monthly and compounded semiannually.

New rates on EE bonds are announced each May and November. These rates apply not just to newly issued bonds but to existing bonds as well. Thus the interest rate on a EE savings bond will vary over the course of time instead of being fixed at the time of purchase, as is the case with other U.S. Treasury securities. For the 6-month period May 1, 2001 – November 1, 2001, EE bonds were being credited with an annualized interest rate of 5.73%.

You can cash in a EE bond at any time after 6 months from the purchase date. However, if you cash in before 5 years have passed, you will be penalized 3 months interest. Bonds can be purchased and cashed in at most banks, credit unions, and savings institutions.

EE bonds are sold at half their face value and are in denominations ranging from $50 through $10,000. Thus a $100 face value bond would sell for $50. The selling price is what counts. The face value basically has no meaning because the value of the bond at any time is completely determined by the changing semiannual interest rate. When you cash in, the amount you get will almost certainly not equal the face value. The only significance of the face value is that if interest rates are so low that the bond value does not equal face value by the time it is 17 years old, the value of the bond will be adjusted upward to equal face value. This amounts to an interest guarantee of about 4% over the 17-year period.

EE bonds earn interest for 30 years. If you keep them longer than this time, you will no longer be earning interest each month. Further information on U.S. Savings Bonds, including the mechanics of purchase, is contained in Section 1 of the *Expenses of Attending School* chapter.

Tax Advantages

U.S. Savings Bonds offer the following 3 tax advantages:

1. Exemption from State and Local Tax

As with all U.S. Government obligations, interest on U.S. EE Savings Bonds is not subject to state or local tax. (However, interest is subject to federal tax.)

2. Deferral of Federal Income Tax

If you wish, you can wait until the year you cash in the bonds to report the interest on your tax return. This deferral is advantageous unless there is a large increase in tax rates. However, if you wish to report the interest each year, you have the option of doing so. This might be the case with bonds owned by a child who pays little or no current income tax.

3. Tax Exemption when Used to Pay for College Tuition

There is an exemption from federal and state income tax when U.S. EE Savings Bonds are cashed in and used to pay for college tuition and fees. However, there are a number of restrictions. Details are contained in Section 1 of the *Expenses of Attending School* chapter.

SECTION 4:
MUNICIPAL BONDS

Municipal bonds are issued by cities, states, counties, or other local governments. The chief feature of such bonds is that the interest they pay is entirely exempt from federal income tax. If the bond is issued by a governmental body in the purchaser's home state, then the interest is also exempt from state income tax.

A bond is simply a loan. The **purchaser** of a bond is lending the issuer a fixed amount of money called the **principal** of the loan. In return, the issuer pays periodic interest at a fixed rate for a certain length of time. After this period of time, the bond reaches its **maturity date** and the issuer returns the principal to the purchaser. Municipal bonds are issued in denominations of $1,000.

General Obligation Bonds are fully guaranteed by the issuing municipality, so that the full taxing authority of the municipality stands behind the bond. **Revenue Bonds** are guaranteed only by the revenue of some income-producing facility. A typical example of this is a toll road bond which is backed by the income which that toll road produces. If the toll road operates at a deficit, the bondholders will suffer because there will not be enough revenue to make the required interest payments.

Certain *private activity* municipal bonds issued after August 7, 1986 might be subjected to alternative minimum tax [see the *Alternative Minimum Tax* chapter]. An individual should seek professional advice before purchasing a sizable amount of such bonds.

For tax purposes, bonds issued by U.S. territories such as Puerto Rico are treated as municipal bonds for federal purposes and U.S. obligations for state purposes. Check the rules in your state.

How Municipal Bonds Are Purchased

When they are issued, municipal bonds are usually sold through brokerage houses. After that, the bonds may be traded on the open market. That is, the original purchaser can sell to someone else who in turn can sell when he wishes, etc. Typically, bonds are resold through brokerage houses, which keep an inventory of certain bonds. They will be willing to buy your bonds from you or sell bonds to you from their inventory. They make their profit by keeping a spread between the price they are willing to pay for a bond and the price at which they are willing to sell.

Due to the large number of different types of municipal bonds, they are not as liquid an investment as stocks or corporate bonds. This is particularly true for small numbers of bonds or bonds issued by obscure municipalities.

The interest rate paid on a bond depends upon the maturity date, the financial strength of the issuer, and the general level of interest rates in the economy. The current market value of a bond rises and falls as the general interest level varies. When interest rates rise, the value of a bond will fall and when interest rates fall the bond value will rise. However, this effect is muted as the maturity date draws close because a bond is worth precisely its face value on the maturity date.

There are also no-load mutual funds which invest in municipal bonds and pass along the tax-free feature to the individual investors. These mutual funds are useful because they provide instant liquidity with no sales or redemption charges. These funds are are discussed further in Section 5.

Reporting Tax-Free Income on Your Tax Return

You are required to report tax-free interest you receive from municipal bonds on line 8b of your Form 1040. The amount you report on this line is not subject to tax, and the IRS currently does not match the amount against any other information it receives as it does with taxable wages, dividends, interest, etc. Rather, Congress wants data on tax-free income mainly to use in designing future tax bills.

However, there are 2 situations in which the IRS might possibly use the information reported on line 8b. First, this amount might affect the amount of tax due if you are receiving social security income [see Section 4 of the *Retirement Plans* chapter]. Second, it might be used to determine if you're wrongly deducting interest on loans used to buy or carry tax-free municipal bonds [see the *Interest* chapter].

SECTION 5:
MUTUAL FUNDS

A mutual fund is an easy way to invest in securities. The fund maintains a diversified portfolio of securities and sells shares in the fund to the general public. When you purchase a share in the fund, you are simply purchasing a proportionate piece of all its securities. The securities held by the fund do not remain constant. The management of the fund will buy and sell securities as it feels such a change will be advantageous.

There are hundreds of different funds. Almost any type of investment philosophy is represented by some fund. The majority of funds maintain a portfolio of common stocks. Some of these stock funds aim at high growth, some at high current yield, and some aim in the middle. Whatever their basic objective, most invest in a wide number of different industries. But there are exceptions to this. For example, you can invest in a fund which only purchases stocks involved in the energy industry.

While mutual funds investing in common stocks have been around a long time, a number of different types of funds have been developed within the past several decades. These new funds invest in tax-free municipal bonds, money-market instruments, high-yielding bonds, etc., depending upon their objective. And these newer funds permit money to be withdrawn much easier than the old type funds — by telephone, telegram, or even by writing a check against the funds in one's account. Further discussion is contained in the next section.

Load vs. No-Load Funds

A *load fund* is one for which you must pay a sales commission (as much as $7^1/2$ percent) in order to purchase shares. A *no-load fund* charges no sales commission.

Most funds are load funds, which testifies to the salesmanship ability of the investment industry. There is no reason to believe that by charging a sales commission a fund will be better able to decide what stocks to purchase. In fact, studies show that, on average, no-load and load funds perform about the same.

No-load funds are typically sold through the mail and a number are advertised in newspapers and financial publications such as the *Wall Street Journal.* A directory of no-load mutual funds, *The Investor's Guide,* can be obtained from the *Mutual Fund Education Alliance*; 1900 Erie Street, Suite 120; Kansas City, MO 64116 — or visit mutual fund sites on the Internet.

There is a middle category, sometimes called *hidden-load* funds, which are basically akin to load funds. However, instead of charging an up-front sales commission, these funds bury their extra charges in some other manner: e.g., by charging a redemption fee or by levying extra annual *distribution fees* (sometimes referred to as *12b-1* fees).

The change to hidden-load funds was a huge marketing success for brokerage houses because investors couldn't spot the hidden fees like they could the up-front sales fees on regular load funds. But, as discussed below, the Securities and Exchange Commission (SEC) has made it much easier to detect the existence of such "hidden" fees.

You should also be aware of the so-called *rolling load* or *load waived* mutual funds, sometimes recommended by financial advisors. These do not have a front-end or back-end load fee. Instead, these funds charge an extra annual fee of about 1% which goes towards paying commissions to whoever advised you to buy the fund. Be sure you know all the fees that will be charged before investing in any particular mutual fund.

You should be aware that many funds charge load fees as well as the hidden fees discussed above.

SEC Requirements Make it Easier to Compare Mutual Funds

There are 3 disclosure requirements which make it easier to compare mutual funds with respect to yields, overall performance, and fees.

1. Newspaper Listings of Mutual Funds Must Indicate the Existence of Extra Fees.

As discussed above, there are many hidden-load mutual funds which attempt to camouflage extra fees by charging redemption fees, extra annual distribution fees, etc. In the past, these extra fees could not be detected just by looking at a newspaper's daily listing of mutual fund prices. Rather, the only sure-fire way of detecting extra fees was to examine the fund's prospectus.

But this situation has changed. Now, the existence of extra charges is indicated in newspaper listings—by the letter *p* for extra distribution fees or the letter *r* for redemption fees.

For example, a newspaper listing might contain the following information:

	NAV	Offer Price
AAA Fund r	6.71	6.71
BBB Fund	p 9.10	N.L.
CCC Fund r	p 10.53	10.53
DDD Fund	11.10	11.56
EEE Fund	8.73	N.L.

In the above example, only the *EEE Fund* is a true no-load fund. This can be spotted by the designation *N.L.* in the *Offer Price* column plus the absence of the letters *r, p,* or *t* (*t* is sometimes used when both *r* and *p* apply). The existence of a load charge in the first 3 funds is indicated by the letters *r* and/or *p*. The load in the *DDD Fund* is indicated by the discrepancy between the figure in the NAV column (the *Net Asset Value,* i.e., price you would receive if selling a share) and the *Offer Price,* which you would pay if buying a share.

To get a more precise picture of the fees charged by a fund, you need to look at the prospectus. This is discussed below.

2. Mutual Funds Must Spell Out All Fees in a Standard Format.

In the past, it was often difficult to get a direct comparison between mutual funds and their fee structures. Sometimes, information on fees would be buried in various places on the inside of a formidable-looking prospectus.

But the SEC (Securities and Exchange Commission) changed this situation. Now, mutual funds are required to lay out their fees in a standardized tabular form and to compute what these fees would add up to on a $1,000 investment over several time periods. This information must be reported on one of the first few pages of the mutual fund's prospectus.

The following is an example of how the fee schedule would look for a typical no-load mutual fund.

A. Shareholder Transaction Expenses

Sales Load Imposed on Purchases	None
Sales Load Imposed on Reinvested Dividends	None
Redemption Fees	None
Exchange Fees	None

B. Annual Fund Operating Expenses

Management and Advisory Expenses	.32%
Investment Advisory Fees	.26%
Shareholder Accounting Costs	None
12b-1 Fees	.10%
Distribution Costs	None
Other Expenses	.06%
Total Operating Expenses	.74%

C. Example

You should pay the following expenses on a $1,000 investment, assuming (i) a 5% annual return, and (ii) redemption at the end of each time period:

1 year	$7
3 years	$24
5 years	$42
10 years	$94

There are several things to observe in the above example. First, Section A has "None" listed on each line for sales and redemption fees. If there are expenses listed on any of these lines, you're not looking at a true *no-load* fund.

Second, Section B contains a listing of the various operating expenses. The significant figure here is the bottom line — total operating expenses. In the above example, the total operating expenses are .74%. This means that for every $100 you have invested, the fund management company takes 74 cents for profit and expenses.

Section C in the above example is basically a restatement of the total operating fees figure summed over various time periods, assuming a 5% increase in value with all dividends reinvested. The only case where this section gives an extra standard of comparison is for load funds, where the sales and redemptions fees can be factored in over various time periods.

The table in the above example reflects all expenses that the fund charges for its services. However, it does not include brokerage fees that the fund pays when it buys or sells securities. These brokerage fees are built into the price performance and are not itemized separately in the prospectus.

3. Mutual Funds Must Advertise Yields the Same Way.

The SEC has instituted uniform reporting rules for advertising in newspapers or other print media. For example, income funds must use a 30-day yield figure computed in a uniform manner if they advertise their returns. And if a stock or bond fund advertises a total return figure (distributions plus increase in value), it must include its average annual total return for the past 1, 5-, and 10-year periods. In theory, this makes it possible to compare funds on a uniform basis. (In the past, funds would use the method producing the highest yield or return figure and tout that figure in their ads.) In practice, this has caused most mutual funds to delete any numerical figures from their ads.

You can call a mutual fund representative to ask for yield or total return figures. If you wind up conversing with a talking computer, then the above rules for print advertising apply. That is, the uniform 30-day yield must be the one quoted and if total return is given, the 1 year, 5-year and 10-year total returns must be provided.

However, if you end up conversing with a human, then anything goes. That is, the human can quote a yield or total return figure which puts the mutual fund in the best light. The uniform 30-day yield figure and the 1, 5-, and 10-year total return figures are required to be provided only if you specifically ask for them.

Open-End Funds

Most funds are *open-end* funds. This means that you always buy shares directly from the fund itself. The purchase price you pay is determined by evaluating the market value of all the securities and assigning a proportionate value to each share. This is called the *net asset value* of the share.

Similarly, you can redeem your shares in the fund any time you wish by selling them back to the fund at the current net asset value. When more people buy than redeem shares, the fund invests the excess cash in new securities. Conversely, when more shares are redeemed than purchased, the fund must sell some of its holdings to meet the excess redemption.

Closed-End Funds

A *closed-end* fund does not sell or redeem shares. It just invests and reinvests the money it already has, without receiving any input of new capital or experiencing any withdrawals. If you wish to buy a share of such a fund, you must find someone who will sell it to you. Similarly, to sell a share you must find a buyer. In practice these funds are sold on a stock exchange or through brokerage houses that make a market in them. Thus you don't have to look for a buyer or seller yourself.

The market value of a closed-end fund is determined by the law of supply and demand. It need not be the same as the net asset value (the proportionate share of the market value of the stocks in the fund). In fact, the market price of closed-end funds often differs from the net asset value. Generally, closed-end funds sell at a discount, that is, at a price less than the net asset value. One partial explanation for this is that because they do not guarantee redemption at net asset value as do open-end funds, the lack of this feature makes them less attractive to investors.

One might think that this discount represents a bargain. But this bargain is in the most part illusory. Unless the discount narrows in the future for some reason, the shares in the fund will not appreciate in price any faster than the value of the securities in the fund. However, you will be receiving a greater portion of the dividends than you would receive if you bought shares of the stocks themselves instead of shares in the fund.

Over the past few years, over 10 billion dollars worth of new closed-end funds have been sold by stockbrokers. When issued, these funds sell at their net asset value rather than at a discount. After a while, a discount generally appears in a loss of value, even if the stocks themselves do not change in price. This loss, when combined with commissions brokers get for selling these funds, generally makes it an unwise move to be an initial purchaser of a closed-end fund.

Tax Aspects of Mutual Funds

As with the purchase of individual shares of common stock, there are two types of taxation that occur with mutual funds. First of all, the stocks in the portfolio of the fund may pay dividends (or interest in the case of bonds). Usually, the fund allows you to receive your proportionate share of these dividends in cash or else it automatically reinvests these dividends in more shares of the fund. Either way, the value of these dividends is ordinary income to you and is taxed at your usual rate. The fund will provide you with an annual statement as to the amount of dividends on which you must pay tax.

The second type of taxation is the tax on capital gains. This can occur in two ways. First of all, the fund itself realizes a capital gain or loss as it sells shares of some securities in order to purchase others. If the fund sells stock at a higher price than the purchase price, then a capital gain is created. The opposite situation produces a capital loss. At least once a year, usually in December, the fund will make a distribution if it has realized a net capital gain on the shares it sold during the year. It may distribute this gain in cash or may automatically reinvest it for you in more shares of the fund. In either event, you must report this capital gain on your tax return.

Of course, a mutual fund may realize a net capital loss in a given year instead of a capital gain. In such a case, you are not allowed to deduct the loss on your own tax return. Instead, the mutual fund is allowed to carry over these losses up to 5 years into the future in order to cancel out future capital gains. For example, if the fund incurs a $50,000 capital loss in one year followed by a $70,000 capital gain in the next year, then the outcome would be a $20,000 capital gains distribution to be reported on shareholders' tax returns the second year.

In addition to tax paid on annual capital gains distributions, you must also pay tax on capital gains if you sell your shares in the mutual fund at a higher price than your purchase price. This is treated the same way as a capital gain arising from the purchase and sale of any other asset. Of course, if you sell at a lower price than the purchase price, then you have a capital loss which can be deducted according to the usual rules for capital losses [see Section 1].

If you purchased shares of the same fund on different dates, when you sell some of these shares it is presumed that you have sold the earliest purchase shares. However, there are exceptions to this rule. If you can identify certain shares as having been purchased on a particular date, then you can use the purchase price on that date as the original cost. Or, you can use the *average cost method* to determine the purchase price. Under this method your purchase price is considered to be the average price paid for all the shares you own. There is another *double-category averaging method* under which you take 2 such averages, one for purchases resulting in long-term gains and another for short-term gains. Shares sold are considered to be taken first from the long-term category unless you specify otherwise to the mutual fund at the time of sale. With either averaging method, you have to indicate on your tax return what you're doing. Consult your mutual fund for further information on electing one of these alternate methods.

If the mutual fund has been reinvesting your dividends or capital gains distributions, the following example shows how to avoid overpaying tax on capital gains when you sell your shares.

Example

You purchase $5,000 worth of shares in a mutual fund. Over a period of years, your shares are credited with $1,000 in dividends and $2,000 in capital gains distributions which are automatically reinvested to purchase more shares of the fund. You pay tax on these dividends and distributions in the years in which they are declared and reinvested. After 5 years, you sell all your shares in the fund (both the original shares and the shares obtained by reinvestment of dividends and capital gains) for $10,000. To determine your final capital gain, you subtract from this $10,000 your original purchase price, $5,000, as well as all dividends and capital gains on which you have already paid tax, $3,000. Thus you must pay a tax on the capital gain of $10,000 – $5,000 – $3,000 = $2,000.

If you had sold your shares for $7,000, then this computation would yield $7,000 – $5,000 – $3,000 = –$1,000. Thus, you would have a capital loss of $1,000 in the year of sale which you deduct according to the usual rules for deducting capital losses.

Mutual Funds That Will Calculate Your Capital Gains Basis for You

The logical thing is for mutual funds to make the capital gains computations for their investors. After all, they have the purchase and sales data in their computers. But the mutual fund industry, because of legal and other concerns, resisted taking this step.

However, a number of mutual funds make basis computations for their investors. These funds will provide you with a printout of your transactions during the year, along with the capital gains or losses produced by the sales. You can then transfer these numbers to Schedule D, instead of having to compute them yourself.

Those mutual funds which compute tax results for their investors generally use the *average cost method* for computing capital gains and losses. However, others may use a different method or even provide a choice of methods on which their tax computations can be based. If you have an existing account, there may be a restriction on the date your account was initiated. If this date was too far in the past, the mutual fund may not be able to perform the necessary computations. In this case, you would need to open up a new account to be able to obtain tax computations in the future, while computing your tax basis from your old records for shares owned prior to this action.

All of the following 5 major no-load mutual companies now provide tax calculations for their investors based on the average cost method: *Dreyfus, Fidelity, T. Rowe Price, Scudder,* and *Vanguard.* The addresses and telephone numbers of these mutual fund companies are given later in this Section.

Tax Considerations in Buying Mutual Funds

The tax rules regarding capital gains distributions suggest a number of important considerations. First of all, you should **not** buy mutual funds shortly before a capital gains distribution is about to be declared. Otherwise, you're simply buying a tax liability.

Example

On November 1, you purchase shares in a mutual fund for $5.00 per share. One month later, a capital gains distribution of 50 cents per share is declared. The price of the mutual fund will automatically decline a corresponding amount so that you now have shares worth $4.50 per share plus the 50 cents per share distribution. But you must now pay tax on this 50 cents per share. Had you purchased your shares after the distribution was declared, you would not have paid any tax. Of course, in the first case, the decline from $5.00 per share to $4.50 per share produces an unrealized capital loss. But until you sell your shares in the fund, this loss gives you no tax benefit. In the meantime, you lose all the interest you could earn on the tax you paid.

Before purchasing a mutual fund, you can check to see if they have realized any capital gains so far that year. This information should be contained in their quarterly reports. Or, you can call the mutual fund for this information.

The disadvantage in buying a tax liability corresponds to an advantage in the opposite situation. That is, you may be able to buy a tax credit. For example, suppose that a mutual fund has incurred capital losses in the past few years. These losses can be carried over into the future to offset capital gains. Thus, if the mutual fund realizes capital gains after you purchase it, no capital gains distribution will be declared until the gains exceed the carried-over losses. In effect, you have bought into a tax credit situation. You will be delaying the payment of capital gains tax until you sell your shares of the mutual fund.

In addition, you should consider not only the *realized* capital gain or loss situation of a mutual fund, but also its *unrealized* capital gains or losses. For example, the current portfolio may have a market price which is lower than the total prices at which the stocks were purchased, so that the fund has a net unrealized loss.

It is better to purchase mutual funds with an unrealized loss than an unrealized gain. As a mutual fund changes its portfolio by selling stocks it owns, these unrealized losses become realized and produce a capital loss. Thus any capital gains the mutual fund achieves will be reduced by these losses. Conversely, if a fund has unrealized gains, then capital gains are produced when the fund sells its stocks, even if their value is no higher than when you bought into the fund. You may wind up with a capital gains distribution even though you haven't made any profit. You can find out the extent of any unrealized capital gains or losses by examining the prospectus or annual report of the mutual fund, or by calling the mutual fund company.

We have seen in the above discussion that it is better to buy mutual funds with realized or unrealized capital losses. In the case of open-end funds, the tax advantage of such funds costs nothing extra because the price of shares in the fund is simply determined by the prices of the stocks in the portfolio. The tax situation of the fund plays no part in determining the price of its shares. This is one of the rare cases in the investment world of getting something for nothing.

How Do You Choose a Mutual Fund?

We have already touched upon the various criteria that are important in selecting a fund in which to invest. You should purchase a no-load fund that invests in the type of securities meeting your general objective, whether it be high current income, long-term capital growth, speculation, etc. You should also look for a fund with unrealized or realized capital losses. And you may wish to select a fund that computes capital gains and losses for you, as discussed above.

Next, you should check the *expense ratio* of the fund. All funds deduct a certain percentage of the net asset value to cover operating expenses and investment advice, and provide a profit to the fund operators. This percentage is generally in the 1% range. However, even among large comparable no-load funds, there can be a substantial difference in the amount of fees charged.

There are no indications that higher fees correlate with better fund performance. This is particularly evident with money-market funds, which all invest in basically the same type of securities. For example, the Vanguard money-market fund, with a low expense charge, has shown one of the largest returns over the past few years. And the funds with the highest fees did poorly.

Note that the expense ratio of a mutual fund does not include brokerage commissions. These are considered a "capital expense" and serve to reduce any capital gains or enlarge capital losses incurred as the fund changes its portfolio. Therefore, you should also check the *turnover rate* of the fund, which is, the percentage of the portfolio that gets changed during the year. For example, a fund with a turnover rate of 20% during a given year has bought and sold stocks representing 20% of its portfolio. The other 80% has not changed. Turnover rates vary widely among funds. By selecting a fund with a low turnover rate, you will in effect be paying less brokerage costs. This could amount to an advantage of several percentage points a year. Also, a lower turnover rate generally results in less realized capital gains producing less taxable income.

Finally, you might want to examine the past performance of the funds in which you are interested. However, this information may be of dubious value. Frankly, there is no compelling evidence that funds which have performed well in the past will continue to perform well in the long-term future.

Selected Mutual Fund Companies

The following is a list of some of the largest mutual fund companies. Each of these companies offers a wide range of different types of no-load mutual funds, including money-market funds, bond funds, stock funds, etc.

T. Rowe Price Funds	**Vanguard Investment Group**	**Dreyfus Funds**
P.O. Box 17630	P.O. Box 1110	144 Glenn Curtis Blvd.
Baltimore, MD 21297-1630	Valley Forge, PA 19482-1110	Uniondale, NY 11556-0144
800-225-5132	800-871-3879	800-782-6620
www.troweprice.com	www.vanguard.com	www.dreyfus.com

Fidelity Investment Group
P.O. Box 770001
Cincinnati, OH 45277-0001
800-FIDELITY
www.fidelity.com

Scudder Funds
P.O. Box 219669
Kansas City, MO 64121-9669
800-728-3337
www.scudder.com

Janus Funds
P.O. Box 173375
Denver, CO 80217-3375
800-975-9932
www.janus.com

The large no-load fund companies are probably the best place to look if you wish to invest in a mutual fund. To start with, no-load funds are a much better deal than load funds. The sales or redemption fee which rewards a stockbroker or sales agent for selling you the fund does not make the fund any smarter in picking investments. In fact, studies show that load and no-load funds perform the same on average, not counting the extra fees.

Among no-load funds, bigger is better when it comes to fees. On average, the larger the total assets in the fund, the lower the operating fees. This means that the large no-load funds run by the mammoth no-load organizations generally have the lowest fees.

In fact, the larger no-load organizations have other advantages as well. For one thing, there is safety in numbers. A large mutual fund run by a major no-load institution does not have the same risk from incompetent or dishonest management that might be present with an isolated mutual fund.

Another advantage is that the large no-load funds generally get high marks for service. In particular, *Vanguard, Fidelity,* and *T. Rowe Price* have all scored near the top in several surveys of investors concerning the quality of services provided.

Where Do You Find Information about Mutual Funds?

It is possible to get information on mutual funds without contacting each mutual fund company directly. You can contact the non-profit *Mutual Fund Education Alliance* for the Guide mentioned near the beginning of this Section. Also, a number of services provide annual data on mutual funds, including their past performance, investment philosophy, expense rate, and turnover rate. These services can be found in the financial reference section of your library. If your library does not have an adequate financial section, then you should check through back issues of *Forbes Magazine* in most libraries. Each August, *Forbes* publishes statistics on all mutual funds currently available. Also, each February, *Money Magazine* gives information, including expense rates, on all the major mutual funds.

The Wall Street Journal and major local newspapers report the prices of mutual funds each day. Strangely, they do not report the most important piece of information needed to evaluate bond funds — namely their yield. Some information can be found in *Money Magazine,* which publishes a monthly list of the yields paid by the larger bond funds.

Each Friday, the *Wall Street Journal* contains an expanded mutual fund listing containing each fund's sales charge, expense ratios, and performance over several time intervals. Other basic information is published on other days of the week.

One piece of information that is not likely to be found in general reference material is the extent of unrealized or realized capital gains or losses. You will probably have to get this information from the mutual fund prospectus or annual report itself.

Special Types of Mutual Funds

Tax-Managed Mutual Funds

A new type of stock-holding mutual fund has become available which minimizes the amount of tax that shareholders need to pay. There are 2 types of taxes that shareholders are called upon to pay. The first is a tax on the distributions the funds make that consists of interest and dividend income earned by the securities held in the portfolio. The second is a a tax on distributions that represent net capital gains earned by the fund when it sells securities at prices higher than when they were purchased.

A *tax-managed mutual fund* reduces these taxes to a minimum by acting as follows: First, the fund invests in stocks that pay very low dividends. This minimizes taxes that become due on income distributions. Second, the fund keeps the selling of stocks in its portfolio to a minimum. And when some stocks need to be sold, those stocks producing the smallest capital gains are chosen. Furthermore, if some capital gains are produced, stocks that have gone down in value are sold to produce offsetting capital losses. In this way, capital gains distributions can be essentially eliminated, along with the attending tax to the shareholders.

Of course, tax cannot be eliminated if you sell shares of the mutual fund at a higher price than your purchase price. Since tax-managed mutual funds invest primarily in low-yielding high growth stocks, substantial capital gains might occur. However, if you hold on to the shares of the mutual fund a long time, tax can be delayed for many years. This is a financial advantage because a delay in payment of tax allows you to earn investment income on the unpaid tax amounts for many years, substantially increasing after-tax yield. And if you should die before the mutual funds are sold, all income tax is escaped because your heirs can sell the shares and pay no income tax at all.

The best examples of tax-managed mutual funds are the ones offered by a pioneer in this type of investment — the Vanguard Group investment company. Its primary tax-managed portfolio is the *Capital Opportunity Portfolio.* This portfolio invests in a diversified sample of stocks selected from the Russell 1000 Index, a benchmark of large- and medium-capitalization stocks. The portfolio emphasizes stocks with low yields to minimize taxable income. In a recent financial statement, the income distributions on the Capital Opportunity Portfolio were averaging a low 1/2 of one percent per year. And the capital gains distributions for the upcoming year were anticipated to be zero.

The Vanguard Group also offers two other tax-managed portfolios. The *Growth and Income Portfolio* invests in substantially all stocks in the Standard and Poor's 500 Composite Stock Price Index. Of course, this means that income distributions must be about the same as the stocks in the index — an average of about 2.25% per year. However, by tax-managed selling as described above, capital gains distributions are kept almost non-existent.

A third Vanguard portfolio invests 50% in intermediate-term municipal bonds and 50% in stocks with low dividend yields selected from the Russell 1000. This keeps taxable income distributions to a minimum, while replacing 50% of the stock holdings in the Capital Appreciation Portfolio by less risky intermediate municipal bonds.

As with all Vanguard funds, operating expenses are far lower than the average of other mutual funds. Operating expenses for the Vanguard tax-managed funds are estimated to be .20% per year.

However, there are two extra redemption fees which do not apply to other Vanguard funds. These fees are designed primarily to discourage short-term investing, so that tax-generating turnover can be minimized. On shares redeemed within one year of purchase, the redemption fee is 2%, and for shares redeemed between one and five years, the redemption fee is 1%. No redemption fee applies to shares held longer than five years. However, the fees are not treated as sales commissions. Rather, they are credited to the portfolios to help defray transaction costs. Thus the fees, while disadvantageous to short-term investors, are actually advantageous to long-term investors.

To get more information about Vanguard tax-managed funds, you can call its toll-free number: 1-800-871-3879.

Municipal Bond Funds

These funds invest in bonds issued by state and local governments. As interest income is distributed to investors, this income is exempt from federal income tax. Most of these funds are set up to provide maximum liquidity. Interest is credited on a daily basis from the date of investment to the date of withdrawal. Usually, this interest is automatically reinvested to purchase additional shares in the fund. If you prefer, you can have monthly interest checks mailed to you.

Investments are made by mailing a check or having your bank wire money to the fund. A number of options are available when it comes to withdrawal. The slowest way to withdraw funds is to request the fund to mail the money to you. More speedy withdrawal methods are provided by most funds. For example, you can call a toll-free number and request that money be wired to your bank account by the next day.

The best withdrawal system, offered by many of the funds, is a checkwriting privilege. These funds have a special arrangement with a bank whereby the bank issues you checks which you write against the balance in your municipal bond fund. The checks must exceed a specified minimum, typically between $100 and $500.

This check-writing arrangement has the extra advantage of your funds earning interest up until the day your check clears. This can be especially useful when paying taxes. Often, governmental agencies will take a long time before they cash checks. You can be earning interest on your money in the meantime.

Opening an account with a municipal bond fund is easy. You fill out a short application form and mail in a check to open your account. Monthly statements are mailed to you showing the activity in your account. Each fund has a minimum amount which must be exceeded in order to open an account and a smaller minimum figure for additional contributions.

Of course, you should realize that the value of your investment will be subject to fluctuation. This is due to the fact that the municipal bonds in the fund rise and fall in value as the general level of interest rates changes in the economy. You can control this somewhat by looking at the average duration of the fund you are considering. The shorter the average duration of the fund, the lower the fluctuation in price.

Most municipal bond funds invest primarily in bonds with a high quality rating. This means there is minimal likelihood the bond will default on any interest payments. But higher quality bonds pay a lower interest rate than lesser quality bonds. Those willing to accept more risk can invest in a high-yield municipal bond fund. This type of fund invests in lower-rated bonds and therefore can pay higher interest than other bond funds. Look at the holdings of a fund to determine risk. All bond funds disclose the percentage of holdings in each ratings class.

Actually, the chance of a typical municipal bond fund suffering a substantial loss due to default is low. For one thing, even medium quality municipal bonds have a good record of meeting their interest payments. And the portfolio diversity offers substantial protection against serious default loss.

Just as there are bond funds that offer a higher risk coupled with a higher yield, there are also lower risk/lower yield funds. In this case it is not the risk of default but the risk of falling prices that is protected against. Shorter-term bonds fall less in value when interest rates rise (and rise less in value when interest rates fall). Thus, municipal bond funds investing in shorter-term bonds carry a lower risk than regular municipal bond funds.

The *Vanguard Municipal Bond Funds* provide an attractive opportunity for those who wish to shift their investment according to changes in the market and changes in their own personal circumstances. These funds maintain three separate regular portfolios — short-term, medium-term, and long-term. The shorter the term, the lower the market risk and the lower the yield. In addition, there is a high-yield portfolio investing in lower-quality bonds. An investor can choose to have his funds apportioned among any of the portfolios he chooses. Then, at any time he chooses, a toll-free telephone call will cause funds to be switched from one of the portfolios to another. The Vanguard Municipal Bond Funds provide check-writing privileges and a lower than average management fee. Further information can be obtained by calling Vanguard's toll-free telephone number, 800-871-3879.

In most states, there are mutual funds that contain only in-state bonds. Income from such funds is exempt not just from federal income tax, but from state income tax as well. Many of the large mutual fund companies offer single-state funds for a number of the larger states. A list of single-state funds, along with toll-free telephone numbers, can be found in the "2001 Mutual Fund Guide" of *Money Magazine*. The list includes funds from over 40 states. You can also search for funds of all varieties at www.morningstar.com, which is an excellent source of information for the mutual fund investor.

Municipal Bond Trusts

A municipal bond trust is a second type of investment which provides tax-free interest through the purchase of municipal bonds. However, in contrast to mutual funds, these trusts do not buy and sell municipal bonds as market conditions change or as more money is invested. Instead, these trusts purchase a single portfolio of bonds that are kept until maturity. Shares of the trust are sold until the full portfolio is paid for, after which no further investments or withdrawals can be made. It is possible to sell one's shares in the trust, although this is not as easily done as withdrawing funds from a mutual fund.

These trusts generally pay a higher interest rate than municipal bond mutual funds because they invest in somewhat lower quality bonds and charge a lower annual expense fee. However, they are subject to an initial sales charge of about 4%. Because of the initial sales charge and relative illiquidity, these trusts are only suitable for the longer-term investor. The portfolios of some municipal bond trusts are insured against default by an insurance company. Municipal bond trusts are sold by most stockbrokers who will be pleased to give you further information upon request.

To escape state and local tax as well as federal tax, there might be a trust investing only in bonds issued in your state. Otherwise, investments in a different state's municipal bonds are subject to your state's income tax. Such trusts are available in a number of states, including California, Connecticut, Florida, Maryland, Massachusetts, Michigan, New Jersey, New York, Ohio, Oregon, Pennsylvania, and Virginia. The rule of thumb for investing in bonds of another state is that you need to get at least $1/2$% more in interest rate to make up for the tax you will pay to your state.

High-Yield Corporate Bond Funds

In the past decade, there has been considerable interest in mutual funds that invest in lower quality bonds (often called *junk bonds*) because these funds make it practical for an individual to earn high interest rates on his money. Because these funds invest in a wide portfolio of bonds, the risk of significant loss due to default is much less than if only a few of these bonds were purchased individually. However, individual bond defaults can lower the total return. And in the past few years, junk bond funds have had periods of significant decreases in value.

Of course, the value of shares in a bond fund is affected by changes in the interest rate. If interest rates fall, the shares will rise in value and if interest rates rise, the share price will fall.

Short-Term Funds

Money-market funds invest in very short-term debt securities, typically with maturities in the 30–60 day range, offered by the nation's leading banks and corporations. These funds operate similarly to an interest-bearing checking account, except that only large-denomination checks can be written. Further details on money-market funds are contained in the next section.

As an alternative to money-market funds, some people keep their money in a *short-term* or *limited-term* bond fund. These funds generally invest in bonds with an average maturity of 2–5 years. This tends to produce a higher interest rate than money-market funds, with substantially less market risk than long-term bond funds.

Most of the large mutual fund companies offer one or more short-term or limited-term bond funds. Also, many fund companies offer *intermediate-term* bond funds. However, these funds generally are similar to long-term funds, with a somewhat lower yield and lower market risk.

SECTION 6:
MONEY-MARKET ACCOUNTS

Money-market accounts are special accounts which pay interest based on the going short-term market rate. These accounts are liquid, allowing you to withdraw your funds at any time. Because the funds pay interest on a short-term basis, there is limited market risk. That is, you generally can't experience a loss of principal because the underlying investment does not go down in value as can happen with longer-term bonds or with stocks.

The going money-market interest rate can vary widely during the course of the year depending upon conditions in the economy.

There are now four basic different types of money-market accounts. Two of these are offered by banks and savings & loans. The other two are offered by mutual funds and stockbrokers. These four types of money-market accounts are discussed below.

Bank and Savings & Loan Money-Market Accounts

These accounts have become enormously popular. You can make an unlimited number of deposits or withdrawals in person or by mail. You can also make up to 6 additional transactions per month including telephone transfers to another account, third party transfers, and check-writing against your account. There is no minimum amount for which checks must be written. However, no more than 3 checks per month can be written without penalty. (The typical penalty is $5 for each extra check or transaction.) The same $100,000 federal insurance that applies to regular accounts applies to these accounts as well.

Each bank or savings & loan is allowed to set its own interest rate that it pays on money-market accounts. Some institutions impose various fees while others impose no fees at all. And the method of computing whether the minimum balance has been breached may vary. Only by exploring these features in addition to the stated interest rates can one account be compared with another.

Fees charged on a money-market account for investment management are deductible as a *miscellaneous deduction* on your 2001 tax return. But ordinary checking account charges are not deductible [IRS Private Letter Ruling 8345067]. The institution managing your money-market account should inform you of any deductible fees charged against your account in the year-end statement it mails to you.

Interest-Bearing Checking Accounts

These accounts, offered by banks and savings & loans, are similar to money-market accounts as described above. However, there is no limitation upon the number of checks that can be written. And the interest rate paid by interest-bearing checking accounts is lower because of government-imposed reserve requirements and the cost of check-processing.

Most interest-bearing checking accounts have a minimum balance requirement, generally in the $500-$1,000 range. If your balance falls below the minimum, you may be hit with a monthly fee and/or checkwriting fees. If your account is likely to remain below the minimum for a period of time, you will probably be better off with an ordinary checking account instead of an interest-bearing checking account.

Asset Management Accounts

An *asset management account* is basically a checking account opened with a stock brokerage house. But unlike ordinary checking accounts, your money is invested in a special money-market fund, earning daily interest on your entire balance. (Even checking accounts which pay interest generally pay far less than current money-market rates.) Also, unlike ordinary money-market funds, there is usually no minimum denomination on the amount for which the checks may be written nor is there a limitation on the number of checks that may be written each month.

One of the chief advantages of asset management accounts is that they provide instant borrowing power to those who own securities. The way it works is this. You deposit with the brokerage company a combination of securities and cash. The cash is deposited in a money-market fund and interest and dividends received on the securities in your account also go into the money-market fund automatically. As checks are written, money is withdrawn from the money-market fund to cover the checks. If that is depleted, you can continue to write checks against the borrowing power of the securities (generally 50%-70% of their value). These are considered loans and interest is charged at a rate based on the going rate for brokerage margin accounts. This rate is lower than the rate charged on typical bank loans. As cash is deposited into your account, your loan is automatically paid down and interest charges reduced.

The interest paid on a margin loan is generally deductible as investment interest on Schedule A of your 1040. You will need to complete Form 4952 to determine if you have a limitation on the deductibility of this interest. Any interest not deductible in the current year may be carried forward to a future year.

In addition to check-writing privileges, you are issued a VISA (or other) charge card. You can use this card to charge purchases in the usual way. You can also use this card to obtain immediate cash at any of the 100,000 bank locations in the world connected with VISA. Many banks will permit you to obtain the full value of your account on the spot. Others place a $5,000 or other daily limit on how much can be withdrawn in this way. The VISA (or other) card is usually a *debit card* rather than a true *credit card*. With a debit card, there is no one-month billing period on charge purchases, as is the case with ordinary credit cards. As soon as the charge slip reaches

the bank, the amount is subtracted from your account. Also, there are stricter reporting requirements should your card be lost, in order for you to avoid liability for
unauthorized purchases.

In the past, asset management accounts were offered mainly by full service
brokerage firms, and required minimum portfolio balances of $20,000 to $100,000.
But now, these accounts are available from hundreds of brokerage firms and banks
across the country. And many require minimum portfolio balances (cash plus securities) of as little as $5,000-$10,000.

Typically, asset management accounts charge annual fees of $50-$125, which generally include all bank charges, check printing fees, annual credit card fees, etc. But
a number of discount brokers charge less. For example, *Charles Schwab Corp.* and
Fidelity Brokerage Services, Inc., two of the largest discount brokerage firms, charge
no annual fee at all for those who place at least one securities trade a year. And these
two firms, among others, have software that allows you to get balance information,
review transactions, and place trades from your own home computer.

Brokerage firms have been heavily promoting asset management accounts since
a new federal settlement rule went into effect in June 1995. Under this rule, stock
and bond trades must be settled so that the brokerage house receives payment within
3 days of the trade, down from 5 days under prior law. Funds from your asset management account can be used to settle a trade immediately, without struggling to get
a check to the brokerage firm within the 3-day limit.

Asset management accounts are a good deal for the consumer. The brokerage
houses do not offer them in order to profit from their operation. The annual fees serve
only to defray the cost of the checking services and bookkeeping expenses. And the
money-market management fees are, if anything, lower than average. Rather, the
chief motivation of the brokerage houses is to get your money and securities under
their wing. That way, when you buy or sell securities generating lucrative commission revenues, you are likely to do it through them.

Money-Market Funds

Money-market funds are mutual funds that pay money-market interest rates. These
funds bear a similarity to money-market accounts offered by banks and savings &
loans, the principal difference being that you do not transact your business in person.
Instead, you mail in your deposits or have them wired by telephone transfer. Your
funds earn daily interest from date of deposit to date of withdrawal.

You can write checks against your account any time you choose. There is no limit
on the number of checks that can be written nor upon the number of transactions you
can make per month. However, money-market funds usually set a minimum amount
for which a check can be written or a telephone transfer can be made — typically
$250 or $500.

Money-market funds also require a minimum amount to open an account. This
varies from fund to fund but there are a number of prominent funds requiring only a
$1,000 minimum deposit. Unlike most bank money-market accounts, you earn full

money-market interest on your entire balance even if it falls below the minimum amount necessary to open an account.

There is no federal deposit insurance on money-market funds. However, they are virtually risk-free because they invest only in short-term securities offered by the most financially secure institutions.

If you are seeking the highest rate, you will have to check out individual institutions to see what rates are currently being offered. A listing of the current rates paid by the major money-market funds is published once a week in *The Wall Street Journal* and other newspapers. The published interest rates are net rates after expenses have been deducted.

When comparing interest rates, be sure to take into account the difference in the way the interest rates are quoted. Banks and savings & loans may quote you the effective annual rate — the actual rate you would earn on funds left on deposit a full year with the result of interest-compounding figured in. Money-market funds, however, generally publish a daily rate which does not include the effect of compounding.

If the daily rate is known, there is a way to approximate the effective annual yield produced by compounding the daily rate over a full year. The extra effective annual yield produced by the daily compounding is approximately equal to $i \times i/2$, where i is the quoted uncompounded interest rate. For example, 8% annual interest yields approximately $8\% + (8\% \times 8\%/2) = 8\% + .32\% = 8.32\%$ when compounded daily. (The mathematically-trained may observe that this approximation works because $i \times i/2$ is the 3d term in the Taylor series expansion for $\exp(i)$, which is the end result of continuously compounding interest rate i for one year, starting with an initial investment of one dollar.) Because the extra compounding effect is proportional to the *square* of the interest rate, it becomes more significant as the interest rate gets higher. For example, if the 8% interest were to rise by 1/4 to 10%, the extra compounding effect would be about $10\% \times 10\%/2 = .5\%$. This is an increase of over 1/2 in the .32% extra compounding term for 8% interest.

Income received from a money-market mutual fund is technically considered a *dividend* rather than *interest* and should be reported as such on your tax return. If you report it as interest, the IRS computer may become confused and send you a dunning notice. Income from bank or S&L money-market accounts is considered *interest.*

The table at the end of this chapter lists a number of leading money-market funds. You can obtain further information and an application form by writing to the fund or calling the telephone number listed in the table.

Most of the organizations that run the regular money-market funds listed in the table also run 2 other types of special money-market funds — tax-exempt funds and government-securities funds. *Tax-exempt money-market funds* invest in short-term securities issued by state and local governments that are exempt from federal income tax. These funds pay less interest than regular money-market funds and are suitable only for those in the highest tax brackets. *Government securities money-market funds* invest in short-term securities issued by the federal government.

Comparing the Different Types of Money-Market Investments

Money-market funds are convenient for those who want the ability to switch into other types of mutual funds via telephone and for those who want to write more than 3 checks per month. Bank money-market accounts, on the other hand, have several advantages of their own. There is no minimum denomination on the three checks per month that can be written, they are convenient for those who prefer in-person rather than mail transactions, and they are insured by the FDIC.

Interest-bearing checking accounts and asset-management accounts are the choice for those who want full checking services. Between these two, interest-bearing checking accounts are generally more convenient because of the ability to make in-person transactions and the typically lower minimum for opening an account. However, asset management accounts pay a higher rate of interest (even when fees are subtracted) and have other features such as instant borrowing power that may make them attractive to those who meet the minimum requirements.

SELECTED MONEY-MARKET FUNDS

Fund	Minimum Initial Deposit	Minimum Subsequent Deposit	Minimum Check Redemption	Telephone Number for Information
Dreyfus Liquid Assets, Inc. P.O. Box 9387 Providence, RI 02940-9387	$2,500	$100 *$500 *Teletransfers	$500	(800) 499-3327
Fidelity Cash Reserves P.O. Box 770001 Cincinnati, OH 45277-0003	2,500	250	500	(800) 544-6666
T. Rowe Price Prime Reserve Fund 100 E. Pratt St. Baltimore, MD 21202	2,500	100	500	(800) 638-5660
Zurich Money Market Fund 222 S. Riverside Plaza, 33rd Floor Chicago, IL 60606	1,000	100	500	(888) 987-8675
Vanguard Prime Money Market Trust P.O. Box 1110 Valley Forge, PA 19482-1110	3,000	100 1,000 by wire	250	(800) 662-7447

16

Moving Expenses

Moving expenses are deductible as an "above the line" *adjustment to income* rather than an *itemized deduction*. This provides a moving expense write-off to those who use the standard deduction, as well as to those who itemized their deductions. It also serves to lower *adjusted gross income,* which can raise the deductions for medical expenses, casualty losses, and miscellaneous deductions, as well as lessen the impact of the deduction and exemption phaseouts applying to higher income taxpayers [see Section 1 of Chapter 1].

However, the moving expense deduction no longer includes write-offs for the cost of meals connected with the move; the cost of lodging or other travel expenses while on pre-move househunting trips; the cost of occupying temporary quarters in the location of the new job; or the cost of expenses connected with the sale, purchase, or lease of your old or new residence. (Although closing costs are no longer deductible as moving expenses, these costs can reduce taxable profit on the sale of your old residence or serve to increase the official purchase price of your new residence [see Section 3 of the *Homeowners* chapter].)

While pre-move househunting trips can no longer be deducted as *moving expenses,* they may be able to be recast as *business-related travel expenses.* For example, suppose a college professor has accepted a position at a new college in a different city, and takes a trip there to search for new housing. If he can engage in sufficient job-related activities while on the trip, his expenses, including food and lodging, can be deducted as business-related travel expenses on Form 2106 or Form 2106-EZ. Such activities might include collaborating or consulting with a faculty member at the new college, using special library materials, participating in a seminar, etc. [see Section 1 of the *Travel* expenses].

One other change that was made was an increase from 35 miles to 50 miles in the extra distance required between your old commute and what your commute to your new job would have been had you stayed in your old residence.

When Can You Deduct Moving Expenses?

If you moved to a new residence in 2001 because you went to work for a new employer or transferred to a new place of employment, you may deduct your moving costs, provided you meet the following two requirements:

1. The distance between your new principal place of work and your old residence must be at least 50 miles farther than the distance between your old place of work and your old residence. (The distance between two points is measured

by the shortest of the more commonly traveled routes between the two points.) If you went to work for the first time or went back to full-time work after a substantial period of part-time work or unemployment, your new principal place of work must be at least 50 miles from your old residence.

2. You must work full-time for at least 39 weeks during the first 12 months following your arrival in the general location of your new place of employment. (Self-employed persons must also work full-time for at least 78 weeks during the first 24 months after arrival in the new job location.)

The 39 weeks of employment need not be consecutive, nor do they have to be for the same employer. It is necessary only that you be employed on a full-time basis within the same general commuting area. Any week during which you work on a full-time basis counts in satisfying the 39-week test. The requirement that your work be full-time is judged by the customary practices in your job. For example, a teacher with a full schedule is working full-time even if the school day is 5 hours or less.

If the work is seasonal, off-season weeks count as weeks of employment as long as your work agreement covers an off-season period of less than 6 months. For example, teachers are not excluded from a moving expense deduction merely because their academic year is less than 39 weeks. Also, you will be considered as working during any week that you are out through no fault of your own. This refers to a temporary absence from work because of illness, strike, shutout, layoff, natural disaster, etc.

If you paid the moving expense but have not met the 39-week test by the time your return is due, you should take a deduction for the moving expense if it appears that you will later meet the 39-week test. However, if you later fail the test, you must report an amount equal to the 2001 moving expense deduction as 2002 taxable income on your 2002 tax return or on an amended 2001 tax return. If you leave the deduction off your 2001 return and later meet the 39-week test during 2002, you will have to amend your 2001 return to get your refund.

A court case emphasizes the fact that you must deduct the moving expenses in the year the move takes place. A nurse, who had not yet worked the required number of weeks at her new job when filing time came along, waited until a later year, after she had worked the required amount of time, to claim the moving expense deduction. However, the Court overruled her deduction. It said she should have claimed the deduction in the year of the move. The only thing she could do now is amend her original return. [Meadows, 66 TC 51]

If you are married and file a joint return and if both you and your spouse are employees, either of you may satisfy the full-time work requirement. However, you may not add the weeks your spouse works to those you work to satisfy the 39-week requirement.

Moving expenses are deductible if paid in connection with the commencement of work at a new principal place of work. It is not necessary that you have a contract or commitment of employment prior to moving to the new location — the moving expense deduction is allowable if employment actually does occur.

Moving expenses are deductible only if reasonable under the circumstances of the particular move. Travel should be by the shortest and most direct route available from your former residence to your new residence by the conventional mode of transportation actually used and in the shortest period of time required to make the move. Additional expenses for circuitous scenic routes or sidetrip stopovers are not deductible.

Which Moving Expenses Can You Deduct?

If you qualify to deduct moving expenses as described above, you may deduct reasonable amounts for the items listed below.

1. **Travel expenses,** including lodging, but not meals, for yourself and your family while en route from your old residence to your new residence. This deduction is allowable for only one trip made by you and members of your household; however, it is not necessary that you and all members of your household travel together or at the same time. Members of your household include your spouse and your dependents for tax purposes; economically independent relatives or others are not included.

2. The cost of **moving household goods,** including automobiles, personal effects, and household pets of both you and members of your family. This includes the cost of transportation from your old to your new residence, plus packing, crating, insurance, and 30 days worth of storage, as well as connecting and disconnecting utilities (but not a telephone). It does not include the cost of automobile registration, driver's license, carpet installation, or appliance installation.

   Transportation of goods to your new residence from some place other than your old residence is deductible to the extent that it does not exceed the cost of transportation from your old residence. However, you cannot deduct the cost of transporting goods purchased en route from your old to your new residence.

If you use your automobile to transport yourself, your family, or your goods, you may take either of these options:

1. Deduct your actual expenses such as gasoline, oil, repairs, etc., but not depreciation. (You must keep a record of each expense in this case.)

2. Deduct 10 cents per mile.

According to an IRS ruling, there is another item you can deduct in addition to the 10 cents per mile or actual operating expenses. Namely, you can deduct a pro rata portion of taxes, such as personal property taxes you pay on the automobile. [Rev Proc 89-66] For example, if 20% of your annual mileage is for moving, you can claim 20% of the taxes as a moving expense.

Limitations

1. The move should be within 1 year from the time you first report to your new job. If the move does not take place within that time, the expenses will not be deductible unless there are extenuating circumstances the IRS finds acceptable (e.g., a child needs to finish school at the old location).

2. If, after you move to your new residence, you are farther from your new job than if you had stayed in your old residence, your moving expense deduction may be disallowed unless you can give a suitable justification for your move, such as lower commuting time or costs.

Exceptions

1. The 39-week full-time employment requirement is waived if you are involuntarily discharged (other than for willful misconduct), transferred because of a request initiated by your employer, or become disabled. However, you must show that you would have satisfied the 39-week test except for being discharged, transferred, or disabled.

2. The 39-week employment requirement need not be met to the extent that you receive reimbursement by your employer for an item of moving expense. In this case, you claim a moving expense deduction to offset your employer's reimbursement included in your gross income.

Reimbursements Received from Employer

You may have received a reimbursement from your employer for moving expenses which you incurred. Your employer is not supposed to include such a reimbursement for deductible expenses in your taxable wages as listed on your yearend Form W-2. (This presumes you have made an adequate accounting to your employer for these expenses.) The amount of the reimbursement will show up in a non-taxable box on your Form W-2. If you do not account to your employer, the entire reimbursement will be included on the Form W-2 in box 12 and designed with a Code P. You can deduct the allowable expenses on Form 3903.

Of course, you can't double-dip by taking a moving expense deduction on an item for which you have received a non-taxable reimbursement.

Where Do You Report Moving Expense?

Moving expenses are claimed as an *adjustment to income* on line 26 of Form 1040. As an adjustment to income, these expenses can be claimed by those who use the standard deduction as well as by those who itemize their deductions [see Section 1 of Chapter 1].

Form 3903 is used to compute the total moving expense deduction to which you are entitled. This total is then entered on line 26 of Form 1040.

Foreign Moves

The rules for deducting storage costs of household goods and personal effects are more liberal for moving to a foreign location than for a domestic move. You can deduct the cost of storage for the entire time the foreign location continues to be your principal place of work. You can also deduct the cost of moving these items to and from storage.

Moving to a Temporary Job

If you move to obtain a temporary post away from home, you cannot deduct both moving costs and the travel costs described in the *Travel* chapter.

> **Example**
>
> *A professor at a midwestern university accepted a one-year temporary appointment with a government agency in Washington, D.C. He returned to his teaching post at the end of the year. There was no quarrel with his deduction for the cost of his meals and lodging during the stay in Washington, D.C. These were legitimate deductions while at a temporary position away from home as described in the Travel chapter. Also, he could deduct the cost of his transportation to and from his temporary post for the same reason.*
>
> *But he was not allowed to deduct, as a moving expense, the cost of transporting his family and his household goods to and from Washington. It was inconsistent with the IRS regulations to allow a moving expense deduction to a place where the taxpayer has been allowed deductions for travel, meals, and lodging while at a temporary post away from home.* [Goldman, 34 AFTR 2nd 74-5046]

─17─
Casualty Losses

If you suffered a casualty or theft loss, you might be entitled to a deduction. At one time, you could deduct all but $100 of each loss that occurred. Now, however, you must also subtract 10% of your adjusted gross income from your total losses when computing the deduction. In particular, only a large amount of losses will yield any deduction at all. The exact procedure for computing your casualty deduction is discussed later in this chapter.

What Is a Casualty?

A **casualty** is the complete or partial destruction or loss of property resulting from an identifiable event that is sudden, unexpected, or unusual in nature.

Note that the elements of suddenness and unexpectedness must be present to justify a deduction. For example, damage to tropical plants caused by a freeze would be deductible in an area where freezes are practically unknown. But if you live in an area where a freeze is not abnormal, the deduction would be disallowed. Similarly, if your driveway is damaged by an unusual freeze or hot spell, this would be deductible. However, the event must be sudden. Damage caused by *progressive deterioration* is not deductible.

Similarly, termite damage is not generally deductible because it is not considered to be a sudden misfortune. Another example occurs with diseases affecting your trees or shrubbery, such as Dutch Elm disease. The Court ruled in 1981 that damage caused by a disease does not qualify for the casualty deduction [Coleman, 76 TC 580]. But a sudden insect invasion might cause a deductible casualty loss if the damage is caused by the insects themselves, rather than by a disease they are carrying. For example, in a 1979 IRS ruling, a deduction was allowed for damage to trees caused by an invasion of pine beetles. [See Revenue Ruling 79-174]

Further illustration of the *suddenness* requirement is given by two cases involving damage due to heavy rainfall. In one case, a deduction was allowed because the rain was concentrated in a short period of time — 14.5 inches in a single week. [Clapp, 321 F 2d 12] But in another 1983 case, a deduction was denied because the damage was caused by excessive precipitation over a 4-month period. Because the damage was not caused by a *sudden event* but rather by *progressive deterioration,* a deduction was disallowed. [Forrest, TC Memo 1983-177]

A casualty deduction can be produced by the negligence of a repair-person. This is illustrated by a 1994 court case in which a person took her car to a service station for routine maintenance. After she picked up her car from the station and drove away, the car "locked up" due to extreme engine temperature. When it was towed to a second service station, it was determined that the first service station must have neglected to replace vital engine fluids. Because this negligence caused a $5,446 casualty loss, the Court permitted a casualty deduction to be claimed. [Wolf, TC Memo 1994-93]

Even if a casualty is caused by the taxpayer's own simple negligence, this does not rule out a deduction. This is illustrated by a 1991 court case concerning an individual who parked his car in an area adjacent to his apartment building. He did so even though he knew the city was doing construction nearby and was towing cars when in the way. When he returned from a 10-day trip, his car was missing. After he finally tracked down the car, he was told the city towed it away and crushed it into scrap metal when it could not find the owner. The court ruled that he could deduct for the loss of his car. Even though he was negligent in parking where towing could be anticipated, this was *simple* negligence rather than *willful* or *wanton* negligence. He could have foreseen his car would be towed, but not that it would be destroyed. The destruction of the car was an unusual, sudden, and unexpected event which was unforeseeable by the taxpayer. [Hamanel, TC Memo, 1991-386]

Examples of deductible casualty losses include:

Damage from a natural disaster, e.g. hurricane, tornado, flood, storm, fire, accident, heavy rains, landslides, extreme dry and wet spells, sudden sinking of land, etc.

Damage from an auto accident to your own automobile. This is deductible even if the accident was your own fault, provided it was not caused on purpose or by willful negligence. You do not deduct payments you make to the owner of another car you damaged in an accident.

Loss from vandalism.

Sonic boom damage.

Damage to your house from boiler explosion, water pipe break, etc.

Smog damage from an unusual, severe concentration of chemicals in the atmosphere. Progressive damage from a long-term smog problem is not deductible.

Loss to personal property caused by accident. For example, one court case allowed a deduction for the loss of a diamond ring jarred loose by a car accident in the person's driveway. Another case allowed a deduction for a ring demolished by a garbage disposal.

Damage from snow, ice, and freezing. Court cases have allowed deductions for damage due to icy road, freezing of an automobile motor, garage wall collapse due to unusual freeze, collapse of eaves due to ice and snow, damage to driveway and brickwork from severe freeze, damage to a house from thawing of collected ice and snow, and damage to trees, shrubs, plants, etc., from extreme winter weather.

Loss from severe drought. Unusual droughts can cause deductible casualty losses. This is illustrated by a 1981 court case involving a married couple who lived in Marin County, California. Because of an unusually severe drought, residents were limited to using only 148 gallons of water a day. As a result, the couple could not water the trees, shrubs, and lawn they had planted on their property, resulting in the complete destruction of these items. Because the Court felt the drought to be unusually sudden and unexpected, it allowed a $2,000 deduction for the decline in property value caused by the destruction of the landscaping.

In another case, decided in 1984, a homeowner claimed a deduction for $10,500 worth of damage caused by drought. The drought had caused the house to settle, producing cracks in the interior walls, ceiling, and driveway. Because the damage was caused by an identifiable event (severe drought) rather than progressive deterioration, the Court allowed the deduction. His case was probably helped by the fact that his part of the country had been declared a national disaster area. [Stevens, TC Memo 1984-365]

If you own property that was damaged in 2001, be sure to claim any damage on your 2001 tax return. If you wait until a later year, your deduction will probably be disallowed and moved to the prior year if your return is examined by the IRS.

This is illustrated by a 1988 court case concerning a married couple whose house had been damaged by a severe drought that occurred in 1981. Some fine cracks were noticed in 1981, but nothing was done until 1982 when more severe damage was noticed — cracks in the front porch, patio, driveway, and walls, gaps between the walls and ceilings, loosened mortar in a brick wall, etc. According to an engineering report, the initial cause for all the damage was due to the soil starting to dry out during the original drought. As the soil dried further, it shrank, causing $30,000 of structural damage to the house.

Their claim of a deduction on their 1982 tax return was disallowed by the Court. The lapse of time between the occurrence of the drought and the damage done in 1982 was *"sufficiently prolonged that it can be said that the loss stemmed from intervening causes, in this case dryness and soil erosion, and consequently should be characterized as progressive deterioration."* This meant the requirement of suddenness necessary to produce a deductible casualty loss was missing. Had a loss been claimed for the damage done in 1981, the story could have been different. According to the Court,

> *"Perhaps petitioners' situation would have been stronger if they had claimed their loss in 1981 when there were visible signs of damage. At that point, the lapse of time would have been much shorter and the impact of the drought clearer so that there would have been a lessened potential for a 'progressive deterioration' characterization of the cause of the loss. But the fact that a loss might have been allowable in another year, not before us, does not support the allowance of the loss in 1982."* [Short, TC Memo 1988-40]

You cannot deduct common, ordinary household misfortunes. For example, you cannot deduct breakage of china or glassware that you drop, the loss of a pet which has run away, or the loss of a ring which has been misplaced.

You can deduct a casualty loss even if you were at fault. In one case, a court allowed a deduction for damage to a lawn due to careless use of a weed poison.

A court case has established that you don't necessarily have to identify the event that caused the casualty loss. In this case, a supermarket cashier noticed that the diamond was missing from a woman's ring as she went through the checkout counter. The woman was sure the diamond was still in the ring earlier that morning when she polished her nails. Apparently it had been dislodged when the woman was doing various chores that morning.

When the ring was examined after the diamond was lost, two of the prongs were missing and the claws on the opposite side of the ring were forced upward. According to expert testimony, this could only have happened if a fairly strong blow had struck the side of the ring. The Court concluded that the *"cause of such a loss was not an ordinary, common, or easily predicted occurrence"* but rather that *"there was a sudden, unexpected, destructive blow to the ring that, although unnoticed by petitioner in her rush to perform her morning's chores, caused damage to the ring's setting and the resulting loss of the diamond."* Even though the precise incident causing the loss could not be pinpointed, the Court allowed a deduction of over $10,000 for the loss of the diamond. [Kielts, TC Memo 1981-329]

Theft Losses

To claim a theft loss, you must establish that an actual robbery, burglary, embezzlement, etc., took place. The mere disappearance of money or property from your person or home is not sufficient proof. You might have misplaced the item, dropped the money, etc. Usually, you need some evidence that another person took the property in question. Of course, if you return home to find your grand piano missing, no one would dispute that a theft had occurred.

You should always report a theft to the police. The first thing the IRS will ask for if it questions a theft deduction on your return is a copy of the report you made to the police.

However, lack of a police report does not automatically rule out a deduction. In a court case several years ago, an individual claimed a $1,700 deduction for the value of a stereo, TV, and diamond ring stolen when his apartment was burglarized. He had not reported the burglary to the police because he did not believe they would be able to recover the property. He felt this way because the police had been unsuccessful in recovering property stolen in a previous burglary. Because the Court believed his testimony that the items were stolen, it allowed a deduction despite the lack of a corroborating police report. [Novik, TC Memo 1981-446]

Thefts can also include oddball losses of money or property caused by criminal activities. For example, in one case, an individual received a deduction for a loss he incurred while betting on a fixed race. [Edwards v Bromberg, 232 F2d 107] In another, a deduction was allowed for payments to a fortuneteller in a place where fortunetelling was a crime in the *theft* category. [Kreiner, TC Memo 1990-587]

How to Compute Your Loss

The amount of your casualty or theft loss is defined to be the decrease in the value of your property caused by the loss. If you incur expenses for restoring the property back to its original condition, this will usually be accepted as being equal to the loss. However, you do not have to replace or repair the damaged property in order to deduct the loss.

The value of your property before the casualty loss would be its resale market value if there is a realistic market for the item. This would be the case for a house, automobile, jewelry, etc. However, using the resale value is not always a reasonable way to set the value of items. For example, used clothing is worth quite a bit more to an individual than its value in the secondhand market.

This is illustrated by a Tax Court case involving a couple whose home and contents were destroyed by fire. The Court rejected the IRS method of evaluating the destroyed property by what it *"would have brought if hawked off by a secondhand dealer or at a forced sale."* Instead it accepted the insurance industry's general valuation method of using the original cost of the items less a depreciation factor of 20% to 25%. [Cornelius, 56 TC 976]

You cannot deduct the cost of repairs or replacements to the extent they represent an improvement over the condition of the property before the casualty or theft. For example, if your watch is stolen, your loss is equal to its used price value. You cannot deduct the cost of a new watch you buy to replace it. Similarly, if your furnace is ruined by a flood, you cannot deduct the cost of a new furnace — only the value of the old furnace.

If you suffer casualty damage, you can establish the amount of the loss by obtaining an appraisal from an experienced and reliable appraiser. You can then deduct the appraiser's fee as a miscellaneous deduction. You should also take photographs where appropriate before the damaged property is repaired.

Your loss cannot exceed the actual price you paid. For example, suppose you purchased your house for $30,000 a number of years ago and then it is totally destroyed by fire. At the time of destruction, the house was worth $125,000. Your casualty loss would be limited to $30,000 plus the cost of any improvements you had made.

You treat your house, land, shrubbery, and other items on your property as one unit. For example, suppose your trees sustain $2,000 worth of damage in a hurricane. You planted these trees yourself many years ago at a cost of $10. You do not have to limit your casualty loss to this $10. Because you are treating the entire property as one unit, the entire $2,000 is the amount of your casualty loss because it doesn't exceed the price you paid for the entire property.

Damage to Trees, Shrubs, and Plants

You are entitled to a casualty deduction for damage due to unexpected ice, snow storms, drought, fire, wind, rain, vandalism, smog, or damage from vehicles. You can deduct the costs of removing damaged trees or shrubs, pruning, bracing, and replanting in order to eventually restore the property to its original state.

However, if there has been extensive damage, another computation procedure may be better. Namely, you can deduct the difference in the value of your property before and after the casualty. This computation procedure may give a larger deduction because damage to landscaping can cause a reduction in property value far greater than the cost of repairing and replanting. You will need to get a qualified appraiser's report to substantiate your claim of decrease in property value.

Casualty deductions for trees and other plant life can be substantial because of the extra value they contribute to property. For example, a recent court decision granted a Florida homeowner a $15,000 deduction for damage to landscaping caused by an unexpected freeze. [Thebaut, TC Memo 1983-699]

The Tax Court, as illustrated by several cases, has been quite sympathetic when trees are destroyed. In one case, a $3,500 deduction was allowed for the loss of 5 cypress trees located 90 feet away from a house after the trees were blown down during a storm. The Court indicated the deduction might have been even higher had there been better testimony as to the loss incurred. [Zardo, TC Memo 1982-84]

In another case, 12 trees were blown down by a tornado. The IRS had denied any deduction because the property contained 10 acres filled with trees and it felt the loss of only 12 of them would cause no measurable decrease in the value of the property. However, the Court noted that 7 of the destroyed trees were on the cleared portion of the lot near the home, and therefore contributed extra value to the property as shade trees. Consequently, it allowed a deduction of over $19,000 for the loss of the trees. [Bowers, TC Memo 1981-658]

In a third case, a fire destroyed trees, shrubs, and grass on a 10.65-acre lot on which a residence was located. The Court allowed the owner to deduct $40,000 for the loss of value to his property caused by the fire. [Beams, TC Memo 1994-301]

And a fourth case is perhaps the most striking of all. In this case, the Court allowed a deduction of $14,900 for the loss of a single prominent oak tree which was done in by a sudden attack of woodborers. [McKean, TC Memo 1981-670]

Insurance Payments Reduce Loss

You must reduce your loss by any reimbursements you receive from your insurance company. However, you only have to subtract insurance payments which are direct compensation for the loss. Indirect payments for living expenses after a house has been damaged or for a rental car after your automobile has been stolen, for example, are not subtracted in computing your loss.

You must reduce your loss by the amount covered by your insurance policy even if you don't file a claim.

The $100 and 10% of Adjusted Gross Income Limitations

After computing your casualty and theft losses, you must make two subtractions in order to obtain your deduction. First, you subtract $100 from the loss caused by each individual incident and total up the remainders. Then, you subtract 10% of your adjusted gross income from the total to obtain your deduction.

Example

The adjusted gross income on your tax return is $50,000. During the year, you had a theft loss of $4,000, of which $1,000 was covered by insurance. Also, a windstorm caused $1,600 damage to your roof, $550 to your fence, and $700 to your shrubbery, none of which was covered by insurance.

	Windstorm		**Theft**	
Roof	$1,600		$4,000	
Fence	550		– 1,000	insurance
Shrubbery	700		$3,000	net loss
	$2,850		– 100	exclusion
	– 100	exclusion	$2,900	
	$2,750			

Total losses ($2,750 + $2,900)...$5,650
Less 10% of adjusted gross income (10% × $50,000)...–5,000
Amount of your deduction ....$ 650

Business Casualties Fully Deductible

The $100 per event and 10% of adjusted gross income subtractions only apply to casualties involving property used for personal purposes. If you suffer a casualty to an item used for professional or business purposes, these subtractions do not apply. Instead, you can deduct the full casualty loss up to your *adjusted basis* in the item. Your *adjusted basis* is equal to the price you paid less any depreciation you were entitled to claim.

When to Deduct Your Casualty Losses

You deduct your loss in the year the casualty or theft actually occurred. If you anticipate that you will be reimbursed by insurance, you subtract the amount of the expected reimbursement from your loss in computing your tax. If the reimbursement does not turn out to be what you expected, you adjust your next year's tax return accordingly by deducting the loss. If you suffer a disaster loss in an area declared by the President as qualifying for federal assistance, you can deduct the loss either in the year the disaster occurred or in the prior year.

However, if the insurance reimbursement that you actually receive is greater than the amount you deducted from the loss in an earlier year, you report the excess amount as income in the year received. You do not file an amended return to reduce the loss in the earlier year.

Casualty and Collision Insurance

You cannot deduct premiums you pay on insurance against fire, theft, or other casualties. Only actual losses due to such casualties are deductible.

Where Do You Deduct Your Losses?

There is a special line on Schedule A for listing your total casualty losses. You also attach Form 4684 on which the amount of your deduction is computed.

18

Will Your Tax Return Be Audited?

SECTION 1:
AUDITS

Your tax return may be examined for a variety of reasons, and the examination may take place in any one of several ways. Before we discuss the reasons and ways a tax return may be selected and examined, it is interesting to note the "modernization" that has taken place within the Internal Revenue Service over the past two years.

The Internal Revenue Service (IRS) restructured their entire organization, which they refer to as "modernizing" America's tax agency. Not only did they change the physical structure of the organization, but the IRS now offers new services to taxpayers. The IRS's new mission statement reflects those changes:

"Provide America's taxpayers top quality service by helping them understand and meet their tax responsibilities and by applying the tax law with integrity and fairness to all."

The IRS is now providing a variety of services to assist with the preparation of tax returns and the payment of tax liabilities if the taxes cannot be paid in full at the time the return is filed. Some of these services include:

- Problem Solving Days
- "e-file" tax returns
- Taxpayer Advocate Services
- IRS web site "Daily Digital" (www.IRS.gov.)
- Paying taxes with a credit card
- Automatic installment agreements for tax liabilities under $25,000
- Revised guidelines for Offers in Compromise
- Local taxpayer assistance services

Basic Procedures for Filing

After you fill out your tax return, you mail it to one of the Service Centers (see the instructions to Form 1040) or you can file your return electronically (e-file). The

IRS's goal is to have everyone filing electronically in the future. Your tax return is subjected to a computer scanning that checks for math errors. If you paid a tax professional or tax service to prepare your return, you can check a box in the signature area on the bottom of page 2 of Form 1040 that allows the tax preparer to talk to a representative at the Service Center to resolve any math discrepancies or changes made by the Service Center during the "processing" of your return. The preparer is also authorized to check on your refund during the period the return is being processed. This does **not** give the preparer power of attorney or authorization to deal with any other tax issues on your behalf.

Non-Audit — The Matching Program

Approximately one year after your tax return is filed, the income you report on your return is matched against information that is provided to the IRS from third parties via electronic filings or magnetic tape. The IRS matches your return against virtually all information provided by third parties, such as: Forms W-2, interest income, dividend income, stockbroker and financial institution information relating to stock and bond sales, and mortgage interest.

Starting in 2000, the IRS required partnerships with more than 100 partners to file returns electronically to enable the IRS the ability to match Schedules K-1 to other tax returns. Therefore, the IRS will be matching Schedules K-1 from partnerships, S-corporations, and trusts to individual returns.

The IRS has a tough policy when the matching program turns up unreported income – an automatic negligence penalty of 20% of the deficiency will be assessed. To escape the penalty, the taxpayer will have to provide "reasonable cause" to show that he or she did not intentionally or carelessly omit income, but rather that there was justification for the omission.

Because the matching program is so effective, you should take care that income and deductions are reported properly on your income tax return. The IRS does not consider the matching program an "audit" of your return because the source of their information is from third parties. Your tax return can still be selected for an "audit" even after you receive and resolve a matching notice from the Service Center. The results of the matching program might trigger a more extensive audit of your return.

Audits

After the return is checked for math or clerical errors, the information on the return is stored on a Master File computer program. It is the Martinsburg (WV) Computing Center that posts returns processed by Service Centers and classifies them into categories, depending on the total income reported and whether it is a business return or a personal return.

A computer program called the Discriminate Function System (DIF) assigns a numeric score to each individual, corporate, and partnership tax return. Your return can be selected for examination if it receives a high DIF score. A high score means there is a significantly greater potential for an examination of your return that might result in a change in your income tax liability. It does not mean there is something wrong with your return.

The DIF numeric score originated with the Taxpayer Compliance Measurement Programs (TCMP). The TCMP audit consisted of a line-by-line audit of a tax return. The last TCMP audit program was in 1988 and Congress has enacted laws since then, these types of intrusive audits in the future. Nevertheless, the IRS uses the last TCMP audit scores from 1988 with statistical upgrades (classified information) to calculate the DIF score for each activity code.

Examination Selection Criteria

Your return can be selected for examination in several ways. The most common ways are as follows:

- Computer Scoring (DIF) – Explained above

- Questionable treatment of an item on the return

- Market Segment Specialization Program

- Information received from other sources on potential noncompliance with the tax laws or inaccurate filing

  - Media

  - Public record

  - Informant

Average Deductions

Although the formula used by the IRS computer to select returns for audit is a closely guarded secret, the basic principle behind the formula is not. The formula is based primarily on the amount and relationship between the deduction claimed and the amount of income shown on the return. If a person's deductions are significantly higher than the average of those with the same income, the computer is likely to select this return for audit. For this reason, it is interesting to know what the average deductions in various categories are in relation to income. The table below lists the average deductions on 1999 returns claiming such deductions, as related to the adjusted gross income on the return. (Data for 2000 returns will not be available until 2002). RIA, A New York-based publisher, has published the following averages:

Adjusted Gross Income	Gifts	Taxes	Interest
$15,000 to 30,000	$ 1,619	$ 2,200	$ 5,866
$30,000 to 50,000	1,774	2,991	6,247
$50,000 to 100,000	2,282	4,918	7,544
$100,000 to 200,000	3,727	9,262	10,806
$200,000 +	19,454	36,592	21,735

Keep in mind that these are averages, and not what the IRS considers acceptable. You are not allowed to use the average amounts in these tables on your own return in place of the actual amounts to which you are entitled. In fact, the IRS computer selects a certain number of returns at random, so simply filing an "average return" will not guarantee that you won't be audited.

Types of Audits

There are three types of audits:

(1) **Correspondence Audit.** Here the IRS will write a letter asking you for further information. All dealings are conducted through the mail. This is the most convenient type of audit because you do not have to travel to the IRS office. Furthermore, you are not forced with making on-the-spot reactions or decisions as in a face-to-face interview.

These types of audits will be increasing in the future for those individuals who file a return with a Schedule A and no business income. Issues are typically interest expense, taxes, charitable contributions, medical expenses, and simple miscellaneous itemized deductions such as union dues and small tools.

(2) **Office Audit.** In this type of audit, you will be requested to pay a visit to your local IRS office and discuss your return with an IRS auditor. The letter requesting such a visit may ask you to bring documentation to support items on your tax return.

You may be able to avoid visiting the IRS office for the audit if it is chiefly a matter of verifying that you actually paid deductions claimed on your tax return. Contact the auditor and ask if you can send in copies of the cancelled checks or other evidence of payment. Then, if he/she agrees, mail in the information so that it reaches IRS before the scheduled time of examination. If everything is in order, you will have saved yourself a trip to the IRS office.

The letter informing you of an audit will specify certain items on your return in which the IRS is interested. These are typically the only items that will be questioned. It is only necessary to bring verification of those items that are questioned to the audit.

Issues are typically Schedule A deductions plus more complicated issues such as travel expenses, employee business expenses, educational expenses, etc. The auditor can expand the "scope" of the examination. The Internal Revenue Manual (IRM) at Section [4.2] 2.6.1 (5-14-1999) states that the examiner must *"access the facts and apply judgement in determining the scope of the examination."*

"Office Audit: The scope of the examination of the return, not requiring pre-contact analysis, is prescribed on a classification checksheet during the classification process. However, the scope of an examination should not be artificially limited to the classified issues if other significant issues are revealed during the examination. Whenever possible, tax examiners should consult with

their manager before raising new issues. The scope of the examination for returns requiring pre-contact analysis will be determined by the auditor."

(3) Field Audit. In this type of audit, the IRS agent comes to your home or office. The IRM states in Section [4.2] 2.7.6 that the place of the examination "will be conducted at the location of where the original books, records and source documents are maintained." Field audits will usually occur only if you operate a business or live in a remote area.

Power of Attorney

You can have a lawyer, a CPA, or an enrolled agent (an individual who has passed a special IRS exam) represent you. You and the Representative should execute Form 2848, Power of Attorney. Form 8821, Tax Information Authorization, can also be executed, which provides limited authority for an individual to act on your behalf.

If you are representing yourself, you can bring a friend or relative. Representatives from commercial preparation firms may accompany you to the audit, but they usually cannot argue your case.

Examiners cannot require the taxpayer's presence at the initial interview per IRC section 7521(c). IRM section [4.2] 2.7.5 (05-14-99) states that "Examiners will use their judgement to determine whether an authorized representative is sufficiently knowledgeable, however examiners should take all reasonable steps to work effectively with authorized representatives."

Which Errors Is the IRS Looking For?

The IRS looks for those mistakes that it thinks taxpayers most likely make. In particular, it sets it sights on those recent changes in the law that, because of their newness, taxpayers might overlook or misunderstand.

On recently filed tax returns, the IRS might be on the lookout for such mistakes as deductions enacted by the Economic Growth and Tax Relief Act of 2001 that will not be fully phased in until later years. For example, there are changes to the Dependent Care Credit that are not effective until 2002, but there is a gradual increase in the Child Care Credit starting in 2001.

Other common errors are deducting excess self-employment retirement contributions, not paying full social security tax on self-employment income, deducting passive losses in excess of passive income, taking home office deductions that exceed business income from the home office, and misapplying the rules regarding distributions from retirement plans including IRA and self-employment retirement plans.

How to Reduce the Odds of an Audit

After the computer assigns a DIF number to all tax returns, the IRM states that the Chief of Planning & Service Programs orders returns so that they are received ratably during the fiscal year. Ratable is defined at IRM [4.1] 3.3 (05-19-99) "as a manner of ordering so that all returns with similar DIF scores, regardless of the filing date, have an equal chance of being delivered to Classification."

IRM [4.1] 3.1.2 (05-19-1999) states, "All individual returns are computer scored under the DIF System. DIF returns are generally ordered in bulk, but some returns are delivered to Examination as Automatics for manual screening without an order being placed. These returns are identified as Automatics by the use of Audit Codes." Exhibit [4.1] 3-1 (05-19-99) provides Audit Codes; some of the most common codes for individuals are:

Audit Code	Explanation
B	Missing Schedules/Forms (Such as Schedule C, D, E, or F, Form 4797, Form 8829 and/or Form 8824)
D	High Income Nonfiler
P	Alternative Minimum Tax – Failed to submit Form 6251
V	Self-employed Tax Returns
W	Alternative Minimum Tax – Form 6251 was filed

The tax returns that are delivered to an Office Audit Group have pre-selected audit issues. An Office Audit Team Manager and a Revenue Agent in a Field Office have the authority to "survey" (this means that the return is not examined, but returned to the Service Center) a tax return if he or she does not find auditable issues on the tax return or if the examiner's inventory of tax returns is too high.

It is important that your tax return be prepared as accurately as possible. The following might bring attention to your return:

1. **Round figures:** Round figures on a tax return imply that the return was filed with estimates. If you must use an estimate, it is appropriate to round the number. If you estimate a number and use an unusual "unrounding" method, this could be construed to be one of the "red flags" for a fraudulently filed income tax return. The best approach is to keep good books and records of all your expenditures and report the actual expense on the return.

2. **Identical numbers:** This might indicate you have miscopied a number two times on the return. Be sure to review your return prior to filing to avoid this type of error.

3. **Incorrect line:** Putting an income item or a deduction on an incorrect line could cause the return to be audited. Review your return prior to filing to avoid this type of error.

4. **Large or unusual deduction:** Attaching supporting documentation, if it is not voluminous, to a return providing substantiation for a large or unusual deduction might convince the examining officer to "survey" the return versus auditing the return. This will not be possible if you file your return electronically.

Common Mistakes:

1. **Schedule A – Medical:** The failure to subtract insurance reimbursements from gross medical expenses

2. **Schedule A – Employee Business Expenses:** Failure to attach Form 2106 to the return

3. **Schedule A – Investment Interest Expense:** Failure to adequately limit investment interest expense to investment income

4. **Alternative Minimum Tax:** Failure to attach Form 6251 to the return or report information properly

5. **Office-in-Home:** Failure to attach Form 8829 to the return

6. **Occupation Information:** The IRS classifies tax returns by using occupational codes. It is recommended to be as accurate as possible in order to avoid confusion. A music teacher should list his or her occupation as a *teacher* rather than as a *musician*.

As mentioned before, not all tax returns are computer-selected under the DIF program. Some returns are selected at random and some are selected because the IRS has special reason to believe they might contain errors.

The number of returns each IRS office requests depends upon the availability of personnel in that office to examine such returns. Thus, a return with a given DIF number might be sent to one local office for examination, while in a different locality, another return with the same DIF number might escape examination because the office in that locality is understaffed. In fact, there is a discrepancy in the percentage of returns audited in various districts. This variation is due partly to a geographical maldistribution of questionable returns and partly to a maldistribution of agents across the country. There is also a discrepancy in the extra tax collected by various IRS offices from those taxpayers that are audited.

There are also occasions when the IRS targets a professional tax preparer related to a "Preparer Project" when the IRS has reason to believe that particular tax return preparer misrepresents information on taxpayers' returns. In this situation, the IRS will try to locate the returns prepared by that preparer and audit all of them.

If you have a tax return prepared by a professional, it is incumbent upon you to review the return prior to filing it to ensure the accuracy and reasonableness of the information on the return. If the return reflects deductions that you did not provide to the preparer — for instance, if the preparer claimed deductions on your return for charitable contributions but you know that you did not make any charitable contributions — you should question the accuracy of the entire tax return.

The IRS hired a substantial number of new examiners in 2001 throughout the country. This should increase the number of 2000 through 2002 tax returns that will be audited.

What If There Is Only One Questionable Item on Your Tax Return?

Suppose your tax return contains only one questionable deduction. Is this sufficient to cause your tax return to be audited? In the past the answer to this question might have been "no." In recent years, however, the IRS has been looking at new ways to audit tax returns. In IRM Section [4.2] 2.6, *Pre-Contact Planning of Examination Activities*, it states "Examiners are expected to examine all large, unusual and questionable items (LUQ). However, it is not intended that examiners should consider every possible issue."

Section [4.2] 2.6.1.1 (05-14-99) explains that the "scope of an examination of a return may be limited to one or two issues if no other items appear worthy of examination." Therefore, it is possible to request that the audit be limited to only one or two items.

When Is an Item Significant Enough to Audit?

The IRM at Section [4.2] 2.3.1 (05-14-99) provides the following factors to be considered when identifying a large, unusual, or questionable item (LUQ):

(A) *Comparative size of the item — an expense item of $6,000 with total expenses of $30,000 would be a large item; however, if total expenses were $300,000, the item would not be generally considered a large item.*

(B) *Absolute size of the item — despite the comparability factor, size by itself maybe significant. For example, a $50,000 item may be significant even though it represents a small percentage of taxable income.*

(C) *Inherent character of the item — although the amount of an item may not be significant, the nature of the item may be significant; e.g., airplane expenses claimed on a plumber's Schedule C.*

(D) *Evidence of intent to mislead — this may include missing, misleading, or incomplete schedules, or incorrectly showing an item on the return.*

(E) *Beneficial effect of the manner in which an item is reported — expenses claimed on a business schedule rather than claimed as an itemized deduction.*

(F) *Relationship to other items — incomplete transactions identified on the tax return. For example, the taxpayer reported sales of stock but no dividend income.*

(G) *Whipsaw Issues — whenever there is a transaction between two parties and characteristics of the transaction will benefit one party and harm the other. Examples include alimony vs. child support, sale vs. rental/royalty, employee vs. independent contractor, gifts vs. income.*

Make Sure Your State Return Agrees with Your Federal Return

The IRS has entered into a cooperative arrangement with most states. Entries on federal and state tax returns are checked against each other for consistency. In the case of a discrepancy, both returns could be flagged for audit. Be sure your tax returns agree with each other to avoid triggering an unnecessary audit. If the IRS audits your federal income tax return, you should amend the state return for all agreed-upon adjustments.

What to Do if You Are Audited

The letter informing you of an office audit will list the items being challenged and the time and place of the audit. If the time is not convenient, you have the right to rearrange the time to fit in with your schedule, although you cannot make extensive delays.

You can request that the audit be moved to a different IRS office if you have sufficient reason (e.g., you moved outside the original district or you work in a different district). Making such a request is a good idea and typically must be done in writing. A substantial delay typically occurs when you transfer your file from one office to another. Also, the new district may not want to audit the return or may not have sufficient auditors and "survey" the return prior to starting the examination.

Note that you are entitled to bring up deductions you overlooked in addition to defending those that the IRS is challenging.

In an Office Audit, the notification letter from the IRS will contain a checklist of the items being questioned on your return. Normally, these will be the only items discussed at the audit. Again, you should bring documentation to support only those items that the IRS has requested and not items not mentioned in the notification. If the auditor's curiosity is aroused by another item, he might be deterred by the fact you haven't brought those documents to the exam. It is possible he will let the matter drop and close the examination rather than force you to return with extra documents. A typical office audit session lasts from one to two hours and the auditor must control his or her inventory by closing cases within a reasonable period of time.

There are two different types of examiners — *Revenue Agents* and *Tax Auditors.* Revenue Agents usually have a college education with a major in accounting or have twenty-hour hours of formal accounting classes. They audit business returns and more complex cases. Tax Auditors, on the other hand, are not required to have taken any accounting or business courses, although they must take some training in accounting before advancing to the journeyman level.

The IRS must follow the tax laws set forth by Congress in the Internal Revenue Code. The IRS also follows Treasury Regulations, other rulings, and procedures that were written to administer the tax laws. The IRS also follows court decisions. However, the IRS can lose cases that involve taxpayers with the same issues and still apply its interpretation of the law to your situation.

If you agree with the proposed changes, you can sign an agreement form and pay any additional tax, interest, and penalties that you might owe. If you are due a refund, you will receive it sooner if you sign the agreement form. You will be paid interest on the refund. If the IRS accepts your return as filed, you will receive a letter stating that the examiner proposed no change to the return.

If you do not agree with the proposed changes, the examiner is required to explain your appeal rights. In an Office Audit, you can request an immediate meeting with the examiner's supervisor to explain your position. If a solution is not agreed upon, you should receive in the mail a letter (known as a *30-day letter*) notifying you of your appeal rights. The Appeals procedure is explained later in this text.

You also have the right to enter into a "partial agreement" with the IRS. This means that you might agree with some adjustments or changes that the IRS proposes on your tax return, but disagree with others. Or, you might disagree with proposed penalties that are being asserted. The revenue agent or office auditor will prepare a report for you to sign for only those adjustments with which you are in agreement. You can appeal those unagreed issues.

One situation where an appeal is particularly effective is when the auditor imposes the negligence penalty. If you believe you were not negligent and have a reasonable cause explanation for the deficiency assessed by the examiner, appealing the assertion of the penalty can often go in your favor. The Appeals Officer has the authority to negotiate penalty issues.

How to Get the IRS to Call Off Repeat Audits

Few things are more irritating than to be audited, to convince the auditor that you're correct, and then to be audited on the very same issue the next year. To prevent this from happening, the IRS has adopted a special policy. Namely, a taxpayer is generally not supposed to be audited on any issue on which he was audited in either of the two preceding years — provided the taxpayer was cleared on that issue in the previous audit. (However, if he was cleared in one of the preceding years and had to pay tax in the other, the current audit can proceed.)

Note that the IRS does not generally check for previous audits. It is up to you to tell the IRS agent about a preceding no-change audit. He should then call off the audit after verifying your story.

No matter what the outcome of an audit, you don't have to face the same auditor the next three years. At your request, an IRS examiner must be replaced if he has examined your return for any of the three preceding tax years, unless there has been an intervening audit by a different examiner. However, this doesn't restrict agents from widening an audit to prior unaudited years.

How Long Does It Take The IRS to Audit Your Return?

The general rule is that the IRS has three years from the due date of your return in which to make an audit. There are several exceptions to this general rule. If you file late, the IRS has 3 years from the actual filing date. If the IRS can prove that at least 25% of gross income was omitted from your return, the statutory date for audit is extended to 6 years. However, if the government can prove fraud, there is no time limit on auditing a return. But if the government decides to prosecute for criminal fraud, it must do so within 6 years. Criminal prosecution for fraud is a rare occurrence, but you do not want to find yourself in this position even if you win your case because of the cost involved in litigating a case.

The IRM instructs its agents to complete an examination as quickly as possible. Except when a return is suspected of fraud or a Form 872, *Consent To Extend The Time to Assess Tax*, is signed by the taxpayer(s) and executed by the IRS, the examination and disposition of income tax returns will be completed within 26 months after the due date of the return (or the date filed in the case of a late filed return). The IRS ordinarily allows 6 months to one year for the examination process. Thus, to complete the examination within 26 months, the IRS must initiate the examination no later than 20 months after the filing date. Thus, if you haven't heard from the IRS by late 2002, your 2000 return will be safe from audit except in unusual circumstances.

The Examination Returns Handbook (IRM 4.2)

The Handbook provides basic procedures, guidance, and requirements for use by Revenue Agents and Tax Auditors in conducting income tax examinations. This Handbook offers interesting glimpses into how agents are instructed to treat taxpayers. The basic premise is that "All examiners must perform their professional responsibilities in a way that supports the IRS Mission. This requires examiners to provide top quality service and to apply the law with integrity and fairness to all."

There is a focus on:

- Customer (Taxpayer) Service Problem Solving

- Timely Action

- Oral and Written Communication

- Taxpayer Rights

- Confidentiality of Taxpayer Information/Taxpayer Privacy

The entire Handbook is located on the IRS website (www.IRS.gov). (Go to the "Site Tree" and locate the "Internal Revenue Manual.")

Appealing Within the IRS

If you feel an auditor is taking an unreasonable position, you can ask to speak to his/her supervisor right then. The supervisor can change the auditor's determination if he agrees with you that your position is reasonable. Otherwise, if you can't come to an agreement at the audit, you can appeal to the Appeals Division of the IRS. The examiner is required to explain your appeal rights under the appeals procedure.

If you do not agree with the proposed changes, the examiner will close his/her case. Within a few weeks of your closing conference, you will receive the following:

- A letter, known as a *30-day letter,* notifying you of your rights to appeal the proposed changes *within 30 days;*

- A copy of the examination report explaining the examiner's proposed changes;

- An agreement or waiver form; and

- A copy of Publication 5.

You generally have 30 days from the date of the 30-day letter to tell the IRS whether you will accept or appeal the proposed changes. The method used to appeal depends upon the dollar amount of the proposed adjustments. You must follow the instructions on the 30-day letter carefully and submit a response (usually written) within 30 days from the date of the letter. Basically, the following rules apply:

- An oral request is sufficient to transfer your case to Appeals in an office audit or correspondence examination cases.

- In a field exam, if the proposed tax is $2,500 or less, a written request is not required.

- For amounts of proposed tax between $2,500 and $10,000, a written request is optional.

- Amounts that exceed $10,000 require a written protest.

It typically takes several months for the case to be transmitted to the Appeals Division. An appeals officer will contact you either by telephone or in writing and schedule a date for the appeals conference. This conference is typically in person at the local IRS Appeals Office that is closest to your home. In some situations, a conference can be held by telephone. This is at the discretion of the Appeals Officer.

How to Stop the Interest From Accruing

If you think you still owe tax at the end of the examination, you can stop the further accrual of the interest by sending the IRS a deposit in the form of a "cash bond."Special procedures must be followed to post the cash bond; you should discuss this with the examiner if this is the procedure you want to follow. In most situations, the IRS must return the money if you request it back. The IRS will not return your deposit if one of the following situations apply:

- The IRS assesses a tax liability

- The IRS determines that, by returning the deposit, it may not be able to collect a future deficiency

- The IRS determines that the deposit should be applied against another tax liability

Deposits do not earn interest.

Tax Court

You can take your case to United States Tax Court if you disagree with the IRS.

The IRS will issue a *notice of deficiency (90-day letter)*. You have 90 days from the date of the notice of deficiency to file a protest in tax court (150 days if it is addressed to you outside the United States). You can represent yourself before the Tax Court or you can be represented by anyone admitted to practice before that Court.

Small case procedures: If your case is $50,000 or less for any one tax year or period, your case can be handled under the small case procedures. You can get more information from the United States Tax Court, 400 Second Street, N.W., Washington D.C. 20217.

Note that even if you don't want to appear in court, it pays to submit the petition anyway. The IRS does not want to send its lawyers into court to adjudicate small issues in a forum that does not involve setting legal precedent. Some time after you file a petition, the IRS will contact you to arrange a settlement. About 90% of small cases are settled without going to trial.

District Court and Court of Federal Claims

Generally, these courts only hear a case once the tax is paid and you have filed a claim for a credit or refund. For further information about procedures for filing suit in either court, contact Clerk of your District Court or of the United States Court of Federal Claims.

Collection Alternatives

Installment Agreements

After you prepare your tax return and discover that money is due with the return, the best solution is to pay the balance due by April 15th. It is important to note that the IRS charges interest from the due date of the return (April 15th for an individual income tax return) plus a failure to pay penalty on the deficiency. The penalty is one-half of 1% of the tax not paid, for each month (or part of a month) it remains unpaid, total penalty not to exceed 25%.

If you are unable to pay the tax, you can file a Form 9465, Installment Agreement Request, with your tax return. Under certain circumstances, depending on the amount due, the IRS is required to enter into an installment agreement without requesting financial information. Those circumstances are as follows:

- **Streamlined Installment Agreement:** If your tax obligation is $10,000 or less and you have a one-time tax deficiency, you can enter into an agreement with the IRS to pay the taxes on a monthly installment agreement without providing financial information.

- **Guaranteed Installment Agreement:** If you owe tax of $25,000 or less, you have filed and paid all other tax periods, you agree to pay within 3 years, and you did not have an installment agreement during the past 5 years, you are guaranteed an installment agreement.

If the IRS accepts the installment agreement, the interest and failure to pay penalty will continue to accrue until the balance is paid in full. But, the failure to pay penalty is reduced to one-quarter of 1% as long as you remain current on the installment agreement.

If the deficiency exceeds $25,000 the IRS will request financial information and, based upon established guidelines, will set the dollar amount they expect you to pay monthly.

Offer in Compromise

In certain circumstances, the IRS might accept an amount that is less than the full amount that you owe. Any one of the following reasons might qualify you for this program:

- There is doubt about the amount that you owe

- There is doubt as to whether you can pay the amount you owe based on your financial situation

- An economic hardship would result if you had to pay the full amount owed

- Regardless of your financial circumstances, payment of the full amount owed would harm voluntary compliance by you or other taxpayers.

Generally, if you submit an Offer in Compromise, the IRS will delay collection activities. The IRS will usually not levy your property while it considers your offer. If the IRS rejects your original offer you can submit a revised offer within 30 days of the rejection. Also, if your offer is rejected you have 30 days to request an appeal with the Appeals Division of the IRS.

Taxpayer Bill of Rights

As part of the *1988 Tax Revision Act,* Congress included a *Taxpayer Bill of Rights.* This was designed to protect against IRS abuses and give the average citizen a reasonable shot when there is a tax dispute with the government.

The following are some of the more important provisions in this *Taxpayer Bill of Rights.*

1. Audits can be tape recorded.

"A taxpayer is permitted, upon advance notice to the IRS, to make an audio recording of an in-person interview at the taxpayer's own expense. IRS employees also are authorized to record taxpayer interviews, provided the taxpayer receives prior notice of such recording and is supplied a copy or a transcript of the recording upon request and payment of the costs of the copy or transcript."

The IRS issued an "administrative pronouncement" in 1989 describing how this provision will work in practice. According to this pronouncement, the taxpayer must give advance notice to the IRS auditor that he intends to make a recording. This notice must be received by the IRS at least 10 calendar days before the audit is scheduled to take place. The taxpayer must provide the equipment with which the recording is made. [IRS Notice 89-51]

However, most tax experts agree that it's not a good idea to tape an audit unless there are unusual circumstances. The person you're recording is likely to become formal and go by the book. You won't be able to deal as effectively to get a favorable compromise settlement.

2. Taxpayer can call a halt in the middle of an audit.

"If a taxpayer clearly states during an interview with the IRS (other than an interview pursuant to an administrative summons) that the taxpayer wishes to consult with [a] representative [e.g. lawyer or CPA], the interview must be suspended to afford the taxpayer a reasonable opportunity to consult with the representative. . . .

"The suspension procedure provided by the provision is to be available to facilitate taxpayers' access to their representatives and not to delay needlessly the interview process. It is intended that in instances of abuse of this process (such as repeated suspensions of interviews to contact different representatives) the IRS may issue an administrative summons."

3. Taxpayer isn't required to appear in person at an audit.

"The bill provides that a taxpayer may be represented during a taxpayer interview by any attorney, certified public accountant, enrolled agent, enrolled actuary, or any other person permitted to represent a taxpayer before the IRS,who is not disbarred or suspended from practice before the IRS and who has a properly executed power of attorney from the taxpayer . . . . Absent an administrative summons, a taxpayer cannot be required to accompany the representative to an interview."

4. Taxpayers can be awarded costs if the IRS is wrong.

"Any person who substantially prevails in any action brought by or against the United States in connection with the determination, collection, or refund of any tax, interest, or penalty may be awarded reasonable litigation costs plus reasonable administrative costs incurred after the earlier of (1) the date of the receipt by the taxpayer of the notice of the decision of the IRS Office of Appeals, or (2) the date of the notice of deficiency."

Taxpayer Bill of Rights 2

This taxpayer bill of rights was signed into law on July 30, 1996. The bill established the position of Taxpayer Advocate (replacing that of Taxpayer Ombudsman).

1. **Taxpayer Advocate Service**
   Publication 1546 (Rev.01-2001) provides the following information relative to the Taxpayer Advocate Program:

   "The Taxpayer Advocate Service is an IRS program that provides an independent system to assure that tax problems, which have not been resolved through normal channels, are promptly and fairly handled. The National Taxpayer Advocate heads the program. Each state and service center has at least one Taxpayer Advocate, who is independent of the local IRS office and reports directly to the National Taxpayer Advocate."

   If you have an ongoing issue that has not been resolved with the IRS through normal processes, or if you have suffered or are about to suffer, a significant hardship as a result of the application of the tax laws, you should:

   1. Call the Taxpayer Advocate's toll-free number: 1-877-777-4778 or contact your local office. A listing of telephone numbers for local offices is listed on the IRS website (www.irs.gov) in Pub 1546;

   2. File Form 911, *Application for Taxpayer Assistance Order (TAO); or*

   3. Visit your local IRS office and request that an IRS employee fill out a Form 911 on your behalf.

2. **Installment Agreements**
   A termination notification is required to notify a taxpayer 30 days before altering, modifying, or terminating an installment agreement and an explanation for the action taken. And, a request can be made for an independent administrative review for an installment agreement termination.

3. **Separate to Joint Return**
   A repeal of the requirement to pay all of the tax as a precondition to switching from married filing separate to a married filing jointly.

4. **Litigation Costs and Attorney Fees**
   There is a shift of burden of proof to the IRS to show substantial justification for its position against a taxpayer if the taxpayer prevails in litigation. A taxpayer can recover attorney's fees if the IRS cannot show substantial justification.

5. **IRS Misconduct**
   There is a provision for a civil penalty against the United States if an officer or employee of the IRS compromises the determination of or collection of tax liability of the taxpayer's representation in exchange for information concerning the taxpayer. The amount recoverable is limited to $500,000 or the sum of the economic damages by the taxpayer, and the cost of litigation.

The IRS is required to report annually to Congress the number of employees reprimanded, terminated, or prosecuted; instances dismissed because of a finding that proper procedures were not followed; and, those initiated but not yet resolved.

IRS Restructuring and Reform Act of 1998 (Taxpayer Bill of Rights 3)

1. Taxpayer Advocate

The law created a dramatic expansion in the power vested by the Taxpayer Advocate. The expansion includes creating a national system of taxpayer advocates serving in local IRS offices. These local advocates work independently from the IRS. A TAO can now be issued for:

- Whether the taxpayer faces an immediate threat

- Whether there has been a delay of more than 30 days in resolving the taxpayer's problem

- Whether the taxpayer faces significant costs, such as legal fees, if the order is not granted

- Whether the taxpayer faces long-term harm if the order is not granted.

2. Innocent Spouse

The new law makes it easier to get innocent spouse relief. Innocent spouse relief is available in situations where the other spouse makes an error or fails to pay his/her tax. The spouse seeking the relief must not have known about the tax problem when the return was signed.

A spouse may now elect separate liability on the amount owed in certain circumstances where there was a divorce or separation.

There is now equitable relief when a spouse would not otherwise qualify for innocent spouse relief or the separate liability provision.

3. Installment Agreements

The new law created a guarantee access to installment agreements in cases where the taxpayer owes $10,000 or less (later increased to $25,000). The failure to pay penalty is cut in half for taxpayers who make an installment agreement with the IRS if the tax return was filed timely and the taxpayer did not receive a notice with intent to levy (penalty reduced from .5% per month to .25%).

4. Appeal Rights for Levies and Liens

There is an expansion of taxpayer rights in situations where the IRS seeks to collect past-due taxes. The taxpayer may request a hearing before an impartial appeals officer within 30 days after the notice of lien has been filed or a notice of intent to levy has been sent. If the taxpayer requests a hearing within the 30-day period, the proposed levy may not take place until after the appeals officer makes a finding. The taxpayer can discuss other collection alternatives, such as an installment agreement or an offer in compromise.

If the appeal is not successful, the taxpayer has 30 days to challenge the findings in Tax Court or U.S. District Court. The IRS cannot levy during this period.

5. Seizure of a Residence

The IRS cannot seize a residence, except rental property, when there is a tax liability of less than $5,000. A taxpayer's principal residence cannot be seized without a court order.

6. Civil Damages for IRS Employee Negligence

A taxpayer can seek civil damages of up to $100,000 if an agency employee negligently disregards the tax code or regulations involving tax collection.

SECTION 2:
PRIVATE IRS RULINGS

You might want to learn in advance the tax consequences of an action you contemplate taking. Many times, the question of whether or not a particular activity falls under the rules for tax-free treatment becomes a matter of judgment. This is especially true when the issue involves determining whether the primary purpose of an activity is for business or personal purposes.

In order to determine how the IRS will treat a particular matter, you can solicit a *Private Letter Ruling* from the IRS. This written opinion, which you attach to your tax return, will then govern the treatment of your particular case by the IRS.

Soliciting a written opinion from the IRS is completely different from merely phoning the information number the IRS provides. It is well established that you cannot legally rely on oral advice from IRS personnel. Past surveys have found substantial error rates in such advice. The error rate is no doubt even higher on specialized or complicated matters. After all, it is unreasonable to expect any given individual to be familiar with all the tax laws as they apply to people in all professions.

What Kind of Questions Will the IRS Rule On?

The IRS has the option of deciding whether or not to issue a ruling. Basically, they will issue a ruling on most matters with the following major exceptions:

1. The IRS will not issue a ruling to specify how much a certain property is worth, to specify the building/land ratio of property for depreciation purposes, or to specify other such "numerical" issues.

2. The IRS will not rule on a hypothetical question, nor on one involving several alternatives. They will not rule on a transaction to be consummated at some indefinite future time. They must be presented with a single definite course of action which is seriously being considered.

3. The IRS will not rule on a transaction or matter having as a major purpose the reduction of federal taxes. In other words, they won't issue a ruling if they feel they are simply being presented with a tax-dodging scheme.

If the ruling request deals with a matter on which the IRS will not issue a ruling, the taxpayer will be so advised. However, the request may be forwarded to the district IRS office for association with the taxpayer's return. The IRS is also reluctant to issue rulings applying changes in the Tax Code until the IRS has had time to issue regulations interpreting the changes.

Preliminary Contact

The National Office of the IRS ordinarily won't discuss a "substantive tax issue" prior to receipt of a written ruling request. However, you can always inquire whether the IRS will rule on a particular question. Any such written inquiry must contain your name and social security number. You can also make inquiries as to procedural questions concerning the request for a ruling.

A ruling request may be withdrawn at any time before the ruling is issued. However, withdrawal won't necessarily prevent the IRS from furnishing its views to the local IRS office where your tax return is filed.

How to Request a Ruling

To request a ruling, you write a letter describing all circumstances addressed to: Internal Revenue Service, Associate Chief Counsel (Income Tax and Accounting), Attn: CC: PA:T, PO Box 7604, Ben Franklin Station, Washington, D.C. 20044. Either you or your attorney, accountant, or enrolled agent will sign the letter.

The request for a ruling should include the following:

1. The names, addresses, and social security or taxpayer account numbers of all interested parties.

2. Location of the IRS district office having audit jurisdiction over the tax return in question.

3. A carefully detailed description of the transaction, including a full and precise statement of the business reasons for the transaction (Statement of Facts).

4. Copies of all relevant documents (photocopies will usually be accepted as true copies of the original documents; originals should not be sent because they won't be returned) and a description of how the attached documents or exhibits bear on the issue in question.

5. A statement whether, to the best of the knowledge of the taxpayer or his representative, the identical issue is pending before any other IRS office and, if so, the office involved.

6. If the request pertains to only one step of a larger transaction, the facts concerning the larger transaction.

7. A statement of the taxpayer's view as to what the tax outcome should be, including reference to relevant authorities in support of this view and whether there are any regulations, rulings, etc., which are contrary to the taxpayer's position, or a statement that none are known (Statement of Law).

8. A statement whether or not the identical issue is being or has been examined in an IRS audit of a prior tax return which has not yet been finally resolved.

9. A separate signed declaration as follows: *"Under penalties of perjury, I have examined this request, including accompanying documents, and to the best of my knowledge and belief, the facts presented in support of the requested ruling or determination letter are true, correct and complete."* This statement does not have to be notarized.

If a ruling request does not contain all the needed information, the IRS will write back and request the missing information. Only one copy of the ruling needs to be sent unless more than one issue is presented. In such a case, duplicate requests should be mailed.

Before a letter ruling is issued, the IRS will usually inform you of its conclusions. If the IRS is going to rule adversely, it will generally offer you the opportunity to withdraw your ruling request.

Optional Statement of Controlling Facts

If you request a ruling, your request might include some information on future actions which you are not certain will take place. If you feel this information is not critical to your case, you would not want the ruling invalidated because of an irrelevant change in plans. In your ruling request, you can make a statement as to what you feel are the "controlling facts." That is, you feel these controlling facts alone should determine the tax outcome. In their ruling, the IRS can then agree with your list of controlling facts or they can make their own list. Any change in facts or circumstances not on the list of controlling facts would then not invalidate the ruling.

Rulings Made Public

The IRS is required to make public all private letter rulings which it issues. Before making a ruling public, the IRS deletes the name of the taxpayer as well as any identifying details or confidential information.

If there is any confidential information which you do not want revealed, you must send a statement to this effect along with your original ruling request with the material you wish to be kept private indicated by brackets (or leave a blank space for the confidential information). If there is no information you wish kept confidential, you must attach a separate statement to your ruling request which states that no information needs to be deleted other than your name, address, and social security number.

The release of IRS rulings is of great assistance to the taxpaying public. At one time, the only information that was made public was contained in rulings which the IRS chose to issue and in reports of cases which wound up in court. Now, it is possible to find out the IRS position on any question about which some taxpayer was concerned enough to request a ruling.

Future editions of this *Tax & Financial Guide* will contain reports of currently issued rulings that are pertinent. This provides new information on many issues for which there is currently no clear guidance.

Can You Rely on Rulings?

If you request and receive a ruling concerning your own tax situation, you can safely rely on that ruling as long as the facts you have described are correct. The IRS won't change its mind in your case. However, you cannot absolutely rely on rulings issued to other people even if the circumstances are the same. That is, the IRS can treat two taxpayers in the same situation differently. However, they do attempt to maintain a consistent policy whenever possible. You must attach to your return a copy of any ruling you have received which is relevant to that return. The IRS wants to make sure that rulings are complied with.

User Fees

The Internal Revenue Service charges a fee to process a request for a letter ruling. These fees are called "user fees" and are intended to reimburse the Service for the cost involved. The user fee for most rulings is $5,000 (there are exceptions for changes of accounting periods: $600; changes in accounting methods: $1,200, etc.). However, there is a *reduced user fee of $500 for:*

1. Requests involving a personal tax issue from taxpayers with gross income of less than $250,000.

2. Requests involving a business-related tax issue (such as home-office expenses, residential rental property issues) from taxpayers with gross income of less than $1,000,000. Taxpayers include partnerships and corporations.

19

Withholding

Withholding from Salary

Every employee is required to have a completed Form W-4 on file with his employer. This form is used by the employer in computing the amount of taxes to be withheld from the employee's paychecks. You need to fill out a new W-4 with your current employer only if you wish to change your withholding. You can probably best determine this after you fill out your tax return. A large refund indicates too much being withheld, while a large amount of tax due indicates that too little tax is being withheld. In such a case where your withholding is off the mark, you should file a new Form W-4 with your employer.

On Form W-4, allowances are claimed based on your dependents, deductions, adjustments to income, child care expenses, and the amount of non-wage income, such as dividends and interest, that you anticipate receiving. There are 2 components to the form — a worksheet for computing the number of withholding allowances you are entitled to claim, and the shorter actual W-4 itself, which is what you file with your employer. You do not file the worksheet, but rather keep it for your own records.

There is also a separate section on the Form W-4 entitled *"Two Earner/Two-Job Worksheet."* This section is used if there are 2 separate incomes (either because an individual has 2 jobs or because a married couple each have jobs) and the total income exceeds a threshold amount specified on the form. Under this section, tables are provided which subtract allowances based on income level and marital status. If these allowances are not subtracted, too little will probably be withheld.

Married couples should use only one worksheet based on their combined exemptions, deductions, etc. The total number of allowances computed on this worksheet is then divided between the husband and wife, who file individual Forms W-4 with their respective employers. The IRS recommends that the higher-earning spouse claim all the withholding allowances on his or her Form W-4, while the other spouse claims none. Married couples who choose a different allocation method will usually experience overwithholding.

Similarly, if you work for more than one employer during the year, you cannot claim the same allowance twice. You should use one worksheet on which you report all your income and allocate the allowances among the W-4's filed with each of your employers.

Individuals whose tax picture is expected to materially change are supposed to file a new withholding form with their employer.

If you claim 10 or more withholding allowances, your employer is required to report this fact to the IRS. In such a case, the IRS may write to you, asking for your computation of the allowances to which you claim you're entitled.

Check your state tax situation also. Some states have not revised their tax structure in line with federal tax reform. This means that your withholding might come out right for your federal tax return, but be too high for your state tax return. In such a case, you should adjust your state withholding allowances separately from your federal withholding allowances. Your federal and state withholding allowances do not have to be the same.

Students with summer jobs may be able to avoid any withholding on their wages. Any student (or other individual) who owed no tax the previous year and expects to owe no tax for the current year qualifies. The exemption from withholding is claimed by writing *"exempt"* on the appropriate line of Form W-4. However, exempt status cannot be claimed by any person who (1) can be claimed as a dependent by a parent or someone else; and (2) expects his total income to be more than $750 and includes more than $250 of unearned income (i.e. interest and dividends). A person satisfying both of these conditions will generally owe income tax. For example, a dependent student who earns $1,500 on a summer job and has $400 in interest income would owe $60 tax. (However, he could *earn* up to $4,550 in wage income and be exempt from tax, as long as he had no *nonwage* income.)

IRS Says You Can Disregard W-4 Worksheet

In keeping the Form W-4 down to only 2 pages (at one time it ran 4 pages), the IRS had to compromise some accuracy for the sake of simplicity. That is, for some persons (in particular, working couples and higher-income persons), withholding based on the current Form W-4 may be off the mark—producing either too large a refund or too much tax due.

The IRS issued an unusual pronouncement about what you can do in such a case. Namely, you can choose to ignore the Form W-4 worksheet section altogether and make your own computation, as long as it more accurately reflects the amount of tax due. [IRS Notice 88-42, IRB 1988-15]

Thus, the IRS has thrown in the towel on trying to come up with a reasonable Form W-4 that gives an accurate estimate of the amount of tax due in all circumstances. The current tax law is just too complicated to make it possible. The approach of adjusting your withholding up or down depending upon your tax refund or amount due may well be the most workable approach for many people.

Backup Withholding on Interest and Dividends

If you fail to furnish a correct social security number to a bank, savings & loan, stock broker, or other financial institution, this could subject you to backup withholding equal to 31% of the interest, dividends, etc., which you earned. Upon your furnishing a correct social security account number, the withholding ceases. This is not a penalty, just extra withholding. You get credit for this withholding when you file your tax return, the same as for amounts withheld from your paychecks.

Estimated Tax Payments

If you have taxable income which is not subject to withholding, you may be required to make quarterly estimated tax payments throughout the year. Generally, you are required to prepay (through withholding and/or estimated tax payments) either:

Option (1). 90% of the tax to be shown on the return for the current year, or

Option (2). 100% of the tax shown on the preceding year's tax return.

If salary withholding equals either (1) or (2), no estimated tax payments are required. Also, no estimated payments are required if the unpaid tax liability for the year is less than $1,000.

For most people, Option (2) is the most convenient to use because it is based on a knowable commodity, namely the amount of tax shown on the prior year's tax return. In contrast, Option (1) requires a prediction as to the tax that will be computed on the next tax return yet to be filed.

Exception: If adjusted gross income exceeded $150,000 ($75,000 for marrieds filing separately) on the preceding year's tax return, the 100% figure in Option (2) is raised to 110% for computing estimated tax liability on your 2001 tax return. This 110% figure increases to 112% for 2002 tax returns, then goes back to 100% for the 2003 tax year and later.

You don't have to verify on your tax return that you have paid the appropriate amount of estimated tax; the IRS computers will check this automatically. If you have not, you will be sent a bill for the amount of penalty due.

Your estimated tax is paid in four installments, the first one being due April 15. You use Form 1040-ES to make your estimated tax payments. This form contains a worksheet for computing the amount due plus four vouchers which you send in with your payments. You do not send in your computation worksheet — only the vouchers indicating the amounts you are paying.

There is an exception which applies if your income is irregular, with more being earned toward the end of the year than toward the beginning. You will escape penalty if your estimated taxes at each quarterly payment date meet the 90% test for your income through the end of the corresponding period — i.e. your estimated taxes are computed as though your income would continue to be earned at the same rate for the rest of the year. This exception is known as the annualized income installment method. To use this exception, you file Form 2210 with your tax return for the year. The IRS can also waive the penalty for an underpayment due to an unexpected calamity, such as loss of records in a fire or serious illness.

If your tax return shows a refund due, you can indicate on the tax form to have part or all of this refund treated as an estimated tax payment for the first quarter of the next year, rather than being paid out to you.

There is a penalty for underpayment of estimated tax. This penalty is adjusted periodically, based on the prime interest rate. This penalty is not deductible.

Yearend Adjustments to Avoid Underpayment Penalty

Don't overlook the following remedy if you discover towards the end of the year that you did not make sufficient estimated tax payments. You can request your employer to withhold extra amounts from your yearend paychecks. Form W-4 is used to make this request. This enables you to move the total prepayment (withholding plus estimated tax) towards the required amount. Your employer must put your new Form W-4 into effect generally no later than 30 days after receiving your revised Form W-4.

Having extra amounts withheld from your yearend paychecks is better than making an extra estimated tax payment near yearend. Your estimated tax payments are generally supposed to be made evenly throughout the year. Even if the total is sufficient to cover your liability, you could be penalized because the early payments were less than the later payments.

However, withholding can be considered spread out evenly no matter when it occurs. This means that amounts withheld late in the year are treated exactly the same as if they were withheld earlier. There is no penalty unless the total for the year is insufficient.

The same situation arises when amounts are withheld from pension distributions you receive. Even if these amounts are all withheld from a large payment made at the end of the year, they are considered to have been spread out evenly over the course of the year.

Similarly, if you have an IRA, you can use it to produce extra withholding. This is done by receiving a *rollover* of funds from your IRA which you can then deposit in a bank account, savings account, etc. [see Section 2 of the *Tax-Sheltered Plans* chapter]. The institution running your IRA will generally withhold 10% of the proceeds (unless you elect to waive this withholding). The amount withheld will be sent to the IRS and credited to your taxes as though it were withheld rateably over the entire year.

To complete the rollover, you must redeposit the funds withdrawn from the IRA back into the same IRA or into a different IRA in your name. This redeposit must be made within 60 days after the original rollover withdrawal was made [see Section 2 of the *Tax-Sheltered Plans* chapter]. To avoid extra taxation, you must not only redeposit the funds you received, but also the amount withheld in taxes.

Example

Near the end of the year, you estimate that your estimated tax plus withholding will be $2,000 short of the required amount. You have an IRA with an account value of $20,000. You make a $20,000 withdrawal and deposit the proceeds into your savings account. Because you are not electing otherwise, the institution running your IRA withholds $2,000 from the distribution, leaving $18,000 to go into your savings account. The $2,000 is treated by the IRS as though it had been withheld evenly throughout the year, and cures the deficit in your estimated tax plus withholding.

> *Within 60 days, you redeposit the $18,000 you received plus an additional $2,000 to cover the withheld amount into the same or a different IRA. This will complete the rollover transaction.*

A similar maneuver can be made if you have a self-employed plan. Funds withdrawn from a self-employed plan can be rolled over within 60 days into another self-employed plan or into an IRA. In this case, the withholding rate on the self-employed plan withdrawal is 20%, rather than 10%. However, if you are under age 59½, you must generally take a complete distribution and terminate your self-employed plan to be able to roll it over into an IRA. Before making a self-employed plan rollover, be sure to check with the sponsors as to the precise withholding rate and rollover restrictions in your individual situation.

—20—

Divorce and Separation

Filing Status

Your marital status on December 31 determines the type of tax return you can file for the year. If, on December 31, you are married and not *legally* separated under a decree of divorce or separate maintenance, you may file a joint return. If you are divorced or legally separated, you may not file a joint return. Instead, you file as a single person. In this case, you may use the lower head-of-household rate if you meet the usual requirements for using this special rate.

A separated couple must have a legal separation under a court decree in order to file as single persons. An informal separation, even under a written agreement, does not count with the following exception:

Exception

Even if you are not divorced or legally separated, you may file as a single person (including as a head-of-household) if you meet all of the following tests:

(1) You do not file a joint return,

(2) You paid more than half the cost to keep up your home for the year,

(3) Your spouse did not live in your home at any time during the last 6 months of the year, and

(4) For over six months of the year, your home was the principal residence of your child or stepchild whom you are entitled to claim as a dependent (or would be entitled except that you relinquished the exemption to your spouse on Form 8332).

Note that the above tests apply to your tax return only. Your spouse must also meet the above tests in order to file as a single person. Otherwise, he or she must file using the higher rates for married individuals filing separately. Of course, you both could file a joint return together if that is preferable, provided you are not divorced or legally separated on December 31.

A couple might be better off taxwise if a joint return is used, especially if only one of them has a significant amount of income. Or, they might be better off filing as single persons. In accord with the above tax rules, this consideration may play a role in deciding whether to turn a separation agreement into a legal separation. This also depends on the law in your state.

Alimony

When a married couple is separated or divorced, one of them may make "alimony" payments to the other. If these payments are made on an informal basis, there is no tax consequence. The payer does not claim the payments as a tax deduction,p nor does the recipient treat the payments as taxable income. However, if all of the following conditions are met, the alimony payments are deducted by the payer and reported as income to the recipient. (This often reduces the total tax bill because the payer is usually in a higher tax bracket than the recipient.)

Conditions Under Which Alimony Is Deducted by Payer and Reported as Income by Recipient

Pre-1985 Rules

Divorce or separation agreements executed prior to 1985 must satisfy the following rules in order for alimony to be deductible:

(1) Payments must be required by an official agreement. This agreement could be part of a divorce, legal separation, or other court decree, or it could simply be a written agreement between the two parties without any court proceedings;

(2) The couple lives apart;

(3) The payments are periodic. They could be fixed monthly amounts, a percentage of annual income, etc. There are several additional requirements that need to be checked out to make sure this periodic condition is satisfied; and

(4) The payments are for the general support of the recipient. Amounts designated specifically for child support do not qualify. Neither do payments to settle loans or other obligations that are part of a property settlement.

Post-1984 Rules

Divorce or separation agreements executed after 1984 must satisfy the following rules in order for alimony to be deductible:

(1) Alimony payments must be required by an official agreement. This agreement could be part of a divorce, legal separation, or other court decree. Or, it could simply be a written agreement between the two parties without any court proceedings.

(2) Alimony payments must be made in cash, check, or money order and there must be no liability to make payments after the death of the recipient spouse. Payments made to a third party on behalf of the spouse (e.g. tuition, medical expenses, health insurance, etc.) can count as alimony if they are made under the terms of the divorce or separation instrument. However, an individual cannot count payments he makes to maintain property he owns (e.g. mortgage payments, taxes, homeowner's insurance) even if such payments are made pursuant to the terms of the divorce or separation instrument. Payment of life insurance premiums will be considered alimony if the payee spouse owns the policy.

(3) Alimony payments cannot be scheduled to decrease upon a child marrying, leaving school, moving out of the house, getting a job, or similar contingency. For example, if the agreement provides for payments of $800 per month, decreasing to $600 after a child marries, only $600 per month will be considered alimony. The remaining $200 per month will be considered nondeductible child support. Similarly, payments cannot be scheduled to decrease upon a child reaching age 18, 21, or local age of majority (give or take 6 months).

Amounts designated specifically for child support do not qualify as alimony. According to a court case, if the full amounts specified in a court decree are not paid, an allocation is made first to child support. For example, suppose you are required to pay $2,000 in child support and $3,000 in alimony for the year, but only pay a total of $2,500. In such a case, $2,000 of the $2,500 would be child support and $500 alimony. This is the case even if you and your spouse were to agree to the lower amount as a reduction in child support, without a written modification in the court decree. [Blair, TC Memo 1988-581]

(4) Alimony payments for the first 3 years must not be excessively front-loaded. The exact requirement is rather complicated to state. However, in all cases, if alimony payments do not decrease by more than $15,000 from either of the first 2 years to the next, this requirement will be satisfied.

This rule (4) applies to payments made under a divorce decree or separation decree or agreement. It does not apply to payments made under only a temporary support decree. The purpose of this rule is to discourage property settlements which typically have a large initial payment from being treated as alimony.

(5) Once a divorce or separation decree is executed, the spouses should not live in the same dwelling. Generally, payments made while living in the same dwelling after a decree is entered do not qualify as alimony, except for a 1-month grace period allowed for the spouses to separate. This restriction does not apply to payments made under a written separation agreement, rather than a divorce or separate maintenance decree. However, in a recent court case, alimony payments made by the husband were allowed as a deduction even though the couple resided in the same house, because the couple was anticipating physical separation. [Benham v. Commissioner, TC Memo 2000-165]

If payments satisfy the above rules, they can be deducted by the payer and become taxable income to the recipient. However, the spouses may designate payments otherwise qualifying as alimony to be nondeductible by the payer and nontaxable to the recipient by so providing in a divorce or separation instrument. An existing instrument can be legally amended to make this provision. The recipient should attach a copy of such a designation to the tax return for each year to which the designation applies.

Alimony Can Be Claimed Even If You Use the Standard Deduction

Alimony payments are claimed as an adjustment to income on line 31a, Form 1040, rather than as an itemized deduction. This means that you can deduct alimony payments whether you claim the standard deduction or itemize your deductions.

Reporting Requirements

There is a special reporting requirement that applies. If you deduct alimony payments on your tax return, you are required to list the recipient's social security number on your return. The IRS can use this to crosscheck that the recipient reports these amounts as taxable income. This reporting requirement applies to all alimony payments, even if made under divorce or separation agreements executed before 1985.

IRA Deduction Based on Alimony Payments

Contributions to an IRA can be based on alimony income. Individuals may be able to contribute up to $2,000 of alimony income to an IRA and deduct this amount on their tax returns [see Section 2 of the *Tax-Sheltered Plans* chapter].

Timing a Divorce

It may be worthwhile to check with your lawyer as to whether an advantage can be obtained by shifting the date of the official divorce. For example, a divorce after 10 years of marriage can sometimes be better than a divorce after 9 years. This can happen when the 10-year period qualifies an individual for spousal Social Security benefits.

Dependency Exemptions

When separate returns are filed, it must be determined which parent is entitled to claim a child as a dependent. The current rule is that the parent (called the *custodial spouse*) having custody of a child for the greater portion of the year is entitled to the dependency exemption. (This assumes that the parents together would have been entitled to the dependency exemption had they been married and filing a joint return.) It makes no difference that the other parent may have furnished most or all of the funds for support of the child.

However, the custodial spouse may release the right to a dependency exemption, in which case the non-custodial spouse can claim the exemption. This release is made by the custodial spouse on Form 8332 which the non-custodial spouse attaches to his or her return. The exemption may be released for a single year, for a number of specified years (for example, alternate years), or permanently. A copy of the release form must be attached to the tax return of the non-custodial spouse each year he or she claims the exemption.

Exception: The non-custodial spouse is entitled to the dependency exemption if so specified under a decree or written agreement executed before 1985. In such a case, no release form is needed. This exception only applies if the non-custodial spouse furnishes at least $600 towards the support of the child.

According to a 1986 IRS ruling, the pre-1985 agreement must **explicitly** assign the dependency exemption to the non-custodial spouse. In this ruling, a man was ordered to pay $300 per month child support in a 1973 divorce agreement. Since the divorce, he had been providing more than half the support of his 3 children and had been claiming dependency exemptions for them. However, even though he had been entitled to the dependency exemptions under the law existing at the time, the divorce agreement did not explicitly specify that he was entitled to the dependency exemptions. Thus, under the new law starting with 1985, because the children lived with their mother, she was now entitled to the dependency exemptions. This could not even be changed by amending the language of the old divorce agreement. The only way he could now claim the exemptions would be for her to release her claim on Form 8332, which he would attach to his tax return each year he claimed the exemptions. [IRS Private Letter Ruling 8609034]

Altering Old Agreements

You may have a divorce or separation agreement with an ex-spouse that results in a total tax bill which is higher than necessary. This is especially true because of the changes in the law governing divorce and alimony. If so, you should seek legal advice to straighten matters out. In many cases, you can amend a pre-1985 divorce or separation agreement so that it comes under the new rules, should that be advantageous. Sometimes, only a wording change will suffice, with no change in the underlying specifics of the agreement. Be aware that the changes must be in writing. Oral modifications will be ignored.

Medical Expenses

Either spouse may claim medical expenses which he or she actually pays for the child. It makes no difference that the other spouse may be claiming the dependency exemption. This assumes that the child receives over half of his total support from his parents.

Because of the 7.5% of income floor on deductible medical expenses [see the *Medical Expenses* chapter], divorced spouses should take care who actually pays the medical bills for a child. For example, suppose the ex-wife earned $20,000 and the ex-husband $50,000. For simplicity, let's say their child ran up a $3,000 bill at the orthodontist and that there are no other medical expenses involved. If the ex-husband paid the bill directly, there is no deduction because his medical expenses floor, 7.5% × $50,000 = $3,750, exceeds the $3,000 expense. However, the ex-wife's medical expense floor is 7.5% × $20,000 = $1,500. If he gave his ex-wife $3,000 and let her pay the bill, she gets a deduction of $3,000 − $1,500 = $1,500, while he has lost nothing in the transaction.

Property Transfer

A house or other property, such as stocks or bonds, may be transferred from one spouse to another as part of a divorce settlement. At one time, the IRS could treat such a transfer as a sale subject to capital gains tax. For example, a husband who transferred to a spouse a house worth $85,000, but which he purchased for $45,000, was liable for capital gains tax on the $40,000 increase in value.

Divorce-related property settlements no longer trigger a capital gains tax at the time of transfer. The transfers are treated as non-taxable events, i.e. a gift. However, the spouse who receives the property must treat it as acquired at the original purchase price. When sold, the difference between the sale price and original purchase price will be subject to capital gains tax. In the example in the preceding paragraph, if the wife were to sell the house for $95,000 in a later year, she would have a capital gain of $50,000. This $50,000 profit would be subject to capital gains tax, unless the house qualifies under the personal residence exception described in the *Homeowner's* chapter. When negotiating a separation agreement, consideration must be given to the tax consequences of the spouse receiving appreciated property.

Legal Fees

The legal fees involved in obtaining a divorce are not generally deductible. However, the portion of such fees which covered tax advice to the individual can be deducted. Also, a spouse may deduct legal costs associated with obtaining or collecting taxable alimony. In any divorce or separation proceeding, your lawyer should provide an itemization which indicates any portion of his fee that is deductible.

Sale of Residence

The exclusion from income of the gain on the sale of your principal residence ($250,000 for single individuals and $500,000 for married couples filing jointly) is discussed in detail in Chapter 9, Section 3. However, there are a few rules to remember for a married couple contemplating separation or divorce.

1. If a married couple files a joint return in the year of sale, either spouse's period of ownership and use of the home as a principal residence (two out of the immediately preceding five years) qualifies them for the $250,000 exclusion.

2. Both spouses must meet the two out of five year requirement to qualify for the $500,000 exclusion.

3. If the residence is transferred to one spouse as part of the property settlement, the use and ownership of the former spouse is counted towards thte other spouse's requirements.

4. If the residence is transferred to one spouse and there is a child residing in the house, the other spouse can exclude the $250,000 in the year of sale even though he/she has not resided in the house for the two out of five year requirement.

5. In some cases, it is better to sell the residence while still married if the gain on the sale will exceed $250,000.

21

Travel

SECTION 1:
BASIC RULES ON DEDUCTING TRAVEL EXPENSES

You can deduct the cost of travel connected with your job or other income-producing activity. This includes travel between two or more job locations the same day, travel to professional or union meetings, travel related to a temporary job, travel to obtain education, travel in connection with an outside business activity, etc. An exception is ordinary commuting expenses, which cannot be deducted except as discussed in Sections 2-4.

There are special rules which apply to various types of deductible travel. These are discussed in later sections. The remainder of this introductory section concerns those general rules which apply to all types of travel.

Where on the Income Tax Form Do You Claim Travel Expenses?

An employee reports his job-related travel expenses on Form 2106 or Form 2106-EZ [see the *Miscellaneous Deductions* chapter]. The total of such expenses is then transferred to line 20 of Schedule A as a *miscellaneous deduction.* As discussed in the *Miscellaneous Deductions* chapter, this total of travel expenses plus other miscellaneous deductions is subjected to a 2% of adjusted gross income floor.

Self-employed persons claim travel expenses on Schedule C or Schedule C-EZ, the same as any other business expense related to their self-employment activity. Thus, these expenses escape the 2% of adjusted gross income floor that applies to miscellaneous deductions; also, non-itemizers as well as itemizers get to deduct their travel expenses.

An employee with an outside business activity should take note of the more favorable treatment accorded self-employed persons when deciding how to treat his or her travel expenses. For example, suppose a college professor incurs unreimbursed travel expenses in attending a convention in his field of expertise. If the professor has self-employment income from consulting or writing, he may have a choice. Instead of treating travel expenses as a miscellaneous deduction connected with his college duties, he may be able to treat these expenses as a Schedule C or Schedule C-EZ write-off connected with his self-employment activity. [See Section 1 of the *Miscellaneous Deductions* chapter for further discussion.]

Which Expenses Are Deductible?

The first point to note is the distinction between travel and transportation expenses. **Transportation** refers to the task of getting from one place to another. But **travel** expenses may include, in addition to transportation expenses, certain living costs.

Let's assume that your travel meets the requirements for deductibility. Then if you are **away from home overnight,** the following are deductible travel expenses:

- Lodging both en route and at your destination

- Meals both en route and at your destination (subject to the 50%-Rule discussed later in this section)

- Transportation costs to and from your destination

- Baggage charges

- Reasonable cleaning and laundry expenses

- Transportation between the airport and your hotel

- Transportation between where you obtain meals and lodging and a temporary work assignment

- Telephone and fax expenses (non-personal)

- Reasonable tips connected with the above expenses

If, on the other hand, you are not away from home overnight, only your transportation costs are deductible. You cannot deduct the cost of meals, lodging, or laundry. You are considered to be traveling away from home overnight if (1) your duties require you to be away from the general area of your tax home substantially longer than an ordinary work day, and (2) you need to get sleep or rest to meet the demands of your work while away from home. Note that this requirement is not satisfied by merely napping in your car. Also, you do not have to be away from your tax home for a whole day or from dusk to dawn as long as your relief from duty is long enough to get necessary sleep or rest. [IRS Publication 463, p. 3]

A special limitation applies to travel by ocean liner or other water transportation. The deduction for such travel cannot exceed twice the highest per diem travel amount allowable to employees of the executive branch of the U.S. government. The non-separately stated cost of meals and entertainment is included in this limitation. If expenses for water transportation include separately stated amounts for meals and entertainment, those amounts are subject to the 50%-Rule before application of the daily limit. [IRS Publication 463, p. 8] However, this limitation does not apply to conventions, seminars, or other meetings held on a cruise ship. Rather, expenses for these activities are limited to $2,000 per year and can only be deducted if all of the cruise ship's ports of call are in the U.S. or in possessions of the U.S. [IRS Publication 463, p 9]

What Does "Away From Home" Mean?

"Home" has a special meaning to the IRS. It means the general area of your principal place of employment, regardless of where you maintain your family residence. For example, if your family residence is in Chicago but you work in Milwaukee, your "tax home" is the Milwaukee area. If you stay overnight in Milwaukee, you are not considered to be away from home overnight. Of course, you probably live and work in the same general area. If so, this general area is considered to be your tax home.

Exactly how much territory the "general area" includes is not well specified. Distinct cities at a distance of 50 miles apart would probably be considered in different areas. However, two points in the same metropolitan area would be considered in the same general area, even if those points were considerably far apart. [Harris, TC Memo 1980-56]

What About Commuting Costs?

In general, the cost of commuting between your residence and your work is not deductible. However, there are exceptions relating to temporary assignments away from your home.

1. If you are on a business trip out of town or if you are on a temporary assignment out of town, you may deduct all your transportation costs between your temporary lodgings and your business destination. You may also deduct all transportation costs from one business destination to another.

2. If you are required to work at a temporary location outside the general area of your home city, you may deduct transportation expenses for daily round trips from your home to the temporary business location. For example, if your home is in Baltimore and you are required to work in Washington, D.C., for a month, you can deduct your commuting expenses.

3. If you have a regular job location outside your residence, you can deduct commuting to an irregular or short-term job site regardless of the distance. [Rev. Rul. 99-7]

See Sections 2-4 for further details.

50%-Rule for Meal Expenses

Meal expenses are not deductible in full. Instead, only 50% of meal (and beverage) expenses can be deducted. All expenses of the meal such as tax, tips, parking, etc., are included under this 50%-Rule. However, transportation to and from a meal is not subject to the reduction.

> **Example 1**
> *While attending an out-of-town professional meeting, you incur the following unreimbursed expenses for dinner: $40 for meal and beverages, $3 for tax, $1 for coat check, and $6 for tip — a total of $50. The cost of taxi fare (including tip) to and from the restaurant is $14.*
> *The $50 total is subject to the 50%-Rule, but not the taxi fare. Thus, the meal yields a deduction of 50% × $50 = $25 plus the entire $14 taxi fare — a total of $39.*

The 50%-Rule is used before application of the 2% of adjusted gross income floor that applies to the total of miscellaneous deductions [see the *Miscellaneous Deductions* chapter]. This is illustrated by the following example:

> **Example 2**
> *An individual's adjusted gross income is $50,000 and his miscellaneous deductions other than travel expenses total $700. In addition, he incurs the following unreimbursed deductible travel expenses during the year:*
>
> | | |
> |---|---|
> | Transportation: | $620 |
> | Lodging: | 300 |
> | Laundry: | 50 |
> | | $970 |
> | | |
> | Meals: | $200 |
>
> *In computing the travel expenses, first apply the 50%-Rule to the meal expenses: 50% × $200 = $100. Thus, the total deductible travel expenses come to $970 + $100 = $1,070. The total of all miscellaneous deductions is then $700 + $1,070 = $1,770. However, this is reduced by 2% of adjusted gross income: 2% × $50,000 = $1,000. This produces a net deduction of $1,770 – $1,000 = $770.*

The above 2 examples illustrate the principles involved in deducting meal expenses, combined with travel and other job-related expenses. In practice, Form 2106 separates these expenses into 2 columns, Column B for meal and entertainment expenses and Column A for other employee business expenses. At the bottom of the form, the total deduction for employee business expenses is obtained by adding the final Column A total plus 50% of the Column B total. In the body of the form, untaxed reimbursements received from your employer are credited against either Column A or Column B expenses and subtracted from the total *expenses* accordingly. For further details, including examples on how to handle expenses on Form 2106, see Section 1 of the *Miscellaneous Deductions* chapter.

Expenses of Spouse

You cannot deduct the expenses of a spouse (or other family member) who simply accompanies you when you travel. To be deductible, the spouse must satisfy the requirements for deducting travel expenses based on the spouse's own job or profession.

If your spouse accompanies you on a trip and the spouse's expenses are not deductible, you do not have to split your expenses down the middle. Instead, you can deduct what it would have cost had you traveled alone. For example, if you and your spouse occupy a double room at a hotel which charges $65 for a single room and $80 for a double room, then you may deduct $65 as your lodging cost.

Recordkeeping

You should keep two kinds of records of your travel expenses–receipts and an expense diary. You do not include these records with the tax return you file. Rather, they are kept in case your return is audited.

Expense Diary

Your diary should contain the following:

1. The place or places of your travel

2. The dates of your departure and return home

3. The business reason for your travel

4. A daily list of your deductible expenses

You should list the amount of each separate expenditure (such as the cost of your transportation or lodging). However, each day the cost of your breakfast, lunch, dinner, and other expenses may be grouped together if they are set forth in reasonable categories such as meals, gasoline and oil, cab fares, telephone calls, etc. Tips may be grouped with the cost of the connected service.

You are not required to record amounts your employer pays directly for any ticket or other travel item. However, if you charge these items to your employer (through a credit card or otherwise), you must make a record of the expenditures.

A receipt, paid bill, or similar evidence is required to support any expenditure of $75 or more and any expenditure for lodging, no matter what the amount (unless a lodging plus meals and incidental expenses per diem method is used, as discussed later). The receipt should show the amount, date, place, and type of expenditure and should be sufficiently detailed to show the different elements of the expenditure. For example, a hotel bill should show as separate items, the costs for lodging, telephone calls, meals, etc. A cancelled check together with a bill will be sufficient. However, a cancelled check or credit card charge slip alone is inadequate. (Receipts are not needed if an allowable per diem expense rate is used, as discussed later.)

If you cannot establish the portion of an expenditure attributable to each person participating in the travel but you have established the amount of the total expenditure, it will ordinarily be allocated to each participant on a pro rata basis.

Your records should be timely. You should write down your expenses in your expense diary at or near the time they are incurred. If the record entries are made later when there is a lack of accurate recall, they will not comply with this rule.

The following is a sample of how a diary should look for attending a 2-day professional convention. The format is copied from an official IRS publication.

Date	Item	Place	Amount	Business Purpose
April 1	Airplane fare (round trip Chicago-Dallas)	Dallas	$460.20	Attend Convention of XYZ Assn.
	Meals and tips		35.10	
	Lodging		62.50	
April 2	Meals and tips		44.50	
	Automobile rental (2 days)		62.00	
	Tips		3.50	
	Registration fee		15.00	

Remark: Pay careful attention to the recordkeeping requirements as illustrated in the above example. Note the **5 different pieces of information required — date, item, place, amount, and business purpose.** If you leave any of these pieces out, your travel expenses could be ruled nondeductible. That's what happened to the taxpayer in the following court case.

> **Example 3**
> *A manufacturer's representative traveled extensively for his job. He kept a diary and produced cancelled checks for his lodging expenses. However, his expenses were ruled nondeductible because his diaries were not adequate. They did not show the location or the business purpose of his away from home business expenses. Even though the cancelled checks might have established the location of his lodging expenses, the Court said that still would not be good enough. He had presented no evidence indicating the business purpose of his trips. The failure to write down a few extra words in his diary turned out to be a very expensive mistake.* [Coursey, TC Memo 1974-43]

The substantiation rules are not so strict for local travel as for travel away from home. In particular, the keeping of a contemporaneous diary would not be mandatory if the traveling were done on a regular basis. This would be the case, say, when someone regularly travels between business locations or commutes to a temporary job. This is illustrated in Example 4 of Section 2.

Reimbursed Expenses

You may receive a reimbursement from your employer for travel expenses which you incur. Usually, you are required to give an expense accounting to your employer. If this accounting satisfies the recordkeeping requirements described above, you do not have to provide any further accounting to the IRS. They will check your employer's records if they wish to see verification of these expenses. If you did not make an adequate accounting to your employer for reimbursed travel expenses or if your expenses exceeded the reimbursement, then you must retain your expense diary and receipts yourself. [See Section 1 of the *Miscellaneous Deductions* chapter for information on how reimbursed expenses are handled on your tax return.]

Your employer may reimburse you on a per diem basis for your combined meals, lodging, and incidental expenses while away from home overnight. As long as the per diem rate does not exceed the *per diem limit,* this will be accepted by the IRS provided the other elements of time, place, and business purpose of the travel are substantiated to the employer. The *per diem limit* is equal to the rate published under the Federal Travel Regulations for government travel, which are updated annually.

Incidental expenses includes such things as laundry, cleaning and pressing of clothing, and tips for services, such as for waiters and porters. It does not include transportation, taxi fares, or the cost of telephone calls or fax services.

The combined per diem rates only apply if you are reimbursed by your employer. If you pay unreimbused expenses out of your pocket, you cannot use these combined per diem rates to determine your deduction.

A complete listing of per diem rates for travel within the 48 contiguous states and the District of Columbia is provided in IRS Publication 1542, *Per Diem Rates (For Travel Within the Continental United States).* This publication is available on the internet at www.irs.gov/forms–pubs/pubs.html.

In lieu of using the maximum per diem rate for each location from IRS Publication 1542, an employer may use the "high-low" method in expensing per diems. According to this simplified method, certain locations are designated as being "high-cost" areas and are characterized with a maximum per diem for lodging and meals and incidental expenses. All other areas are "low-cost" areas. For 2001, a high-cost locality has a maximum per diem of $201, and a low-cost locality has a maximum per diem of $124. Accordingly, travel in any high-cost location is eligible for a per diem of $201, and travel in all other localities warrants a per diem of $124. If an employer uses this method for an employee at any time during a calendar year, this method must be used for that employee for the entire year for travel within the continental United States.

The following is a list of the high cost-of-living areas in the continental U.S. from IRS Publication 1542. The areas include not just the cities themselves, but also the surrounding metropolitan counties. (For areas outside the continental U.S., the allowable per diem rate is the one used by federal employees when they travel.)

In some cases, a city is listed followed by a time period in parentheses. In these cases, the $201 rate applies only during this time period.

High Cost-of-Living Areas ($201 per Day) for Travel During 2001

California:	Palo Alto/San Jose/Sunnyvale (1/1-5/31); San Francisco; Tahoe City
Colorado:	Aspen (1/1-4/30); Silverthorne/Keystone; Telluride (1/1-3/31); Vail (1/1-3/31; 7/1-12/31)
D.C.:	Washington
Florida:	Key West (1/1-4/30)

Illinois:	Chicago
Louisiana:	New Orleans/St. Bernard (1/1-5/31)
Maryland:	Ocean City (6/15-10/31); Washington Suburbs
Massachusetts:	Boston; Cambridge; Martha's Vineyard (6/1-10/15)
Michigan:	Mackinac Island; Traverse City (6/1-9/30)
Montana:	Big Sky (1/1-4/30; 11/1-12/31)
New Jersey:	Cape May (6/1-11/30); Ocean City (6/15-9/15); Piscataway/Belle Mead; Princeton/Trenton
New York:	The Bronx/Brooklyn/Queens; Manhattan; Nassau County/Great Neck; Suffolk County; White Plains
Pennsylvania:	Hershey (6/1-9/15); Philadelphia
Utah:	Park City (1/1-3/31); (12/15-12/31)
Virginia:	Wintergreen; Washington Suburbs

There are many cities that are exceptions to the $201 and $124 per diem limits discussed above. The following is a list of cities that are major exceptions, along with the per diem allowances permitted for travel during 2001. [IRS Publication 1542] Again, where a time period is enclosed in parentheses, the amount following the parentheses applies to that time period only.

Arizona:	Flagstaff (5/1-10/31): $101
California:	Los Angeles: $145; Monterey (5/1-10/31): $136; Oakland: $156; Sunnyvale, Palo Alto/San Jose: $185; San Diego: $145; San Francisco: $205; Santa Barbara: $137
Colorado:	Boulder: $132; Denver: $128
Connecticut:	Bridgeport: $143
Delaware:	Wilmington: $133
Florida:	Key West (1/1-4/30): $211; Miami (1/1-4/15): $131; Tampa/St. Petersburg (1/1-4/30): $143
Georgia:	Atlanta: $131
Illinois:	Chicago: $176
Louisiana:	New Orleans/St. Bernard (1/1-5/31): $181
Maryland:	Annapolis: $132; Baltimore: $152; Columbia: $152
Massachusetts:	Andover: $147; Plymouth (6/15-10/15): $130
Michigan:	Detroit: $155; Pontiac/Troy/Auburn Hills: $132
Minnesota:	Minneapolis-St. Paul: $141
Missouri:	Kansas City/Clay County: $127; St. Louis: $136
New Jersey:	Princeton-Trenton: $181
New Mexico:	Santa Fe: $136

New York:	The Bronx/Brooklyn/Queens: $216
North Carolina:	Research Triangle Park/Durham: $127
Ohio:	Cleveland: $128
Pennsylvania:	King of Prussia/Ft. Washington/Bala Cynwyd: $126; Pittsburgh: $125
Texas:	Dallas: $135; Ft. Worth: $132; San Antonio: $133
Washington:	Seattle: $155

Your employer might provide you with a per diem rate only for the cost of your meals and incidental expenses. This is discussed later in this chapter.

Suppose your employer reimburses you at a rate within the above guidelines and that you provide him with substantiation as to time, place, and business purpose. In this case, there is nothing more for you to do. Your employer should not include such reimbursements in taxable income on your year-end Form W-2 and you do not claim any deduction on your tax return. If your expenses were less than the reimbursement, you wind up with a "profit" of the difference, which is not subject to tax.

If you receive a per diem rate that is higher than the amount specified by the IRS, your employer will include the excess in taxable income on your year-end Form W-2. Note that this applies only to *per diems*. If your employer reimburses you for your *actual* expenses, there is no taxable income as long as you provide adequate substantiation to your employer.

If your out-of-pocket expenses exceed the reimbursement, you can claim the difference as a miscellaneous deduction. This is done by listing your total expenses on Form 2106 and then subtracting the amount of the reimbursement as directed on that Form. For a more thorough discussion on handling reimbursed expenses, see Section 1 of the *Miscellaneous* chapter. Also included there is an explanation of the proper use of Form 2106.

There is also a standard reimbursement rate for automobile travel. The IRS will accept a standard reimbursement rate of up to $34\frac{1}{2}$ cents per mile for business-related travel. Provided you have made adequate substantiation to your employer, he should not include the reimbursement in taxable income reported on your year-end Form W-2 and you claim no deduction. Section 1 of the *Miscellaneous* chapter contains a more thorough discussion on how to handle reimbursed expenses in more complicated situations.

Under a 1990 IRS ruling, an employer can sometimes reimburse an employee at a higher tax-free rate than the standard mileage allowance ($34\frac{1}{2}$ cents per mile in 2001). This is done by making estimates of depreciation and operating costs actually incurred. However, the reimbursement must cover at least 5,000 business miles driven by the given employee and satisfy some other requirements. [Rev. Proc. 90-34]

Excess Reimbursement

You might receive a reimbursement which exceeds either the per diem standard rates or the actual amounts you spent, whichever basic reimbursement method your employer uses. For example, your employer may have given you an advance, anticipating more extensive travel than you actually undertook. In such a case, your employer may require you to return the excess reimbursement. If not, the excess is considered to be taxable income to you and will be included as such on your year-end Form W-2.

Also, your employer is required by the IRS to withhold income tax and social security tax on this excess. These taxes must be taken out of a future paycheck of yours within a reasonable period of time. Only the excess reimbursement not given back to your employer is treated as taxable income. The portion of the reimbursement that is justified by your travel remains free of tax, assuming you make proper substantiation to your employer. [Rev. Proc. 2000-39]

Example 4

You took a 4-day business trip to Chicago during February 2001. Instead of keeping track of your meals, lodging, and incidental expenses, you rely upon a $194 per diem reimbursement from your employer.

The $194 per diem exceeds the IRS-approved per diem of $176 by $18, or $72 for the 4-day period. You do not have to return this excess $72 to your employer. Rather, your employer will include this $72 in taxable income by including it in the amount reported as "wages" on your year-end W-2 Form. As such, it will be subjected to income tax and social security withholding. The remaining amount, $176 × 4 = $704, will be included in the non-taxable "Employee Information" box on your Form W-2.

What If You Didn't Apply for Reimbursement?

One of the basic rules of tax policy is that an employee cannot deduct job-related expenses he paid if he could have received a reimbursement from his employer for these expenses. It makes no difference if the employee failed to put in a claim for these expenses. As long as he was entitled to a reimbursement, he cannot claim a deduction on his personal tax return.

With regard to this issue, the IRS pays particular attention to job-related travel expenses. Such expenses are often reimbursed by employers. If there is any reason to believe that an individual could have received a reimbursement, he might be required to provide evidence that he was ineligible to be reimbursed for travel expenses. Otherwise, his deduction might be disallowed.

For this reason, it sometimes pays to file a request with your employer for reimbursement, even if you're convinced the request will be denied. This is particularly true if you have received reimbursement in the past for similar expenses. The difficulty of deducting expenses when there is an indication of possible reimbursement is illustrated by several court cases.

In one case, an ROTC teacher at a midwestern college made various trips connected with his employment, many of them to attend enclaves and other activities as faculty advisor to a campus student group. When he claimed a deduction for travel expenses not covered by a reimbursement, the IRS objected. He had made similar trips the prior year for which he received a reimbursement from the college. But for the year in question, he offered no explanation as to why he received no reimbursement. Whether or not he actually received a reimbursement was not the issue. The Court disallowed the deduction because no evidence was presented that the expenses would not have been reimbursed by the college if asked. [Register, TC Memo 1988-390]

In a second case, an employee was entitled to reimbursement for job-related out-of-town travel but not for local travel. When he claimed a travel deduction on his tax return, the IRS objected. The employee's record book was not sufficiently detailed to determine which trips were out-of-town and which were local. Consequently, there was no way to tell to what extent the cost of these trips was eligible for reimbursement. For this reason, the Court ruled out any deduction whatever. [Primas, TC Memo 1988-352]

And in a third case, an engineer set up his own corporation which contracted with the U.S. Department of Energy to perform physical audits on energy conversion facilities. In performing these audits, he incurred $12,167 in travel expenses. Because the Department of Energy did not make advance payments, the engineer paid these expenses out of his own pocket. His corporation could not pay these expenses because it did not have any funds during the year. The Court ruled that the engineer was not entitled to a deduction. The travel expenses were an obligation of the corporation, not the engineer personally. In the Court's words, . . . *"it is clear that petitioner would have been reimbursed had there been available corporation funds. The fact that he was not reimbursed does not change the nature of the expenditures made on behalf of the corporation into ordinary and necessary expenses of petitioner."* [Thomas, TC Memo 1988-505]

What If You Are Missing Records or Receipts?

You are supposed to keep a contemporaneous diary and receipts, as described at the beginning of this section. However, legally speaking, this is not a strict necessity. You are entitled to offer other evidence in support of your deduction, as long as the 5 basic pieces of information (date, item, place, amount, and business purpose) are attested to. For example, the Congressional tax-writing committee specifically noted that *"testimony from a disinterested, unrelated party describing the taxpayer's activities, may be of sufficient probative value that it should not be automatically excluded from consideration."* It also noted that records created at a later date might have some value, but would have far less *"probative value"* than *"written evidence arising at or near the time of the expenditure."*

As a matter of fact, the courts have not been impressed with travel records in which entries were not made in a timely fashion. Four cases illustrate this situation. In the first case, a salesman presented a spiral notebook in which, he claimed, he had made entries on a day-to-day basis concerning his travel expenses. However, the Court took a look at the notebook and promptly threw the case out. The pages were too clean and there was too little wear at the wire ring bindings for a notebook handled frequently. And the ink was suspiciously uniform in color and intensity. [Wilson, TC Memo 1979-2]

The second case centered upon the adequacy of a travel diary. In this case, the Court was convinced that the diary was *"an accurate, contemporaneous record of the date and amounts of expenditures."* But, the Court stated, *"we believe that, in certain instances, the place and business purpose of petitioner's travel were recorded in later years. In such instances, petitioner's diary does not satisfy the adequate records requirement with respect to those elements."* Because of this inadequacy, about 60% of the claimed travel deduction was disallowed. [Benke, TC Memo 1979-195]

The third case illustrates the pitfall of recording suspiciously uniform numbers in the diary. An individual who traveled quite a bit on business presented a diary of his expenses, as required. But for each day he was away during the year, his diary listed meal expenses of exactly $20. The Court found *"it hard to believe that petitioner's expenses remained so perfectly consistent throughout that year."* The Court concluded that the diary simply represented an after-the-fact estimate of expenses rather than a contemporaneous diary of actual expenses incurred. Because of this, it disallowed his meal expenses altogether. [Bowman, TC Memo 1979-432]

And the fourth case makes it clear that your diary should be handwritten, not typed. The only record which was presented to the Court was a neatly-typed statement listing mileage, motel costs, and meal costs. This indicated the entries were not made in a timely fashion and no deduction was allowed. [Johnston, TC Memo, 1980-477, affd]

When some receipts are missing, the matter is not as serious. In the past, IRS agents have been known to disallow a deduction whenever a required receipt was missing. But in recent instructions to its agents, the IRS suggested going a bit easier on this requirement. According to these instructions,

> *"If a taxpayer cannot precisely document the amounts spent for expenses while away from home for a business purpose, examiners may establish that reasonable amounts were spent for such items if taxpayers can clearly establish the following:*
>
> *(a.) Time: Dates of departure and return for each trip away from home, and number of days away from home;*
>
> *(b.) Place: Destinations or locality of travel, for example, name of city or town.;*
>
> *(c.) Business Purpose: Business reason for travel or nature of business benefit derived or expected to be derived; and*
>
> *(d.) Proof that Expenditures were Incurred: A reasonable showing based upon secondary evidence, including oral testimony, that out-of-pocket expenses were paid."* [Internal Revenue Manual, Section 4.2.7.4.2, "Reasonable Determinations"]

However, despite the liberal wording of item (d.), this should not be taken as a go-ahead to ignore the receipt-keeping requirement. IRS agents are only permitted, not required, to allow deductions without the required receipts. And this is only suggested when not too much is missing. If there is substantial disregard of the receipt-keeping rule, the IRS will probably disallow any deductions and perhaps even assess a negligence penalty in flagrant cases.

Standard Per Diem Meal Allowance

There is a standard per diem meal allowance you can use while traveling away from home. You have the option of using this per diem rate or keeping track of your actual expenses. This per diem rate only applies to the cost of meals, not to other travel expenses such as lodging, transportation, etc.

The standard per diem meal allowance for 2001 is $30. However, for many *higher cost* areas, a different per diem applies. Depending upon the area, the per diem for these areas is either $34, $38, $42, or $46.

The applicable per diem allowances are the ones you use to compute your total meals-while-away-from-home expenses. After this total is listed on Form 2106 or Form 2106-EZ, it is subjected to the 50%-reduction factor discussed earlier in this Section.

Self-employed persons can also use the applicable meal per diem. However, the 50%-factor still applies. For example, in a low-cost area where the $30 allowance applies, this would amount to a per diem of 50% × $30 = $15. Self-employed persons do not use Form 2106, but rather report their travel expenses on Schedule C or Schedule C-EZ.

A complete listing of standard per diem meal allowance rates for travel within the 48 contiguous states and the District of Columbia can be found in IRS Publication 1542, *Per Diem Rates (for Travel Within the Continental United States)*. As stated previously, this publication is available on the internet at www.irs.gov/forms–pubs/pubs.html. The table below gives a list of major high cost areas.

Meal Per Diems in Higher Cost Areas

Arizona:	Grand Canyon: $42; Phoenix/Scottsdale: $42
California:	Contra Costa County: $42; Death Valley: $46; Los Angeles $46, Mammoth Lakes: $46; Marin County: $42; Monterey: $42; Napa: $42; Palm Springs: $42; Sacramento: $42; San Diego: $46; San Francisco: $46; San Mateo/Redwood City: $42; Santa Cruz: $42; Santa Rosa: $42; Solano County: $42; South Lake Tahoe: $42; Sunnyvale/Palo Alto/San Jose: $46; Tahoe City; $42; Truckee: $42; Yosemite National Park: $46
Colorado:	Aspen: $46: Boulder: $42; Crested Butte: $42; Denver: $42; Telluride: $42; Vail $46
Connecticut:	Hartford: $42
D.C.:	Washington: $46
Delaware:	Lewes: $42
Florida:	Ft. Lauderdale: $42; Fort Myers: $42; Fort Pierce: $46; Key West: $46; Miami: $42; Orlando: $42; Palm Beach: $46

Idaho:	Ketchum: $42; Sun Valley: $42
Illinois:	Chicago: $46
Indiana:	Indianapolis: $42
Louisiana:	New Orleans/St. Bernard: $42
Maine:	Rockport: $42
Maryland:	Annapolis: $42; Baltimore: $42; Columbia: $42; Ocean City: $46; St. Michaels: $42
Massachusetts:	Boston: $46; Cambridge: $46; Martha's Vineyard: $46; Nantucket: $46
Michigan:	Detroit: $46; Mackinac Island: $46; Traverse City: $42
Minnesota:	Duluth: $42; Minneapolis/St Paul: $46
Missouri:	Kansas City/Clay County: $42; St. Louis: $46
Montana:	Big Sky: $46
Nevada:	Stateline: $42
New Hampshire:	Hanover/Sullivan County: $42; Newington: $42; Portsmouth: $42
New Jersey:	Atlantic City: $42; Cape May: $42; Cherry Hill/Camden/ Moorestown: $42; Newark: $42; Princeton/Trenton: $42
New Mexico:	Santa Fe: $46
New York:	Albany: $42; The Bronx/Brooklyn/Queens: $46; Buffalo: $42; Manhattan: $46; Nassau County/Great Neck: $42; Rochester: $42; Staten Island: $42; Tarrytown: $42; White Plains: $42
North Carolina:	Research Triangle Park/Durham: $42
Ohio:	Cincinnati: $46; Cleveland: $42
Oregon:	Ashland: $42
Pennsylvania:	Harrisburg: $34; Hershey: $42; King of Prussia/Fort Washington/Bala Cynwyd: $42; Philadelphia: $46; Pittsburgh: $46; Warminster: $42; Wayne: $42
Rhode Island:	Newport: $42; Providence: $42
South Carolina:	Charleston-Berkeley: $42;, Hilton Head: $42; Myrtle Beach: $42
Tennessee:	Nashville: $42
Texas:	Dallas: $46; Galveston: $42; Houston: $42; San Antonio: $42
Utah:	Park City: $46; Salt Lake City: $42
Vermont:	Manchester: $46
Virginia:	Charlottesville: $42; Wintergreen: $46
Washington:	Friday Harbor: $42; Seattle: $46
Wisconsin:	Milwaukee: $42
Wyoming:	Jackson: $42

(For some reason, there is no comparable per diem rate individuals can use for lodging or other expenses. You use actual cost. The combined per diem rates discussed earlier in this Section only apply to an employer who has a reimbursement plan for his employees. These amounts cannot be automatically claimed on the tax return of a self-employed person.)

For a given year, you must either use the standard meal allowance for all travel during the year or else deduct your actual meal expenses throughout the year.

If you receive a specific per diem meal reimbursement from your employer which falls short of the IRS allowance, you can deduct the difference between the IRS allowance and your employer's allowance. This only applies if the employer allowance is a straight per diem rate not based on an accounting of your actual expenses.

If you use the per diem rate, you still must substantiate the other basic elements for deductible travel — namely time, place, and business purpose. However, if you neglected to keep a diary, the per diem amounts might be useful.

> ### Example 5
> *You attended a 3-day professional convention in Chicago, Illinois, at which you presented a paper. You did not create any diary of your expenses. However, you have receipts for your airplane ticket and your hotel bill. Technically, you have not met the precise recordkeeping requirements for deducting your travel expenses because you have no diary of your expenses. However, you have enough secondary evidence (see the preceding subsection) to establish the time, place, and business purpose of your travel. Because you have no record of your meal expenses, you could use the standard allowance of $46 per day for meals if you wish.*

The standard meal allowances are subjected to the same 50%-Rule, described earlier in this Section, that applies to meal expenses in general. For example, suppose an individual travels away from home for 10 days, with the standard meal allowance yielding: 10 × $42 = $420. Under the 50%-Rule, the amount actually claimed as a miscellaneous deduction for these meals would be 50% × $420 = $210.

Meal Allowance for Partial Days

The per diem meal allowances apply to full 24-hour days that are spent away from home overnight. On the day that travel begins or ends, when less than 24 hours is spent away, you have to prorate the appropriate meal allowance. Under a liberal IRS ruling, there are now 2 basic proration methods that you can use.

According to the first method, the meal allowance may be prorated using the method prescribed by the Federal Travel Regulations. Currently, this method allows 75% of the meal allowance for each partial day that an employee or self-employed person is traveling on business.

Under a second method, the meal allowance may be prorated using any method that is consistently applied and in accordance with reasonable business practice. For example, if an employee travels away from home 9 a.m. one day to 5 p.m. the next day, a method of proration that results in an amount equal to no more than 2 times the federal M&IE rate will be treated as being in accordance with reasonable business practice (even though only 1+ times the federal M&IE rate would be allowed under Federal Travel Regulations). [Rev. Proc. 2000-39]

Foreign Travel

The usual per diem rates do not apply to Alaska, Hawaii, or any locations outside the U.S. The standard allowance for these areas is the federal per diem rate paid government employees when traveling. In many foreign places, this can produce a very high figure. Following are examples of the meal allowance rates in some notable cities: Melbourne $75, Brussels $79, Montreal $64, Paris $80, Berlin $88, Rome $106, Osaka $111, Tokyo $108, Madrid $69, Stockholm $98, London $90. These rates can vary from month to month, so you should either call the IRS or go to the following web site, www.state.gov/m/a/als/prdm/ to get the federal per diem amount for a particular foreign location to which you are traveling.

Miscellaneous Travel

The following sections describe special rules that apply to various types of job-related travel. However, don't overlook miscellaneous travel not covered by any of these specific situations. As long as the travel is a non-reimbursable "ordinary and necessary" expense connected with your job, it is deductible [see Chapter 1, Section 2].

This is emphasized by several court cases. The first concerned a teacher of the handicapped who deducted transportation costs for taking his students on trips to various activities in the community. He was not required to take the students on these trips, but that did not matter. According to the Court,

> *"Although there is no proof that Mr. Gudmundsson was obligated by his employer to take the students on these trips, we know of no requirement that there must be an underlying legal obligation to make an expenditure before it can qualify as an 'ordinary and necessary' business expense. . . The arrangement of such activities for his students is in accord with what a teacher of the handicapped might do and the expenses incurred therein are clearly business expenses [and therefore deductible]."* [Gudmundsson, TC Memo 1978-299]

The second case concerned an assistant principal at a high school who was responsible for student discipline and attendance, computer scheduling and grading, student transportation, and other duties. He was expected, although not required, to attend job-related meetings and seminars and to serve on school and civic committees.

During the year, he attended many meetings at different locations at which he discussed the problems which his school and other schools in the county were experiencing. The IRS and the Court both agreed that he was entitled to deduct his transportation costs in attending these meetings. The Court allowed him a $600 deduction, indicating it would have been higher had his recordkeeping been better. [Wilhelm, TC Memo 1978-327]

And a third case involved a Professor of Management and Marketing at a university in the South. During the course of a year, he made about 100 trips by automobile in connection with his professional duties. These included 31 trips to a library 100 miles away which had extensive materials not available in his home town, 44 trips in connection with seminars he ran at a local hotel, 13 trips to the airport to pick up visiting speakers, 2 trips to attend a Board of Regents meeting, and 8 trips to conduct surveys on grocery prices. The Court ruled that all of these trips could be deducted. His total deduction for auto travel during the year amounted to $1,939. [Stearns, TC Memo 1984-97]

Travel to Libraries

Traveling to a library for employment-related purposes is a common occurrence. If the library is located within your general home area, the rules discussed in Sections 2 and 3 apply. That is, you will be entitled to a deduction if you visit more than one business location during the day, or if the library is an irregular or short-term destination as discussed in Section 3.

On the other hand, if the library (or other business destination) is located outside your general home area, the rules allow you to deduct your transportation costs even if it is the only business activity that day. Such travel falls under the *temporary job away from home* category discussed in Section 4.

However, a recent court case shows that to be deductible, you must be able to point to a business reason for traveling to the out-of-town library. A community college English teacher took courses at a college 160 miles from home. The IRS did not challenge the deduction for traveling to and from the college for days on which he attended class. This was a legitimate educational expense [see Chapter 13, *Expenses of Attending School*].

However, he also traveled to the distant college on days he had no class in order to do research in the library. The Court did not allow a deduction for this travel. The only reason the teacher gave for using this particular library was that he was familiar with the layout and it was near his parents' home. According to the Court, there *"were other libraries closer to petitioner's home, that were more extensive in their collection of books and periodicals pertaining to subject matter useful for petitioner's job."* Thus, travel to the library was for *"personal convenience"* rather than for a valid business purpose. [Ginkel, TC Memo 1980-424]

This case offers an important tip to those who travel to a library distant from home. They should have a solid reason why the library was chosen over one closer to home, especially if the closer one has a more extensive collection. For example, the smaller library might have certain materials not found in the larger one. Or, materials in the larger library's collection might typically be off the shelf due to heavy use by faculty and students.

Section 2:
More Than One Job Location

If you work in more than one location during a given day, you can deduct the cost of transportation from one location to another. This applies whether or not you are working for the same employer at both locations or for different employers. You cannot deduct the cost of traveling from your home to the day's first place of employment (unless it is a temporary work location), nor from the final place of employment back home.

Example 1

Atkins is employed at the State University where he is a Professor of Poultry Science. On Monday and Wednesday nights, he goes from the University to the local office of the CROA (Chicken Raisers of America) where he is employed to teach a course in Chicken Management to interested farmers. Along the way, he stops off at a restaurant for dinner. He may deduct the cost of his transportation from the University to the CROA. However, he cannot deduct the cost of dinner because he is not away from home overnight.

Example 2

Baker is a Professor of Computer Science and teaches primarily at the main campus of a State University. However, on Tuesday and Thursday, she teaches in the morning at the main campus and in the afternoon she teaches at a second campus in a different location. She may deduct the cost of transportation from one location to the other. If she stops off at an intermediate point, she deducts what the transportation cost would have been had she traveled directly.

Example 3

Mrs. Chu teaches Chemistry five days a week. On Saturdays she works at a chemical firm. She cannot deduct any transportation costs because she did not visit two different locations during the same day.

Example 4

Friend was a part-time lecturer at various colleges in the Louisville area. He regularly drove between his jobs at the main campus of a local university, a branch location of a different university, and a community college.

Friend was allowed to deduct the $301 he had claimed as a deduction for traveling between these business locations on the same day. It did not matter that he didn't keep a contemporaneous diary. He established the deduction by convincing the judge that the traveling took place. Because his trips were made on a regular weekly basis, it was possible to determine the deduction to which he was entitled without reference to a diary.

Example 5

Beards was an associate professor at a Community College in a large northeastern city. The College had 5 buildings located in various parts of the city and she found it necessary to travel from one building to another, usually by taxi, during the course of a day.

Beards was permitted to deduct the cost of traveling from one College building to another the same day. This constituted deductible travel between job locations on the same day. [Beards, TC Memo 1984-438]

The above case concerned traveling from one college building to another the same day. Although these buildings were not located on the same "campus," the following case would indicate that travel in such a situation would still be deductible. This case involved travel between different locations on the same Air Force base. However, this is the same type of situation as occurs when a college teacher uses his auto to get from one building to another located on the same campus.

Example 6

Brandt was a flight engineer assigned to work at an Air Force base for a period of 44 days. He needed to transport himself from one part of the base to another in connection with the duties he was expected to perform. However, after 2 days, he found the motor pool transportation to be unreliable and rented an automobile for the remainder of his stay.

Brandt was permitted to deduct the cost of his rental automobile. He used the auto to travel from one business location to another. Even though the locations were on the same Air Force base, this made no difference. Because the existing motor pool transportation was inadequate and the Air Force would not reimburse him for his transportation, the Court allowed the deduction. [Brandt, TC Memo 1982-180]

Example 7

Smith drives to his office on the campus of a large University. Later in the morning, he drives several miles to and from a library on the other side of town. In the afternoon, he drives to the airport and back to pick up a visiting faculty member at the airport. None of his travel expenses is reimbursable by the school. The cost of these side trips is a deductible business expense.

Example 8

Davis was employed as a minister for a newly-founded church in a northeastern state. The congregation rented a parsonage adjacent to the church building, in which Davis resided. Because the church could not provide Davis with sufficient compensation, he obtained a job teaching at a Bible College in another town. He claimed a deduction for the cost of commuting between his two jobs, one at the church where he lived and the other at the college where he taught.

> *The Court denied his deduction. His principal place of business was the college where he earned the vast majority of his livelihood. When an individual's residence is located at a minor place of business (in this case, the church), the transportation between his residence and his principal place of employment is considered a non-deductible commuting expense.* [Davis, TC Memo 1984-302]

Travel between one's home and principal place of business is not deductible. However, as the next example shows, if one's home is the *principal place of business,* then travel to a secondary business location is deductible.

Example 9
Curphey owned and managed a number of residential rental properties as a side business. His management activities were conducted out of a home office from which he periodically traveled to the various rental properties. Because his home office was the principal place of business for his rental activities, this was considered to be deductible business travel rather than personal commuting. [Curphey, 73 TC 766]

The rules for qualification of the home office as the "principal place of business" have changed significantly. Thus, one's principal place of business now includes a place of business that is used by the taxpayer for the administrative or management activities of any trade or business of the taxpayer if there is no other fixed location of such trade or business where the taxpayer conducts substantial administrative or management activities of the trade or business. [I.R.C.§ 280A(c)(1)] See Chapter 3, *Home Office,* for more information.

According to this additional definition of "principal place of buinsess," a professor who has an office at a university and an office at home would not be able to call his home office his "principal place of business," because he would be able to perform managerial tasks in his office at the university. However, if the same professor established a home office from which he had a separate trade or business, such as writing books, he could deduct expenses for travel related to that business. Note, though, that the same professor, even having established a separate trade or business for his home office, still could not deduct travel expenses incurred between his home and the university, because this is considered a commuting expense.

If you work at two places in one day away from home, whether or not for the same employer, you can deduct the expense of getting from one work place to the other. However, if for some personal reason you do not go directly from one location to the other, you cannot deduct more than the amount it would have cost you to go directly from the first location to the second. Transportation expenses you have in going between home and a part-time job on a day off from your main job are nondeductible commuting expenses. [IRS Publication 463, p. 14]

Example 10
Parker makes several trips during the day between his home and his office at school. His expenses are not deductible — he is commuting each time.

Example 11

Jones works regularly at two different locations in the same city. He drives from home to one of the locations and then back home again. Later, he drives to and from the second location. None of his expenses is deductible. This was spelled out in a court case involving a doctor who drove to and from his office and later drove to and from his hospital. Both of his trips were ruled to be nondeductible commuting. [Shea, TC Memo 1979-303]

Example 12

Chandler was the principal of a high school in the Massachusetts town where he lived. Two nights a week, after returning home for dinner, he drove 37 miles to Boston where he taught a college accounting course. Because Boston was outside the general location of his home, he could deduct the entire cost of driving from his home to Boston and back. [Chandler, 226 F 2nd 467]

Example 13

A professor taught in a large Texas city during the week. On weekends, he often traveled 150 miles to an out-of-town location in order to oversee a launderette business which he owned. He was permitted to deduct travel expenses connected with his secondary business out-of-town. Because he was away from home overnight, this included meals and lodging in addition to transportation expenses.

SECTION 3:
COMMUTING TO A TEMPORARY JOB NEAR HOME

Before 1990, the cost of commuting to a temporary job could be deducted only if the temporary job was located outside the general area of your regular job. Now, however, this deduction is available even if the temporary job is in the same general area. Even so, the restrictions are stricter than for commuting to a temporary job away from home [see Section 4].

According to a recent IRS ruling, daily transportation expenses incurred in going between a taxpayer's residence and a work location are deductible under the following circumstances:

(1) A taxpayer may deduct daily transportation expenses in going between the taxpayer's residence and a temporary work location outside the metropolitan area where the taxpayer lives and normally works. However, unless paragraph (2) or (3) below applies, daily transportation expenses incurred in going between the taxpayer's residence and a temporary work location within that metropolitan area are nondeductible commuting expenses.

(2) If a taxpayer has one or more regular work locations away from the taxpayer's residence, the taxpayer may deduct daily transportation expenses incurred in going between the taxpayer's residence and a temporary work location in the same trade or business, regardless of the distance.

(3) If a taxpayer's residence is the taxpayer's principal place of business within the meaning of section 280A(c)(1)(A), the taxpayer may deduct daily transportation expenses incurred in going between the residence and another work location in the same trade or business, regardless of whether the other work location is regular or temporary and regardless of the distance.

For purposes of paragraphs (1), (2), and (3), the following rules apply in determining whether a work location is temporary. If employment at a work location is realistically expected to last (and does in fact last) for 1 year or less, the employment is temporary in the absence of facts and circumstances indicating otherwise. If employment at a work location is realistically expected to last for more than 1 year or less, the employment is not temporary, regardless of whether it actually exceeds 1 year. If employment at a work location initially is realistically expected to last for 1 year or there is no realistic expectation that the employment will last for 1 year or less, but at some later date the employment is realistically expected to exceed 1 year, that employment will be treated as temporary (in the absence of facts and circumstances indicating otherwise) until the date that the taxpayer's realistic expectation changes, and will be treated as not temporary after that date. [Rev Rule 99-7]

If the above conditions are satisfied, you can deduct the cost of commuting to the temporary job. If you drive to the job, you can use the standard allowance (34½ cents per mile in 2001) if you wish [see the *Automobile Expenses* chapter].

Example 1

Richards is a professor at a state university. During the summer, he teaches a 4-week course at a satellite location in the same city as the main campus.

Rule: Richards may deduct the cost of commuting to the satellite location. Both the requirements that he have a regular job location (the main campus) and that the job to which he is commuting be temporary are satisfied.

Example 2

Jackson is a teacher at a community college. During one semester, instead of teaching at the community college, he teaches at a different institution located in the same general area.

Rule: Jackson can deduct the commuting costs, as long as the teaching assignment at the second institution is temporary in the sense that Jackson intends to return to the original community college at the end of the semester. Thus, if Jackson has actually changed jobs, the second teaching assignment would not be temporary, and no deductions would be allowed.

Example 3

Trafton is a Professor of Urban Studies in a large city. On days when he does not teach, he travels from his home to various city offices and building sites as part of research he is doing. He also travels occasionally to several libraries in different locations in the city.

Rule: Because he has a regular job location, his commuting costs to these temporary worksites are deductible.

Example 4

Whitworth is a research associate in astronomy at a large university. He spends most of his time in his office, but sometimes travels to an off-campus observatory where the telescope is located. Trips to the observatory are not made weekly, nor do they follow any particular pattern.

Rule: Whitworth can deduct the cost of traveling between his office and the observatory, as expenses incurred when commuting between two job locations are deductible. However, when Whitworth travels from his home to the observatory, the commuting costs are deductible only if the observatory is considered to be a temporary work location.

Example 5

Marley is a chemistry instructor at a community college. As a sideline, he operates as on on-site computer repairer. He does not have any steady customers, but gets his clients mostly from ads placed in the newspaper.

Rule: If Marley uses a home office that qualifies as the principal place of business for his computer repair business [see the Home Office Chapter], *he can deduct the cost of traveling between his home and the locations where he repairs computers.*

In any event, the cost of traveling from one job or business location to another (away from your home) is deductible, whether or not in the same trade or business. This is discussed in Section 2.

SECTION 4:
TEMPORARY JOB AWAY FROM HOME

If you have a temporary job *away from home*, you qualify to deduct your travel expenses. Your temporary job can last up to one year. Thus, if you live away from home, you deduct not just transportation, but also meals, lodging, and laundry.

The rules in this section apply if both of the following conditions are satisfied. First, your temporary job must be **located away from home.** Second, the temporary job must qualify as being **temporary** in the eyes of the law.

Job Located Away From Home

You must show that you have some fixed home base in a different location than your temporary job. To take a common example, suppose you have a regular job at which you worked prior to the temporary job and to which you return after the temporary job. Suppose further that you rent your house out during the period you are away. These two conditions are generally sufficient to establish a fixed home base.

When Is a Job Temporary?

According to the law, there is a one-year cutoff on when a job can be considered temporary. Jobs extending 1 year or less can generally be considered temporary, while jobs extending over one year are *indefinite* rather than *temporary*.

However, an IRS ruling [Rev. Rul. 93-86] has clarified that it is the *initial expectation* that counts more than the actual period the job lasts. Specifically, the ruling states:

(1) If employment away from home in a single location is realistically expected to last (and does in fact last) for 1 year or less, the employment will be treated as temporary in absence of facts and circumstances indicating otherwise.

(2) If employment away from home in a single location is realistically expected to last for more than 1 year or there is no realistic expectation that the employment will last for less than a year, the employment will be treated as indefinite, regardless of whether it actually exceeds 1 year.

(3) If employment away from home in a single location initially is realistically expected to last for less than a year, but at some later date the employment is realistically expected to exceed 1 year, that employment will be treated as temporary (in the absence of facts and circumstances indicating otherwise) until the date that the taxpayer's realistic expectation changes.

The Ruling then illustrates the above text with 3 situations:

Situation 1: Taxpayer A is regularly employed in City 1. He accepted work in City 2, which is 250 miles from City 1. He realistically expected the work in City 2 to be completed in 6 months and planned to return to City 1 at that time. In fact, the employment lasted 10 months, after which time he returned to City 1.

Taxpayer A realistically expected that the work in City 2 would last only 6 months, and it did in fact last less than 1 year. Because he had always intended to return to City 1 at the end of his employment in City 2, the City 2 employment is temporary. Thus, A's travel expenses in City 2 are deductible.

Situation 2. The facts are the same as in Situation 1, except that Taxpayer B realistically expected the work in City 2 to be completed in 18 months, but in fact it was completed in 10 months.

Taxpayer B's employment in City 2 is indefinite because he realistically expected that the work in City 2 would last longer than 1 year, even though it actually lasted less than 1 year. Thus, B's travel expenses in City 2 are nondeductible.

Situation 3. The facts are the same as in Situation 1, except that Taxpayer C realistically expected the work in City 2 to be completed in 9 months. After 8 months, however, C was asked to remain for 7 more months (for a total actual stay of 15 months).

For the first 8 months, Taxpayer C realistically expected that the work in City 2 would last only 9 months. However, after 8 months it was no longer realistic to expect that the work would last less that 1 year. Therefore, C's employment in City 2 is temporary for the first 8 months and indefinite for the remaining 7 months. Thus, C's travel expenses in City 2 during the first 8 months are deductible, but his travel expenses thereafter are nondeductible.

Which Expenses Can You Deduct?

If your temporary job is located away from home and you do not return home overnight, you may deduct the cost of meals, lodging, cleaning and laundry, and commuting between where you obtain your meals and lodging and your temporary job. Your meal expenses are subject to the 50%-Rule discussed in Section 1. That is, you can deduct only 50% of your unreimbursed meal expenses.

You should pay special attention to the per diem meal rates allowed by the IRS. For example, at $42 per day, an individual at a temporary position away from home for a full year would be able to claim $42 × 365 = $15,330 in meal expenses for the year. Applying the 50%–reduction factor, his deduction for meals alone would be 50% × $15,330 = $7,665. And to top it off, he wouldn't even have to keep any records of his food costs. (As discussed in Section 1, the per diem meal allowances are much greater in many foreign locations.)

In addition to expenses at the location of your temporary job, you can also deduct the initial and final transportation costs of traveling between your permanent home and your temporary residence, as well as the daily commuting between your permanent home and your temporary job, as discussed in Sections 3 and 4.

Temporary Academic Position

Faculty members at academic institutions commonly accept visiting positions at other institutions for a temporary period of time. The following 1979 IRS ruling issued to a college teacher spells out exactly what can be deducted.

IRS Private Letter Ruling #7917044

"You are regularly employed as a professor in the Department of Aeronautics and Astronautics at X University. Y offered you a temporary appointment as a professor in its Aerospace Engineering Department. The appointment which you accepted is of fixed duration commencing October 15, 1978, and ending September 1, 1979. When this temporary appointment terminates, you intend to return to your tenured professorial position at X University.

"In order to discharge your appointment, you will have to travel across country and set up a temporary residence in the vicinity of Y. During the term of the appointment your permanent residence is being rented to unrelated parties.

"In light of these facts you request a ruling finding the following expenses deductible to the extent not reimbursed by your temporary employer:

1. Travel expenses to and from the temporary work site;

2. Local transportation costs at the temporary work site;

3. Lodging at the temporary work site;

4. Meals at the temporary work site [now subject to the 50%-Rule described in Section 1–ed.];

5. Incidental expenses at the temporary work site;

6. Travel expenses to and from the temporary work site twice during the appointment (i.e. Christmas and Easter);

7. Costs for transportation of personal and professional articles with which to set up housekeeping at the temporary work site.

"Although your wife will be accompanying you, no deductions will be claimed for any of the above travel expenses which would be applicable to her.

". . .if your records will establish the recordkeeping and substantiation elements required by [the law], you may claim a deduction for reasonable amounts expended for meals [now subject to the 50%-Rule-ed.] *and lodging plus other incidental expenses such as laundry you incur as a result of your temporary employment. In addition, your expenses for transportation are deductible to the extent they are reasonable in amount and were incurred in the pursuit of your temporary assignment in going between your place of lodging and place of temporary employment.*

"In view of these holdings and. . .the regulations you will not be entitled to a deduction for moving expenses. [See the end of the *Moving Expenses* chapter which explains that moving expenses cannot be claimed in connection with a temporary job.—ed.]

"The cost of any trips back and forth to the city of your residence are personal expenses and nondeductible under section 262 of the Code. Such travel expenses bear no relation to the execution of your duties at Y, nor in any way benefit your temporary employer. . . . [According to the current rules, you can deduct the initial cost of traveling to the location of the temporary job and the final trip back to the permanent home. Additionally, on your days off, you can deduct your travel expenses, including meals and lodging, while traveling from the area of your temporary place of work to your hometown and back to work. You can claim these expenses up to the amount it would have cost you for meals and lodging had you stayed at your temporary place of work. (IRS Publication 463, p. 14) —ed.] *Similarly, since you will be only temporarily away from your tax home, such expenses as you incur for transportation of personal and professional articles with which to set up housekeeping at Y, are nondeductible personal or living expenses."*

Example 1

Professor Jones teaches History at a well-known university in Princeton, New Jersey. He takes a leave of absence in order to accept a position as visiting professor at a minor university in New Haven, Connecticut. In September, he drives with his family from Princeton to New Haven to assume his duties there. He returns to Princeton in June. He rents his house in Princeton to a faculty member who was visiting there for the school year. While in New Haven, he and his family live in a rented house five miles from the university he is visiting. He commutes daily by automobile.

Rule: Professor Jones has taken a temporary position away from home. He can deduct the cost of his transportation between Princeton and New Haven and the cost of his daily commuting between the rented house and his office in New Haven. While in New Haven, he may also deduct his lodging, laundry, and 50% of the cost of his meals. The expenses of his wife and children are non-deductible.

Example 2

Mr. Black teaches at a special education elementary school in New York City and lives in a nearby suburb. He takes a 10-month leave of absence in order to accept an offer of organizing and setting up a new special education school in New Haven, Connecticut, during one school year. He commutes daily from his home in the New York suburbs to his office in New Haven.

Rule: Mr. Black has a temporary position in a different general location than that of his tax home. He deducts his daily commuting costs to and from New Haven. He cannot deduct the cost of meals or other living expenses because he is not away from home overnight.

Example 3. Several Temporary Positions

Professor Brown teaches Physics at a university in Pennsylvania. He accepts a position as a Visiting Professor of Physics at a west coast university in the San Francisco area. He teaches for the academic year plus summer school, his appointment lasting from October 1 through August 30 of the following year. He vacations in Canada during the month of September, after which he travels to a New Mexico university where he has a visiting position in connection with a government funded special semester in his field of expertise. He returns back to his original university to resume his duties for the spring semester.

Professor Brown claims that his tax home is Pennsylvania and that both of his visiting positions qualify as temporary positions. He claims that he is entitled to his transportation costs from Pennsylvania to San Francisco, from New Mexico to Pennsylvania, and what it would have cost him to travel from San Francisco to New Mexico had he traveled directly. In addition, he claims as deductions his cost of lodging, commuting expenses between his temporary homes and temporary jobs, and 50% of the cost of his meals. He does not claim any deduction for expenses incurred while vacationing in Canada.

Rule: Brown's positions in California and New Mexico were both temporary positions away from home. In similar cases (not involving academic personnel), the courts have allowed such deductions. (However, it is not certain that the results of these cases would be the same under current law.)

Example 4. Temporary Position Plus Trip Back Home on Weekends

Professor Dodd's regular job is in Chicago. He takes a 5-month leave of absence to accept a temporary position in St. Louis. His family remains in Chicago. On weekends, he travels back to Chicago to visit his family.

Rule: He is entitled to deduct his living expenses (lodging, commuting, laundry, and 50% of the cost of his meals) while in St. Louis. He cannot deduct his living costs while he is back home in Chicago. However, he may deduct the cost of transportation of returning home for the weekend, provided this cost does not exceed what it would have cost him for food and lodging had he stayed in St. Louis. If the cost of transportation is in excess of this, he may deduct only what he could have deducted for food and lodging in St. Louis.

Example 5

Cass was a Professor of Economics at a university in the East. He accepted an appointment under a "distinguished scholar" program to spend the academic year at a well-known university in Southern California. His stipend qualified as a fellowship grant under the rules that applied at the time.

Cass took a leave of absence from his regular position, rented out his house, and moved — together with his wife, 17-year old son, 11-year old daughter, and dog — out West for the academic year. He was permitted to deduct his living expenses during this stay in California. The issue that arose at trial was how much was spent on food for Professor Cass.

Cass proved by production of receipts that the total food expenses for his family amounted to $4,390. Of this amount, it was agreed that $173 was clearly deductible for lunches Professor Cass ate on campus. Of the remaining $4,217, $3,307 was for food purchased at the supermarket and $910 for restaurant meals. It was in allocating what part of this $4,217 worth of food was consumed by Professor Cass that the dispute arose.

Cass claimed that about 1/3 of this $4,217 was allocable to food that he ate. He testified that making this type of allocation was right up his alley as an economist. His methodology for making the allocation here was to apportion the cost of food for each family member according to that person's body weight.

However, the court did not buy this method. It ruled, *"Petitioner's allocation is, to say the least, creative. However, if it proposes to approach a scientific approximation of the amount of food consumed by each member of the household, it is flawed, e.g., it ignores factors such as the relative metabolic rate of each person. Any parent having a teenage child can attest to the fact that a teenager eats as much as, or more than, the parent regardless of weight.*

"Of course the best proof would be to have receipts directly related to petitioner's own food consumption. Understandably, in a situation such as the one before us now, such a requirement would be onerous. Thus, we will make an estimation which we deem best reflects or approximates the true costs involved. In the absence of proof of a more precise method, we deem it best to employ the simplest approach available. Accordingly, we allocate one-fourth of the total contested food expenses ($4,217) to petitioner, discounting the grocery expenses ($3,307) by 5% to account for dog food. Thus, petitioners may deduct $1,185.91 of the $4,390 food costs as a food expense." (Note that under current law, only 50% of the cost of food would be deductible.) [Cass, 86TC 1275]

Example 6. Married People Living Apart

Professor and Professor Lighthouse, a married couple, both have regular teaching positions in cities 400 miles apart. They live in the cities where they work on weekdays, but one of them visits the other on weekends. Because neither of their positions is temporary, they are not entitled to deduct any transportation or living expenses. Each person's tax home is considered to be the city where that person works. A weekend trip to visit a spouse is a personal non-deductible activity. However, if one of their positions were temporary and in a different location than the person's permanent home, expenses as described in Example 4 would be deductible.

Example 7

Mr. and Mrs. Felton moved to a midwestern city where he enrolled as a student at the State university located there. After obtaining his degree, he obtained a position on the faculty of the same university.

Mrs. Felton also enrolled at the university and obtained a master's degree in economics. After teaching for several years in the same locality, she obtained a temporary appointment as a Visiting Lecturer at a university 100 miles away. Later, she was promoted to a full-time position on the faculty, as a Lecturer for half a year and then as Assistant Professor upon attainment of her Ph.D. degree.

Mrs. Felton did not move her personal residence. She arranged her schedule so she could spend 5 nights a week back home with her husband, making 2 round trips per week between where she worked and her permanent residence. She rented a room the 2 nights a week she stayed near her job.

Mrs. Felton was able to deduct her travel expenses during the time she was a Visiting Lecturer (a time span of less than 1 year). At the point in time when Mrs. Felton obtained the full-time faculty position, she was no longer allowed to deduct her travel expenses, because she was no longer temporarily away from home. [Felton, TC Memo 1982-11]

Example 8

An individual sought a ruling from the IRS in the following situation. He was currently doing research and writing from his home. Apparently, he had no other source of employment at the time. He received an appointment as a Visiting Professor for one academic year at a college in a different location. Following his appointment, he expected to return back home.

The IRS ruled that his permanent tax home was where he was currently doing his research and writing. His position as a Visiting Professor constituted a temporary job away from home. Thus, he could deduct his travel expenses, including the cost of commuting, meals [now subject to the 50%-Rule], lodging, and laundry while at his temporary teaching position. [IRS Private Letter Ruling 8449013]

Example 9

Andrews operated two businesses. One of them was a pool construction business located in Massachusetts and the other a horse breeding business located in Florida. About 50% of his time was spent in Massachusetts, while the remaining 50% was spent in Florida.

When Andrews deducted his living expenses in Florida as travel expenses while away from home, the IRS objected. The IRS asserted that Andrews was not away from home while in Florida. Rather, Andrews had 2 tax homes, one in Massachusetts and one in Florida. According to the IRS, this meant Andrews was not "away from home" in either location, ruling out a deduction for his living expenses.

After the IRS position was upheld by the Tax Court, Andrews took his case to the Court of Appeals in his area. This higher court overturned the previous decision and ruled in favor of Andrews.

The Court of Appeals turned back to basics. The basic reason behind allowing a deduction for travel expenses while away from home is to compensate for the duplicate living expenses that must be incurred. In this case, Andrews did incur extra expenses because he had to maintain 2 homes, one in Massachusetts and one in Florida. This meant that he should be allowed a deduction for travel expenses while away from home. In turn, this required a determination of which location was his tax home and which was not. He could not have two separate tax homes despite the decision of the lower court.

The Court of Appeals did not choose which location was Andrews' tax home. It sent the case back to the lower court for this determination, to be based mainly on the amount of time spent, the amount of business activity, and the amount of income earned at both locations. Whichever place was ruled to be Andrews' tax home, Andrews' could deduct his living expenses while at the other location. [Andrews, 67 AFTR2d 91-881]

College Teachers can apply the reasoning in the above case, provided their situation is similar. For example, suppose a college teacher teaches during the academic year at one place but spends his summer at another. If there is sufficient business reason for him to be at his summer location and there are duplicate living expenses, a deduction can be claimed for his living expenses away from home. Sufficient business reasons might be a summer teaching job or a location that provided access to research materials not available at home.

Example 10. Student Working at Summer Job

Hantzsis was a student at a major law school in the Boston area. During the summer of her second year of law school, she accepted a 10-week job as a legal assistant at a New York law firm. While in New York, she rented a small apartment in which she lived. Her husband, a faculty member at a Boston-area university, remained in Boston.

Mrs. Hantzsis viewed her employment in New York as a temporary job away from home. Thus, she claimed a deduction for her transportation between Boston and New York and for meals and lodging while living in New York. The Tax Court allowed the deduction. The amount allowed was surprisingly large — $3,080 just for meals and the rental of a small apartment for the 10 weeks spent in New York.

However, an Appeals Court overruled the Tax Court, disallowing the deduction. It ruled that Boston was not her tax home because she did not work there. Thus, she was not entitled to an away-from-home travel deduction while in New York. In order for her to be allowed a deduction, she would need to "establish the existence of some sort of business relation both to the location she claims as 'home' and to the location of her temporary employment sufficient to support a finding that her duplicative expenses are necessitated by business exigencies." Presumably, had she held even a part-time job in Boston, her deduction for living expenses in New York would have been allowed. [Hantzsis, 47 AFTR 2d 81-721]

Example 11

Kaster was a certified welder who worked at various jobs in the northeastern quarter of Ohio and a small portion of northwestern Pennsylvania. He and his family lived in Titusville, 120 miles east of Cleveland, from which he commuted to his various jobsites. He and his family had lived in Titusville their entire lives.

In July 1981, Kaster obtained work at a nuclear power plant in Perry, Ohio. He expected he would work only two months at the power plant. This was based on his previous work record, which showed a large number of short-term jobs during the previous several years. However, the power plant did not advise him of the expected duration of this particular job and Kaster could not know exactly how long his job would last.

Kaster was subject to immediate layoff at any time. Welders were not generally notified that they were to be laid off until the day that the layoff occurred. However, under the "last hired, first fired" method of determining layoffs, the longer he worked at that job, the less likely he was to be edged out by a fellow employee in the event of a layoff. In fact, his job lasted for 27 months until November 1983 before he was laid off.

The IRS agreed that Titusville was Kaster's tax home and that the job at Perry to which he commuted was away-from-home. The only question that remained was determining for which period of time the job was temporary and for which period indefinite.

Kaster claimed a deduction on his 1982 tax return for an entire year of commuting between his Titusville home and his job at Perry. His total commuting mileage for the year was 50,000 miles, for which he claimed a deduction of $7,178. In order for this claim to be allowed, it would be necessary to determine that his job at Perry was temporary rather than indefinite during the entire 1982 year.

When the IRS audited Kaster's tax return, it allowed a deduction for only part of the year. The IRS said that Kaster's job at Perry was temporary for the first 12 months from July 1981 to July 1982. After that, the job became indefinite, ruling out a deduction. [Kaster, TC Memo 1985-580]

Duplicate Expenses Test

When in doubt, the Tax Court in recent decisions has referred back to the original justification in allowing deductions for living expenses while at a temporary job away from home, namely to provide relief to those who incur extra *"duplicate living expenses"* because of their situation. When no extra expenses are incurred, the Court is sometimes reluctant to permit a deduction. Another factor the Court has been looking for is secondary evidence such as auto registration, voter registration, bank accounts, etc., which point to where a person considers his permanent home to be. The following court case illustrates both of these considerations.

Example 12

For 5 years, Thomas Crain and his wife lived with his parents in a house in Hot Springs, Arkansas. During this time, he worked as an electrician in various places near Hot Springs, obtaining his job assignments through his union. Then he received an assignment near Baton Rouge, Louisiana, which lasted for about 10 months. Despite the impermanence of his job in Louisiana, the Court denied a temporary job-away-from-home deduction.

The Court pointed to the absence of any extra living expenses beyond what would have been normal had they stayed in Hot Springs. During their absence, the Court noted,

"*Petitioners did not pay any rent to Thomas' parents, nor did they contribute any money to them for the purchase of groceries, the payment of utility bills, or the payment of other expenses associated with the upkeep of a home . . . The purpose of allowing the deduction of living expenses while a taxpayer is 'away from home' is 'to mitigate the burden of the taxpayer who, because of exigencies of his trade or business, must maintain two places of abode and thereby incur additional and duplicate living expenses. . . .'*

"*There is no evidence in the record which supports petitioners' contention that they have incurred the requisite increased or duplicate living expenses by maintaining the house [in] Hot Springs, Arkansas.*"

The Court also noted the extent to which they settled into their new location, stating

"We think it pertinent that in Baton Rouge, Mr. and Mrs. Crain rented and lived in an apartment and maintained an account in a local bank. Mrs. Crain held a Louisiana driver's license, registered to vote in that state, and held a job there during at least part of their stay. Mr. Crain also registered to vote in Louisiana and served as a reserve deputy sheriff in Baton Rouge." [Crain, TC Memo 1985-498]

Travel Expenses While Under a Fellowship Grant

A person at a temporary position away from home might have been paid under a grant qualifying for the exemption from Social Security tax as described in the *Tax-Free Grants* chapter. Sometimes, the IRS will contend there is no temporary job in such a case. Rather, it claims the taxpayer is simply studying or doing research under a fellowship grant. Because there is no temporary job, the IRS claims there can be no deduction for expenses incurred at a temporary job away from home.

One can counter such an objection by the IRS by claiming that the expenses were incurred as an *educational expense while on temporary leave of absence from one's regular job* (see the *Expenses of Attending School* chapter). Usually, in the process of denying that a job exists, the IRS contends that the grant is provided simply for the educational benefit of the recipient. Thus, the same travel and living expenses that were denied as a *temporary job* deduction can become an *educational expense* deduction. In fact, there is an IRS ruling concerning teachers' sabbaticals which supports this viewpoint. [Rev Rul 64-176] However, don't expect the IRS to point this out to you if your deduction is challenged in an audit. You must be prepared to point this out to them.

Exactly how you list your claimed deduction on your tax return could be an important factor. This is underscored by the following court case.

Example 13

A teacher received a $10,000 grant from the small liberal arts College in the Midwest where he taught. Such grants were awarded after 7 years of employment. The teacher pursued a Ph.D. program at a major University with the grant. During the period he attended the University, he was not employed at the College which provided the grant, nor was he under any obligation to return to the College after he completed his Ph.D. work.

While at the University, he claimed a deduction of $2,006 for his living expenses. The issue arose at trial as to the category under which this deduction was being claimed. Was the deduction being claimed as a business expense or an educational expense?

The IRS asserted that the teacher was claiming the $2,006 deduction as a business expense. If so, it could object to the deduction because the teacher was not actually employed when the expenses were incurred. To support its assertion, the IRS pointed to the fact that the expenses were claimed on the part of Form 2106, labeled "Employee Business Expenses."

However, the teacher asserted that the deduction was being claimed as an educational expense. As discussed in Section 5 of the Expenses of Attending School chapter, one can deduct educational expenses even while not currently employed, as long as one is considered to be temporarily on leave of absence from his profession. The teacher claimed that the only reason he listed the expenses under the "Employee Business Expenses" section of Form 2106 was that there was no special place for the listing of Educational Expenses on Form 2106.

The judge ruled in favor of the teacher, allowing him to deduct the $2,006 as an educational expense. It agreed that the teacher's claim for a refund hinged on how he had claimed these expenses, i.e. as business expenses or educational expenses. But the teacher had placed the IRS on notice that his deduction was claimed in connection with his education because under the occupation line on Form 2106 he had listed "Scholarship Grant." He had not listed his occupation as "teacher" nor linked the expenses to his job by naming the college where he taught. Because there was no special place for the listing of educational expenses on Form 2106, the teacher had acted sufficiently to identify that the amounts were being deducted as educational expenses connected with his studies rather than as business expenses connected with a job. [Pelowski, DC Ohio, 1985 CCH ¶9217 and other similar cases]

Sabbaticals

A sabbatical leave of absence is governed by the same basic rules that apply to temporary jobs as discussed above. Thus, the costs of travel, meals, lodging, commuting, cleaning, and laundry while away from home are generally deductible. This is spelled out by the following IRS ruling:

IRS Private Letter Ruling #7828042

"This is in reply to your letter with enclosures of January 12, 1978, which concerns the treatment, for federal income tax purposes of certain expenses incurred while away from your permanent place of employment on a temporary employment assignment.

"You are regularly employed as a Professor of Industrial Systems Engineering at X University. During your sabbatical you are working for the Federal Government as a Visiting Mathematical Scientist at Y Agency which is located in the metropolitan Washington, D.C., area. This assignment is of fixed duration commencing October 1, 1977, and ending September 29, 1978. Your Department Chairman at X University attests that you are a university employee on temporary government assignment for which you are paid by the University. The government agency where you are temporarily employed then reimburses the University for that part of your salary designated in your Assignment Agreement which is not covered by sabbatical pay and certain sponsored research which you continue to carry out. This latter research is separately funded under a federal grant program and although you will be working on the project during your temporary employment at Y Agency, the University continues to administer the grant project.

"You have rented out your condominium apartment for part of the time you will be away. During this temporary employment assignment, you are incurring certain expenses which you believe may be deductible for federal income tax purposes. Specifically, you ask whether you may deduct the cost of meals, rental of a temporary apartment, and the cost of commuting between where you obtain your meals, your temporary apartment and Y Agency. Y Agency has paid your round-trip travel expenses between the city of your permanent employment and your temporary post.

". . . Assuming that your appointment with Y Agency is temporary for the term described and that upon expiration of the appointment you will return to your permanent employment at X University, we conclude that while temporarily employed in the metropolitan Washington, D.C. area, you will be traveling away from home for purposes of section 162 of the Code.

"Accordingly, if your records will establish the recordkeeping and substantiation elements required . . ., you may claim a deduction for reasonable amounts expended for meals [now subject to the 50%-Rule] *and lodging plus other incidental expenses such as laundry you incur as a result of your temporary employment. In addition, your expenses for transportation are deductible to the extent they are reasonable in amount and were incurred in the pursuit of your temporary assignment in going between your place of lodging and place of temporary employment."*

Example 14

A Professor and Chairman of the Department of Anesthesiology at a New York medical school took a 6-month sabbatical from his duties. He spent this period in Washington, D.C., where he served as an unpaid advisor to a Senate subcommittee on health-related issues. He rented an apartment while in Washington and traveled back to New York regularly to take care of certain job-related matters there.

The IRS ruled that he could deduct his living expenses in Washington and his travel back and forth between New York and Washington. According to the IRS, *"an appearance or communication by an employee or self-employed individual in connection with legislation or proposed legislation shall be considered to be with respect to legislation of direct interest to such person if the legislation is in the field in which he specializes in his business and if the appearance or communication is made pursuant to an invitation extended to him individually for the purpose of receiving his expert testimony. Expenses incurred by an employee or self-employed individual in connection with such an appearance or communication, including traveling expenses properly allocable thereto, represent ordinary and necessary business expenses and are, therefore, deductible . . . "* [IRS Private Letter Ruling 8727010]

Example 15

Michael and Nancy McColloch were both teachers in Colorado — he, an Assistant Professor of Philosophy at a large State university and she, an elementary school teacher at a public school. During one school year, they both took sabbaticals from their respective teaching positions which they spent in Ireland, accompanied by their 4 children.

The IRS did not object to Michael deducting his expenses while on sabbatical. The matter before the Court was whether or not Nancy could deduct hers.

Nancy used her sabbatical to study

> *"the use of storytelling in elementary curricula of selected high school systems and to learn from Irish storytellers the essentials of their art . . . She chose to take her sabbatical in Ireland because of its rich tradition in storytelling and because many fine storytellers still live there. Further, through the library at Trinity College in Dublin, Mrs. McCulloch had access to an outstanding collection of storytelling literature. In her opinion, Ireland was the best English speaking place to learn storytelling."*

While in Ireland, she spent most weekday mornings at the library, reading collections of stories and books that detailed the importance of storytelling in the elementary school classroom. In the afternoon and evening, in addition to caring for her children, she did more reading and research. In the course of her studies, she prepared an annotated bibliography for use both in a handbook that she was preparing for other teachers and for her master's thesis.

Upon her return from Ireland,

> *"Mrs. McCulloch relied heavily on storytelling in her teaching. She told her students stories two to three times each week, and although each story lasted only approximately one-half hour, she used the story as the focal point for many of her lessons. She built handwriting and spelling lessons around the stories and had the children list the adverbs and adjectives that they heard in the stories. She also based some of her social studies lessons on the stories she told.*
>
> *"Mrs. McCulloch benefited professionally from her sabbatical in a number of ways. She found that her intensive study of Irish stories enabled her to learn other stories more easily and to relate these stories to her students. As a result of her experience in Ireland, she was able to tell 15 stories well, could learn 50 more at a week's notice, and knew hundreds more. In addition, she learned research techniques which enabled her to gain access to stories in Colorado.*
>
> *"Mrs. McCulloch shared her skills by conducting a workshop and by telling stories in an enrichment program for gifted and talented children. She recommended stories to other teachers and shared with them the bibliography she prepared in Ireland. She also made a videotape which has been used, with impressive results, to train other teachers."*

The Court ruled that the primary purpose of her sabbatical was to improve her teaching skills. Thus, she could deduct her travel expenses including her living costs during her stay in Ireland. [McColloch, TC Memo 1988-84]

The above discussion and examples concern sabbaticals during which a teacher studies or does research at a distant location. In such a case, the usual rules for deducting business travel expenses apply. Another type of sabbatical occurs when a teacher travels extensively and claims that the travel itself is a form of education. This type of travel is no longer deductible, as discussed in Section 8 of this chapter.

The expenses of renting out a home while on sabbatical or other leave of absence are deductible. This is discussed further in Section 4 of the *Homeowners* chapter.

SECTION 5:
TRAVEL TO LOOK FOR EMPLOYMENT

You can deduct expenses connected with looking for a new job, whether or not you are successful. However, you can only deduct job-hunting costs if you are looking for work in your current profession. You cannot deduct the expenses of looking for work in a new profession even if you are successful.

If you take a trip to look for a new job in your own profession, you can deduct all your travel expenses. If the trip combines the search for a job with sightseeing or other personal activity, you can deduct your travel expenses provided that the **primary purpose** of your trip was to look for a job. Of course, any expense directly connected with your sightseeing activity is not deductible. [See Example 8 of the *Automobile Expenses* chapter for an illustration of deducting auto expenses while looking for a job.]

Example
Whitman takes a 2-day trip to New York to interview for a new job. While in New York, he rides the Staten Island ferry and does some other incidental sightseeing. He can deduct the entire cost of his trip including transportation, meals [subject to the 50%-Rule], and lodging. He can't deduct the fare for the Staten Island ferry or other direct sightseeing expenses.

SECTION 6:
TRAVEL TO PROFESSIONAL CONVENTIONS

If you attend a convention which is directly connected with your profession, you may deduct the cost of travel, including meals and lodging, if you are away from home overnight, as well as direct convention expenses such as registration fees. This includes professional conventions, conventions of learned societies, union conventions, etc., but not conventions of fraternal organizations. Also excluded now are conventions which provide investment information rather than relate directly to an individual's job or business.

If your spouse accompanied you (and your spouse had no business purpose for being there), you may deduct what it would have cost had you gone alone. Thus, if the hotel rate is $80 for a double and $65 for a single room, you may deduct $65 as the cost of the room. Likewise, you may deduct 34½ cents per mile for your automobile expenses whether or not your spouse traveled with you.

For conventions held outside the North American area, it must be "reasonable" for the convention to be held abroad. For example, a foreign convention of an international professional society would qualify, but a convention of the Iowa Engineering Association held in France would not.

If you stay an extra day or two in order to obtain a lower air fare, you can deduct your travel expenses for this extra period to the extent money is saved on the overall trip. This point of view was expressed in a recent IRS ruling [IRS Private Letter Ruling 9237014]. This ruling concerned the tax exemption for expenses reimbursed by an employer, but the reasoning applies also to a self-employed person or employee paying expenses out of his own pocket.

> **Example**
> *You go out of town to attend a deductible 3-day convention from Wednesday through Friday. Ordinarily, you would have returned home on Saturday morning. However, you decided to stay over an extra day to do some sightseeing, returning home on Sunday. Because you are staying over a Saturday night, you qualify for a reduced excursion fare.*
>
> *Because your expenses for the extra day are offset by the airfare savings, you can deduct the cost of your entire trip, including lodging and meals for the extra day. However, if the airfare savings does not entirely offset the extra day's expenses, you can only deduct what it would have cost you had you returned home on Saturday morning.*

While the IRS ruling referred to above applied to an extra day's stay to obtain a lower airfare, the same reasoning would apply in similar situations. For example, it would apply if you extend a stay abroad in order to qualify for a low-cost charter flight.

Many convention trips include some sightseeing or other personal activity. Section 7 discusses how to treat travel which combines business with personal activities.

SECTION 7:
TRAVEL WHICH COMBINES BUSINESS WITH PLEASURE

A. *Travel Within the United States*

If your trip was entirely for business, your ordinary and necessary travel expenses may be deducted. If your trip was solely personal, no part of your travel expenses are deductible, even if you engaged in some business activity at your destination.

You may travel to a business destination, and extend your stay for nonbusiness reasons, make a nonbusiness side trip, or engage in other nonbusiness activities. In this case, your travel expenses are deductible only if the trip was related **primarily** to your profession.

Regardless of whether the primary purpose of your trip was business or pleasure, an expense that is properly attributable to a business purpose, such as a registration fee at a professional convention, is deductible.

Whether a trip is primarily for business or is primarily personal in nature depends on the facts and circumstances in each case. However, the length of time spent in business or personal activities is an important factor in determining the primary purpose of the trip.

Example 1

Jones is a Professor of Chemistry at a university in Iowa. He attends the annual convention of the American Chemical Society in San Francisco. The convention consists primarily of papers presented by various members of the society on research in chemistry. Jones attends the convention for five days and spends most of his time during the day attending sessions of the convention. He rides a few cable cars for fun and does some other incidental sightseeing.

Rule: The travel is primarily for business. He may deduct the cost of transportation between Iowa and San Francisco, lodging, and 50% of the cost of meals both while in transit and at the convention. His sightseeing costs are not deductible.

Example 2

Same as in Example 1, except that instead of returning directly from San Francisco to Iowa, Dr. Jones flies to Los Angeles for a day to visit his brother. He then returns to Iowa from Los Angeles.

Rule: Jones can claim that his was primarily a business trip to attend the convention. The side trip to Los Angeles was not his primary purpose in taking the trip. Jones may deduct his lodging and 50% of the cost of meals in San Francisco, plus what the cost of transportation would have been had he traveled directly between Iowa and San Francisco instead of stopping over in Los Angeles. He cannot deduct expenses incurred while in Los Angeles.

Example 3

Mr. Burns teaches high school in Atlanta and travels to St. Louis to attend the convention of the teacher's union to which he belongs. He does little or no sightseeing.

Rule: Travel to union conventions is a legitimate business expense. Therefore his transportation, lodging, and 50% of the cost of his meals while in St. Louis are deductible.

Example 4

Cooper teaches Psychology at a New Mexico high school. After the school term is over, he and his family take a month-long camping trip in California. He leaves his family at Yosemite National Park for two days to attend a meeting of the American Society for Teachers of Psychology in San Francisco.

Rule: His trip was primarily for personal activities connected with his camping trip. However, he may deduct any expenses directly connected with his attendance at the convention. Thus, his living expenses in San Francisco and the cost of transportation between Yosemite and San Francisco are deductible.

B. Travel Outside the United States

Different rules govern travel inside the U.S. and travel outside the U.S. For combined business-with-pleasure travel **inside** the U.S., you may deduct all of your travel expenses (except those specifically connected with personal activities such as sightseeing) as long as you can establish that the primary purpose of your travel was of a business or professional nature.

For combined business-with-pleasure travel **outside** the U.S. where the primary purpose of the travel is for business purposes, you must meet one of the following conditions in order to deduct all of your travel expenses:

1. **You were outside the U.S. a week or less.** In counting the days, do not count the day of departure from the U.S., but do count the day of return to the U.S.

2. **You were reimbursed** by or received a travel expense allowance from your employer (and you are not a managing executive nor related to your employer).

3. **You spent less than 25 percent of the total time outside the U.S. on non-business activities.**

4. **You had no substantial control over arranging the trip.** You are not considered to have control merely because you have control over timing the trip.

5. **You can establish that a personal vacation was not a major consideration.**

Even if you satisfy one of the above conditions for a trip taken primarily for business, you still cannot deduct expenses which are strictly personal in nature, such as sightseeing expenses. Similarly, if you extend your stay just to engage in some personal activity, your living expenses during such an extension are not deductible. However, if you spend time on personal activities during the middle of a business trip, your living expenses during such a period can still be deductible.

Example

You traveled to Paris primarily for business purposes connected with your profession. You left Denver Tuesday and flew to New York. On Wednesday, you flew nonstop from New York to Paris, arriving Thursday morning. Thursday and Friday were spent on business activities and from Saturday until Tuesday you were sightseeing. You flew back to New York, arriving Wednesday afternoon. On Thursday, you flew back to Denver. Because the day of departure from the United States does not count, you were not outside the United States for more than a week. You may deduct what it would have cost you to fly from Denver to Paris, stay there Thursday and Friday, and return on Saturday. The cost of your stay in Paris from Saturday through Tuesday is not deductible because it is not attributable to a business purpose.

However, suppose that your professional activities had temporarily ceased on Friday afternoon, resuming on Monday and Tuesday. In this case, the fact that you spent Saturday and Sunday sightseeing would not disqualify your living expenses during such days from being deductible. You had to stay in Paris during the weekend for the business purpose of being able to continue your professional activities on Monday and Tuesday. Of course, you still cannot deduct your sightseeing expenses.

Allocating Expenses

If you do not meet one of the five conditions listed above for travel outside the U.S., your expenses must be allocated between business and nonbusiness activities. Generally, the amount of your travel expense outside the United States incurred in getting to and from your business destination that is not deductible is determined by multiplying the total travel expenses by the total number of nonbusiness days outside the United States, and dividing the result by the total number of days outside the United States. For this purpose you must count both the day of your departure from, and return to, the United States. The allocation to business or nonbusiness activity is generally made on a day by day basis according to the following rules.

Transportation days. If you travel a reasonably direct route without interruption to your business destination, each day en route outside the United States is considered a business day. If your travel is interrupted by a substantial nonbusiness diversion, or if you do not travel a reasonably direct route, you count as business days only the number of days you would have been outside the United States if you had traveled to your business destination by a reasonably direct route without interruption, using the same means of transportation.

Presence required. Any day that your presence is required in a particular place for a specific and bona fide business purpose is counted as a business day, even though your presence is required for only a part of the day and if, during the normal working hours of the day, you spend more time in nonbusiness activities than in business activities.

If your principal activity during normal working hours is in pursuit of your business, the day is counted as a business day. Any day that you are prevented from engaging in the conduct of your business as a principal activity because of circumstances beyond your control is also counted as a business day.

Weekends, holidays, and other necessary standby days are counted as business days if they fall between business days. But if they are at the end of your business activity and you remain at your business destination for nonbusiness or personal reasons, they are not business days.

If the nonbusiness activity occurred between the point of departure from the United States and your business destination, you allocate what it would have cost you to travel (including meals and lodging) between the place where your travel outside the United States begins and the place of your nonbusiness activity, and return to the United States, using the same mode of travel as you actually used.

Example

You live in New York and flew to Brussels on Monday, May 31 for professional activities that began at noon Tuesday, June 1, and were over at noon Friday, June 4. That evening you flew to Dublin, Ireland, where you visited with friends until the afternoon of June 17, when you flew home to New York. The primary reason for the trip was for business purposes. If you had not stopped in Dublin, you would have arrived home the evening of June 4. You were outside the United States more than a week, and you are unable to show that you had no substantial control over arranging the trip, or that a personal vacation was not a major consideration in making the trip. May 31 through June 4 (5 days) are business days and June 5 through June 17 (13 days) are nonbusiness days. Your expenses while in Dublin are nondeductible. In addition, 13/18 of the cost of the round-trip airline fare from New York to Dublin is not deductible. You may deduct the cost of lodging and 50% of the cost of your meals while in Brussels, to the extent they are not lavish or extravagant, all other necessary travel expenses while in Brussels, and that portion of your roundtrip transportation cost (including meals) from New York to Brussels, that exceeds 13/18 of the round-trip plane fare between New York and Dublin.

If the nonbusiness activity was at or beyond your business destination, you would allocate your total travel expenses (including meals and lodging en route) from the place where travel outside the United States began to the place of business activity and return to the United States.

Example

Assume the same facts as in the example above, except that instead of going to Dublin for your vacation, you fly to Venice, Italy, for a vacation, and arrive back in New York on the evening of June 17. (Note that in this example, Venice is further from New York than Brussels, whereas in the preceding example Dublin was closer to New York than Brussels.) You may not deduct any part of the cost of your trip from Brussels to Venice.

> *You may deduct 5/18 of the round-trip plane fare from New York to Brussels (including 50% of the cost of meals en route), plus lodging and 50% of the cost of your meals while in Brussels to the extent they are not lavish or extravagant, and any other ordinary and necessary business expenses incurred while you were in Brussels.*

Other allocation method. You may use a different allocation method if it more clearly reflects the proportion of your time spent on business activity.

Converting a Personal Trip Into a Deductible Business Trip

Sometimes, it is possible to convert a trip with personal motives into a deductible business trip. The following 2 court cases should prove an inspiration to those who attempt to accomplish this objective.

Example

Habeeb was an assistant professor at a Medical School in the South. For six years in a row, he made an annual trip to Egypt where he visited his mother and other relatives who lived there. The court case involves one of these years when Habeeb claimed that his trip qualified for a tax-deduction because it was made primarily for business purposes. The court opinion describes his trip as follows:

"The trip lasted 45 days and travel was by a chartered flight because it was cheaper. During his stay in Egypt petitioner delivered 5 lectures at the University of Alexandria and 2 lectures at the University of Cairo. These lectures involved subjects within petitioner's expertise, such as 'Antigenicity of Proteins' and 'Chemistry of Antibodies.' The lecture dates span the 14-day period from July 4 to July 18. Petitioner testified that he was invited to give these lectures, but also admitted on cross-examination that he had volunteered his services. He received no compensation or expense reimbursement for such lectures. Petitioner testified that he had numerous discussions with students, professors, and other lecturers while in Egypt for the purpose of exchanging ideas, keeping abreast, reviewing articles, and generally to avoid the isolation which one would experience if one did not travel. Petitioner's testimony on this score was general and nonspecific."

Habeeb had three strikes against him. First, he had volunteered to give the lectures and received no pay or expense reimbursement from the universities he visited. Second, the trip had a strong personal component because he was visiting his mother and other relatives. And third, he spent less than 1/3 of his time, 14 out of 45 days, for business purposes.

In spite of these three negative points, the Court decided that his trip was undertaken primarily for business purposes and therefore a portion of his expenses could be deducted. The written opinion of the Court shows how it reached this conclusion.

"Even though petitioner may have solicited the invitations to lecture, there is no question that he did give the lectures; and additionally, it has been established that petitioner is well-respected for his specialized learning, his writings, and his lectures, and that his lectures helped to maintain that reputation.

"The first question to be answered is whether the trip to Egypt was primarily personal in nature. If so, [IRS regulations] would require disallowance of the travel deduction even though some business activities took place during the trip. Two weeks of the approximate 6-week trip were spent delivering a series of lectures, for which petitioner devoted substantial time and effort in preparation. Even though petitioner might have chosen some other country for some of his lectures had it not been for his mother and father in Egypt, the trip does not, for that reason become 'primarily personal.' It is true that the presence of close relatives at the place of destination may raise a question of disguised personal motive for a trip or series of trips. [See William R. Kenney, 66 TC 122] *But if an adequate business justification exists, the fact that trips are repeated to the same destination, where the taxpayer has relatives or friends does not, ipso facto, obliterate the business character of the trip.*

"As to the overall time spent on the trip, it is to be noted that petitioner took a 45-day charter flight because it was cheaper. [Although IRS regulations state] that the amount of time spent on personal versus business activities is 'an important factor' in determining primary purpose, it is believed that under the totality of facts and circumstances here present, the trip was taken primarily for the business purpose of maintaining petitioner's reputation in the field of his specialty." [Habeeb, TC Memo 1976-259]

Example

Professor Rezazadeh was a widely educated individual with a degree in aeronautical engineering, a master of laws in international law, and a Ph.D. in political science and economics. During the year in question, he was on the faculty of the political science department at a small university in the midwest.

Professor Rezazadeh was scheduled to present a paper on local government in the nation of Columbia at a national conference being held in Nebraska. Preparing such a paper required extensive research in Bogota, Columbia. However, he did not have time in his schedule to travel to Columbia for this research.

As luck would have it, his wife was born in Columbia and had a number of relatives in Bogota with whom she could stay. And while not an expert in political science, she was knowledgeable of the research process because she had written a dissertation while obtaining her Ph.D. in psychology. So Mrs. Rezazadeh traveled to Columbia for 60 days, performing the research her husband needed.

The IRS denied a deduction for this travel. Pointing to the fact she was visiting and staying with relatives the entire period, it determined that the trip was more for pleasure than for business. However, the Court overruled the IRS and allowed a travel deduction, stating that the Rezazadehs

> "... *presented evidence that Mrs. Rezazadeh spent 50 of the 60 days she was in Bogota, including weekends and holidays, doing research, which included collecting, studying, organizing, and tabulating over 700 pages of material. While Mrs. Rezazadeh did spend some time visiting relatives while she was in Bogota, the Court is satisfied that her trip to Bogota was primarily for business and not personal purposes. Accordingly, the Rezazadehs are entitled to deduct those business-related travel expenses that have been properly substantiated."*
>
> While Mrs. Rezazadeh qualified for a travel deduction, she did no record-keeping and had only her round trip airplane ticket as corroboration. As a result, she was only entitled to a $901 deduction for the cost of her ticket. [Rezazadeh, T.C. Memo 1996-245]

SECTION 8:
EDUCATIONAL TRAVEL

There are two basic types of travel for educational purposes. The first is travel to one or more locations in order to obtain education there. In this case, travel expenses are deductible providing the education qualifies as described in the *Expenses of Attending School* chapter.

The second is travel of a type that the travel itself is of educational value. Travel of this type is no longer deductible.

Example 1

A scholar of French literature travels to Paris to take courses that are offered only at the Sorbonne or to study, doing specific library research that cannot be done elsewhere. Assuming that the cost of his studies is deductible as educational expenses, his associated travel costs are deductible. [See the *Expenses of Attending School* chapter. Also see Sections 1–4 of this chapter for other examples where travel expenses connected with research can be deducted as an *employee business expense.*]

Example 2

A French language teacher travels to France in order to improve his general knowledge of the French language and customs. He doesn't spend any significant amount of time doing specific scholarly research or taking classes. His travel is considered to be for personal purposes. Expenses for this type of travel are no longer deductible.

Section 9:
Discount Rates for Teachers

Some hotel and motel chains, such as Hilton and Holiday Inn, offer discounts specifically for teachers. It is also commonplace to find discounts for government employees, which may include teachers who work for a state by teaching in public schools or colleges.

Even if a hotel doesn't have a standard discount policy for teachers, the management often has authority to give a discount. Sometimes, they'll give a teacher their standard corporate discount rate when asked. You can find out a hotel's general policy by calling the free 800 number for that hotel. Dial the 800 information number (1-800-555-1212) and ask for the chain you are interested in. When you call the 800 number, the operator can make reservations anywhere in the country for that hotel chain. However, the operator may not be aware of all the discounts available at each hotel. To get the most complete information, it's best to call the specific hotel.

Many motel and hotel chains give discounts to members of certain "senior citizen" organizations. For example, most Holiday Inns, Sheratons, Travelodges, and Marriotts will give a discount to members of the American Association of Retired Persons (AARP) or National Retired Teachers Association (NRTA). Also, many chains, such as Quality Inn, Travelodge, Econolodge and Hampton Inn, offer discounts designed specifically for senior citizens.

Another avenue of approach is to ask if the hotel or motel has a "super-saver" or other special discount rate. This can sometimes cut the cost by up to 50%. However, some of these discounts aren't advertised or mentioned by the reservation department — you have to know to ask if there's a discount rate that applies to you.

You should also inquire about discounts if you rent an auto on your trip. Some auto rental companies give discounts to seniors with proof of age or to government workers, including teachers who work at a public institution.

Despite their names, memberships in the National Retired Teachers Association and the American Association of Retired Persons are open to those age 50 or over, whether or not they are retired. These organizations charge an annual fee of $10 or less. [Addresses: NRTA, 601 E St., N.W., Washington, D.C. 20049; AARP, 601 E St., N.W., Washington, D.C. 20049]

—22—
Miscellaneous Deductions

SECTION 1:
BASIC RULES

This chapter describes the items that can be claimed under the category of *miscellaneous deductions* on Schedule A. As discussed in Section 2, this includes all deductible job-related expenses. And as discussed in Section 3, *miscellaneous deductions* also include such items as investment-related expenses and expenses connected with tax computation (e.g. the cost of this book).

2% of Adjusted Gross Income (AGI) Floor

There is a 2% of adjusted gross income floor on *miscellaneous deductions*. That is, to determine your deduction for *miscellaneous expenses* on Schedule A, you must subtract 2% of your adjusted gross income (AGI) from the total of your allowable expenses. Schedule A builds in this subtraction (on line 26) in the computation procedure for determining your total itemized deductions.

Example 1

Johnson computes adjusted gross income of $50,000 on his tax return. He has allowable miscellaneous expenses of $1,500. His miscellaneous deduction is computed as follows:

Total Expenses:	$1,500
less 2% of AGI (2% × $50,000):	− 1,000
Deduction:	$ 500 (entered on line 26 of Schedule A)

There are a few specialized miscellaneous deductions which escape application of the 2% floor. Included in this category are gambling losses up to the amount of gambling winnings, certain expenses for handicapped workers, and jury duty pay turned over to your employer [see the end of Section 3].

Where Do You Claim Job-Related Expenses?

You report your job-related expenses either on Form 2106 or on Form 2106-EZ. Form 2106-EZ is the simple version of Form 2106 and can be used if you satisfy the requirements listed below.

Form 2106-EZ

Form 2106-EZ is a one-page version of the longer Form 2106, with fewer lines to be filled out. You may use this form for your deductible job-related expenses if you satisfy all of the following requirements:

1. You did not get reimbursed by your employer for any expenses, except when included as taxable wages on your Form W-2.

2. If you are claiming vehicle expenses,

   a. You own your vehicle, and

   b. You are using the standard mileage rate, and you also used the standard mileage rate in the year you first drove the vehicle for business or job-related purposes.

There are two sections you fill out on Form 2106-EZ. The *Figure Your Expenses* section contains 5 lines for listing different categories of expenses and for taking into account the 50%-reduction on meals and entertainment [see the *Travel and Entertainment* chapters]. Your deductible expenses are then totaled on line 6, with the total transferred to line 20 of Schedule A. On Schedule A, this amount is combined with your other miscellaneous deductions and subjected to the 2% of AGI floor, as described at the beginning of this chapter.

The other section, *Information on Your Vehicle,* only needs to be filled out if you are claiming vehicle expenses. This section contains a version of the 6 basic questions on auto expenses as described in the *Automobile Expenses* chapter.

Form 2106

Form 2106 is used when you are deducting job-related expenses and do not qualify or do not choose to use Form 2106-EZ . On page 1 of this form, you list your expenses broken down into several categories. On page 2, you give the basic data and answer the basic questions concerning your deductible use of your automobile.

Page 1 is separated into 2 columns, one for meals and entertainment and the other for the remainder of your expenses. This separation is made so that the 50%-Rule for meals and entertainment [see the *Travel* or *Entertainment* chapters] can be factored into the computation.

Page 1 of Form 2106 is divided into 3 sections, called "Steps." In Step 1, you report the amounts of your job-related expenses, broken down into several categories as listed on the form.

If your employer **did not reimburse** you for any of your job-related expenses, you skip Step 2, proceeding directly to Step 3. In Step 3, your total of job-related expenses is computed. The total is then entered as a miscellaneous deduction on line 20 of Schedule A and, when combined with your other miscellaneous deductions, subjected to the 2% of AGI floor as described above.

Reimbursed Expenses

You may have included expenses in Step 1 for which you received a reimbursement from your employer. Your employer is now generally required to report these reimbursements on the year-end Form W-2 he gives you. Your employer may report these reimbursements in either of two ways:

Case 1. The **reimbursements are not included** in taxable income on your W-2 Form; or

Case 2. The **reimbursements are included** in taxable income on your Form W-2.

Case 1. Reimbursements Not Included in Taxable Income

This is the situation that leads to the most favorable treatment. Reimbursements received from your employer are listed separately on your Form W-2 but are **not included** in the taxable income figure. Or, these reimbursements are simply not listed on your Form W-2 at all. This situation can arise when you are reimbursed by receiving a per diem allowance or where you give your employer a detailed summary of your costs with copies of receipts attached.

A. If you **did not claim** any of these expenses as deductions in Step 1 of Form 2106, you're done. Neither the expenses nor the reimbursements appear on your tax return — producing a net result of zero.

B. If you **did claim** these expenses as deductions in Step 1 of Form 2106, you list the reimbursements in Step 2 of Form 2106. The reimbursements are then subtracted from the expenses on line 8 of Form 2106 — again producing a net result of zero.

Case 1 arises when your employer does not report reimbursements as taxable income received by you. There are 2 requirements that must be satisfied in order for your employer to be able to treat reimbursements this way. First, you must have provided your employer with satisfactory written substantiation for the expenses you incurred. [See Section 1 of the *Travel* chapter for what constitutes satisfactory substantiation.] Second, you must return, in a timely manner, excess reimbursements received for days not traveled or mileage not driven. [See Section 1 of the *Travel* chapter, in particular Examples 4 and 5, along with the surrounding material, for a discussion of this requirement.]

If these 2 conditions are not satisfied, your employer is supposed to include the reimbursements in your taxable income as discussed in Case 2.

If you have received reimbursements from your employer, be sure to examine your year-end Form W-2 . You'll want to make sure your employer has reported these reimbursements the correct way. Those reimbursements that qualify under the rules described above should not be included as taxable income in the *"Wages"* box on your Form W-2. If they are, you should request that your employer file an amended

Form W-2 correcting the error. (This will produce a reduction in adjusted gross income, which can be better than an itemized deduction for reasons discussed in Section 1 of Chapter 1.)

Case 2. Reimbursements Included in Taxable Income

As discussed above, there are circumstances under which your employer will report reimbursements you receive for job-related expenses as taxable income on your Form W-2. In this case, you just claim the expenses as a miscellaneous deduction using Step 1 of Form 2106. This situation generally arises when your employer gives you a fixed amount for expenses or does not require detail of how you spent that money.

As a miscellaneous deduction, these expenses will be subjected to the 2% of adjusted gross income subtraction that applies, as discussed earlier in this chapter. The disadvantage is that if your total miscellaneous deductions are not sufficiently large, you might get no deduction for these expenses at all. This means you would wind up paying extra tax on the amount of reimbursements received from your employer, without any offsetting deduction. This result was intended by Congress when it changed the law. It wanted to treat reimbursement plans harshly in this way if the 2 requirements specified in the Case 1 explanation above were not satisfied.

Example 2
Jones has deductible employee business expenses totaling $1,000, for which he receives a full reimbursement from his employer. None of these expenses is for meals or entertainment.

Case 1. Jones provides an adequate accounting of the expenses to his employer.
As a result, Jones' employer does not include the reimbursement as taxable income on the Form W-2 it issues to Jones at year-end.
In this case, there's nothing for Jones to do. He does not claim the expenses on his tax return, nor does the reimbursement show up as taxable income on his tax return — a net result of zero.

Case 2. Jones does not provide an adequate accounting to his employer.
As a result, Jones' employer does include the reimbursement as taxable income on Jones' year-end Form W-2 .
In this case, Jones must claim the $1,000 in expenses as a deduction on his own tax return. The expenses are reported on Form 2106 and then claimed as a miscellaneous deduction on line 20 of Schedule A. On Schedule A, this $1,000, when combined with other miscellaneous deductions, is subjected to the 2% of AGI floor that applies. If the 2% floor negates the deduction or if Jones uses the standard deduction, he's out of luck. He winds up with $1,000 in extra taxable income with no offsetting deduction.

Meal and Entertainment Expenses

An extra complication arises from the *50%-Rule* on meal and entertainment expenses. Under this rule, only 50% of these expenses can be claimed as a deduction [see the *Travel* and the *Entertainment* chapters].

The IRS handles this by dividing Form 2106 into 2 columns. Column B is used for meal and entertainment expenses, while Column A is used for all other employee business expenses.

The computation procedure given by Steps 1–3, as discussed earlier in this Section, is applied to each column separately. Thus, reimbursements for meal and entertainment expenses are subtracted from the total expenses given in Column B, while other reimbursements are subtracted from the total expenses given in Column A. The resulting 2 remainders, one for Column B expenses and one for Column A expenses, appear separately on line 8 of Form 2106.

The bottom line is obtained by adding the Column A result plus 50% of the Column B result. This is the amount you carry over to line 20 of Schedule A as a miscellaneous deduction.

Example 3

Smith has deductible employee business expenses totaling $3,000: $900 for meals and entertainment plus $2,100 for other expenses. His employer has a policy of reimbursing employees for 2/3 of their expenses. Under this policy, Smith receives a reimbursement of $2,000 (2/3 × $900 = $600 for meals and entertainment, plus 2/3 x $2,100 = $1,400 for other expenses). Because Smith made an adequate accounting to his employer, the employer does not include the reimbursement in taxable income reported on Smith's year-end Form W-2 .

The computation of Smith's employee business expense deduction on Form 2106 proceeds as follows:

		Column A Other than Meals and Entertainment	**Column B** Meals and Entertainment
Step 1.	Expenses:	$2,100	$900
Step 2.	Reimbursements not included in taxable income on Form W-2 :	– 1,400	– 600
Step 3.	Remainder:	$ 700	$300

Deduction: $700 + (50% × $300) = $850.

Smith transfers the $850 deduction computed above to line 20 of Schedule A. (On Schedule A, this $850, when combined with other miscellaneous deductions, is subjected to the 2% of AGI floor that applies.)

Example 4

Same as Example 3, except that Smith did not make an adequate accounting to his employer. Because of this, the employer includes the $2,000 in taxable income reported on Smith's Form *W-2. As in the Case 2 discussion in Example 2, Step 2 of Form 2106 is omitted. Thus, the amounts in Step 3 are equal to amounts in Step 1:*

	Column A Other than Meals and Entertainment	Column B Meals and Entertainment
Step 1. Expenses:	$2,100	$900
Step 2. (Omitted)		
Step 3. (Equal to Step 1):	$2,100	$900

Deduction: $2,100 + (50% × $900) = $2,550.

Smith transfers the $2,550 deduction computed above to line 20 of Schedule A. On Schedule A, this $2,550, when combined with other miscellaneous deductions, is subjected to the 2% of AGI floor that applies.

The outcome in Example 4 is inferior to that in Example 3 in two ways. First, if Smith cannot use the full miscellaneous deduction as computed in the example, either because of the 2% of AGI floor or because he uses the standard deduction, the result in Example 4 is a disaster. In the absence of any deduction, Smith simply winds up with almost $2,850 in extra taxable income in the Example 4 situation, i.e. the $2,000 amount in the Form W-2 plus the $850 deduction cost.

Second, even if the deductions are fully usable (because the 2% floor is already exceeded by other miscellaneous expenses), Example 4 produces an inferior result. In Example 3, the net result was an $850 reduction in taxable income produced by the computed deduction. But in Example 4, Smith has $2,000 extra taxable income produced by the reimbursement coupled with a $2,550 deduction — producing a net reduction in taxable income of $550.

The lesser reduction in taxable income produced in Example 4 is due to the fact that Smith absorbs the full impact of the 50%-reduction factor applying to the $900 expenses for meals and entertainment. In Example 3, only the unreimbursed $300 was subject to this factor on Smith's tax return. (The employer is then stuck with the rest of the 50%-reduction factor when it deducts the reimbursed amounts paid out on its tax return.)

In Example 3, $600 of the reimbursement was applied toward the $900 spent for meals and entertainment because the employer's basic policy was to reimburse 2/3 of all expenses. This meant that Smith had to reduce the remaining unreimbursed $300 by using the 50% factor when computing his total deduction. The same type of percentage allocation is made even if there is no explicit reimbursement policy. Thus, the above example would apply if the same $2,000 reimbursement were received by

Smith without any specification as to how the employee calculated this reimbursement amount. [Temp Reg. 1.62-IT(e)]

However, if the employer's policy is to reimburse different categories of expenses differently, the reimbursement is allocated accordingly. The next example illustrates a situation where the reimbursement could be considered to cover all of the meal and entertainment costs. This is the most favorable situation because there is no 50%-reduction factor that applies to the unreimbursed expenses the employee is allowed to deduct.

Example 5

Parker takes a 4-day business-related trip, incurring meal expenses of $250, lodging expenses of $500, and other travel expenses of $600. Parker's employer reimburses employees for business travel, except that meals are limited to $75 per day and lodging to $100 per day. Thus, the total reimbursement is $250 for meals plus $400 + $600 = $1,000 for lodging and other travel expenses, a total of $1,250. Parker's employer does not include this $1,250 reimbursement in taxable income reported on Parker's year-end Form W-2.

		Column A Other than Meals and Entertainment	Column B Meals and Entertainment
Step 1.	Travel Expenses:	$1,100	$250
	Additional Expenses:	+ 800	
	Total Expenses:	$1,900	$250
Step 2.	Reimbursements not included in taxable income on W-2 Form:	– $1,000	– $250
Step 3.	Remainder:	$ 900	$ 0

Deduction: $900 + (50% × $0) = $900

Escaping the 2% of AGI Floor

The 2% of AGI floor only affects items claimed as *Miscellaneous Deductions* on Schedule A. It does not apply to items connected with a self-employment activity which can be claimed on either Schedule C, *Profit (or Loss) from Business or Profession* (or on the simplified Schedule C-EZ) or on Schedule E, *Supplemental Income and Loss.* You might be able to claim an item on Schedule C or C-EZ as a *Business Expense* rather than on Schedule A as a *Miscellaneous Deduction.* This might "save" all or part of the deduction from being hit by the 2% floor on miscellaneous deductions. Or, you might be able to claim the item as a rental expense on page 1 of Schedule E or on page 2 as an expense related to a partnership where your share of income is subject to self-employment tax. Again, all or part of the deduction would be "saved." Furthermore, if it is claimed on page 2, it could further reduce self-employment taxes.

For example, suppose an employee earns extra income from his own consulting business. Certain items such as books, periodicals, professional dues, etc., may be reasonably attributed to either his regular job or his consulting business. By claiming these items as a business expense on Schedule C or Schedule C-EZ instead of as a job-related expense on Schedule A, the 2% of AGI floor is sidestepped. This will lower taxes, including self-employment taxes, unless the total of other miscellaneous deductions already exceeds the 2% of AGI floor. (In that case, further miscellaneous deductions will have the same tax-lowering effect as any other deduction.)

To illustrate, suppose an individual's adjusted gross income is $50,000 and he has miscellaneous deductions totaling $1,500. After subtracting 2% of adjusted gross income (2% × $50,000 = $1,000), his deduction on Schedule A is $1,500 – $1,000 = $500. If he has an additional expense of $100 for, say, dues to a professional society, his miscellaneous expenses would total $1,600 instead of $1,500 and his deduction would be equal to $1,600 – $1,000 = $600. Thus, the extra $100 expense would lower taxable income by an extra $100 ($600 – $500), the same as any other deduction.

However, if he had no other miscellaneous deductions, claiming the $100 as a miscellaneous deduction would do him no good. The 2% of AGI floor would just reduce the amount to $0. In such a case, claiming the $100 on Schedule C, Schedule C-EZ, or Schedule E, rather than on Schedule A, would save the deduction.

SECTION 2:
EMPLOYMENT RELATED EXPENSES

The following employment-related expenses are deductible as *miscellaneous deductions:*

Travel Expenses [see Chapter 21]

Auto Expenses [see Chapter 10]

Educational Expenses [see Chapter 23]

Entertainment Expenses [see Chapter 24]

Home Office [see Chapter 3]

Research Expenses [see Chapter 29]

Books, Supplies, & Equipment [see Chapter 2]

Job-Hunting Expenses. These expenses are deductible whether or not you are successful in obtaining a job. However, you must be looking for a job in your same profession, not a different one. An IRS ruling indicates that a part-time teaching position is sufficient to establish membership in a profession. The ruling permitted an attorney who lectured part-time at a law school to deduct the cost of looking for a full-time teaching position. [Rev. Rul. 78-93]

Deductible expenses include employment agency fees, travel expenses, resume typing costs, job counseling fees, newspapers or other publications to check want ads, etc. Also, don't overlook entertainment expenses incurred in your hunt for a job. For example, taking a friend to lunch for the purpose of getting him to help you obtain a job where he works would be deductible, subject to the 50%-Rule described in the *Entertainment* chapter.

Required Physical. You may deduct the cost of a physical examination or TB test which was required by your school. These may be deducted as a business expense if you wish to avoid subjecting them to the 7.5% floor on medical deductions [see the *Medical Expenses* chapter].

Payment of Substitute. If your school requires you to pay a substitute teacher when you are absent, you may deduct this expense as a *Miscellaneous Deduction*. [Rev. Rul. 76-286]

Dues to Professional Organizations or Teachers' Unions. Agency shop fees required of a nonmember in lieu of union dues are also deductible.

Extracurricular Activities. Do you travel on school business, coach a school athletic team, sponsor a school organization, visit students' homes, lead student tours, etc.? You can deduct expenses connected with these activities if they are a legitimate part of your profession.

Preparing Master's Thesis or Doctoral Dissertation. You may deduct expenses for such things as typing, research, tuition, clerical help, etc., which are connected with writing a thesis or dissertation. However, you must qualify under the rules described in the *Expenses of Attending School* chapter.

Telephone Expenses. You can deduct the cost of business-related long distance calls made from your home telephone. You can no longer deduct any portion of the basic monthly service charge for your principal residential telephone [see the *Books, Supplies, & Equipment* chapter]. However, if you have a separate line that is used 100% for business, you may deduct the basic monthly charge for this second telephone number.

SECTION 3: OTHER MISCELLANEOUS DEDUCTIONS

In addition to the employment-related expenses discussed in the preceding section, the following items can be claimed as miscellaneous deductions:

Investment Expenses. You can deduct the costs associated with managing your investments. These include safe deposit boxes to store investments, burglar alarms to protect investment items, telephone calls, miscellaneous supplies, investment fees (but not bank fees charged for the privilege of writing checks even on interest-bearing accounts), etc. It also includes travel associated with managing your investments — e.g. to stock brokers for advice, to manage rental property, to place items in your safe deposit box, etc.

Postage. Don't forget to put down a few dollars for the cost of postage connected with your job, investment activities, tax form filing, etc. Even Jimmy Carter didn't overlook this deduction when he was President. His tax return included a $15.53 deduction for the cost of mailing tax records between Georgia and the White House.

Tax Guide. You may deduct the cost of this book and any other book or professional service which aids you in the preparation of your tax return or in tax planning for the future.

If you are reporting self-employment income on Schedule C or Schedule C-EZ, an appropriate portion of the cost of tax aids can be deducted on Schedule C or Schedule C-EZ [Rev. Rul. 92-29, I.R.B. 1992-16, reversing IRS Private Letter Ruling 9126014]. For example, if you use a $39 tax guide 60% for preparing items reported on Schedule C or Schedule C-EZ, you deduct 60% × $39 = $23 on Schedule C or Schedule C-EZ. The remaining $16 could be deducted as an itemized deduction on Schedule A. [The advantage of claiming items on Schedule C or Schedule C-EZ rather than on Schedule A is discussed at the end of Section 1.] Of course, there's no objective way to determine precisely how you have used a tax guide, so you can make any reasonable allocation you feel is justified.

A similar policy applies to those who use Schedule E for reporting rental income and royalties. A portion of the cost of tax guides or services attributable to the preparation of Schedule E can be deducted on Schedule E.

Legal Expenses are deductible to the extent they are connected with income-producing investment activities or tax advice. Your lawyer should show a breakdown on his bill indicating the amount of his fees that can be properly claimed as a miscellaneous deduction. (Legal expenses connected with a self-employment business activity are deducted on Schedule C or Schedule C-EZ.)

Periodicals. You may deduct magazines, newspapers, etc., connected with your income-producing investment activities. Such publications might include *The Wall Street Journal, Barrons, Forbes Magazine,* etc. For information on how to handle subscription fees for periods longer than one year, see the *Books, Supplies & Equipment* chapter.

IRA & Self-Employed Plan Fees. You may have an IRA or self-employed plan which levies a setup fee or annual maintenance fee. Such a fee can be claimed as a miscellaneous deduction if separately itemized and paid from your personal bank account (rather than paid out of the IRA or Self-Employed Plan). On the other hand, brokerage fees for buying and selling securities in the IRA or self-employed plan are not deductible.

Appraisal fees to value a deductible charitable donation or casualty loss may be deducted.

Items Exempted from 2% of AGI Floor

There are a few special-purpose items which the law specifies to be miscellaneous deductions **not** subject to the 2% of AGI subtraction. These include:

Impairment-related work expenses incurred by a handicapped individual in order to be able to work. This would include such items as special tools and attendant care services at work.

Deductible gambling losses up to the amount of gambling winnings that are included in taxable income.

Jury duty pay which you are required to turn over to your employer because you are receiving a salary while serving as a juror. Unlike the preceding 3 items which are claimed as miscellaneous deductions on line 27 of Schedule A, this jury duty pay is claimed as an *adjustment* to *income* on line 32 of Form 1040. You write *"jury pay"* on the dotted line next to line 32.

Deductions connected with certain specialized investment activities — namely, the expenses of short sales, deductions for amortizable premiums on bonds you own, deductions for an unrecovered investment in a terminated annuity, and deductions that arise under the *"claim of right"* doctrine when you return funds that were received erroneously in a prior year.

Bad Debts

If you have loaned money but were never paid back, you may be allowed a *bad debt* deduction, provided two basic conditions are satisfied.

First, the loan must constitute a valid legally enforceable obligation to pay a fixed determinable sum of money (not property). And second, the debt must have become worthless during the year for which you claim the bad debt deduction.

To show that the loan meets the first requirement of being a valid debt, you should have a note or other written evidence of the debt. This is particularly important in the case of loans to relatives or friends, where you may have to convince the IRS that the money you have is a *loan* rather than a *gift*. One way to do this is to use a standard promissory note form obtainable from your local stationery store. Or, a simple IOU might do. The IOU could say, for example, *"I promise to repay to Lender upon demand the sum of $5,000, together with interest at an annual rate of 10%."*

To establish that the debt has become worthless, you need evidence that you are unable to collect the amounts due you. You should send correspondence asking for payment and keep records of any telephone calls and bounced checks. A return letter from the borrower stating that he can't pay should be obtained, if possible. This should all be done within a single calendar year so you can pinpoint that year as the one in which the debt became worthless.

It is not just a loan between individuals that can give rise to a bad debt. Any type of loan qualifies, as long as a valid debtor-creditor relationship is created.

Example

You contract to have a new roof put on your house and place a $1,000 deposit for the work. Before any work is done, the roofer goes bankrupt and cannot work on your house or return the deposit.

You claim $1,000 as a bad debt deduction. When you paid the $1,000 in return for a promise to work on your roof, a valid debtor-creditor relationship was created. And the bankruptcy pinpointed the time when the debt became worthless.

The discussion here concerns non-business bad debts arising from your own personal activities. If a bad debt arises from a trade or business of yours, it falls into the *business bad debt* category and can offset other ordinary income.

A non-business bad debt is treated the same as a short-term capital loss and is claimed in Part 1 of Schedule D with the bad debt amount being listed in Column f as though it were a short-term capital loss. Thus, in the absence of other capital gains or losses, the deduction for a non-business bad debt would be limited to $3,000, with any remainder carried over to future years. This limitation doesn't apply to business bad debts, which are claimed on Schedule C or Schedule C-EZ.

23

Expenses of Attending School

The law provides several options for deducting or crediting the expenses of attending school. This chapter covers not only the circumstances under which the cost of education can be deducted or credited against tax, but also special rules for the creation of tax-deferred or tax-free savings accounts that may be used for the education expenses of the taxpayer of his or her family.

SECTION 1:
PAYMENT PLANS FOR COVERING COLLEGE EXPENSES

Educational Reimbursements Received from Employer

Some employers have a plan under which employees are reimbursed for the cost of undergraduate courses which they take. As long as the plan meets certain non-discrimination rules, reimbursements for educational expenses are tax-free, whether or not the education is job-related. There is a ceiling of $5,250 per year on the amount of tax-free educational benefits an employee can receive. For 2001, graduate courses do not qualify unless taken by someone in an undergraduate program. For 2002 and later years, graduate courses qualify.

The above restrictions do not apply to educational expenses which the employee could have deducted (according to the rules described in this chapter) had he paid the expenses himself. Also, these restrictions do not generally apply to graduate assistants who receive tax-free aid under a qualified educational reimbursement plan [see Section 2 of the *Tax-Free Grants* chapter], nor do they apply to non-discriminatory tuition remission plans for faculty dependents.

Tuition Plans for College Faculty Family Members

Many universities and colleges have plans under which faculty family members receive free college tuition. The value of this fringe benefit is exempt from tax if it is generally applied to all employees — not restricted just to faculty members.

However, tuition remission will be considered a tax-free fringe benefit only for education below the graduate level. Tuition remission at the graduate level can still qualify for tax-free treatment, though, if it falls under the usual fellowship or scholarship rules [see the *Tax-Free Grants* chapter].

417

Tax-free treatment applies to reciprocal agreements between colleges providing free tuition to children of faculty members attending any of the colleges.

Don't Reduce the College Aid Your Child Is Entitled to Receive

Parents often make mistakes in qualifying their children for college financial aid. Generally, you will apply for such aid by filling out a financial aid form supplied to you by the college. You will be required to list your assets and your income for the year preceding the one your child enters college.

When computing the amount of aid (in the form of loans and grants) your child needs, it is generally assumed the child will contribute each year about 35% of his assets and up to 70% of the income he earned the previous year. Contributions from parents are calculated at lower percentages than for the child's, typically 5% – 12% of assets and 25% – 50% of pretax income.

The above figures suggest several things. First, it is sometimes unwise for a parent to transfer college funds into a child's name. For example, if a parent gives a child $1,000, the child will be expected to contribute $350 of this amount towards the next year's tuition. If the parent keeps the $1,000 himself, the required contribution would be $50 – $120 instead.

Second, care should be taken that assets or income in the year preceding college do not appear unrepresentatively large. In this connection, here are some things to look out for.

1. Don't create unnecessary capital gains. If you have stocks, bonds, etc., which have substantially risen in value, be careful which year you sell them. The year before your child enters college is the critical one. If you create the capital gain in this year, it will reduce the financial aid your child will receive. You will be better off selling the assets in the year in which your child enters the junior year of high school than in the next year.

2. Don't reduce contributions to or take money out of pension programs such as IRAs, self-employed plans, tax-sheltered annuities, deferred compensation plans, etc., in anticipation of college costs. Money in such plans is intended to support you during retirement and is not expected to be used for your child's education. Thus, this money will reduce financial aid if withdrawn from the pension program and considered as just a monetary asset, but will not reduce financial aid if left untouched. Note that money withdrawn early from a pension program may also be subject to extra penalty taxes [see the *Tax-Sheltered Plans* chapter].

3. Consolidate consumer loans with a home-equity loan. As discussed in the *Interest* chapter, home-equity loans produce deductible interest and are usually lower in cost than non-deductible consumer loans such as auto loans or credit card loans. The astute taxpayer will be better off repaying all his consumer loans by a loan taken out on his house. This also improves the financial aid situation because colleges typically ignore consumer loans, but reduce assets by home loans.

4. Don't make unusually large gifts to your child. Let your child purchase his computer, stereo, etc., with his own funds from working, savings, etc. This will increase the amount of financial aid available, because the aid formula takes more of your child's assets than it does of yours.

Of course, a complete analysis would depend on whether the financial aid is in the form of a scholarship or a loan. Loans are not as advantageous because they have to be repaid. A tax savings obtained by shifting assets to a child might well be worth a decrease in the amount that can be borrowed, but a loss in scholarship funds would be more serious.

If a student no longer qualifies to be claimed as a dependent by his parents, this may actually prove to be an advantage. Without the parents' income being counted on the student's financial aid form, the student might qualify for additional loans and grants. This situation often arises in the case of graduate students who have some income from teaching assistantships or other sources, especially when they are age 24 or older [see Section 5 of Chapter 1].

Rules for Student Aid

The rules for computing student aid have been undergoing a significant change. Recent federal rule changes, anti-trust legislation, and new competition for top students have all altered the financial aid picture.

The most significant federal rule change is that the aid formula no longer includes the equity value of a family residence among the assets available to pay for college. This applies to federal grants and U.S. guaranteed student loans. It also applies to aid from most public institutions, which usually base their awards on the federal formula.

The situation is different for private colleges. High-cost colleges, in particular, typically use their own aid formulas.

Another difference involves divorced couples. The federal aid formula only takes into account the income of the custodial spouse and that person's new spouse if remarried. Income of divorced non-custodial parents doesn't count (although payments such as child support are taken into account). However, private schools typically take into account the incomes of both divorced parents. This often reduces the amount of aid awarded.

In the past, competing private colleges would agree to use the same formula when determining how much aid should be given. But anti-trust litigation has disrupted this practice. Now, colleges can differ widely on the amount of aid their students will receive. There are cases where a student has been offered $20,000 more aid at one college than at another nearby competing institution.

You might also be able to negotiate an increase in a college's initial offer of financial aid. This will have more likelihood of success if a larger offer is received from another institution. It might also be possible to point out where the school's financial aid formula might not fit your situation, for example when a divorced spouse refuses to make any college contributions.

The above is only a general discussion of the financial aid picture. You should check with the colleges you're interested in to obtain more precise information.

Tax-Free EE Savings Bond Tuition Plan

Congress has authorized a tax-free savings plan to provide for future college tuition payments using U.S. Series EE Savings Bonds. The way it works is this.

You purchase Savings Bonds now and hold them until a later year in which your child attends college. You then cash in the bonds and use the money to pay tuition and required fees. All interest earned on the bonds is excluded from federal and state taxation. No tax is paid during the years the bonds are accumulating income, nor in the year of redemption.

The rules governing newly purchased U.S. EE Savings Bonds have been changed. These bonds now earn interest equal to 90% of the yield on 5-year Treasury Securities — based on the average of the yield for the preceding six months. Each May and November, the yield is recalculated and applied to the following 6-month period. (Further details on U.S. Savings Bonds are contained in Section 3 of the *Investing Your Money* chapter.)

If you purchase these bonds with the intent of making tuition payments, but your child (heaven forbid) decides not to go to college, you haven't made a big mistake. You can still cash in the bonds, but will have to pay tax on the accumulated interest in the year the bonds are redeemed. However, U.S. Savings Bonds are still exempt from state and local income tax, no matter how the proceeds are used.

To qualify for the exclusion, the purchaser must be at least age 24 at the time of purchase. Bonds purchased by a child or purchased by a parent and later transferred to the child are not eligible. Also, the bonds must actually be purchased — rollovers of Series E Bonds into Series EE Bonds do not qualify.

Under this program, the bonds must be used to pay for tuition (including fees) of the purchaser, his spouse, or his dependents. Thus, bonds purchased by a grandparent (or other relative) will generally be ineligible for the exclusion. To take advantage of the exclusion, a grandparent would have to give the money to the parent so he could purchase the bonds in his name. Married couples must file a joint tax return in the year the bonds are redeemed in order to claim the exclusion.

The interest excluded from tax in the year the bonds are redeemed cannot exceed the cost of tuition (including fees), reduced by any scholarships, fellowships, employer-provided assistance, or any other tuition reduction amounts. The tuition must be for an accredited college, university, junior college, or other qualified post-secondary school. Expenses for other education-related costs such as room, board, or books do not qualify. Also excluded is tuition for courses on sports, games, or hobbies, unless the courses are required as part of a degree or certificate granting program.

If the amount of tuition paid during a year equals or exceeds the amount of bonds redeemed that year, all the interest is excluded from tax.

Example 1

Frank pays $6,000 in 2001 to purchase U.S. EE Savings bonds. In a later year, he redeems the bonds for $10,000. (The $10,000 redemption includes the original $6,000 purchase price plus $4,000 in interest.) That same year, he pays $12,000 in college tuition for his child. Because the $12,000 in tuition exceeds the $10,000 in bond redemptions, the entire $4,000 in interest is excluded from tax.

If the amount of tuition and fees is less than the amount of bonds redeemed that year, only a fraction of the interest is excluded from tax. This is the case even if the tuition and fees exceed the interest earned on the bonds. The reason for this is that the fraction is computed by dividing the tuition and fees by the total amount redeemed. This latter amount includes both interest and principal.

> ### Example 2
> *Same as Example 1, except that the tuition is only $8,000 instead of $12,000. Because this $8,000 in tuition is less than the total redemption amount of $10,000, only $8,000/$10,000 = 80% of the interest is excludible. Thus, Jones excludes 80% x $4,000 = $3,200 of the interest from tax. The remaining $4,000 – $3,200 = $800 is taxable.*

If a Hope Tax Credit or Lifetime Learning Credit is claimed for a student's expenses, a special restriction applies. These expenses reduce the amount of tuition and fees which can be covered by U.S. Bond redemptions on a tax-free basis.

Income Limitation

The full benefits described above are available only to those whose *Modified Adjusted Gross Income* does not exceed $55,750 for single persons or $83,650 for married couples filing a joint return. *Modified Adjusted Gross Income* for these purposes is obtained from adjusted gross income by adding in the following items:

1. Deductible IRA contributions

2. Foreign income excluded from tax

3. The partial exclusion for social security benefits received

4. Adjustments to limitations of passive losses and credits

5. Interest on EE bonds excluded from tax to pay for qualified college tuition and fees.

The $55,750 and $83,650 limitation figures are the ones applying in 2001. Note that the limitations apply in the year bonds are redeemed to pay for educational expenses. It makes no difference what the income figures are in the year the bonds are purchased.

Phase-Out Ranges

There is a phase-out range higher than the amounts described above where a partial exclusion is permitted. The phase-out ranges are incorporated into the following tables:

	Modified Adjusted Gross Income	Eligibility
Single	Below $55,750	Full Exclusion
	$55,750–$70,750	Partial Exclusion
	Above $70,750	No Exclusion
Married filing jointly	Below $83,650	Full Exclusion
	$83,650–$113,650	Partial Exclusion
	Above $113,650	No Exclusion
Married filing separately		No Exclusion

(Above figures will be adjusted next year for inflation)

The way the partial exclusion is computed in the phase-out ranges above is illustrated by the following example.

Example 3

Same as Example 1, except that Frank had modified adjusted gross income on his joint return of $90,000 in the year the bonds are redeemed. This places him into the phase-out range in the above table. Frank's phase-out percentage is equal to ($90,000 – $83,650) ÷ $30,000 = 21%. This percentage is applied to the tax-free interest figure computed in Example 1. Thus, 21% x $4,000 = $840 of the interest is taxable. The remaining $4,000 – $840 = $3,160 is excluded from tax.

U.S. Savings Bonds can be bought at most banks and savings institutions. Also, you can get a brochure on these bonds by writing to *Office of Public Affairs, U.S. Treasury Department, Savings Bonds Division, Washington, D.C. 20226.* The brochure contains an order form for purchasing bonds directly from the government. If you want to know the current interest rate being paid, you can call toll-free 1-800-US BONDS. There is a limit of $30,000 (issue price) on the amount of U.S. Savings Bonds that can be purchased by any one individual during a single year.

Here's a little-known trick when buying a savings bond. Wait until the end of the month to make your purchase. Savings bonds earn interest from the **beginning** of the month of purchase. A savings bond purchased at the end of a month is treated exactly the same as one purchased at the beginning. While waiting until the end of the month to buy a bond, you can earn a month's extra interest in a money-market or other savings account.

Hope Tax Credit

The 1997 *Tax Reduction Act* introduced a new tax credit which covers part of the cost of the first two years of college education.

The Hope Tax Credit may be claimed for college tuition and fees of a taxpayer's family (i.e. the taxpayer, his spouse, or eligible dependents). "College" includes not just ordinary colleges and universities, but other postsecondary education including trade schools, as long as the student is pursuing a degree, certificate, or other recognized credential. For the credit to apply, the student must be enrolled at least half-time in one of the first two years of college or other postsecondary education. The enrollment must be for at least one academic period (e.g. semester, trimester, quarter) beginning during the year for which the credit is claimed.

The maximum tax credit that can be claimed for a student in any one year is $1,500 (100% of the first $1,000 of tuition expenses plus 50% of the next $1,000 of tuition expenses). This maximum credit applies when tuition and fees exceed $2,000. For expenses up to $1,000, the credit is equal to the full amount of the expenses. This credit applies to each student who qualifies. For example, if a family had two children in the first two years of college, the maximum credit would be $3,000. The credit can be claimed in no more than two years for each student.

The allowable credit is phased out beginning when the taxpayer's AGI (modified for this purpose) reaches $40,000 ($80,000 for married taxpayers filing jointly). The credit is completely eliminated when AGI reaches $50,000 ($100,000 for married taxpayers filing jointly) The credit is reduced by the extent to which AGI exceeds $40,000 ($80,000 for married filing jointly) as a percentage of the $10,000 ($20,000 for married filing jointly) phase-out range. No credit can be claimed by married persons filing a separate return.

The Hope Credit only applies to tuition and fees. It does not apply to room and board, books, equipment, student activities, etc.

In the case of a dependent child, either the parent or the child, but not both, may claim the credit in a particular year. If the parent claims the child as a dependent, tuition and fees payments are treated as if made by the parent. In this case, only the parent, not the child, can claim the Hope Credit on his or her tax return. If the parent cannot use the credit because his AGI is too high, it may pay to not claim a child as a dependent and let the child claim the credit for tuition and fees he pays on his or her tax return. (This will only work if the child has sufficient taxable income against which the credit can be offset.)

For 2001, you cannot claim the Hope Credit against tuition and fees to the extent these expenses are paid with a Pell Grant or other tax-free scholarship, a tax-free distribution from an Education IRA, or tax-free educational assistance provided by an employer. Effective for 2002, this rule is repealed with respect to Education IRA distributions.

Generally, the credit is available only for payments of tuition and fees that cover an academic period beginning in the same year as the payments are made. An exception occurs if you make payments in one year which apply to an academic period beginning in January, February, or March of the following year. For example, you can claim a tax credit for payments made in 2001 which apply to a semester beginning in the first three months of 2002 on your 2001 tax return.

Lifetime Learning Credit

Like the Hope Credit discussed above, the Lifetime Learning Credit can be claimed for tuition and fees of a taxpayer's family at a college or other postsecondary institution. However, unlike the Hope Credit, the student need not be enrolled in a degree or certificate program, i.e. taking just one course during the year qualifies. Also, there is no limit on the number of years for which a Lifetime Learning Credit can be claimed. For example, an individual could take a college course (undergraduate or graduate) each year for the rest of his life and be eligible for the credit each year.

The Lifetime Learning Credit is equal to 20% of payments made for tuition and fees not to exceed $5,000, up to a maximum credit of $1,000 per year. This $1,000 limit applies to the total tuition and fees paid for all family members. This is different from the Hope Credit, where there is a per-student limit, not an overall limit. Beginning in 2003, the credit will increase to a maximum of $2,000 (20% × $10,000).

If a taxpayer is claiming a Hope Tax Credit for a particular student, none of that student's expenses for that year can be covered by the Lifetime Learning Credit. Also, you cannot claim the Lifetime Learning Credit against tuition and fees to the extent these expenses are paid with a Pell Grant or other tax-free scholarship, a tax-free distribution from an Educational IRA, or tax-free educational assistance provided by an employer.

The same AGI limitations that apply to the Hope Credit apply to the Lifetime Learning Credit.

Either the parent or the child, but not both, may claim the credit for a child's expenses in a particular year. If the parent claims the child as a dependent, tuition and fees payments are treated as if made by the parent. In this case, only the parent, not the child, can claim the Lifetime Learning Credit on his or her tax return.

Generally, the credit is available only for payments of tuition and fees that cover an academic period beginning in the same year as the payments are made. However, you may claim the credit for payments made after July 1, 2000, if applied to an academic period beginning in January, February, or March of the next year.

For 2001, the Hope and Lifetime Learning credits may reduce the alternative minimum tax as well as the regular tax.

Education IRAs

Education IRAs, recently renamed *Coverdell Education Savings Accounts,* are yet another tax break for covering college expenses. As the name indicates, Education IRAs work like other IRAs (see Section 2 of the *Tax-Sheltered Plans* chapter). You open up a special Education IRA account with a bank, savings institution, mutual fund, etc., which accepts such accounts. As with other IRAs, amounts deposited in the account grow tax-free until distributed. No tax is paid as the earnings on the account compound year after year. However, with Education IRAs, there is no deduction when contributions are made, and distributions are tax-free only when used for appropriate college or other post-secondary expenses.

For 2001, taxpayers may deposit up to $500 per year (increasing to $2,000 in 2002) into a specially designated Education IRA account for a child who is under age 18 at the time of deposit. Parents, grandparents, other family members, friends, and a child himself may contribute to a child's Education IRA, provided that the total contributions to all such IRAs for the child during the year do not exceed the dollar threshold.

Contributions in 2001 to an Education IRA and a *Qualified State Tuition Program* on behalf of the same beneficiary are not allowed. A penalty tax will be assessed if the IRS discovers such an overlap.

There is an Adjusted Gross Income (AGI) limitation on who can contribute to an Education IRA. An individual can contribute the full $500 if his AGI on a joint return is less than $150,000. No contribution is allowed when AGI exceeds $160,000, with a partial contribution allowed for AGI between $150,000 and $160,000. On single returns, the $150,000 figure becomes $95,000, and the $160,000 figure becomes $110,000. In 2002, the maximum contribution increases from $500 to $2,000 and the phase-out range for married taxpayers filing a joint return increases from $190,000 to $220,000 (the single phase-out remains increased from $95,000 to $110,000).

Frankly, the above AGI limitations seem to have little importance because they apply only to the contributor. If the parents' income is too large to qualify, a grandparent, friend, or the child himself can make the contribution, with a compensating gift or allowance from the parents. The gift should not be made at the same time as the contribution.

There is no limit on the number of Education IRAs that can be established with a given child as beneficiary. However, the total contributions to all Education IRAs in a single beneficiary's name cannot exceed the $500 threshold per year.

There is a separate $500 limit for each child. For example, if a parent has three children, he can contribute $500 in 2001 to Education IRAs in each of their names, for a total of $1,500.

Distributions from Education IRAs

The beneficiary named in the Education IRA may withdraw funds tax-free to pay for expenses at a college, university, or other qualifying postsecondary institution. (After 2001, tax-free withdrawals may be made for elementary or secondary school expenses as well.) The expenses which qualify include tuition, fees, books, supplies, and equipment required for the enrollment or attendance at the institution. There is no minimum enrollment required to make such withdrawals. Even taking a single course would qualify.

Amounts can also be withdrawn tax-free from an Education IRA to pay for room and board, provided the student is enrolled at least half-time in a program leading to a degree or other recognized credential. The amount allowed would be the school's posted room and board charge, $1,500 per year for a student living at home, or $2,500 per year for a student living off-campus and not at home. Note that the range of items covered by an Education IRA is much greater than just the tuition and fees covered by the Hope Tax Credit or the Lifetime Learning Credit discussed earlier in this Section.

If a student receives a tax-free distribution from an Education IRA in a particular year, none of that student's expenses that year can be claimed as a basis for the Hope Credit or the Lifetime Learning Credit. However, the student may waive tax-free treatment for the distribution so that one of these tax credits can be claimed by himself or his parents. After 2001, a taxpayer may claim a Hope or Lifetime Learning Credit and exclude from income Education IRA distributions as long as the distributions are used for the same educational expenses for which a credit was claimed.

The designated beneficiary may withdraw funds from his Education IRA even if the funds are not used for his education. In this case, tax is due on the fraction of the withdrawal attributable to earnings on funds in the account. For example, if $2,000 has been contributed to the IRA, and it's now worth $5,000 because of $3,000 investment earnings, $3,000/$5,000 = 3/5 of any withdrawal is subject to ordinary income tax. In addition, a 10% penalty tax generally applies to this amount, except in the case of death or disability.

Distributions from an Education IRA may be rolled over tax-free into another Education IRA for the same beneficiary or certain family members of the beneficiary. The list of eligible family members includes the beneficiary's children and their descendants, stepchildren and their descendants, siblings and their children, parents and grandparents, stepparents, and spouses of all the foregoing.

The annual contribution limit on Education IRAs does not apply to these rollover contributions. For example, an older brother who has $3,000 left in his Education IRA after graduation from college can roll over the full $3,000 to an Education IRA for his younger sister, without paying any tax on the transfer. The institution running the IRA may simply be able to redesignate the beneficiary, without any movement of funds required.

When a beneficiary reaches age 30, any amount remaining in an Education IRA must be distributed and tax paid on the earnings portion as discussed above. However, tax can be avoided if, prior to that age, the IRA is rolled over for the benefit of another family member as described in the preceding paragraph.

Qualified Tuition Programs (Section 529 Plans)

Many states have adopted some type of *Qualified State Tuition Plan*. Under such a plan, the parents generally contribute a certain amount to a state-run plan when their child is young. Later, when the child attends a public (or in some cases private) institution in that state, part or all of his college expenses are covered by the state-run plan. Most state plans will now pay for out-of-state tuition. If the child doesn't attend college or goes to a college in a different state, there is usually a refund made of at least the original contribution; plus, in most cases, interest on the amount contributed. In this case, the state imposes a penalty on the withdrawal.

Beginning in 2002, qualified tuition programs will no longer be limited to state programs, but will include prepaid tuition programs established and maintained by eligible private institutions. One transfer between plans will be allowed every twelve months and the penalty for distributions from a plan that are not used for educational expenses will be eliminated.

When money in the plan is eventually used to pay college expenses, tax will be owed at the child's tax rate, generally 15%. (After 2001, no tax is imposed on withdrawals from a state-maintained program.) This tax is owed only on that fraction of the payout representing investment earnings rather than family contributions. However, any matching money that a state may provide under its Tuition Plan will generally be considered a tax-free scholarship (see the *Tax-Free Grants* chapter).

College expenses that the IRS permits states to cover under their tuition plans includes tuition, fees, room and board, books, supplies, and equipment required for enrollment at a college, university, or other eligible postsecondary institution. This list of permissible items does not mean a given state's plan need include anything beyond tuition benefits.

If a student uses amounts from a qualified state tuition plan to pay for college, he or his parents can still claim a Hope Credit or Lifetime Learning Credit, but not on the same amounts. However, if contributions are made to a qualified state tuition plan on behalf of a child, no contributions may be made that same year to an Education IRA in the name of that child. An individual is allowed to redeem U.S. Savings Bonds tax-free under the rules described earlier in this Section and transfer the money to a qualified state tuition plan on behalf of himself, his spouse, or a dependent.

Obviously, the above is only a sketch of qualified tuition plans and their federal tax consequences. You would need to get the particulars of any plan before making your investment decisions. Generally speaking, the plan will be a good deal if you can't earn a higher after-tax rate by investing the money yourself rather than contributing to the plan.

For example, suppose current tuition at public colleges in your state is $5,000 per year. If you can buy into a prepaid tuition plan that guarantees 4 years of college tuition for, say, $20,000, it's a good deal. To do better, you would have to earn an after-tax rate of return averaging more than the average annual inflation rate for college tuition. Considering that this inflation rate has consistently been outstripping the consumer price index inflation rate, this might be difficult to do.

The above simplified example ignores such things as any diminution in benefits if your child doesn't attend college. However, it also ignores the risk-reduction value of such a plan. The peace of mind that comes from knowing future college costs are covered is worth a lot to many persons. Also for some, prepayment of tuition provides the appropriate climate of commitment for encouraging a child in pre-college academic pursuits.

If your child doesn't attend college, some plans only refund to you the amount of your original contributions, while others add interest. Also, some plans allow the entire plan to be transferred to other family members who choose to go to college.

There is a trap in state tuition plans if you anticipate your child will qualify for financial aid. The financial aid can be significantly reduced, depending upon the tuition plan. Under some plans, the financial aid might be reduced dollar for dollar by any amounts paid under the tuition plans.

Under some plans, the amounts paid by the tuition plans might be considered assets of the child, rather than of the parent. This is detrimental because under federal aid formulas, a student is expected to contribute up to 35% of his assets toward college costs each year. Families are expected to contribute a much smaller percentage of their assets. Thus, contributing to the state tuition plan will reduce the amount of federal aid for a student whose family's financial status qualifies the student for such aid.

Baccalaureate Bonds

Instead of prepaid tuition plans, many states are offering special college tuition bonds, sometimes called *baccalaureate bonds.* These bonds are basically similar to other municipal bonds issued by state and local governments [see Section 4 of the *Investing your Money* chapter]. In particular, interest paid on the bonds is exempt from federal income tax and from state income tax in the state of issue.

However, there are generally special features of these bonds that make them tailor-made for those wishing to save for future tuition payments. First, they are *zero-coupon bonds,* which means that all interest is paid on the date of maturity, like U.S. savings bonds. For example, a parent might purchase a 15-year bond for $1,000 when his child is age 2. On the maturity date 15 years after purchase, the bond would be cashed in for, say, $3,500, depending upon the prevailing interest rate. With no tax due, the $3,500 could be used toward making tuition payments (or for some other purpose).

The second feature is that these bonds are easy to purchase directly from the state in reasonably small denominations of $1,000 or less. Ordinary municipal bonds are issued in round lots of $5,000 or more and must be purchased from a commercial broker who charges a commission at the time of purchase.

The basic interest rate on college tuition bonds is set at an appropriate market rate. However, unlike state tuition plans, there is no guarantee that the funds received at maturity will be sufficient to cover tuition. However, what gives some of these tuition bond plans an edge are extra features that they provide. The following is a list of some features to look for that appear in some of these plans.

1. **Extra Interest.** In addition to the interest based on the going market rate, some states pay extra interest when the bond proceeds are used to pay tuition. This can run from an extra interest rate of 1/2% to 4%, or more.

2. **Extra Endowment Funds.** Some states plan to set up an endowment fund to go along with their tuition bond plan. Money from the endowment fund would supplement tuition payments made from proceeds of the tuition bonds.

3. **Extra Financial Aid.** Many states have a financial aid program providing loans or grants to college students, based on a needs analysis. To avoid the savings disincentive caused by this needs analysis, some states will exclude, say, the first $25,000 in proceeds from tuition bonds, when computing how much money a family has available to go towards tuition.

4. **Indexed Interest Rate.** At least one state has considered setting the interest rate on tuition bonds each year to equal the average increase in college costs. This

would make it similar to a tuition prepayment plan, except that the student would not be restricted on which school to attend.

The best time to buy baccalaureate bonds is when they are first issued by the state. However, it still may be possible to buy bonds at a later date. Often, there is at least one brokerage house which participated in the original offering and which makes a current market in the bonds. (You may be able to get such information from your state Treasurer's Office.) However, you'll have to pay extra to cover the broker's commission, even if you are able to find the type of bond you are interested in purchasing.

It should be cautioned that some states issue baccalaureate bonds only in long-term maturities. This means you should not delay in checking out the situation in your state. For example, in a state that issues bonds with maturities of 14 years or more, you'd have to act before your child enters elementary school in order to use funds from the matured bond to pay for the freshman year of college.

New Deduction for Qualified Tuition and Related Expenses

Beginning in 2002, a new deduction for qualified tuition and related expenses is available to individuals and their dependents to attend an accredited post-secondary education institution. In 2002, the deduction is limited to $3,000 and is available only to taxpayers with adjusted gross income not exceeding $65,000 ($130,000 for joint filers). This deduction is not available if a Hope or Lifetime Learning Credit is claimed for the student.

Paying for College by Cashing in Stocks

If you are planning to cash in stocks which have gone up in value and use the money towards your child's education, there may be a better way to proceed. First, transfer the stocks into your child's name and then have your child sell the stocks himself. This will move the capital gain from your tax bracket into your child's lower bracket. This applies also to mutual fund shares which have risen in value. (However, the stocks should not be given so far in advance that they distort the child's net worth picture on financial aid forms. As discussed near the beginning of this Chapter, this could lower the amount of financial aid your child will receive.)

Example

You purchased stock for $5,000 which is now worth $15,000. If you sell the stock, you will have a capital gain of $15,000 – $5,000 = $10,000. Using the 20% capital gain rate, this will produce a tax of 20% x $10,000 = $2,000 on the sale. On the other hand, if you transfer the stock to your child, the $5,000 purchase price transfers to the child as his "basis" in the stock. When he sells stock for $15,000, he incurs the same capital gain of $10,000. But because he is likely to be in the 10% capital gains tax bracket, the tax on this gain is only 10% x $10,000 = $1,000. This represents a tax-saving of $2,000 – $1,000 = $1,000.

If you have stock that has depreciated since you purchased it, it's better to sell it yourself rather than first transferring it to your child. Because your child takes a tax basis at the depreciated value, in the event the child sells the stock for a loss, your depreciation would be lost forever.

SECTION 2:
WHEN DO EDUCATIONAL EXPENSES QUALIFY FOR DEDUCTION?

The expenses of attending school are deductible provided that certain conditions are satisfied. These conditions are designed to permit an individual to deduct schooling which aids him in his or her **current** occupation, but to rule out schooling which prepares him or her for a **new** career. For example, a teacher can deduct the cost of a summer refresher course, but a college student cannot deduct the cost of education for preparing himself for a new career.

When Are the Expenses of Attending School Deductible?

You may deduct the cost of attending school if your attendance is for any one of the following purposes:

(1) Maintaining or improving skills required in your present employment;

(2) Keeping your current employment, status, or salary; or

(3) Meeting the express requirements of your current employer.

However, there are two exceptions. Your expenses **cannot** be deducted if either:

Rule A. The courses are required in order to meet the minimum educational requirements for your employment; or

Rule B. The education would qualify you for a new trade or business. A change of duties is not considered as being a new trade or business if the new duties involve the same general work that you did previously.

You may have several purposes for attending school. If Rule A or B listed immediately above is among your reasons, you may not deduct your educational expenses.

There is one further requirement. You must be considered a current member of your profession at the time you incur the educational expenses. This does not mean you must actually be employed at the time. If you were employed prior to the education and intend to resume employment in the same general profession, your expenses may still be deductible. This is explained further in the section below entitled "Temporary v. Indefinite Absence from Profession."

Education Which Maintains or Improves Skills

If you incur expenses for education which maintains or improves your professional skills, these expenses are deductible provided they are not disqualified under either the *minimum requirements* of Rule A or the *new trade or business* of Rule B. To qualify, the education must be in subject matter related to your teaching, research, or other professional duties. For example, a German teacher would be allowed to deduct expenses for taking a course in German literature. The education in question may be day courses, refresher courses, vocational courses, research on a dissertation, or any other educational activity. In the following example, 2 physical education teachers were permitted to deduct a portion of their membership fees in racquetball clubs, because the facilities were used to improve their teaching skills.

Example

A married couple were both physical education teachers at different schools in neighboring cities. They each taught a variety of courses covering different athletic activities, including racquetball and handball.

During the year in question, they paid for memberships in 4 different facilities with racquetball courts. She learned to play racquetball at one of the facilities to which she belonged; she also attended some clinics which taught her how to play racquetball so she could teach the activity to her students.

He already knew how to play racquetball and handball, but he observed clinics in these sports and, from time to time, gave some instruction to students of his who also belonged to the facilities. The clinics were conducted by a professional and he picked up some teaching techniques for use in his classroom. He also played racquetball against handball and vice versa; he used this mixed-sport for a special education class he taught where he matched children with impaired vision (who used a racquet) against those without impaired vision (who used their hands).

The Court ruled that the above activities involved the *"maintenance or improvement of skills required in petitioners' employments as physical education teachers. We believe that the business aspect of the foregoing activities predominates over the personal pleasure or general fitness aspect of petitioners' activities at the Facilities."*

However, the Court complained that it did *"not have any information as to how much of their time at the Facilities was essentially for pleasure or for general physical or mental well-being, rather than being specially connected with their job-related activities."* As a result, it allowed a deduction of only $200, 17% of the total cost of the memberships. Had the couple presented better information on which a more favorable allocation could have been made, their deduction would have been higher. [Cohn, TC Memo 1985-480]

The example below shows just how impartial the American Judicial System can be. A college teacher who was in prison for murdering his wife took the IRS to Court. He convinced the Court that he should be able to deduct educational expenses incurred by himself and his wife, before she was murdered. And how did he get out of prison to present his case? He didn't. The Tax Court trial judge and IRS lawyers traveled to the prison so the trial could take place there.

> **Example**
> *Friend was an English teacher, working at several colleges in the Louisville area. His wife, before he murdered her, was also an English teacher. During the year in question, both he and his wife took English courses at a university.*
> *The Court allowed Friend a deduction for the educational expenses of himself and his (ex)wife. The courses they took were in the same field as their teaching assignments. Thus, they were undertaken in order to maintain and improve their respective job skills, and were deductible. Apparently, it did not matter that Friend's wife might not have lived long enough to actually make use of the education she received.* [Friend, TC Memo 1990-144]

Education which contributes to your general education but is not directly related to your professional duties does not qualify for deduction. For example, a mathematics teacher would not ordinarily be allowed a deduction for taking a course in political science. However, if there is an employment-related reason for you to take courses outside your area of expertise, your expenses can be deductible. This is illustrated by the following IRS ruling.

> **Example**
> *Because of shifting enrollments, a college encouraged its faculty members to take courses in the business economics area. In response to this encouragement, a Professor of American History took courses in the Labor and Industrial Relations Program at another institution. The IRS noted that "surveys have shown that many colleges. . .have been experiencing a decline in the number of History Majors and an increase in the number of Business-Economics Majors." Thus, his education was sufficiently related to his professional duties to qualify for deduction.* [IRS Private Letter Ruling 8030093]

Education Which Maintains Your Current Employment, Status, or Salary

You may deduct expenses for education which meets the express requirements for maintaining your employment, status, or rate of compensation, provided the education does not fall under the *minimum requirements* of Rule A or the *new trade or business* of Rule B. For example, suppose a teacher has already met the minimum requirements for employment, but the school board requires that periodic refresher courses or other education be taken to retain employment. These expenses are deductible. Similarly, educational expenses are deductible if the education is required in order to avoid demotion or other loss of status. Thus, a teacher can deduct required courses if the requirement is imposed not on the teacher's right to enter the profession (disqualified by Rule A), but on his right to continue in it.

A teacher may be required to obtain further education in order to participate in the normal increases provided by a set salary schedule or by, for example, an across-the-board cost of living increase. Expenses incurred in meeting this type of requirement are deductible.

Education Which Meets the Express Requirements of Your Employer

You may deduct expenses which meet the express requirements of your employer as long as the requirements have been imposed for a bona fide purpose. Again, the education must not fall under the *minimum requirements* of Rule A or the *new trade or business* of Rule B. The requirements must be identifiable. General encouragement alone will not constitute an express requirement. Even if your employer fails to enforce the rule, you can still normally take the deduction.

Example

From 1953 to 1958, Robertson was an Assistant Professor in the Department of Economics at the University of Nebraska. He had received an M.A. in 1948 and had all the requirements for a Ph.D. except for his doctoral dissertation. At the time he was first appointed, there was no requirement that a staff member have a Ph.D. as a requirement to the granting of tenure. However, in 1958 there was such a policy, so Robertson was told that his employment would be terminated unless he obtained a Ph.D. He took a one-year leave of absence in 1958 in order to complete his dissertation.

Ruling: *The costs incurred in returning to school to finish his dissertation were deductible. He had met the minimum requirements which were in effect at the time he was appointed and his schooling was for the purpose of maintaining his current employment.* [Robertson, 37 TC 1153]

SECTION 3:
WHEN ARE DEDUCTIONS DISALLOWED
UNDER RULE A?

Rule A states that you cannot deduct education which is required in order to meet the minimum requirements for employment in a new job [see the first page of this Chapter]. You may accept a job for which you do not meet the minimum educational qualifications, but you are hired temporarily or provisionally pending fulfillment of those requirements. If you then take courses in order to meet these qualifications (even though you may also qualify under (1), (2), or (3) on the first page of this Chapter), you may not deduct your expenses. However, if you meet the minimum educational requirements that are in effect when you are first employed in a job, and those qualifications are raised later, you may deduct expenses for courses taken to satisfy the new minimum qualifications.

What Are Minimum Educational Requirements?

The IRS has issued the following regulation defining what is meant by minimum educational requirements for teachers.

"The minimum educational requirements for qualification of a particular individual in a position in an educational institution is the minimum level of education (in terms of aggregate college hours or degree) which under the applicable laws or regulations in effect at the time this individual is first employed in such position, is normally required of an individual initially being employed in such a position. If there are no normal requirements as to the minimum level of education required for a position in an educational institution, then an individual in such a position shall be considered to have met the minimum educational requirements for qualification in that position when he becomes a member of the faculty of the educational institution. The determination of whether an individual is a member of the faculty of an educational institution must be made on the basis of the particular practices of the institution. However an individual will ordinarily be considered to be a member of the faculty of an institution if (a) he has tenure or his years of service are being counted toward obtaining tenure; (b) the institution is making contributions to a retirement plan (other than Social Security or a similar program) in respect of his employment; or (c) he has a vote in faculty affairs." [Reg. Sec. 1.162-5(b) (2)(ii)]

Example 1

An individual obtained employment in August 1981 as a Professor of Physical Education. At the time, he was enrolled in a doctorate program at a university in a different location. He completed his dissertation about a year later, obtaining his Ph.D. degree in December 1982. A contingency clause was written into his second year contract to complete the doctorate. However when he was employed, he had already met the minimum requirements for his position as a regular faculty member.

The IRS ruled that he could deduct all his expenses in working toward his doctorate after he became employed. This included tuition as well as *"the reasonable expenses of editing, typing, photocopying, telephone, photography, graphics, mailing, supplies and any reasonable expenses that were incurred as incident to the preparation of [his] doctoral dissertation to obtain [his] graduate doctoral degree." He was also permitted to deduct his travel expenses, including meals and lodging, for a 2^1/2-month trip back to the institution where he was enrolled in the doctorate program. The trip was needed to enable him to finish some experimental animal work and to use some specialized equipment which was located there.* [IRS Private Letter Ruling 8340025]

Example 2

Wilkins, who holds a master's degree, obtains temporary employment as an instructor at a university. He undertakes graduate courses as a candidate for a doctoral degree. He may become a regular faculty member only if he obtains a doctoral degree. He can continue his position as instructor only as long as he shows satisfactory progress towards obtaining that degree.

The graduate courses Wilkins takes are necessary to meet the minimum educational requirements for qualification in his trade or business. Thus, the expenditures for these courses are not deductible.

Example 3

Jungreis worked for the University of Minnesota on a part-time basis as a graduate teaching assistant in the zoology department. Because he then had only a bachelor of science degree, he was not qualified for a position as a regular faculty member of the University. He was enrolled as a student in the graduate school and was a candidate for a Doctor of Philosophy degree in zoology which was required to qualify him as a regular full-time faculty member. The University required Jungreis to be enrolled as a graduate student before he could be eligible for an appointment as a graduate teaching assistant.

While serving under an appointment as a graduate teaching assistant, he was required to be making satisfactory progress toward a graduate degree to maintain his appointment. The employment as a graduate teaching assistant was a temporary position which terminated upon receipt of the Ph.D.

Jungreis claimed he was entitled to deduct expenses relating to his graduate school education because they were required for him in order to maintain his position as a teaching assistant. He claimed he had already met the minimum requirements, i.e., a bachelor's degree, which were required of him in his current position.

The Tax Court disallowed his deduction. It ruled that the position at an educational institution for which an individual must meet the minimum educational requirements before he can get a deduction is a permanent position on the faculty of the institution. In this case, the minimum education required for permanent employment in the University's zoology department is a Ph.D. Jungreis was enrolled in a program to meet those minimum requirements; hence his expenses were not deductible. [Jungreis, 55 TC 581]

Example 4

Damm, after working as a registered civil engineer for 5 years, enrolled in graduate school at a leading California university. He obtained his master's degree and continued as a student in the Ph.D. program for an additional year. He then left school and obtained a job as a lecturer in Engineering at a state college. After several years of full-time teaching, he returned to the university for 2 years and completed his Ph.D. studies. He then returned to teaching, first at the state college for a year and then at a university in the midwest.

When Damm deducted his education expenses for the period he was completing his Ph.D. studies, the IRS objected. It referred back to the Jungreis decision [Example 3], claiming that Damm had not met the minimum requirements for the position of permanent college faculty member, namely the Ph.D. degree.

But the Court did not agree with the IRS, permitting the deduction to stand. It contrasted Damm's situation with that of Jungreis as follows:

> *"Jungreis was a teaching assistant, he taught part time, his salary was less than that of the regular faculty members, his work was different from that of regular faculty members, his service did not count toward tenure, and from the outset he could not hold his job for any period unless for that period he was enrolled as a student and making satisfactory progress toward a graduate degree. We concluded that Jungreis was essentially an apprentice, rather than a teacher. Damm, by contrast, was a full-time teacher doing what regular faculty members did in the classroom, he was paid the same as regular faculty members, up to two years of his service could count toward tenure, and his job did not depend on a condition precedent."*

The Court also pointed out that the state college

> *"did not normally require a doctorate degree as a minimum level of education for lecturers or for faculty members in general. We concluded that Damm, who had already been awarded the baccalaureate degree and the master's degree, met the minimum educational requirements for lecturers and for faculty members in general at [the state college]. From the foregoing, we concluded that Damm's educational expenses are not rendered nondeductible by the minimum educational expenses test."* [Damm, TC Memo 1981-203]

SECTION 4:
WHEN ARE DEDUCTIONS DISALLOWED UNDER RULE B?

Rule B states that you may not deduct expenses for education which will qualify you for a new trade or business. In the case of an employee, a change of duties does not constitute a new trade or business if the new duties involve the same type of work that he was formerly doing. Furthermore, all teaching and related duties are considered to involve the same general type of work. For example, none of the following changes are considered to constitute a new trade or business:

a. *change from elementary to secondary classroom teacher*

b. *change from teaching one subject to teaching another*

c. *change from teaching to guidance counselor*

d. *change from teacher to principal*

Note that the above does not explicitly state that you can deduct the expenses for education required to make the above changes. It only states that these education expenses are not automatically excluded from being deductible. However, the following examples taken from government rulings and regulations indicate that expenses undertaken to meet the requirements for such changes are generally deductible.

Example 1

Green, who had a master's degree, was an Education Professor at a college. He became eligible for appointment as President of a junior college within the same educational system. The next year, the requirement for this position was raised from a master's degree to a doctorate. In order to be retained on the eligibility list, Green earned a doctorate in education. Note that prior to getting the additional education, Green had met the minimum educational requirements. His appointment as President of a junior college would not be a new trade or business, but merely a change of duties in his accustomed type of work. Hence, his expenses in obtaining a doctorate were deductible. [Rev. Rul. 68-580]

Example 2

Schwerm was employed as a discussion leader in a local college's adult education program. Discussion topics included family relationships, self-awareness, and coping with problems such as stress, retirement, etc. She enrolled in a graduate program for a master's degree in Educational Psychology, thinking this course of study would aid her in becoming a better discussion leader. After obtaining her master's degree, she entered an internship program to train her to become a school counselor.

The Court ruled that she could deduct the expenses of both the master's degree program and the internship program. Even though the internship program was qualifying her for the new position of school counselor, the Court ruled that her positions as discussion leader and school counselor were part of the same trade or business. (In fact, she would perform similar guidance services in both these positions.) [Schwerm, TC Memo 1986-16]

Note that the above examples show situations in which Rule B did not apply. For teachers, the only case where Rule B is likely to apply is if courses taken were in a completely different field.

Law School Expenses

Rule B eliminates a deduction for education which **qualifies** you for a new trade or profession. It does not matter if you actually make the switch into the new trade or profession. As long as the education enables you to make the switch, a deduction is ruled out. This is best illustrated by a number of cases involving individuals attempting to deduct the expenses of attending law school. In several of these cases, the individual involved did not intend to become a lawyer, but rather to use the law school education in his current profession. But because the education **qualified** him for the new profession of being a lawyer, Rule B prevented a deduction.

One case involved an insurance adjuster who intended to use the legal training in his same line of work [Gates, TC Memo 1977-236]. Another case involved a college teacher of mathematics who intended to switch to teaching law, a change of duties which usually qualifies for deduction [Bouchard, TC Memo 1977-273]. A third case involved someone who performed quasi-legal activities for a corporation prior to and after law school [McDermott, TC Memo 1977-31]. A fourth case concerned a contracts manager who never took the bar examination and used his law school only to aid in legal negotiations connected with his job [Rehe, TC Memo 1980-316]. A fifth case concerned an Associate Professor of Communication who was studying law because his primary teaching responsibility was a course on the legal aspects of mass communication [IRS Private Letter Ruling 8432028]. And a sixth case involved a Philosophy Professor who studied law while on sabbatical [Watkins, TC Memo 1990-206].

In all of the above cases, it was ruled that the profession of being a lawyer was different than the employment they had before or during their law school attendance. Because their law degree *qualified* them for this new profession, they were not permitted to deduct their educational expenses whether or not they actually entered the new profession.

Where an individual already holds a law degree and is a member of the bar, education consisting of a one-year advanced graduate program in law in the area of his specialty is deductible. [IRS Private Letter Ruling 9112003]

SECTION 5:
TEMPORARY VS. INDEFINITE ABSENCE
FROM PROFESSION

An additional requirement for deductibility is that the education be undertaken when you are a current member of your profession. If you are actively teaching, on vacation, or on a temporary leave of absence, you are considered to be a current member of the teaching profession. But if you leave your profession for an **indefinite period** of time, you may not deduct expenses related to that profession. This is the case even if you return to the profession at a later date.

If you temporarily leave your profession for a **fixed period** of time to take courses that maintain or improve your skills, these expenses are eligible for deduction. It is not necessary that you be on official leave of absence or even that you plan to return to the same job. However, you must plan to resume employment in the same field you left.

The IRS had been following the general policy of considering any period exceeding one year as an indefinite period of time. Thus, education requiring an absence from work for more than a year was considered non-deductible. However, the Tax Court has thrown out this one-year policy as being arbitrary and unjustified. In several court cases, they have permitted a deduction for full-time study lasting 2 or 3 years. These cases are discussed below.

Deduction for Graduate School Education

The court cases permitting a deduction for extended periods of education all involved graduate students returning to school after a period of employment. The key to qualifying for deduction was that their education was sufficiently related to their profession. The extended length of time required to complete the education was no barrier.

Example 1

Mrs. H. held a master's degree in the field of nursing education. She held positions first as an Assistant Professor at a community college and then as a consultant to an educational organization. Mrs. H. left her employment to undertake a 3-year doctoral program in nursing education. When she left her job, she did not have any specific intent to return. However, after receiving her doctoral degree, she did in fact return to work for the same educational organization that she had worked for earlier.

The IRS did not dispute that the education was for the purpose of improving her skills as a nursing educator. However, it maintained that her 3-year absence from the profession ruled out a deduction.

The Court did not agree with the IRS. It found nothing in the law which placed "an arbitrary limitation on the self-improvement process." Rather, "the 3-year period of study was an appropriate period in which to accomplish her educational objective." [Hitt, TC Memo 1978-66]

Example 2

Over a period of 10 years, Mr. P. was employed by various public school systems in New England. He served as school teacher, curriculum coordinator, and finally principal of an elementary school.

Mr. P. resigned his position as principal and undertook full-time graduate studies in the field of educational administration. He received his Ph.D. three years later. Upon graduation, he wrote letters to various universities, colleges, and school systems seeking employment in a teaching or administrative capacity. However, he met with little success. In spite of continuing his job-seeking efforts for a number of years, he was unable to secure employment except for a few minor part-time positions. In fact, at the time his case came to trial, he was still unemployed.

Mr. P. claimed a deduction for the cost of his schooling. However, the IRS challenged the deduction, reasoning that his extended absence from work meant he was not a member of his profession at the time of his education.

However, the Court upheld the deduction. His graduate studies were of definite as opposed to indefinite duration. Moreover, they were directly related to his profession as an educator and educational administrator. The fact that he was unable to obtain a regular job upon graduation was not held against him. To establish that he continued being a member of his profession, it sufficed that he actively pursue employment in that profession, not that he actually obtain employment. [Picknally, TC Memo 1977-321]

Example 3

For several years, Wyatt was a teacher of secretarial skills in a secondary school in Kansas. From 1963 to 1967, she was employed as a secretary, working for various employers. In March 1967, she accepted an offer to begin teaching again in August 1967. Even though she still had a valid teaching certificate, she took graduate school courses in education in the spring and summer of 1967 preparatory to her resumption of teaching.

> The Court held that Wyatt left the teaching profession in 1963 for an indefinite period. At the time she incurred the expenses for her education, she was not engaged in the profession of teaching even though she had accepted a teaching position to begin later. Her expenses were not deductible because they did not improve her skills in the profession she was engaged in at the time she took the courses. [Wyatt, 56 TC 517]

If you leave your profession temporarily, you should still list that profession on the *Occupation* line on your tax form. A court decision denied an education deduction to a registered nurse who went back to school after a long period of time during which she was unemployed. The denial was based on the Court's conclusion that she was no longer in the nursing profession when she undertook the education. It stated that the fact she did not consider herself a nurse at the time was "*demonstrated by the fact that she listed her occupation on her federal income tax returns for those years to be that of a student and housewife.*" [Cannon, TC Memo 1980-224]

However, you should take care how you fill out the *occupation* line at the top of Form 2106 so that it is clear that you are claiming an *educational deduction* rather than a *job-related travel deduction* [see Example 13 in Section 4 of the *Travel* chapter for details].

Court Gives Green Light to Deducting MBA Expenses

The following court case applies to those pursuing advanced degrees in business schools. Often these students have returned to school after a stint in the working world. As this court case shows, the expenses of obtaining education in these circumstances will generally be deductible.

Example 4
Sherman was a civilian employee with the military. He held a managerial job, being in charge of a regional "Plans and Programs Office." He left this employment after two years to attend Harvard University as a candidate for a master's degree in business administration (MBA). After a two-year period, he received his degree and became Director of Planning and Research in a private corporation.
    As in the previous two examples, the IRS asserted first that he had not established any "trade or business" in which he was improving his skills by attending school. And second, his absence from employment beyond one year automatically excluded his deduction in any event.
    Once again, the Court sided with the taxpayer against the IRS. Sherman had established himself in a trade or business, namely "*the business of being an employee who was an administrator and planner.*" And the MBA program improved his skills in this "business." As in Examples 1 and 2, the Court rejected the one-year limitation placed by the IRS on deductible education. The 2-year program was of fixed duration and entirely reasonable for the purpose of obtaining an MBA degree.
[Sherman, TC Memo 1977-301]

Finally, in a private letter ruling, the IRS itself allowed an education deduction for schooling extending more than one year. In this ruling, an administrator planned a leave of absence from his job extending 2 academic years in order to pursue a master's degree. He was paid his full salary while at school, but received no reimbursements for tuition, fees, or other educational costs. Despite the extended term of the schooling, the IRS ruled that the taxpayer could deduct his educational expenses on his tax returns. [IRS Private Letter Ruling 8813049]

SECTION 6:
WHICH EXPENSES ARE DEDUCTIBLE?

If your education qualifies for deduction, you may deduct tuition, fees, books, supplies, photocopying, and other related costs (e.g., required physical examination, tutor's fees, etc.). If your education includes writing a thesis or dissertation, you may deduct associated costs such as typing, research expenses, etc.

Transportation Expenses To and From School

You may deduct transportation expenses for qualified educational activities that you incur in going between:

1. the general area of your principal place of employment and a school located **beyond the general area;** or

2. your place of employment and a school **within the same general area.** However, if you return home before going to school, you may deduct the expense in going from home to school only to the extent it does not exceed the transportation expense you would have incurred had you gone from work to school.

Example
You live and work in Newark, New Jersey, and go to New York City three times a week to attend night classes at a university there. If your educational expenses are deductible, you may deduct your round trip transportation expenses, including tolls and parking fees.

Example
You attend night classes at a college located in the same city as your job. (Assume that you can deduct your educational expenses.) You go directly to the college after work. You may deduct the cost of going from your job to the college.

You may not deduct the cost of local transportation between your residence and school on a non-working day. This expense is in the nature of a personal commuting expense.

You cannot deduct transportation between your residence and school during a period of unemployment. This is illustrated by the following court case.

Court Case

An unemployed teacher took college courses, using local transportation to travel the 30 miles between her home and the college. She deducted $1,178 for educational expenses, including $564 for transportation. The IRS allowed the deduction to the extent it covered tuition, fees, and books, but disallowed the $564 travel costs on the grounds they were personal commuting costs.

The Tax Court agreed with the IRS. Because she was unemployed, her travel did not fall into the deductible category described in the preceding example. Also, her schooling was not temporary employment, so that the examples in Section 3 of the *Travel* chapter were inapplicable. The Court simply considered her expenses to serve her personal convenience by allowing her to reside at some distance from her school. Note also that because her education did not require her to be away from home overnight, the provisions of the next subsection do not apply. [Zimmerman 71 TC 367]

Travel Expenses While Away from Home Overnight

Perhaps you attend school out of town to obtain education that qualifies for deduction. In this case, you are governed by the rules for deducting travel expenses as described in the *Travel* chapter. The IRS describes as follows the general situation concerning travel away from home overnight to obtain education:

"If an individual travels away from home primarily to obtain education the expenses of which are deductible (as an education expense) his expenditures for travel, meals, and lodging while away from home are deductible. However, if as an incident of such trip the individual engages in some personal activity such as sightseeing, social visiting, or entertaining, or other recreation, the portion of the expenses attributable to such personal activity constitutes nondeductible personal or living expenses and is not allowable as a deduction. If the individual's travel away from home is primarily personal, the individual's expenditures for travel, meals and lodging (other than meals and lodging during the time spent in participating in deductible educational pursuits) are not deductible. Whether a particular trip is primarily personal or primarily to obtain education the expenses of which are deductible under this section depends upon all the facts and circumstances of each case. An important factor to be taken into consideration in making the determination is the relative amount of time devoted to personal activity as compared with the time devoted to educational pursuits." [Reg. Sec. 1.162-5(e)(1)]

Example

You work in Newark, New Jersey. You went to Chicago to take a 1-week course, the cost of which is deductible, and while there, you took a sightseeing trip, entertained some personal friends, and took a sidetrip to Pleasantville for a day. Your transportation expenses to Chicago and back are deductible, but your transportation expenses to Pleasantville are not. You may deduct only the meals [subject to the 50%-Rule described in Section 1 of the Travel chapter] and lodging allocable to your educational activities. [IRS Pub. 17]

Example

You work in Newark and you went to a university in California to take a course, the cost of which is deductible. The course was one-fourth of a full program of study and you spent the rest of your time on personal activities. Your trip is considered to have been primarily personal unless you can show otherwise. You may not deduct the cost of your transportation to California, but you may deduct one-fourth the cost of your meals [reduced further by the 50%-Rule] and lodging while attending the university. [Reg. Sec. 1.162-5(e)(2)]

Example

Jorgensen was an English teacher at a large Californis high school. One summer, she enrolled in a 3-week university extension course to study abroad in Greece. The Court allowed her to deduct her expenses because she taught Greek mythology in her English classes.

Later that year, she enrolled in a 2-week course to study abroad in Southeast Asia. A deduction for this travel was allowed because she had many Asian students in her classes. As the Court ruled, Jorgensen "has applied what she learned in the Southeast Asia course to understand better her Asian students' responses in class and to work more effectively with them. [Jorgensen's] experiences in Asia serve as a basis for further intelligent and respectful discussion with her students about their cultures." [Jorgensen, TC Memo 2000-138]

If your travel was outside of the United States, see Section 8b of the *Travel* chapter.

Where Do You Deduct Educational Expenses?

Educational expenses incurred by an employee in connection with his job are claimed on Form 2106 or Form 2106-EZ, *Employee Business Expenses.* The total of expenses computed on either of the forms is claimed on line 20 of Schedule A as a *miscellaneous deduction,* and when aggregated with other miscellaneous deductions, subjected to a 2% of Adjusted Gross Income floor. Section 1 of the *Miscellaneous Deductions* chapter discusses claiming employee business expenses in more complete detail. It also shows how to handle the situation where a full or partial reimbursement is received from an employer.

Educational expenses connected with a self-employment activity are claimed on Schedule C or Schedule C-EZ. This has the advantage of escaping the 2% floor and being available to those who claim the standard deduction as well as to those who itemize.

You cannot deduct your educational expenses to the extent you receive a tax-exempt scholarship to defray such expenses. For example, if your educational expenses are $1,500, toward which you receive a $500 scholarship, your deduction would be $1,500 − $500 = $1,000. [Rev. Ru.l 83-3]

You break down your educational expenses into categories as provided on Form 2106 or Form 2106-EZ. On either form, lines 1–3 are used for travel expenses and Line 5 is used for deductible meal expenses. Line 4 is for all other expenses such as tuition, fees, books, etc. You should also keep records and supporting evidence to substantiate each element of expenditure, in case your return is audited.

Further information on the requirements for deducting and keeping records of travel expenses is contained in the *Travel* chapter.

24

Entertainment Expenses

Many college teachers entertain as part of their job. They may take a visiting colleague out to lunch or dinner. Or, they may host a dinner or reception in their home in honor of such a visitor. The question then becomes whether or not the expense of such entertainment can be deducted.

There has been no direct guidance on this question in any published court case or IRS ruling. And the basic Tax Code section under which entertainment expenses are deducted offers little illumination. It states only:

"In the case of an individual, there shall be allowed as a deduction all the ordinary and necessary expenses paid or incurred during the taxable year. . . for the production or collection of income."

Thus, to qualify for deduction, entertainment must be an *ordinary and necessary* activity connected with your job. The word *ordinary* refers to an expense connected with a common and accepted practice in your job. For example, a professor could regard the expense of taking a visiting colloquium speaker out to dinner as an ordinary expense if this is typically done on his campus. On the other hand, the expense of treating a class to ice cream cones would not be an ordinary expense because it is not common practice to do so.

The term *necessary* in this context does not have its usual meaning of "compulsory." Here, a necessary expense is one that is *appropriate and helpful* in the conduct of your job.

Employees sometimes have a difficult time convincing the IRS that an entertainment expense qualifies for deduction. The IRS generally expects the employer to pick up the bill for all job-related expenses. Of course, college teachers are in a special category. They often have to dig into their own pockets to pay for job-related items for which an employee in private industry would receive a reimbursement.

It is not necessary for there to be an absolute requirement to entertain. As long as the entertainment in question is a general practice in one's institution and is appropriate and helpful to the job, a deduction can be justified. Of course, a statement that such entertainment is required as part of the job would boost one's case. However, it is not an absolute requirement.

The *ordinary and necessary* rule discussed above applies to the most common type of business entertaining, namely dining out in a restaurant. This includes having drinks at a bar or cocktail lounge provided there is no distracting floor show or other entertainment. It also includes the cost of *quiet business meals* served to your guests at home.

There is an additional rule that applies. This rule states that entertainment (including meals and beverages except when traveling away from home) must either (1) be *directly related to the active conduct of the taxpayer's trade or business,* or (2) take place either directly before, at the same time as, or directly after a *substantial and bona fide business discussion* associated with the active conduct of the taxpayer's trade or business. Exactly how this rule applies to college teachers is unclear at this time because there still have not yet been any rulings on this issue.

The above discussion indicates that the cost of hosting a dinner party for an out-of-town visitor can be a deductible entertainment expense. But how about dinner parties attended only by in-town guests? The presumption is that such parties are simply personal gatherings rather than deductible business activities. However, a court case shows how this presumption might be overcome, namely, by pointing to parties for which no deduction was claimed. A newspaper publisher held dinner parties to which he invited people from politics, business, journalism, publishing, theater, and other fields. He did not have specific business to transact with these individuals. Rather, *"the purpose of the dinners was to provide an opportunity to discuss developments and ideas with people who were prominent in their professions."* The publisher claimed a deduction for about a dozen of these dinner parties. Had these been the only parties given by the publisher, they would have been considered merely social gatherings. But he had hosted many other dinner parties for which no deduction was claimed. Because of this, the Court was able to accept the publisher's contention that the relatively few parties for which he claimed a deduction were business-related rather than being just social gatherings. [Howard, TC Memo 1981-250]

Whose Expenses Can Be Deducted?

When your entertainment activities are deductible, the letter of the law only allows you to deduct your own meal to the extent it exceeds what you would ordinarily have spent. However, in practice, the IRS almost always lets you deduct the full cost of your own meal in addition to that of the person you are entertaining. The IRS also recognizes that when entertaining an out-of-town visitor, it may be impractical to leave out his or her spouse. In such a case, the expenses of the spouse will be deductible also. Furthermore, if your spouse is included because the visitor's spouse is present, these expenses can also be deducted. However, all expenses are subject to the 50%-Rule discussed below.

To be deductible, entertainment expenses should not be reimbursable by the employer. This is illustrated by a court case in which an engineer was denied a $122 deduction for lunches and dinners with professional colleagues. The Court agreed that such costs might qualify for deduction. In this case, however, the engineer testified that his employer would have reimbursed him for the costs if he had asked. An employee cannot deduct expenses which he pays if his employer would have reimbursed him for those expenses. [Narain, TC Memo 1983-701]

50%-Rule for Entertainment Expenses

Entertainment expenses are not deductible in full on your tax return. Instead, only 50% of the cost of entertainment (including meals and beverages) can be deducted. All expenses associated with the entertainment such as tax, tips, parking, etc., are included under this 50%-Rule. However, transportation to and from the place of entertainment is not subject to the 50%-Rule.

Exception. The 50%-Rule does not apply to expenses which are reimbursed by an employer, provided the reimbursement is not included as taxable income on the employee's Form W-2.

The 50%-Rule for entertainment expenses is exactly the same as the 50%-Rule for meal expenses described in Section 1 of the *Travel* chapter. Also see Section 1 of the *Miscellaneous Deductions* chapter, which shows how the 50%-Rule is applied when expenses are reported on Form 2106 or Form 2106-EZ.

Lunch and Dinner

Sometimes, an individual attends lunch or dinner meetings in connection with his professional duties. The cost of attending such meetings can be deductible if they are sufficiently business-related. In one court case, Example 1 below, the Court even allowed a deduction for luncheon meetings which consisted of discussions of recent journal articles. This court case opens the door for college teachers to deduct for "luncheon meetings" with colleagues organized for similar purposes.

Example 1

Beltran was an anesthesiologist at a hospital in Maryland. He periodically joined a group of other anesthesiologists in "Journal Club" luncheons held at various local restaurants. The purpose of these luncheons was for the anesthesiologists "to discuss the latest professional journals they had read."

The Tax Court ruled that the cost of these luncheons was a legitimate professional expense. Thus, the cost could be claimed as a "business meal" deduction. The court allowed the full amount claimed by the anesthesiologist — about $400 over a two-year period. [Beltran, TC Memo 1982-153]

Example 2

A Vocational Education Coordinator belonged to several vocational organizations which often met over lunch or dinner. The IRS ruled that these meetings were directly related to his professional duties. Therefore, he was entitled to deduct the portion of the cost of any such meal which was in excess of what he would have normally spent. Because he ordinarily simply ate a sack lunch at his school or ate dinner at home, this would cover almost the entire cost of the meals. [IRS Private Letter Ruling 8006004]

While this ruling forced the educational coordinator to subtract what he ordinarily would have spent from the cost of the meals at those meetings, in practice the IRS is not so strict. If a business meal qualifies for deduction, the full cost (subject to the 50%-Rule) will almost always be allowed.

Example 3

Didsbury was a Professor at a college in the East. In addition to his college-related duties, he served on the planning committee of a Society dedicated to the study of world affairs. The Society periodically held conferences and published papers based on these conferences. Didsbury, in addition to participating in the planning of the conferences, helped edit the conference volumes and had some responsibility for obtaining speakers. He received $6,000 in income from the Society for teaching a course in connection with a conference and for his writing and editing activities.

About once a week, Didsbury met with potential speakers over lunch or dinner to discuss their participation in one of the Society's conferences. He picked up the check each time, but did not receive reimbursement from the Society.

The IRS did not challenge his right to a deduction for the lunches and dinners. These were legitimate expenses connected with his business activity of "Lecture-Writing" for the Society. The issue that arose at trial was the adequacy of the records he maintained to support his $1,565 entertainment deduction for these meal expenses.

Didsbury had an adequate collection of receipts, credit card slips, and contemporaneous diary notes to verify the date, amount, and restaurant where each of the meals occurred. However, he did not write down his relationship to the person entertained or the business purpose of the entertainment. Furthermore, he did not always write down the name of the person entertained. In some cases, he just wrote down the initials of the person on the credit card slip and in a few cases had no such notation at all.

However, at the time of trial, he was able to create a listing of the meals, along with the name of the person entertained and an indication of the person's business relationship (e.g. "possible conference participant, conference planning, work draft manuscripts, etc."). This listing was based on his receipts and diary book, plus his own recollections.

The IRS claimed that the documentation was not sufficient because of the lack of contemporaneous recording of all the elements required to substantiate the deduction. However, the Court sided with Didsbury, allowing the entire $1,565 deduction. Didsbury did have contemporaneous records concerning date, place, and amount. And the law permits missing pieces to be substantiated by adequate corroboration. To determine whether the corroboration in this case was adequate, the Court went back to the original Senate committee report explaining the requirements:

> *"Where the taxpayer fails to maintain adequate records with respect to any of the described aspects of an expense, that aspect must be substantiated by the taxpayer's own statement corroborated by sufficient evidence. The taxpayer's own uncorroborated statement will not constitute substantiation with respect to any such aspect. The evidence required may vary with respect to each aspect of an item claimed as a deduction. Thus, circumstantial evidence, such as the nature of the business activities of the taxpayer and of the person entertained, may be sufficient to corroborate the taxpayer's statement regarding business purpose and business relationship, whereas more direct*

> *evidence, such as the testimony of witnesses, would be required to substantiate amount, time, place, date, and description."* [S. Rept. No. 1881, 87th Cong., 2d Sess. (1962), 1962-3 C.B. 878]

In this case, the Court ruled that Didsbury's listing constituted sufficient alternate evidence of the nature of the *"business activities of the taxpayer and the person entertained."* It was not simply an *"uncorroborated statement."* Rather, it was corroborated by the fact that it fit with the receipts and other contemporaneous recordkeeping which Didsbury had maintained. [Didsbury, T.C. Memo 1989-1]

Each of the above examples concerned an individual deducting for lunch or dinner meetings with other persons with whom he ordinarily did not work. But what about meetings with co-workers? Can you deduct for lunch or dinner meetings attended just by those whom you regularly see at work? The following court case indicates that the answer is yes, as long as the meetings are not too frequent. That is, you can't simply use the entertainment deduction to write off all your lunches even if business is always discussed. However, occasional lunches with co-workers can qualify for an entertainment expense deduction.

Example 4

Moss was a partner in a law firm in Chicago. The partners and other employees met over lunch at a nearby restaurant each day to give each other advice on handling current matters and to discuss other business. This was the most convenient time to meet because the courts were in recess at this time and all the lawyers would generally be free to attend.

When Moss attempted to deduct his share of the daily lunches, the IRS objected. The Tax Court upheld this objection. It ruled that even though the lunches served a business purpose, the frequency of these lunches meant they became a normal personal expense.

However, 9 of the Tax Court judges signed a concurring opinion that the deduction was only ruled out in this case because of the frequency of the lunches. As the justice who wrote the opinion noted,

> *"I do not view this opinion as disallowing the cost of meals in all instances where only partners, co-workers, etc., are involved. We have here findings that the partners met at lunch because it was 'convenient' and 'convenient' 5 days a week, 52 weeks a year."*

The concurring opinion thus indicates that occasional meetings with co-workers could qualify for the entertainment expense deduction. The line between occasional and regular is not spelled out. That would depend on the particular facts and circumstances.

While only 9 of 19 Tax Court judges signed the concurring opinion, the position of the other 10 is not indicated. Because it is likely that at least one of these 10 would join the other 9 were it necessary to rule on this issue, it is reasonable to treat this as representing the viewpoint of the Tax Court. [Moss. 80 TC 1073]

Moss appealed to the U. S. Court of Appeals in his district. But the Appeals Court upheld the decision denying the deduction. However, its 1985 written opinion gives additional information as to where to draw the line when deciding the deductibility of lunches with co-workers.

First of all, the purpose of the deduction is to compensate persons who "spend more money on business meals because they are business meals than they would spend on their meals if they were not working." Thus, if you are planning to deduct a business lunch, you should go to a more expensive restaurant than the ones to which you ordinarily go. Of course, if you ordinarily bring your own lunch or dine cheaply at the cafeteria where you work, then going out to lunch at a restaurant automatically satisfies this criterion. In the Moss case, they always ate at the same modestly-priced cafe, so there was no evidence that their business lunches were costing them any more than personal lunches would have cost.

Second, the business purpose of lunching together is to provide, in the Court's phrase, "social lubrication" conducive to the transacting of business. This extra social lubrication would not ordinarily be needed if you are lunching with an office-mate or someone else you work with closely. On the other hand, discussing business matters with someone you don't know as well might provide the helpful social lubrication conducive to the business-related matters being discussed. In the Moss case, the lawyers eating lunch together were part of a small 8-lawyer firm who "did not need a daily lunch to cement relationships among them."

And finally, the Appeals Court agreed with the Tax Court that deducting the cost of daily meals was pushing it too far, even had there been more business justification. According to the Court, "It is all a matter of degree and circumstance (the expense of a testimonial dinner, for example, would be deductible on a morale-building rationale); and particularly of frequency. Daily — for a full year — is too often, perhaps even for entertainment of clients." [Moss. 80 TC 1073]

The following court case concerns the deduction for business lunches claimed by the manager of a computer department. In this case, entertainment for improving the morale of an individual's subordinates was ruled nondeductible, while the cost of business lunches with outside vendors was ruled deductible because her employer *"expected her to incur any such expenses which would help the firm's business."*

Example 5

Dunkelberger was a computer-aided design manager at a computer company in California. She incurred 2 types of entertainment expenses in connection with her job.

First, she spent money entertaining the persons under her supervision. On her tax return, she claimed the $160.88 cost of giving periodic lunch parties for persons she supervised as expressions of gratitude for good work, as well as the $310.61 cost of having a Christmas party, and the $294 cost of providing them with candy and doughnuts so that they would have higher morale in an often stressful work environment. The Court ruled that these expenses were not deductible because they were not a "condition of employment." It stated,

"Petitioner testified that the costs of meals, parties, doughnuts, candy, and flower expenses, all for the benefit of persons under her supervision, were necessary expenditures in order to maintain high morale of these persons in the often stressful business setting. While it is certainly an understandable goal to inspire high productivity among fellow employees, we are unable to find that these expenditures were ordinary and necessary expenditures of petitioner as an employee. Petitioner did not establish that she was required to incur such outlays. She was not reimbursed for these expenditures, and we are not convinced that her employer expected or required petitioner to incur these expenditures as a condition of employment. In order for petitioner to deduct these expenditures as employee business expenses, she must show that these expenses were a condition to her employment."

Second, Dunkelberger claimed the $805 cost of taking vendors of computer equipment to lunch where the exchange of information and the negotiation of contracts would take place. The Court ruled that these expenses were deductible, stating,

"In order for petitioner to deduct business entertainment or meals, she must show that the expenses were appropriate or helpful to the trade or business, and that they had a reasonably proximate relationship to the operation of her business. Where the taxpayer is an employee, she must show that the employer required or expected her to incur and to bear the expenses without reimbursement. Petitioner has demonstrated that the business lunch expenses were ordinary and necessary and arose out of the conduct of petitioner's employment as a manager. Her management team expected her to incur any such expenses which would help the firm's business. [Dunkelberger, TC Memo 1992-723]

Recordkeeping Requirement

You are supposed to record the following information for all entertaining which you claim as a deduction:

1. The **amount** of each separate item of entertaining, except that incidental items like taxi fares or telephone calls can be aggregated together.

2. The **date** of the expenditure.

3. The **place** of entertainment, including the name and location of restaurants where dining occurred.

4. The **business purpose** of the entertainment. (A sentence or two describing the nature of your business conversation would be appropriate.)

5. The **occupation** or other information concerning the persons being entertained, including name, title, or other designations sufficient to establish their business relationship to you.

You should record the above information in a timely manner. That is, you should write it down soon after the entertainment occurred, not reconstruct it from memory at a later date. You do not have to record information in your record book that duplicates information shown on a receipt as long as your records and receipts complement each other in an orderly manner.

If your timely-kept records and receipts do not contain all 5 items of information specified above, this does not automatically rule out a deduction. You may be allowed to present other evidence which corroborates your claim as to the missing items. This is more likely to be acceptable in the case of items (4) and (5) than for the first three items. A good illustration of this is provided in Example 4 of this chapter.

You must also keep a receipt, cancelled check, or other documentary evidence substantiating any expenditure of $75 or more. This was increased from $25 to $75 per IRS Notice 95-50.

Where Do You Deduct Entertainment Expenses?

Unreimbursed entertainment expenses are claimed by employees as an *employee business expense* on Form 2106 or Form 2106-EZ [see Section 1 of the *Miscellaneous Deductions* chapter for information on how to report your expenses on Form 2106 or Form 2106-EZ]. The total computed on either of these forms is carried over to Schedule A, where it is claimed as a miscellaneous deduction. The total of miscellaneous deductions is then subjected to the 2% of Adjusted Gross Income floor.

Self-employed persons claim entertainment expenses on line 24b of Schedule C or, after applying the 50%-Rule, on line 2 of Schedule C-EZ. (This has the advantage of escaping the 2% floor and being available to those who claim the standard deduction as well as those who itemize.)

An employee who receives a reimbursement that is not included as taxable income on his Form W-2 can simply ignore the reimbursement and expenses for tax purposes, provided the appropriate records are maintained. For situations where a partial or taxable reimbursement is received, see Section 1 of the *Miscellaneous Deductions* chapter.

25

Retirement Plans

SECTION 1:
INTRODUCTION

The chances are good that you participate in some sort of retirement plan other than Social Security. This plan may be entirely funded by contributions from your employer or it may be funded by both employer contributions and employee contributions. In almost all cases, contributions required of employees are simply withheld from their paychecks.

In addition to simply providing a savings vehicle for later years, retirement plans are a significant tax-shelter. As explained in Section 3, tax might be avoided on the contributions paid into the plan. And no tax is paid on the annual income earned by funds in the retirement plan. Thus, these funds earn income compounding at a higher effective rate than they could earn in the hands of a taxpaying individual.

To illustrate, compare placing $1,000 into a retirement plan with placing $1,000 into the hands of an individual in the 30% tax bracket (federal plus state). Let's suppose each $1,000 is invested at 8% interest compounded annually. The retirement plan earns interest at the full 8% rate. However, the individual earns a net interest rate of only 5.6% after paying taxes. The $1,000 in the individual's hands would grow to $3,905 after 25 years. But the $1,000 in the retirement plan would grow to $6,848, an increase of 75%, subject, of course, to income tax when withdrawn.

SECTION 2:
PAYMENTS FROM RETIREMENT PLANS

When you receive annuity payments from your retirement plan, your employer will furnish information concerning the tax status of these payments. A portion of each payment reflecting your own contributions on which you have already paid tax is not subject to further taxation. The remaining portion is taxable. Thus, you are taxed when you receive amounts reflecting contributions made by your employer, as well as investment income.

Your employer can compute the tax-free portion of your annuity payments in 2 ways — using either the *General Rule* or the *Simplified General Rule.* The Simplified General Rule is not only simpler, but better — generally producing a larger tax-free amount than that produced by the General Rule.

If your employer uses the General Rule, it may pay you to make the computation yourself using the Simplified General Rule. This is done by using the worksheet found in IRS Publication 575, obtainable from the IRS. This rule may generally be used retroactively by filing an amended return within the usual 3-year deadline [see Section 1 of Chapter 1]. If your computation produces a different figure than that reported by your employer on Form W-2P, you should attach a statement to your tax return explaining your computation.

The portion of each payment you receive that is exempt from tax is based on your life expectancy. That is, if you live precisely as long as predicted by the actuarial tables, the total amounts exempted from tax will be equal to the total contributions you made during the years you worked.

However, if you live beyond the age predicted in the life-expectancy tables, you must pay tax on the full amount of each annuity payment from that time on. That way, the total amounts exempted from tax will be equal to the total contributions you made.

On the other hand, there is a little known provision that applies if you die before your predicted life expectancy. In that situation, the total amounts you have exempted from tax will be less than your total contributions. The law provides that the difference between these 2 totals can then be deducted on your final tax return for the year in which you die.

Because, mercifully, you won't be filling out this tax return yourself, your spouse or other heirs should be aware of this provision. The amount of this final deduction could be quite large. And there is even a carryback rule that sometimes applies if this final deduction exceeds the taxable income for the final year. In such a case, professional assistance will be needed to make the appropriate computation.

Lump-Sum Distributions

There is a special transfer provision of the law which applies to a lump-sum distribution from your retirement plan. Under this transfer provision, any distribution (or part of a distribution) can be rolled over, in whole or in part, to another tax-sheltered plan. This new tax-sheltered plan can be an Individual Retirement Account (IRA) which you set up. Or it might be a qualified plan, run by your employer or new employer, which accepts such rollovers. However, a 20%-withholding provision applies if you obtain control of the money when it is distributed from your retirement plan. This withholding can be avoided by having your employer directly transfer funds to the IRA or other receiving plan so you don't have control of the money. Details are discussed in Section 2 of the *Tax-Sheltered Plans* chapter.

Special Transition Rule for Individuals Born Before 1936

There is a special transition rule for individuals born before 1936. They can choose to apply the prior law 10-year averaging rule to a distribution using 1986 tax rates if they wish.

The 10-year averaging rule taxes the distribution as though it were spread out over a 10-year period. The major cases when the 10-year averaging rule is advantageous are where it is desired to spend the major portion of funds within several years after distribution, the distribution is less than $200,000 and you expect to be in a higher tax bracket in the future, or if your health is so poor that life expectancy is short and a spouse is not your beneficiary.

However, a once-in-a-lifetime rule still applies. That is, if the 10-year averaging rule is used on a lump-sum distribution received after 1986, no use of a special averaging rule is permitted for any future lump-sum distributions.

Capital Gains Treatment for Pre-1974 Contributions

If you were born before 1936 and were a participant in your retirement plan before 1974, you have another option that applies to the *pre-1974 portion* of a lump-sum distribution. This *pre-1974 portion* is determined by multiplying the taxable amount of the distribution by the number of pre-1974 years of participation and dividing by the total number of years of participation. (This amount will be shown on Form 1099-R which you will receive from your employer.) You then have 2 choices. You can apply the maximum 20% capital gains rate to the pre-1974 portion and apply 10-year averaging to the remainder. Or, you can group the pre-1974 portion with the remaining portion and apply 10-year averaging to the entire amount. Your choice should be made after computing the consequences of both choices and determining which is the more advantageous in your particular situation.

The special option for treating the pre-1974 portion of a lump-sum distribution falls under the same once-in-a-lifetime rule that applies to the 10-year averaging option. That is, if any of these 3 options is used for a lump-sum distribution received after 1986, none of these options can be used for any future lump-sum distributions.

If 10-year averaging is used, the appropriate tax calculations are made on Form 4972.

Extra 10% Tax on Distributions before Age 59½

In general, an individual who receives a distribution from a pension plan prior to reaching age 59½ is subject to an additional "penalty tax" equal to 10% of the taxable portion of the distribution. This 10% tax is in addition to any income tax due on such distributions. However, there is no additional tax on the portion of the distribution that is a return of non-deductible employee contributions.

The 10% penalty tax is waived if either (i) you die and your beneficiaries get the money, (ii) you become disabled, (iii) you leave your job and take your pension entitlement in the form of an annuity payable in equal periodic amounts over a lifetime, (iv) you leave your job after reaching age 55, (v) you use the distribution to pay for medical bills in excess of 7.5% of your adjusted gross income, or (vi) you roll over the distribution tax-free into an IRA or other pension plan The penalty is also waived for distributions to first-time home buyers and for certain higher education expenses.

Due to the complexity of the rules, professional advice should be sought before making any lump-sum distribution decisions. Also, special rules apply if you are covered by a retirement plan of a company of which you are at least a 5% owner.

Special rules apply to employees of the federal government. These are contained in Publication 721, *Tax Guide to U.S. Civil Service Retirement Benefits*, available from the IRS.

Section 3:
Contributions to Retirement Plans

Employer's Contributions

Your employer's contributions to your retirement plan are not taxable at the time the contributions are made, provided (as is usually the case) the IRS has approved the plan as qualifying for this benefit.

Employee's Contributions

An employee's contributions to his retirement plan are taxable. That is, the taxable wages figure reported on his Form W-2 includes his full salary before his contributions to the retirement plan are taken out. He must pay tax based on this full figure and can get no deduction for his contributions to the retirement plan.

This situation is inherently unfair. To illustrate this unfairness, compare the situations of the following two persons:

A earns $52,000 per year. He is required to participate in a retirement plan to which both he and his employer contribute $1,000 per year. Effectively, A's annual salary is $51,000 plus the $2,000 which is contributed to his retirement system.

B, on the other hand, earns an annual salary of $51,000. His retirement plan is entirely funded by his employer who makes a contribution of $2,000 per year. Thus, like A, B has an annual salary of $51,000 plus the $2,000 retirement contribution. The employers of both A & B have precisely the same expense — $53,000 per year.

However, there is one important difference. A must pay tax based on his official $52,000 salary while B pays tax only on $51,000. For no good reason, A is required to pay more tax than B. However, when A and B retire, B must pay tax on the full amount of his retirement pay (see Section 2). A does not have to pay tax on that amount which represents a return of his contributions to the plan. Thus, the net result is A pays tax on the additional $1,000 in the year he earns it while B defers paying tax on his amount until he receives it in the form of retirement benefits. Meanwhile, B has been able to earn interest on the difference for many years. This amount could be multiplied many times over, especially if retirement is far away. In addition, B's tax rate is likely to be lower during retirement than when he is working.

The only distinction in the two situations described above is a semantic one, namely whether contributions are **designated** as being made by the employee or the employer. But Congress has specifically made this semantic distinction the criterion for deduction. The employee must pay tax on any amounts designated as salary even if these amounts are put into a retirement plan as an employee contribution without passing through his hands. However, he does not have to pay tax on amounts put into a qualified retirement plan if these payments are designated as employer contributions.

Private employers are well aware of this distinction. They usually designate all contributions to a retirement plan to be employer contributions. This produces the best tax result for the employee without costing the employer anything extra. In fact, keeping pension plan contributions outside the employee's official salary can even benefit the employer by lowering worker's compensation premiums, social security contributions, and other payments based on salary.

Public institutions are another matter. Their pension plans are often part of a large system established by state or local law. For example, teachers in public institutions typically are covered under the same general retirement plan applying to all state employees. These plans often require contributions to be made both by employer and employee.

Exception. A number of IRS rulings have highlighted an exception to the general rule that employee contributions are included in taxable income. This exception applies when a state or local government retirement plan requires employee contributions, but a school district, college education board, or other subdivision agrees to "pick up" the employee contribution. The IRS uses a Congressional committee's report to describe the situation as follows:

> *"However, some state and local government plans designate certain amounts as being employee contributions even though statutes authorize or require the relevant governmental units or agencies to pick up some or all of what would otherwise be the employee's contribution. In other words, the governmental unit pays all or part of the employee's contribution but does not withhold this amount from the employee's salary. In this situation, the portion of the contribution which is 'picked-up' by the government is, in substance, an employer contribution for purposes of Federal tax law, notwithstanding the fact that for certain purposes of State Law the contribution may be designated as an employee contribution. Accordingly,... in the case of a government pick-up plan... the portion of the contribution which is paid by the government, with no withholding from the employee's salary, will be treated as an employer contribution under the tax law."* [H. Rep. 93-807]

A number of IRS rulings have made it relatively easy to qualify under the above pick-up rule. First, the IRS issued a Revenue Ruling stating that pick-up plans need only satisfy the following two criteria:

"(1) the employer must specify that the contributions, although designated as employee contributions, are paid by the employer in lieu of contributions by the employee; and

"(2) the employee must not be given the option of choosing to receive the contributed amounts directly instead of having them paid by the employer to the pension plan." [Rev. Rul. 81-36]

Then, an IRS Chief Council Memorandum liberalized the interpretation of criterion (2). According to this memorandum, criterion (2)

"must not be interpreted to prohibit 'pick-up' of amounts that are, in substance, employer contributions. This rationale suggests that criteria (2) should only be applied to cases in which an employee is considered to have the option to choose to receive the amounts directly rather than having them contributed to a plan because the employee is in fact controlling the amounts and, therefore, the contributions are not, in substance, employer contributions.

"An option that would be impermissible under criteria (2) is one in which the employee will currently receive the amounts unless he must annually opt to have these amounts contributed on his behalf to the employer's pension plan. In this case the employee, not the employer, is in fact controlling the contributions."

However, a one-time nonrevocable election whether or not to participate in a pension plan is all right. According to the memorandum,

"it is our opinion that the nonexercise of a one-time election to opt out of a plan or the one-time, nonrevocable election to begin early participation in a plan does not vest in the employee enough control of the employer contribution to taint the amounts contributed on the employee's behalf." [G.C.M. 38820]

For example, under this policy, the IRS issued a private ruling approving a pick-up plan which provided that an employee became a participant when first hired unless he filed a written notice of election not to participate within a 30-day period. [IRS Private Letter Ruling 8209038]

There is no restriction on how the contributions are to be picked up. According to an IRS Private Letter Ruling,

"The employer may pick up these contributions by a reduction in cash salary of the employee or by an offset against future salary increase or by a combination of reduction in salary and offset against a future salary increase." [IRS Private Letter Ruling 8206146]

As the above discussion indicates, it has become quite easy for governmental units to establish pick-up plans. Essentially, all they need to do is pass the appropriate statute authorizing the pick-up. Practically speaking, this is just a bookkeeping change, costing the employer nothing while saving the employee many hundreds of dollars in taxes. In fact, many pick-up plans involving government employees, including teachers, have been established in states across the country during the past few years. Presumably, other states will be giving this no-cost benefit to their employees in the near future.

Special Rules for School Employees

There is another alternative available to schools and certain other non-profit organizations. Instead of qualifying under the usual retirement plan rules, they can set up their retirement plan under the special tax-sheltered annuity regulations that apply only to these types of organizations. [See Section 4 of the *Tax-Sheltered Plans* chapter.] To qualify, the retirement plan must provide that all contributions to the plan are non-transferable and non-forfeitable. This means that amounts credited to the account of an employee cannot be assigned over to someone else, nor can they be forfeited because the employee terminates his employment or for any other reason. Also, certain *non-discrimination* rules apply that require retirement plans not to overly benefit higher-salaried employees when compared with lower-salaried employees.

Under the tax-sheltered annuity regulations, an employee can make an agreement with his employer to reduce his salary by an amount equal to his contribution to the retirement plan. Then, the institution contributes this amount to the retirement plan. The net result is that the employee's contribution is transformed into an employer's contribution. The employee's Form W2 shows the reduced amount as his taxable wages. Because his official salary is reduced, the employee escapes tax on the amount of his contribution to the plan.

Of course, as discussed in Section 2, tax must be paid later when this amount is received in the form of retirement benefits. In the meantime, the tax that was not paid can be invested to earn interest for many years. In effect, the deferral of tax gives the same benefit as obtaining a long-term interest-free loan from the government. Over the long run, this can amount to a substantial benefit.

Private institutions have little trouble qualifying their plans under the tax-sheltered annuity regulations. Public institutions are another matter. Often, their employees are included in the same retirement system that applies to all state employees. These state plans typically require that both the employer and employee contribute to the plan. And, as discussed earlier, amounts designated as being contributed by the employee are included in taxable wages.

However, a court case shows that even if the state retirement system designates amounts as *employee* contributions, this may not rule out a deduction. The administration of the educational organization may be able to *redesignate* these amounts as *employer* contributions, exempting them from tax. This case involved the retirement system applying to employees of the state of North Dakota. According to North Dakota law, both employer and employee were required to contribute 4% of the employee's salary to the state retirement system. The Court ruled that the State Board of Higher Education, under its broad administrative authority, had the power to authorize salary reduction agreements transforming employee contributions into employer contributions, despite the state statute requiring contributions from the employee. [University of North Dakota, 44 AFTR 2d 79-5392]

The TIAA-CREF Retirement System

TIAA-CREF (Teachers Insurance and Annuity Association/College Retirement Equities Fund) are organizations founded by the Carnegie Foundation. Their basic function is to provide a universal retirement plan which allows faculty members to transfer their retirement plan from one institution to another without losing any benefits.

Most private colleges and a number of public colleges use the TIAA-CREF system as the basic retirement system for their employees. It is also used by a number of other eligible non-profit institutions.

In addition to being used as basic retirement plans, the TIAA-CREF system can be used to provide *Supplemental Retirement Annuities (SRAs)* as a voluntary tax-sheltered annuity choice [see Section 4 of the *Tax-Sheltered Plans* chapter]. Most colleges and universities make this choice available to their employees, even if their basic retirement plan is not run by TIAA-CREF. This organization has undergone numerous changes over the past few years because they are no longer classified as a not-for-profit organization for federal income tax purposes. The investment choices they offer cover the spectrum from money market accounts to international equity funds. The company still focuses on the educational community, although they have expanded their constituency to individuals and for-profit companies.

1. TIAA Fund. The TIAA Fund is invested primarily in fixed income securities such as bonds, mortgages, and direct loans to business and industry. The fund operates more like an insurance annuity fund than a mutual fund. That is, your account is credited each year with interest earned by the fund. Money invested when rates are high will continue to earn higher interest than money invested when rates are low. By operating in this fashion, TIAA guarantees there will be no loss of principal and that annual interest will never fall below 3%. In fact, the interest rates paid by the fund in recent years have been much higher than this. For example, new investments in TIAA have recently been earning about 7%.

2. TIAA Real Estate Fund. This fund looks for favorable long-term returns through capital appreciation and rental income. Real Estate investments have traditionally been less volatile than stocks and have tended to provide a good hedge against inflation. Since inception, this fund has an annual return of approximately 8.8%.

3. CREF Stock Fund. This is the basic CREF fund that has been in existence for decades. Money is invested in a wide portfolio of stocks. About 60% of the fund is invested in an indexed portfolio which mirrors the behavior of basic stock market averages. The other 40% is invested in foreign stocks and in domestic stocks selected by the fund managers.

4. CREF Money-Market Fund. This acts like a typical money-market fund [see Section 7 of the *Investing Your Money* chapter]. That is, the fund invests in short-term high-quality debt instruments such as U.S. Treasury Bills, certificates of deposit, short-term commercial loans, etc. Money-market funds are the safest type of investment other than short-term securities issued by or guaranteed by the U.S. Government. However, money-market interest rates are almost always lower than longer-term rates.

5. CREF Bond Market Fund. This fund invests primarily in investment-grade fixed-income securities. This includes U.S. Government securities, publicly-traded corporate bonds, and mortgage-backed securities which are guaranteed by the U.S. Government or have a sufficiently high investment rating.

6. CREF Inflation-Linked Bond Account. This fund invests in U.S. Treasury Inflation-Indexed Securities [see Section 3 of the *Investing Your Money* chapter] and similar securities indexed to inflation.

7. CREF Social Choice Fund. This fund invests in a portfolio of stocks and fixed-income securities. According to the prospectus, this fund *"will seek to invest in companies conducting their activities in a manner that recognizes acceptable standards for addressing specified social concerns."* This fund has not invested in any company which (1) has an operation in Northern Ireland which does not follow a code prohibiting religious discrimination, (2) produces nuclear energy, (3) has a significant portion of its business involved in the manufacture of weapons, or (4) produces and markets alcoholic beverages or tobacco products. Currently, the fund states that its Finance Committee *"will seek to adopt practical criteria permitting systematic exclusion of investments in companies that fail to adhere to sound environmental policies and practices."*

8. Global Equities Fund. This fund invests in a diversified portfolio consisting primarily of foreign and U.S. stocks. The fund is weighted so that a majority of the assets in the fund are invested in foreign securities.

9. Growth Fund. This fund invests in stocks which are believed to have the potential for significant capital appreciation. This includes substantial holdings of small or medium size companies in new and emerging areas of the economy. This fund is for those who choose to tolerate greater risk and fluctuation in value in exchange for the potential of higher returns over time.

10. Equity Index Fund. This is essentially an *index fund.* It invests in stocks chosen to mirror the performance of the Russell 3000 index. This index tracks the performance of the 3000 largest publicly traded companies, weighted according to market value.

You can choose any allocation you want among the above funds. You can have all your money invested in one fund, or specify the percentages if you divide up the money among several funds. The same percentage need not be chosen for each fund. For example, you can have 60% of your money invested in one fund, 30% in another, and 10% in a third.

While most participating organizations will make all funds available to their employees, they do not have to do so. They can prohibit allocations to the CREF Bond Market and/or Social Choice Funds altogether, but may not do so for the CREF Stock or Money-Market Funds. This applies to CREF funds used as part of a basic retirement plan. It does not apply to voluntary SRAs [see Section 4 of the *Tax-Sheltered Plans* chapter], which always offer all of the TIAA-CREF funds as investment options.

Transferability

You are permitted to transfer funds from one of the CREF funds to the TIAA Fund or to any of the other available CREF funds at any time you choose. The only restriction is that the amount transferred must be at least $1,000. There is even a toll-free Automated Telephone Service (800-842-2252) which you can call to make the transfer. You can also call to change your allocation of future premiums.

Also, TIAA-CREF will allow you to transfer money out of any of the CREF Funds into any other funds offered by the College (or other non-profit institution) for which you work. However, each College must decide whether and to what extent it will permit this type of transfer.

For transfers out of the TIAA Fund, there is a restriction. You cannot make an immediate transfer as you can with CREF funds. Instead, the money must be taken out in staged withdrawals over a 10-year period. This restriction applies when TIAA is used as part of a basic retirement plan. It does not apply to SRA tax-sheltered annuities [see Section 4 of the *Tax-Sheltered Plans* chapter]. Transfers out of TIAA must be made in a minimum denomination of $10,000, unless there is not this much in the account.

You will have to check with the personnel office where you work to find out which options are available to you. If all the options are not available, be sure to check whether they have been rejected, or are still under consideration. These options are relatively new and many colleges have not yet decided which to allow.

The transferability options will prove valuable to those who wish to tailor an investment strategy for their retirement funds.

Example

Mann is 40 years old when he starts participation in the TIAA-CREF system. He wishes to have half of his money in a no-risk investment and the other half in the stock market. As he nears retirement, he wishes to change the mix so he is 75% in the no-risk investment and only 25% in the stock market.

Mann designates 50% of contributions to be invested in the CREF Stock Fund and the other 50% in the CREF Money Market Fund. The money market fund invests in short-term high-quality securities. This protects it not only from the risk of default, but also from the risk of inflation. (The inflation risk is negated because short-term interest rates track the movement of inflation so your funds will grow in general pace with inflation. This is not the case with either the TIAA Fund or the CREF Bond Fund, which are adversely affected if the inflation rate climbs.)

After 10 years, let's say the stock market has been kind to Mann. Because of the rise in value, his account in the CREF Stock Market Fund is now worth 2 times the money in his CREF Money Market Fund. To return to his basic investment strategy, he can use a transfer to return to a 50/50 allocation.

As Mann nears retirement, he can further use the transfer option to work his portfolio towards the 75/25 allocation he desires in retirement.

Cashability

CREF will allow participants to withdraw all or part of the accumulated account in a CREF fund upon retirement or terminating employment. However, each employer has the authority to permit or restrict such withdrawals. Many are reluctant to allow full withdrawals, partly out of paternalistic concern that the employee will squander the funds, leaving him with inadequate retirement support.

You will need to check if your employer has made a decision as to what type of lump sum withdrawals, if any, will be permitted under the TIAA-CREF options. Such withdrawals would come under the rules described in Sections 2 and 4 of the *Tax-Sheltered Plans* chapter. In particular, note there the rules for rolling over funds into an IRA or other plan, and the extra 10% penalty tax that applies to withdrawals before age 59½ in the absence of a rollover.

Comparing TIAA-CREF with Other Plans

Contributions to TIAA-CREF are non-transferable and non-forfeitable. Thus, TIAA-CREF satisfies the basic tax-sheltered annuity regulations described above. Most institutions which use the TIAA-CREF system permit their employees to make a reduction-of-salary agreement to shelter their contributions from tax. However, some institutions do not permit such agreements, either because local law does not allow it, because the bookkeeping requirements cannot be met, or for other reasons.

Many institutions permit employees to make tax-sheltered contributions to TIAA-CREF in addition to the regular required contributions to the basic retirement plan. This is the case even if TIAA-CREF is not used for the basic retirement plans. These additional contributions are subject to certain limitations provided for in the law. Details are discussed in Section 4 of the *Tax-Sheltered Plans* chapter.

Some institutions offer their employees a choice between the TIAA-CREF system and a second retirement plan sponsored by the institution. Often, this second plan is a state or local retirement system that applies to all government employees. In such cases, there can be substantial differences between the two plans. The TIAA-CREF system may permit reduction-of-salary agreements to defer tax on employee contributions, while the state or local retirement system may not.

However, this tax advantage could be outweighed by other advantages of the state or local system. Benefits paid by TIAA-CREF are actuarially computed to correspond precisely to the amounts that have been contributed to your account and the investment experience of the funds. But state and local systems are often not based on such actuarial computations. Especially in times of high inflation, governmental pension plans often pay out benefits far more than that which an actuarial computation would yield. This is particularly true when cost-of-living adjustments are provided for.

Often, employees who anticipate changing jobs within a few years will be better off with a plan like TIAA-CREF because it provides for no forfeiture of amounts in the employee's account. This is not the case with many other pension plans. Employees who do not anticipate changing jobs will have to make a careful evaluation of the features of each of the plans being offered to determine which is more favorable in their case.

Retirement Options

Under TIAA, an annuity can be selected which essentially pays a fixed monthly amount until death, based on the size of the employee's account and his age at retirement. Or, an annuity can be chosen which starts at a lower level and increases annually to compensate, roughly, for the increase in the cost of living. A number of options are available to provide that payments continue to a spouse after the death of the employee. Of course, any options which provide payments to a spouse reduce the amount of the original annuity according to the appropriate actuarial computation.

Amounts in CREF are used to purchase a variable annuity upon retirement. Monthly payments are made which vary according to the dividend and interest payments made by the securities and the rise and fall in market value. Options providing benefits to a beneficiary apply to these variable annuities also.

Supreme Court Unisex Ruling

In 1983, the Supreme Court issued a ruling concerning payments from *defined contribution* pension plans. These are pension plans under which each year, money is credited to an individual's account. At retirement, an annuity is purchased based solely on the amount in the individual's account, including investment income earned on the contributions. The plans run by TIAA and CREF are defined contribution plans. Pension plans which promise a certain monthly benefit based on final salary are **not** defined contribution plans.

Historically, two different life-expectancy tables were used to calculate the annuity payments which the funds in an individual's account would purchase — one table for women and the other for men. Because women, on average, live longer than men, their annuity payments would be expected to continue over a longer period of time. Therefore, the monthly payments they received were less than the payments received by men to compensate for the expectation that more payments would be made.

However, the Supreme Court ruled that this policy violated antidiscrimination requirements of the law. As of August 1, 1983, employers must use one unisex mortality table in computing the annuity payments an individual is to receive based on the value of the funds accumulated in his retirement account after this date. That is, there can be no different treatment of men and women as there had been in the past. If women as a class live longer than men, they will simply receive more total benefits than men.

The U.S. Court of Appeals for the Second Circuit extended the Supre ruling to cover all individuals in the TIAA-CREF system retiring after May 1, 1980. It ruled that the pensions of such individuals should be adjusted to conform to a unisex mortality table applied to the entire value of their account. In October 1984, the Supreme Court declined to review this Court of Appeals decision, thereby letting it stand as law. Although the Second Circuit Court of Appeals only has jurisdiction over a limited geographical area, TIAA-CREF announced that it would apply the decision nationwide.

TIAA-CREF has computed the difference that a switch to unisex mortality tables makes. Pension payments to men generally decrease while pension payments to women generally increase. However, the amount of change depends on the type of annuity which is selected.

There are two basic types of annuities — single-life and joint-life annuities. A *single-life annuity* makes payments to the individual until he/she dies. A *joint-life annuity* continues payments to the surviving spouse until the spouse dies.

Single-life annuities are the ones most affected by the switch to unisex tables. TIAA single-life annuities are lowered $4\frac{1}{2}\%$ for men and raised $4\frac{1}{2}\%$ for women. CREF annuities are lowered 8% for men and raised 8% for women.

Single-life annuities can also be chosen which guarantee that payments continue for 10 or 20 years (to a beneficiary) if the individual dies before that time. For a 10-year guaranteed period, the men's loss/women's gain is $2\frac{1}{2}\%$ for TIAA and 6% for CREF. For a 20-year guaranteed period, the figures are 1% for TIAA and $2\frac{1}{2}\%$ for CREF.

Joint-life annuities which continue payments to the surviving spouse at the same rate or at a $\frac{2}{3}$ reduction are unaffected by the switch to unisex tables. If annuity payments to the spouse are $\frac{1}{2}$ the payments to the individual, the TIAA change is 2% and the CREF change is $3\frac{1}{2}\%$. (All of the above figures are based on an assumption that both husband and wife are 65 years old.)

Those who participate in the TIAA-CREF Retirement System should take note of the above percentage changes when making a selection of payout option. For example, men who select the single-life annuity option are hit the hardest; so from an actuarial point of view, this option is the least preferable. The joint-life option is the most favorable, with no reduction in benefits if the surviving spouse receives full or $\frac{2}{3}$ benefits.

The opposite is true for women. Under the single-life option, women get an increase in benefits of as much as 8%; while under the joint-life option with full or $\frac{2}{3}$ survivor benefits there is no increase. Keep in mind that a spouse would have to waive his/her rights to the assets in order for a married individual to obtain a single-life annuity.

Of course, non-actuarial considerations may play a larger role in an individual's decision on which payout option to use. For example, a man may still want to choose a straight single-life option if he has no heirs he wishes to provide for. Also, the actuarial tables are based on average life expectancies from which a person may have reason to believe he will deviate. The health, family history, or living habits of an individual may indicate a different life expectancy than average. In such a case, this may point to a particular payout option. For example, the joint-life option is statistically preferable for a female in ill health with a healthy husband even though the single-life option benefits from the switch to unisex mortality tables.

The IRS has issued new regulations dealing with minimum distribution elections. For 2001, the use of the new rules is elective if the plan has been amended. For 2002, the new rules are mandatory and any elections made under prior regulations will have to be changed to conform with the new regulations. The new regulations require a distribution based on a uniform table that accounts for the account owner's age and an age ten years younger. This method in essence creates a joint-life annuity and the only deviation from the use of this table is where a spouse is more than ten years younger. In this case, the old joint-life tables will be used to determine the amount to be distributed.

The Supreme Court ruling applies to all defined benefit plans, so they will be affected similarly to TIAA-CREF. However, only employer-provided annuities are required to use unisex tables. If a pension plan pays a lump-sum benefit and allows the individual to purchase an annuity from a commercial insurance company of his choice, the Supreme Court ruling does not apply.

SECTION 4:
SOCIAL SECURITY

Tax on Social Security Benefits

As income levels exceed certain trigger points, social security benefits become subject to income tax. The lower trigger points are $32,000 on a joint return and $25,000 on a single return. The upper trigger points are $44,000 on a joint return and $34,000 on a single return. The trigger points for marrieds filing separately who live with their spouse anytime during the year are $0.

As income rises above the lower trigger point ($32,000 on joint returns, but not exceeding the upper limit of $44,000), up to 50% of social security benefits are subject to income tax. The exact procedure for computing how much of social security benefits is complex. Here's how it works. Start with Adjusted Gross Income (AGI). Add to this any untaxed income from either municipal bonds or foreign earned income. Then add in half the social security benefits. If the total is less than the lower trigger point, no benefits are taxed. If the total exceeds the lower trigger point but is less than the upper trigger point, half this excess is taxed except that no more than half the social security benefits can be subjected to tax.

As income rises above the upper trigger point ($44,000 on joint returns), an 85% rate starts to apply to a portion of the social security benefits. To make the actual computation of social security benefits subject to tax, fill out the worksheet in the instruction booklet accompanying your tax forms. The taxable amount of social security benefits is then reported on line 20b of Form 1040.

The obvious effect of the tax on social security benefits is to lower the net benefit for those who exceed the trigger points. A less obvious but equally strong effect is that for some, an increase in other income triggers an extra tax on social security benefits. For example, suppose a single person has $22,000 AGI plus $6,000 social security benefits. His AGI + ½ of social security benefits equal $25,000. Because this places him right at the lower trigger point, no tax is paid on his social security benefits. He simply computes his tax on the $22,000 of Adjusted Gross Income.

But now suppose he earns an extra $3,000 in taxable income, bringing his AGI to $25,000. The total of his AGI + ½ of social security benefits equals $28,000. This exceeds the $25,000 trigger point by $3,000, so half this excess, ½ × $3,000 = $1,500, is subjected to tax. He must pay tax on $25,000 + $1,500 = $26,500. Thus, the extra $3,000 in earnings triggers an increase in taxable income of $4,500. In effect, his marginal tax bracket on extra earnings has been increased by 50%!

A similar effect would occur if instead of an extra $3,000 in earnings, he earned an extra $3,000 in tax-exempt income. This would trigger a tax on $1,500 of benefits just as in the preceding computation. Effectively, instead of being totally exempt from tax, half of this "tax-exempt" income is subject to tax.

Note that many states which tie their state income tax computation to the federal tax computation make an exception in the case of Social Security benefits. In these states, all Social Security benefits are completely exempt from state income tax.

Tax Rules for Household Employees

Under the tax law, no Social Security tax is due on domestic workers unless total 2001 wages exceed $1,300. (For these purposes, wages do not include the value of food, lodging, or clothing, nor do they include reimbursements for public transportation up to a maximum of $65 per month.) When wages exceed $1,300, social security and medicare taxes need to be paid at the regular rates of 6.2% and 1.45% = 7.65% for both employer and employee. You can withhold the employee's share from his salary or you can choose to pay both portions yourself. The social security tax applies to the first $80,400 of wages paid. The medicare tax applies to the total of all wages paid.

In addition to the social security tax, there can be a liability for federal and state unemployment taxes. This tax is assessed if you pay more than $1,000 per quarter in wages. The federal tax is paid with your quarterly estimates and reported on Schedule H, discussed below. Most states use the $1,000 per quarter test for unemployment taxes. If you are required to pay this state tax, you will need to register as an employer with your state. The state will send you their forms to compute and pay this tax, usually paid quarterly.

The amount you owe for 2001 is computed on Schedule H, *Household Employment Taxes,* which you attach to your 2001 Form 1040 that you file by April 15, 2002. This schedule is also used for computing any unemployment tax that is due, as well as for listing any amounts you may have withheld from the domestic employee's paychecks. Estimated tax penalties apply to underpayments of estimated tax due to employment taxes reported on Schedule H.

Schedule H can be obtained as part of "Package H (Form 1040)," available from the IRS. Package H contains about 10 pages of instructions along with a blank copy of Schedule H. You will need to get an *Employee Identification Number* (EIN) from the IRS to enter on your Schedule H and any Forms W-2 you may issue to domestic employees of yours. This number can be obtained by completing and filing Form SS-4, which you obtain from the IRS.

One complication of using Schedule H is that income tax shown on your Form 1040 is increased by the amount of Social Security taxes, unemployment taxes, and withholding for domestic workers you employ. If the amounts withheld from your paychecks just cover the tax on your wages and investment income, there will be a shortage. To avoid penalties, you must make up the difference by increasing the amounts withheld from your paycheck or by making *estimated tax payments* four times a year [see the *Withholding* chapter]. This only applies to amounts paid after 1997. Prior to 1998, there was no penalty for insufficient withholding or estimated tax payments to the extent the insufficiency was due to amounts reported on Schedule H.

You don't have to withhold income tax from your domestic employee's wages unless your employee asks you to withhold and you agree. In this case, the employee must give you a completed Form W-4 and you must issue a Form W-2 specifying the total amounts withheld.

There is a special exception to the Social Security tax rules for domestic workers who have not yet reached age 18 as of the first of the year. Namely, no social security tax is due, no matter how much the workers earn. This exception extends for the entire year during which an employee reaches his 18th birthday. However, for an employee who is a non-student, this exception does not apply if his principal occupation is domestic work.

No Limit on Base for Medicare Tax

In 1990, social security tax was levied on all wages up to the social security wage base, then $51,300. The rate of tax was 7.65% paid by the employee and a matching 7.65% paid by the employer. The 7.65% rate actually consisted of 2 components — 6.2% for retirement (and disability) benefits plus 1.45% for medicare.

For 2001, the **wage base** for the retirement portion has risen to $80,400. However, there is no longer a wage base cutoff for the 1.45% medicare portion. In other words, earned income from $0 – $80,400 is subject to a social security tax rate of 7.65% and income above $80,400 is subject to a rate of 1.45%. These rates apply both to the employee's contribution and to the employer's.

Grant recipients should consult the *Tax-Free Grants* chapter to determine if their grants qualify for exemption from social security tax. If so, they should notify their employer. Otherwise, employers might automatically withhold payroll taxes on the amount of th grants.

Self-Employed Persons

Self-employed persons must pay both the employee's portion and the employer's portion of the social security tax. However, if the person also has wages as an employee, the $80,400 upper limit on earnings subject to the social security retirement tax applies to the total earned income. Thus, in particular, when a person has employee wages exceeding $80,400 for 2001, he/she does not owe any further social security retirement tax on any self-employment income he earns. However, because there is no upper limit on the amount of earnings subject to the medicare tax (1.45% for employee and 1.45% for employer), a self-employed person must pay medicare tax of 1.45% + 1.45% = 2.9% on all his self-employment earnings.

Self-employed persons compute social security tax on their self-employment earnings on Schedule SE. The total tax due is then entered on line 52 of Form 1040. However, this tax is partly alleviated by the deduction for one-half the social security tax that is claimed on line 27 of Form 1040 [see Section 1 of the *Outside Business Activity* chapter].

Excess Social Security Retirement Tax

The basic social security retirement tax rate is 6.2% of an individual's wages up to a maximum annual wage level of $80,400 for 2001. Thus, the maximum social security retirement taxes an individual employee can pay for 2001 is 6.2% × $80,400 = $4,984.80. (This does not include the 1.45% medicare tax which applies to all income without regard to the $80,400 limit.)

If all your wages come from one employer, there is nothing for you to do. If your annual wages exceed $80,400, your employer will only take out the maximum $4,984.80 in social security retirement taxes (plus the medicare tax that is due). If your employer makes a mistake and withholds too much, he will have to make an adjustment and refund the excess to you.

However, if you have annual wages from 2 or more employers which total more than $80,400, too much will be withheld. For example, if you earn $50,000 from each of 2 employers, each employer will withhold 6.2% × $50,000 = $3,100, a total of $6,200 in social security retirement taxes. This exceeds the social security retirement maximum for 2001 by $6,200 − $4,984.80 = $1,215.20.

In this situation, you can claim the excess social security taxes withheld as a credit on your income tax return. The amount of the credit is computed on a worksheet in the instruction booklet accompanying your tax forms. The amount of the credit is then entered on line 61 of Form 1040. This credit does not apply to the medicare portion of your social security tax because the $80,400 wage base does not apply. You must pay the 1.45% medicare tax on the full amount of any earned income you receive, with no excess payments generating a tax credit.

A similar situation arises if you have self-employment earnings in addition to wages from an employer. If the total earnings exceed $80,400, the basic computations would cause too much social security retirement tax to be withheld. However, in this case, Schedule SE, *Self-Employment Tax,* handles the situation. It simply cuts off the social security retirement tax when total earnings reach $80,400. You don't have to fill out anything extra on Form 1040 as you do when excess amounts are withheld from 2 or more employers.

Checking Your Social Security Account

Form SSA7004 can be filled out to obtain a statement which includes an estimate of what your social security benefits will be when you retire. The statement will include a year-by-year breakdown of how much Social Security earnings were credited to your account. You can use this to correct your earnings record if there are inaccuracies. You can obtain this form by calling 1-800-772-1213, or go to www.ssa.gov/reach.htm.

Social Security Numbers Required for Children

You must have social security numbers for children if you wish to claim them as dependents on your 2001 tax return. You list these numbers in 6c on Form 1040. Call your local social security office to get application forms.

There's a simple way to get a social security number for a newborn. In most places, you can get the number issued automatically by having a box on the birth record checked. The information will then be sent to the Social Security Administration, which will issue a number within a few months.

You should anticipate needing social security numbers in advance of filing your tax return. The IRS states it will no longer accept *"Applied For"* as a substitute.

26

Outside Business Activity

SECTION 1:
BASIC RULES

In addition to your regular job, you or your spouse may have an outside "business" activity, e.g. writing, tutoring, consulting, refereeing, reviewing, art, photography, etc. If this activity produces extra income, it becomes taxable along with the rest of your income. As discussed in Sections 2 and 3, there are a number of ways to ease the tax burden on this outside income.

Of particular note are the remarkable *self-employed plans*. With such plans, those with self-employment income can often **shelter up to 100% of such income from tax** [see Section 3 of the *Tax-Sheltered Plans* chapter for details].

On the other hand, the activity might produce a loss. When a loss is produced, the question arises whether the activity qualifies as a business activity or is simply a hobby. Losses produced by a business activity are fully deductible, while losses produced by a hobby are not. Section 4 discusses the rules for deducting losses in more detail.

The methods described in this chapter apply only to income which is earned as a result of your labor. Investment income, income from rents, etc., do not qualify. Furthermore, such income must be self-employment income earned when you are working for yourself or income received from a corporation which you own.

Example
Jones, in addition to his regular job, does consulting work for an industrial company in the city where he lives. He arranges it so that he is not considered an employee of the company for which he works. Rather, he is a self-employed professional contracting out his services. Alternatively, he could form the Jones Consulting Firm (whose only employee is Jones) which contracts with the company for the services of Jones. Actually, the industrial company is quite happy with this arrangement. It doesn't have to pay social security, unemployment insurance, or worker's compensation premiums as it has to do on its regular employees. In fact, Jones' remuneration as a private contractor may be higher than it would be as an employee because of these savings.

Who Is an Employee?
You cannot call yourself a private contractor just because you and the party engaging your services agree. There is a definite body of law as to when a person

471

is an employee and when he is a private contractor. The basic definition of an employee is one who performs services subject to control by an employer *"not only as to the result to be accomplished by the work, but also as to the details and means by which that result is accomplished. That is, an employee is subject to the will and control of the employer not only as to what is to be done, but also as to how and when it shall be done."* Of course, the preceding definition is not sufficiently precise to determine borderline cases. There may be specific IRS guidelines which apply in your case. If not, the particular circumstances of your situation will determine your status. You can get a ruling from the IRS in any doubtful situation by filling out a special questionnaire for that purpose.

It's possible to work for an organization as a self-employed private contractor, even while working as an employee for the same organization. This is illustrated by the following court case.

Court Case

Reece was a tenured faculty member in the School of Business at a large midwestern university. As such, he was a salaried employee of the university, with a teaching commitment of 9 months per year.

In addition to his faculty duties, he organized and led short seminars for business executives throughout the year. These seminars were held under the auspices of the Division of Executive Education of the same university where he taught. He contracted with this Division, being paid on a per seminar basis. He prepared the syllabus and all course materials for these seminars. For giving these seminars, he received $27,788, with no fringe benefits.

The Court ruled that his activities conducting the seminars were undertaken as a private contractor. This was a separate activity from that of his employee duties as a faculty member. This meant that Reece was permitted to deduct 20% × $27,788 = $5,558, which he contributed to a self-employed plan. [Reece, TC Memo 1992-335]

IRS Crackdown on Self-Employed Persons

The IRS has a general preference that individuals be labeled *employees* rather than *self-employed persons*. It's easier to tax an employee because both income tax and social security tax are withheld from his paychecks. However, self-employed persons are responsible for sending in their tax payments themselves. In fact, studies have shown that underreporting of self-employment income is a significant problem.

As a consequence, the IRS sometimes targets individuals who classify income as self-employment income when it feels this income might better be classified as wages. The IRS instructs its computers to look for tax returns reporting self-employment income from only one source. That is, it is targeting tax returns of individuals who have received only one Form 1099 reporting self-employment income.

Generally, payments totalling $600 or more during the year must be reported to the recipient and the IRS on a Form 1099. Thus, an individual with self-employment income exceeding $600 from only one source might find himself targeted by the IRS.

Of course, this targeting device by the IRS is a crude one. As discussed later in this Section, a person can have self-employment income even if it comes only from a single source. And even if income is reclassified, this does not necessarily mean that extra tax will be due, although the tax return may have to be revised.

To prevent unwanted communications from the IRS, it would be wise to avoid having just one source of self-employment reported to the IRS. If possible, try to earn at least $600 from a second source, so the IRS will receive 2 separate reports of self-employment income.

If you have 2 sources of self-employment income, but one of them amounts to less than $600, there is still something you can do. While only annual payments of $600 or more *must* be reported by a payer to the IRS on a Form 1099, this does not mean smaller amounts should not be reported. You can ask payers of amounts less than $600 to file a Form 1099 on you, even though they are not required to do so. In any event, keeping good records should get you through an IRS audit (see Chapter 18, *Will Your Tax Return Be Audited?*).

Basic Forms of Organization

There are four basic forms of business organizations:

(1) Sole Proprietorship (i.e. Self-Employed)

(2) Partnership

(3) Corporation

(4) Limited Liability Company

1. Sole Proprietorship (i.e. Self-Employed)

This is how most people in business for themselves operate. It just means you are self-employed. No special form of organization or legal paraphernalia is required. If you are performing services for a fee such as consulting, reviewing, etc., and are not an employee of the party for whom you perform these services, you are automatically operating a sole proprietorship.

Income and expenses due to self-employment are reported on Schedule C or Schedule C-EZ. In addition to income tax, self-employment income is subject to social security tax at the rate of 15.3% until earned income from all sources exceeds $80,400. Thereafter, the rate is 2.9% [see Section 4 of the *Retirement Plans* chapter]. However, there is no social security tax if self-employment income for the year is less than $400. The self-employment social security tax is computed on Schedule SE.

On Form 1040, there is a special way of handling self-employment earnings. It is important to be aware of this provision or the **Deduction for One-Half of Self-Employment Tax** could easily be overlooked.

The reason this deduction was instituted is the way social security tax is now treated. For employees, both the employer and the employee pay 7.65% social security tax on the first $80,400 of 2001 wages — a total rate of 15.3%. For self-employment income, the basic rate on the first $80,400 is 15.3%. While the total rate is 15.3% in each case, there is still a fundamental inequity. The employee pays no income tax on the 7.65% of salary paid by the employer. But the basic rules would subject the self-employed to income tax on the entire amount of his earnings up to $80,400, unreduced by any social security tax paid.

On 2001 tax returns, there is a special *adjustment to income* which self-employed persons claim on line 27 of Form 1040. This adjustment reduces taxable income by one-half of the social security tax on the self-employment income. This basically equalizes the social security treatment of employees and the self-employed because the adjustment is equal to the half of total social security tax payments (paid by the employer) which is not subject to income tax.

As an *adjustment to income* rather than an *itemized deduction,* the deduction for self-employment income tax can be claimed on line 27 both by those who use the standard deduction as well as by those who itemize their deductions. Adjustments to Income also serve to lower *adjusted gross income*, which can result in increased deductions for medical expenses and miscellaneous expenses [see Section 1 of Chapter 1].

(In addition to the deduction on line 27, there is one more technical adjustment required to equalize the treatment of employees and self-employed. On Schedule SE, self-employment income is reduced by 7.65% before calculating the amount of self-employment social security tax due. This technical adjustment compensates for the fact that an employee is not only exempt from income tax on the social security paid by his employer, but is also exempt from social security tax on this employer's social security payment amount as well. You need not understand this technical adjustment — the computation is made automatically as Schedule SE is filled out.)

2. Partnership

A partnership is similar to a sole proprietorship except that it involves two or more people sharing a business. Each shares in the profits and each is responsible for any liabilities incurred by the business. If one of the partners absconds with all of the company's funds, the remaining partners are personally liable for the debts of the partnership.

3. Corporation

A corporation is a distinct legal entity which is owned by one or more stockholders. The stockholders have no personal liability by virtue of their ownership. Thus, unlike a partnership, if the company gets into financial difficulties, the stockholders are not required to pay the corporation's liabilities out of their own pockets.

There are two basic types of corporations.

(a) S-Corporation. A corporation with 75 or fewer stockholders may, under certain circumstances, elect S-corporation status. Any profit or loss from the corporation passes directly through to the stockholders as though it were ordinary income from any other source. However, the stockholders still benefit from the limited liability protection offered by corporate status.

(b) Regular Corporation. Profits and losses accrue to the corporation itself. The corporation pays tax on any profits. The stockholders pay tax only when they receive dividends or upon the sale or liquidation of the business.

4. Limited Liability Company

Limited Liability Companies (LLCs) are a relatively new invention. Like S-Corporations, they provide limited liability and direct pass-through of profits and losses for tax purposes, but operate under a simpler structure like partnerships. The main advantage is that certain technical restrictions applying to S-Corporations do not apply to LLCs.

During the past few years, most state legislatures have passed laws approving the use of LLCs. The rules vary from state to state, so professional assistance will be needed when setting up an LLC.

As explained later, more tax-saving benefits are available to regular corporations than to S-corporations or any other form of business organization. However, there are two disadvantages. First, if the business consistently loses money, the stockholders are not always able to get a direct write-off of the losses against their other income. Second, there might be a double taxation involved — first the corporation tax — then the tax on dividends. However, this disadvantage need not always occur. For example, if you are able to pay out all of the profits as salary to yourself, there is no double taxation because the corporation has no net income.

Estimated Tax

If you are a sole proprietor, partner, or shareholder in a corporation, you may have net income on which no tax is being withheld. In this situation, you might have to make estimated tax payments during the year. Otherwise, you may have to pay a penalty in addition to the regular amount of tax due (see the *Withholding* chapter).

Consultants

A consultant should have a high degree of independence in his work in order to be considered *self-employed* rather than an *employee* of the firm for which he consults. An illustration of such a situation is contained in an IRS private letter ruling. This ruling authorized a consultant to consider himself as self-employed rather than an employee. The IRS noted that he did not have any formal schedule of duties and consulted only on an irregular basis when matters came up in an area in which he had special competence. Also, as the IRS told the consultant, the company *"will not exercise supervision over you in the performance of your consulting duties, nor will it require compliance with detailed orders or instructions."* [IRS Private Letter Ruling 7912055]

At one time, consultants generally had to be available to work for more than one client in order to be considered self-employed. Individuals who agreed to work for only one company were usually considered to be employees of that company. However, some IRS rulings have changed this policy.

In 1982, the IRS issued a ruling concerning an engineer who retired from the company where he worked. Upon retirement, he set up his own laboratory and entered into a consulting contract with the company for which he had worked. His contract precluded him from working for any other company. The IRS ruled that he was a self-employed consultant. The terms of the contract and the nature of his duties were such that he could not be considered an employee of the company. This meant his status was that of a self-employed individual, despite the fact he was not available to perform services for any other company. [Rev. Rul. 82-210]

The policy in the above IRS ruling was upheld by a 1983 Court of Appeals decision. The Court ruled that the proper focus of an inquiry as to self-employment status is *"not upon the number of clients or customers an activity generates but upon the nature of that activity that produced those clients or customers."* In the case at hand, it ruled that an individual had self-employment income even though he was performing services for only one client. [Steffens, 52 AFTR 2d 83-5227]

It should be noted that even if consulting activities cannot be considered self-employment, they might still come under the shelter of a corporation owned by the individual. While this requires extra expense and trouble, it could be beneficial in sheltering income from tax. This is discussed later in this chapter.

Technical Service Specialists

The IRS issued a ruling in 1987 that applies to services performed under an arrangement with a *technical service firm.* This type of firm acts as a broker between technical service specialists — engineers, designers, drafters, computer programmers, systems analysts, etc. — and companies who need their services. In the past, such technical service specialists were generally considered to be self-employed independent contractors. This meant they could benefit from self-employed plans and other advantages accorded self-employed persons, as described in Section 2.

In general, if it is common industry practice to treat a category of workers as self-employed individual contractors instead of employees, the IRS will go along with this classification as long as the appropriate annual tax-reporting forms have consistently been filed. This is the basis under which the technical service specialists described in the preceding paragraph could classify themselves as self-employed. However, the 1986 Tax Reform Act specifically declared this *common industry practice* principle to no longer apply to such technical service specialists.

With the *common industry practice* umbrella now being denied technical service specialists, most of them no longer qualify for self-employed status. In general, under the basic rules governing the self-employed/employee distinctions, they will be considered employees, usually of the technical service firm acting as broker [Rev. Rul. 87-41].

Two IRS rulings illustrate the 2 basic different situations that arise. One ruling concerned a systems engineer hired by a technical services firm. While working for one of the firm's clients, he did not perform similar services for others, did not advertise his services elsewhere, and had no investment in equipment which he used. This indicated he was an employee, not a private contractor. [IRS Private Letter Ruling 8903040]

The other ruling was issued to an aeronautical engineer, similarly hired by a technical services firm to serve one of its clients. However, in this case, the engineer did work for others about half the time during the period he was also working for the client. Furthermore, he had an investment in equipment (computer, drill presses, vertical mill, metal lathe, machinist tool chest, etc.) which he used in his home office.

In addition, he represented to the public that he was in business for himself by advertising, maintaining a business listing, sponsoring a sports team in his area, and through the use of business cards, stationery, and checks with his own business name upon them. In this case, the worker was ruled to be a private contractor rather than an employee. [IRS Private Letter Ruling 8830047]

Authors

Income which authors receive is usually considered self-employment income. This is the case even if the individual works at a regular job. For example, the IRS has ruled that income received by a college teacher from writing textbooks is self-employment income when the writing of the books is not part of the basic contract with the college. This IRS ruling, excerpted below, is instructive because it applies to the typical situation encountered by college faculty who do writing on the side.

IRS Revenue Ruling 55-385

"In the instant case, a professor, employed by a state university to perform full-time teaching services at the university, is engaged in sideline activities involving public lecturing and the writing of several books. One of his books is a college textbook which he revises from time to time under contract with the publisher; another is a laboratory manual which he has devised for the use of students at the university where he teaches and which he sells direct to them. He receives royalties from the publisher from the sale of his textbook. During the past year, the publisher made him an advance on his royalties with respect to the preparation of a current revision of the textbook. Although the books and lectures are in the general field of education, they are the result of his own initiative and are not instigated pursuant to his employment contract with the university.

"... In the instant case, it is held that... the royalties and other income received by him from those sideline activities are to be taken into account in computing his net earnings from self-employment."

A basic question is whether an author is in the *trade or business* of writing or has just written a once-in-a-lifetime book. Royalties from writing a book are treated differently depending upon this distinction. Authors in the *trade or business* of writing report their income (and expenses) on Schedule C or Schedule C-EZ. This means they may be liable for the social security tax on self-employed individuals, as computed on Schedule SE. However, they can shelter a portion of their net self-employment income by placing it into a self-employed plan.

Royalties from a *once-in-a-lifetime* book do not count as self-employment income. [Rev. Rul. 68-498] Such royalties can be entered on Schedule E, *Rents and Royalties,* with the total of such income being recorded on line 17 of Form 1040. No social security tax is paid on royalties reported on Schedule E. However, such income does not qualify for a self-employed plan.

To qualify as a "trade or business," the writing of a book should be part of a *continuing and regular* activity. This is illustrated by an IRS ruling issued to a teacher who had written several books. IRS stated that,

> *"If an individual writes only one book as a sideline and never revises it, he would not be considered to be 'regularly engaged' in an occupation or profession and his royalties therefrom would not be considered net earnings from self-employment. However, when an individual prepares new editions of the book from time to time, and writes other books and materials, such activities reflect the conduct of a trade or business."* [IRS Private Letter Ruling 8137103]

A recent court case, however, illustrates that an author need not necessarily have written a previous book to be considered in the trade or business of writing. In this case, a lawyer who moonlighted as a photographer worked on a book of nature photographs. A lower court had agreed with the IRS that the photographer could not already be in the *trade or business* of writing because of his lack of previous work. But the Court of Appeals held that as long as he was engaged in a substantial ongoing activity with a profit-making objective, this constituted a *trade or business.* [Snyder, 49 AFTR 2d 82-1061]

On the other hand, sometimes you can write more than one book and still not be in the trade or business of writing, provided the writing is spread out enough. This is illustrated by a recent court case. In this case, a college professor coauthored the fifth edition of a textbook on textiles, receiving royalty payments each succeeding year. Five years later, she contracted to work on the sixth edition. The Court ruled that the royalty payments on the fifth edition were not self-employment income. Until she signed the contract, she was under no obligation to work on the sixth edition. And according to the Court, *"the five year hiatus . . . persuades us that her authoring activities were not engaged in regularly."* This meant she was not subject to social security tax on this income because she was not in the trade or business of being an author. [Langford, TC Memo 1988-300]

As the above shows, there is no hard and fast rule that determines how royalties must be handled in all cases. In borderline cases, you are best advised to treat the royalties in the manner most advantageous to you. If your other wages do not exceed the social security wage base, then by reporting your royalties on Schedule E instead of on Schedule C or C-EZ as income from a trade or business, you will save on social security taxes. On the other hand, if you want to tax-shelter the income in a self-employed plan, you would have to report the royalties on Schedule C or Schedule C-EZ as income from a trade or business. (Note that, as discussed in Section 3 of the *Tax-Sheltered Plans* chapter, by using a *Defined-Benefit Plan,* you might actually be able to shelter 100% of this royalty income from tax.)

Work Done While Outside the U.S.

Authors should take particular notice of the foreign earned income exclusion. Under this exclusion, $78,000 or more per year of payments received for writing a book can be totally exempted from tax. This exclusion applies as long as the writing was done outside the U.S., even if the work is published and sold only in the U.S. However, the author must be abroad for at least a year and the payments must occur no later than the year following the year in which the work was performed. See the *Foreign Income* chapter for further details.

Deducting vs. Capitalizing Expenses

Under the 1986 Tax Reform Act, authors were required to *capitalize* expenses incurred in writing a book over the period of time they expected it to be sold using the *income-forecast method* [see the 1989 edition of this *Tax & Financial Guide*]. This meant that to make the appropriate allocation, it was necessary to be a forecaster (like a weatherman or perhaps, more appropriately, an astrologer). That is, one had to predict what percentage of income from the book would be produced in each future year it would be sold.

The same rules were applied to artists, photographers, inventors, etc. Under the 1986 Tax Reform Act, they could not just deduct all their expenses in the year these expenses were incurred. Rather, they too had to capitalize these expenses over the period of time during which they received income from sale of the artwork, pictures, inventions, etc.

When waves of protest were made (many by prominent authors and artists), Congress changed the rules back to what they had been. More specifically, writers, photographers, and artists are exempted from the requirement to capitalize their expenses. Instead, they can deduct their business-related expenses in the year these expenses are paid.

This provision applies not only to future tax returns, but applies retroactively as well. That is, if you capitalized expenses on previous tax returns, you may go back and amend these returns to deduct all expenses in the year paid.

The tax-writing committee of Congress makes it clear that this new provision applies specifically only to expenses that are

   * *"paid or incurred by an individual engaged in the business of being a writer, photographer, or artist."*

Thus, for example, inventors would still be required to capitalize their expenses.

For these purposes, *"a writer is defined as any individual whose personal efforts create or may reasonably be expected to create a literary manuscript, musical composition (including any accompanying words), or dance score."* The IRS still has not yet interpreted the phrase *"literary manuscript, musical composition (including any accompanying words), or dance score."* The IRS could interpret this to include any written work, based on the usual definition of *"writer."* Or, it might possibly take a narrower view of the word *"literary manuscript."* For example, it's possible an IRS agent might deem, say, an engineering textbook as not being a *"literary manuscript."* Further information on this issue will be contained in future editions of this *Tax & Financial Guide* if it becomes available.

Under the starred provision above, a photographer can deduct expenses for creating a *photograph, photographic negative, or transparency.* And, an artist is defined as *"any individual whose personal efforts create or may reasonably be expected to create a picture, painting, sculpture, etching, drawing, cartoon, graphic design, or original print edition."*

An IRS ruling spells out the key criteria that will be used in deciding if the production of an item is considered sufficiently *"artistic"* to qualify expenses to be deducted as incurred. According to this ruling,

> *"The originality and uniqueness of the item created (or to be created) and the predominance of aesthetic value over utilitarian value of the item created (or to be created) will be considered in determining whether a qualified creative expense is paid or incurred by an artist. Thus, for example, any expense that is paid or incurred in producing jewelry, silverware, pottery, furniture, and other similar household items generally will not be considered as being paid or incurred in the business of an individual being an artist."* [Notice 89-67]

The ability to currently deduct instead of capitalize expenses does not apply to any expense paid by an individual in his capacity as an employee. In addition, it does not apply to *"any expense that is related to printing, photographic plates, motion picture films, video tapes, or similar items."*

Profit-Making Intention

One further requirement for the deductibility of expenses is that there be an *intention to make a profit*. Writing a book without expectation of profit is considered a hobby activity and expenses can only be deducted to the extent there is income. However, if there is **intent** to make a profit, expenses can be written off even if income from the book does not cover the expenses. This is discussed in Section 4.

Of course, if expenses are related to one's regular job instead of being incurred to produce a profit-making book, there is no problem. For example, a professor who incurs research expenses in connection with his job may claim these expenses concurrently as a miscellaneous deduction. It is only when the expenses are incurred to produce a book as a separate business activity that the question of deductibility arises.

An individual whose writing activities produce substantial income might consider incorporating. In effect, the corporation contracts with the publisher to produce a book. After publication, royalties are paid to the corporation which in turn pays out the money in salary and fringe benefits to the author. As discussed later in this section, incorporation can provide certain tax benefits unavailable otherwise.

Assigning Royalties to a Child — A Tax-Reduction Technique

An IRS ruling shows how authors who receive royalties from books they have written can shift some of this income to a lower-bracket child, relative, etc., whom they wish to aid financially.

Ordinarily, a person must pay tax on income he earns — e.g. he cannot shift part of his salary to a child to lower his taxes. But once an author has written a book and contracted with a publisher to receive royalty payments, the contract takes on a life of its own. If the author then assigns part or all of the contract over to, say, a child, royalties can be taxed to the child. Because the child will be in a lower (perhaps zero) tax bracket than the parent, this results in a net tax savings. (However, for amounts in excess of $1,500 per year, this income-shifting technique won't work anymore for dependent children under the age of 14. In such a situation, these amounts would be taxed to the parent in any event [see Section 5 of Chapter 1].)

In this ruling, an author entered into an agreement to deliver a manuscript to a publisher. Under the agreement, the publisher was granted the exclusive right to publish the work and take out a copyright in its name. The publisher agreed to publish the work at its expense and to pay royalties on all copies sold.

The author proposed to assign to his child all of his interest in the royalty contract. He asked the IRS if royalties paid under the contract could then be taxed to his child rather than himself.

The IRS ruled in the author's favor. Because he was assigning the contract itself, not simply turning over the royalty payments to his child, the income derived from the contract became taxable to the child rather than to the parent. It was the same as if he had given any other type of property such as stocks or bonds to his child. As long as the income-producing property (in this case, the royalty contract) is legally turned over to the child, income from such property can be taxable to the child, not to the parent. [IRS Private Letter Ruling 8444073]

In the above ruling, the author also agreed to later revise the book at the request of the publisher. However, if the author did make such revisions, the IRS said this would be considered rendering personal services to the publisher. Because no additional compensation for the revisions was provided for, a portion of royalty payments received after such revisions were made would be considered *compensation for personal services,* taxable to the author.

Authors (or editors of compiled works of others) who wish to take advantage of the above tax-shifting arrangement should take note of the above distinction between *royalties* and *compensation* when drawing up a contract with a publisher. A contract for the publisher to purchase a manuscript from an author or editor in return for royalties can be transferred to a child, parent, etc., as a tax-shifting maneuver. But to the extent the contract calls for services to be rendered to the publisher rather than a sale of a manuscript, payment for such services is taxable to the one who renders the services.

Also, be sure a publisher you select will be amenable to transferring the contract. If the contract is assignable only with the permission of the publisher and the publisher refuses to go along, you're out of luck. [Miedaner, 81 TC 272]

The above income-shifting technique works not just for royalties on a book, but also for royalties from the sale of an invention, musical work, etc. Also, more complicated arrangements can be made than the simple transfer of all royalties to a child described in the above ruling. For example, partial transfers can be made. This is illustrated by a court case in which an inventor sold his invention to a company in return for royalties. He later transferred a 25% interest in the contract each to a son and to a daughter. The Court ruled that royalties from the transferred portion of the contract were taxable to the son and daughter. [Heim v. Fitzpatrick, 262 F 2d 887]

Also, a royalty contract can be transferred to a trust to provide flexibility. The trust, for example, might invest the royalty money, with investment income paid out to a child and taxed to him. The actual funds in the trust could revert at a later time to the original author, inventor, etc. [IRS Private Letter Ruling 8337055]

In the above type of arrangements, take note of the fact that tax-shifting is not generally allowed on amounts used for basic items of support for a minor child such as food, shelter, or clothing. But money spent on extras such as music lessons, summer camp, etc., does not generally fall under this restriction [see the *Income-Shifting* chapter for further details]. Also, tax-shifting is not allowed for amounts in excess of $1,500 shifted to a dependent child under age 14 [see Section 5 of Chapter 1].

Teachers and Academic Employees

In almost all cases, teachers are considered to be employees of the schools or other organizations where they teach. Exceptions exist where the teacher is hired on a short-term, part-time basis, and is under minimal supervision.

For example, the IRS has ruled in each of the following situations that the teachers were private contractors, not employees:

1. Artists were hired to give workshops in their specialties at an art and craft school. They prepared the course descriptions and were free to decide what material to present and how to present it. [IRS Private Letter Ruling 8832029]

2. Music teachers contracted to teach at a music conservatory. The teachers controlled the time and manner in which the lessons were given and kept a percentage of the lesson fees as compensation. [Rev. Rul. 70-338]

3. Teachers of childbirth classes at a health care corporation. [IRS Private Letter Ruling 8822076]

4. A swimming coach hired by a non-profit organization which operated a swim team. [IRS Private Letter Ruling 8814007]

5. Referees at school athletic contests who were paid by the game. [IRS Private Letter Ruling 8904017]

6. Music tutors hired by a school board. The tutors taught at school, at home, or at other locations convenient to the students, and were paid an hourly fee out of a pool funded partly by the students and partly by the school board. In making its ruling, the IRS was mainly influenced by the lack of control exercised by the school board over the tutors, relative to either the lessons taught, the hours worked, or the methods used. [IRS Private Rulings 9337019, 9337022]

Adjunct Professors

The IRS issued a private letter ruling in 1989 to a university, stating that adjunct professors which it had hired were to be considered employees, rather than private contractors. The university provided all the materials and classroom space necessary for the courses taught by the adjunct professors. And the university established the times the courses were taught, chose the textbooks which were used, and gave instructions on the standards which the teachers were to maintain. Also, the adjunct professors were performing work that was an integral part of the university because the degrees received by the students were awarded by the university, not by the adjunct professors. The students were not private pupils of the teachers, but rather were enrolled in the university. [IRS Private Letter Ruling 8925001]

The above paragraph is only a brief summary of some of the basic circumstances that were extensively detailed in the lengthy ruling issued to the university. While indicative of basic negative IRS thinking on the issue, it does not follow that the same result would necessarily occur in all cases of adjunct professors hired by other universities under different arrangements.

In particular, the university in the ruling had several classes of adjunct professors, one of which it treated as employees. This was a factor in causing the IRS to rule that other adjunct professors, being in the same general situation, should be treated as employees also. This also caused the IRS to deny *"Section 530 Relief,"* which provides that employers who have, over a long period of time, consistently been treating a certain class of individuals as private contractors, can continue to do so if there was a reasonable basis to do so to begin with. A university which has not treated any class of adjunct professors as employees might possibly be able to make a successful *"Section 530 Relief"* argument, depending upon the particular circumstances of the case.

Lecturing Fees and Honorariums

Often, an individual who gives a talk in the field of his expertise will get a small fee or honorarium. Giving an occasional lecture will not produce enough income to bother with tax-sheltering. In fact, this would not even be considered a *trade or business* activity, so that the income would not qualify for a self-employed plan. In this case, the income would be reported on Form 1040, line 21, *Other Income.*

However, when there are substantial lecturing activities or when the lecturing activities are taken together with other activities such as writing or consulting, the income becomes self-employment income reportable on Schedule C or Schedule C-EZ. This is illustrated by an IRS ruling issued to a teacher-author-lecturer. He had received two $100 honorariums for talks and had received $1,000 from the publication of a book and various newspaper articles. The IRS ruled that the activities, taken together, constituted a *trade or business* activity and the income qualified for self-employed plan tax-sheltering. [IRS Private Letter Ruling 7904059]

Another benefit of listing self-employment income on Schedule C or Schedule C-EZ, in addition to offering self-employed plan sheltering, is that related expenses can be claimed on Schedule C or Schedule C-EZ. This reduces adjusted gross income by the full amount of the expenses. In contrast, expenses connected with income reported as *Other Income* on line 21 of Form 1040 must be claimed on Schedule A. If the standard deduction is used or if miscellaneous deductions do not exceed 2% of adjusted gross income, no deduction is produced by these expenses [see the *Miscellaneous Deductions* chapter].

Reporting Income and Expenses on Schedule C or Schedule C-EZ

At one time, Schedule C was used for all self-employment activities. Schedule C contains places for listing self-employment income and expenses broken down into various categories from *Advertising* to *Wages paid to others*.

However, now there is a second choice. You can still file Schedule C just as in the past. But there is another alternative to Schedule C, namely the simplified Schedule C-EZ.

Schedule C-EZ is intended for those with only a small amount of expenses and income. The main simplification is that you only have to report the total amount of expenses. You don't have to break this amount into various categories on Schedule C-EZ as you do on Schedule C.

There are a number of conditions you must meet to be able to use Schedule C-EZ. Basically, you must have had expenses totalling less than $2,500, did not show a net loss from your self-employment activity, had only one self-employment activity, had no employees, do not claim a home office, and aren't required to use Form 4562. A more precise statement of these conditions is found at the top of Schedule C-EZ.

Net Operating Losses

If your self-employment activity produces a loss as computed on Schedule C, this loss is entered on line 12 of Form 1040. If you report wages and other earned income exceeding this amount, the self-employment loss serves to reduce the taxable income on which you pay taxes.

However, if the self-employment loss exceeds other wages and earned income, the tax write-off value of this loss can be wasted. To prevent this from happening, you are allowed to *carry back* this loss 2 years into the past or *carry over* the loss up to 20 years in the future.

Generally speaking, you perform the following steps to see if you are eligible to carry over or carry back a net operating loss:

(1) Total your wages and other trade or business earned income. Do not include investment earnings such as interest or dividends.

(2) Subtract expenses connected with earning this income such as deductible employee expenses like travel, professional dues, etc.

(3) Subtract your net operating loss.

If the result of the above 3 steps is negative (meaning the net operating loss exceeds the other net income), the carry back or carry over provision can apply. In such a case, you are advised to seek professional assistance. In effect, the loss is assigned to either past years or future years when it can be used to reduce taxes. This means that revised tax returns have to be filed for these years. You can obtain further information by obtaining a copy of Publication 536 from the IRS.

SECTION 2:
TAX BENEFITS

Let us suppose you are either self-employed (i.e. a sole proprietor) or else you are the sole stockholder in a corporation which employs you. We assume there are no other employees who work for you or the corporation. Here's a list of some of the benefits which might apply. Certain of these benefits apply only if you incorporate. Others are available to the self-employed as well.

The importance of fringe benefits such as pension and medical plans lies in their tax-free status. Pure salary or self-employment income is always taxable. However, qualifying fringe benefits are not taxed either to you or to the business which pays them. That is, these fringe benefits are not reported as income on your tax return, yet they are taken off as a deduction by the business which pays for them.

1. Tax-Deferred Pension and Profit-Sharing Plans

If you think of private pension or profit-sharing plans as just being a method of forced savings for retirement, you are missing perhaps the most important element of such plans. In reality, they are among the most powerful tax-saving devices allowed under the current income tax laws. Furthermore, funds placed into such plans do not necessarily have to remain untouched until retirement, but may in some circumstances be withdrawn earlier.

The basic idea behind such plans is described in the *Tax-Sheltered Plans* chapter. Namely, instead of being received as salary and taxed in your highest tax bracket, money can be placed into such plans with no tax paid. The investment income earned by money placed into such plans compounds entirely tax-free until the funds are later drawn out and used for your benefit.

Upon retirement at an age you have specified, money in a pension plan can be used to purchase an annuity or can be withdrawn in a lump sum. (With corporation plans, you may also be able to withdraw all your money plus investment earnings if you cease to work for the corporation or upon dissolution of the corporation.) There is a special averaging rule you can use for computing your tax when all the money in the plan is distributed to you in one lump sum. Using this rule, you can average the money received in a lump sum distribution over a 10-year period (depending upon your age), disregarding all other income. The tax on the rest of your income is computed in the usual way without taking into account the lump sum distribution [see the *Retirement* chapter].

An example of the value of tax-deferral is contained in Section 1 of the *Tax-Sheltered Plans* chapter. This example shows how one dollar placed in a tax-deferred pension or profit sharing plan can be equal to three dollars or more outside such a plan.

Self-employed persons can set up a tax-sheltered plan. At one time, corporation pension plans had more generous limitations than self-employed plans. However, this disparity has been eliminated. self-employed plans now have the same contribution limits as regular pension plans [see Section 3 of the *Tax-Sheltered Plans* chapter].

Thus, an individual will generally be able to contribute close to 20% of his 2001 self-employed earned income to a regular self-employed plan.

Those with self-employment income can actually do much better than this by setting up a *Defined-Benefit Plan*. Under these rules, they can often **shelter up to 100% of this income from tax** [see Section 3 of the *Tax-Sheltered Plans* chapter for further details].

2. Medical Reimbursement Plan

Suppose you set up a corporation which hires you as its employee. The corporation agrees to pay all the medical (including dental) expenses of its employees and their spouses and children. The corporation receives a deduction, but you pay no tax on these amounts. Essentially, you are receiving a tax deduction of 100% of the medical expenses you pay for yourself and your family. This is better than the usual medical expense deduction because there is no initial 7.5% exclusion. This includes regular health insurance as well as a portion of long-term care insurance premiums (the amount depends on your age in 2001: $220 for age 40 or less; $410 for ages 40-49; $2200 for ages 60-69; and $2750 for age over 70).

A self-employed individual can't be directly covered by this type of medical plan. However, he can set up a plan to cover all his other employees (including relatives) and their dependents. Thus, a self-employed person can employ his spouse to help out in the business and set up a medical plan which pays for all medical expenses of his spouse and his spouse's dependents, including himself. He gets a business deduction for the medical expenses paid under the plan, but there is no tax to the recipient spouse. In this way, the self-employed person receives the equivalent of a tax deduction for 100% of his family's medical expenses without the ordinary 7.5% exclusion. (Professional assistance should be obtained to set up such a plan in a valid legal manner.)

Under a special provision in the law, a self-employed individual can deduct 60% of the cost of health insurance for himself and his family in 2001. This applies just to health insurance, not ordinary medical expenses. (The remaining 40% of insurance expenses falls under the usual rules for deducting medical expenses on Schedule A.) However, no deduction is allowed for any month he is covered on a subsidized basis by a health plan of an employer for whom either he or his spouse works. Also, the deduction cannot exceed the net earnings from the individual's self-employment. This deduction is claimed on line 28 of Form 1040. (A similar deduction for medical insurance paid to a stockholder in an S corporation of a partner in a partnership is allowable. However, the partnership or S corporation is not allowed a deduction for the premiums under the tax law.)

3. Ability to Escape the 2% of Adjusted Gross Income Floor that Applies to Miscellaneous Deductions

As discussed in the *Miscellaneous Deductions* chapter, a 2% of adjusted gross income floor applies to the total of itemized *miscellaneous deductions* claimed on Schedule A. The *miscellaneous deductions* category includes job-related expenses such as books, supplies, travel, equipment, home office, educational expenses, etc.

It also includes expenses connected with tax preparation (e.g. the cost of this *Tax & Financial Guide*) as well as with investment activities.

Self-employed persons can escape this 2% floor to the extent they can treat items as business deductions on Schedule C or Schedule C-EZ connected with their self-employment activity rather than as itemized deductions. For example, a college professor with an outside consulting business might be able to attribute the cost of journals, books, home office, travel to meetings, professional dues, etc., to this consulting business. As such, they could be claimed on Schedule C or Schedule C-EZ to escape the 2% of adjusted gross income floor. [See the end of Section 1 of the *Miscellaneous Deductions* chapter for a more complete discussion of this matter.]

Operating in corporate form provides the same benefit as discussed above for self-employed persons. A corporation can deduct as a business expense such items as books, supplies, travel, tax preparation, etc. The 2% floor does not apply to corporation business expenses.

4. Ability to Elect the Standard Deduction and Still Deduct Business Expenses

As an employee, you may deduct expenses connected with your job only if you itemize your deductions. However, self-employed persons can subtract their business expenses from their gross income and still claim the standard deduction. If you are the sole owner-employee of a corporation, you still get the same effect because the corporation pays and deducts the expense. You can still claim the standard deduction on your salary received from the corporation.

5. Benefit of Lower Tax Rate

This benefit applies only to regular corporations. Income can be retained by the corporation instead of being paid out as salary. Tax is then paid at the rate that applies to corporation profits — the first $50,000 of profit is taxed at only 15%, the next $25,000 at 25%. The 34% corporation tax rate only applies to profits in excess of $75,000. (There is an exception. The lower 15% and 25% rates cannot be used by a *personal service corporation*. This is a corporation engaged in the performance of services in the fields of health, law, engineering, architecture, accounting, actuarial science, the performing arts, or consulting — substantially all the stock of which is owned by its employees.)

6. Tax-Sheltered Accumulation of Funds

Excess funds left in the corporation can benefit from a tax-shelter of their own. Corporations pay only a small tax on dividends received from investments in other corporations. Thus, corporation funds can be used to purchase shares of preferred stock yielding high dividends which are mostly free from tax. There are even special mutual funds geared for corporations to take advantage of this tax shelter.

There is a limit of $250,000 on the amount of funds that can be accumulated by a corporation without having to give a business justification for the accumulation. This limit is reduced to $150,000 for *personal service corporations* [see item 5 above].

The ability to accumulate and tax-shelter funds only applies to corporations involved in an active business. If a corporation receives over 60% of its income from passive sources such as dividends, interest, rents, etc., the IRS may label it a *personal holding company.* As such, it would be subject to a much higher tax rate than that applying to other corporations.

7. Ability to Delay Tax by Choosing Proper Fiscal Year

Corporations sometimes qualify to use a fiscal year different than the calendar year. This can serve to defer the payment of tax. For example, let's say the corporation qualifies for a fiscal year beginning March 1 and that your salary is paid annually on February 28. Then on February 28, 2002, you receive pay for amounts earned primarily in 2001. If you report this amount on your 2002 return, you have effectively delayed paying tax for almost a year. This enables you to earn a year's worth of interest on the delayed payment. As a note, S corporations and partnerships, including limited liability companies, are generally required to report on a calendar year basis.

8. Reducing Social Security Tax

It's possible to reduce the amount of social security tax by using a corporation to shelter income earned by someone with earnings less than the social security wage base ($80,400 for 2001).

For example, suppose an individual has wages of $30,000 and self-employment earnings of $25,000. When the individual fills out his tax return, he must pay self-employment social security tax (computed on Schedule SE) on the $25,000.

But now suppose that the self-employment activity is incorporated, with the corporation paying wages to the individual of $15,000 and with the remaining $10,000 constituting the profits of the corporation. In this situation, extra social security tax is paid only on the $15,000 wages (half withheld from wage payments and the other half paid by the corporation), with the remaining $10,000 free from social security tax. This results in a tax savings of about $1,500.

The above situation reverses when earnings exceed the social security wage base. For example, suppose you have wages of $90,000 plus self-employment earnings of $25,000. In this case, the self-employment income reported on Schedule C or C-EZ would be subject only to the medicare tax of $2.9\% \times \$25,000 = \$725$, because the maximum social security tax has already been withheld from your wages. If you were to incorporate the self-employment activity and pay yourself $25,000 in wages, the Corporation would have to pay extra social security tax of $7.65\% \times \$25,000 = \$1,193$, an increase in tax of $\$1,913 - \$725 = \$1,188$. (You would not wind up paying the employee portion of social security tax on the $25,000 because it would be cancelled by the *excess social security* credit claimed on line 61 of Form 1040.)

Disadvantages of Being in Business for Yourself

There are a number of disadvantages in being self-employed or operating under the umbrella of a corporation. Some of these are listed below.

More Forms to Fill Out

Self-employed persons must file an extra form, Schedule C or Schedule C-EZ, listing their business income and expenses. Corporations also must file income tax returns of their own. In addition, there are other miscellaneous forms which may have to be filed from time to time.

Legal, Accounting, and Incorporation Fees

There are fees required to incorporate, as well as legal or accounting fees. There are do-it-yourself books which will enable you to carry through the incorporation yourself for under $100. However, most people will be well advised to seek professional guidance even if it requires additional fees for advice or services. In addition, you will want professional assistance in setting up medical reimbursement plans or pension and profit-sharing plans, even if this assistance is just selecting the appropriate standard form to use.

Social Security, Unemployment Taxes, and Worker's Compensation

You may be liable for these taxes depending on your situation.

Caution. We have only briefly touched upon some of the aspects of being in business for yourself to acquaint you with the potential for tax-savings. Especially if you contemplate incorporation, you should consult a lawyer to determine how to take advantage of the tax benefits which apply in your particular case. He or she can also advise you of any extra conditions you must satisfy. For example, the IRS may require you to have a "business purpose" for incorporating in addition to just the tax benefits involved. Also, restrictions on *personal service corporations* might apply in your case.

However, you should not be overly intimidated by the legal complications. Businesspersons, doctors, and other professionals have learned how to take advantage of the benefits which the law allows and which the general taxpayer subsidizes. If you have an outside source of income, you should explore doing the same for yourself.

Section 3:
Paying Family Members for Assistance

If you have an income-producing outside business activity, perhaps you can place your children, spouse, or even a live-in friend on the payroll. As discussed below, this might serve to lower the overall amount of taxes that will be paid. The following discussion concerns business activities being operated as a sole proprietorship. The situation is a bit different for corporations because of extra expenses that may be involved.

Payments to Children

One way to lower the taxes due on income produced by an outside business activity is to pay your children for assisting you. You get a deduction for the you pay them, while they might pay no tax at all on the amounts received because of the standard deduction to which they are entitled.

The IRS has specifically ruled that a parent can deduct payments to a child for services if such services would be deductible if performed by someone else. According to this ruling, *"to do otherwise would be tantamount to penalizing the father for employing his own child, inasmuch as a deduction would be allowable if he employed someone else's child under the same circumstances."* The payments can be for any type of normal services required in a business — cleaning, telephone answering, clerical work, business errands, etc.

A number of court cases illustrate this deduction. For example, one court case permitted a medical professor a $1,500 per year deduction for payments made to his teenage children. The children performed miscellaneous clerical tasks in connection with a small private practice the father ran out of his home. [Moriarty, TC Memo 1984-249] In another case, an engineer paid his children for chores performed in connection with his consulting practice. The IRS objected that the wages violated child labor laws and therefore could not be deducted. But the Court found that these laws were designed to protect children from being hired out to do work in a factory or mercantile establishment where their health or welfare would be imperiled. Because this did not apply in this case, a deduction was allowed. [Denman, 48 TC 439] Finally, in a case discussed at the end of this chapter, a consultant was permitted to deduct salary payments to his children, even though his children failed to include the income on their tax returns.

Not only is the salary of a child working in a parent's business deductible, but it is also exempt from social security tax as long as the child is under age 18. (Non-business wages paid to a child under age 21 are also exempt from social security tax, but cannot be deducted by the parent.) However, the salary should be in the form of actual wages. You cannot deduct the value of meals or lodging which you provide to an unemancipated minor child in return for services. [Rev. Rul. 73-393]

Of course, the IRS sometimes takes a skeptical view of payments made to children because of the potential for abuse. But if the payments are made in a businesslike manner, with suitable records kept, a deduction should be upheld even if the children are young. This is illustrated by a court case involving a family who owned a mobile home park. The family consisted of the parents plus 3 children, with the youngest child being only 7 years old. The children were paid for a variety of chores they performed in the business including cleaning, ground maintenance, answering the telephone, clerical work, and assisting in minor repairs. The Court allowed over $15,000 to be deducted over a 3-year period as being reasonable compensation to the children — including $4,000 for the services performed by the 7-year old. [Eller 77 TC 934]

Payments to a Spouse

Payments made to a spouse for services in an outside business can lower the overall tax bill, although not in the same income-shifting way as payments to a child as described above. The reason income-shifting doesn't work is that payments which are deducted as salary to a spouse become taxable income to that spouse. Thus, on a joint return, there is no change in the amount of tax due.

However, the following provisions in the law can all cause payments to a spouse to lower the overall tax bill.

1. IRA & Self-Employed Plan Contributions

Each spouse may be entitled to contribute up to the first $2,000 of earned income to an IRA [see Section 2 of the *Tax-Sheltered Plans* chapter]. If the spouse has no earned income in 2001, this opportunity is lost. Also, if you have a self-employed plan, contributions can be made on behalf of your spouse, based on your spouse's salary.

2. Household Services & Child Care Tax Credit

The expenses to which the household services and child care tax credit is applied cannot exceed the earned income of the spouse with the lower earnings, except when one of the spouses is a full-time student [see the *Household Services & Child Care* chapter]. Thus, there is generally no tax credit allowed when one spouse has no earned income. In such a situation, placing a spouse on the payroll makes the couple eligible for the tax credit.

The maximum amount of expenses to which the credit can be applied is $2,400 for one qualifying dependent or $4,800 for two or more qualifying dependents. In the latter case, paying a spouse $4,800 might allow the couple to claim the maximum credit. This maximum credit depends upon the couple's adjusted gross income — ranging from $1,440 for those with adjusted gross income less than $10,000 to $960 for those with adjusted gross income over $28,000.

3. Obtaining a Full Medical Deduction

Ordinarily, only medical expenses in excess of 7.5% of adjusted gross income are deductible. However, a sole proprietor who employs his spouse can generally set up a plan to pay all the medical expenses of his spouse (and other employees) and the spouse's dependents (including himself). In this way, he gets a business deduction for 100% of his family's medical expenses with no 7.5% limitation [see Section 2 for further details].

Disadvantage

There is also a potential disadvantage to hiring a spouse, namely the extra social security tax that must be paid on the spouse's wages. At one time, wages paid to a spouse in the employ of the other spouse were exempt from social security tax. Now, however, a spouse's wages earned for working in the other spouse's business are subjected to social security tax, the same as for an unrelated employee. This is usually a disadvantage, but can prove to be a benefit to some spouses who need to accumulate enough quarters of coverage to qualify for social security benefits in their own names.

How Payments Should Be Made

If you want to establish that payments made to a spouse, child, or friend represent pay for services rendered, you should make the payments in the form of wages. This is illustrated by an IRS Private Letter Ruling where the wife of a veterinarian worked for her husband, performing such duties as being a receptionist 2 days a week, purchasing office supplies, laundering blankets and towels, and reconciling business bank accounts.

The husband filed a Schedule C for his business earnings. In the years in question, the husband took a deduction for the wife's wages on his Schedule C. The amount of the wages was computed according to the number of hours worked. In each year, a Form W-2 was issued to the wife and the income was reported on the couple's joint return. However, no actual payment was made to the wife for her services. Instead, the husband deposited all income from his business into a joint bank account held with the wife.

In his view, the amount representing wages to his wife would end up in the same bank account no matter what. However, this depositing of funds was not sufficient to establish that wages had been paid. The IRS ruled that *"in order for a deduction for wages to be allowed, actual payment must be made, and a deposit into a joint account does not constitute actual payment."* Thus, the husband could not deduct these payments as salary, nor was the wife able to make an IRA contribution based on these payments. [IRS Private Letter Ruling 8707004]

Payments to a Live-In Friend

Support of a live-in friend can be converted into a tax deduction if the friend performs work in a secondary business activity. In one case, a man and woman lived together in a relationship which, in the Court's delicate phrasing, was *"other than platonic."* She assisted him in the acquisition and management of various investments and rental properties which he owned. He, in turn, provided funds for food, shelter, etc., for the household which included himself, his non-platonic friend, her child, and her dog.

The Court ruled that he could deduct $2,500 for the value of the work which she performed. Of course, the $2,500 would have to be reported as taxable income to her as well as social security tax paid on her earnings. But assuming she was in a lower tax bracket than he, a net tax savings could still be achieved. [Bruce, TC Memo 1983-121]

SECTION 4:
OUTSIDE ACTIVITIES PRODUCING A LOSS

An activity such as art, photography, music, writing, etc., might generate expenses in excess of income received. It is desirable to be able to deduct the loss on your tax return. However, to do this, the activity must qualify as a **business activity** as opposed to simply a **hobby.**

What Is a Business Activity?

A **business activity** is one engaged in with the **objective of making a profit.** This does not need to be the only objective or even the most important objective.

However, it should be a basic and dominant objective. That is, the activity should be conducted in a manner aimed at making a profit.

It is important to note what the law does not require. When the law was first drafted, the House bill required that the taxpayer show a reasonable expectation of realizing a profit. However, this was changed to only require that the activity be engaged in for profit, not that there be a reasonable expectation of making one. For example, the odds might be heavily stacked against a photographer earning enough income to exceed his expenses. But in his own mind, he might feel he could buck the odds and earn money at it. As long as he conducted his activities with the intention and expectation of making a profit, this would suffice even if others might not expect him to succeed.

The intent to make a profit need not be an immediate one. It is recognized that many business activities result in early losses until the business can become established. This is all right as long as there is an aim to make an overall profit. That is, one should expect that over the period of years the activity is engaged in, the total income will exceed the total expenses.

Note that there is no requirement that the taxpayer not enjoy what he is doing. Just because an activity such as music, art, photography, etc., might be pleasurable does not rule out a deduction.

Presumption in Favor of the Taxpayer

The law contains the following provision: If the activity has produced a profit in any 3 of the preceding 5 years, it will be presumed to be a business activity. Any losses will be deductible.

The IRS can challenge the above presumption if special circumstances are involved. For example, an activity which produced very small profits in 3 years and huge losses the other 2 could be challenged by the IRS.

If the "business" activity has been going on less than 5 years, the above test cannot be applied. Instead, you are permitted to wait until 5 years have passed to see if a profit is produced in at least 3 of the years. If so, the activity is presumed to have been a business activity for each of the first 5 years of existence.

What Happens if a Profit Is Not Made in 3 Out of the Last 5 Years?

If the above 3 out of 5 year test is not satisfied, this does not mean a business deduction is ruled out. It just means there is no automatic presumption of a business activity. In such a case, the taxpayer must, if challenged, show that the activity is engaged in for profit. (The profit can be expected to come from earnings generated by the activity or from the appreciation in value of assets used in the activity.) The principal indicator is the manner in which the activity is carried out. In case of dispute, the IRS suggests that the following factors be examined in order to determine if an activity is a business activity. [Reg 1.183-2 (b)]:

A. Has the activity been carried out in a businesslike manner, e.g. have appropriate records, receipts, etc., been kept?

B. Does the taxpayer have enough expertise to run a profitable enterprise?

C. Has enough time and effort been expended in carrying on the activity?

D. Has the taxpayer been successful in other business endeavors?

E. What is the history of profits or losses from the activity?

F. What is the taxpayer's financial status, e.g. does he need to earn a profit or is he looking for a tax write-off instead?

G. Have there been any profits earned in the past or can assets used in the business be expected to increase in value?

H. Are there significant elements of recreation or pleasure involved?

Note that the above list of factors does not constitute a set of formal criteria. There do not necessarily have to be favorable answers to all or even a majority of them.

If you are trying to qualify a money-losing activity as a business, you should conduct yourself in as businesslike a manner as possible. Any of the following would be helpful:

1. Establish a separate bank account for the activity.

2. Advertise your services to the public.

3. Consult financial or other experts for the purpose of setting up a profitable operation.

4. Keep businesslike records of income and expenses.

5. Write down a projection showing how you anticipate future profits.

6. Operate the activity under a trade name.

7. Have business cards and stationery printed.

Another thing you can do is time your expenses and income to show a profit for a given year. By turning a profit in 3 out of 5 years, you establish the presumption in your favor.

Activities Never Showing a Profit

As mentioned above, in order to qualify an activity as a business, it is not necessary to actually show a profit — just have the intention of making one. This was dramatically illustrated in the following court case. In spite of 20 straight losing years, a professor's wife established that her artistic activities constituted a business endeavor, enabling her to deduct her losses.

Court Case. Professor's Wife Gets Deduction in Spite of 20 Straight Losing Years

Mrs. C. was the wife of a professor at a well-known university in California. For a period of twenty years, she engaged in artistic activities, mainly painting and sculpture. She devoted a substantial amount of time to these activities and held no other job except as a housewife. She exhibited her work at local galleries several times a year, sent announcements of her shows to a small mailing list, and for a short time even ran a gallery of her own. When dissatisfied with the sale of her paintings, she also began making posters and books with the hope that these items would meet with more commercial success.

However, although she occasionally sold some of her work, at no time during the 20 years did the income from her artwork exceed her expenses. The IRS challenged Mrs. C.'s deduction for the losses produced by her artistic activities. No doubt, the IRS challenge was induced by her 20-year string of losses.

The Court, however, felt that the 20 straight losing years did not rule out a strong profit motive. It examined the case further to see if, despite her actual losses, she had sufficient interest and expectation to show a profit. Referring to the list A-H discussed earlier in this section, the Court noted that the factors A, B, C were in her favor — the businesslike way she maintained records, the training she obtained in art school, and the considerable time and effort she expended on her activities. On the other hand, the financial factors D, E, F, G, and factor H all weighed against her.

But the Court did not feel that her lack of financial success was determinative. After hearing her testimony, it felt she was truly attempting to establish herself as a financially successful artist. Mrs. C. went to considerable effort to sell her works and even to change media to achieve commercial success. As for her losses, it noted that "a history of losses is less persuasive in the art field than it might be in other fields because the archetypical 'struggling artist' must first achieve public acclaim before her serious work will command a price sufficient to provide her with profit. . . . Petitioner has a relatively large inventory, she had considerable training, she devotes substantial time to her artwork, she has sold some paintings in the past, and is attempting to sell more. It is certainly conceivable, in our view, that she may someday sell enough of her paintings to enable her to recoup the losses which have meanwhile been sustained in the intervening years."

As a result of the above analysis, the Court found her artistic endeavors to be a business activity entitling her to deduct the losses on her tax return. [West and Churchman, 68 TC 696]

Similarly, an artist was allowed to deduct a loss on her tax return despite a string of 10 straight losing years. The court concluded that while she had *"not sold as much as could be hoped due to certain conditions in the art world, we believe that [she] sought recognition and profit."* [Waitzkin, TC Memo 1992-216]

As the above shows, it is not necessary to show a profit — even if over an extended period of time — to qualify to deduct losses. In fact, it is not even required that any income at all be received. This is illustrated by the following court case concerning an engineer who attempted to develop an invention in his spare time.

Court Case.   Engineer Gets Deduction for Invention That Was Never Produced

Maximoff held a position as Senior Engineer, performing design work for radar warning receivers. During his spare time, he worked on developing a miles per gallon indicator for passenger automobiles. He thought there would be a good market for such a device because of the high price of gasoline. He produced a test set-up combined with a miles per gallon indicator for development purposes.

However, Maximoff encountered unforeseen complexities that would run up the cost of the device. Furthermore, when he contacted General Motors regarding his device, he was told that General Motors had started the development of the same device with a team of engineers. He felt that he would be unable to compete with the corporation's production team. Although he had taken out patents in the past, he did not receive a patent for his miles per gallon indicator. He did not reach a point in development of the device where marketing or sales activity could be realistically attempted. He generated no income from this project.

Maximoff claimed a deduction of $5,747 for expenses connected with his work on the device. This included supplies, postage, rent, telephone, utilities, typing, dues, publications, and auto expenses.

The IRS objected to the deduction, claiming that Maximoff's work on the device was a hobby, rather than a trade or business. According to the Court, the IRS made much of the fact that the project was dropped before the device was fully developed or marketed.

However, the Court regarded this fact as working towards the benefit of Maximoff, not against him. According to the Court opinion, Maximoff

> *"explained that he dropped the project [after] realizing that he could not compete with General Motors research resources and also that the high cost of the indicator he was developing would prohibit successful marketing. We believe that the abandonment of the project at this point shows that petitioner was interested in a money-making activity rather than just a recreational hobby or an activity designed to generate tax losses. The record is clear that petitioner was concerned about his future income in view of his uncertain continued employment due to his post-retirement age and was interested in producing some income . . . While no income was generated from this project, this factor is not determinative. Experimental activity may yield little, if any, return during the developmental stages, although it has the potential of producing significant income. Petitioner was involved in the activity of inventing with continuity and regularity during the taxable year in issue as well as subsequently through at least the time of trial. Accordingly, we find petitioner was engaged in a trade or business [and therefore could deduct his expenses]."*
> [Maximoff, TC Memo 1987- 155]

In the next court case, a professor was able to claim deductions connected with a consulting business he operated on the side, despite the apparent overall lack of profit. In this case, the Court regarded it as a favorable factor that his consulting work was closely related to his university work. This was evidence of expertise that would lead to the expectation that a profit could be achieved.

Court Case

Hutchinson was employed as a Professor at a major state university in the Midwest. He taught courses in management information systems, production, operations research, and quantitative methods.

Hutchinson was an expert in the field of computer applications to the automation of industrial processes. In addition to his university salary, Hutchinson earned income as a consultant to a number of clients, mostly industrial companies. The clients sought assistance from him in exploring the need for an automated computer system design in their businesses.

During the year, Hutchinson had about $20,000 in consulting income. Part of this amount constituted payments for software programs he sold to his clients. The primary program he used in his consulting was a form of artificial intelligence which generated a tailor-made computer program for the client, based on the user's answers to various computer-generated questions.

Hutchinson claimed expenses of over $27,000 incurred in his consulting business. Of this amount, $8,000 was paid to the developer of the basic computer package which he sold as part of his consulting services. The remainder included such items as travel, supplies, books, postage, etc. Also included were payments made to his 2 college-aged sons for helping run time-consuming computer programs and compiling business records.

The basic question to be answered by the Court was whether his consulting activities were truly a separate business activity, undertaken with the objective of making a profit. This would permit him to deduct all his expenses on Schedule C, even if exceeding the income he earned.

Two possible negative factors were the fact that the expenses he claimed exceeded the income received and the intimate connection that his university work had with the subject matter on which he consulted. However, the Court ruled that his objective was indeed to make a profit. And the connection between his university work and consulting activities was regarded as a positive, rather than a negative factor. It showed he had the expertise that could be expected to be put to profitable business use. In the Court's words,

> *"We conclude that petitioner was engaged in a trade or business. Petitioner devoted large quantities of time and effort to his software consulting and sales business. Petitioner did not merely dabble in software consulting—he approached it in a business-like fashion. Furthermore, his business was integrally related to the courses he taught. . . in that much of the knowledge petitioner gained in the classroom was put to work in his software consulting. . . . Although petitioner finds his activities personally rewarding, his objective was to make a profit."*

The other main point of interest was the deductibility of the payments made to Hutchinson's children. The IRS objected that these payments were not fully reflected as income on the children's own tax returns, thereby ruling out a deduction by the father. However, the Court did not agree. The payments to his children were entirely for legitimate services performed in his consulting business, therefore deductible. As to the issue of the lack of inclusion on the children's tax returns, that did not affect the father's return. In the Court's succinct phrasing, that issue "is not before us today." [Hutchinson, TC Memo 1989-114]

27

Foreign Income

Congress has provided the following important tax break for citizens or residents of the U.S. who work in a foreign country. Income which you earn while outside the U.S. can be excluded from U.S. income tax provided all of the following conditions are met:

(1) The income was *earned income* received for services performed;

(2) The income was for services performed while either:

    a. You were outside the U.S. for at least 330 days out of any period of 12 consecutive months; or

    b. You were a bona fide resident of a foreign country or countries for an uninterrupted period that includes a full calendar year;

(3) Your tax home was in a foreign country; and

(4) You were not an employee of the United States government or one of its agencies, paid from U.S. government funds.

In (1) above, *earned income* means compensation derived from personal services rendered. This includes wages, salaries, professional fees, and the like. It also includes self-employment income to the extent produced by personal services rather than capital investment. Unearned income such as dividends, interest, alimony, etc., does not qualify, nor do amounts received as a pension or annuity.

To qualify for a tax exclusion, the earned income need not be paid by a foreign institution or company but simply needs to be earned while you are outside the U.S. For example, a bank president was allowed an exclusion under a similar provision in prior law for management services he performed by mail and telephone for his bank while on extended leave abroad. [Rev Rul 72-423]

On the other hand, a U.S. scholar who receives a grant or scholarship to study abroad is generally subject to U.S. income tax on the full payment. Such income is usually not considered to be *earned income* for services rendered as required under condition 1. [Rev Rul 89-67]

In (2b) above, the residency requirement does not demand that you be outside the U.S. for the full term of foreign residency. Vacations or business trips to the U.S. or elsewhere do not destroy the period of foreign residency. In fact, the only time that condition (2b) would need to be invoked instead of (2a) would be when a foreign stay is interrupted by an extended trip back to the U.S. To establish yourself as a bona fide resident of a foreign country, you should be working there for an indefinite or extended period of time lasting at least one full calendar year and set up permanent-style quarters for yourself and your family.

In (3) above, the term *tax home* has the same meaning as in Sections 1 and 4 of the *Travel* chapter. That is, your tax home is the location of your principal permanent place of employment. The reason Congress included the tax home condition in addition to Condition (2) was to rule out claiming away-from-home travel expenses in addition to the foreign income exclusion. Because the *tax home* must be in the foreign country to qualify for the foreign income exclusion, it would be a contradiction to also claim *away-from-home* expenses.

As discussed in Section 4 of the *Travel* chapter, special rules apply in determining whether an individual's tax home shifts when he takes a temporary job away from home. Employment expected to last one year or less is generally considered to be *temporary,* and the tax home would not shift. Employment lasting more than one year is considered *indefinite* and the tax home would shift to the location of this indefinite employment.

Example 1

A history professor took a one-year sabbatical leave from the university where he worked. He traveled to a foreign country in order to do research, the results of which he intended to publish in scholarly journals and in a book he was writing. His stay in the foreign country lasted from June 24, 1984 to June 29, 1985 — a period exceeding one year. While on sabbatical, he received money both from the National Endowment for the Humanities (NEH) and from the university where he worked.

The IRS ruled that the research he performed constituted labor for which he was being compensated, hence the money he received from both NEH and the university while abroad constituted earned income. Thus, Condition (1) on the previous page was satisfied. Also, NEH regulations specified that recipients of its grants were not classified as employees of the United States so that Condition (4) was satisfied. Condition (2) was clearly satisfied because the professor was outside the U. S. for the required 330-day period. The only remaining question was whether Condition (3), the tax home requirement, was satisfied.

The IRS ruled that he did satisfy the tax home requirement. The professor clearly intended to return to his university after his sabbatical year was over, so in that sense he was going to be away only "temporarily." But since his actual stay abroad during which he was doing research exceeded one year, this was sufficient to establish that his tax home shifted to the foreign country during the period he was away.

Since he satisfied all 4 of the foreign income conditions, the IRS ruled that the professor could exclude from taxable income both the money he received from NEH and from his university while away. [IRS Private Letter Ruling 8619051]

In Example 1, the professor's research sabbatical actually exceeded one year, if only by 5 days. If the stay is less than 1 year, the *tax home* generally will not move, ruling out the foreign income exclusion. This is illustrated by the next 1992 Tax Court case.

Example 2

Gelhar was a professor of Civil Engineering at a well-known private university in the Northeast. The university granted him a one-year leave of absence extending from June 1 of one year until June 1 of the next. During this period, he rented out his furnished house to an unrelated party.

For the first part of the sabbatical, Gelhar visited Belgium, Sweden, Switzerland, France, Greece, and Singapore. The second part, from January 1 until his return home at the end of May, was spent in Australia and New Zealand. While in these 2 countries, Gelhar worked for the University of Western Australia and an agency of the Australian Government and carried out other professional work.

The Court ruled that Gelhar had not established a tax home *outside the U.S. His longest stay in a foreign location was the 5 months spent in Australia. According to the Court, this was clearly a* temporary *position which would not cause relocation of his tax home. Since he had not established a tax home in a foreign country, he could not claim the foreign income exclusion.* [Gelhar, TC Memo 1992-162]

It should be pointed out that the law concerning tax homes refers to *employment* lasting more than one year. An individual who stayed abroad for more than one year but was considered employed abroad for less than one year might fail the *tax home* test. The professor in Example 1 was on a research sabbatical so he had no trouble establishing that he was actually working during the entire period abroad. The teacher referred to in Example 2 ran into trouble partly because, while *living* abroad for one year, he did not actually *teach* for the entire one-year period.

In condition (4) above, all that's required is that you are not a direct employee of the U.S. Government or of one of its agencies. Thus, amounts paid in inconvertible foreign currency to a Fulbright lecturer in Japan were treated as being paid by a U.S. federal agency, even though they were disbursed by a binational organization, the U.S. Educational Commission. [Dowd 37 TC 399] If you are a *private contractor* [see the *Outside Business Activity* chapter] rather than an *employee,* then condition (4) will be satisfied. This is the conclusion of a Tax Court where an engineer was hired by an agency of the U.S. government to oversee the rehabilitation of several provinces of Ecuador damaged by "El Nino," a severe weather pattern with strong winds and currents that caused coastal flooding. Because he was hired as a private contractor rather than an employee, he satisfied condition (4) and was permitted to claim the foreign income exclusion. [deTorres, TC Memo 1993-161]

Limitation

If you satisfy Conditions (1) – (4) above, you can exclude income earned outside the U.S. up to a maximum of $78,000 in 2001 ($80,000 in 2002). If you are not outside the U. S. for the entire year, the maximum exclusion is prorated according to how many days you were actually away. A separate exclusion allowance applies to the earned income of your spouse. If your income exceeds the maximum exclusion amount, an additional exclusion is provided for certain housing costs paid by your employer and therefore taxable to you.

The exclusion is computed based on when the services were performed. For example, if you receive income in 2001 for services performed outside the U.S. in 2000, you exclude this income on your 2001 tax return, even if you are not outside the U.S. when the payments are received. However, you cannot exclude amounts received two or more calendar years after the services are performed. For example, you can't exclude amounts received in 2002 for services performed in 2000.

If you are planning a stay outside the U.S., you should obtain a copy of Publication 54 from the IRS. This publication will explain the rules governing foreign income in fuller detail and illustrate how to claim the foreign income exclusion on the appropriate form.

Sabbatical Pay

College faculty members often spend their sabbaticals abroad. As shown in the earlier example, if their stay in a foreign country lasts more than 1 year, the foreign income exclusion comes into play. However, in some cases, the IRS might argue that sabbatical pay received from one's school while abroad was actually earned in prior years when the individual was teaching in the U.S., thereby disqualifying it from exclusion.

To guard against an IRS challenge, college faculty should submit a proposal to their university stressing the academic work they are going to perform while abroad. Often, colleges treat such proposals as a mere formality. But such a document, when shown to the IRS, can be strong evidence that the sabbatical pay is not a reward for previously performed work, but rather is pay for academic work performed while abroad, thereby possibly qualifying for the foreign earned income exclusion.

An important distinction should be made between two types of sabbaticals. The first is a sabbatical undertaken to study or do research for your own educational development. The second is a sabbatical undertaken to work on publishable research as part of your professional responsibilities. Payments received from your school while on the first type of sabbatical are more open to challenge as having been "earned" in prior years. Payments while on the second type of sabbatical are more likely to be considered as "earned while abroad."

Of course, in real life, the distinction between the two types of sabbaticals is not so clear cut. However, an individual teacher has an opportunity to make this distinction when he/she applies for sabbatical leave. He/she should stress the *accomplishment* rather than the *study* aspect of his sabbatical in his/her official letter to his /her school requesting a sabbatical leave. This letter then becomes the leading document describing the nature of the sabbatical.

Authors Can Exclude Royalties

Royalties or other payments which an author receives for writing are considered earned income. The situation is similar for artists, composers, inventors, etc. Any payment received for work produced by the personal efforts of these individuals is considered earned income. However, if part of the income is due to capital investment, that part might not be included in earned income. This would not apply, typically, to authors, artists, or composers, but might apply to inventors with significant investment in equipment.

The above represents an opportunity for authors, inventors, etc., to exclude income from tax. For example, suppose an individual plans to write a book. He waits until he is out of the country to do his writing. (In fact, this might be an especially good time to do such writing for, say, a professor on sabbatical or other leave of absence.) If his stay abroad qualifies under the rules in this chapter, payments he receives for his work can be excluded from tax, even though these payments come from an American publisher and the book is sold only in the U.S.

However, note the requirement that to be excluded, payments for work done during a given year must be made no later than the end of the following year. This is a severe restriction, especially for authors who usually have to wait at least a year after they have completed their work before it is published and royalties commence. Hence, an author should try to obtain as much as he can in the way of pre-publication payments. For those planning to write a book while abroad, the ability to receive advance payments qualifying for the earned income exclusion could become an important factor in choosing a publisher.

However, the advance royalties should not be repayable in the event the book does not sell as well as anticipated. Otherwise, the IRS could claim the amounts paid were just loans, not payments for work performed. [IRS Private Letter Ruling 8131016]

Denial of Double Benefits

You cannot claim any deduction or tax credit to the extent attributable to foreign income that is excluded from tax. For example, you can't deduct travel expenses connected with your foreign employment. However, such items as medical expenses, charitable contributions, mortgage interest, etc., would still be deductible.

How to Claim the Foreign Income Exclusion

The foreign income exclusion is elected on Form 2555 which you attach to your tax return. There is also a simpler Form 2555-EZ that you can use instead of Form 2555, provided you satisfy the following conditions:

(1) you had foreign earned wages/salaries not exceeding the earned income ceiling limitation,

(2) you did not have any self-employment income or business/moving expenses, and

(3) you do not claim the foreign tax credit or the foreign housing exclusion.

If you submit a suitable statement to your employer that you will qualify for the foreign income exclusion, your employer should not withhold taxes on payments made to you. You can use Form 673 in lieu of the statement. The form can be obtained by writing to the Foreign Operations District, Internal Revenue Service, Washington, D.C. 20225.

In order to receive the benefit of the exclusion you must file a tax return containing Form 2555 to claim the foreign income exclusion even if all your income is excluded from tax. The election can be claimed on an original tax return or on an amended return. [Reg. Sec. 1.911-7(a)(2)]

It is entirely possible for foreign income to be exempt from U.S. income tax as described in this chapter at the same time it is exempt from a foreign country's tax under a treaty with the U.S.

Extension of Time to File

For those who are out of the country on April 15, there is an automatic 2-month extension until June 15 for filing tax returns and paying the tax due. However, this only applies to those whose tax homes are in a foreign country. If additional time is needed, an extension until August 15 can be obtained by filing Form 4868 before June 15. The same rules apply for filing this form as for those who did not spend time outside the U.S. [see Section 1 of Chapter 1]. On Form 4868 you must estimate and pay the amount of tax you expect to owe. If you do not pay the tax due for the year in full with the extension, interest will be charged dating back to April 15 on any amounts due. Also, an additional late payment charge will be assessed of one-half of one percent (dating back to April 15), if the amount you owe with Form 1040 exceeds 10% of the total tax liability for the year shown on that form.

If you have not yet met the 330-day test or the bona fide resident test by the date your tax return is due but expect to do so and thereby owe no tax or receive a refund, you should file for a special extension on Form 2350. This will give you until 30 days after the date on which you meet the applicable test to file your tax return. Further details on the Foreign Income Exclusion may be found in Publication 54, *Tax Guide for U.S. Citizens and Resident Aliens Abroad,* obtainable from the IRS.

Extra Moving Expense Deduction

If you move to a location outside the United States that is a new *principal place of work,* you can claim a moving expense deduction as described in the *Moving Expenses* chapter. Note that the limitations on the amounts that can be deducted for foreign moves are substantially higher than for domestic moves. However, you can't deduct moving expenses to a foreign location to the extent your expenses are associated with foreign earned income you excluded. Moving expenses from or to the U.S. are reported on Form 3903-F whereas expenses of returning from a foreign country to the U.S. are reported on Form 3903. Moving expenses back to the U.S. can be deducted unless they are *inextricably linked* to the tax-exempt foreign income. Thus, an individual's deduction was disallowed because of an agreement made with his employer before he left the U.S. that his return moving expenses would be reimbursed upon completion of his foreign assignment. This was a sufficient link between the moving expenses and the foreign income to rule out a deduction. [D.J. Butka, 91 TC 110]

Payment of Foreign Taxes

The United States has a number of treaties with foreign countries that generally exempt you from their tax for a period of six months to three years, if you are temporarily visiting a foreign country for the purpose of teaching or research. Such countries include Australia, Austria, Belgium, Canada, Denmark, Finland, France, Germany, Greece, Ireland, Italy, Japan, Luxembourg, Netherlands, New Zealand, Norway, Pakistan, Republic of South Africa, Sweden, Switzerland, and United Kingdom countries.

Effect of Foreign Income Exclusion on Other Tax Breaks

A number of tax benefits are phased out when adjusted gross income exceeds a certain level. When you claim the foreign income exclusion, you reduce adjusted gross income, thereby enhancing the range of these tax breaks.

However, for the sole purpose of computing the following tax breaks, the foreign income exclusion is added back to adjusted gross income: tax on social security payments, adoption expense exclusion and credit, deduction for regular IRAs, student loan deduction, child tax credit, education savings accounts, education tax credits, and the exclusion for savings bond interest used for education. (Also added back is income excluded from tax because it was earned in Puerto Rico or U.S. island possessions.)

28

Tax-Free Grants

SECTION 1:
BASIC RULES

Special rules apply to scholarship and fellowship grants which an individual receives. **Degree candidates** are able to exempt from income tax amounts used for tuition and related instructional expenses such as fees, books, supplies, and equipment. (However, amounts used for room, board, or other living expenses are subject to income tax.) **Non-degree candidates** get no income tax exemption on amounts received under a grant.

Both degree and non-degree candidates may be exempt from social security tax on their grants. This exemption is discussed in Section 3.

Definitions

A **scholarship** generally means an amount paid to enable a student to pursue his studies at an educational institution.

A **fellowship** generally means an amount paid to aid an individual in the pursuit of study or research.

The term *scholarship or fellowship* does not include money which is given by a friend or relative, motivated by philanthropic or family considerations. Such money, however, will probably qualify to be a tax-free gift.

Some educational institutions participate in a program whereby tuition is not charged for the child of a faculty member at one of the other participating institutions. As discussed in the *Expenses of Attending School* chapter, such tuition remission is generally exempt from tax.

Also, if a grant meets either of the following 2 conditions, it will generally **not** be considered a scholarship or fellowship and will be taxable income:

(i)   The grant is paid as compensation for past, present, or future services; or

(ii) The grant is paid to enable you to pursue studies or research primarily for the benefit of the grantor.

Difference Between a Gift and a Grant

Gifts which you receive are better than grants because they are entirely tax-free, while scholarship and fellowship grants are subject to the limitations described in Section 2. However, you can't simply call a grant a gift. To be regarded as a gift, you must show that the donor was motivated by family or philanthropic reasons that were directed solely to the recipient. In other words, unless a grant you receive is given by a relative or a charity, you will not be able to treat it as a gift.

Prizes and Awards

Prior to 1987, certain prizes and awards made in recognition of past achievements (e.g. the Nobel Prize, Pulitzer Prize, etc.) were exempt from tax entirely. However, starting in 1987, this exemption was eliminated, except where the recipient assigns the prize or award to a governmental unit or tax-exempt charitable organization.

SECTION 2
INCOME TAX EXEMPTION FOR
SCHOLARSHIPS & FELLOWSHIPS

Degree Candidates

Students who are candidates for a degree may exempt from income tax amounts under a scholarship or fellowship grant used for *"qualified tuition* and *related expenses."* This includes tuition and fees required by the school, plus books, supplies, and equipment required for courses of instruction. It does not include amounts used for other expenses such as room and board or for optional supplies and equipment. This is illustrated by the following example adapted from an example in a proposed IRS regulation.

> **Example**
>
> *On September 2, 2001, A receives a scholarship from University U for the academic year 2001-2002. A is enrolled in a writing course at the University. Suggested supplies for the writing course include a word processor, but students in the course are not required to obtain a word processor. Any amount used for suggested supplies is not an amount used for qualified tuition and related expenses for purposes of this section. Thus, A may not include the cost of a word processor in determining the amount received by A as a qualified scholarship.*
> [Prop Reg. § 1.117-6(c)(6) Ex.(1)]

It is up to the student to keep records of scholarship or fellowship amounts used for qualified tuition, fees, and required supplies or equipment. These amounts are tax-free; the remainder is taxable income.

One piece of good news is that scholarship and fellowship grants, to the extent they are taxable, are considered to be **earned income** for the purpose of computing the standard deduction, rather than **unearned income.** As discussed in Section 5 of

Chapter 1, tax is due if there is unearned income which exceeds $750. But an individual receiving only earned income up to $4,500 for 2001 (the amount of the standard deduction for singles) need not even file a tax return.

The exclusion from income tax does not apply to any portion of amounts received as a scholarship or fellowship grant representing payment for teaching, research, or other services required as a condition for receiving the grant. Such portions are included in taxable income, even if used for tuition or course-related expenses. (Note that this exception applies even if the teaching, research, or other service is required of all candidates for a particular degree.)

If only part of a scholarship or fellowship grant represents payment for services, it is up to the grantor to make the appropriate allocation. According to the IRS,

> *"Factors to be taken into account in making this allocation include, but are not limited to, compensation paid by*
>
> *(i) The grantor for similar services performed by students with qualifications comparable to those of the scholarship recipient, but who do not receive scholarship or fellowship grants;*
>
> *(ii) The grantor for similar services performed by full-time or part-time employees of the grantor who are not students; and*
>
> *(iii) Educational organizations, other than the grantor of the scholarship or fellowship, for similar services performed either by students or other employees."* [Prop Reg. § 1.117-6(d)(3)]

This is illustrated by the following examples adapted from a proposed IRS regulation.

Example

D receives a qualified scholarship from University X. As a condition to receiving the scholarship, D performs services as a teaching assistant for X. Such services are required of all candidates for a degree at X. The amount of D's scholarship from X is equal to the compensation paid by X to teaching assistants who are part-time employees and not students at X. D's scholarship from X represents payment for services. Thus, the entire amount of D's scholarship from X must be included in D's gross income as wages. [Prop Reg. § 1.117-6(d)(5) Ex.(4)]

Example

E receives a $6,000 scholarship for attending University Y. As a condition to receiving the scholarship, E performs services as a researcher for Y. Other researchers who are not scholarship recipients receive $2,000 for similar services for the year. Therefore, Y allocates $2,000 of the scholarship amount to compensation for services performed by E. Thus, the portion of the scholarship that represents payment for services, $2,000, must be included in E's gross income as wages. However, if E establishes expenditures of $4,000 for qualified tuition and related expenses, $4,000 of E's scholarship is excludable from E's gross income as a qualified scholarship. [Prop Reg. § 1.117-6(d)(5) Ex.(5)]

The question of whether a stipend is considered payment for services rendered or a scholarship/fellowship grant hinges on whether or not the primary purpose of the grant was for the benefit of the grantor. In the proposed regulation, the IRS spells this out as follows:

"For purposes of this section, a scholarship or fellowship grant represents payment of services when the grantor requires the recipient to perform services in return for the granting of the scholarship or fellowship. A requirement that the recipient pursue studies, research, or other activities primarily for the benefit of the grantor is treated as a requirement to perform services. A requirement that a recipient furnish periodic reports to the grantor for the purpose of keeping the grantor informed as to the general progress of the individual, however, does not constitute the performance of services. A scholarship or fellowship grant conditioned upon either past, present, or future teaching, research, or other services by the recipient represents payment for services under this section." [Prop Reg. § 1.117-6(d)(2)]

Tuition Remission Exempt From Tax

Graduate teaching and research assistants often have part or all of their tuition waived. Under a special provision in the law, the value of the tuition waived for such graduate assistants is exempt from tax, provided the remaining monetary stipend is equal to or exceeds fair pay for the services performed.

Example

F is employed as a teaching assistant at University L. F receives a salary from L that represents reasonable compensation for the position of teaching assistant. In addition to salary, F receives a tuition waiver. F includes the salary in gross income. The waiver does not represent payment for services and, therefore, is not includable in F's gross income.

Example

Jones receives a research assistantship paying $8,000 for the academic year. In addition to the monetary award, his tuition is waived. As an out-of-state resident, he would have had to pay $5,000 for tuition without such a waiver. Other researchers without research assistantships that include a tuition waiver are paid $10,000 for similar services.

Jones has received $13,000 in money and tuition benefits. Of this, $10,000 is considered taxable income for services rendered. The remaining $3,000 is exempt from tax as a tuition-related scholarship grant.

Withholding from Grants

A scholarship or fellowship grant awarded to a student might be partly tax-exempt and partly taxable, even if no services are rendered to the grantor. In this situation, making this partition is the duty of the recipient. Neither the grantor nor the school is required to file a form with the IRS reporting on the taxable portion of the grant. And, because such grants are not considered wages, there should be no withholding of income tax or social security on any payments under the grant. Essentially, students are being placed on the honor system with regard to reporting taxable amounts of scholarships or fellowships.

An exception to this rule occurs to the extent amounts received under the grant represent payment for teaching, research, or other services by the student required as a condition for receiving the scholarship or tuition remission. In such a case, the school is required to make the allocation between the taxable and tax-free amounts (as discussed earlier in this Section) and issue an appropriate Form W-2 reporting the amount regarded as wages.

Teaching and Research Assistants

Teaching assistants almost always must include their teaching stipends in taxable income. These stipends are considered to be pay for services rendered, rather than a tax-free scholarship or fellowship.

The status of research assistants is not so clear. The IRS tends to assume that research stipends primarily represent pay in return for research services rendered. This is the situation, for example, when there is a specific project on which the grantor wants the researcher to work.

But other research assistantships are designed primarily to facilitate the education of the recipient, rather than to yield a specified research product [see the examples below]. In this case, the research stipend does not represent *wages,* but is in the nature of a *scholarship or fellowship,* tax-free to the extent it is used for tuition and related expenses.

In general, the determination whether research assistantships constitute wages for services or scholarships primarily to aid the student in his studies is based upon an analysis of all the factors in a particular case. The Tax Court confronted this issue in a case concerning two research assistants in the Department of Economics at a large Midwestern University. One of the assistants was in the Ph.D. program, while the other was pursuing a master's degree only. Both of them worked on research projects under the direction of a professor in the Economics Department. Funds for their assistantships came both from the National Science Foundation and from the general research budget of the University.

The Court reasoned that one of the objectives of graduate education at the University was to develop the research skills of its students. These skills cannot be acquired simply by completing the regular course work, but require actual participation in some sort of research project or other similar *creative component.* The Court concluded that the amounts received by the assistants *"were not intended as compensation for services, but rather were intended to facilitate their graduate education."*

The Court pointed to 6 factors which supported its conclusion. (These 6 factors need not all apply in every case.) First, each assistant derived *"clear and unmistakable educational benefits"* from his research assistantship. Second, they worked longer than the 20 hours per week that was required, without additional compensation. This was *"inconsistent with a true employment relationship where one might reasonably expect to be compensated for overtime."* Third, the review of their research by their Professors was informal and irregular. In substance, their Professors *"served more in the capacity of an advisor than a supervisor, and there was a distinct absence of an employer-employee relationship in the traditional sense."* Fourth, the assistants were not required to turn over the results of the research to any persons outside the Economics Department, nor was there any contractual commitment to perform specific research activities. Fifth, the assistantships were regarded by the University and the students as a means of providing financial aid so the students could complete their studies. And sixth, *"many of the trappings associated with an employment relationship"* were absent in this case. The University did not contribute to a health plan, made no Worker's Compensation or Unemployment Insurance contributions, did not withhold social security or taxes, etc.

The Court found that the payments received by the research assistants were only educational in nature and were *"not intended to compensate petitioners for services rendered as an employee or any other capacity."* This meant that none of the stipend was wages, but rather a scholarship or fellowship, tax-free to the extent allowed under existing law. [Langley and O'Riley, TC Memo 1982-460]

Even if a research assistant did some teaching, he can still get an exemption for a stipend covering just his research activities. This is illustrated by the following IRS Private Letter Ruling issued to a Mechanical Engineering Ph.D. candidate:

> *"... The information submitted discloses that you are an instructor and a candidate for the degree of Ph.D. in the Mechanical Engineering Department at X. You have been awarded a research grant through X, by the ***** covering a period of approximately one year beginning September 15, 1983. During this time you will perform research at a ***** research center as a portion of your dissertation research for the Ph.D. degree. You have indicated that the research that you perform for X satisfies a specifically stated requirement and that equivalent services are required of all candidates for the same degree. The research will not be performed in your capacity as an instructor at X.*
>
> *"Your research is to be performed under the guidance of a 'principal investigator' that has been approved by *****. The grantee is required to submit to the grantor semi-annual status reports and a final technical report during the course of the grant. The research performed is not carried out during the course of a specific project of the grantor and the grant is not awarded based on past or future services to be rendered by you to X or *****.*
>
> *"Based upon the information submitted we conclude that the stipend that you receive from ***** under the research grant will be excludable from gross income under section 117(a) of the Code. . ."* [to the extent used for tuition and related expenses, ed.] [PLR 8451053]

Despite the above discussion, the IRS has been known to take a hard-line position on the taxation of research assistantships. For example, it has been known to require Universities to withhold income taxes on the full amount of all research assistantships, no matter what the specifics of the services required. If an individual feels his assistantship should be tax-free, he would still be able to get the amounts withheld refunded to him by filing a tax return as discussed in the next subsection.

Where to Claim the Income Tax Exclusion for a Scholarship or Fellowship

Sometimes, an institution will simply report the entire amount of a scholarship or fellowship as taxable income on year-end Forms W-2 which it sends to you and the IRS. (This is especially true in the case of research assistants, as discussed above.) In this case, the official procedure calls for you to subtract the tax-free amount of the grant from the figure shown on your Form W-2 and report the difference on the *Wages* line of your tax return.

However, this has caused numerous grant recipients a lot of trouble because it has flagged their tax returns for audit . The IRS has a "Matching Program" to verify that the amount reported on Forms W-2 matches the amount reported as *Wages* on an individual's tax return. If the figures do not match, the return will be singled out for examination. This can result not only in the tax-free status of the grant being called into question, but also other items as well [see Section 9 of Chapter 1].

If the Form W-2 sent to you by your employer includes amounts which qualify as a tax-free grant, the following procedure is best. Report the full amount shown on your Form W-2 as *Wages* on your tax return. Then list the tax-free amount of your grant as a negative amount on line 21, *Other Income*. The net tax result will be the same as if you had omitted the tax-free amount of the grant from your total wages, but you won't have stirred up the IRS computer by creating an arithmetical discrepancy.

Note that there are two additional advantages to including tax-free grants in taxable income and then subtracting these amounts on line 21. First, you cannot be accused of fraud for failing to report income. Second, you have subjected the question of your grant's tax status to the statute of limitations. You should attach a statement to your return showing the amounts received and the letter of award to you or other description of the grant.

In the late 1980's, about 20,000 graduate students got most unwelcome letters from the IRS because they did not claim tax-exemption for their grants as we recommend above. These letters told the students that they owed back taxes, plus interest and penalties, on stipends they received going back to 1984 and 1985. These stipends were exempt from tax under the law that applied at the time.

Why did the IRS take this action? The basic reason was the way the graduate students handled their stipends on their tax returns. While the colleges reported the stipends on Forms W-2 (with copies sent to the IRS), the students just omitted reporting their stipends on the basic Form 1040 line for wages, salaries, etc.

This made the IRS computers very unhappy. As we have reported in previous issues of this *Tax & Financial Guide*, the IRS has been getting much more efficient with its matching program, under which amounts reported on an individual's tax return are compared with compensation amounts reported on Forms W-2 and dividends, interest, etc., reported on Forms 1099 [see Section 9 of Chapter 1]. When the IRS computer found that the students had not reported as income amounts shown on Forms W-2, it kicked out their returns, sending them to local IRS offices for examination.

Many of these local offices across the country took a hard-line attitude. Because their computer found a discrepancy, they demanded that students pay back taxes, plus interest and penalties, on their stipends.

This caused much protest from the graduate students involved and from their colleges and universities. When this unfair treatment of graduate students began to receive more public attention, the IRS threw in the towel. It announced [IRS News Release 88-65] that it would reimburse students who paid taxes on research and teaching stipends to the extent these stipends qualified for exemption from tax.

The 20,000 graduate students who were harassed by the IRS could have almost certainly avoided trouble if they had handled their stipends as we have advised in annual editions of this *Tax & Financial Guide*. As discussed above, we advise reporting on line 7 of Form 1040 all income which is shown as wages or other taxable compensation on Forms W-2 you receive from your employer. Then, subtract any amounts that should be tax-free by entering a negative entry on line 21, *Other Income*. This method of handling tax-free income showing up on a Form W-2 is not spelled out in any official IRS instructions (or other Tax Guides we've seen) but has been recommended by the IRS in other similar situations. And in the more than 10 years we've been recommending similar methods of avoiding the matching program trap (depending upon the layout of the tax return that year), our editorial staff has not received a single letter indicating IRS objection to using this type of reporting procedure. If the 20,000 graduate students who received dunning letters had been properly advised of this reporting method, a lot of trouble (including hiring lawyers, filing Tax Court appeals, borrowing to pay back taxes, or just diverting attention from studies) would have been avoided.

SECTION 3:
EXEMPTION FROM SOCIAL SECURITY TAX

Although a grant or fellowship may be subject to income tax because it does not qualify under the rules for exemption of scholarships previously discussed, this does not necessarily subject the grant to employment taxes, i.e. social security tax or self-employment tax.

More specifically, a grant qualifies for exemption from social security tax if the *primary purpose* of the grant is to further the education and training of the recipient in his individual capacity, rather than being for the benefit of the grantor. This means that the money received under the grant is not classified as wages. And social security tax is only levied against wages, not against any other type of income even if this income is subject to income tax [IRS Private Letter Rulings 7929051, 7929066, 8047019, and 8109026; IRS Notice 87-31; Rev Rul 60-376].

The exemption from social security tax on the entire amount of the grant can be worth a substantial amount of money. For example, a person whose only earnings are $3,000 per month under a 12-month grant would save about $2,700 in social security taxes, a substantial tax-free benefit. Even where the social security tax wage base is exceeded, the 1.45% medicare portion of the social security tax has no upper cutoff limit [see Section 4 of the *Retirement Plans* chapter].

The exclusion of grants from social security tax is illustrated by a 1994 Tax Court case concerning a geologist who received a postdoctoral fellowship from a well-known university in the East. The fellowship provided funds and office space to individuals to allow them to conduct independent scientific research. According to the Court,

> *"The fellows choose their own subjects and determine how best to conduct their research; they do not, however, earn a degree or credit leading to a degree for their endeavors. They have no teaching or other responsibilities, and [the university] has no legal right to, or interest in, the fruit of the recipients' labors. The fellows are not required to observe office hours, and they are not required to report to a supervisor."*

As discussed earlier in this Section, grants with the above characteristics are generally considered to be fellowships as opposed to wages for services rendered. In fact, this is how the university treated the grant, reporting it on a Form 1099 as *"nonemployee compensation."* Because these were not wages, no social security tax was taken out or paid by the university.

The geologist paid income tax on the grant as required by the rules, as described in Section 2. However, this was not good enough for the IRS. The IRS wanted the geologist to pay social security tax as though he were a self-employed person. But the Court ruled otherwise. Because the grant did not represent wages, no social security tax was due either as an employee or as a self-employed person. [Spiegelman, 102 TC 394]

Recipients of grants qualifying for tax-free treatment should request that the institution administering the grant withhold no social security taxes. In fact, if the grant qualifies for tax-free treatment, the institution is legally required to do this.

The following discussion contains examples of grants awarded before 1986. The issue with these grants is whether or not they qualify for *tax-free treatment*. Under the law that applied at that time, this referred to exemption from income tax as well as social security tax. Under the current law, grants no longer enjoy an income tax exemption, unless received by a student as discussed in Section 2. However, the reasoning for the exemption should still apply for employment tax exemption. This means that if the phrase *"tax-free"* is taken to mean *"free from social security tax,"* these examples can be taken to be representative of grants awarded under current law.

Due to the individual nature of each type of grant, it is not possible to predict with accuracy how grants will be treated. The finest of differences may cause one grant to be ruled taxable and another tax-free.

This is illustrated by two IRS rulings concerning grants from the National Endowment for the Humanities. The first ruling concerned a grant made to junior college professors *"to increase their understanding of the subjects they teach and to improve their teaching ability."* The second ruling concerned a grant to a professor of English literature so he could *"study the interaction of the sciences and literature with a view toward writing a book on the taxpayer's conclusion."* If anything, the first grant would seem to better qualify under the tax-free criterion of furthering *the education and training of the recipient in his individual capacity.* The second grant would seem more likely to yield a concrete result that could be regarded as *benefiting the grantor.*

However, the IRS ruled just the opposite. It decided that the first grant was taxable because a non-exclusive right to reproduce publishable matter arising from the grant made the grant primarily for the benefit of the grantor. The second grant did not have this feature and was ruled to qualify for tax-free treatment. [IRS Private Letter Rulings 8021120 and 8008056]

NSF Grants

For scientists, the most common type of research grant comes from the NSF (National Science Foundation). The Tax Court has, on the two occasions when the issue came to trial, denied tax-free status for NSF research grants. In 1977, the Tax Court ruled against a computer scientist. In an ironic twist, the computer scientist's expertise and the fact that his work was considered valuable were used against him by the court. [Findler, TC Memo, 1976-352] (A similar conclusion was reached in a different case involving a mathematics professor. In that case, the grant proposal specified that the recipient would spend 1/3 of his time during the academic year on the project funded by the grant, such services to be paid by the university. This linking of the work performed under the summer grant and his ordinary academic-year work was a decidedly negative factor. [Carroll, 60 TC 96]) But in 1978, the IRS issued a private ruling to a scientist giving him permission to claim tax-free status for his NSF grant. Although the IRS ruling was devoid of detailed reasoning, it is worthwhile to take a look at the two grants in question.

1976 Court Case — Tax-Free Status for NSF Grant Denied

A professor of Computer Science applied for and received an NSF grant to work on the development of a new kind of programming language. As is the usual case, the grant was actually awarded to the university, with the professor as principal investigator. Funds from the grant were used to pay him for a 6-month period when he was on sabbatical.

The professor claimed that his grant qualified for tax-free status. However, the Court denied his claim. It appeared to be influenced by 3 major considerations.

First, it pointed out that the grant actually covered a longer period of time than the 6-month period during which direct payments were received from the grant. Over this longer period of time, the professor was to be working on the same project as part of his regular duties as a Computer Science professor and paid his normal salary from university funds. This indicated to the Court that the payments should not be considered as a fellowship. It stated,

". . . it was not the intent of Congress that grants which were in effect continuing salary payments to the recipient while on leave from his regular job be considered as fellowship grants. Here, part of petitioner's regular job and part

of the activity he undertook during the school year while he was performing his other functions at the university was research on the project for which NSF had made a grant. When he went on sabbatical leave and pursued this research full-time instead of part-time, the nature of his research work was unchanged. He was still pursuing the research as a part of his work as a professor and in accordance with the NSF grant."

Second, the Court seemed impressed by the usefulness of the research. Ironically, this worked against the professor because it meant that NSF and the university would receive "benefit" from the research. The Court stated,

"NSF seeks to further research which it finds to be in the public interest. Because it found that the research proposal by the petitioner met that standard, NSF made funds available to support such research. The university is interested in encouraging the members of its faculty to perform research, and for that reason it undertook to administer the grant made by NSF and to make its facilities available for the performance of such research."

Finally, the Court held the professor's experience and competence against him. The fact that he was already an expert in the field was evidence that the grant was not for the purpose of providing him with training or education. It stated that because he

"had so many years of work in the area with which his research dealt, it is not even shown by this record that his education was enhanced by the research he did. In any event, in this case the facts as a whole show that the funds were made available for petitioner's project because NSF wished to have it performed by him, and that the payments made to petitioner from the NSF funds were for the services he performed on the research project. Here, an essential element of having the research proposal approved was the qualifications of petitioner to perform the important research he had outlined. The grant was made to support the proposed research which NSF determined should be performed."

1978 IRS Ruling — Exclusion Allowed for NSF Grant

A scientist solicited an official opinion from the IRS as to whether his NSF grant qualified for exclusion. In response, the IRS issued him a private letter ruling. This private ruling does not set legal precedent, but because the IRS attempts to be consistent in its interpretation of the law, it is still of considerable interest. As is customary, the IRS ruling is published with all mention of taxpayer's name or other identifying information deleted.

IRS Private Letter Ruling 7817011

We are writing in reply to a letter dated July 8, 1977, submitted on your behalf by — and prior correspondence. You request a ruling regarding the treatment for . . . tax purposes of amounts received by you under the circumstances described below.

You received a grant from the National Science Foundation for research in your field. The grant was established for the purpose of recognizing and encouraging the work of younger scientists whose capabilities and accomplishments show exceptional promise of significant future achievements. Your grant is administered by Princeton University.

At the time you received the grant, you were on the faculty of_____. Since the beginning of the grant period, you have been on leave from your faculty position. You teach no classes and participate in no administrative duties. You have no schedule other than that which you set for yourself, and you receive no supervision from the University.

You choose your own research problems, however, when you publish the results of your work, you are required to acknowledge the support of the National Science Foundation. You must also publish a "disclaimer" that the views presented are your own and not those of the National Science Foundation. You are not required to submit any reports of the progress of your work to the University or the National Science Foundation. . . .

In Biederdorf v. Commissioner, 60 T.C. 114 (1973), the United States Tax Court held that a postdoctoral fellowship grant awarded to a licensed physician and funded by the National Institutes of Health was excludable from the recipient's gross income. Seventy-five to eighty percent of his time was spent performing research which was of only incidental value to the grantor, and there was no requirement for future employment services as a condition for receiving the grant. A similar result was reached in Bailey v. Commissioner, 60 T.C. 447 (1973).

Revenue Ruling 58-498, 1958-2 C.B. 47, provides that amounts paid as grants to high school and college teachers to attend summer institutes for science [qualify for tax-free treatment]. The grantees were not affiliated with the National Science Foundation (the grantor) nor did they incur any independent obligation to any educational institution by accepting the stipend.

Based upon our analysis of the authorities cited above and the information submitted by you, we conclude that [your grant qualifies for tax-free treatment].

A copy of this ruling should be attached to your income tax return when it is filed.

A copy of this letter is being sent to your representative pursuant to the power of attorney on file with this office.

As the above discussion indicates, the tax-free status of a research grant is often a borderline question which can be decided in either direction, depending upon who does the deciding. However, an instructive pattern has emerged from various cases on this issue.

First, let us compare the Court Case above in which an exclusion was denied to a Computer Science Professor with the IRS Ruling described earlier in which tax-free treatment was approved for a Professor of English. The difference seems to lie mostly in the more specific nature of the Computer Science proposal than the English proposal. The grant to the English Professor was awarded for the purpose of *"study with a view towards writing a book."* There was no mention of any concrete results that it was hoped would be attained. The NSF grant to the Computer Science Professor, on the other hand, was made on the basis of a specific research proposal to develop a particular type of programming language. The court felt that NSF *"wished to have the research performed"* and therefore received *benefit* from the research.

It is also interesting to compare the two NSF Grants discussed above. The first grant was awarded to an established scientist by NSF in order to *"further research which it finds to be in the public interest."* Because of the existing expertise of the researcher and the desired end product of the research, the grant was considered to be for the primary purpose of *benefiting the grantor* rather than *furthering the education and training of the recipient.*

The second NSF grant, on the other hand, had the stated purpose of *"recognizing and encouraging the work of younger scientists whose capabilities and accomplishments show exceptional promise of significant future achievements."* In this case, the purpose of *furthering the education and training of the recipient in his individual capacity* predominated over the purpose of benefiting the grantor.

Two 1983 examples illustrate that when asked to rule, the IRS generally looks for some special feature of the grant which will make it fully taxable.

In the first of these rulings, the IRS denied tax-exemption for a research grant received by a professor at an unnamed college. This research grant provided not just summer support, but also provided 1/4 support during the academic year so that the professor could receive a reduced teaching load to carry on his research. The ruling was devoid of detailed reasoning. However, the fact that the grant covered not just the summer months but also part of the regular academic year was clearly a negative factor—indicating the grant was more in the nature of pay for services rendered than for the educational benefit of the recipient. [IRS Private Letter Ruling 8336021]

The second ruling concerned a summer-only NSF grant to a professor for 2/9 of his academic year salary. Under this grant, however, the NSF retained the right to receive a portion of royalties from copyrights produced during the life of the grant and for 3 years thereafter. The grant also gave the NSF the rights to patentable inventions arising from work done under these grants. As discussed earlier in this section, the retention of rights by the grantor to work produced under a grant is an important indicator to the IRS that the grant is for the purpose of benefiting the grantor rather than the recipient. Hence, it ruled that this NSF grant did not qualify for tax-free treatment. [IRS Private Letter Ruling 8330749]

The above discussion indicates that the official IRS policy on tax-free grants is to be tough about allowing tax-free treatment. In fact, 4 more recent IRS Private Letter Rulings have all denied tax exemptions for various NSF grants with no obvious special features which were awarded to college faculty members. In each case, the IRS ruled that the grant was primarily for the benefit of the grantor (NSF) rather than the recipient. In 3 of these rulings, the IRS used the following same language (including reference to a 1970 court case, *Turem vs. Commissioner*) describing why it considered the grant to *"benefit"* the NSF:

> *"A grant in support of basic research is made because the National Science Foundation decides that the results of the research are desired and in the public interest. A grant for basic research sets forth the budget to be followed,*

including the allocation of the amounts to be paid as salary to the principal investigator and others working on the project. On the other hand, a fellowship grant is always made to an individual and is awarded to enhance the applicant's competence. Although a recipient of a fellowship grant may engage in research as an incident of his study and development, the objective of the grant is to further his study and not to achieve the research.

"In Turem v. Commissioner, 54 T.C. 1494 (1970), the court found that governmental grants resulted in grantor benefit by inducing recipients to engage in educational activity beneficial to governmental agencies in the attainment of their objectives, even though the general public was expected to be the ultimate beneficiary of the petitioner's education. Thus, Turem stands for the proposition that grantor benefit need not be in the form of monetary gain or services rendered directly to the grantor." [IRS Private Letter Rulings 8521084, 8521029, 8524071, 8528012]

The above discussion suggests that grant recipients are wise to avoid formal confrontation with the IRS, if possible. However, the basic legal situation remains. That is, each grant is judged separately on its merits as to whether or not it is primarily for the benefit of the grantor or the recipient.

As the above discussion indicates, there are no rigid rules to apply which will determine whether or not a grant is exempt from social security tax. Even the Court has admitted that the tax status of a grant must be decided *"on a case by case basis by considering the facts and circumstances"* in the given situation. However, the above discussion suggests how to improve the chances of obtaining tax-free status for a grant. Namely, the **study** aspect of the research should be stressed as opposed to the **result** aspect. Funds for study tend to be regarded as benefiting the recipient, while funds to obtain specific results tend to be regarded as benefiting the grantor.

Grants Requiring Future Services

A grant should not be conditioned upon the performance of future services. For example, if a faculty member accepted a grant which requires him to return to his school after the grant period is over, this would disqualify the grant from tax-free status. This fact was emphasized in several court cases and IRS rulings. [IRS Private Letter Rulings 7828044, 7907079, 8439055, 8439086, Stephens, TC Memo 1978-449]

Teaching & Research Assistants

The income tax treatment of teaching and research assistantships has been discussed in Section 2. The social security tax treatment of these grants is governed by a different rule. Specifically, amounts paid for services paid by a school, college, or university are exempt from social security tax if the services are performed by a student who is enrolled and regularly attending classes at such school, college, or university. Thus, teaching and research assistantships are usually exempt from social security tax.

Refund of Prior Social Security Tax

Of course, the optimum situation is for the institution administrating your grant to simply refrain from withholding social security tax. However, institutions tend to be conservative and withhold from all grants so the IRS can't come after them for amounts they failed to withhold. If social security tax (also known as FICA) was withheld on money you received from a grant which qualified for tax-free treatment, you are entitled to a refund of the amounts withheld. To get this refund, you should first contact your employer. According to IRS Regulation 31.6413(a)(3), your employer can refund the amount overwithheld, and apply to the IRS for a refund of the overpayment it made to the IRS.

If your employer won't agree to the refund, you can apply directly to the IRS. This situation is covered in a ruling which describes the exact procedure to follow to obtain the refund. [PLR 8109026] This ruling was issued to an individual who received a grant on which social security tax was incorrectly withheld. Because many individuals are in the same situation, we quote the relevant portion of this ruling in its entirety.

". . . We conclude that the stipend you receive is excludable from gross income to the extent of $300.00 per `month for the number of months of the internship, not to exceed the 36 month limitation of Code section 117(b) (2) (B).

"Because FICA payments have been withheld on this amount, you are entitled to a recovery.

"Section 31. 6402 (a)-2 (a) of the Employment Tax Regulations provides that any person who pays to the district director more than the correct amount of employee tax under section 3101 or employer tax under section 3111 of the Federal Insurance Contributions Act (FICA) may file a claim for refund of the overpayment or may claim a credit for the overpayment. The employer may file a claim for refund on Form 843 or take a credit for the overpayment on any subsequent return. Claims filed by an employer for refund, credit, or abatement of employee tax collected from an employee must include a statement by the employee that the employer has repaid him/her the amount of the overcollection or has obtained the employee's written consent to the allowance of the refund or credit. If the claim for credit or refund is for a calendar year prior to the calendar year in which the claim is made, the employer must obtain a statement that the employee has not and will not claim a refund or credit of the amount of the overcollection. This is the preferable method for recovery.

"If the employer does not correct the error, the employee may file a claim for refund or credit of an overcollection of FICA tax where: (1) the employer collects more than the correct amount of employee social security tax and pays it to the district director, and (2) the employee has not claimed reimbursement through credit against, or refund of, his income tax (or if so claimed, the claim has been rejected), and (3) the employee does not receive reimbursement in any manner from such employer and does not authorize the employer to file a claim and receive refund or credit. The employee may file a claim for refund of the overpayment on Form 843. Each employee who makes

such a claim must submit along with the claim a statement setting forth (a) the extent, if any, to which the employer has reimbursed the employee in any manner for the over-collection, and (b) the amount, if any, of credit or refund of such overpayment collected by the employer. If the employee is unable to obtain the employer's statement, the employee must make the statement to the best of his knowledge and belief and include an explanation of his inability to obtain the statement from the employer.

"The statement to accompany an employer's and employee's claim for credit or refund of employee tax under section 3101 or employer tax under section 3111 made with respect to payments erroneously reported on a return as wages paid to an employee must include (1) the identification number of the employer, (2) the name and account number of the employee, (3) the period covered by the return, (4) the amount of payments actually reported as wages for the employee, and (5) the amount of wages which should have been reported for the employee. No particular form is prescribed for making such statement, but if printed forms are desired, Form 941c may be used."

Although not mentioned in the above ruling, the 3-year statute of limitations applies to the filing of a refund claim. That is, the refund claim generally should be filed within 3 years of the date the employer filed the erroneous social security withholding tax form with the government.

29

Research Expenses of College Teachers

SECTION 1:
DEDUCTION FOR RESEARCH EXPENSES

College teaching is one of the most misunderstood professions that exists today. Most people do not understand the difference between the job of teaching elementary or high school and that of teaching college. They do not understand that many college teachers must do more than just teach their classes, consult with students, and serve on administrative committees. College teachers are expected to keep abreast of advances in their field by reading journals, attending seminars, traveling to conventions, etc. Furthermore, in many colleges and universities, faculty members are required to be scholars in their own right. They must do original research and communicate their results by publishing articles in journals, writing books, giving colloquium and seminar talks, corresponding with colleagues, discussing topics with their fellow teachers and graduate students, etc.

College teachers often incur expenses in doing their research. They may spend money on attending meetings in their specialties, subscribing to journals, buying books, buying equipment or supplies, etc.

Fortunately, the tax regulations now specifically recognize the integral part that research plays in the duties of many professors. This was not always the case. For example, in one 1962 case, the Tax Court denied a deduction to a professor of English at a distinguished college in California. The professor had claimed a deduction for expenses incurred doing research on *Translators and Translations into English from 1475 to 1640.* The court ruled that the purpose of his research activity was "to increase his prestige as a scholar" and not to fill a requirement of his job. Since he was already tenured, he did not have to perform this research to keep his job. For this reason, his expenses were ruled nondeductible. [Davis, 38 TC 175]

However, in 1963, the IRS issued an important ruling which is excerpted below. This ruling declared that a college professor can deduct expenses he incurs in connection with his research, provided this research is expected of him in his capacity as a professor. He does not have to show that he will be fired or suffer a salary decrease if he does not do the research.

521

Special IRS Ruling on Professors' Research (Revenue Ruling 63-275)

"Advice has been requested concerning the deductibility for federal income tax purposes of research expenses, including traveling expenses incurred by college and university professors in their capacity as educators.

"The facts presented are that the duties of a professor, with or without tenure, encompass not only the usual lecture and teaching duties but also the communication and advancement of knowledge through research and publication. Appointments are commonly made to college and university faculties with the expectation that the individuals will carry on independent research in their fields of competence and will put that research to use in advancing the body of learning in that area by teaching, lecturing, and writing. It is customary, therefore, for professors to engage in research for the above purposes. Where the research is undertaken with a view to scholarly publication, the expenses for such purposes can not usually be considered to have been incurred for the purpose of producing a specific income-producing asset.

"Based on the facts presented, it is held that research expenses, including traveling expenses properly allocable thereto, incurred by a professor for the purpose of teaching, lecturing, or writing and publishing in his area of competence, as a means of carrying out the duties expected of him in his capacity as a professor and without expectation of profit apart from salary, represent ordinary and necessary business expenses incurred in that capacity and are, therefore, deductible. The responsibility rests with each professor to show that the amounts claimed are reasonable in relation to the research performed and that the research is in his area of competence; that is, that the research directly relates to the general field in which the professor is performing services as an educator."

The above ruling applies to college faculty members whose duties include research. However, for others in a position where research is not part of their professional responsibilities, deductions may be disallowed. In one case, for example, a high school physics teacher was not permitted to deduct the cost of a trip taken to do research on solar eclipses. The Court held that he failed to show that this research was related to his job of teaching high school physics. [Feldman, TC Memo 1967-91]

If a professor's research leads to profit such as the writing of a book, then of course he may not take a double deduction for his expenses. That is, he cannot deduct his expenses under this chapter on Schedule A and also deduct the same expenses on Schedule C or Schedule C-EZ as business expenses incurred in the production of his book.

What Research Expenses Are Deductible?

(a) **Travel.** As the above ruling expressly states, you may deduct travel costs connected with your research activities. The rules governing travel expenses described in the *Travel* chapter apply here. Thus, you may deduct not only the cost of transportation, but also of lodging, laundry, and 50% of the cost of meals while away from home overnight.

Example: Sabbatical to Do Research

Jones is a Professor of Art History at a major university in California. He is one of the world's leading experts on the history of Albanian lithography. Jones spends his sabbatical year at Princeton and returns home after the year is over. During his absence, he rents out his California home. While at Princeton, he does research in the history of Modern Albanian lithography and uses Princeton's special collection of Albanian lithographs. He also collaborates with several other scholars in his field who are on the Princeton faculty.

Jones is entitled to deduct travel expenses connected with his sabbatical at Princeton. This includes not only his transportation costs between California and New Jersey, but also such living expenses as lodging, laundry, and commuting costs while away from California, plus 50% of the cost of his meals. The same deduction and recordkeeping rules apply as for any type of travel expense. See the Travel chapter for details, including Section 4 which contains examples of teachers at a temporary position away from home.

(b) Home Office or Laboratory. If you use a home office or laboratory for research or other professional duties, see Chapter 3, *"Home Office."* You might be able to deduct a portion of your house expenses such as rent, depreciation, utilities, etc.

(c) Books, Equipment, and Supplies Necessary for Your Job.

(d) Publication Costs. You can deduct expenses incurred in getting material published. This is confirmed by a Tax Court case concerning a research associate. He had a number of articles published in scientific journals at no cost to himself. But he wrote one paper that he couldn't get published, apparently because it criticized work by another prominent researcher. So the research associate published the work himself at a cost of $1,400 for 1,000 copies.

The IRS refused to allow a deduction for the $1,400 spent on publishing the paper. It argued that since research papers are customarily published at no expense to the author, the cost involved in publishing the paper himself was not an "ordinary and necessary" business expense.

However, the Court allowed the deduction, calling the IRS reasoning too narrow. It stated,

> *"We are satisfied that petitioner's employer expected (although it did not require) its research associates to communicate the results of their research. To be sure, petitioner's employer anticipated that such communication would be accomplished through publication in scientific journals without cost to the author. However, the facts herein indicate, albeit not with crystal clarity, that*

with respect to the particular article in question, the normal channel of communication was not available to petitioner because the article contained critical comment of a person who was in a position to control its acceptance for publication. Such being the case, petitioner's only viable alternative to discharge his reasonably perceived responsibility to disseminate the results of his work was to finance personally the publication thereof. In this respect, he was in a position not unlike the handicapped person who, because of his handicap, is required to incur an expense which nonhandicapped persons similarly situated would not customarily incur."

However, the Court did not allow a deduction for the cost of mailing a different paper to experts in his field because he could have had his employer pay for these mailing costs. An employee is not entitled to deduct expenses for which he could have been reimbursed by his employer. [Drury, TC Memo 1977-199]

(e) Miscellaneous Expenses. Be on the alert for other deductible expenses you incur in connection with your research activities such as telephone calls, clerical help, special laboratory apparel, etc.

Example

Rottman is a Professor of American History at a university in Washington, D.C. He is the author of a number of books and papers on recent American history. Rottman teaches in the mornings and spends many of his afternoons doing research at the Library of Congress and the Smithsonian Institution. He also spends time tape-recording interviews with ex-government officials in connection with his research. He has an office at home that he uses for his book writing activities.

Rottman can deduct the expenses he incurs in connection with his research activities. This may include travel expenses, home office expenses, and incidental costs for such things as photocopying, tapes, supplies, etc. He also may be able to claim deductions for his tape recorder, typewriter, home office furniture, etc. (see the *Travel, Home Office,* and *Depreciation* chapters).

There is another item which Rottman can deduct. He can pay his children or spouse for assisting him in his research (e.g., transcribing tapes, typing, filing etc.). This then becomes a deductible business expense as discussed in the next subsection.

Paying Your Children or Spouse for Assistance

Suppose your children assist you with your research activities. Perhaps they perform clerical work, clean laboratory equipment, help you conduct a survey, etc. If you had paid other people for these services, you would have been able to deduct their salaries as a business expense. Under these circumstances, you can pay your children a reasonable salary and deduct this amount as a business expense. This will lower the overall tax bill since your children are in a lower (often zero) tax bracket.

Similarly, you can pay your spouse for assistance with your research activities. This will not bring the payments into a lower bracket but may still lower the overall tax due because of the effects of the IRA deduction, the child care tax credit, and the ability to set up a tax-deductible medical plan for your family. [See Section 3 of the *Outside Business Activity* chapter.]

Where Do You Deduct Your Research Expenses?

Research expenses are treated the same as other business expenses. Employees report their job-related expenses on Form 2106 or Form 2106-EZ. These expenses then become a miscellaneous deduction on Schedule A which, when combined with other miscellaneous deductions, is subject to a 2% of adjusted gross income floor [see the *Miscellaneous Deductions* chapter]. Self-employed individuals report all their income and expenses on Schedule C or Schedule C-EZ.

SECTION 2:
RESEARCH TAX CREDIT

This credit generally applies when costs for research and experimentation exceed the average costs for these items in previous years. The actual computation of the credit is complicated and can be accomplished by referring to IRS Publication 535 and Form 6765, available from your local IRS office or on the IRS website.

What Kind of Research Expenses Qualify for the Credit?

The **research tax credit** is meant to apply to research and experimentation *"performed in a field of laboratory science (such as physics or biochemistry), engineering or technology."* The research must be undertaken for the purpose of discovering information that is technological in nature. It must relate to a new or improved function, performance, reliability, or quality; research relating to style, taste, cosmetic, or seasonal design factors does not qualify.

Specifically excluded is research in connection with literary, historical, or similar projects. Also excluded is research in the social sciences (including economics, business management, and behavioral sciences), arts, or humanities.

The credit applies to costs for the development or improvement of a pilot model, product, formula, invention, or similar property. It does not apply to the cost of management or consumer surveys, routine improvements of existing products, production planning, engineering follow-through during production, or routine data collection.

The costs of developing new or significantly improved computer software can qualify for the credit. The software should relate to research or production that is technological in nature. Software for bookkeeping, payroll, personnel management, etc., does not qualify. Also, the software should be innovative, involve significant economic risk, and not be commercially available from an outside source.

The following expenses qualify for the credit: (i) wages or self-employment earned income, (ii) supplies used in the conduct of the research, and (iii) payments for computer time.

Land or property of a character subject to the allowance for depreciation does not qualify. [See Chapter 4, Section 3, *"Depreciation"*] Also excluded are the costs of activities indirectly connected with the research such as bookkeeping, quality control, market testing, routine data collection, etc., and expenses for research conducted outside the U.S.

Who Can Claim the Research Credit?

The credit can only be claimed by the taxpayer on whose behalf the research is conducted. It cannot be claimed by an individual for research activities performed for another party, whether *"funded by any grant, contract, or otherwise."* This would apparently rule out the credit for expenses incurred by an employee conducting research in connection with his job. (But if substantial rights in the research are retained by the taxpayer, expenses qualify for the credit except to the extent the taxpayer is entitled to payment for performing the research.)

However, research expenses connected with an outside activity would qualify. The activity must be an ongoing business activity undertaken with the aim of making a profit, rather than just a hobby [see the *Outside Business Activity* chapter]. For example, research expenses connected with inventing a new or improved product would qualify as long as the aim is to make money by bringing the product to market. The research must be performed in connection with an existing business. Expenses paid to develop a product whose sale would constitute a new trade or business don't qualify for the credit.

A taxpayer can also deduct the cost of qualified research expenses he contracts with another party to perform on his behalf for business purposes. In this case, 35% of the cost of the contract is deemed to be overhead not qualifying for the credit.

30

Alternative Minimum Tax

Under our basic tax system, individuals are entitled to reduce their taxable income by using various deductions, credits, exclusions, etc. A consequence of this system is that some wealthy individuals with high incomes were paying little or no income tax. In fact, newspapers periodically ran stories on the number of people with income over $1,000,000 who legally paid no tax whatever.

Congress has been sensitive to this issue. Many taxpayers have been displeased with a system under which they paid sizable chunks of their earnings in taxes while some millionaires paid nothing. To remedy this situation, Congress added an extremely complex provision, the *alternative minimum tax,* as part of the 1986 Tax Reform Act.

The Tax Reduction Act of 2001 increased the alternative minimum tax exemption from $45,000 to $49,000 for married couples filing joint returns; from $33,750 to $35,750 for singles or heads of households; and from $22,500 to $24,500 for married couples filing separately. The increase will be in effect for the 2001 through 2004 tax returns.

To check whether you are subject to the alternative minimum tax, first add up the following *preferences* and *adjustments*:

1. State and local taxes deducted on Schedule A.

2. Personal exemptions.

3. Miscellaneous deductions exceeding 2% of your adjusted gross income (AGI).

4. Your medical expense deduction on Schedule A (using a 10% of AGI reduction, as compared to the 7.5% subtraction normally used to calculate the medical expense deduction on Schedule A for regular tax).

5. Tax-exempt interest on private activity bonds issued after August 7, 1986.

6. The "bargain element" of certain incentive stock options when exercised by an employee.

7. Interest claimed on Schedule A on a mortgage, taken out after June 30, 1982 on a primary or second residence, to the extent it was not used to purchase, build, or substantially rehabilitate the residence. (For mortgages refinanced after June 30, 1982 for an amount in excess of your original mortgage, only the interest on this excess is counted.)

8. Certain excess deductions from taxable income produced by tax-shelter type investments in oil, gas, minerals, farming, real estate, etc.

9. A portion of your deduction for certain accelerated depreciation. The tax preference is the difference between depreciating an asset over the alternative minimum tax useful lives as 150% declining balance method and the regular MACRS useful lives at a 200% declining balance method. See Publication 946 for tables that may be used to figure AMT depreciation.

10. Deferred amounts resulting from installment sales of either (i) real estate used in a trade or business, or (ii) rental real estate when the sales price exceeds $150,000.

If your taxable income income minus the sum of these items is less than the "exemption amount," you will not be subject to the alternative minimum tax described earlier in this chapter. However, the exemption is phased-out at a rate of 25 cents on the dollar when alternative minimum taxable income (i.e. taxable income plus the items listed above) exceeds these levels:

- $112,500 for single taxpayers;

- $150,000 for married taxpayers filing jointly; and

- $75,000 for married taxpayers filing separately.

Example
A single taxpayer has AMTI of $192,500 for the year. His $35,750 initial exemption is reduced by $20,000 [($192,500 – $112,500) × 25% phase-out rate]. His AMT exemption is $13,750 ($33,750 exemption – $20,000 reduction).

If you are not exempt from the alternative minimum tax, you may want to seek professional assistance. Essentially what happens is that the sum of your regular taxable income plus adjustments and preferences is subject to tax at rates of 26% – 28%, replacing the income tax computed in the regular way.

However, tax computations and planning become quite complex when the alternative minimum tax is involved. The above is only a brief sketch of the actual rules designed to alert those with unusually large deductions, exclusions, etc., to the existence of the alternative minimum tax.

An individual may be ensnared by the alternative minimum tax because of an unusual situation in only one year. If so, the tax result may not be so bad. It may be possible to recapture the extra tax on later years' tax returns by use of a special tax credit that applies in this situation. For example, alternative minimum tax generated from the sale of incentive stock options, or from the difference between regular depreciation and AMT depreciation may be allowed as a credit against your tax in a later year. Other AMT preferences and adjustments, such as personal exemptions, and miscellaneous deductions exceeding 2% of your adjusted gross income, medical expenses deducted on Schedule A (after the 10% subtraction) are not items that will give rise to the tax credit in future periods. You should seek professional assistance if the 10 items listed above exceed the exemption less any phase-out, and to learn more about which preferences and adjustments will generate a tax credit in future periods.

Because the alternative minimum tax is beginning to reach moderate income taxpayers, many personal tax credits such as the dependent care credit, education credits and child credit could reduce regular tax liability to a point where the taxpayer would be liable for the AMT. For 2001 the law permits these nonrefundable, personal credits to offset AMT as well. However, for later years, the potential of these personal credits creating an AMT liability is real.

APPENDIX:
SAMPLE TAX RETURN

The following sample tax return is intended to illustrate the full spectrum of professional deductions. It is not meant to represent a "typical" tax return.

A few of the forms used in these examples are 2000 tax forms because the 2001 versions were not finalized by the IRS at the time the *Tax & Financial Guide* went to press. Significant differences between these 2000 tax forms and the 2001 tax forms are not anticipated.

Form 1040 Department of the Treasury—Internal Revenue Service
U.S. Individual Income Tax Return 2001 (99) IRS Use Only—Do not write or staple in this space.

For the year Jan. 1–Dec. 31, 2001, or other tax year beginning , 2001, ending , 20

OMB No. 1545-0074

Label (See instructions on page 19.) Use the IRS label. Otherwise, please print or type.

L A B E L H E R E	

Your first name and initial: **JAY A.** Last name: **DOE**

Your social security number: **123 45 6789**

If a joint return, spouse's first name and initial: **SUSAN B.** Last name: **DOE**

Spouse's social security number: **987 65 4321**

Home address (number and street). If you have a P.O. box, see page 19. **3215 MAIN ST.** Apt. no.

▲ **Important!** ▲
You **must** enter your SSN(s) above.

City, town or post office, state, and ZIP code. If you have a foreign address, see page 19. **PITTSBURGH, PA 18246**

Presidential Election Campaign (See page 19.)

Note. Checking "Yes" will not change your tax or reduce your refund.
Do you, or your spouse if filing a joint return, want $3 to go to this fund? . . . ▶

	You	Spouse
	☑ Yes ☐ No	☐ Yes ☑ No

Filing Status

Check only one box.

1 ☐ Single
2 ☑ Married filing joint return (even if only one had income)
3 ☐ Married filing separate return. Enter spouse's social security no. above and full name here. ▶ _____
4 ☐ Head of household (with qualifying person). (See page 19.) If the qualifying person is a child but not your dependent, enter this child's name here. ▶ _____
5 ☐ Qualifying widow(er) with dependent child (year spouse died ▶). (See page 19.)

Exemptions

6a ☑ **Yourself.** If your parent (or someone else) can claim you as a dependent on his or her tax return, **do not** check box 6a . . . .
b ☑ **Spouse** . . . .

No. of boxes checked on 6a and 6b: **2**

c **Dependents:**

(1) First name	Last name	(2) Dependent's social security number	(3) Dependent's relationship to you	(4) ☑ if qualifying child for child tax credit (see page 20)
ALEC	DOE	333 44 5555	SON	☑
MOLLY	DOE	777 88 9999	DAUGHTER	☑
				☐
				☐
				☐
				☐

If more than six dependents, see page 20.

No. of your children on 6c who:
• lived with you **2**
• did not live with you due to divorce or separation (see page 20)
Dependents on 6c not entered above
Add numbers entered on lines above ▶ **4**

d Total number of exemptions claimed

Income

Attach Forms W-2 and W-2G here. Also attach Form(s) 1099-R if tax was withheld.

If you did not get a W-2, see page 21.

Enclose, but do not attach, any payment. Also, please use Form 1040-V.

7	Wages, salaries, tips, etc. Attach Form(s) W-2	7	147,814
8a	**Taxable** interest. Attach Schedule B if required	8a	15,466
b	Tax-exempt interest. **Do not** include on line 8a . . .	8b	7,143		
9	Ordinary dividends. Attach Schedule B if required	9	8,895
10	Taxable refunds, credits, or offsets of state and local income taxes (see page 22) . .	10	
11	Alimony received	11	
12	Business income or (loss). Attach Schedule C or C-EZ	12	7,281
13	Capital gain or (loss). Attach Schedule D if required. If not required, check here ▶ ☐	13	18,111
14	Other gains or (losses). Attach Form 4797	14	
15a	Total IRA distributions . 15a	b Taxable amount (see page 23)	15b	
16a	Total pensions and annuities 16a	b Taxable amount (see page 23)	16b	
17	Rental real estate, royalties, partnerships, S corporations, trusts, etc. Attach Schedule E	17	
18	Farm income or (loss). Attach Schedule F	18	
19	Unemployment compensation	19	
20a	Social security benefits 20a	b Taxable amount (see page 25)	20b	
21	Other income. List type and amount (see page 27) _____	21	
22	Add the amounts in the far right column for lines 7 through 21. This is your **total income** ▶	22	197,567

Adjusted Gross Income

23	IRA deduction (see page 27)	23	
24	Student loan interest deduction (see page 28)	24	
25	Archer MSA deduction. Attach Form 8853	25	
26	Moving expenses. Attach Form 3903	26	2,421
27	One-half of self-employment tax. Attach Schedule SE .	27	371
28	Self-employed health insurance deduction (see page 30)	28	
29	Self-employed SEP, SIMPLE, and qualified plans . .	29	5,500
30	Penalty on early withdrawal of savings	30	
31a	Alimony paid b Recipient's SSN ▶	31a	
32	Add lines 23 through 31a	32	8,292
33	Subtract line 32 from line 22. This is your **adjusted gross income** . . . . . ▶	33	189,275

For Disclosure, Privacy Act, and Paperwork Reduction Act Notice, see page 72. Cat. No. 11320B Form **1040** (2001)

Form 1040 (2001)

Tax and Credits	34	Amount from line 33 (adjusted gross income)	34	189,275
	35a	Check if: ☐ **You** were 65 or older, ☐ Blind; ☐ **Spouse** was 65 or older, ☐ Blind.		
Standard Deduction for—		Add the number of boxes checked above and enter the total here . . . . ▶ 35a		
• People who checked any box on line 35a or 35b **or** who can be claimed as a dependent, see page 31.	b	If you are married filing separately and your spouse itemizes deductions, or you were a dual-status alien, see page 31 and check here . . . . . . ▶ 35b ☐		
	36	**Itemized deductions** (from Schedule A) **or** your **standard deduction** (see left margin) .	36	29,891
	37	Subtract line 36 from line 34	37	159,384
• All others: Single, $4,550	38	If line 34 is $99,725 or less, multiply $2,900 by the total number of exemptions claimed on line 6d. If line 34 is over $99,725, see the worksheet on page 32	38	11,600
Head of household, $6,650	39	**Taxable income.** Subtract line 38 from line 37. If line 38 is more than line 37, enter -0- .	39	147,784
Married filing jointly or Qualifying widow(er), $7,600	40	**Tax** (see page 33). Check if any tax is from **a** ☐ Form(s) 8814 **b** ☐ Form 4972 . . .	40	34,245
	41	**Alternative minimum tax** (see page 34). Attach Form 6251 . . . . ▶	41	
Married filing separately, $3,800	42	Add lines 40 and 41	42	34,245

	43	Foreign tax credit. Attach Form 1116 if required	43	
	44	Credit for child and dependent care expenses. Attach Form 2441	44	960
	45	Credit for the elderly or the disabled. Attach Schedule R . .	45	
	46	Education credits. Attach Form 8863	46	
	47	Rate reduction credit. See the worksheet on page 36	47	
	48	Child tax credit (see page 37)	48	
	49	Adoption credit. Attach Form 8839	49	
	50	Other credits from: **a** ☐ Form 3800 **b** ☐ Form 8396 **c** ☐ Form 8801 **d** ☐ Form (specify)	50	

	51	Add lines 43 through 50. These are your **total credits** . . . . ▶	51	960
	52	Subtract line 51 from line 42. If line 51 is more than line 42, enter -0- . . . . . ▶	52	33,285
Other Taxes	53	Self-employment tax. Attach Schedule SE	53	741
	54	Social security and Medicare tax on tip income not reported to employer. Attach Form 4137 . .	54	
	55	Tax on qualified plans, including IRAs, and other tax-favored accounts. Attach Form 5329 if required .	55	
	56	Advance earned income credit payments from Form(s) W-2	56	
	57	Household employment taxes. Attach Schedule H	57	679
	58	Add lines 52 through 57. This is your **total tax** . . . . ▶	58	34,705

Payments	59	Federal income tax withheld from Forms W-2 and 1099 . .	59	35,148	
	60	2001 estimated tax payments and amount applied from 2000 return .	60		
If you have a qualifying child, attach Schedule EIC.	61a	**Earned income credit (EIC)**	61a		
	b	Nontaxable earned income . [61b]			
	62	Excess social security and RRTA tax withheld (see page 51) .	62		
	63	Additional child tax credit. Attach Form 8812	63		
	64	Amount paid with request for extension to file (see page 51) .	64		
	65	Other payments. Check if from **a** ☐ Form 2439 **b** ☐ Form 4136	65		
	66	Add lines 59, 60, 61a, and 62 through 65. These are your **total payments** . . . . ▶	66		35,148

Refund	67	If line 66 is more than line 58, subtract line 58 from line 66. This is the amount you **overpaid**	67	443
Direct deposit? See page 51 and fill in 68b, 68c, and 68d.	68a	Amount of line 67 you want **refunded to you**	68a	443
	▶ b	Routing number	▶ c Type: ☐ Checking ☐ Savings	
	▶ d	Account number		
	69	Amount of line 67 you want **applied to your 2002 estimated tax** ▶	69	
Amount You Owe	70	**Amount you owe.** Subtract line 58 from line 66. For details on how to pay, see page 52 ▶	70	
	71	Estimated tax penalty. Also include on line 70	71	

Third Party Designee

Do you want to allow another person to discuss this return with the IRS (see page 53)? ☐ **Yes.** Complete the following. ☑ **No**

Designee's name ▶	Phone no. ▶ ( )	Personal identification number (PIN) ▶	

Sign Here

Under penalties of perjury, I declare that I have examined this return and accompanying schedules and statements, and to the best of my knowledge and belief, they are true, correct, and complete. Declaration of preparer (other than taxpayer) is based on all information of which preparer has any knowledge.

Joint return? See page 19.
Keep a copy for your records.

Your signature	Date	Your occupation **COLLEGE TEACHER**	Daytime phone number ( )
Spouse's signature. If a joint return, **both** must sign.	Date	Spouse's occupation **THERAPIST**	

Paid Preparer's Use Only

Preparer's signature ▶	Date	Check if self-employed ☐	Preparer's SSN or PTIN
Firm's name (or yours if self-employed), address, and ZIP code ▶		EIN	
		Phone no. ( )	

Form **1040** (2001)

534

SCHEDULES A&B
(Form 1040)

Department of the Treasury
Internal Revenue Service (99)

Schedule A—Itemized Deductions

(Schedule B is on back)

▶ Attach to Form 1040. ▶ See Instructions for Schedules A and B (Form 1040).

OMB No. 1545-0074

2001

Attachment
Sequence No. 07

Name(s) shown on Form 1040
JAY A. & SUSAN B. DOE

Your social security number
123 : 45 : 6789

Medical and Dental Expenses		Caution. Do not include expenses reimbursed or paid by others.		
	1	Medical and dental expenses (see page A-2)	1	11,920
	2	Enter amount from Form 1040, line 34. ⌊2⌋ 189,275		
	3	Multiply line 2 above by 7.5% (.075)	3	14,196
	4	Subtract line 3 from line 1. If line 3 is more than line 1, enter -0-	4	0
Taxes You Paid (See page A-2.)	5	State and local income taxes	5	6,211
	6	Real estate taxes (see page A-2)	6	1,352
	7	Personal property taxes	7	
	8	Other taxes. List type and amount ▶	8	
	9	Add lines 5 through 8	9	7,563
Interest You Paid (See page A-3.) Note. Personal interest is not deductible.	10	Home mortgage interest and points reported to you on Form 1098	10	7,598
	11	Home mortgage interest not reported to you on Form 1098. If paid to the person from whom you bought the home, see page A-3 and show that person's name, identifying no., and address ▶	11	
	12	Points not reported to you on Form 1098. See page A-3 for special rules	12	
	13	Investment interest. Attach Form 4952 if required. (See page A-3.)	13	150
	14	Add lines 10 through 13	14	7,748
Gifts to Charity If you made a gift and got a benefit for it, see page A-4.	15	Gifts by cash or check. If you made any gift of $250 or more, see page A-4	15	4,040
	16	Other than by cash or check. If any gift of $250 or more, see page A-4. You **must** attach Form 8283 if over $500	16	312
	17	Carryover from prior year	17	
	18	Add lines 15 through 17	18	4,352
Casualty and Theft Losses	19	Casualty or theft loss(es). Attach Form 4684. (See page A-5.)	19	
Job Expenses and Most Other Miscellaneous Deductions (See page A-5 for expenses to deduct here.)	20	Unreimbursed employee expenses—job travel, union dues, job education, etc. You **must** attach Form 2106 or 2106-EZ if required. (See page A-5.) ▶	20	15,560
	21	Tax preparation fees	21	
	22	Other expenses—investment, safe deposit box, etc. List type and amount ▶ IRA FEE-10; TAX GUIDE-39; SAFE DEP BOX-55; PUBLICATIONS-184	22	288
	23	Add lines 20 through 22	23	15,848
	24	Enter amount from Form 1040, line 34. ⌊24⌋ 189,275		
	25	Multiply line 24 above by 2% (.02)	25	3,786
	26	Subtract line 25 from line 23. If line 25 is more than line 23, enter -0-	26	12,062
Other Miscellaneous Deductions	27	Other—from list on page A-6. List type and amount ▶	27	
Total Itemized Deductions	28	Is Form 1040, line 34, over $132,950 (over $66,475 if married filing separately)? ☐ **No.** Your deduction is not limited. Add the amounts in the far right column for lines 4 through 27. Also, enter this amount on Form 1040, line 36. ☑ **Yes.** Your deduction may be limited. See page A-6 for the amount to enter.	28	29,891

For Paperwork Reduction Act Notice, see Form 1040 instructions. Cat. No. 11330X Schedule A (Form 1040) 2001

Page A-6 of Instructions

protect property held for earning income. But **do not** include any personal expenses. List the type and amount of each expense on the dotted lines next to line 22. If you need more space, attach a statement showing the type and amount of each expense. Enter one total on line 22.

Examples of expenses to include on line 22 are:

● Certain legal and accounting fees.

● Clerical help and office rent.

● Custodial (for example, trust account) fees.

● Your share of the investment expenses of a regulated investment company.

● Certain losses on nonfederally insured deposits in an insolvent or bankrupt financial institution. For details, including limits that apply, see **Pub. 529.**

● Casualty and theft losses of property used in performing services as an employee from **Form 4684**, lines 32 and 38b, or **Form 4797**, line 18b(1).

● Deduction for repayment of amounts under a claim of right if $3,000 or less.

Other Miscellaneous Deductions

Line 27

Only the expenses listed next can be deducted on this line. List the type and amount of each expense on the dotted lines next to line 27. If you need more space, attach a statement showing the type and amount of each expense. Enter one total on line 27.

● Gambling losses, but only to the extent of gambling winnings reported on Form 1040, line 21.

● Casualty and theft losses of income-producing property from **Form 4684,** lines 32 and 38b, or **Form 4797,** line 18b(1).

● Federal estate tax on income in respect of a decedent.

● Amortizable bond premium on bonds acquired before October 23, 1986.

● Deduction for repayment of amounts under a claim of right if over $3,000. See **Pub. 525** for details.

● Certain unrecovered investment in a pension.

● Impairment-related work expenses of a disabled person.

For more details, see **Pub. 529.**

Total Itemized Deductions

Line 28

Use the worksheet below to figure the amount to enter on line 28 if the amount on Form 1040, line 34, is over $132,950 if single, married filing jointly, head of household, or qualifying widow(er); $66,475 if married filing separately.

Itemized Deductions Worksheet—Line 28 *Keep for Your Records*

1. Add the amounts on Schedule A, lines 4, 9, 14, 18, 19, 26, and 27 . . . . **1.** _31,731_

2. Add the amounts on Schedule A, lines 4, 13, and 19, plus any gambling and casualty or theft losses included on line 27 . . . . **2.** _150_

> ⚠️ **CAUTION** Be sure your total gambling and casualty or theft losses are clearly identified on the dotted lines next to line 27.

3. Is the amount on line 2 less than the amount on line 1?

☐ **No.** 🛑 Your deduction is not limited. Enter the amount from line 1 above on Schedule A, line 28.

☒ **Yes.** Subtract line 2 from line 1 . . . . **3.** _31,581_

4. Multiply line 3 above by 80% (.80) . . . . **4.** _25,265_

5. Enter the amount from Form 1040, line 34 . . . . **5.** _189,275_

6. Enter: $132,950 if single, married filing jointly, head of household, or qualifying widow(er); $66,475 if married filing separately . . . . . . **6.** _132,950_

7. Is the amount on line 6 less than the amount on line 5?

☐ **No.** 🛑 Your deduction is not limited. Enter the amount from line 1 above on Schedule A, line 28.

☒ **Yes.** Subtract line 6 from line 5 . . . . **7.** _56,325_

8. Multiply line 7 above by 3% (.03) . . . . **8.** _1,690_

9. Enter the **smaller** of line 4 or line 8 . . . . **9.** _1,690_

10. **Total itemized deductions.** Subtract line 9 from line 1. Enter the result here and on Schedule A, line 28 . . . . **10.** _29,891_

536

OMB No. 1545-0074   Page **2**

Name(s) shown on Form 1040. Do not enter name and social security number if shown on other side.	Your social security number
JAY A. & SUSAN B. DOE	123 ⋮ 45 ⋮ 6789

Schedule B—Interest and Ordinary Dividends

Attachment Sequence No. **08**

Part I Interest

(See page B-1 and the instructions for Form 1040, line 8a.)

1 List name of payer. If any interest is from a seller-financed mortgage and the buyer used the property as a personal residence, see page B-1 and list this interest first. Also, show that buyer's social security number and address ▶

		Amount
FIDELITY S & L		9,154
U.S. TREASURY NOTE		5,100
CREDIT UNION		32
ALLIED CORP BONDS		7,330
FIRST NATIONAL BANK	**1**	2,050

Note. If you received a Form 1099-INT, Form 1099-OID, or substitute statement from a brokerage firm, list the firm's name as the payer and enter the total interest shown on that form.

2 Add the amounts on line 1	**2**	15,466
3 Excludable interest on series EE and I U.S. savings bonds issued after 1989 from Form 8815, line 14. You **must** attach Form 8815	**3**	
4 Subtract line 3 from line 2. Enter the result here and on Form 1040, line 8a ▶	**4**	15,466

Note. If line 4 is over $400, you must complete Part III.

Part II Ordinary Dividends

(See page B-1 and the instructions for Form 1040, line 9.)

5 List name of payer. Include only ordinary dividends. If you received any capital gain distributions, see the instructions for Form 1040, line 13 ▶

		Amount
VANGUARD INDEX FUND		4,314
IBM		1,650
AA MONEY MARKET FUND		2,931

Note. If you received a Form 1099-DIV or substitute statement from a brokerage firm, list the firm's name as the payer and enter the ordinary dividends shown on that form.

6 Add the amounts on line 5. Enter the total here and on Form 1040, line 9 . ▶	**6**	8,895

Note. If line 6 is over $400, you must complete Part III.

Part III Foreign Accounts and Trusts

(See page B-2.)

You must complete this part if you **(a)** had over $400 of taxable interest or ordinary dividends; **(b)** had a foreign account; or **(c)** received a distribution from, or were a grantor of, or a transferor to, a foreign trust.

	Yes	No
7a At any time during 2001, did you have an interest in or a signature or other authority over a financial account in a foreign country, such as a bank account, securities account, or other financial account? See page B-2 for exceptions and filing requirements for Form TD F 90-22.1		✔
b If "Yes," enter the name of the foreign country ▶		
8 During 2001, did you receive a distribution from, or were you the grantor of, or transferor to, a foreign trust? If "Yes," you may have to file Form 3520. See page B-2		✔

For Paperwork Reduction Act Notice, see Form 1040 instructions.

SCHEDULE C
(Form 1040)

Department of the Treasury
Internal Revenue Service   (99)

Profit or Loss From Business
(Sole Proprietorship)

▶ Partnerships, joint ventures, etc., must file Form 1065 or Form 1065-B.

▶ Attach to Form 1040 or Form 1041.   ▶ See Instructions for Schedule C (Form 1040).

OMB No. 1545-0074

2001

Attachment
Sequence No. **09**

Name of proprietor	Social security number (SSN)
JAY A. DOE	123 45 6789

A	Principal business or profession, including product or service (see page C-1 of the instructions) **CONSULTING**	B Enter code from pages C-7 & 8 ▶ 5 4 1 9 5 0

C	Business name. If no separate business name, leave blank. **J. D. CONSULTING SERVICES**	D Employer ID number (EIN), if any

E   Business address (including suite or room no.) ▶ ....
City, town or post office, state, and ZIP code

F   Accounting method: (1) ☑ Cash   (2) ☐ Accrual   (3) ☐ Other (specify) ▶ ....

G   Did you "materially participate" in the operation of this business during 2001? If "No," see page C-2 for limit on losses   . ☑ Yes   ☐ No

H   If you started or acquired this business during 2001, check here   . . . . ▶ ☐

Part I   Income

1	Gross receipts or sales. **Caution.** If this income was reported to you on Form W-2 and the "Statutory employee" box on that form was checked, see page C-2 and check here . . . . . . ▶ ☐	1	18,740
2	Returns and allowances	2	
3	Subtract line 2 from line 1	3	18,740
4	Cost of goods sold (from line 42 on page 2)	4	
5	**Gross profit.** Subtract line 4 from line 3	5	18,740
6	Other income, including Federal and state gasoline or fuel tax credit or refund (see page C-3) . . .	6	
7	**Gross income.** Add lines 5 and 6 . . . . ▶	7	18,740

Part II   Expenses. Enter expenses for business use of your home **only** on line 30.

8	Advertising	8	300	19 Pension and profit-sharing plans	19	
9	Bad debts from sales or services (see page C-3) . .	9		20 Rent or lease (see page C-4):		
				a Vehicles, machinery, and equipment .	20a	
10	Car and truck expenses (see page C-3)	10		b Other business property . .	20b	
11	Commissions and fees . .	11	713	21 Repairs and maintenance . .	21	
12	Depletion	12		22 Supplies (not included in Part III) .	22	721
13	Depreciation and section 179 expense deduction (not included in Part III) (see page C-3) . .	13		23 Taxes and licenses	23	932
				24 Travel, meals, and entertainment:		
14	Employee benefit programs (other than on line 19) . .	14		a Travel	24a	315
15	Insurance (other than health) .	15	1,137	b Meals and entertainment 530		
16	Interest:			c Enter nondeductible amount included on line 24b (see page C-5) . 265		
a	Mortgage (paid to banks, etc.) .	16a		d Subtract line 24c from line 24b .	24d	265
b	Other	16b	610	25 Utilities	25	
17	Legal and professional services	17	1,250	26 Wages (less employment credits) .	26	
18	Office expense	18	316	27 Other expenses (from line 48 on page 2)	27	1,225

28	**Total expenses** before expenses for business use of home. Add lines 8 through 27 in columns . ▶	28	7,784
29	Tentative profit (loss). Subtract line 28 from line 7	29	10,956
30	Expenses for business use of your home. Attach **Form 8829**	30	3,675
31	**Net profit or (loss).** Subtract line 30 from line 29. ● If a profit, enter on **Form 1040, line 12,** and also on **Schedule SE, line 2** (statutory employees, see page C-5). Estates and trusts, enter on Form 1041, line 3. ● If a loss, you **must** go to line 32.	31	7,281
32	If you have a loss, check the box that describes your investment in this activity (see page C-6). ● If you checked 32a, enter the loss on **Form 1040, line 12,** and also on **Schedule SE, line 2** (statutory employees, see page C-5). Estates and trusts, enter on Form 1041, line 3. ● If you checked 32b, you **must** attach **Form 6198.**	32a ☐ All investment is at risk. 32b ☐ Some investment is not at risk.	

For Paperwork Reduction Act Notice, see Form 1040 instructions.   Cat. No. 11334P   Schedule C (Form 1040) 2001

Part III   Cost of Goods Sold (see page C-6)

33   Method(s) used to
value closing inventory: **a** ☐ Cost   **b** ☐ Lower of cost or market   **c** ☐ Other (attach explanation)

34   Was there any change in determining quantities, costs, or valuations between opening and closing inventory? If
"Yes," attach explanation . . . . ☐ **Yes**   ☐ **No**

35 Inventory at beginning of year. If different from last year's closing inventory, attach explanation . .	**35**	
36 Purchases less cost of items withdrawn for personal use	**36**	
37 Cost of labor. Do not include any amounts paid to yourself	**37**	
38 Materials and supplies	**38**	
39 Other costs	**39**	
40 Add lines 35 through 39	**40**	
41 Inventory at end of year	**41**	
42 **Cost of goods sold.** Subtract line 41 from line 40. Enter the result here and on page 1, line 4 . .	**42**	

Part IV   **Information on Your Vehicle.** Complete this part **only** if you are claiming car or truck expenses on
line 10 and are not required to file Form 4562 for this business. See the instructions for line 13 on page
C-3 to find out if you must file.

43   When did you place your vehicle in service for business purposes? (month, day, year) ▶ ..../......../...... .

44   Of the total number of miles you drove your vehicle during 2001, enter the number of miles you used your vehicle for:

a   Business .... **b** Commuting .... **c** Other ....

45   Do you (or your spouse) have another vehicle available for personal use? . . . . ☐ **Yes**   ☐ **No**

46   Was your vehicle available for personal use during off-duty hours?   . . . . ☐ **Yes**   ☐ **No**

47a   Do you have evidence to support your deduction?   . . . . ☐ **Yes**   ☐ **No**

b   If "Yes," is the evidence written? . . . . ☐ **Yes**   ☐ **No**

Part V   **Other Expenses.** List below business expenses not included on lines 8–26 or line 30.

COMPUTER SERVICES	950
DELIVERY CHARGES	211
POSTAL SERVICES	64

48 **Total other expenses.** Enter here and on page 1, line 27	**48**	**1,225**

SCHEDULE D
(Form 1040)

Department of the Treasury
Internal Revenue Service (99)

Capital Gains and Losses

▶ Attach to Form 1040.   ▶ See Instructions for Schedule D (Form 1040).

▶ Use Schedule D-1 to list additional transactions for lines 1 and 8.

OMB No. 1545-0074

20**01**

Attachment
Sequence No. **12**

Name(s) shown on Form 1040
JAY A. & SUSAN B. DOE

Your social security number
123 45 6789

Part I   Short-Term Capital Gains and Losses—Assets Held One Year or Less

(a) Description of property (Example: 100 sh. XYZ Co.)	(b) Date acquired (Mo., day, yr.)	(c) Date sold (Mo., day, yr.)	(d) Sales price (see page D-5 of the instructions)	(e) Cost or other basis (see page D-5 of the instructions)	(f) Gain or (loss) Subtract (e) from (d)
1 100 sh ABC	1/14/01	10/6/01	14,152	21,310	(7,158)
200 sh DEF	7/11/00	6/10/01	7,120	6,844	276

2 Enter your short-term totals, if any, from Schedule D-1, line 2 . . . . **2**

3 Total short-term sales price amounts. Add lines 1 and 2 in column (d) **3**   21,272

4 Short-term gain from Form 6252 and short-term gain or (loss) from Forms 4684, 6781, and 8824 . . . . **4**

5 Net short-term gain or (loss) from partnerships, S corporations, estates, and trusts from Schedule(s) K-1 . . . . **5**

6 Short-term capital loss carryover. Enter the amount, if any, from line 8 of your 2000 Capital Loss Carryover Worksheet . . . . **6** (   )

7 **Net short-term capital gain or (loss).** Combine lines 1 through 6 in column (f). **7**   (6,882)

Part II   Long-Term Capital Gains and Losses—Assets Held More Than One Year

(a) Description of property (Example: 100 sh. XYZ Co.)	(b) Date acquired (Mo., day, yr.)	(c) Date sold (Mo., day, yr.)	(d) Sales price (see page D-5 of the instructions)	(e) Cost or other basis (see page D-5 of the instructions)	(f) Gain or (loss) Subtract (e) from (d)	(g) 28% rate gain or (loss) * (see instr. below)
8 300 sh JKL	5/4/00	6/2/01	14,211	10,100	4,111	
400 sh TUV	6/10/99	10/6/01	11,014	12,152	(1,138)	
200 sh XYZ	7/4/00	9/5/01	8,150	10,012	(1,862)	
LAND—5 ACRES	6/2/95	4/12/01	42,000	20,540	21,460	

9 Enter your long-term totals, if any, from Schedule D-1, line 9 . . . . **9**

10 Total long-term sales price amounts. Add lines 8 and 9 in column (d) **10**   75,375

11 Gain from Form 4797, Part I; long-term gain from Forms 2439 and 6252; and long-term gain or (loss) from Forms 4684, 6781, and 8824 . . . . **11**

12 Net long-term gain or (loss) from partnerships, S corporations, estates, and trusts from Schedule(s) K-1. . . . . **12**

13 Capital gain distributions. See page D-1 of the instructions **13**   2,422

14 Long-term capital loss carryover. Enter in both columns (f) and (g) the amount, if any, from line 13 of your 2000 Capital Loss Carryover Worksheet . . . . . . **14** (   ) (   )

15 Combine lines 8 through 14 in column (g) **15**

16 **Net long-term capital gain or (loss).** Combine lines 8 through 14 in column (f) **16**   24,993
Next: Go to Part III on the back.

*28% rate gain or loss includes all "collectibles gains and losses" (as defined on page D-6 of the instructions) and up to 50% of the eligible gain on qualified small business stock (see page D-4 of the instructions).

For Paperwork Reduction Act Notice, see Form 1040 instructions.   Cat. No. 11338H   **Schedule D (Form 1040) 2001**

Schedule D (Form 1040) 2001

Part III — Taxable Gain or Deductible Loss

| 17 | Combine lines 7 and 16 and enter the result. If a loss, go to line 18. If a gain, enter the gain on Form 1040, line 13, and complete Form 1040 through line 39 . . . . | **17** | **18,111** |

Next: • If both lines 16 and 17 are gains **and** Form 1040, line 39, is more than zero, complete Part IV below.
• Otherwise, skip the rest of Schedule D and complete Form 1040.

| 18 | If line 17 is a loss, enter here and on Form 1040, line 13, the **smaller** of **(a)** that loss or **(b)** ($3,000) (or, if married filing separately, ($1,500)). Then complete Form 1040 through line 37 | **18** |( ) |

Next: • If the loss on line 17 is more than the loss on line 18 **or** if Form 1040, line 37, is less than zero, skip **Part IV** below and complete the **Capital Loss Carryover Worksheet** on page D-6 of the instructions before completing the rest of Form 1040.
• Otherwise, skip **Part IV** below and complete the rest of Form 1040.

Part IV — Tax Computation Using Maximum Capital Gains Rates

| 19 | Enter your unrecaptured section 1250 gain, if any, from line 17 of the worksheet on page D-7 of the instructions . . . . . | **19** | | |

If line 15 or line 19 is more than zero, complete the worksheet on page D-9 of the instructions to figure the amount to enter on lines 22, 29, and 40 below, and skip all other lines below. Otherwise, go to line 20.

20	Enter your taxable income from Form 1040, line 39	**20**	**147,784**	
21	Enter the **smaller** of line 16 or line 17 of Schedule D	**21**	**18,111**	
22	If you are deducting investment interest expense on Form 4952, enter the amount from Form 4952, line 4e. Otherwise, enter -0-	**22**	**0**	
23	Subtract line 22 from line 21. If zero or less, enter -0-	**23**	**18,111**	
24	Subtract line 23 from line 20. If zero or less, enter -0-	**24**	**129,673**	
25	Figure the tax on the amount on line 24. Use the Tax Table or Tax Rate Schedules, whichever applies	**25**		**30,623**
26	Enter the **smaller** of: • The amount on line 20 **or** • $45,200 if married filing jointly or qualifying widow(er); $27,050 if single; $36,250 if head of household; or $22,600 if married filing separately	**26**	**45,200**	

If line 26 is greater than line 24, go to line 27. Otherwise, skip lines 27 through 33 and go to line 34.

27	Enter the amount from line 24	**27**		
28	Subtract line 27 from line 26. If zero or less, enter -0- and go to line 34	**28**		
29	Enter your qualified 5-year gain, if any, from line 7 of the worksheet on page D-8 . .	**29**		
30	Enter the **smaller** of line 28 or line 29	**30**		
31	Multiply line 30 by 8% (.08)	**31**		
32	Subtract line 30 from line 28	**32**		
33	Multiply line 32 by 10% (.10)	**33**		

If the amounts on lines 23 and 28 are the same, skip lines 34 through 37 and go to line 38.

34	Enter the **smaller** of line 20 or line 23	**34**	**18,111**	
35	Enter the amount from line 28 (if line 28 is blank, enter -0-) . . .	**35**	**0**	
36	Subtract line 35 from line 34	**36**	**18,111**	
37	Multiply line 36 by 20% (.20)	**37**		**3,622**
38	Add lines 25, 31, 33, and 37	**38**		**34,245**
39	Figure the tax on the amount on line 20. Use the Tax Table or Tax Rate Schedules, whichever applies	**39**		**36,147**
40	**Tax on all taxable income (including capital gains). Enter the smaller of line 38 or line 39 here and on Form 1040, line 40**	**40**		**34,245**

⊛

Schedule D (Form 1040) 2001

Schedule SE (Form 1040) 2001	Attachment Sequence No. **17**		Page **2**

Name of person with **self-employment** income (as shown on Form 1040) JAY A. DOE	Social security number of person with **self-employment** income ▶	123 : 45 : 6789

Section B—Long Schedule SE

Part I Self-Employment Tax

Note. If your only income subject to self-employment tax is **church employee income,** skip lines 1 through 4b. Enter -0- on line 4c and go to line 5a. Income from services you performed as a minister or a member of a religious order **is not** church employee income. See page SE-1.

A   If you are a minister, member of a religious order, or Christian Science practitioner **and** you filed Form 4361, but you had $400 or more of **other** net earnings from self-employment, check here and continue with Part I . . . . . ▶ ☐

1	Net farm profit or (loss) from Schedule F, line 36, and farm partnerships, Schedule K-1 (Form 1065), line 15a. **Note.** Skip this line if you use the farm optional method. See page SE-3 . .	**1**	
2	Net profit or (loss) from Schedule C, line 31; Schedule C-EZ, line 3; Schedule K-1 (Form 1065), line 15a (other than farming); and Schedule K-1 (Form 1065-B), box 9. Ministers and members of religious orders, see page SE-1 for amounts to report on this line. See page SE-2 for other income to report. **Note.** Skip this line if you use the nonfarm optional method. See page SE-3.	**2**	7,281
3	Combine lines 1 and 2	**3**	7,281
4a	If line 3 is more than zero, multiply line 3 by 92.35% (.9235). Otherwise, enter amount from line 3	**4a**	6,724
b	If you elect one or both of the optional methods, enter the total of lines 15 and 17 here . . .	**4b**	
c	Combine lines 4a and 4b. If less than $400, **do not** file this schedule; you do not owe self-employment tax. **Exception.** If less than $400 and you had **church employee income,** enter -0- and continue ▶	**4c**	6,724
5a	Enter your **church employee income** from Form W-2. **Caution.** See page SE-1 for definition of church employee income **5a**		
		5b	
b	Multiply line 5a by 92.35% (.9235). If less than $100, enter -0-	**6**	6,724
6	**Net earnings from self-employment.** Add lines 4c and 5b		
7	Maximum amount of combined wages and self-employment earnings subject to social security tax or the 6.2% portion of the 7.65% railroad retirement (tier 1) tax for 2001	**7**	80,400 00
8a	Total social security wages and tips (total of boxes 3 and 7 on Form(s) W-2) and railroad retirement (tier 1) compensation **8a** 76,000		
b	Unreported tips subject to social security tax (from Form 4137, line 9) **8b**		
c	Add lines 8a and 8b	**8c**	76,000
9	Subtract line 8c from line 7. If zero or less, enter -0- here and on line 10 and go to line 11 . ▶	**9**	4,400
10	Multiply the **smaller** of line 6 or line 9 by 12.4% (.124)	**10**	546
11	Multiply line 6 by 2.9% (.029)	**11**	195
12	**Self-employment tax.** Add lines 10 and 11. Enter here and on **Form 1040, line 53**	**12**	741
13	Deduction for one-half of self-employment tax. Multiply line 12 by 50% (.5). Enter the result here and on **Form 1040, line 27** **13** 371		

Part II Optional Methods To Figure Net Earnings (See page SE-3.)

Farm Optional Method. You may use this method **only if:**
- Your gross farm income¹ was not more than $2,400 **or**
- Your net farm profits² were less than $1,733.

14	Maximum income for optional methods	**14**	1,600 00
15	Enter the **smaller** of: two-thirds (⅔) of gross farm income¹ (not less than zero) **or** $1,600. Also include this amount on line 4b above	**15**	

Nonfarm Optional Method. You may use this method **only if:**
- Your net nonfarm profits³ were less than $1,733 and also less than 72.189% of your gross nonfarm income⁴ **and**
- You had net earnings from self-employment of at least $400 in 2 of the prior 3 years.

Caution. You may use this method no more than five times.

16	Subtract line 15 from line 14	**16**	
17	Enter the **smaller** of: two-thirds (⅔) of gross nonfarm income⁴ (not less than zero) **or** the amount on line 16. Also include this amount on line 4b above	**17**	

¹From Sch. F, line 11, and Sch. K-1 (Form 1065), line 15b.   ³From Sch. C, line 31; Sch. C-EZ, line 3; Sch. K-1 (Form 1065), line 15a; and Sch. K-1 (Form 1065-B), box 9.
²From Sch. F, line 36, and Sch. K-1 (Form 1065), line 15a.   ⁴From Sch. C, line 7; Sch. C-EZ, line 1; Sch. K-1 (Form 1065), line 15c; and Sch. K-1 (Form 1065-B), box 9.

Schedule SE (Form 1040) 2001

Form **2441**	**Child and Dependent Care Expenses**	OMB No. 1545-0068
Department of the Treasury Internal Revenue Service (99)	▶ Attach to Form 1040. ▶ See separate instructions.	**2001** Attachment Sequence No. **21**

Name(s) shown on Form 1040	Your social security number
JAY A. & SUSAN B. DOE	123 : 45 :6789

Before you begin: You need to understand the following terms. See **Definitions** on page 1 of the instructions.

● **Dependent Care Benefits**   ● **Qualifying Person(s)**   ● **Qualified Expenses**   ● **Earned Income**

Part I **Persons or Organizations Who Provided the Care**—You **must** complete this part.
(If you need more space, use the bottom of page 2.)

1	(a) Care provider's name	(b) Address (number, street, apt. no., city, state, and ZIP code)	(c) Identifying number (SSN or EIN)	(d) Amount paid (see instructions)
	KID'S CARE	2400 IRON AVE. PITTSBURGH, PA 15219	77-1111111	5,120

Did you receive **dependent care benefits?**	**No** ──────▶ Complete only Part II below.
	Yes ──────▶ Complete Part III on the back next.

Caution. If the care was provided in your home, you may owe employment taxes. See the instructions for Form 1040, line 57.

Part II **Credit for Child and Dependent Care Expenses**

2   Information about your **qualifying person(s).** If you have more than two qualifying persons, see the instructions.

(a) Qualifying person's name		(b) Qualifying person's social security number	(c) Qualified expenses you incurred and paid in 2001 for the person listed in column (a)
First	Last		
ALEC	DOE	333 : 44 : 5555	1,484
MOLLY	DOE	777 : 88 : 9999	3,636

3	Add the amounts in column (c) of line 2. **Do not** enter more than $2,400 for one qualifying person or $4,800 for two or more persons. If you completed Part III, enter the amount from line 24	3	4,800
4	Enter your **earned income**	4	83,281
5	If married filing a joint return, enter your spouse's earned income (if your spouse was a student or was disabled, see the instructions); **all others,** enter the amount from line 4	5	71,814
6	Enter the **smallest** of line 3, 4, or 5	6	4,800
7	Enter the amount from Form 1040, line 34 . . . . [7	189,275]		

8   Enter on line 8 the decimal amount shown below that applies to the amount on line 7

If line 7 is:			If line 7 is:				
Over	But not over	Decimal amount is	Over	But not over	Decimal amount is		
$0—10,000		.30	$20,000—22,000		.24		
10,000—12,000		.29	22,000—24,000		.23		
12,000—14,000		.28	24,000—26,000		.22	8	× . 20
14,000—16,000		.27	26,000—28,000		.21		
16,000—18,000		.26	28,000—No limit		.20		
18,000—20,000		.25					

9	Multiply **line 6** by the decimal amount on line 8. Enter the result here and on Form 1040, line 44. But if this amount is more than the amount on Form 1040, line 42, minus any amount on line 43, **or** you paid 2000 expenses in 2001, see the instructions for the amount to enter on line 44	9	960

For Paperwork Reduction Act Notice, see page 3 of the instructions.   Cat. No. 11862M   Form **2441** (2001)

SCHEDULE H (Form 1040) Department of the Treasury Internal Revenue Service (99)	**Household Employment Taxes** (For Social Security, Medicare, Withheld Income, and Federal Unemployment (FUTA) Taxes) ▶ Attach to Form 1040, 1040NR, 1040NR-EZ, 1040-SS, or 1041. ▶ See separate instructions.	OMB No. 1545-0074 20**00** Attachment Sequence No. **44**

Name of employer JAY A. DOE	Social security number 123 : 45 : 6789
	Employer identification number 6 | 2 : 6 | 2 | 6 | 2 | 6 | 2 | 6

A Did you pay **any one** household employee cash wages of $1,200 or more in 2000? (If any household employee was your spouse, your child under age 21, your parent, or anyone under age 18, see the line A instructions on page 3 before you answer this question.)

    ☑ **Yes.** Skip lines B and C and go to line 1.
    ☐ **No.** Go to line B.

B Did you withhold Federal income tax during 2000 for any household employee?

    ☐ **Yes.** Skip line C and go to line 5.
    ☐ **No.** Go to line C.

C Did you pay **total** cash wages of $1,000 or more in **any** calendar **quarter** of 1999 or 2000 to household employees? (**Do not** count cash wages paid in 1999 or 2000 to your spouse, your child under age 21, or your parent.)

    ☐ **No.** **Stop.** Do not file this schedule.
    ☐ **Yes.** Skip lines 1-9 and go to line 10 on the back.

Part I	Social Security, Medicare, and Income Taxes

1	Total cash wages subject to social security taxes (see page 3) . .	**1** 4,220	
2	Social security taxes. Multiply line 1 by 12.4% (.124)	**2**	523
3	Total cash wages subject to Medicare taxes (see page 3)	**3** 4,220	
4	Medicare taxes. Multiply line 3 by 2.9% (.029)	**4**	122
5	Federal income tax withheld, if any	**5**	
6	**Total social security, Medicare, and income taxes** (add lines 2, 4, and 5)	**6**	645
7	Advance earned income credit (EIC) payments, if any	**7**	
8	**Net taxes** (subtract line 7 from line 6)	**8**	645

9 Did you pay **total** cash wages of $1,000 or more in **any** calendar **quarter** of 1999 or 2000 to household employees? (**Do not** count cash wages paid in 1999 or 2000 to your spouse, your child under age 21, or your parent.)

    ☐ **No.** **Stop.** Enter the amount from line 8 above on Form 1040, line 56. If you are not required to file Form 1040, see the line 9 instructions on page 4.

    ☑ **Yes.** Go to line 10 on the back.

For Paperwork Reduction Act Notice, see Form 1040 instructions.   Cat. No. 12187K   Schedule H (Form 1040) 2000

Schedule H (Form 1040) 2000

Page **2**

Part II   Federal Unemployment (FUTA) Tax

		Yes	No
10	Did you pay unemployment contributions to only one state? 10	✔	
11	Did you pay all state unemployment contributions for 2000 by April 16, 2001? Fiscal year filers, see page 4 11	✔	
12	Were all wages that are taxable for FUTA tax also taxable for your state's unemployment tax? . . . 12	✔	

Next: If you checked the **"Yes"** box on **all** the lines above, complete Section A.

If you checked the **"No"** box on **any** of the lines above, skip Section A and complete Section B.

Section A

13	Name of the state where you paid unemployment contributions ▶	**PA**
14	State reporting number as shown on state unemployment tax return ▶	221122112

15	Contributions paid to your state unemployment fund (see page 4) .	15	228	
16	Total cash wages subject to FUTA tax (see page 4)		16	4,220

17	**FUTA tax.** Multiply line 16 by .008. Enter the result here, skip Section B, and go to line 26 . .	17	34

Section B

18   Complete all columns below that apply (if you need more space, see page 4):

(a) Name of state	(b) State reporting number as shown on state unemployment tax return	(c) Taxable wages (as defined in state act)	(d) State experience rate period		(e) State experience rate	(f) Multiply col. (c) by .054	(g) Multiply col. (c) by col. (e)	(h) Subtract col. (g) from col. (f). If zero or less, enter -0-.	(i) Contributions paid to state unemployment fund
			From	To					

19	Totals	19		
20	Add columns (h) and (i) of line 19	20		
21	Total cash wages subject to FUTA tax (see the line 16 instructions on page 4)		21	
22	Multiply line 21 by 6.2% (.062)		22	
23	Multiply line 21 by 5.4% (.054)	23		
24	Enter the **smaller** of line 20 or line 23		24	
25	**FUTA tax.** Subtract line 24 from line 22. Enter the result here and go to line 26		25	

Part III   Total Household Employment Taxes

26	Enter the amount from line 8	26	645
27	Add line 17 (or line 25) and line 26	27	679

28   Are you required to file Form 1040?

☑ **Yes.**   **Stop.** Enter the amount from line 27 above on Form 1040, line 56. **Do not** complete Part IV below.

☐ **No.**   You may have to complete Part IV. See page 4 for details.

Part IV   Address and Signature—Complete this part **only** if required. See the line 28 instructions on page 4.

Address (number and street) or P.O. box if mail is not delivered to street address

Apt., room, or suite no.

City, town or post office, state, and ZIP code

Under penalties of perjury, I declare that I have examined this schedule, including accompanying statements, and to the best of my knowledge and belief, it is true, correct, and complete. No part of any payment made to a state unemployment fund claimed as a credit was, or is to be, deducted from the payments to employees.

▶ _____   ▶ _____

Employer's signature   Date

Schedule H (Form 1040) 2000

Form **2106-EZ**	**Unreimbursed Employee Business Expenses**	OMB No. 1545-1441
Department of the Treasury Internal Revenue Service (99)	▶ **Attach to Form 1040.**	20**01** Attachment Sequence No. **54A**

Your name JAY A. DOE	Occupation in which you incurred expenses **COLLEGE TEACHER**	Social security number 123 : 45 : 6789

You May Use This Form Only if All of the Following Apply.

- You are an employee deducting expenses attributable to your job.
- You **do not** get reimbursed by your employer for any expenses (amounts your employer included in box 1 of your Form W-2 are not considered reimbursements).
- If you are claiming vehicle expense, you are using the standard mileage rate for 2001.

Caution: *You can use the standard mileage rate for 2001 **only if: (a)** you owned the vehicle and used the standard mileage rate for the first year you placed the vehicle in service **or (b)** you leased the vehicle and used the standard mileage rate for the portion of the lease period after 1997.*

Part I   **Figure Your Expenses**

1	Vehicle expense using the standard mileage rate. Complete Part II and multipy line 8a by 34½¢ (.345)	**1**	891
2	Parking fees, tolls, and transportation, including train, bus, etc., that **did not** involve overnight travel or commuting to and from work	**2**	304
3	Travel expense while away from home overnight, including lodging, airplane, car rental, etc. **Do not** include meals and entertainment	**3**	4,831
4	Business expenses not included on lines 1 through 3. **Do not** include meals and entertainment	**4**	6,779
5	Meals and entertainment expenses: $ _____5,510_____ x 50% (.50) (Employees subject to Department of Transportation (DOT) hours of service limits: Multiply meal expenses by 60% (.60) instead of 50%. For details, see instructions.)	**5**	2,755
6	**Total expenses.** Add lines 1 through 5. Enter here and **on line 20 of Schedule A (Form 1040).** (Fee-basis state or local government officials, qualified performing artists, and individuals with disabilities: See the instructions for special rules on where to enter this amount.)	**6**	15,560

Part II   **Information on Your Vehicle.** Complete this part **only** if you are claiming vehicle expense on line 1.

7   When did you place your vehicle in service for business use? (month, day, year) ▶ ......4...... / ......7...... / ......96......
8   Of the total number of miles you drove your vehicle during 2001, enter the number of miles you used your vehicle for:
a   Business ....2,583...........   b Commuting ....7,051...........   c Other ....2,216...........
9   Do you (or your spouse) have another vehicle available for personal use? . . . . ☑ Yes ☐ No
10   Was your vehicle available for personal use during off-duty hours? . . . . ☑ Yes ☐ No
11a   Do you have evidence to support your deduction? . . . . ☑ Yes ☐ No
  b   If "Yes," is the evidence written? . . . . ☑ Yes ☐ No

General Instructions

Section references are to the Internal Revenue Code.

A Change To Note

The standard mileage rate has been increased to 34½ cents for each mile of business use in 2001.

Purpose of Form

You may use Form 2106-EZ instead of Form 2106 to claim your unreimbursed employee business expenses if you meet all the requirements listed above Part I.

Recordkeeping

You cannot deduct expenses for travel (including meals, unless you used the standard meal allowance), entertainment, gifts, or use of a car or other listed property, unless you keep records to prove the time, place, business purpose, business relationship (for entertainment and gifts), and amounts of these expenses. Generally, you must also have receipts for all lodging expenses (regardless of the amount) and any other expense of $75 or more.

Additional Information

For more details about employee business expenses, see:

Pub. 463, Travel, Entertainment, Gift, and Car Expenses

Pub. 529, Miscellaneous Deductions

Pub. 587, Business Use of Your Home (Including Use by Day-Care Providers)

Pub. 946, How To Depreciate Property

For Paperwork Reduction Act Notice, see back of form.   Cat. No. 20604Q   Form **2106-EZ** (2001)

Form **3903**	**Moving Expenses**		OMB No. 1545-0062
(Rev. October 2001) Department of the Treasury Internal Revenue Service	▶ **Attach to Form 1040.**		Attachment Sequence No. **62**

Name(s) shown on Form 1040	Your social security number
JAY A. & SUSAN B. DOE	123 : 45 : 6789

Before you begin: See the **Distance Test** and **Time Test** in the instructions to find out if you can deduct your moving expenses. If you are a member of the armed forces, see the instructions to find out how to complete this form.

1	Enter the amount you paid for transportation and storage of household goods and personal effects (see instructions)	**1**	2,104
2	Enter the amount you paid for travel and lodging expenses in moving from your old home to your new home. **Do not** include the cost of meals (see instructions)	**2**	317
3	Add lines 1 and 2	**3**	2,421
4	Enter the total amount your employer paid you for the expenses listed on lines 1 and 2 that is **not** included in the wages box (box 1) of your W-2 form. This amount should be identified with code **P** in box 12 of your W-2 form	**4**	
5	Is line 3 **more than** line 4?		
	☐ **No.** You **cannot** deduct your moving expenses. If line 3 is less than line 4, subtract line 3 from line 4 and include the result on the "Wages, salaries, tips, etc." line of Form 1040.		
	☑ **Yes.** Subtract line 4 from line 3. Enter the result here and on the "Moving expenses" line of Form 1040. This is your **moving expense deduction**	**5**	2,421

General Instructions

A Change To Note

Beginning in 2001, the standard mileage rate for using your vehicle to move to a new home is 12 cents a mile.

Purpose of Form

Use Form 3903 to figure your moving expense deduction for a move related to the start of work at a new principal place of work (workplace) that is either:

• Within the United States or its possessions or

• Outside the United States or its possessions and you are a U.S. citizen or resident alien.

If you qualify to deduct expenses for more than one move, use a separate Form 3903 for each move.

For more details, see **Pub. 521,** Moving Expenses.

Who May Deduct Moving Expenses

If you move to a new home because of a new principal workplace, you may be able to deduct your moving expenses whether you are self-employed or an employee. But you must meet both of the tests explained next.

Distance Test

Your new principal workplace must be at least 50 miles farther from your old home than your old workplace was. For example, if your old workplace was 3 miles from your old home, your new workplace must be at least 53 miles from that home. If you did not have an old workplace, your new workplace must be at least 50 miles from your old home. The distance between the two points is the shortest of the more commonly traveled routes between them.

TIP: *To see if you meet the distance test, use the worksheet on this page.*

Time Test

If you are an employee, you must work full time in the general area of your new workplace for at least 39 weeks during the 12 months right after you move. If you are self-employed, you must work full time in the general area of your new workplace for at least 39 weeks during the first 12 months and a total of at least 78 weeks during the 24 months right after your move.

What If You Do Not Meet the Time Test Before Your Return Is Due? If you expect to meet the time test, you may deduct your moving expenses in the year you move. Later, if you do not meet the time test, you must either:

• Amend your tax return for the year you claimed the deduction by filing **Form 1040X,** Amended U.S. Individual Income Tax Return **or**

• For the year you cannot meet the time test, report as income the amount of your moving expense deduction that reduced your income tax for the year you moved.

Distance Test Worksheet *(Keep for Your Records)*		
1. Enter the number of miles from your **old home** to your **new workplace**	**1.**	314 miles
2. Enter the number of miles from your **old home** to your **old workplace**	**2.**	12 miles
3. Subtract line 2 from line 1. If zero or less, enter -0- . . .	**3.**	302 miles
Is line 3 at least 50 miles?		
☑ **Yes.** You meet this test.		
☐ **No.** You do not meet this test. You **cannot** deduct your moving expenses. **Do not** complete Form 3903.		

For Paperwork Reduction Act Notice, see back of form.	Cat. No. 12490K	Form **3903** (Rev. 10-2001)

Form **8829**	**Expenses for Business Use of Your Home**
	▶ File only with Schedule C (Form 1040). Use a separate Form 8829 for each home you used for business during the year.
Department of the Treasury Internal Revenue Service (99)	▶ See separate instructions.

OMB No. 1545-1266

2001

Attachment Sequence No. **66**

Name(s) of proprietor(s)
JAY A. DOE

Your social security number
123 : 45 : 6789

Part I   Part of Your Home Used for Business

1	Area used regularly and exclusively for business, regularly for day care, or for storage of inventory or product samples. See instructions	1	625
2	Total area of home	2	3,750
3	Divide line 1 by line 2. Enter the result as a percentage	3	16.67 %

• For day-care facilities not used exclusively for business, also complete lines 4–6.
• All others, skip lines 4–6 and enter the amount from line 3 on line 7.

4	Multiply days used for day care during year by hours used per day	4	hr.
5	Total hours available for use during the year (365 days × 24 hours). See instructions	5	8,760 hr.
6	Divide line 4 by line 5. Enter the result as a decimal amount	6	.
7	Business percentage. For day-care facilities not used exclusively for business, multiply line 6 by line 3 (enter the result as a percentage). All others, enter the amount from line 3 ▶	7	16.67 %

Part II   Figure Your Allowable Deduction

8	Enter the amount from Schedule C, line 29, **plus** any net gain or (loss) derived from the business use of your home and shown on Schedule D or Form 4797. If more than one place of business, see instructions	8	10,956

See instructions for columns (a) and (b) before completing lines 9–20.

		(a) Direct expenses	(b) Indirect expenses		
9	Casualty losses. See instructions	9			
10	Deductible mortgage interest. See instructions	10		9,118	
11	Real estate taxes. See instructions	11		1,622	
12	Add lines 9, 10, and 11	12		10,740	
13	Multiply line 12, column (b) by line 7	13		1,790	
14	Add line 12, column (a) and line 13			14	1,790
15	Subtract line 14 from line 8. If zero or less, enter -0-			15	9,166
16	Excess mortgage interest. See instructions	16			
17	Insurance	17		176	
18	Repairs and maintenance	18		413	
19	Utilities	19		2,787	
20	Other expenses. See instructions	20		2,130	
21	Add lines 16 through 20	21		5,506	
22	Multiply line 21, column (b) by line 7	22		918	
23	Carryover of operating expenses from 2000 Form 8829, line 41	23			
24	Add line 21 in column (a), line 22, and line 23			24	1,231
25	Allowable operating expenses. Enter the **smaller** of line 15 or line 24			25	1,231
26	Limit on excess casualty losses and depreciation. Subtract line 25 from line 15			26	7,935
27	Excess casualty losses. See instructions	27			
28	Depreciation of your home from Part III below	28		654	
29	Carryover of excess casualty losses and depreciation from 2000 Form 8829, line 42	29			
30	Add lines 27 through 29			30	654
31	Allowable excess casualty losses and depreciation. Enter the **smaller** of line 26 or line 30			31	654
32	Add lines 14, 25, and 31			32	3,675
33	Casualty loss portion, if any, from lines 14 and 31. Carry amount to **Form 4684**, Section B			33	
34	Allowable expenses for business use of your home. Subtract line 33 from line 32. Enter here and on Schedule C, line 30. If your home was used for more than one business, see instructions ▶			34	3,675

Part III   Depreciation of Your Home

35	Enter the **smaller** of your home's adjusted basis or its fair market value. See instructions	35	124,620
36	Value of land included on line 35	36	31,155
37	Basis of building. Subtract line 36 from line 35	37	93,465
38	Business basis of building. Multiply line 37 by line 7	38	15,578
39	Depreciation percentage. See instructions	39	4.2 %
40	Depreciation allowable. Multiply line 38 by line 39. Enter here and on line 28 above. See instructions	40	654

Part IV   Carryover of Unallowed Expenses to 2002

41	Operating expenses. Subtract line 25 from line 24. If less than zero, enter -0-	41	
42	Excess casualty losses and depreciation. Subtract line 31 from line 30. If less than zero, enter -0-	42	

For Paperwork Reduction Act Notice, see page 4 of separate instructions.   Cat. No. 13232M   Form **8829** (2001)

Form **4562**	**Depreciation and Amortization**	OMB No. 1545-0172
Department of the Treasury Internal Revenue Service (99)	**(Including Information on Listed Property)** ▶ See separate instructions. ▶ Attach this form to your return.	**2000** Attachment Sequence No. **67**

Name(s) shown on return	Business or activity to which this form relates	Identifying number
JAY A. & SUSAN B. DOE		123-45-6789

Part I Election To Expense Certain Tangible Property (Section 179)

Note: *If you have any "listed property," complete Part V before you complete Part I.*

1	Maximum dollar limitation. If an enterprise zone business, see page 2 of the instructions . .	**1**	$20,000
2	Total cost of section 179 property placed in service. See page 2 of the instructions	**2**	3,727
3	Threshold cost of section 179 property before reduction in limitation	**3**	$200,000
4	Reduction in limitation. Subtract line 3 from line 2. If zero or less, enter -0-	**4**	0
5	Dollar limitation for tax year. Subtract line 4 from line 1. If zero or less, enter -0-. If married filing separately, see page 2 of the instructions	**5**	20,000

(a) Description of property	(b) Cost (business use only)	(c) Elected cost
6 BOOKS, CALCULATOR, FAX, ANSWERING MACH.	897	897

7	Listed property. Enter amount from line 27 . . . . **7**	2,830	
8	Total elected cost of section 179 property. Add amounts in column (c), lines 6 and 7 . . .	**8**	3,727
9	Tentative deduction. Enter the smaller of line 5 or line 8	**9**	3,727
10	Carryover of disallowed deduction from 1999. See page 3 of the instructions	**10**	
11	Business income limitation. Enter the smaller of business income (not less than zero) or line 5 (see instructions)	**11**	20,000
12	Section 179 expense deduction. Add lines 9 and 10, but do not enter more than line 11 . .	**12**	3,727
13	Carryover of disallowed deduction to 2001. Add lines 9 and 10, less line 12 ▶ **13**		

Note: *Do not use Part II or Part III below for listed property (automobiles, certain other vehicles, cellular telephones, certain computers, or property used for entertainment, recreation, or amusement). Instead, use Part V for listed property.*

Part II MACRS Depreciation for Assets Placed in Service Only During Your 2000 Tax Year (Do not include listed property.)

Section A—General Asset Account Election

14	If you are making the election under section 168(i)(4) to group any assets placed in service during the tax year into one or more general asset accounts, check this box. See page 3 of the instructions . . . . ▶ ☐

Section B—General Depreciation System (GDS) (See page 3 of the instructions.)

(a) Classification of property	(b) Month and year placed in service	(c) Basis for depreciation (business/investment use only—see instructions)	(d) Recovery period	(e) Convention	(f) Method	(g) Depreciation deduction
15a 3-year property						
b 5-year property						
c 7-year property						
d 10-year property						
e 15-year property						
f 20-year property						
g 25-year property			25 yrs.		S/L	
h Residential rental property			27.5 yrs.	MM	S/L	
			27.5 yrs.	MM	S/L	
i Nonresidential real property			39 yrs.	MM	S/L	
				MM	S/L	

Section C—Alternative Depreciation System (ADS) (See page 5 of the instructions.)

16a Class life					S/L	
b 12-year			12 yrs.		S/L	
c 40-year			40 yrs.	MM	S/L	

Part III Other Depreciation (Do not include listed property.) (See page 5 of the instructions.)

17	GDS and ADS deductions for assets placed in service in tax years beginning before 2000 .	**17**	281
18	Property subject to section 168(f)(1) election	**18**	
19	ACRS and other depreciation	**19**	654

Part IV Summary (See page 6 of the instructions.)

20	Listed property. Enter amount from line 26	**20**	32
21	**Total.** Add deductions from line 12, lines 15 and 16 in column (g), and lines 17 through 20. Enter here and on the appropriate lines of your return. Partnerships and S corporations—see instructions	**21**	4,694
22	For assets shown above and placed in service during the current year, enter the portion of the basis attributable to section 263A costs . . **22**		

For Paperwork Reduction Act Notice, see page 9 of the instructions.   Cat. No. 12906N   Form **4562** (2000)

Form 4562 (2000)   Page **2**

Part V	Listed Property (Include automobiles, certain other vehicles, cellular telephones, certain computers, and property used for entertainment, recreation, or amusement.)

Note: *For any vehicle for which you are using the standard mileage rate or deducting lease expense, complete only 23a, 23b, columns (a) through (c) of Section A, all of Section B, and Section C if applicable.*

Section A—Depreciation and Other Information (Caution: *See page 7 of the instructions for limits for passenger automobiles.*)

23a Do you have evidence to support the business/investment use claimed? ☑ Yes ☐ No   23b If "Yes," is the evidence written? ☑ Yes ☐ No

(a) Type of property (list vehicles first)	(b) Date placed in service	(c) Business/ investment use percentage	(d) Cost or other basis	(e) Basis for depreciation (business/investment use only)	(f) Recovery period	(g) Method/ Convention	(h) Depreciation deduction	(i) Elected section 179 cost
24 Property used more than 50% in a qualified business use (See page 6 of the instructions.):								
COMPUTER	6/00	90 %	3,144	2,830				2,830
		%						
		%						
25 Property used 50% or less in a qualified business use (See page 6 of the instructions.):								
VIDEO CAMERA	9/92	40 %	962	385	12-YR	S/L – HY	32	
		%				S/L –		
		%				S/L –		
26 Add amounts in column (h). Enter the total here and on line 20, page 1.						**26**	32	
27 Add amounts in column (i). Enter the total here and on line 7, page 1							**27**	2,830

Section B—Information on Use of Vehicles

Complete this section for vehicles used by a sole proprietor, partner, or other "more than 5% owner," or related person.
If you provided vehicles to your employees, first answer the questions in Section C to see if you meet an exception to completing this section for those vehicles.

		(a) Vehicle 1		(b) Vehicle 2		(c) Vehicle 3		(d) Vehicle 4		(e) Vehicle 5		(f) Vehicle 6	
28	Total business/investment miles driven during the year (**do not** include commuting miles— see page 1 of the instructions)												
29	Total commuting miles driven during the year												
30	Total other personal (noncommuting) miles driven												
31	Total miles driven during the year. Add lines 28 through 30.												
		Yes	No	Yes	No	Yes	No	Yes	No	Yes	No	Yes	No
32	Was the vehicle available for personal use during off-duty hours?												
33	Was the vehicle used primarily by a more than 5% owner or related person? .												
34	Is another vehicle available for personal use?												

Section C—Questions for Employers Who Provide Vehicles for Use by Their Employees

Answer these questions to determine if you meet an exception to completing Section B for vehicles used by employees who **are not** more than 5% owners or related persons. See page 8 of the instructions.

		Yes	No
35	Do you maintain a written policy statement that prohibits all personal use of vehicles, including commuting, by your employees?		
36	Do you maintain a written policy statement that prohibits personal use of vehicles, except commuting, by your employees? See page 8 of the instructions for vehicles used by corporate officers, directors, or 1% or more owners		
37	Do you treat all use of vehicles by employees as personal use?		
38	Do you provide more than five vehicles to your employees, obtain information from your employees about the use of the vehicles, and retain the information received?		
39	Do you meet the requirements concerning qualified automobile demonstration use? See page 8 of the instructions . .		

Note: *If your answer to 35, 36, 37, 38, or 39 is "Yes," do not complete Section B for the covered vehicles.*

Part VI	**Amortization**

(a) Description of costs	(b) Date amortization begins	(c) Amortizable amount	(d) Code section	(e) Amortization period or percentage	(f) Amortization for this year
40 Amortization of costs that begins during your 2000 tax year (See page 8 of the instructions.):					
41 Amortization of costs that began before 2000				**41**	
42 Total. Add amounts in column (f). See page 9 of the instructions for where to report . . .				**42**	

✪

Form **4562** (2000)

Child Tax Credit Worksheet

Before you begin: You will need any of the following forms that you are filing.
  √ Form 2555, Foreign Earned Income
  √ Form 2555-EZ, Foreign Earned Income Exclusion
  √ Form 4563, Exclusion of Income for Bona Fide Residents of American Samoa

Part 1

1. Number of qualifying children: ____2____ × $500. Enter the result. | **1** | **1,000**

2. Enter the amount from Form 1040, line 34, or Form 1040A, line 19. | **2** | **189,275**

3. **1040 filers:** Enter the total of any—
   - Exclusion of income from Puerto Rico, and
   - Amounts from Form 2555, lines 43 and 48; Form 2555-EZ, line 18; and Form 4563, line 15.

   1040A filers: Enter -0-. | **3** | **0**

4. Add lines 2 and 3. Enter the result. | **4** | **189,275**

5. Enter the amount shown below for your filing status.
   - Married filing jointly - $110,000
   - Single, head of household, or qualifying widow(er) - $75,000
   - Married filing separately - $55,000 | **5** | **110,000**

6. Is the amount on line 4 more than the amount on line 5?

   ☐ **No.** Leave line 6 blank. Enter -0- on line 7.

   ☒ **Yes.** Subtract line 5 from line 4.
   If the result is not a multiple of $1,000, increase it to the next multiple of $1,000 (for example, increase $425 to $1,000, increase $1,025 to $2,000, etc.). | **6** | **80,000**

7. Multiply the amount on line 6 by 5% (.05). Enter the result. | **7** | **4,000**

8. Is the amount on line 1 more than the amount on line 7?

   ☒ **No.** (STOP)
   You cannot take the child tax credit on Form 1040, line 47, or Form 1040A, line 30. You also cannot take the additional child tax credit on Form 1040, line 62, or Form 1040A, line 39. Complete the rest of your Form 1040 or 1040A.

   ☐ **Yes.** Subtract line 7 from line 1. Enter the result. *Go to Part 2 on the next page.* | **8** |

SUPPLEMENT #1
JOB-RELATED TRAVEL EXPENSES AWAY FROM HOME OVERNIGHT
(FORM 2106-EZ, LINES 3 AND 5)

1. Sabbatical at University of San Francisco to do research:
    September 1 – December 30

    Meals ($42/day x 121 days) $5082
    Round-trip airplane fare.......................................$ 406
    Lodging..2518
    Cleaning and laundry 146
    Daily bus fares between temporary home and job....170

2. Trip to attend meeting of American Physics Society:
    May 10 – May 16 in Los Angeles, CA

    Meals $314
    Round-trip airplane fare.......................................$ 458
    Lodging..486
    Taxi Fares 35

3. Trip to interview for new job in same line of work:
    January 7 – January 9 in Albany, NY

    Meals ($38/day x 3 days) $114
    Round-trip airplane fare.......................................$ 356
    Lodging..226
    Airport Limousine..30

TOTAL OTHER THAN MEALS & ENTERTAINMENT
(Form 2106-EZ, Line 3)....................................$4831

TOTAL MEALS & ENTERTAINMENT
(Form 2106-EZ, Line 5) $5510

SUPPLEMENT #2
JOB-RELATED TRAVEL EXPENSES — OTHER THAN FOR TRAVEL, MEALS & ENTERTAINMENT (FORM 2106-EZ, LINE 4)

A.   Books & Equipment

Listed Property (Form 4562, Part V)

1.   Home computer (including peripherals)
     used 90% for job-related research:

> Date of purchase: 6/13/2001
> Purchase price: $3144
> Expensing deduction: 90% x $3144.........................$2830

2.   Video camera, required by employer,
     purchased 9/14/1992 for $962 used
     40% for job-related purposes:

> Depreciation deduction using 12-year
> listed property table percentage (8.34%)
> for item in ninth year of use:
>> Basis for Depreciation:
>> $962 x 40% = $385
>> Deduction for 2001: $385 x 8.34%.........................$32
>> (Included on Form 4562, Line 20)

Non-listed Property Purchased in 2001:

1.   Books..$ 382
2.   Calculator 36
3.   Answering machine..78
4.   Fax machine ....<u>401</u>

> Expensing Deduction $897
> (Form 4562, Line 6)

Nonlisted Property Purchased in 1992-2000 ....$<u>281</u>
     (Form 4562, Line 17)

TOTAL DEDUCTION FOR
JOB-RELATED BOOKS & EQUIPMENT $4040

SUPPLEMENT #2 (continued)

B. Educational Expenses:

Expenses connected with attending seminar in
Advanced Mechanics at University of Pittsburgh
to learn new material for use in job-related research.
(This seminar was not needed to meet the minimum
requirements for holding my job nor for a new job.):

Tuition	$ 840
Texbook	65
Supplies	20
Laboratory Fee	30
TOTAL EDUCATIONAL EXPENSES	$ 955

C. Other Expenses:

Dues to National Education Association	$ 80
Dues to A.A.U.P.	95
Dues to American Physics Society	110
Subscriptions to professional journals	244
Supplies used in teaching — paper, pens, record book, etc.	283
Laboratory apparel (including cleaning)	75
Laboratory equipment	157
Required physical exam	125
Payment to substitute teacher	265
Employment agency fee to obtain job	350
TOTAL "OTHER EXPENSES"	$1784
GRAND TOTAL (FORM 2106-EZ, LINE 4	$6779

SUPPLEMENT #3
JOB-RELATED AUTO MILEAGE (FORM 2106-EZ, LINE 8a)

1. Travel between two different jobs:
    18 miles per week for 20 weeks .... 360 miles

2. Travel to temporary job away from home
    in city 51 miles from home:
    2 weeks x 3 days/week x 102 miles 612

3. Travel to temporary job 16 miles from home:
    6 weeks x 5 days/week x 32 miles 960

4. Travel to attend seminar on Advanced Mechanics......... 269

5. Travel to libraries to do research 962

6. Travel to pick up official visitors at airport.................... 120

TOTAL   .... 2583 miles

SUPPLEMENT #4
SCHEDULE C DEDUCTION

Home Office (1 room of 6-room house, used exclusively for job-related purposes)

Home Expenses:

Mortgage interest	$9118
Property taxes	1622
Gas for heating	1405
Electricity for light and air conditioning	1382
Homeowner's insurance	176
Cleaning service	2130
Repair of roof	<u>413</u>
	$16,246

Home expenses attributable to office:

1/6 x $16,246	$2,708
Plus: Painting the office	313
*Depreciation	<u>654</u>

TOTAL HOME OFFICE DEDUCTION $3675
    SCHEDULE C, LINE 30

*Depreciation Calculation:
    Purchase price of house (excluding land): $393,465
    Date of purchase: 7/12/90
    Basis of home office: 1/6 x $93,465 = $15,578
    Depreciation deduction for 2001:
       4.28% x $15,578 = $654

(Depreciation included on Form 4562, Line 19)

Note: This Home Office Supplement is not needed by self-employed persons, who list home office expenses on Form 8829.

INDEX